Pro Angular 6

Third Edition

Adam Freeman

Pro Angular 6

Adam Freeman
London, UK

ISBN-13 (pbk): 978-1-4842-3648-2   ISBN-13 (electronic): 978-1-4842-3649-9
https://doi.org/10.1007/978-1-4842-3649-9

Library of Congress Control Number: 2018960245

Managing Director, Apress Media LLC: Welmoed Spahr
Acquisitions Editor: Joan Murray
Development Editor: Laura Berendson
Coordinating Editor: Mark Powers

Cover designed by eStudioCalamar

Cover image designed by Freepik (www.freepik.com)

Distributed to the book trade worldwide by Springer Science+Business Media New York, 233 Spring Street, 6th Floor, New York, NY 10013. Phone 1-800-SPRINGER, fax (201) 348-4505, e-mail orders-ny@springer-sbm.com, or visit www.springeronline.com. Apress Media, LLC is a California LLC and the sole member (owner) is Springer Science + Business Media Finance Inc (SSBM Finance Inc). SSBM Finance Inc is a **Delaware** corporation.

For information on translations, please e-mail editorial@apress.com, for reprint, paperback, or audio rights, please email bookpermissions@springernature.com.

Apress titles may be purchased in bulk for academic, corporate, or promotional use. eBook versions and licenses are also available for most titles. For more information, reference our Print and eBook Bulk Sales web page at www.apress.com/bulk-sales.

Any source code or other supplementary material referenced by the author in this book is available to readers on GitHub via the book's product page, located at www.apress.com/9781484236482. For more detailed information, please visit http://www.apress.com/source-code.

Printed on acid-free paper

Dedicated to my lovely wife, Jacqui Griffyth. (And also to Peanut.)

Table of Contents

About the Author xxiii

About the Technical Reviewer xxv

■Part I: Getting Started with Angular 1

■Chapter 1: Getting Ready... 3

What Do You Need to Know? 3

What Is the Structure of This Book? 4

Part 1: Getting Started with Angular 4

Part 2: Angular in Detail 4

Part 3: Advanced Angular Features...4

Are There Lots of Examples?.. 4

Where Can You Get the Example Code? 6

How Do You Set Up Your Development Environment? 6

Contacting the Author.. 6

Summary.. 6

■Chapter 2: Your First Angular App... 7

Preparing the Development Environment.. 7

Installing Node.js 7

Installing the angular-cli Package 8

Installing Git...8

Installing an Editor...9

Installing a Browser...9

Creating and Preparing the Project 10

    Creating the Project 10

    Adding the Bootstrap CSS Package 10

    Starting the Development Tools 11

    Editing the HTML File 12

Adding Angular Features to the Project 15

    Preparing the HTML File 15

    Creating a Data Model 16

    Preparing the Template 18

    Preparing the Component 18

    Putting the Application Together 20

Adding Features to the Example Application 22

    Adding the To-Do Table 23

    Creating a Two-Way Data Binding 26

    Adding To-Do Items 28

Summary 30

■Chapter 3: Putting Angular in Context 31

Understanding Where Angular Excels 32

    Understanding Round-Trip and Single-Page Applications 32

    Comparing Angular to jQuery 33

Comparing Angular to React and Vue.js 34

Understanding the MVC Pattern 34

    Understanding Models 36

    Understanding Controllers/Components 38

    Understanding Views/Templates 38

Understanding RESTful Services 39

Common Design Pitfalls 41

    Putting the Logic in the Wrong Place 41

    Adopting the Data Store Data Format 41

    Just Enough Knowledge to Cause Trouble 42

Summary 42

▓Chapter 4: An HTML and CSS Primer 43

Preparing the Example Project 43

Understanding HTML 45

Understanding Void Elements 46

Understanding Attributes 46

Applying Attributes Without Values 46

Quoting Literal Values in Attributes 47

Understanding Element Content 47

Understanding the Document Structure 47

Understanding Bootstrap 49

Applying Basic Bootstrap Classes 50

Using Bootstrap to Style Tables 53

Using Bootstrap to Create Forms 54

Using Bootstrap to Create Grids 55

Summary 61

▓Chapter 5: JavaScript and TypeScript: Part 1 63

Preparing the Example Project 64

Understanding the Basic Workflow 66

Using Statements 66

Defining and Using Functions 67

Defining Functions with Parameters 69

Defining Functions That Return Results 70

Using Functions As Arguments to Other Functions 71

Using Variables and Types 72

Using Variable Closure 73

Using the Primitive Types 74

Using JavaScript Operators 76

Using Conditional Statements 77

The Equality Operator vs. the Identity Operator 78

Explicitly Converting Types 79

Working with Arrays **81**

    Using an Array Literal 81

    Reading and Modifying the Contents of an Array 81

    Enumerating the Contents of an Array.. 82

    Using the Spread Operator 83

    Using the Built-in Array Methods 83

Summary **85**

■Chapter 6: JavaScript and TypeScript: Part 2 .... **87**

Preparing the Example Project **87**

Working with Objects **88**

    Using Object Literals 89

    Using Functions as Methods.. 89

    Defining Classes 90

Working with JavaScript Modules **93**

    Creating and Using Modules 94

Useful TypeScript Features **97**

    Using Type Annotations 97

    Using Tuples 102

    Using Indexable Types 103

    Using Access Modifiers 103

Summary **105**

■Chapter 7: SportsStore: A Real Application **107**

Preparing the Project **107**

    Installing the Additional NPM Packages 108

    Preparing the RESTful Web Service... 109

    Preparing the HTML File 111

    Creating the Folder Structure 112

    Running the Example Application 112

    Starting the RESTful Web Service.. 113

Preparing the Angular Project Features 113

    Updating the Root Component.. 113

    Updating the Root Module 114

    Inspecting the Bootstrap File.. 114

Starting the Data Model 115

    Creating the Model Classes.. 115

    Creating the Dummy Data Source 116

    Creating the Model Repository 117

    Creating the Feature Module 118

Starting the Store 119

    Creating the Store Component and Template 119

    Creating the Store Feature Module.. 120

    Updating the Root Component and Root Module... 121

Adding Store Features the Product Details 122

    Displaying the Product Details.. 122

    Adding Category Selection 124

    Adding Product Pagination 126

    Creating a Custom Directive... 130

Summary... 133

▨ **Chapter 8: SportsStore: Orders and Checkout**.. **135**

Preparing the Example Application 135

Creating the Cart 135

    Creating the Cart Model... 135

    Creating the Cart Summary Components 137

    Integrating the Cart into the Store.. 139

Adding URL Routing... 142

    Creating the Cart Detail and Checkout Components 143

    Creating and Applying the Routing Configuration... 144

    Navigating Through the Application... 145

    Guarding the Routes.. 148

Completing the Cart Detail Feature 150

Processing Orders 153

    Extending the Model 153

    Collecting the Order Details 156

Using the RESTful Web Service 160

    Applying the Data Source 161

Summary 163

■ Chapter 9: SportsStore: Administration 165

Preparing the Example Application 165

    Creating the Module 165

    Configuring the URL Routing System 168

    Navigating to the Administration URL 169

Implementing Authentication 171

    Understanding the Authentication System 171

    Extending the Data Source 172

    Creating the Authentication Service 173

    Enabling Authentication 174

Extending the Data Source and Repositories 177

Creating the Administration Feature Structure 181

    Creating the Placeholder Components 181

    Preparing the Common Content and the Feature Module 182

    Implementing the Product Feature 185

    Implementing the Orders Feature 189

Summary 191

■ Chapter 10: SportsStore: Progressive Features and Deployment 193

Preparing the Example Application 193

Adding Progressive Features 193

    Installing the PWA Package 193

    Caching the Data URLs 194

    Responding to Connectivity Changes 195

Preparing the Application for Deployment.. 197

    Creating the Data File 197

    Creating the Server..198

    Changing the Web Service URL in the Repository Class...200

Building and Testing the Application 200

    Testing the Progressive Features 202

Containerizing the SportsStore Application.. 203

    Installing Docker...203

    Preparing the Application 203

    Creating the Docker Container 204

    Running the Application...205

Summary.. 207

▨Part II: Angular in Detail 209

▨Chapter 11: Creating an Angular Project... 211

Creating a New Angular Project 211

Understanding the Project Structure... 212

    Understanding the Source Code Folder...214

    Understanding the Packages Folder..216

Using the Development Tools 220

    Understanding the Development HTTP Server 221

    Understanding Hot Model Replacement..222

    Using the Linter 223

Understanding How an Angular Application Works 226

    Understanding the HTML Document..226

    Understanding the Application Bootstrap 227

    Understanding the Root Angular Module...228

    Understanding the Angular Component..229

    Understanding Content Display 229

Starting Development in an Angular Project 230

    Adding the Bootstrap CSS Framework 231

    Creating the Data Model 231

    Creating a Component and Template 234

    Configuring the Root Angular Module 236

Summary 236

Chapter 12: Using Data Bindings 237

Preparing the Example Project 238

Understanding One-Way Data Bindings 239

    Understanding the Binding Target 241

    Understanding the Expression 242

    Understanding the Brackets 243

    Understanding the Host Element 244

Using the Standard Property and Attribute Bindings 244

    Using the Standard Property Binding 244

    Using the String Interpolation Binding 246

    Using the Attribute Binding 247

Setting Classes and Styles 249

    Using the Class Bindings 249

    Using the Style Bindings 254

Updating the Data in the Application 258

Summary 260

Chapter 13: Using the Built-in Directives 261

Preparing the Example Project 262

Using the Built-in Directives 264

    Using the ngIf Directive 264

    Using the ngSwitch Directive 267

    Using the ngFor Directive 270

    Using the ngTemplateOutlet Directive 280

Understanding One-Way Data Binding Restrictions 283

    Using Idempotent Expressions 283

    Understanding the Expression Context.. 286

Summary... 289

■Chapter 14: Using Events and Forms... 291

Preparing the Example Project.. 292

    Importing the Forms Module 292

    Preparing the Component and Template 293

Using the Event Binding 294

    Understanding Dynamically Defined Properties 296

    Using Event Data 298

    Using Template Reference Variables 300

Using Two-Way Data Bindings... 302

    Using the ngModel Directive... 304

Working with Forms 305

    Adding a Form to the Example Application... 305

    Adding Form Data Validation 308

    Validating the Entire Form 318

Using Model-Based Forms 325

    Enabling Model-Based Forms Feature 325

    Defining the Form Model Classes.. 326

    Using the Model for Validation.. 329

    Generating the Elements from the Model... 333

Creating Custom Form Validators.. 334

    Applying a Custom Validator... 335

Summary... 337

■Chapter 15: Creating Attribute Directives 339

Preparing the Example Project.. 340

Creating a Simple Attribute Directive 343

    Applying a Custom Directive... 344

Accessing Application Data in a Directive 345

Reading Host Element Attributes 345

Creating Data-Bound Input Properties 348

Responding to Input Property Changes 351

Creating Custom Events 353

Binding to a Custom Event 355

Creating Host Element Bindings 356

Creating a Two-Way Binding on the Host Element 358

Exporting a Directive for Use in a Template Variable 361

Summary 364

■Chapter 16: Creating Structural Directives 365

Preparing the Example Project 366

Creating a Simple Structural Directive 367

Implementing the Structural Directive Class 368

Enabling the Structural Directive 371

Using the Concise Structural Directive Syntax 373

Creating Iterating Structural Directives 374

Providing Additional Context Data 377

Using the Concise Structure Syntax 379

Dealing with Property-Level Data Changes 380

Dealing with Collection-Level Data Changes 381

Querying the Host Element Content 392

Querying Multiple Content Children 395

Receiving Query Change Notifications 397

Summary 399

■Chapter 17: Understanding Components 401

Preparing the Example Project 402

Structuring an Application with Components 403

Creating New Components 404

Defining Templates 408

Completing the Component Restructure 419

Using Component Styles 420

Defining External Component Styles 422

Using Advanced Style Features 423

Querying Template Content 430

Summary 433

■Chapter 18: Using and Creating Pipes 435

Preparing the Example Project 436

Understanding Pipes 439

Creating a Custom Pipe 441

Registering a Custom Pipe 442

Applying a Custom Pipe 443

Combining Pipes 444

Creating Impure Pipes 445

Using the Built-in Pipes 449

Formatting Numbers 450

Formatting Currency Values 453

Formatting Percentages 456

Formatting Dates 458

Changing String Case 461

Serializing Data as JSON 463

Slicing Data Arrays 463

Summary 465

■Chapter 19: Using Services 467

Preparing the Example Project 468

Understanding the Object Distribution Problem 469

Demonstrating the Problem 469

Distributing Objects as Services Using Dependency Injection 474

Declaring Dependencies in Other Building Blocks 480

Understanding the Test Isolation Problem 487

    Isolating Components Using Services and Dependency Injection 488

Completing the Adoption of Services 491

    Updating the Root Component and Template 491

    Updating the Child Components 492

Summary 494

Chapter 20: Using Service Providers **495**

Preparing the Example Project 496

Using Service Providers 498

    Using the Class Provider 500

    Using the Value Provider 508

    Using the Factory Provider 510

    Using the Existing Service Provider 513

Using Local Providers 514

    Understanding the Limitations of Single Service Objects 514

    Creating Local Providers in a Component 515

    Understanding the Provider Alternatives 517

    Controlling Dependency Resolution 522

Summary 524

Chapter 21: Using and Creating Modules **525**

Preparing the Example Project 526

Understanding the Root Module 528

    Understanding the imports Property 530

    Understanding the declarations Property 530

    Understanding the providers Property 531

    Understanding the bootstrap Property 531

Creating Feature Modules 533

    Creating a Model Module 535

    Creating a Utility Feature Module 540

    Creating a Feature Module with Components 545

Summary 550

■Part III: Advanced Angular Features 551

■Chapter 22: Creating the Example Project 553

Starting the Example Project 553

Adding and Configuring the Bootstrap CSS Package 553

Creating the Project Structure 554

Creating the Model Module 554

Creating the Product Data Type 554

Creating the Data Source and Repository 554

Completing the Model Module 556

Creating the Core Module 557

Creating the Shared State Service 557

Creating the Table Component 557

Creating the Form Component 559

Completing the Core Module 561

Creating the Messages Module 562

Creating the Message Model and Service 562

Creating the Component and Template 563

Completing the Message Module 563

Completing the Project 564

Summary 566

■Chapter 23: Using Reactive Extensions 567

Preparing the Example Project 568

Understanding the Problem 569

Solving the Problem with Reactive Extensions 571

Understanding Observables 572

Understanding Observers 574

Understanding Subjects 575

Using the Async Pipe 577

Using the Async Pipe with Custom Pipes 578

Scaling Up Application Feature Modules 580

Going Beyond the Basics 582

    Filtering Events 583

    Transforming Events 584

    Receiving Only Distinct Events 587

    Taking and Skipping Events 589

Summary 591

■Chapter 24: Making Asynchronous HTTP Requests 593

Preparing the Example Project 594

    Configuring the Model Feature Module 595

    Creating the Data File 595

    Updating the Form Component 596

    Running the Example Project 596

Understanding RESTful Web Services 597

Replacing the Static Data Source 598

    Creating the New Data Source Service 598

    Configuring the Data Source 600

    Using the REST Data Source 601

    Saving and Deleting Data 603

Consolidating HTTP Requests 606

Making Cross-Origin Requests 607

    Using JSONP Requests 608

Configuring Request Headers 610

Handling Errors 613

    Generating User-Ready Messages 614

    Handling the Errors 615

Summary 617

▓Chapter 25: Routing and Navigation: Part 1 619

Preparing the Example Project 620

Getting Started with Routing 622

Creating a Routing Configuration 623

Creating the Routing Component 625

Updating the Root Module 625

Completing the Configuration 626

Adding Navigation Links 627

Understanding the Effect of Routing 630

Completing the Routing Implementation 632

Handling Route Changes in Components 632

Using Route Parameters 635

Navigating in Code 641

Receiving Navigation Events 643

Removing the Event Bindings and Supporting Code 645

Summary 648

▓Chapter 26: Routing and Navigation: Part 2 649

Preparing the Example Project 649

Adding Components to the Project 653

Using Wildcards and Redirections 656

Using Wildcards in Routes 656

Using Redirections in Routes 659

Navigating Within a Component 661

Responding to Ongoing Routing Changes 662

Styling Links for Active Routes 664

Fixing the All Button 668

Creating Child Routes 669

Creating the Child Route Outlet 670

Accessing Parameters from Child Routes 673

Summary 676

■Chapter 27: Routing and Navigation: Part 3 677

Preparing the Example Project 677

Guarding Routes 679

Delaying Navigation with a Resolver 680

Preventing Navigation with Guards 687

Loading Feature Modules Dynamically 700

Creating a Simple Feature Module 701

Loading the Module Dynamically 702

Guarding Dynamic Modules 705

Targeting Named Outlets 708

Creating Additional Outlet Elements 709

Navigating When Using Multiple Outlets 711

Summary 713

■Chapter 28: Using Animation 715

Preparing the Example Project 716

Disabling the HTTP Delay 716

Simplifying the Table Template and Routing Configuration 717

Getting Started with Angular Animation 719

Enabling the Animation Module 720

Creating the Animation 720

Applying the Animation 724

Testing the Animation Effect 727

Understanding the Built-in Animation States 729

Understanding Element Transitions 730

Creating Transitions for the Built-in States 730

Controlling Transition Animations 732

Understanding Animation Style Groups 737

Defining Common Styles in Reusable Groups 738

Using Element Transformations 739

Applying CSS Framework Styles 741

Summary 743

■**Chapter 29: Angular Unit Testing**..**745**

Preparing the Example Project..746

Running a Simple Unit Test 748

Working with Jasmine...749

Testing an Angular Component 751

Working with the TestBed Class 751

Testing Data Bindings..755

Testing a Component with an External Template..758

Testing Component Events 760

Testing Output Properties 762

Testing Input Properties...764

Testing with Asynchronous Operations..766

Testing an Angular Directive..768

Summary...770

Index...**771**

About the Author

Adam Freeman is an experienced IT professional who has held senior positions in a range of companies, most recently serving as chief technology officer and chief operating officer of a global bank. Now retired, he spends his time writing and long-distance running.

About the Technical Reviewer

Fabio Claudio Ferracchiati is a senior consultant and a senior analyst/developer using Microsoft technologies. He works for BluArancio (`www.bluarancio.com`). He is a Microsoft Certified Solution Developer for .NET, a Microsoft Certified Application Developer for .NET, a Microsoft Certified Professional, and a prolific author and technical reviewer. Over the past ten years, he's written articles for Italian and international magazines and coauthored more than ten books on a variety of computer topics.

Getting Started with Angular

CHAPTER 1

■ ■ ■

Getting Ready

Angular taps into some of the best aspects of server-side development and uses them to enhance HTML in the browser, creating a foundation that makes building rich applications simpler and easier. Angular applications are built around a design pattern called *Model-View-Controller* (MVC), which places an emphasis on creating applications that are

- *Extendable*: It is easy to figure out how even a complex Angular app works once you understand the basics—and that means you can easily enhance applications to create new and useful features for your users.

- *Maintainable*: Angular apps are easy to debug and fix, which means that long-term maintenance is simplified.

- *Testable*: Angular has good support for unit and end-to-end testing, meaning that you can find and fix defects before your users do.

- *Standardized*: Angular builds on the innate capabilities of the web browser without getting in your way, allowing you to create standards-compliant web apps that take advantage of the latest features (such as HTML5 APIs) and popular tools and frameworks.

Angular is an open source JavaScript library that is sponsored and maintained by Google. It has been used in some of the largest and most complex web apps around. In this book, I show you everything you need to know to get the benefits of Angular in your own projects.

What Do You Need to Know?

Before reading this book, you should be familiar with the basics of web development, have an understanding of how HTML and CSS work, and have a working knowledge of JavaScript. If you are a little hazy on some of these details, I provide refreshers for the HTML, CSS, and JavaScript I use in this book in Chapters 4, 5, and 6. You won't find a comprehensive reference for HTML elements and CSS properties, though, because there just isn't the space in a book about Angular to cover all of HTML.

© Adam Freeman 2018
A. Freeman, *Pro Angular 6*, https://doi.org/10.1007/978-1-4842-3649-9_1

3

What Is the Structure of This Book?

This book is split into three parts, each of which covers a set of related topics.

Part 1: Getting Started with Angular

Part 1 of this book provides the information you need to get ready for the rest of the book. It includes this chapter and primers/refreshers for key technologies, including HTML, CSS, and TypeScript, which is a superset of JavaScript used in Angular development. I also show you how to build your first Angular application and take you through the process of building a more realistic application, called SportsStore.

Part 2: Angular in Detail

Part 2 of this book takes you through the building blocks provided by Angular for creating applications, working through each of them in turn. Angular includes a lot of built-in functionality, which I describe in depth, and provides endless customization options, all of which I demonstrate.

Part 3: Advanced Angular Features

Part 3 of this book explains how advanced features can be used to create more complex and scalable applications. I demonstrate how to make asynchronous HTTP requests in an Angular application, how to use URL routing to navigate around an application, and how to animate HTML elements when the state of the application changes.

Are There Lots of Examples?

There are *loads* of examples. The best way to learn Angular is by example, and I have packed as many of them as I can into this book. To maximize the number of examples in this book, I have adopted a simple convention to avoid listing the contents of files over and over again. The first time I use a file in a chapter, I'll list the complete contents, just as I have in Listing 1-1. I include the name of the file in the listing's header and the folder in which you should create it. When I make changes to the code, I show the altered statements in bold.

Listing 1-1. A Complete Example Document

```
import { NgModule } from "@angular/core";
import { BrowserModule } from "@angular/platform-browser";
import { ProductComponent } from "./component";
import { FormsModule, ReactiveFormsModule } from "@angular/forms";
import { PaAttrDirective } from "./attr.directive";

@NgModule({
    imports: [BrowserModule, FormsModule, ReactiveFormsModule],
    declarations: [ProductComponent, PaAttrDirective],
    bootstrap: [ProductComponent]
})
export class AppModule { }
```

This listing is taken from Chapter 15. Don't worry about what it does; just be aware that this is a complete listing, which shows the entire contents of the file. When I make a series of changes to the same file or when I make a small change to a large file, I show you just the elements that change, to create a *partial listing*. You can spot a partial listing because it starts and ends with an ellipsis (. . .), as shown in Listing 1-2.

Listing 1-2. A Partial Listing

```
...
<table class="table table-sm table-bordered table-striped">
    <tr><th></th><th>Name</th><th>Category</th><th>Price</th></tr>
    <tr *ngFor="let item of getProducts(); let i = index" pa-attr>
        <td>{{i + 1}}</td>
        <td>{{item.name}}</td>
        <td pa-attr pa-attr-class="bg-warning">{{item.category}}</td>
        <td pa-attr pa-attr-class="bg-info">{{item.price}}</td>
    </tr>
</table>
...
```

Listing 1-2 is a later listing from Chapter 15. You can see that just the body element, and its content, is shown and that I have highlighted a number of statements. This is how I draw your attention to the part of the listing that has changed or emphasize the part of an example that shows the feature or technique I am describing. In some cases, I need to make changes to different parts of the same file, in which case I omit some elements or statements for brevity, as shown in Listing 1-3.

Listing 1-3. Omitting Statements for Brevity

```
import { ApplicationRef, Component } from "@angular/core";
import { Model } from "./repository.model";
import { Product } from "./product.model";
import { ProductFormGroup } from "./form.model";

@Component({
    selector: "app",
    templateUrl: "app/template.html"
})
export class ProductComponent {
    model: Model = new Model();
    form: ProductFormGroup = new ProductFormGroup();

    // ...other members omitted for brevity...

    showTable: boolean = true;
}
```

This convention lets me pack in more examples, but it does mean it can be hard to locate a specific technique. To this end, all of the chapters in which I describe Angular features in Parts 2 and 3 begin with a summary table that describes the techniques contained in the chapter and the listings that demonstrate how they are used.

Where Can You Get the Example Code?

You can download the example projects for all the chapters in this book from `https://github.com/Apress/pro-angular-6`. The download is available without charge and includes all of the supporting resources that are required to re-create the examples without having to type them in. You don't have to download the code, but it is the easiest way of experimenting with the examples.

How Do You Set Up Your Development Environment?

Chapter 2 introduces Angular by creating a simple application, and, as part of that process, I tell you how to create a development environment for working with Angular.

Contacting the Author

If you have problems making the examples in this chapter work or if you find a problem with the book, then you can e-mail me at `adam@adam-freeman.com`, and I will try my best to help.

Summary

In this chapter, I outlined the content and structure of this book. The best way to learn Angular development is by example, so in the next chapter, I jump right in and show you how to set up your development environment and use it to create your first Angular application.

CHAPTER 2

■ ■ ■

Your First Angular App

The best way to get started with Angular is to dive in and create a web application. In this chapter, I show you how to set up your development environment and take you through the process of creating a basic application, starting with a static mock-up of the functionality and applying Angular features to create a dynamic web application, albeit a simple one. In Chapters 7–10, I show you how to create a more complex and realistic Angular application, but for now, a simple example will suffice to demonstrate the major components of an Angular app and set the scene for the other chapters in this part of the book.

Don't worry if you don't follow everything that happens in this chapter. Angular has a steep learning curve, so the purpose of this chapter is just to introduce the basic flow of Angular development and give you a sense of how things fit together. It won't all make sense right now, but by the time you have finished reading this book, you will understand every step I take in this chapter and much more besides.

Preparing the Development Environment

There is some preparation required for Angular development. In the sections that follow, I explain how to get set up and ready to create your first project. There is wide support for Angular in popular development tools, and you can pick your favorites.

Installing Node.js

Many of the tools used for Angular development rely on Node.js—also known as Node—which was created in 2009 as a simple and efficient runtime for server-side applications written in JavaScript. Node.js is based on the JavaScript engine used in the Chrome browser and provides an API for executing JavaScript code outside of the browser environment.

Node.js has enjoyed success as an application server, but for this book, it is interesting because it has provided the foundation for a new generation of cross-platform development and build tools. Some smart design decisions by the Node.js team and the cross-platform support provided by the Chrome JavaScript runtime have created an opportunity that has been seized upon by enthusiastic tool writers. In short, Node.js has become essential for web application development.

It is important that you download the same version of Node.js that I use throughout this book. Although Node.js is relatively stable, there are still breaking API changes from time to time that may stop the examples I include in the chapters from working.

The version I have used is 8.11.3, which is the current Long-Term Support release at the time of writing. There may be a later version available by the time you read this, but you should stick to the 8.11.3 release for the examples in this book. A complete set of 8.11.3 releases, with installers for Windows and macOS and binary packages for other platforms, is available at `https://nodejs.org/dist/v8.11.3`.

© Adam Freeman 2018
A. Freeman, *Pro Angular 6*, https://doi.org/10.1007/978-1-4842-3649-9_2

When you install Node.js, make sure you select the option to add the Node.js executables to the path. When the installation is complete, run the following command:

```
node -v
```

If the installation has gone as it should, then you will see the following version number displayed:

```
v8.11.3
```

The Node.js installer includes the Node Package Manager (NPM), which is used to manage the packages in a project. Run the following command to ensure that NPM is working:

```
npm -v
```

If everything is working as it should, then you will see the following version number:

```
5.6.0
```

Installing the angular-cli Package

The angular-cli package has become the standard way to create and manage Angular projects during development. In the original version of this book, I demonstrated how to set up an Angular project from scratch, which is a lengthy and error-prone process that is simplified by angular-cli. To install angular-cli, open a new command prompt and run the following command:

```
npm install --global @angular/cli@6.0.8
```

Notice that there are two hyphens before the global argument. If you are using Linux or macOS, you may need to use sudo, like this:

```
sudo npm install --global @angular/cli@6.0.8
```

Installing Git

The Git revision control tool is required to manage some of the packages required for Angular development. If you are using Windows or macOS, then download and run the installer from https://git-scm.com/downloads. (On macOS, you may have to change your security settings to open the installer, which has not been signed by the developers.)

Git is already installed on most Linux distributions. If you want to install the latest version, then consult the installation instructions for your distribution at https://git-scm.com/download/linux. As an example, for Ubuntu, which is the Linux distribution I use, I used the following command:

```
sudo apt-get install git
```

Once you have completed the installation, open a new command prompt and run the following command to check that Git is installed and available:

```
git --version
```

This command prints out the version of the Git package that has been installed. At the time of writing, the latest version of Git for Windows and Linux is 2.17, and the latest version of Git for macOS is 2.16.3.

Installing an Editor

Angular development can be done with any programmer's editor, from which there is an endless number to choose. Some editors have enhanced support for working with Angular, including highlighting key terms and good tool integration. If you don't already have a preferred editor for web application development, then Table 2-1 describes some popular options for you to consider. I don't rely on any specific editor for this book, and you should use whichever editor you are comfortable working with.

Table 2-1. *Popular Angular-Enabled Editors*

Name	Description
Sublime Text	Sublime Text is a commercial cross-platform editor that has packages to support most programming languages, frameworks, and platforms. See `www.sublimetext.com` for details.
Atom	Atom is a free, open source, cross-platform editor that has a particular emphasis on customization and extensibility. See `atom.io` for details.
Brackets	Brackets is a free open source editor developed by Adobe. See `brackets.io` for details.
WebStorm	WebStorm is a paid-for cross-platform editor that integrates many tools so that you don't have to use the command line during development. See `www.jetbrains.com/webstorm` for details.
Visual Studio Code	Visual Studio Code is a free, open source, cross-platform editor from Microsoft, with an emphasis on extensibility. See `code.visualstudio.com` for details.
Visual Studio	Visual Studio is Microsoft's flagship developer tool. There are free and commercial editions available, and it comes with a wide range of additional tools that integrate into the Microsoft ecosystem.

When choosing an editor, one of the most important considerations is the ability to filter the content of the project so that you can focus on a subset of the files. There can be a lot of files in an Angular project, and many have similar names, so being able to find and edit the right file is essential. Editors make this possible in different ways, either by presenting a list of the files that are open for editing or by providing the ability to exclude files with specific extensions.

Installing a Browser

The final choice to make is the browser that you will use to check your work during development. All the current-generation browsers have good developer support and work well with Angular. I have used Google Chrome throughout this book, and this is the browser I recommend you use as well.

Creating and Preparing the Project

Once you have Node.js, `angular-cli`, an editor, and a browser, you have enough of a foundation to start the development process.

Creating the Project

To create the project, select a convenient location and use a command prompt to run the following command to create a new project called `todo`:

```
ng new todo
```

The ng command is provided by the `angular-cli` package, and `ng new` sets up a new project. The installation process creates a folder called `todo` that contains all of the configuration files that are needed to start Angular development, some placeholder files to start development, and the NPM packages required for developing, running, and deploying Angular applications. (There are a large number of NPM packages, which means that project creation can take a while.)

■ **Tip** You can download the example project for this chapter—and for all the other chapters in this book—from `https://github.com/Apress/pro-angular-6`.

Adding the Bootstrap CSS Package

The ng new command creates a project with almost everything that is required for this chapter. The exception is the Bootstrap CSS package, which I use to style the HTML content throughout this book. Run the following commands to navigate to the `todo` folder created by the ng new command and add the Bootstrap package to the project:

```
cd todo
npm install bootstrap@4.1.1
```

To configure the Angular development tools to use the Bootstrap CSS file, add the entry shown in Listing 2-1 to the `styles` section of the `angular.json` file, which was added to the `todo` folder by the ng new command when the project was created.

Listing 2-1. Configuring CSS in the angular.json File in the todo Folder

```
...
{
  "$schema": "./node_modules/@angular/cli/lib/config/schema.json",
  "version": 1,
  "newProjectRoot": "projects",
  "projects": {
    "todo": {
      "root": "",
      "sourceRoot": "src",
```

```
"projectType": "application",
"prefix": "app",
"schematics": {},
"architect": {
  "build": {
    "builder": "@angular-devkit/build-angular:browser",
    "options": {
      "outputPath": "dist/todo",
      "index": "src/index.html",
      "main": "src/main.ts",
      "polyfills": "src/polyfills.ts",
      "tsConfig": "src/tsconfig.app.json",
      "assets": [
        "src/favicon.ico",
        "src/assets"
      ],
      "styles": [
        "src/styles.css",
        "node_modules/bootstrap/dist/css/bootstrap.min.css"
      ],
      "scripts": []
    },
...
```

As I explain in Chapter 11, the angular.json file is used to configure the project tools, and the statement shown in the listing incorporates the Bootstrap CSS file into the project so that it will be included in the content sent to the browser.

Starting the Development Tools

Everything is in place, so it is time to test the Angular development tools. Run the following command from the todo folder:

```
ng serve --port 3000 --open
```

This command starts the Angular development tools, which go through an initial build process to prepare the application for the development session. This process takes a moment and will generate output similar to this:

```
** Angular Live Development Server is listening on localhost:3000, open your browser on
http://localhost:3000/ **

Hash: ebb64e6046efff317389
Time: 6767ms
chunk {main} main.js, main.js.map (main) 10.8 kB [initial] [rendered]
chunk {polyfills} polyfills.js, polyfills.js.map (polyfills) 227 kB [initial] [rendered]
chunk {runtime} runtime.js, runtime.js.map (runtime) 5.22 kB [entry] [rendered]
chunk {styles} styles.js, styles.js.map (styles) 15.7 kB [initial] [rendered]
chunk {vendor} vendor.js, vendor.js.map (vendor) 3.06 MB [initial] [rendered]
[wdm]: Compiled successfully.
```

Don't worry if you see slightly different output, just as long as you see the "compiled successfully" message once the preparations are complete.

The development tools in the project include an HTTP server. Once the build process is completed, a new browser window will open, and you will see the content shown in Figure 2-1, which shows the placeholder content added to the project when it was created.

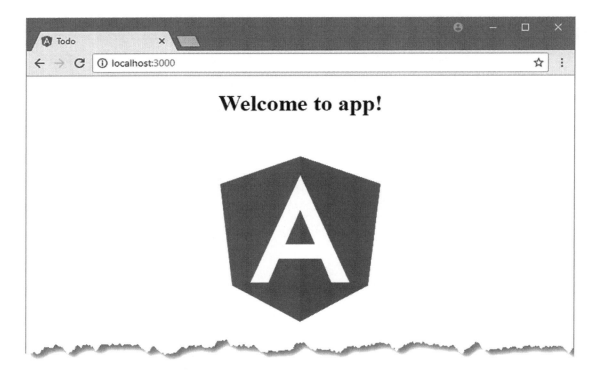

Figure 2-1. *The placeholder HTML content*

Editing the HTML File

I am going to start by removing the placeholder content added to the project when it was created so that I can start with an HTML file that contains static content that I will later enhance using Angular. Edit the index.html file in the todo/src folder to replace the contents with those shown in Listing 2-2.

Listing 2-2. The Contents of the index.html File in the src Folder

```
<!DOCTYPE html>
<html>
<head>
  <title>ToDo</title>
  <meta charset="utf-8" />
</head>
<body class="m-1 p-1">
```

```
<h3 class="bg-primary text-white p-3">Adam's To Do List</h3>

<div class="my-1">
  <input class="form-control" />
  <button class="btn btn-primary mt-1">Add</button>
</div>

<table class="table table-striped table-bordered">
  <thead>
    <tr>
      <th>Description</th>
      <th>Done</th>
    </tr>
  </thead>
  <tbody>
    <tr><td>Buy Flowers</td><td>No</td></tr>
    <tr><td>Get Shoes</td><td>No</td></tr>
    <tr><td>Collect Tickets</td><td>Yes</td></tr>
    <tr><td>Call Joe</td><td>No</td></tr>
  </tbody>
</table>
</body>
</html>
```

The Angular development tools include a feature that automatically updates the browser when there is a change in the project. As soon as you save the index.html file, the server will detect the change and update the application, reflecting the new content, as shown in Figure 2-2.

■ **Tip** When you are making changes to a series of files, there may be times when the browser won't be able to load and execute the example application, especially in later chapters where the examples are more complex. For the most part, the development HTTP server will trigger a reload in the browser, and everything will be fine, but if it gets stuck, you may have to manually reload the browser to get going again.

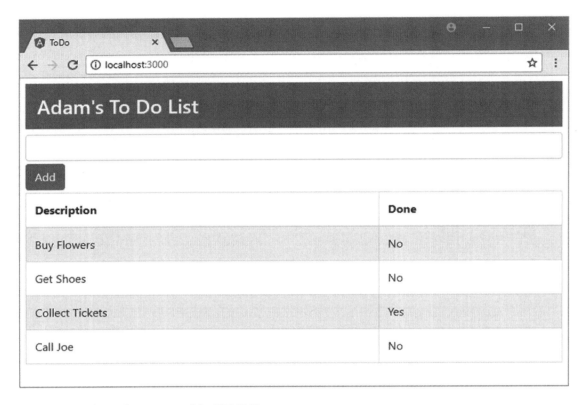

Figure 2-2. *Editing the contents of the HTML file*

The HTML elements in the index.html file show how the simple Angular application I create in this chapter will look. The key elements are a banner with the user's name, an input element and an Add button that add a new to-do item to the list, and a table that contains all the to-do items and indicates whether they have been completed.

I used the excellent Bootstrap CSS framework to style HTML content. Bootstrap is applied by assigning elements to classes, like this:

```
...
<h3 class="bg-primary text-white p-3">Adam's To Do List</h3>
...
```

This h3 element has been assigned to three classes. The bg-primary class sets the background color of the element to the primary color of the Bootstrap theme. There are other theme colors available, including bg-secondary, bg-info, and bg-danger. The p-1 class adds a fixed amount of padding to all edges of the element, ensuring that the text has some space around it. The text-white class sets the text color to white, which increases the contrast with the background color. You will see HTML elements added to these classes and others throughout this book as I apply Bootstrap, and I provide a brief overview of the classes that I use most in Chapter 4.

In the next section, I'll remove the HTML from the file, cut it up into smaller pieces, and use it to create a simple Angular application.

Adding Angular Features to the Project

The static HTML in the index.html file acts as a placeholder for the basic application. The user should be able to see the list of to-do items, check off items that are complete, and create new items. In the sections that follow, I add basic Angular features to the project to bring the to-do application to life. To keep the application simple, I assume that there is only one user and that I don't have to worry about preserving the state of the data in the application, which means that changes to the to-do list will be lost if the browser window is closed or reloaded. (Later examples, including the SportsStore application developed in Chapters 7–10, demonstrate persistent data storage.)

Preparing the HTML File

The first step toward adding Angular to the application is to prepare the index.html file, as shown in Listing 2-3.

Listing 2-3. Preparing for Angular in the index.html File in the src Folder

```
<!DOCTYPE html>
<html>
<head>
    <title>ToDo</title>
    <meta charset="utf-8" />
</head>
<body class="m-1">
    <todo-app>Angular placeholder</todo-app>
</body>
</html>
```

This listing replaces the content of the body element with a todo-app element. There is no todo-app element in the HTML specification, and the browser will ignore it when parsing the HTML file, but this element will be the entry point into the world of Angular and will be replaced with my application content. When you save the index.html file, the browser will reload the file and show the placeholder message, as shown in Figure 2-3.

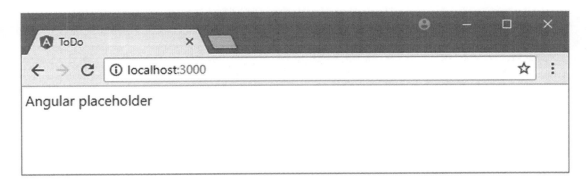

Figure 2-3. *Preparing the HTML file*

Creating a Data Model

When I created the static mock-up of the application, the data was distributed across all the HTML elements. The user's name is contained in the header, like this:

```
...
<h3 class="bg-primary text-white p-3">Adam's To Do List</h3>
...
```

The details of the to-do items are contained within td elements in the table, like this:

```
...
<tr><td>Buy Flowers</td><td>No</td></tr>
...
```

The next task is to pull all the data together to create a data model. Separating the data from the way it is presented to the user is one of the key ideas in the MVC pattern, as I explain in Chapter 3.

■ **Tip**   I am simplifying here. The model can also contain the logic required to create, load, store, and modify data objects. In an Angular app, this logic is often at the server and is accessed by a web service. See Chapter 3 for further details and Chapter 24 for examples.

Angular applications are typically written in TypeScript. I introduce TypeScript in Chapter 6 and explain how it works and why it is useful. TypeScript is a superscript of JavaScript, but one of its main advantages is that it lets you write code using the latest JavaScript language specification with features that are not yet supported in all of the browsers that can run Angular applications. One of the packages that angular-cli added to the project in the previous section was the TypeScript compiler, which is set up to generate browser-friendly JavaScript files automatically when a change to a TypeScript file is detected.

To create a data model for the application, I added a file called model.ts to the todo/src/app folder (TypeScript files have the .ts extension) and added the code shown in Listing 2-4.

Listing 2-4. The Contents of the model.ts File in the src/app Folder

```
var model = {
    user: "Adam",
    items: [{ action: "Buy Flowers", done: false },
    { action: "Get Shoes", done: false },
    { action: "Collect Tickets", done: true },
    { action: "Call Joe", done: false }]
};
```

One of the most important features of TypeScript is that you can just write "normal" JavaScript code as though you were targeting the browser directly. In Listing 2-4, I used the JavaScript object literal syntax to assign a value to a global variable called model. The data model object has a user property, which provides the name of the application's user, and an items property, which is set to an array of objects with action and done properties, each of which represents a task in the to-do list.

This is the most important aspect of using TypeScript: you don't have to use the features it provides, and you can write entire Angular applications using just the JavaScript features that are supported by all browsers, like the code in Listing 2-4.

But part of the value of TypeScript is that it converts code that uses the latest JavaScript language features into code that will run anywhere, even in browsers that don't support those features. Listing 2-5 shows the data model rewritten to use JavaScript features that were added in the ECMAScript 6 standard (known as ES6).

Listing 2-5. Using ES6 Features in the model.ts File in the src/app Folder

```
export class Model {
    user;
    items;

    constructor() {
        this.user = "Adam";
        this.items = [new TodoItem("Buy Flowers", false),
                      new TodoItem("Get Shoes", false),
                      new TodoItem("Collect Tickets", false),
                      new TodoItem("Call Joe", false)]
    }
}

export class TodoItem {
    action;
    done;

    constructor(action, done) {
        this.action = action;
        this.done = done;
    }
}
```

This is still standard JavaScript code, but the class keyword was introduced in a later version of the language than most web application developers are familiar with because it is not supported by older browsers. The class keyword is used to define types that can be instantiated with the new keyword to create objects that have well-defined data and behavior.

Many of the features added in recent versions of the JavaScript language are syntactic sugar to help programmers avoid some of the most common JavaScript pitfalls, such as the unusual type system. The class keyword doesn't change the way that JavaScript handles types; it just makes it more familiar and easier to use for programmers experienced in other languages, such as C# or Java. I like the JavaScript type system, which is dynamic and expressive, but I find working with classes more predictable and less error-prone, and they simplify working with Angular, which has been designed around the latest JavaScript features.

■ **Tip** Don't worry if you are not familiar with the features that have been added in recent versions of the JavaScript specification. Chapters 5 and 6 provide a primer for writing JavaScript using the features that make Angular easier to work with, and Chapter 6 also describes some useful TypeScript-specific features.

The export keyword relates to JavaScript modules. When using modules, each TypeScript or JavaScript file is considered to be a self-contained unit of functionality, and the export keyword is used to identify data or types that you want to use elsewhere in the application. JavaScript modules are used to manage the dependencies that arise between files in a project and avoid having to manually manage a complex set of script elements in the HTML file. See Chapter 7 for details of how modules work.

Preparing the Template

I need a way to display the data values in the model to the user. In Angular, this is done using a *template*, which is a fragment of HTML that contains instructions that are performed by Angular. The angular-cli setup for the project created a template file called app.component.html in the src/app folder. I edited this file and added the markup shown in Listing 2-6 to replace the placeholder content. The name of the file follows the standard Angular naming conventions, which I explain later.

Listing 2-6. The Contents of the app.component.html File in the src/app Folder

```
<h3 class="bg-primary p-1 text-white">{{ getName() }}'s To Do List</h3>
```

I'll add more elements to this file shortly, but a single h3 element is enough to get started. Including a data value in a template is done using double braces—{{ and }}—and Angular evaluates whatever you put between the double braces to get the value to display.

The {{ and }} characters are an example of a *data binding*, which means they create a relationship between the template and a data value. Data bindings are an important Angular feature, and you will see more of them in this chapter as I add features to the example application (and I describe them in detail in Part 2 of this book). In this case, the data binding tells Angular to invoke a function called getName and use the result as the contents of the h3 element. The getName function doesn't exist anywhere in the application at the moment, but I'll create it in the next section.

Preparing the Component

An Angular *component* is responsible for managing a template and providing it with the data and logic it needs. If that seems like a broad statement, it is because components are the part of an Angular application that does most of the heavy lifting. As a consequence, they can be used for all sorts of tasks.

At the moment, I have a data model that contains a user property with the name to display, and I have a template that displays the name by invoking a getName function. What I need is a component to act as the bridge between them. The angular-cli setup created a placeholder component file called app.component.ts to the todo/src/app folder, which I edited to replace the original content with the code shown in Listing 2-7.

Listing 2-7. The Contents of the app.component.ts File in the src/app Folder

```
import { Component } from "@angular/core";
import { Model } from "./model";

@Component({
    selector: "todo-app",
    templateUrl: "app.component.html"
})
export class AppComponent {
    model = new Model();

    getName() {
        return this.model.user;
    }
}
```

This is still JavaScript, but it relies on features that you may not have encountered before but that underpin Angular development. The code in the listing can be broken into three main sections, as described in the following sections.

Understanding the Imports

The `import` keyword is the counterpart to the `export` keyword and is used to declare a dependency on the contents of a JavaScript module. The `import` keyword is used twice in Listing 2-7, as shown here:

```
...
import { Component } from "@angular/core";
import { Model } from "./model";
...
```

The first `import` statement is used in the Listing to load the `@angular/core` module, which contains the key Angular functionality, including support for components. When working with modules, the `import` statement specifies the types that are imported between curly braces. In this case, the `import` statement is used to load the `Component` type from the module. The `@angular/core` module contains many classes that have been packaged together so that the browser can load them all in a single JavaScript file.

The second `import` statement is used to load the `Model` class from a file in the project. The target for this kind of import starts with `./`, which indicates that the module is defined relative to the current file.

Notice that neither `import` statement includes a file extension. This is because the relationship between the target of an import statement and the file that is loaded by the browser is managed by a *module loader*, which I configure in the "Putting the Application Together" section.

Understanding the Decorator

The oddest-looking part of the code in the listing is this:

```
...
@Component({
    selector: "todo-app",
    templateUrl: "app.component.html"
})
...
```

This is an example of a *decorator*, which provides metadata about a class. This is the `@Component` decorator, and, as its name suggests, it tells Angular that this is a component. The decorator provides configuration information through its properties, which in the case of `@Component` includes properties called `selector` and `templateUrl`.

The `selector` property specifies a CSS selector that matches the HTML element to which the component will be applied: in this case, I have specified the `todo-app` element, which I added to the `index.html` file in Listing 2-3. When an Angular application starts, Angular scans the HTML in the current document and looks for elements that correspond to components. It will find the `todo-app` element and know that it should be placed under the control of this component.

The `templateUrl` property is to specify the component's template, which is the `app.component.html` file for this component. In Part 2, I describe the other properties that can be used with the `@Component` decorator and the other decorators that Angular supports.

Understanding the Class

The final part of the listing defines a class that Angular can instantiate to create the component.

```
...
export class AppComponent {
    model = new Model();

    getName() {
        return this.model.user;
    }
}
...
```

These statements define a class called AppComponent that has a model property and a getName function, which provide the functionality required to support the data binding in the template from Listing 2-6.

When a new instance of the AppComponent class is created, the model property will be set to a new instance of the Model class defined in Listing 2-5. The getName function returns the value of the user property defined by the Model object.

Putting the Application Together

I have the three key pieces of functionality required to build a simple Angular application: a model, a template, and a component. When you saved the change to the app.component.ts file, there was enough functionality in place to bring the three pieces together and display the output shown in Figure 2-4.

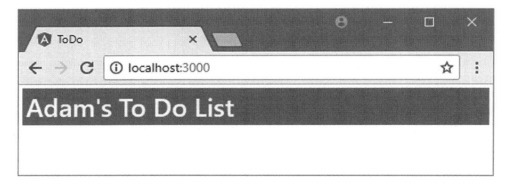

Figure 2-4. *Simple Angular functionality in the example application*

One advantage of using angular-cli to create a project is that you don't have to worry about creating the basic files required by an Angular application. The drawback is that skipping over these files means you will miss out on some important details that are worth exploring.

Angular applications require a *module*. Through an unfortunate naming choice, there are two types of module used in Angular development. A *JavaScript module* is a file that contains JavaScript functionality that is used through the import keyword, which I describe in Chapter 6. The other type of module is an *Angular module*, which is used to describe an application or a group of related features. And just to complicate matters, every application has a *root module*, which is the Angular module that provides Angular with the information that it needs to start the application.

When angular-cli set up the project, it created a file called app.module.ts, which is the conventional file name for the root module, in the todo/src/app folder and added the code shown in Listing 2-8.

Listing 2-8. The Default Contents of the app.module.ts File in the src/app Folder

```
import { BrowserModule } from '@angular/platform-browser';
import { NgModule } from '@angular/core';
import { AppComponent } from './app.component';

@NgModule({
    declarations: [AppComponent],
    imports: [BrowserModule],
    providers: [],
    bootstrap: [AppComponent]
})
export class AppModule { }
```

The purpose of the Angular module is to provide configuration information through the properties defined by the @NgModule decorator. I explain how Angular modules work in detail in Chapter 21, but for the moment, it is enough to know that the decorator's imports property tells Angular that the application depends on features required to run an application in the browser and that the declarations and bootstrap properties tell Angular about the components in the application and which one should be used to start the application (there is only one component in this simple example application, which is why it is the only value for both properties).

To create a to-do application, I need to use the Angular features for working with form elements, which are defined in an Angular module called @angular/forms. To enable these features, make the changes shown in Listing 2-9 to the app.module.ts file.

Listing 2-9. Enabling Forms Supports in the app.module.ts File in the src/app Folder

```
import { BrowserModule } from '@angular/platform-browser';
import { NgModule } from '@angular/core';
import { FormsModule } from "@angular/forms";
import { AppComponent } from './app.component';

@NgModule({
  declarations: [AppComponent],
  imports: [BrowserModule, FormsModule],
  providers: [],
  bootstrap: [AppComponent]
})
export class AppModule { }
```

Angular applications also need a *bootstrap file*, which contains the code required to start the application. The bootstrap file is called main.ts, and it is created in the todo/src folder with the code shown in Listing 2-10. No changes are required to the main.ts file for this chapter.

Listing 2-10. The Contents of the main.ts File in the src Folder

```
import { enableProdMode } from '@angular/core';
import { platformBrowserDynamic } from '@angular/platform-browser-dynamic';

import { AppModule } from './app/app.module';
import { environment } from './environments/environment';

if (environment.production) {
  enableProdMode();
}

platformBrowserDynamic().bootstrapModule(AppModule)
  .catch(err => console.log(err));
```

Although this book focuses on applications that run in a web browser, Angular is intended to work in a range of environments. The code statements in the bootstrap file select the platform that will be used and load the root module, which is the entry point into the application.

■ **Tip**   Calling the `platformBrowserDynamic().bootstrapModule` method is for browser-based applications, which is what I focus on in this book. If you are working on different platforms, such as the Ionic mobile development framework, then you will have to use a different bootstrap method specific to the platform you are working with. The developers of each platform that supports Angular provide details of their platform-specific bootstrap method.

The browser executed the code in the bootstrap file, which fired up Angular, which in turn processed the HTML document and discovered the `todo-app` element. The `selector` property used to define the component matches the `todo-app` element, which allowed Angular to remove the placeholder content and replace it with the component's template, which was loaded automatically from the `app.component.html` file. The template was parsed; the {{ and }} data binding was discovered, and the expression it contains was evaluated, calling the `getName` method and displaying the result shown in the figure. It may not be that impressive, but it is a good start, and it provides a foundation on which to add more features.

■ **Tip**   In any Angular project, there is a period where you have to define the main parts of the application and plumb them together. During this period, it can feel like you are doing a lot of work for little return. This period of initial investment *will* ultimately pay off, I promise. You will see a larger example of this in Chapter 7 when I start to build a more complex and realistic Angular application; there is a lot of initial setup and configuration required, but then the features start to quickly snap into place.

Adding Features to the Example Application

Now that the basic structure of the application is in place, I can add the remaining features that I mocked up with static HTML at the start of the chapter. In the sections that follow, I add the table containing the list of to-do items and the `input` element and button for creating new items.

Adding the To-Do Table

Angular templates can do more than just display simple data values. I describe the full range of template features in Part 2, but for the example application, I am going to use the feature that allows a set of HTML elements to be added to the DOM for each object in an array. The array, in this case, is the set of to-do items in the data model. Listing 2-11 adds a method to the component that provides the template with the array of to-do items.

Listing 2-11. Adding a Method in the app.component.ts File in the src/app Folder

```
import { Component } from "@angular/core";
import { Model } from "./model";

@Component({
    selector: "todo-app",
    templateUrl: "app.component.html"
})
export class AppComponent {
    model = new Model();

    getName() {
        return this.model.user;
    }

    getTodoItems() {
        return this.model.items;
    }
}
```

The getTodoItems method returns the value of the items property from the Model object. Listing 2-12 updates the component's template to use the new method.

Listing 2-12. Displaying the To-Do Items in the app.component.html File in the src/app Folder

```
<h3 class="bg-primary p-1 text-white">{{ getName() }}'s To Do List</h3>

<table class="table table-striped table-bordered">
    <thead>
        <tr><th></th><th>Description</th><th>Done</th></tr>
    </thead>
    <tbody>
        <tr *ngFor="let item of getTodoItems(); let i = index">
            <td>{{ i + 1 }}</td>
            <td>{{ item.action }}</td>
            <td [ngSwitch]="item.done">
                <span *ngSwitchCase="true">Yes</span>
                <span *ngSwitchDefault>No</span>
            </td>
        </tr>
    </tbody>
</table>
```

The additions to the template rely on several different Angular features. The first is the `*ngFor` expression, which is used to repeat a region of content for each item in an array. This is an example of a *directive*, which I describe in Chapters 12–16 (directives are a big part of Angular development, which is why there they are described in several chapters). The `*ngFor` expression is applied to an attribute of an element, like this:

```
...
<tr *ngFor="let item of getTodoItems(); let i = index">
...
```

This expression tells Angular to treat the `tr` element to which it has been applied as a template that should be repeated for every object returned by the component's `getTodoItems` method. The `let item` part of the expression specifies that each object should be assigned to a variable called `item` so that it can be referred to within the template.

The `ngFor` expression also keeps track of the index of the current object in the array that is being processed, and this is assigned to a second variable called `i`.

```
...
<tr *ngFor="let item of getTodoItems(); let i = index">
...
```

The result is that the `tr` element and its contents will be duplicated and inserted into the HTML document for each object returned by the `getTodoItems` method; for each iteration, the current to-do object can be accessed through the variable called `item`, and the position of the object in the array can be accessed through the variable called `i`.

■ **Tip**   It is important to remember the * character when using *ngFor. I explain what it means in Chapter 16.

Within the `tr` template, there are two data bindings, which can be recognized by the {{ and }} characters, as follows:

```
...
<td>{{ i + 1 }}</td>
<td>{{ item.action }}</td>
...
```

These bindings refer to the variables that are created by the `*ngFor` expression. Bindings are not just used to refer to property and method names; they can also be used to perform simple JavaScript operations. You can see an example of this in the first binding, where I sum the `i` variable and 1.

■ **Tip**   For simple transformations, you can embed your JavaScript expressions directly in bindings like this, but for more complex operations, Angular has a feature called *pipes*, which I describe in Chapter 18.

The remaining template expressions in the tr template demonstrate how content can be generated selectively.

```
...
<td [ngSwitch]="item.done">
    <span *ngSwitchCase="true">Yes</span>
    <span *ngSwitchDefault>No</span>
</td>
...
```

The [ngSwitch] expression is a conditional statement that is used to insert different sets of elements into the document based on a specified value, which is the item.done property in this case. Nested within the td element are two span elements that have been annotated with *ngSwitchCase and *ngSwitchDefault and that are equivalent to the case and default keywords of a regular JavaScript switch block. I describe ngSwitch in detail in Chapter 13 (and what the square brackets mean in Chapter 12), but the result is that the first span element is added to the document when the value of the item.done property is true, and the second span element is added to the document when item.done is false. The result is that the true/false value of the item.done property is transformed into span elements containing either Yes or No. When you save the changes to the template, the browser will reload, and the table of to-do items will be displayed, as shown in Figure 2-5.

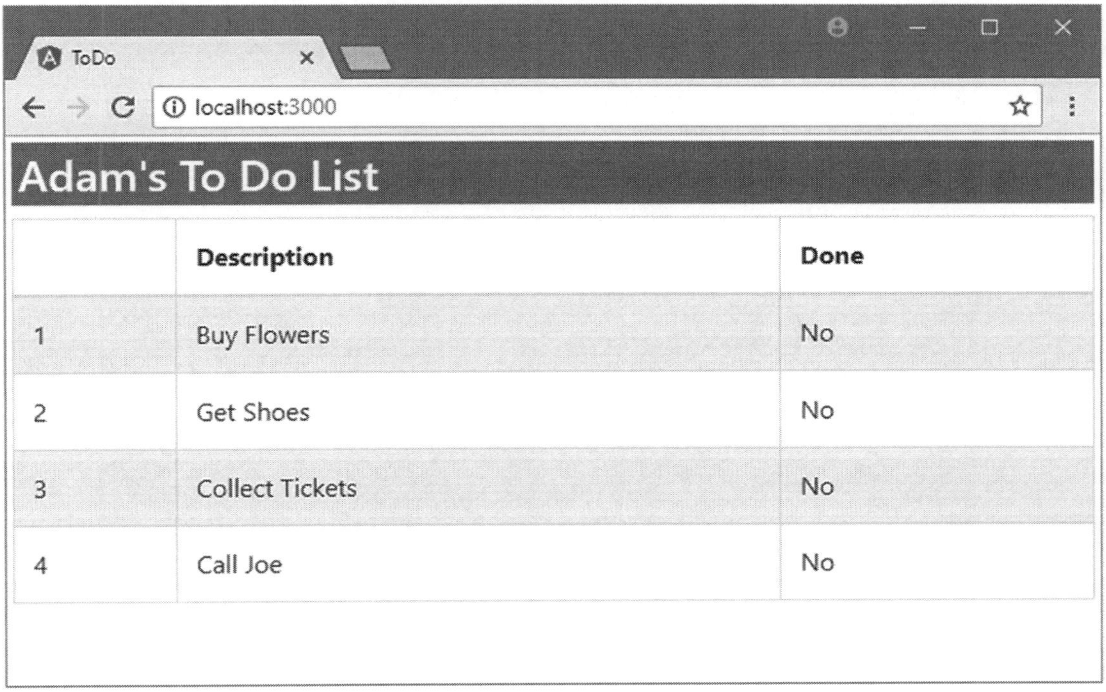

Figure 2-5. *Displaying the table of to-do items*

If you use the browser's F12 developer tools, you will be able to see the HTML content that the template has generated. (You can't do this looking at the page source, which just shows the HTML sent by the server and not the changes made by Angular using the DOM API.)

You can see how each to-do object in the model has produced a row in the table that is populated with the local item and i variables and how the switch expression shows Yes or No to indicate whether the task has been completed.

```
...
<tr>
    <td>2</td>
    <td>Get Shoes</td>
    <td><span>No</span></td>
</tr>
...
```

Creating a Two-Way Data Binding

At the moment, the template contains only *one-way data bindings*, which means they are used to display a data value but are unable to change it. Angular also supports *two-way data bindings*, which can be used to display a data value and change it, too. Two-way bindings are used with HTML form elements, and Listing 2-13 adds a checkbox input element to the template that will let users mark a to-do item as complete.

Listing 2-13. Adding a Two-Way Binding in the app.component.html File in the src/app Folder

```
<h3 class="bg-primary p-1 text-white">{{getName()}}'s To Do List</h3>

<table class="table table-striped table-bordered">
    <thead>
        <tr><th></th><th>Description</th><th>Done</th></tr>
    </thead>
    <tbody>
        <tr *ngFor="let item of getTodoItems(); let i = index">
            <td>{{i + 1}}</td>
            <td>{{item.action}}</td>
            <td><input type="checkbox" [(ngModel)]="item.done" /></td>
            <td [ngSwitch]="item.done">
                <span *ngSwitchCase="true">Yes</span>
                <span *ngSwitchDefault>No</span>
            </td>
        </tr>
    </tbody>
</table>
```

The ngModel template expression creates a two-way binding between a data value (the item.done property in this case) and a form element. When you save the changes to the template, you will see a new column that contains checkboxes appear in the table. The initial value of the checkbox is set using the item.done property, just like a regular one-way binding, but when the user toggles the checkbox, Angular responds by updating the specified model property.

To demonstrate how this works, I have left the column that contains the Yes/No display of the done property value generated using the ngSwitch expression in the template. When you toggle a checkbox, the corresponding Yes/No value changes as well, as illustrated in Figure 2-6.

Figure 2-6. *Changing a model value using a two-way data binding*

This reveals an important Angular feature: the data model is *live*. This means that data bindings—even one-way data bindings—are updated when the data model is changed. This simplifies web application development because it means you don't have to worry about ensuring that you display updates when the application state changes.

Filtering To-Do Items

The checkboxes allow the data model to be updated, and the next step is to remove to-do items once they have been marked as done. Listing 2-14 changes the component's getTodoItems method so that it filters out any items that have been completed.

Listing 2-14. Filtering To-Do Items in the app.component.ts File in the src/app Folder

```
import { Component } from "@angular/core";
import { Model } from "./model";

@Component({
    selector: "todo-app",
    templateUrl: "app.component.html"
})
export class AppComponent {
    model = new Model();

    getName() {
        return this.model.user;
    }

    getTodoItems() {
        return this.model.items.filter(item => !item.done);
    }
}
```

27

This is an example of a *lambda function*, also known as a *fat arrow function*, which is a more concise way of expressing a standard JavaScript function. The arrow in the lambda expressions is read as "goes to" such as "`item` goes to not `item.done`." Lambda expressions are a recent addition to the JavaScript language specification, and they provide an alternative to the conventional way of using functions as arguments like this:

```
...
return this.model.items.filter(function (item) { return !item.done });
...
```

Whichever way you choose to define the expression passed to the `filter` method, the result is that only incomplete to-do items are displayed. Since the data model is live and changes are reflected in data bindings immediately, checking the checkbox for an item removes it from view, as shown in Figure 2-7.

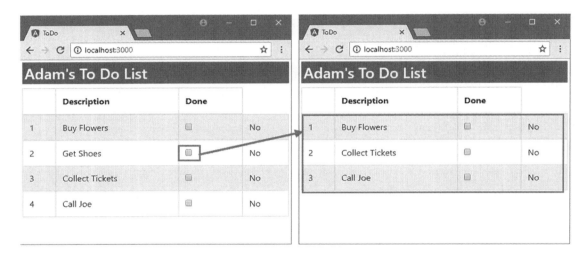

Figure 2-7. *Filtering the to-do items*

Adding To-Do Items

The next step is to build on the basic functionality to allow the user to create new to-do items and store them in the data model. Listing 2-15 adds new elements to the component's template.

Listing 2-15. Adding Elements in the app.component.html File in the src/app Folder

```
<h3 class="bg-primary p-1 text-white">{{getName()}}'s To Do List</h3>
<div class="my-1">
    <input class="form-control" #todoText />
    <button class="btn btn-primary mt-1" (click)="addItem(todoText.value)">
        Add
    </button>
</div>
<table class="table table-striped table-bordered">
    <thead>
        <tr><th></th><th>Description</th><th>Done</th><th></th></tr>
    </thead>
```

```
<tbody>
    <tr *ngFor="let item of getTodoItems(); let i = index">
        <td>{{i + 1}}</td>
        <td>{{item.action}}</td>
        <td><input type="checkbox" [(ngModel)]="item.done" /></td>
        <td [ngSwitch]="item.done">
            <span *ngSwitchCase="true">Yes</span>
            <span *ngSwitchDefault>No</span>
        </td>
    </tr>
</tbody>
</table>
```

The input element has an attribute whose name starts with the # character, which is used to define a variable to refer to the element in the template's data bindings. The variable is called todoText, and it is used by the binding that has been applied to the button element.

```
...
<button class="btn btn-primary mt-1" (click)="addItem(todoText.value)">
...
```

This is an example of an *event binding*, and it tells Angular to invoke a component method called addItem, using the value property of the input element as the method argument. Listing 2-16 implements the addItem method in the component.

■ **Tip** Don't worry about telling the bindings apart at the moment. I explain the different types of binding that Angular supports in Part 2 and the meaning of the different types of brackets or parentheses that each requires. They are not as complicated as they first appear, especially once you have seen how they fit into the rest of the Angular framework.

Listing 2-16. Adding a Method in the app.component.ts File in the src/app Folder

```
import { Component } from "@angular/core";
import { Model, TodoItem } from "./model";

@Component({
    selector: "todo-app",
    templateUrl: "app.component.html"
})
export class AppComponent {
    model = new Model();

    getName() {
        return this.model.user;
    }

    getTodoItems() {
        return this.model.items.filter(item => !item.done);
    }
```

```
addItem(newItem) {
    if (newItem != "") {
        this.model.items.push(new TodoItem(newItem, false));
    }
}
}
```

The import keyword can be used to import multiple classes from a module, and one of the import statements in the listing has been updated so that the TodoItem class can be used in the component. Within the component class, the addItem method receives the text sent by the event binding in the template and uses it to create a new TodoItem object and add it to the data model. The result of these changes is that you can create new to-do items by entering text in the input element and clicking the Add button, as shown in Figure 2-8.

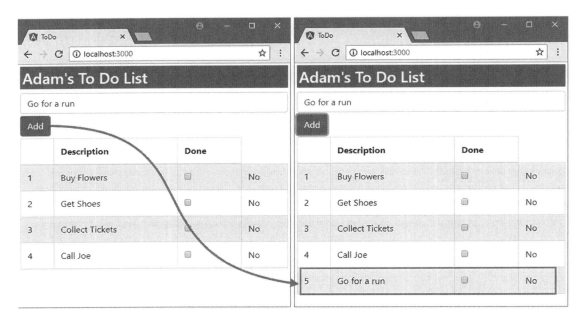

Figure 2-8. *Creating a to-do item*

Summary

In this chapter, I showed you how to create your first simple Angular app, moving from an HTML mock-up of the application to a dynamic app that lets the user create new to-do items and mark existing items as complete.

Don't worry if not everything in this chapter makes sense. What's important to understand at this stage is the general shape of an Angular application, which is built around a data model, components, and templates. If you keep these three key building blocks in mind, then you will have a context for everything that follows. In the next chapter, I put Angular in context.

CHAPTER 3

■ ■ ■

Putting Angular in Context

In this chapter, I put Angular in context within the world of web app development and set the foundation for the chapters that follow. The goal of Angular is to bring the tools and capabilities that have been available only for server-side development to the web client and, in doing so, make it easier to develop, test, and maintain rich and complex web applications.

Angular works by allowing you to *extend* HTML, which can seem like an odd idea until you get used to it. Angular applications express functionality through custom elements, and a complex application can produce an HTML document that contains a mix of standard and custom markup.

The style of development that Angular supports is derived through the use of the *Model-View-Controller* (MVC) pattern, although this is sometimes referred to as Model-View-*Whatever*, since there are countless variations on this pattern that can be adhered to when using Angular. I am going to focus on the standard MVC pattern in this book since it is the most established and widely used. In the sections that follow, I explain the characteristics of projects where Angular can deliver significant benefit (and those where better alternatives exist), describe the MVC pattern, and describe some common pitfalls.

THIS BOOK AND THE ANGULAR RELEASE SCHEDULE

Google has adopted an aggressive release schedule for Angular. This means that there is an ongoing stream of minor releases and a major release every six months. Minor releases should not break any existing features and should largely contain bug fixes. The major releases can contain substantial changes and may not offer backward compatibility.

It doesn't seem fair or reasonable to ask readers to buy a new edition of this book every six months, especially since the majority of Angular features are unlikely to change even in a major release. Instead, I am going to post updates following the major releases to the GitHub repository for this book, `https://github.com/Apress/pro-angular-6`.

This is an experiment for me (and for Apress), and I don't yet know what form those updates may take—not least because I don't know what the major releases of Angular will contain—but the goal is to extend the life of this book by supplementing the examples it contains.

I am not making any promises about what the updates will be like, what form they will take, or how long I will produce them before folding them into a new edition of this book. Please keep an open mind and check the repository for this book when new Angular versions are released. If you have ideas about how the updates could be improved as the experiment unfolds, then e-mail me at `adam@adam-freeman.com` and let me know.

© Adam Freeman 2018
A. Freeman, *Pro Angular 6*, https://doi.org/10.1007/978-1-4842-3649-9_3

Understanding Where Angular Excels

Angular isn't the solution to every problem, and it is important to know when you should use Angular and when you should seek an alternative. Angular delivers the kind of functionality that used to be available only to server-side developers, but entirely in the browser. This means Angular has a lot of work to do each time an HTML document to which Angular has been applied is loaded—the HTML elements have to be compiled, the data bindings have to be evaluated, components and other building blocks need to be executed, and so on, building support for the features I described in Chapter 2 and those that I describe later in this book.

This kind of work takes time to perform, and the amount of time depends on the complexity of the HTML document, on the associated JavaScript code, and—critically—on quality of the browser and the processing capability of the device. You won't notice any delay when using the latest browsers on a capable desktop machine, but old browsers on underpowered smartphones can really slow down the initial setup of an Angular app.

The goal, therefore, is to perform this setup as infrequently as possible and deliver as much of the app as possible to the user when it is performed. This means giving careful thought to the kind of web application you build. In broad terms, there are two kinds of web application: *round-trip* and *single-page*.

Understanding Round-Trip and Single-Page Applications

For a long time, web apps were developed to follow a *round-trip* model. The browser requests an initial HTML document from the server. User interactions—such as clicking a link or submitting a form—led the browser to request and receive a completely new HTML document. In this kind of application, the browser is essentially a rending engine for HTML content, and all of the application logic and data resides on the server. The browser makes a series of stateless HTTP requests that the server handles by generating HTML documents dynamically.

A lot of current web development is still for round-trip applications, not least because they require little from the browser, which ensures the widest possible client support. But there are some serious drawbacks to round-trip applications: they make the user wait while the next HTML document is requested and loaded, they require a large server-side infrastructure to process all the requests and manage all the application state, and they require a lot of bandwidth because each HTML document has to be self-contained (leading to a lot of the same content being included in each response from the server).

Single-page applications take a different approach. An initial HTML document is sent to the browser, but user interactions lead to Ajax requests for small fragments of HTML or data inserted into the existing set of elements being displayed to the user. The initial HTML document is never reloaded or replaced, and the user can continue to interact with the existing HTML while the Ajax requests are being performed asynchronously, even if that just means seeing a "data loading" message.

Most current apps fall somewhere between the extremes, tending to use the basic round-trip model enhanced with JavaScript to reduce the number of complete page changes, although the emphasis is often on reducing the number of form errors by performing client-side validation.

Angular gives the greatest return from its initial workload as an application gets closer to the single-page model. That's not to say you can't use Angular with round-trip applications—you can, of course—but there are other technologies that are simpler and better suit discrete HTML pages, either working directly with the Document Object Model (DOM) API or using a library to simplify its use, such as jQuery. In Figure 3-1 you can see the spectrum of web application types and where Angular delivers benefit.

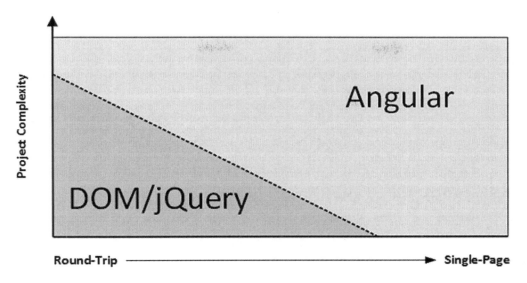

Figure 3-1. *Angular is well-suited to single-page web apps*

Angular excels in single-page applications and especially in complex round-trip applications. For simpler projects, using the DOM API directly or a library like jQuery is generally a better choice, although nothing prevents you from using Angular in all of your projects.

The single-page application model is the sweet spot for Angular, not just because of the initialization process but because the benefits of using the MVC pattern (which I describe later in this chapter) really start to manifest themselves in larger and more complex projects, which are the ones pushing toward the single-page model.

■ **Tip** Another phrase you may encounter is progressive web applications (PWAs). Progressive applications continue to work even when disconnected from the network and have access to features such as push notifications. PWAs are not specific to Angular, but I demonstrate how to use simple PWA features in Chapter 10.

Comparing Angular to jQuery

Angular and jQuery take different approaches to web app development. jQuery is all about explicitly manipulating the browser's Document Object Model (DOM) to create an application. The approach that Angular takes is to co-opt the browser into being the foundation for application development.

jQuery is, without any doubt, a powerful tool—and one I love to use. jQuery is robust and reliable, and you can get results pretty much immediately. I especially like the Fluid API and the ease with which you can extend the core jQuery library. But as much as I love jQuery, it isn't the right tool for every job any more than Angular is. It can be hard to write and manage large applications using jQuery, and thorough unit testing can be a challenge.

Angular also uses the DOM to present HTML content to users but takes an entirely different path to building applications, focusing more on the data in the application and associating it to HTML elements through dynamic data bindings.

The main drawback of Angular is that there is an up-front investment in development time before you start to see results—something that is common in any MVC-based development. This initial investment is worthwhile, however, for complex apps or those that are likely to require significant revision and maintenance.

So, in short, use jQuery (or use the DOM API directly) for low-complexity web apps where unit testing isn't critical and you require immediate results. Use Angular for single-page web apps, when you have time for careful design and planning and when you can easily control the HTML generated by the server.

Comparing Angular to React and Vue.js

There are two main competitors to Angular: React and Vue.js. There are some low-level differences between them, but, for the most part, all of these frameworks are excellent, all of them work in similar ways, and all of them can be used to create rich and fluid client-side applications.

The main difference between these frameworks is the developer experience. Angular requires you to use TypeScript to be effective, for example. If you are used to using a language like C# or Java, then TypeScript will be familiar and avoids dealing with some of the oddities of the JavaScript language. Vue.js and React don't require TypeScript but lean toward mixing HTML, JavaScript, and CSS content together in a single file, which not everyone enjoys.

My advice is simple: pick the framework that you like the look of the most and switch to one of the others if you don't get on with it. That may seem like an unscientific approach but there isn't a bad choice to make, and you will find that many of the core concepts carry over between frameworks even if you switch.

Understanding the MVC Pattern

The term *Model-View-Controller* has been in use since the late 1970s and arose from the Smalltalk project at Xerox PARC where it was conceived as a way to organize some early GUI applications. Some of the fine detail of the original MVC pattern was tied to Smalltalk-specific concepts, such as *screens* and *tools*, but the broader ideas are still applicable to applications, and they are especially well-suited to web applications.

The MVC pattern first took hold in the server-side end of web development, through toolkits like Ruby on Rails and the ASP.NET MVC Framework. In recent years, the MVC pattern has been seen as a way to manage the growing richness and complexity of client-side web development as well, and it is in this environment that Angular has emerged.

The key to applying the MVC pattern is to implement the key premise of a *separation of concerns*, in which the data model in the application is decoupled from the business and presentation logic. In client-side web development, this means separating the data, the logic that operates on that data, and the HTML elements used to display the data. The result is a client-side application that is easier to develop, maintain, and test.

The three main building blocks are the *model*, the *controller*, and the *view*. In Figure 3-2, you can see the traditional exposition of the MVC pattern as it applies to server-side development.

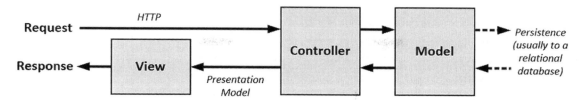

Figure 3-2. *The server-side implementation of the MVC pattern*

I took this figure from my *Pro ASP.NET Core MVC 2* book, which describes Microsoft's server-side implementation of the MVC pattern. You can see that the expectation is that the model is obtained from a database and that the goal of the application is to service HTTP requests from the browser. This is the basis for round-trip web apps, which I described earlier.

Of course, Angular exists in the browser, which leads to a twist on the MVC theme, as illustrated in Figure 3-3.

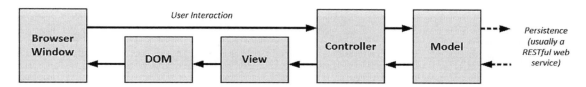

Figure 3-3. *A client-side implementation of the MVC pattern*

The client-side implementation of the MVC pattern gets its data from server-side components, usually via a RESTful web service, which I describe in Chapter 24. The goal of the controller and the view is to operate on the data in the model to perform DOM manipulation so as to create and manage HTML elements that the user can interact with. Those interactions are fed back to the controller, closing the loop to form an interactive application.

Angular uses slightly different terminology for its building blocks, which means that the MVC model implemented using Angular looks more like Figure 3-4.

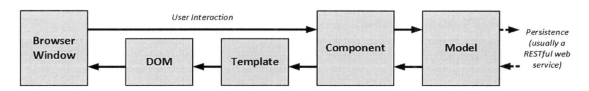

Figure 3-4. *The Angular implementation of the MVC pattern*

The figure shows the basic mapping of Angular building blocks to the MVC pattern. To support the MVC pattern, Angular provides a broad set of additional features, which I describe throughout the book.

▪ **Tip**   Using a client-side framework like Angular doesn't preclude using a server-side MVC framework, but you'll find that an Angular client takes on some of the complexity that would have otherwise existed at the server. This is generally a good thing because it offloads work from the server to the client, and that allows for more clients to be supported with less server capacity.

PATTERNS AND PATTERN ZEALOTS

A good pattern describes an approach to solving a problem that has worked for *other* people on *other* projects. Patterns are recipes, rather than rules, and you will need to adapt any pattern to suit your specific projects, just like a cook has to adapt a recipe to suit different ovens and ingredients.

The degree by which you depart from a pattern should be driven by need and experience. The time you have spent applying a pattern to similar projects will inform your knowledge about what does and doesn't work for you. If you are new to a pattern or you are embarking on a new kind of project, then you should stick as closely as possible to the pattern until you truly understand the benefits and pitfalls that await you. Be careful not to reform your entire development effort around a pattern, however, since wide-sweeping disruption usually causes productivity losses that undermine whatever outcome you were hoping the pattern would give.

Patterns are flexible tools and not fixed rules, but not all developers understand the difference, and some become *pattern zealots*. These are the people who spend more time talking about the pattern than applying it to projects and consider any deviation from their interpretation of the pattern to be a serious crime. My advice is to simply ignore this kind of person because any kind of engagement will just suck the life out of you, and you'll never be able to change their minds. Instead, just get on with some work and demonstrate how a flexible application of a pattern can produce good results through practical application and delivery.

With this in mind, you will see that I follow the broad concepts of the MVC pattern in the examples in this book but that I adapt the pattern to demonstrate different features and techniques. This is how I work in my own projects—embracing the parts of patterns that provide value and setting aside those that do not.

Understanding Models

Models—the *M* in MVC—contain the data that users work with. There are two broad types of model: *view models*, which represent just data passed from the component to the template, and *domain models*, which contain the data in a business domain, along with the operations, transformations, and rules for creating, storing, and manipulating that data, collectively referred to as the *model logic*.

■ **Tip** Many developers new to the MVC pattern get confused with the idea of including logic in the data model, believing that the goal of the MVC pattern is to separate data from logic. This is a misapprehension: the goal of the MVC framework is to divide an application into three functional areas, each of which may contain both logic *and* data. The goal isn't to eliminate logic from the model. Rather, it is to ensure that the model contains logic only for creating and managing the model data.

You can't read a definition of the MVC pattern without tripping over the word *business*, which is unfortunate because a lot of web development goes far beyond the line-of-business applications that led to this kind of terminology. Business applications are still a big chunk of the development world, however, and if you are writing, say, a sales accounting system, then your business domain would encompass the process related to sales accounting, and your domain model would contain the accounts data and the logic by which accounts are created, stored, and managed. If you are creating a cat video website, then you still have a business domain; it is just that it might not fit within the structure of a corporation. Your domain model would contain the cat videos and the logic that will create, store, and manipulate those videos.

Many Angular models will effectively push the logic to the server side and invoke it via a RESTful web service because there is little support for data persistence within the browser, and it is simply easier to get the data you require over Ajax. I explain how Angular can be used with RESTful web services in Chapter 24. For each element in the MVC pattern, I'll describe what should and should not be included. The model in an application built using the MVC pattern *should*

- Contain the domain data

- Contain the logic for creating, managing, and modifying the domain data (even if that means executing remote logic via web services)

- Provide a clean API that exposes the model data and operations on it

The model *should not*

- Expose details of how the model data is obtained or managed (in other words, details of the data storage mechanism or the remote web service should not be exposed to controllers and views)

- Contain logic that transforms the model based on user interaction (because this is the component's job)

- Contain logic for displaying data to the user (this is the template's job)

The benefits of ensuring that the model is isolated from the controller and views are that you can test your logic more easily (I describe Angular unit testing in Chapter 29) and that enhancing and maintaining the overall application is simpler and easier.

The best domain models contain the logic for getting and storing data persistently and the logic for create, read, update, and delete operations (known collectively as CRUD) or separate models for querying and modifying data, known as the Command and Query Responsibility Segregation (CQRS) pattern.

This can mean the model contains the logic directly, but more often the model will contain the logic for calling RESTful web services to invoke server-side database operations (which I demonstrate in Chapter 8 when I build a realistic Angular application and which I describe in detail in Chapter 24).

ANGULAR VS. ANGULARJS

The original AngularJS was popular but awkward to use and required developers to deal with some arcane and oddly implemented features that made web application development more complex than it needed to be. Angular, starting with Angular 2 and continuing to the Angular 6 release described in this book, is a complete rewrite that is easier to learn, is easier to work with, and is much more consistent. It is still a complex framework, as the size of this book shows, but creating web applications with Angular is a more pleasant experience than with AngularJS.

The differences between AngularJS and Angular are so profound that I have not included any migration details in this book. If you have an AngularJS application that you want to upgrade to Angular, then you can use the upgrade adapter, which allows code from both versions of the framework to coexist in the same application. See `https://angular.io/guide/upgrade` for details. This can ease the transition, although AngularJS and Angular are so different that my advice is to make a clean start and switch to Angular for a ground-up rewrite. This isn't always possible, of course, especially for complex applications, but the process of migrating while also managing coexistence is a difficult one to master and can lead to problems that are hard to track down and correct.

Understanding Controllers/Components

Controllers, which are known as *components* in Angular, are the connective tissue in an Angular web app, acting as conduits between the data model and views. Components add business domain logic required to present some aspect of the model and perform operations on it. A component that follows the MVC pattern *should*

- Contain the logic required to set up the initial state of the template

- Contain the logic/behaviors required by the template to present data from the model

- Contain the logic/behaviors required to update the model based on user interaction

A component *should not*

- Contain logic that manipulates the DOM (that is the job of the template)

- Contain logic that manages the persistence of data (that is the job of the model)

Understanding View Data

The domain model isn't the only data in an Angular application. Components can create *view data* (also known as *view model data* or *view models*) to simplify templates and their interactions with the component.

Understanding Views/Templates

Views, which are known as *templates* in Angular, are defined using HTML elements that are enhanced by data bindings. It is the data bindings that make Angular so flexible, and they transform HTML elements into the foundation for dynamic web applications. I explain the different types of data bindings that Angular provides in detail in Part 2. Templates *should*

- Contain the logic and markup required to present data to the user

Templates *should not*

- Contain complex logic (this is better placed in a component or one of the other Angular building blocks, such as directives, services, or pipes)
- Contain logic that creates, stores, or manipulates the domain model

Templates *can* contain logic, but it should be simple and used sparingly. Putting anything but the simplest method calls or expressions in a template makes the overall application harder to test and maintain.

Understanding RESTful Services

The logic for domain models in Angular apps is often split between the client and the server. The server contains the persistent store, typically a database, and contains the logic for managing it. In the case of a SQL database, for example, the required logic would include opening connections to the database server, executing SQL queries, and processing the results so they can be sent to the client.

You don't want the client-side code accessing the data store directly—doing so would create a tight coupling between the client and the data store that would complicate unit testing and make it difficult to change the data store without also making changes to the client code.

By using the server to mediate access to the data store, you prevent tight coupling. The logic on the client is responsible for getting the data to and from the server and is unaware of the details of how that data is stored or accessed behind the scenes.

There are lots of ways of passing data between the client and the server. One of the most common is to use *Asynchronous JavaScript and XML* (Ajax) requests to call server-side code, getting the server to send JSON and making changes to data using HTML forms.

This approach can work well and is the foundation of *RESTful web services*, which use the nature of HTTP requests to perform CRUD operations on data.

> ■ **Note** REST is a style of API rather than a well-defined specification, and there is disagreement about what exactly makes a web service RESTful. One point of contention is that purists do not consider web services that return JSON to be RESTful. Like any disagreement about an architectural pattern, the reasons for the disagreement are arbitrary and dull and not at all worth worrying about. As far as I am concerned, JSON services *are* RESTful, and I treat them as such in this book.

In a RESTful web service, the operation that is being requested is expressed through a combination of the HTTP method and the URL. So, for example, imagine a URL like this one:

```
http://myserver.mydomain.com/people/bob
```

There is no standard URL specification for a RESTful web service, but the idea is to make the URL self-explanatory, such that it is obvious what the URL refers to. In this case, it is obvious that there is a collection of data objects called people and that the URL refers to the specific object within that collection whose identity is bob.

■ **Tip** It isn't always possible to create such self-evident URLs in a real project, but you should make a serious effort to keep things simple and not expose the internal structure of the data store through the URL (because this is just another kind of coupling between components). Keep your URLs as simple as possible and keep the mappings between the URL format and the structure of the data within the server.

The URL identifies the data object that I want to operate on, and the HTTP method specifies what operation I want to be performed, as described in Table 3-1.

Table 3-1. *The Operations Commonly Performed in Response to HTTP Methods*

Method	Description
GET	Retrieves the data object specified by the URL
PUT	Updates the data object specified by the URL
POST	Creates a new data object, typically using form data values as the data fields
DELETE	Deletes the data object specified by the URL

You don't have to use the HTTP methods to perform the operations I describe in the table. A common variation is that the POST method is often used to serve double duty and will update an object if one exists and create one if not, meaning that the PUT method isn't used. I describe the support that Angular provides for Ajax and for easily working with RESTful services in Chapter 24.

IDEMPOTENT HTTP METHODS

You can implement any mapping between HTTP methods and operations on the data store, although I recommend you stick as closely as possible to the convention I describe in the table.

If you depart from the normal approach, make sure you honor the nature of the HTTP methods as defined in the HTTP specification. The GET method is *nullipotent*, which means the operations you perform in response to this method should only retrieve data and not modify it. A browser (or any intermediate device, such as a proxy) expects to be able to repeatedly make a GET request without altering the state of the server (although this doesn't mean the state of the server won't change between identical GET requests because of requests from other clients).

The PUT and DELETE methods are *idempotent*, which means that multiple identical requests should have the same effect as a single request. So, for example, using the DELETE method with the /people/bob URL should delete the bob object from the people collection for the first request and then do nothing for subsequent requests. (Again, of course, this won't be true if another client re-creates the bob object.)

The POST method is neither nullipotent nor idempotent, which is why a common RESTful optimization is to handle object creation *and* updates. If there is no bob object, using the POST method will create one, and subsequent POST requests to the same URL will update the object that was created.

All of this is important only if you are implementing your own RESTful web service. If you are writing a client that consumes a RESTful service, then you just need to know what data operation each HTTP method corresponds to. I demonstrate consuming such a service in Chapter 8 and describe the Angular features for HTTP requests in more detail in Chapter 24.

Common Design Pitfalls

In this section, I describe the three most common design pitfalls that I encounter in Angular projects. These are not coding errors but rather problems with the overall shape of the web app that prevent the project team from getting the benefits that Angular and the MVC pattern can provide.

Putting the Logic in the Wrong Place

The most common problem is logic put into the wrong component such that it undermines the MVC separation of concerns. Here are the three most common varieties of this problem:

- Putting business logic in templates, rather than in components

- Putting domain logic in components, rather than in the model

- Putting data store logic in the client model when using a RESTful service

These are tricky issues because they take a while to manifest themselves as problems. The application still runs, but it will become harder to enhance and maintain over time. In the case of the third variety, the problem will become apparent only when the data store is changed (which rarely happens until a project is mature and has grown beyond its initial user projections).

■ **Tip** Getting a feel for where logic should go takes some experience, but you'll spot problems earlier if you are using unit testing because the tests you have to write to cover the logic won't fit nicely into the MVC pattern. I describe the Angular support for unit testing in Chapter 29.

Knowing where to put logic becomes second nature as you get more experience in Angular development, but here are the three rules:

- Template logic should prepare data only for display and never modify the model.

- Component logic should never directly create, update, or delete data from the model.

- The templates and components should never directly access the data store.

If you keep these in mind as you develop, you'll head off the most common problems.

Adopting the Data Store Data Format

The next problem arises when the development team builds an application that depends on the quirks of the server-side data store. In a well-designed Angular application that gets its data from a RESTful service, it is the job of the server to hide the data store implementation details and present the client with data in a suitable data format that favors simplicity in the client. Decide how the client needs to represent dates, for example, and then ensure you use that format within the data store—and if the data store can't support that format natively, then it is the job of the server to perform the translation.

Just Enough Knowledge to Cause Trouble

Angular is a complex framework that can be bewildering until you get used it. There are lots of different building blocks available, and they can be combined in different ways to achieve similar results. This makes Angular development flexible and means you will develop your own style of problem-solving by creating combinations of features that suit your project and working style.

Becoming proficient in Angular takes time. The temptation is to jump into creating your own projects before understanding how the different parts of Angular fit together. You might produce something that works without really understanding why it works, and that's a recipe for disaster when you need to make changes. My advice is to go slow and take the time to understand all the features that Angular provides. By all means, start creating projects early, but make sure you really understand how they work and be prepared to make changes as you find better ways of achieving the results you require.

Summary

In this chapter, I provided some context for Angular. I explained how Angular supports the MVC pattern for app development, and I gave a brief overview of REST and how it is used to express data operations over HTTP requests. I finished the chapter by describing the three most common design problems in Angular projects. In the next chapter, I provide a quick primer for HTML and the Bootstrap CSS framework that I use for examples throughout this book.

CHAPTER 4

An HTML and CSS Primer

Developers come to the world of web app development via many paths and are not always grounded in the basic technologies that web apps rely on. In this chapter, I provide a brief primer for HTML and introduce the Bootstrap CSS library, which I use to style the examples in this book. In Chapters 5 and 6, I introduce the basics of JavaScript and TypeScript and give you the information you need to understand the examples in the rest of the book. If you are an experienced developer, you can skip these primer chapters and jump right to Chapter 7, where I use Angular to create a more complex and realistic application.

Preparing the Example Project

For this chapter, I need only a simple example project. I started by creating a folder called HtmlCssPrimer, created a file called package.json within it, and added the content shown in Listing 4-1.

■ **Tip**   You can download the example project for this chapter—and for all the other chapters in this book—from https://github.com/Apress/pro-angular-6.

Listing 4-1. The Contents of the package.json File in the HtmlCssPrimer Folder

```json
{
  "dependencies": {
    "bootstrap": "4.1.1"
  },

  "devDependencies": {
    "lite-server": "2.3.0"
  },

  "scripts": {
    "start": "npm run lite",
    "lite": "lite-server"
  }
}
```

© Adam Freeman 2018
A. Freeman, *Pro Angular 6*, https://doi.org/10.1007/978-1-4842-3649-9_4

Run the following command within the HtmlCssPrimer folder to download and install the NPM packages specified in the package.json file:

```
npm install
```

Next, I created a file called index.html in the HtmlCssPrimer folder and added the content shown in Listing 4-2.

Listing 4-2. The Contents of the index.html File in the HtmlCssPrimer Folder

```
<!DOCTYPE html>
<html>
<head>
    <title>ToDo</title>
    <meta charset="utf-8" />
    <link href="node_modules/bootstrap/dist/css/bootstrap.min.css"
        rel="stylesheet" />
</head>
<body class="m-1">

    <h3 class="bg-primary text-white p-3">Adam's To Do List</h3>

    <div class="my-1">
        <input class="form-control" />
        <button class="btn btn-primary mt-1">Add</button>
    </div>

    <table class="table table-striped table-bordered">
        <thead>
            <tr>
                <th>Description</th>
                <th>Done</th>
            </tr>
        </thead>
        <tbody>
            <tr><td>Buy Flowers</td><td>No</td></tr>
            <tr><td>Get Shoes</td><td>No</td></tr>
            <tr><td>Collect Tickets</td><td>Yes</td></tr>
            <tr><td>Call Joe</td><td>No</td></tr>
        </tbody>
    </table>
</body>
</html>
```

This is the HTML content I used in Chapter 2 to mock up the appearance of the example application. Run the following command in the HtmlCssPrimer folder to start the development HTTP server:

```
npm start
```

A new browser tab or window will open and show the content in Figure 4-1.

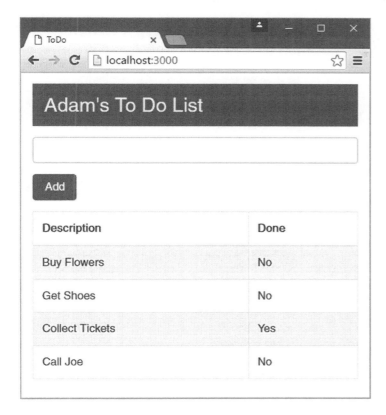

Figure 4-1. *Running the example application*

Understanding HTML

At the heart of HTML is the *element*, which tells the browser what kind of content each part of an HTML document represents. Here is an element from the example HTML document:

```
...
<td>Buy Flowers</td>
...
```

As illustrated in Figure 4-2, this element has three parts: the start tag, the end tag, and the content.

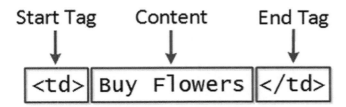

Figure 4-2. *The anatomy of a simple HTML element*

45

The *name* of this element (also referred to as the *tag name* or just the *tag*) is td, and it tells the browser that the content between the tags should be treated as a table cell. You start an element by placing the tag name in angle brackets (the < and > characters) and end an element by using the tag in a similar way, except that you also add a / character after the left-angle bracket (<). Whatever appears between the tags is the element's content, which can be text (such as Buy Flowers in this case) or other HTML elements.

Understanding Void Elements

The HTML specification includes elements that are not permitted to contain content. These are called *void* or *self-closing* elements, and they are written without a separate end tag, like this:

```
...
<input />
...
```

A void element is defined in a single tag, and you add a / character before the last angle bracket (the > character). The input element is the most commonly used void element, and its purpose is to allow the user to provide input, through a text field, radio button, or checkbox. You will see lots of examples of working with this element in later chapters.

Understanding Attributes

You can provide additional information to the browser by adding *attributes* to your elements. Here is an element with an attribute from the example document:

```
...
<link href="node_modules/bootstrap/dist/css/bootstrap.min.css" rel="stylesheet" />
...
```

This is a link element, and it imports content into the document. There are two attributes, which I have emphasized so they are easier to see. Attributes are always defined as part of the start tag, and these attributes have a *name* and a *value*.

The names of the two attributes in this example are href and rel. For the link element, the href attribute specifies the content to import, and the rel attribute tells the browser what kind of content it is. The attributes on this link element tell the browser to import the bootstrap.min.css file and to treat it as a style sheet, which is a file that contains CSS styles.

Applying Attributes Without Values

Not all attributes are applied with a value; just adding them to an element tells the browser that you want a certain kind of behavior. Here is an example of an element with such an attribute (not from the example document; I just made up this example element):

```
...
<input class="form-control" required />
...
```

This element has two attributes. The first is class, which is assigned a value just like the previous example. The other attribute is just the word required. This is an example of an attribute that doesn't need a value.

Quoting Literal Values in Attributes

Angular relies on HTML element attributes to apply a lot of its functionality. Most of the time, the values of attributes are evaluated as JavaScript expressions, such as with this element, taken from Chapter 2:

```
...
<td [ngSwitch]="item.done">
...
```

The attribute applied to the td element tells Angular to read the value of a property called done on an object that has been assigned to a variable called item. There will be occasions when you need to provide a specific value rather than have Angular read a value from the data model, and this requires additional quoting to tell Angular that it is dealing with a literal value, like this:

```
...
<td [ngSwitch]="'Apples'">
...
```

The attribute value contains the string Apples, which is quoted in both single and double quotes. When Angular evaluates the attribute value, it will see the single quotes and process the value as a literal string.

Understanding Element Content

Elements can contain text, but they can also contain other elements, like this:

```
...
<thead>
    <tr>
        <th>Description</th>
        <th>Done</th>
    </tr>
</thead>
...
```

The elements in an HTML document form a hierarchy. The html element contains the body element, which contains content elements, each of which can contain other elements, and so on. In the listing, the thead element contains tr elements that, in turn, contain th elements. Arranging elements is a key concept in HTML because it imparts the significance of the outer element to those contained within.

Understanding the Document Structure

There are some key elements that define the basic structure of an HTML document: the DOCTYPE, html, head, and body elements. Here is the relationship between these elements with the rest of the content removed:

```
<!DOCTYPE html>
<html>
<head>
    ...head content...
</head>
<body>
    ...body content...
</body>
</html>
```

Each of these elements has a specific role to play in an HTML document. The DOCTYPE element tells the browser that this is an HTML document and, more specifically, that this is an *HTML5* document. Earlier versions of HTML required additional information. For example, here is the DOCTYPE element for an *HTML4* document:

```
...
<!DOCTYPE HTML PUBLIC "-//W3C//DTD HTML 4.01//EN"
    "http://www.w3.org/TR/html4/strict.dtd">
...
```

The html element denotes the region of the document that contains the HTML content. This element always contains the other two key structural elements: head and body. As I explained at the start of the chapter, I am not going to cover the individual HTML elements. There are too many of them, and describing HTML5 completely took me more than 1,000 pages in my HTML book. That said, Table 4-1 provides brief descriptions of the elements I used in the index.html file in Listing 4-2 to help you understand how elements tell the browser what kind of content they represent.

UNDERSTANDING THE DOCUMENT OBJECT MODEL

When the browser loads and processes an HTML document, it creates the *Document Object Model* (DOM). The DOM is a model in which JavaScript objects are used to represent each element in the document, and the DOM is the mechanism by which you can programmatically engage with the content of an HTML document.

You rarely work directly with the DOM in Angular, but it is important to understand that the browser maintains a live model of the HTML document represented by JavaScript objects. When Angular modifies these objects, the browser updates the content it displays to reflect the modifications. This is one of the key foundations of web applications. If we were not able to modify the DOM, we would not be able to create client-side web apps.

Table 4-1. *HTML Elements Used in the Example Document*

Element	Description
DOCTYPE	Indicates the type of content in the document
body	Denotes the region of the document that contains content elements
button	Denotes a button; often used to submit a form to the server
div	A generic element; often used to add structure to a document for presentation purposes
h3	Denotes a header
head	Denotes the region of the document that contains metadata
html	Denotes the region of the document that contains HTML (which is usually the entire document)
input	Denotes a field used to gather a single data item from the user
link	Imports content into the HTML document
meta	Provides descriptive data about the document, such as the character encoding
table	Denotes a table, used to organize content into rows and columns
tbody	Denotes the body of the table (as opposed to the header or footer)
td	Denotes a content cell in a table row
th	Denotes a header cell in a table row
thead	Denotes the header of a table
title	Denotes the title of the document; used by the browser to set the title of the window or tab
tr	Denotes a row in a table

Understanding Bootstrap

HTML elements tell the browser what kind of content they represent, but they don't provide any information about how that content should be displayed. The information about how to display elements is provided using *Cascading Style Sheets* (CSS). CSS consists of a comprehensive set of *properties* that can be used to configure every aspect of an element's appearance and a set of *selectors* that allow those properties to be applied.

One of the main problems with CSS is that some browsers interpret properties slightly differently, which can lead to variations in the way that HTML content is displayed on different devices. It can be difficult to track down and correct these problems, and CSS frameworks have emerged to help web app developers style their HTML content in a simple and consistent way.

The most widely used framework is Bootstrap, which consists of a set of CSS classes that can be applied to elements to style them consistently and JavaScript code that performs additional enhancement. I use the Bootstrap CSS styles in this book because they let me style my examples without having to define custom styles in each chapter. I don't use the Bootstrap JavaScript features at all in this book.

I don't want to get into too much detail about Bootstrap because it isn't the topic of this book, but I do want to give you enough information so you can tell which parts of an example are Angular features and which are Bootstrap styling. See `http://getbootstrap.com` for full details of the features that Bootstrap provides.

Applying Basic Bootstrap Classes

Bootstrap styles are applied via the class attribute, which is used to group together related elements. The class attribute isn't just used to apply CSS styles, but it is the most common use, and it underpins the way that Bootstrap and similar frameworks operate. Here is an HTML element with a class attribute, taken from the index.html file:

```
...
<button class="btn btn-primary mt-1">Add</button>
...
```

The class attribute assigns the button element to three classes, whose names are separated by spaces: btn, btn-primary, and mt-1. These classes correspond to styles defined by Bootstrap, as described in Table 4-2.

Table 4-2. *The Three Button Element Classes*

Name	Description
btn	This class applies the basic styling for a button. It can be applied to button or a elements to provide a consistent appearance.
btn-primary	This class applies a style context to provide a visual cue about the purpose of the button. See the "Using Contextual Classes" section.
mt-1	This class adds a gap between the top of the element and the content that surrounds it. See the "Using Margin and Padding" section.

Using Contextual Classes

One of the main advantages of using a CSS framework like Bootstrap is to simplify the process of creating a consistent theme throughout an application. Bootstrap defines a set of *style contexts* that are used to style related elements consistently. These contexts, which are described in Table 4-3, are used in the names of the classes that apply Bootstrap styles to elements.

Table 4-3. *The Bootstrap Style Contexts*

Name	Description
primary	This context is used to indicate the main action or area of content.
secondary	This context is used to indicate the supporting areas of content.
success	This context is used to indicate a successful outcome.
info	This context is used to present additional information.
warning	This context is used to present warnings.
danger	This context is used to present serious warnings.
muted	This context is used to de-emphasize content.
dark	This context is used to increase contrast by using a dark color.
white	This context is used to increase contrast by using white.

Bootstrap provides classes that allow the style contexts to be applied to different types of elements. Here is the primary context applied to the h3 element, taken from the index.html file created at the start of the chapter:

```
...
<h3 class="bg-primary text-white p-3">Adam's To Do List</h3>
...
```

One of the classes that the element has been assigned to is bg-primary, which styles the background color of an element using the style context's color. Here is the same style context applied to a button element:

```
...
<button class="btn btn-primary mt-1">Add</button>
...
```

The btn-primary class styles a button or anchor element using the style context's colors. Using the same context to style different elements will ensure their appearance is consistent and complementary, as shown in Figure 4-3, which highlights the elements to which the style context has been applied.

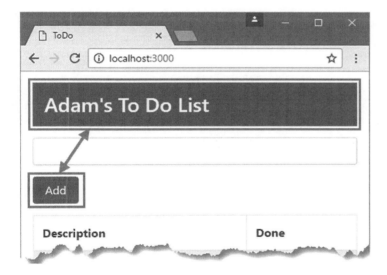

Figure 4-3. *Using style contexts for consistency*

Using Margin and Padding

Bootstrap includes a set of utility classes that are used to add padding (space between an element's inner edge and its content) and margin (space between an element's edge and the surrounding elements). The benefit of using these classes is that they apply a consistent amount of spacing throughout the application.

The names of these classes follow a well-defined pattern. Here is the body element from the index.html file created at the start of the chapter, to which margin has been applied:

```
...
<body class="m-1">
...
```

The classes that apply margin and padding to elements follow a well-defined naming schema: first, the letter m (for margin) or p (for padding), then a hyphen, and then a number indicating how much space should be applied (0 for no spacing, or 1, 2, or 3 for increasing amounts). You can also add a letter to apply spacing only to specific sides, so t for top, b for bottom, l for left, r for right, x for left and right, and y for top and bottom).

To help put this scheme in context, Table 4-4 lists the combinations used in the index.html file.

Table 4-4. *Sample Bootstrap Margin and Padding Classes*

Name	Description
p-1	This class applies padding to all edges of an element.
m-1	This class applies margin to all edges of an element.
mt-1	This class applies margin to the top edge of an element.
mb-1	This class applies margin to the bottom edge of an element.

Changing Element Sizes

You can change the way that some elements are styled by using a size modification class. These are specified by combining a basic class name, a hyphen, and lg or sm. In Listing 4-3, I have added button elements to the index.html file, using the size modification classes that Bootstrap provides for buttons.

Listing 4-3. Using Button Size Modification Classes in the index.html File in the HtmlCssPrimer Folder

```
<!DOCTYPE html>
<html>
<head>
    <title>ToDo</title>
    <meta charset="utf-8" />
    <link href="node_modules/bootstrap/dist/css/bootstrap.min.css"
        rel="stylesheet" />
</head>
<body class="m-1">

    <h3 class="bg-primary text-white p-3">Adam's To Do List</h3>

    <div class="my-1">
        <input class="form-control" />
        <button class="btn btn-lg btn-primary mt-1">Add</button>
        <button class="btn btn-primary mt-1">Add</button>
        <button class="btn btn-sm btn-primary mt-1">Add</button>
    </div>

    <table class="table table-striped table-bordered">
        <thead>
            <tr>
                <th>Description</th>
                <th>Done</th>
            </tr>
        </thead>
```

```
    <tbody>
        <tr><td>Buy Flowers</td><td>No</td></tr>
        <tr><td>Get Shoes</td><td>No</td></tr>
        <tr><td>Collect Tickets</td><td>Yes</td></tr>
        <tr><td>Call Joe</td><td>No</td></tr>
    </tbody>
    </table>
</body>
</html>
```

The btn-lg class creates a large button, and the btn-sm class creates a small button. Omitting a size class uses the default size for the element. Notice that I am able to combine a context class and a size class. Bootstrap class modifications work together to give you complete control over how elements are styled, creating the effect shown in Figure 4-4.

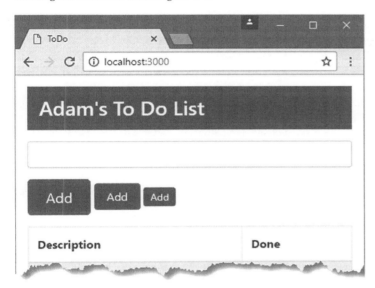

Figure 4-4. *Changing element size*

Using Bootstrap to Style Tables

Bootstrap includes support for styling table elements and their contents, which is a feature I use throughout this book. Table 4-5 lists the key Bootstrap classes for working with tables.

Table 4-5. *The Bootstrap CSS Classes for Tables*

Name	Description
table	Applies general styling to a table element and its rows
table-striped	Applies alternate-row striping to the rows in the table body
table-bordered	Applies borders to all rows and columns
table-hover	Displays a different style when the mouse hovers over a row in the table
table-sm	Reduces the spacing in the table to create a more compact layout

All these classes are applied directly to the table element, as shown in Listing 4-4, which highlights the Bootstrap classes applied to the table in the index.html file.

Listing 4-4. Using Bootstrap to Style Tables

```
...
<table class="table table-striped table-bordered">
    <thead>
        <tr>
            <th>Description</th>
            <th>Done</th>
        </tr>
    </thead>
    <tbody>
        <tr><td>Buy Flowers</td><td>No</td></tr>
        <tr><td>Get Shoes</td><td>No</td></tr>
        <tr><td>Collect Tickets</td><td>Yes</td></tr>
        <tr><td>Call Joe</td><td>No</td></tr>
    </tbody>
</table>
...
```

■ **Tip**   Notice that I have used the thead element when defining the tables in Listing 4-4. Browsers will automatically add any tr elements that are direct descendants of table elements to a tbody element if one has not been used. You will get odd results if you rely on this behavior when working with Bootstrap because most of the CSS classes that are applied to the table element cause styles to be added to the descendants of the tbody element.

Using Bootstrap to Create Forms

Bootstrap includes styling for form elements, allowing them to be styled consistently with other elements in the application. In Listing 4-5, I have expanded the form elements in the index.html file and temporarily removed the table.

Listing 4-5. Defining Additional Form Elements in the index.html File in the HtmlCssPrimer Folder

```
<!DOCTYPE html>
<html>
<head>
    <title>ToDo</title>
    <meta charset="utf-8" />
    <link href="node_modules/bootstrap/dist/css/bootstrap.min.css"
        rel="stylesheet" />
</head>
<body class="m-2">
    <h3 class="bg-primary text-white p-3">Adam's To Do List</h3>
    <form>
        <div class="form-group">
```

```
        <label>Task</label>
        <input class="form-control" />
    </div>
    <div class="form-group">
        <label>Location</label>
        <input class="form-control" />
    </div>
    <div class="form-group">
        <input type="checkbox" />
        <label>Done</label>
    </div>
    <button class="btn btn-primary">Add</button>
</form>
</body>
</html>
```

The basic styling for forms is achieved by applying the form-group class to a div element that contains a label and an input element, where the input element is assigned to the form-control class. Bootstrap styles the elements so that the label is shown above the input element and the input element occupies 100 percent of the available horizontal space, as shown in Figure 4-5.

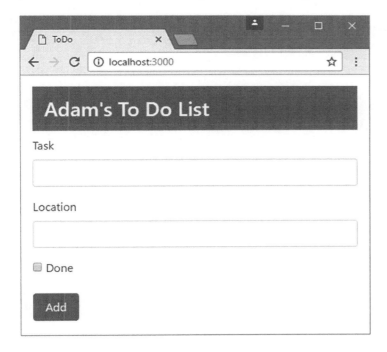

Figure 4-5. *Styling form elements*

Using Bootstrap to Create Grids

Bootstrap provides style classes that can be used to create different kinds of grid layout, ranging from one to twelve columns and with support for responsive layouts, where the layout of the grid changes based on the width of the screen. Listing 4-6 replaces the content of the example HTML file to demonstrate the grid feature.

Listing 4-6. Using a Bootstrap Grid in the index.html File in the HtmlCssPrimer Folder

```
<!DOCTYPE html>
<html>
<head>
    <title>ToDo</title>
    <meta charset="utf-8" />
    <link href="node_modules/bootstrap/dist/css/bootstrap.min.css"
          rel="stylesheet" />
    <style>
        .row > div {
                    border: 1px solid lightgrey; padding: 10px;
                    background-color: aliceblue; margin: 5px 0;
                    }
    </style>
</head>
<body class="m-2">
    <h3>Grid Layout</h3>
    <div class="container">
        <div class="row">
            <div class="col-1">1</div>
            <div class="col-1">1</div>
            <div class="col-2">2</div>
            <div class="col-2">2</div>
            <div class="col-6">6</div>
        </div>

        <div class="row">
            <div class="col-3">3</div>
            <div class="col-4">4</div>
            <div class="col-5">5</div>
        </div>

        <div class="row">
            <div class="col-6">6</div>
            <div class="col-6">6</div>
        </div>

        <div class="row">
            <div class="col-11">11</div>
            <div class="col-1">1</div>
        </div>

        <div class="row">
            <div class="col-12">12</div>
        </div>
    </div>
</body>
</html>
```

The Bootstrap grid layout system is simple to use. A top-level div element is assigned to the container class (or the container-fluid class if you want it to span the available space). You specify a column by applying the row class to a div element, which has the effect of setting up the grid layout for the content that the div element contains.

Each row defines 12 columns, and you specify how many columns each child element will occupy by assigning a class whose name is col- followed by the number of columns. For example, the class col-1 specifies that an element occupies one column, col-2 specifies two columns, and so on, right through to col-12, which specifies that an element fills the entire row. In the listing, I have created a series of div elements with the row class, each of which contains further div elements to which I have applied col-* classes. You can see the effect in the browser in Figure 4-6.

■ **Tip** Bootstrap doesn't apply any styling to the elements within a row, which I why I have used a style element to create a custom CSS style that sets a background color, sets up some spacing between rows, and adds a border.

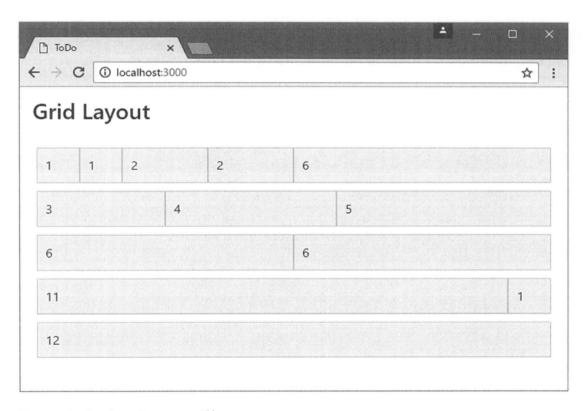

Figure 4-6. *Creating a Bootstrap grid layout*

Creating Responsive Grids

Responsive grids adapt their layout based on the size of the browser window. The main use for responsive grids is to allow mobile devices and desktops to display the same content, taking advantage of whatever screen space is available. To create a responsive grid, replace the col-* class on individual cells with one of the classes shown in Table 4-6.

Table 4-6. *The Bootstrap CSS Classes for Responsive Grids*

Bootstrap Class	Description
col-sm-*	Grid cells are displayed horizontally when the screen width is greater than 576 pixels.
col-md-*	Grid cells are displayed horizontally when the screen width is greater than 768 pixels.
col-lg-*	Grid cells are displayed horizontally when the screen width is greater than 992 pixels.
col-xl-*	Grid cells are displayed horizontally when the screen width is greater than 1200 pixels.

When the width of the screen is less than the class supports, the cells in the grid row are stacked vertically rather than horizontally. Listing 4-7 demonstrates a responsive grid in the index.html file.

Listing 4-7. Creating a Responsive Grid in the index.html File in the HtmlCssPrimer Folder

```
<!DOCTYPE html>
<html>
<head>
    <title>ToDo</title>
    <meta charset="utf-8" />
    <link href="node_modules/bootstrap/dist/css/bootstrap.min.css"
        rel="stylesheet" />
    <style>
        #gridContainer {padding: 20px;}
        .row > div {
                    border: 1px solid lightgrey; padding: 10px;
                    background-color: aliceblue; margin: 5px 0;
                    }
    </style>

</head>
<body class="m-1">

    <h3>Grid Layout</h3>
    <div class="container">
        <div class="row">
            <div class="col-sm-3">3</div>
            <div class="col-sm-4">4</div>
            <div class="col-sm-5">5</div>
        </div>

        <div class="row">
            <div class="col-sm-6">6</div>
            <div class="col-sm-6">6</div>
        </div>
```

```
        <div class="row">
            <div class="col-sm-11">11</div>
            <div class="col-sm-1">1</div>
        </div>
    </div>
</body>
</html>
```

I removed some grid rows from the previous example and replaced the col-* classes with col-sm-*. The effect is that the cells in the row will be stacked horizontally when the browser window is greater than 576 pixels wide and stacked horizontally when it is smaller, as shown in Figure 4-7.

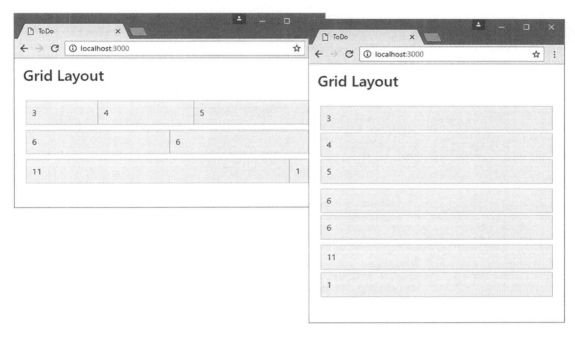

Figure 4-7. *Creating a responsive grid layout*

Creating a Simplified Grid Layout

For most of the examples in this book that rely on the Bootstrap grid, I use a simplified approach that displays content in a single row and requires only the number of columns to be specified, as shown in Listing 4-8.

Listing 4-8. Using a Simplified Grid Layout in the index.html File in the HtmlCssPrimer Folder

```
<!DOCTYPE html>
<html>
<head>
    <title>ToDo</title>
    <meta charset="utf-8" />
    <link href="node_modules/bootstrap/dist/css/bootstrap.min.css"
        rel="stylesheet" />
</head>
```

59

```
<body class="m-1">
    <h3 class="bg-primary text-white p-3">Adam's To Do List</h3>
    <div class="container-fluid">
        <div class="row">
            <div class="col-4">
                <form>
                    <div class="form-group">
                        <label>Task</label>
                        <input class="form-control" />
                    </div>
                    <div class="form-group">
                        <label>Location</label>
                        <input class="form-control" />
                    </div>
                    <div class="form-group">
                        <input type="checkbox" />
                        <label>Done</label>
                    </div>
                    <button class="btn btn-primary">Add</button>
                </form>
            </div>
            <div class="col-8">
                <table class="table table-striped table-bordered">
                    <thead>
                        <tr>
                            <th>Description</th>
                            <th>Done</th>
                        </tr>
                    </thead>
                    <tbody>
                        <tr><td>Buy Flowers</td><td>No</td></tr>
                        <tr><td>Get Shoes</td><td>No</td></tr>
                        <tr><td>Collect Tickets</td><td>Yes</td></tr>
                        <tr><td>Call Joe</td><td>No</td></tr>
                    </tbody>
                </table>
            </div>
        </div>
    </div>
</body>
</html>
```

This listing uses the col-4 and col-8 classes to display two div elements side by side, allowing the form and the table that displays the to-do items to be displayed horizontally, as illustrated in Figure 4-8.

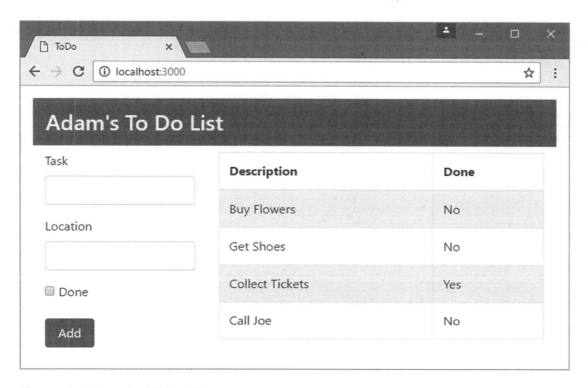

Figure 4-8. *Using a simplified grid layout*

Summary

In this chapter, I provided a brief overview of HTML and the Bootstrap CSS framework. You need to have a good grasp of HTML and CSS to be truly effective in web application development, but the best way to learn is by firsthand experience, and the descriptions and examples in this chapter will be enough to get you started and provide just enough background information for the examples ahead. In the next chapter, I continue the primer theme and introduce the basic features of JavaScript that I use in this book.

CHAPTER 5

■ ■ ■

JavaScript and TypeScript: Part 1

In this chapter I provide a quick tour of the most important basic features of the JavaScript language as they apply to Angular development. I don't have the space to describe JavaScript completely, so I have focused on the essentials that you'll need to get up to speed and follow the examples in this book. In Chapter 6, I describe some of the more advanced JavaScript features that you will need and some of the additional features provided by TypeScript.

The JavaScript language is managed through a standard process that defines new features. Modern browsers have started to implement features from the ECMAScript 6 (also known as ES6) standard, and ECMAScript 7 (ES7) is making its way into service as I write this. The new standards broaden the features available to JavaScript developers and make using JavaScript more consistent with more conventional languages such as C# or Java.

Modern browsers update themselves, which means that a Google Chrome user, for example, is likely to have a recent release of the browser that implements at least some of the most recent JavaScript features. Sadly, older browsers that don't update themselves are still in widespread use, which means you can't rely on modern features being available for use in your application.

There are two ways to approach this problem. The first is to use only the core JavaScript features that you can rely on being present in the browsers that your application targets. The second is to use a compiler that processes your JavaScript files and converts them into code that can run on older browsers. It is the second approach that Angular takes and that I describe in this chapter. Table 5-1 summarizes this chapter.

Table 5-1. *Chapter Summary*

Problem	Solution	Listing
Create JavaScript functionality	Use JavaScript statements	5
Create groups of statements that are executed on command	Use functions	6, 7, 10–12
Define functions that can handle more or fewer arguments than parameters	Use default or rest parameters	8, 9
Express functions more concisely	Use arrow functions	13
Store values and objects for later use	Declare variables using the let or var keyword	14–16
Store basic data values	Use the JavaScript primitive types	17–20
Control the flow of JavaScript code	Use conditional statements	21
Determine whether two objects or values are the same	Use the quality and identity operators	22–23
Explicitly convert types	Use the to<type> methods	24–26
Store related objects or values together in sequence	Use an array	27–33

© Adam Freeman 2018
A. Freeman, *Pro Angular 6*, https://doi.org/10.1007/978-1-4842-3649-9_5

```
┌─────────────────────────────────────────────────────────────────────────┐
│              USING "PLAIN" JAVASCRIPT FOR ANGULAR                         │
└─────────────────────────────────────────────────────────────────────────┘
```

When Angular 2 was introduced, the use of TypeScript was optional, and it was possible to write Angular applications using plain JavaScript. The result was awkward and required some contorted code to re-create the effect of key TypeScript features, but it was possible, and Google provided a complete set of API documents for both TypeScript and plain JavaScript developers.

The support for working with plain JavaScript development has been reduced with each subsequent release, with the effect that there is no guidance for programmers who are reluctant to adopt TypeScript.

My advice is to embrace the complete Angular experience, even though it can take some time and effort to master TypeScript. The result will be a better development experience, containing code that is more concise, easier to read, and simpler to maintain. This is the approach I have taken in this book, and every example assumes that this is the path you are following.

Preparing the Example Project

To create the example project for this chapter, open a new command prompt, navigate to a convenient location, and run the command shown in Listing 5-1.

■ **Tip** You can download the example project for this chapter—and for all the other chapters in this book—from `https://github.com/Apress/pro-angular-6`.

Listing 5-1. Creating the Example Project

```
ng create JavaScriptPrimer
```

This command creates a project called JavaScriptPrimer that is set up for Angular development. I don't do any Angular development in this chapter, but I am going to use the Angular development tools as a convenient way to demonstrate different JavaScript and TypeScript features. To prepare, I replaced the contents of the `main.ts` file in the `src` folder with the single JavaScript statement shown in Listing 5-2.

■ **Tip** Pay attention to the extension of the file. Even though this chapter uses only JavaScript features, it relies on the TypeScript compiler to convert them into code that will run in any browser. That means the `.ts` file must be used, which then allows the TypeScript compiler to create the corresponding `.js` file that will be used by the browser.

Listing 5-2. Replacing the Contents of the main.ts File in the src Folder

```
console.log("Hello");
```

Run the command shown in Listing 5-3 in the `JavaScriptPrimer` folder to start the Angular development compiler and HTTP server.

Listing 5-3. Starting the Development Tools

```
ng serve --port 3000 --open
```

A new browser tab or window will open but will be empty, as shown in Figure 5-1, because I replaced the contents of the main.ts file and the browser has nothing to display.

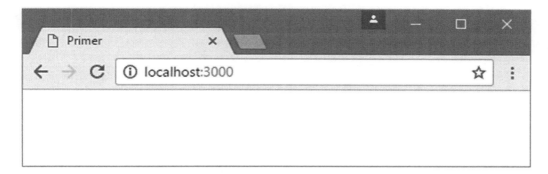

Figure 5-1. *Running the example application*

All the results for the examples in this chapter are displayed in the browser's JavaScript console. Open the browser's F12 developer tools (so called because they are typically opened by pressing the F12 key) and look at the Console tab, which is shown in Figure 5-2.

Figure 5-2. *The Google Chrome JavaScript console*

The JavaScript console shows the result of the call to the `console.log` function from Listing 5-2. Rather than show a screenshot of the browser's JavaScript console for each example, I'll just show the text result, like this:

```
Hello
```

Understanding the Basic Workflow

Writing the word *Hello* to the JavaScript console is a simple example, but there is a lot going on behind the scenes. To get a sense of the development workflow, add the statement shown in Listing 5-4 to the `main.ts` file.

Listing 5-4. Adding a Statement in the main.ts File in the src Folder

```
console.log("Hello");
console.log("Apples");
```

When you save the change to the `main.ts` file, the following process occurs:

1. The TypeScript compiler will detect the change to the `main.ts` file and compile it to generate a new `main.js` file that can run in any browser. The code that is produced is combined with the other JavaScript code produced by the compiler into a single file called a *bundle*.

2. The development HTTP server detects the change to the bundle file and signals the browser to reload the HTML document.

3. The browser reloads the HTML document and starts processing the elements it contains. It loads the JavaScript files specified by the `script` elements in the HTML document, including one that specifies the bundle file that contains the statements from the `main.ts` file.

4. The browser executes the statements that were originally in the `main.ts` file, which writes out two messages to the browser's JavaScript console.

The overall result is that you will see the following messages displayed:

```
Hello
Apples
```

This may seem like a large number of steps for a simple application, but this process allows TypeScript features to be used and automatically takes care of detecting changes, running the compiler, and updating the browser.

Using Statements

The basic JavaScript building block is the *statement*. Each statement represents a single command, and statements are usually terminated by a semicolon (`;`). The semicolon is optional, but using them makes your code easier to read and allows for multiple statements on a single line. In Listing 5-5, I have added a pair of statements to the JavaScript file.

Listing 5-5. Adding JavaScript Statements in the main.ts File in the src Folder

```
console.log("Hello");
console.log("Apples");
console.log("This is a statement");
console.log("This is also a statement");
```

The browser executes each statement in turn. In this example, all the statements simply write messages to the console. The results are as follows:

```
Hello
Apples
This is a statement
This is also a statement
```

Defining and Using Functions

When the browser receives JavaScript code, it executes the statements it contains in the order in which they have been defined. This is what happened in the previous example. The browser loader loaded the main.js file, and the statements it contains were executed one by one, all of which wrote a message to the console.

You can also package statements into a *function*, which won't be executed until the browser encounters a statement that *invokes* the function, as shown in Listing 5-6.

Listing 5-6. Defining a JavaScript Function in the main.ts File in the src Folder

```
let myFunc = function () {
    console.log("This is a statement");
};

myFunc();
```

Defining a function simple: use the `let` keyword followed by the name you want to give the function, followed by the equal sign (=) and the `function` keyword, followed by parentheses (the (and) characters). The statements you want the function to contain are enclosed between braces (the { and } characters).

In the listing, I used the name `myFunc`, and the function contains a single statement that writes a message to the JavaScript console. The statement in the function won't be executed until the browser reaches another statement that calls the `myFunc` function, like this:

```
...
myFunc();
...
```

Executing the statement in the function produces the following output:

```
This is a statement
```

Other than demonstrating how functions are defined, this example isn't especially useful because the function is invoked immediately after it has been defined. Functions are much more useful when they are invoked in response to some kind of change or event, such as user interaction.

```
┌─────────────────────────────────────────────────────────────────────┐
│                  THE OTHER WAY TO DEFINE FUNCTIONS                    │
└─────────────────────────────────────────────────────────────────────┘
```

There are two ways in which you can define functions in JavaScript. The approach I used in Listing 5-6 is known as a *function expression*. The same function can also be defined like this:

```
...
function myFunc() {
    console.log("This is a statement");
}
...
```

This is known as a *function declaration*. The result is the same: a function called myFunc that writes a message to the console. The difference is how the functions are processed by the browser when a JavaScript file is loaded. Function declarations are processed before the code in a JavaScript file is executed, which means you can use a statement that calls a function before it is defined, like this:

```
...
myFunc();

function myFunc() {
    console.log("This is a statement");
}
...
```

This works because the browser finds the function declaration when it parses the JavaScript file and sets up the function before the remaining statements are executed, a process known as *function hoisting*. Function expressions, however, are not subject to hoisting, which means that this code will *not* work:

```
...
myFunc();

let myFunc = function() {
    console.log("This is a statement");
};
...
```

This code will generate an error reporting that myFunc is not a function. Developers who are new to JavaScript tend to prefer using function declarations because the syntax is more consistent with languages like C# or Java. The technique you use is entirely up to you, although you should aim to be consistent throughout your project to make your code easier to understand.

Defining Functions with Parameters

JavaScript allows you to define parameters for functions, as shown in Listing 5-7.

Listing 5-7. Defining Functions with Parameters in the main.ts File in the src Folder

```
let myFunc = function(name, weather) {
    console.log("Hello " + name + ".");
    console.log("It is " + weather + " today");
};

myFunc("Adam", "sunny");
```

I added two parameters to the myFunc function, called name and weather. JavaScript is a dynamically typed language, which means you don't have to declare the data type of the parameters when you define the function. I'll come back to dynamic typing later in the chapter when I cover JavaScript variables. To invoke a function with parameters, you provide values as arguments when you invoke the function, like this:

```
...
myFunc("Adam", "sunny");
...
```

The results from this listing are as follows:

```
Hello Adam.
It is sunny today
```

Using Default and Rest Parameters

The number of arguments you provide when you invoke a function doesn't need to match the number of parameters in the function. If you call the function with fewer arguments than it has parameters, then the value of any parameters you have not supplied values for is undefined, which is a special JavaScript value. If you call the function with more arguments than there are parameters, then the additional arguments are ignored.

The consequence of this is that you can't create two functions with the same name and different parameters and expect JavaScript to differentiate between them based on the arguments you provide when invoking the function. This is called *polymorphism*, and although it is supported in languages such as Java and C#, it isn't available in JavaScript. Instead, if you define two functions with the same name, then the second definition replaces the first.

There are two ways that you can modify a function to respond to a mismatch between the number of parameters it defines and the number of arguments used to invoke it. *Default parameters* deal with the situation where there are fewer arguments than parameters, and they allow you to provide a default value for the parameters for which there are no arguments, as shown in Listing 5-8.

Listing 5-8. Using a Default Parameter in the main.ts File in the src Folder

```
let myFunc = function (name, weather = "raining") {
    console.log("Hello " + name + ".");
    console.log("It is " + weather + " today");
};

myFunc("Adam");
```

69

The weather parameter in the function has been assigned a default value of raining, which will be used if the function is invoked with only one argument, producing the following results:

```
Hello Adam.
It is raining today
```

Rest parameters are used to capture any additional arguments when a function is invoked with additional arguments, as shown in Listing 5-9.

Listing 5-9. Using a Rest Parameter in the main.ts File in the src Folder

```
let myFunc = function (name, weather, ...extraArgs) {
    console.log("Hello " + name + ".");
    console.log("It is " + weather + " today");
    for (let i = 0; i < extraArgs.length; i++) {
        console.log("Extra Arg: " + extraArgs[i]);
    }
};

myFunc("Adam", "sunny", "one", "two", "three");
```

The rest parameter must be the last parameter defined by the function, and its name is prefixed with an ellipsis (three periods, . . .). The rest parameter is an array to which any extra arguments will be assigned. In the listing, the function prints out each extra argument to the console, producing the following results:

```
Hello Adam.
It is sunny today
Extra Arg: one
Extra Arg: two
Extra Arg: three
```

Defining Functions That Return Results

You can return results from functions using the return keyword. Listing 5-10 shows a function that returns a result.

Listing 5-10. Returning a Result from a Function in the main.ts File in the src Folder

```
let myFunc = function(name) {
    return ("Hello " + name + ".");
};

console.log(myFunc("Adam"));
```

This function defines one parameter and uses it to produce a result. I invoke the function and pass the result as the argument to the console.log function, like this:

```
...
console.log(myFunc("Adam"));
...
```

Notice that you don't have to declare that the function will return a result or denote the data type of the result. The result from this listing is as follows:

```
Hello Adam.
```

Using Functions As Arguments to Other Functions

JavaScript functions can be passed around as objects, which means you can use one function as the argument to another, as demonstrated in Listing 5-11.

Listing 5-11. Using a Function as an Arguments to Another Function in the main.ts File

```
let myFunc = function (nameFunction) {
    return ("Hello " + nameFunction() + ".");
};

console.log(myFunc(function () {
    return "Adam";
}));
```

The myFunc function defines a parameter called nameFunction that it invokes to get the value to insert into the string that it returns. I pass a function that returns Adam as the argument to myFunc, which produces the following output:

```
Hello Adam.
```

Functions can be chained together, building up more complex functionality from small and easily tested pieces of code, as shown in Listing 5-12.

Listing 5-12. Chaining Functions Calls in the main.ts File in the src Folder

```
let myFunc = function (nameFunction) {
    return ("Hello " + nameFunction() + ".");
};

let printName = function (nameFunction, printFunction) {
    printFunction(myFunc(nameFunction));
}

printName(function () { return "Adam" }, console.log);
```

This example produces the same result as Listing 5-11.

Using Arrow Functions

Arrow functions—also known as fat arrow functions or lambda expressions—are an alternative way of defining functions and are often used to define functions that are used only as arguments to other functions. Listing 5-13 replaces the functions from the previous example with arrow functions.

Listing 5-13. Using Arrow Functions in the main.ts File in the src Folder

```
let myFunc = (nameFunction) => ("Hello " + nameFunction() + ".");

let printName = (nameFunction, printFunction) => printFunction(myFunc(nameFunction));

printName(function () { return "Adam" }, console.log);
```

These functions perform the same work as the ones in Listing 5-12. There are three parts to an arrow function: the input parameters, then an equal sign and a greater-than sign (the "arrow"), and finally the function result. The `return` keyword and curly braces are required only if the arrow function needs to execute more than one statement. There are more examples of arrow functions later in this chapter.

Using Variables and Types

The `let` keyword is used to declare variables and, optionally, assign a value to the variable in a single statement. Variables declared with `let` are scoped to the region of code in which they are defined, as shown in Listing 5-14.

Listing 5-14. Using let to Declare Variables in the main.ts File in the src Folder

```
let messageFunction = function (name, weather) {
    let message = "Hello, Adam";
    if (weather == "sunny") {
        let message = "It is a nice day";
        console.log(message);
    } else {
        let message = "It is " + weather + " today";
        console.log(message);
    }
    console.log(message);
}

messageFunction("Adam", "raining");
```

In this example, there are three statements that use the `let` keyword to define a variable called `message`. The scope of each variable is limited to the region of code that it is defined in, producing the following results:

```
It is raining today
Hello, Adam
```

This may seem like an odd example, but there is another keyword that can be used to declare variables: `var`. The `let` keyword is a relatively new addition to the JavaScript specification that is intended to address some oddities in the way `var` behaves. Listing 5-15 takes the example from Listing 5-14 and replaces `let` with `var`.

Listing 5-15. Using var to Declare Variables in the main.ts File in the src Folder

```
let messageFunction = function (name, weather) {
    var message = "Hello, Adam";
    if (weather == "sunny") {
        var message = "It is a nice day";
        console.log(message);
    } else {
        var message = "It is " + weather + " today";
        console.log(message);
    }
    console.log(message);
}

messageFunction("Adam", "raining");
```

When you save the changes in the listing, you will see the following results:

```
It is raining today
It is raining today
```

The problem is that the var keyword creates variables whose scope is the containing function, which means that all the references to message are referring to the same variable. This can cause unexpected results for even experienced JavaScript developers and is the reason that the more conventional let keyword was introduced.

USING LET AND CONST

The let keyword is used to define a variable, and the const keyword is used to define a constant value that will not change. It is good practice to use the const keyword for any value that you don't expect to modify so that you receive an error if any modifications are attempted. This is a practice that I rarely follow, however—in part because I am still adapting to not using the var keyword and in part because I write code in a range of languages and there are some features that I avoid because they trip me up when I switch from one to another. If you are new to JavaScript, then I recommend trying to use const and let correctly and avoiding following my poor behavior.

Using Variable Closure

If you define a function inside another function—creating *inner* and *outer* functions—then the inner function is able to access the variables of the outer function, using a feature called *closure*, as demonstrated in Listing 5-16.

Listing 5-16. Using Variable Closure in the main.ts File in the src Folder

```
let myFunc = function(name) {
    let myLocalVar = "sunny";
    let innerFunction = function () {
        return ("Hello " + name + ". Today is " + myLocalVar + ".");
    }
    return innerFunction();

};
console.log(myFunc("Adam"));
```

The inner function in this example is able to access the local variables of the outer function, including its name parameter. This is a powerful feature that means you don't have to define parameters on inner functions to pass around data values, but caution is required because it is easy to get unexpected results when using common variable names like counter or index, where you may not realize that you are reusing a variable name from the outer function. This example produces the following results:

```
Hello Adam. Today is sunny.
```

Using the Primitive Types

JavaScript defines a basic set of primitive types: string, number, and boolean. This may seem like a short list, but JavaScript manages to fit a lot of flexibility into these three types.

> ■ **Tip** I am simplifying here. There are three other primitives that you may encounter. Variables that have been declared but not assigned a value are undefined, while the null value is used to indicate that a variable has no value, just as in other languages. The final primitive type is Symbol, which is an immutable value that represents a unique ID but that is not widely used at the time of writing.

Working with Booleans

The boolean type has two values: true and false. Listing 5-17 shows both values being used, but this type is most useful when used in conditional statements, such as an if statement. There is no console output from this listing.

Listing 5-17. Defining boolean Values in the main.ts File in the src Folder

```
let firstBool = true;
let secondBool = false;
```

Working with Strings

You define string values using either the double quote or single quote characters, as shown in Listing 5-18.

Listing 5-18. Defining string Variables in the main.ts File in the src Folder

```
let firstString = "This is a string";
let secondString = 'And so is this';
```

The quote characters you use must match. You can't start a string with a single quote and finish with a double quote, for example. There is no output from this listing. JavaScript provides `string` objects with a basic set of properties and methods, the most useful of which are described in Table 5-2.

Table 5-2. *Useful string Properties and Methods*

Name	Description
length	This property returns the number of characters in the string.
charAt(index)	This method returns a string containing the character at the specified index.
concat(string)	This method returns a new string that concatenates the string on which the method is called and the string provided as an argument.
indexOf(term, start)	This method returns the first index at which term appears in the string or -1 if there is no match. The optional start argument specifies the start index for the search.
replace(term, newTerm)	This method returns a new string in which all instances of term are replaced with newTerm.
slice(start, end)	This method returns a substring containing the characters between the start and end indices.
split(term)	This method splits up a string into an array of values that were separated by term.
toUpperCase() toLowerCase()	These methods return new strings in which all the characters are uppercase or lowercase.
trim()	This method returns a new string from which all the leading and trailing whitespace characters have been removed.

Using Template Strings

A common programming task is to combine static content with data values to produce a string that can be presented to the user. The traditional way to do this is through string concatenation, which is the approach I have been using in the examples so far in this chapter, as follows:

```
...
let message = "It is " + weather + " today";
...
```

JavaScript also supports *template strings*, which allow data values to be specified inline, which can help reduce errors and result in a more natural development experience. Listing 5-19 shows the use of a template string.

Listing 5-19. Using a Template String in the main.ts File

```
let messageFunction = function (weather) {
    let message = `It is ${weather} today`;
    console.log(message);
}

messageFunction("raining");
```

Template strings begin and end with backticks (the ` character), and data values are denoted by curly braces preceded by a dollar sign. This string, for example, incorporates the value of the weather variable into the template string:

```
...
let message = `It is ${weather} today`;
...
```

This example produces the following output:

```
It is raining today
```

Working with Numbers

The number type is used to represent both *integer* and *floating-point* numbers (also known as *real numbers*). Listing 5-20 provides a demonstration.

Listing 5-20. Defining number Values in the main.ts File in the src Folder

```
let daysInWeek = 7;
let pi = 3.14;
let hexValue = 0xFFFF;
```

You don't have to specify which kind of number you are using. You just express the value you require, and JavaScript will act accordingly. In the listing, I have defined an integer value, defined a floating-point value, and prefixed a value with 0x to denote a hexadecimal value.

Using JavaScript Operators

JavaScript defines a largely standard set of operators. I've summarized the most useful in Table 5-3.

Table 5-3. *Useful JavaScript Operators*

Operator	Description
++, --	Pre- or post-increment and decrement
+, -, *, /, %	Addition, subtraction, multiplication, division, remainder
<, <=, >, >=	Less than, less than or equal to, more than, more than or equal to
==, !=	Equality and inequality tests
===, !==	Identity and nonidentity tests
&&, ||	Logical AND and OR (|| is used to coalesce null values)
=	Assignment
+	String concatenation
?:	Three-operand conditional statement

Using Conditional Statements

Many of the JavaScript operators are used in conjunction with conditional statements. In this book, I tend to use the if/else and switch statements. Listing 5-21 shows the use of both, which will be familiar if you have worked with pretty much any programming language.

Listing 5-21. Using the if/else and switch Conditional Statements in the main.ts File

```
let name = "Adam";

if (name == "Adam") {
    console.log("Name is Adam");
} else if (name == "Jacqui") {
    console.log("Name is Jacqui");
} else {
    console.log("Name is neither Adam or Jacqui");
}

switch (name) {
    case "Adam":
        console.log("Name is Adam");
        break;
    case "Jacqui":
        console.log("Name is Jacqui");
        break;
    default:
        console.log("Name is neither Adam or Jacqui");
        break;
}
```

The results from the listing are as follows:

```
Name is Adam
Name is Adam
```

The Equality Operator vs. the Identity Operator

The equality and identity operators are of particular note. The equality operator will attempt to coerce (convert) operands to the same type to assess equality. This is a handy feature, as long as you are aware it is happening. Listing 5-22 shows the equality operator in action.

Listing 5-22. Using the Equality Operator in the main.ts File in the src Folder

```
let firstVal = 5;
let secondVal = "5";

if (firstVal == secondVal) {
    console.log("They are the same");
} else {
    console.log("They are NOT the same");
}
```

The output from this script is as follows:

```
They are the same
```

JavaScript is converting the two operands into the same type and comparing them. In essence, the equality operator tests that values are the same irrespective of their type. To help guard against this kind of error, the TypeScript compiler will generate a warning, although it will still generate the JavaScript code since this type of comparison is legal:

```
Operator '==' cannot be applied to types 'number' and 'string'.
```

If you want to test to ensure that the values *and* the types are the same, then you need to use the identity operator (===, three equal signs, rather than the two of the equality operator), as shown in Listing 5-23.

Listing 5-23. Using the Identity Operator in the main.ts File in the src Folder

```
let firstVal = 5;
let secondVal = "5";

if (firstVal === secondVal) {
    console.log("They are the same");
} else {
    console.log("They are NOT the same");
}
```

In this example, the identity operator will consider the two variables to be different. This operator doesn't coerce types. The result from this script is as follows:

```
They are NOT the same
```

Explicitly Converting Types

The string concatenation operator (+) has a higher precedence than the addition operator (also +), which means JavaScript will concatenate variables in preference to adding. This can cause confusion because JavaScript will also convert types freely to produce a result—and not always the result that is expected, as shown in Listing 5-24.

Listing 5-24. String Concatenation Operator Precedence in the main.ts File

```
let myData1 = 5 + 5;
let myData2 = 5 + "5";

console.log("Result 1: " + myData1);
console.log("Result 2: " + myData2);
```

The result from this script is as follows:

```
Result 1: 10
Result 2: 55
```

The second result is the kind that causes confusion. What might be intended to be an addition operation is interpreted as string concatenation through a combination of operator precedence and over-eager type conversion. To avoid this, you can explicitly convert the types of values to ensure you perform the right kind of operation, as described in the following sections.

Converting Numbers to Strings

If you are working with multiple number variables and want to concatenate them as strings, then you can convert the numbers to strings with the toString method, as shown in Listing 5-25.

Listing 5-25. Using the number.toString Method in the main.ts File in the src Folder

```
let myData1 = (5).toString() + String(5);
console.log("Result: " + myData1);
```

Notice that I placed the numeric value in parentheses, and then I called the toString method. This is because you have to allow JavaScript to convert the literal value into a number before you can call the methods that the number type defines. I have also shown an alternative approach to achieve the same effect, which is to call the String function and pass in the numeric value as an argument. Both of these techniques have the same effect, which is to convert a number to a string, meaning that the + operator is used for string concatenation and not addition. The output from this script is as follows:

```
Result: 55
```

There are some other methods that allow you to exert more control over how a number is represented as a string. I briefly describe these methods in Table 5-4. All of the methods shown in the table are defined by the number type.

Table 5-4. *Useful Number-to-String Methods*

Method	Description
toString()	This method returns a string that represents a number in base 10.
toString(2)toString(8) toString(16)	This method returns a string that represents a number in binary, octal, or hexadecimal notation.
toFixed(n)	This method returns a string representing a real number with the n digits after the decimal point.
toExponential(n)	This method returns a string that represents a number using exponential notation with one digit before the decimal point and n digits after.
toPrecision(n)	This method returns a string that represents a number with n significant digits, using exponential notation if required.

Converting Strings to Numbers

The complementary technique is to convert strings to numbers so that you can perform addition rather than concatenation. You can do this with the Number function, as shown in Listing 5-26.

Listing 5-26. Converting Strings to Numbers in the main.ts File in the src Folder

```
let firstVal = "5";
let secondVal = "5";

let result = Number(firstVal) + Number(secondVal);
console.log("Result: " + result);
```

The output from this script is as follows:

```
Result: 10
```

The Number function is strict in the way that it parses string values, but there are two other functions you can use that are more flexible and will ignore trailing non-number characters. These functions are parseInt and parseFloat. I have described all three methods in Table 5-5.

Table 5-5. *Useful String to Number Methods*

Method	Description
Number(str)	This method parses the specified string to create an integer or real value.
parseInt(str)	This method parses the specified string to create an integer value.
parseFloat(str)	This method parses the specified string to create an integer or real value.

Working with Arrays

JavaScript arrays work like arrays in most other programming languages. Listing 5-27 shows how you can create and populate an array.

Listing 5-27. Creating and Populating an Array in the main.ts File in the src Folder

```
let myArray = new Array();
myArray[0] = 100;
myArray[1] = "Adam";
myArray[2] = true;
```

I have created a new array by calling new Array(). This creates an empty array, which I assign to the variable myArray. In the subsequent statements, I assign values to various index positions in the array. (There is no console output from this listing.)

There are a couple of things to note in this example. First, I didn't need to declare the number of items in the array when I created it. JavaScript arrays will resize themselves to hold any number of items. The second point is that I didn't have to declare the data types that the array will hold. Any JavaScript array can hold any mix of data types. In the example, I have assigned three items to the array: a number, a string, and a boolean.

Using an Array Literal

The array literal style lets you create and populate an array in a single statement, as shown in Listing 5-28.

Listing 5-28. Using the Array Literal Style in the main.ts File in the src Folder

```
let myArray = [100, "Adam", true];
```

In this example, I specified that the myArray variable should be assigned a new array by specifying the items I wanted in the array between square brackets ([and]). (There is no console output from this listing.)

Reading and Modifying the Contents of an Array

You read the value at a given index using square braces ([and]), placing the index you require between the braces, as shown in Listing 5-29.

Listing 5-29. Reading the Data from an Array Index in the main.ts File in the src Folder

```
let myArray = [100, "Adam", true];
console.log("Index 0: " + myArray[0]);
```

You can modify the data held in any position in a JavaScript array simply by assigning a new value to the index. Just as with regular variables, you can switch the data type at an index without any problems. The output from the listing is as follows:

```
Index 0: 100
```

Listing 5-30 demonstrates modifying the contents of an array.

Listing 5-30. Modifying the Contents of an Array in the main.ts File in the src Folder

```
let myArray = [100, "Adam", true];
myArray[0] = "Tuesday";
console.log("Index 0: " + myArray[0]);
```

In this example, I have assigned a `string` to position 0 in the array, a position that was previously held by a `number` and produces this output:

```
Index 0: Tuesday
```

Enumerating the Contents of an Array

You enumerate the content of an array using a `for` loop or using the `forEach` method, which receives a function that is called to process each element in the array. Both approaches are shown in Listing 5-31.

Listing 5-31. Enumerating the Contents of an Array in the main.ts File in the src Folder

```
let myArray = [100, "Adam", true];

for (let i = 0; i < myArray.length; i++) {
    console.log("Index " + i + ": " + myArray[i]);
}

console.log("---");

myArray.forEach((value, index) => console.log("Index " + index + ": " + value));
```

The JavaScript `for` loop works just the same way as loops in many other languages. You determine how many elements there are in the array by using the `length` property.

The function passed to the `forEach` method is given two arguments: the value of the current item to be processed and the position of that item in the array. In this listing, I have used an arrow function as the argument to the `forEach` method, which is the kind of use for which they excel (and you will see used throughout this book). The output from the listing is as follows:

```
Index 0: 100
Index 1: Adam
Index 2: true
```

```
Index 0: 100
Index 1: Adam
Index 2: true
```

Using the Spread Operator

The spread operator is used to expand an array so that its contents can be used as function arguments or combined with other arrays. In Listing 5-32, I used the spread operator to expand an array so that its items can be combined into another array.

Listing 5-32. Using the Spread Operator in the main.ts File in the src Folder

```
let myArray = [100, "Adam", true];
let otherArray = [...myArray, 200, "Bob", false];

for (let i = 0; i < otherArray.length; i++) {
  console.log(`Array item ${i}: ${otherArray[i]}`);
}
```

The spread operator is an ellipsis (a sequence of three periods), and it causes the array to be unpacked.

```
...
let otherArray = [...myArray, 200, "Bob", false];
...
```

Using the spread operator, I am able to specify myArray as an item when I define otherArray, with the result that the contents of the first array will be unpacked and added as items to the second array. This example produces the following results:

```
Array item 0: 100
Array item 1: Adam
Array item 2: true
Array item 3: 200
Array item 4: Bob
Array item 5: false
```

Using the Built-in Array Methods

The JavaScript Array object defines a number of methods that you can use to work with arrays, the most useful of which are described in Table 5-6.

Table 5-6. *Useful Array Methods*

Method	Description
concat(otherArray)	This method returns a new array that concatenates the array on which it has been called with the array specified as the argument. Multiple arrays can be specified.
join(separator)	This method joins all the elements in the array to form a string. The argument specifies the character used to delimit the items.
pop()	This method removes and returns the last item in the array.
shift()	This method removes and returns the first element in the array.
push(item)	This method appends the specified item to the end of the array.
unshift(item)	This method inserts a new item at the start of the array.
reverse()	This method returns a new array that contains the items in reverse order.
slice(start,end)	This method returns a section of the array.
sort()	This method sorts the array. An optional comparison function can be used to perform custom comparisons.
splice(index, count)	This method removes count items from the array, starting at the specified index. The removed items are returned as the result of the method.
unshift(item)	This method inserts a new item at the start of the array.
every(test)	This method calls the test function for each item in the array and returns true if the function returns true for all of them and false otherwise.
some(test)	This method returns true if calling the test function for each item in the array returns true at least once.
filter(test)	This method returns a new array containing the items for which the test function returns true.
find(test)	This method returns the first item in the array for which the test function returns true.
findIndex(test)	This method returns the index of the first item in the array for which the test function returns true.
foreach(callback)	This method invokes the callback function for each item in the array, as described in the previous section.
includes(value)	This method returns true if the array contains the specified value.
map(callback)	This method returns a new array containing the result of invoking the callback function for every item in the array.
reduce(callback)	This method returns the accumulated value produced by invoking the callback function for every item in the array.

Since many of the methods in Table 5-6 return a new array, these methods can be chained together to process a filtered data array, as shown in Listing 5-33.

Listing 5-33. Processing a Data Array in the main.ts File in the src Folder

```
let products = [
    { name: "Hat", price: 24.5, stock: 10 },
    { name: "Kayak", price: 289.99, stock: 1 },
    { name: "Soccer Ball", price: 10, stock: 0 },
    { name: "Running Shoes", price: 116.50, stock: 20 }
];

let totalValue = products
    .filter(item => item.stock > 0)
    .reduce((prev, item) => prev + (item.price * item.stock), 0);

console.log("Total value: $" + totalValue.toFixed(2));
```

I use the filter method to select the items in the array whose stock value is greater than zero and use the reduce method to determine the total value of those items, producing the following output:

```
Total value: $2864.99
```

Summary

In this chapter, I provided a brief primer on the JavaScript, focusing on the core functionality that will get you started with the language. Some of the features that I described in this chapter are recent additions to the JavaScript specification and require the TypeScript compiler to convert them to code that can run in older browsers. I continue this theme in the next chapter and introduce some of the more advanced JavaScript features that are used in Angular development.

CHAPTER 6

■ ■ ■

JavaScript and TypeScript: Part 2

In this chapter, I describe some of the more advanced JavaScript features that are useful for Angular development. I explain how JavaScript deals with objects, including support for classes, and I explain how JavaScript functionality is packaged into JavaScript modules. I also introduce some of the features that TypeScript provides that are not part of the JavaScript specification and that I rely on for some of the examples later in the book. Table 6-1 summarizes the chapter.

Table 6-1. *Chapter Summary*

Problem	Solution	Listing
Create an object by specifying properties and values	Use the new keyword or use an object literal	1–3
Create an object using a template	Define a class	4, 5
Inherit behavior from another class	Use the extends keyword	6
Package JavaScript features together	Create a JavaScript module	7
Declare a dependency on a module	Use the import keyword	8–12
Declare the types used by properties, parameters, and variables	Use TypeScript type annotations	13–18
Specify multiple types	Use union types	19–21
Create ad hoc groups of types	Use tuples	22
Group values together by key	Use indexable types	23
Control access to the methods and properties in a class	Use the access control modifiers	24

Preparing the Example Project

For this chapter, I continue using the JavaScriptPrimer project from Chapter 5. No changes are required to prepare for this chapter, and running the following command in the JavaScriptPrimer folder will start the TypeScript compiler and the development HTTP server:

```
ng serve --port 3000 --open
```

© Adam Freeman 2018
A. Freeman, *Pro Angular 6*, https://doi.org/10.1007/978-1-4842-3649-9_6

A new browser window will open, but it will be empty because I removed the placeholder content in the previous chapter. The examples in this chapter rely on the browser's JavaScript console to display messages. If you look at the console, you will see the following result:

```
Total value: $2864.99
```

Working with Objects

There are several ways to create objects in JavaScript. Listing 6-1 gives a simple example to get started.

■ **Note** Some of the examples in this chapter cause the TypeScript compiler to report errors. The examples still work, and you can ignore these messages, which arise because TypeScript provides some extra features that I don't describe until later in this chapter.

Listing 6-1. Creating an Object in the main.ts File in the src Folder

```
let myData = new Object();
myData.name = "Adam";
myData.weather = "sunny";

console.log("Hello " + myData.name + ".");
console.log("Today is " + myData.weather + ".");
```

I create an object by calling new Object(), and I assign the result (the newly created object) to a variable called myData. Once the object is created, I can define properties on the object just by assigning values, like this:

```
...
myData.name = "Adam";
...
```

Prior to this statement, my object doesn't have a property called name. When the statement has executed, the property does exist, and it has been assigned the value Adam. You can read the value of a property by combining the variable name and the property name with a period, like this:

```
...
console.log("Hello " + myData.name + ".");
...
```

The result from the listing is as follows:

```
Hello Adam.
Today is sunny.
```

Using Object Literals

You can define an object and its properties in a single step using the *object literal* format, as shown in Listing 6-2.

Listing 6-2. Using the Object Literal Format in the main.ts File in the src Folder

```
let myData = {
    name: "Adam",
    weather: "sunny"
};

console.log("Hello " + myData.name + ". ");
console.log("Today is " + myData.weather + ".");
```

Each property that you want to define is separated from its value using a colon (:), and properties are separated using a comma (,). The effect is the same as in the previous example, and the result from the listing is as follows:

```
Hello Adam.
Today is sunny.
```

Using Functions as Methods

One of the features that I like most about JavaScript is the way you can add functions to objects. A function defined on an object is called a *method*. Listing 6-3 shows how you can add methods in this manner.

Listing 6-3. Adding Methods to an Object in the main.ts File in the src Folder

```
let myData = {
    name: "Adam",
    weather: "sunny",
    printMessages: function () {
        console.log("Hello " + this.name + ". ");
        console.log("Today is " + this.weather + ".");
    }
};
myData.printMessages();
```

In this example, I have used a function to create a method called printMessages. Notice that to refer to the properties defined by the object, I have to use the this keyword. When a function is used as a method, the function is implicitly passed the object on which the method has been called as an argument through the special variable this. The output from the listing is as follows:

```
Hello Adam.
Today is sunny.
```

Defining Classes

Classes are templates that are used to create objects that have identical functionality. Support for classes is a recent addition to the JavaScript specification intended to make working with JavaScript more consistent with other mainstream programming languages, and classes are used throughout Angular development. Listing 6-4 shows how the functionality defined by the object in the previous section can be expressed using a class.

Listing 6-4. Defining a Class in the main.ts File in the src Folder

```
class MyClass {

    constructor(name, weather) {
        this.name = name;
        this.weather = weather;
    }

    printMessages() {
        console.log("Hello " + this.name + ". ");
        console.log("Today is " + this.weather + ".");
    }
}

let myData = new MyClass("Adam", "sunny");
myData.printMessages();
```

JavaScript classes will be familiar if you have used another mainstream language such as Java or C#. The class keyword is used to declare a class, followed by the name of the class, which is MyClass in this case.

The constructor function is invoked when a new object is created using the class, and it provides an opportunity to receive data values and do any initial setup that the class requires. In the example, the constructor defines name and weather parameters that are used to create variables with the same names. Variables defined like this are known as *properties*.

Classes can have methods, which defined as functions, albeit without needing to use the function keyword. There is one method in the example, called printMessages, and it uses the values of the name and weather properties to write messages to the browser's JavaScript console.

■ **Tip**   Classes can also have static methods, denoted by the static keyword. Static methods belong to the class rather than the objects they create. I have included an example of a static method in Listing 6-14.

The new keyword is used to create an object from a class, like this:

```
...
let myData = new MyClass("Adam", "sunny");
...
```

This statement creates a new object using the MyClass class as its template. MyClass is used as a function in this situation, and the arguments passed to it will be received by the constructor function defined by the class. The result of this expression is a new object that is assigned to a variable called myData. Once you have created an object, you can access its properties and methods through the variable to which it has been assigned, like this:

```
...
myData.printMessages();
...
```

This example produces the following results in the browser's JavaScript console:

```
Hello Adam.
Today is sunny.
```

JAVASCRIPT CLASSES VS PROTOTYPES

The class feature doesn't change the underlying way that JavaScript handles types. Instead, it simply provides a way to use them that is more familiar to the majority of programmers. Behind the scenes, JavaScript still uses its traditional type system, which is based on prototypes. As an example, the code in Listing 6-4 can also be written like this:

```
var MyClass = function MyClass(name, weather) {
    this.name = name;
    this.weather = weather;
}

MyClass.prototype.printMessages = function () {
    console.log("Hello " + this.name + ". ");
    console.log("Today is " + this.weather + ".");
};

var myData = new MyClass("Adam", "sunny");
myData.printMessages();
```

Angular development is easier when using classes, which is the approach that I have taken throughout this book. A lot of the features introduced in ES6 are classified as syntactic sugar, which means they make aspects of JavaScript easier to understand and use. The term *syntactic sugar* may seem pejorative, but JavaScript has some odd quirks, and many of these features help developers avoid common pitfalls.

Defining Class Getter and Setter Properties

JavaScript classes can define properties in their constructor, resulting in a variable that can be read and modified elsewhere in the application. Getters and setters appear as regular properties outside of the class, but they allow the introduction of additional logic, which is useful for validating or transforming new values or generating values programmatically, as shown in Listing 6-5.

Listing 6-5. Using Getters and Setters in the main.ts File in the src Folder

```
class MyClass {
    constructor(name, weather) {
        this.name = name;
        this._weather = weather;
    }

    set weather(value) {
        this._weather = value;
    }

    get weather() {
        return `Today is ${this._weather}`;
    }

    printMessages() {
        console.log("Hello " + this.name + ". ");
        console.log(this.weather);
    }
}

let myData = new MyClass("Adam", "sunny");
myData.printMessages();
```

The getter and setter are implemented as functions preceded by the get or set keyword. There is no notion of access control in JavaScript classes, and the convention is to prefix the names of internal properties with an underscore (the _ character). In the listing, the weather property is implemented with a setter that updates a property called _weather and a getter that incorporates the _weather value in a template string. This example produces the following results in the browser's JavaScript console:

```
Hello Adam.
Today is sunny
```

Using Class Inheritance

Classes can inherit behavior from other classes using the extends keyword, as shown in Listing 6-6.

Listing 6-6. Using Class Inheritance in the main.ts File in the src Folder

```
class MyClass {
    constructor(name, weather) {
        this.name = name;
        this._weather = weather;
    }

    set weather(value) {
        this._weather = value;
    }
```

```
    get weather() {
        return `Today is ${this._weather}`;
    }

    printMessages() {
        console.log("Hello " + this.name + ". ");
        console.log(this.weather);
    }
}

class MySubClass extends MyClass {

    constructor(name, weather, city) {
        super(name, weather);
        this.city = city;
    }

    printMessages() {
        super.printMessages();
        console.log(`You are in ${this.city}`);
    }
}

let myData = new MySubClass("Adam", "sunny", "London");
myData.printMessages();
```

The extends keyword is used to declare the class that will be inherited from, known as the *superclass* or *base class*. In the listing, the MySubClass inherits from MyClass. The super keyword is used to invoke the superclass's constructor and methods. The MySubClass builds on the MyClass functionality to add support for a city, producing the following results in the browser's JavaScript console:

```
Hello Adam.
Today is sunny
You are in London
```

Working with JavaScript Modules

JavaScript modules are used to manage the dependencies in a web application, which means you don't need to manage a large set of individual code files to ensure that the browser downloads all the code for the application. Instead, during the compilation process, all of the JavaScript files that the application requires are combined into a larger file, known as a *bundle*, and it is this that is downloaded by the browser.

■ **Note**   Older versions of Angular relied on a module loader, which would send separate HTTP requests for the JavaScript files required by an application. Changes to the development tools have simplified this process and switch to using bundles created during the build process.

Creating and Using Modules

Each TypeScript or JavaScript file that you add to a project is treated as a module. To demonstrate, I created a folder called `modules` in the `src` folder, added to it a file called `NameAndWeather.ts`, and added the code shown in Listing 6-7.

Listing 6-7. The Contents of the NameAndWeather.ts File in the src/modules Folder

```
export class Name {
    constructor(first, second) {
        this.first = first;
        this.second = second;
    }

    get nameMessage() {
        return `Hello ${this.first} ${this.second}`;
    }
}

export class WeatherLocation {
    constructor(weather, city) {
        this.weather = weather;
        this.city = city;
    }

    get weatherMessage() {
        return `It is ${this.weather} in ${this.city}`;
    }
}
```

The classes, functions, and variables defined in a JavaScript or TypeScript file can be accessed only within that file by default. The `export` keyword is used to make features accessible outside of the file so that they can be used by other parts of the application. In the example, I have applied the `export` keyword to the `Name` and `WeatherLocation` classes, which means they are available to be used outside of the module.

■ **Tip** I have defined two classes in the `NameAndWeather.ts` file, which has the effect of creating a module that contains two classes. The convention in Angular applications is to put each class into its own file, which means that each class is defined in its own module and that you will see the `export` keyword is the listings throughout this book.

The `import` keyword is used to declare a dependency on the features that a module provides. In Listing 6-8, I have used `Name` and `WeatherLocation` classes in the `main.ts` file, and that means I have to use the `import` keyword to declare a dependency on them and the module they come from.

Listing 6-8. Importing Specific Types in the main.ts File in the src Folder

```
import { Name, WeatherLocation } from "./modules/NameAndWeather";

let name = new Name("Adam", "Freeman");
let loc = new WeatherLocation("raining", "London");
```

```
console.log(name.nameMessage);
console.log(loc.weatherMessage);
```

This is the way that I use the `import` keyword in most of the examples in this book. The keyword is followed by curly braces that contain a comma-separated list of the features that the code in the current files depends on, followed by the `from` keyword, followed by the module name. In this case, I have imported the `Name` and `WeatherLocation` classes from the `NameAndWeather` module in the `modules` folder. Notice that the file extension is not included when specifying the module.

When the changes to the `main.ts` file are saved, the Angular development tools build the project and see that the code in the `main.ts` file depends on the code in the `NameAndWeather.ts` file. This dependency ensures that the `Name` and `WeatherLocation` classes are included in the JavaScript bundle file, and you will see the following output in the browser's JavaScript console, showing that code in the module was used to produce the result:

```
Hello Adam Freeman
It is raining in London
```

Notice that I didn't have to include the `NaneAndWeather.ts` file in a list of files to be sent to the browser. Just using the `import` keyword is enough to declare the dependency and ensure that the code required by the application is included in the JavaScript file sent to the browser.

(You will see errors warning you that properties have not been defined. Ignore those warnings for the moment; I explain how they are resolved later in the chapter.)

UNDERSTANDING MODULE RESOLUTION

You will see two different ways of specifying modules in the `import` statements in this book. The first is a relative module, in which the name of the module is prefixed with `./`, like this example from Listing 6-8:

```
...
import { Name, WeatherLocation } from "./modules/NameAndWeather";
...
```

This statement specifies a module located relative to the file that contains the `import` statement. In this case, the `NameAndWeather.ts` file is in the `modules` directory, which is in the same directory as the `main.ts` file. The other type of import is nonrelative. Here is an example of a nonrelative import from Chapter 2 and one that you will see throughout this book:

```
...
import { Component } from "@angular/core";
...
```

The module in this `import` statement doesn't start with `./`, and the build tools resolve the dependency by looking for a package in the `node_modules` folder. In this case, the dependency is on a feature provided by the `@angular/core` package, which is added to the project when it is created by the `ng new` command.

Renaming Imports

In complex projects that have lots of dependencies, it is possible that you will need to use two classes with the same name from different modules. To re-create this situation, I created a file called DuplicateName.ts in the src/modules folder and defined the class shown in Listing 6-9.

Listing 6-9. The Contents of the DuplicateName.ts File in the src/modules Folder

```
export class Name {

    get message() {
        return "Other Name";
    }
}
```

This class doesn't do anything useful, but it is called Name, which means that importing it using the approach in Listing 6-8 will cause a conflict because the compiler won't be able to differentiate between the two classes with that name. The solution is to use the as keyword, which allows an alias to be created for a class when it is imported from a module, as shown in Listing 6-10.

Listing 6-10. Using a Module Alias in the main.ts File in the src Folder

```
import { Name, WeatherLocation } from "./modules/NameAndWeather";
import { Name as OtherName } from "./modules/DuplicateName";

let name = new Name("Adam", "Freeman");
let loc = new WeatherLocation("raining", "London");
let other = new OtherName();

console.log(name.nameMessage);
console.log(loc.weatherMessage);
console.log(other.message);
```

The Name class in the DupliateName module is imported as OtherName, which allows it to be used without conflicting with the Name class in the NameAndWeather module. This example produces the following output:

```
Hello Adam Freeman
It is raining in London
Other Name
```

Importing All of the Types in a Module

An alternative approach is to import the module as an object that has properties for each of the types it contains, as shown in Listing 6-11.

Listing 6-11. Importing a Module as an Object in the main.ts File in the src Folder

```
import * as NameAndWeatherLocation from "./modules/NameAndWeather";
import { Name as OtherName } from "./modules/DuplicateName";
```

```
let name = new NameAndWeatherLocation.Name("Adam", "Freeman");
let loc = new NameAndWeatherLocation.WeatherLocation("raining", "London");
let other = new OtherName();

console.log(name.nameMessage);
console.log(loc.weatherMessage);
console.log(other.message);
```

The `import` statement in this example imports the contents of the `NameAndWeather` module and creates an object called `NameAndWeatherLocation`. This object has `Name` and `Weather` properties that correspond to the classes defined in the module. This example produces the same output as Listing 6-10.

Useful TypeScript Features

TypeScript is a superset of JavaScript, providing language features that build on those that are provided by the JavaScript specification. In the sections that follow, I demonstrate the most useful TypeScript features for Angular development, many of which I have used in the examples in this book.

■ **Tip** TypeScript supports more features than I describe in this chapter. I introduce some additional features as I use them in later chapters, but for a full reference, see the TypeScript home page at `www.typescriptlang.org`.

Using Type Annotations

The headline TypeScript feature is support for type annotations, which can help reduce common JavaScript errors by applying type checking when the code is compiled, in a way that is reminiscent of languages like C# or Java. If you have struggled to come to terms with the JavaScript type system (or didn't even realize that there was one), then type annotations can go a long way to preventing the most common errors. (On the other hand, if you like the freedom of regular JavaScript types, you may find TypeScript type annotations restrictive and annoying.)

To show the kind of problem that type annotations solve, I created a file called `tempConverter.ts` in the `JavaScriptPrimer` folder and added the code in Listing 6-12.

Listing 6-12. The Contents of the tempConverter.ts in the src Folder

```
export class TempConverter {

    static convertFtoC(temp) {
        return ((parseFloat(temp.toPrecision(2)) - 32) / 1.8).toFixed(1);
    }
}
```

The `TempConverter` class contains a simple static method called `convertFtoC` that accepts a temperature value expressed in degrees Fahrenheit and returns the same temperature expressed in degrees Celsius.

There are assumptions in this code that are not explicit. The convertFtoC method expects to receive a number value, on which the toPrecision method is called to set the number of floating-point digits. The method returns a string, although that is difficult to tell without inspecting the code carefully (the result of the toFixed method is a string).

These implicit assumptions lead to problems, especially when one developer is using JavaScript code written by another. In Listing 6-13, I have deliberately created an error by passing the temperature as a string value, instead of the number that the method expects.

Listing 6-13. Using the Wrong Type in the main.ts File in the src Folder

```
import { Name, WeatherLocation } from "./modules/NameAndWeather";
import { Name as OtherName } from "./modules/DuplicateName";
import { TempConverter } from "./tempConverter";

let name = new Name("Adam", "Freeman");
let loc = new WeatherLocation("raining", "London");
let other = new OtherName();

let cTemp = TempConverter.convertFtoC("38");

console.log(name.nameMessage);
console.log(loc.weatherMessage);
console.log(`The temp is ${cTemp}C`);
```

When the code is executed by the browser, you will see the following message in the browser's JavaScript console (the exact working may differ based on the browser you are using):

```
temp.toPrecision is not a function
```

This kind of issue can be fixed without using TypeScript, of course, but it does mean that a substantial amount of the code in any JavaScript application is given over to checking the types that are being used. The TypeScript solution is to make type enforcement the job of the compiler, using type annotations that are added to the JavaScript code. In Listing 6-14, I have added type annotations to the TempConverter class.

Listing 6-14. Adding Type Annotations in the tempConverter.ts File in the src Folder

```
export class TempConverter {

    static convertFtoC(temp: number) : string {
        return ((parseFloat(temp.toPrecision(2)) - 32) / 1.8).toFixed(1);
    }
}
```

Type annotations are expressed using a colon (the : character) followed by the type. There are two annotations in the example. The first specifies that the parameter to the convertFtoC method should be a number.

```
...
static convertFtoC(temp: number) : string {
...
```

98

The other annotation specifies that the result of the method is a string.

```
...
static convertFtoC(temp: number) : string {
...
```

When you save the changes to the file, the TypeScript compiler will run. Among the errors that are reported will be this one:

```
Argument of type 'string' is not assignable to parameter of type 'number'.
```

The TypeScript compiler has examined that the type of the value passed to the convertFtoC method in the main.ts file doesn't match the type annotation and has reported an error. This is the core of the TypeScript type system; it means you don't have to write additional code in your classes to check that you have received the expected types, and it also makes it easy to determine the type of a method result. To resolve the error reported to the compiler, Listing 6-15 updates the statement that invokes the convertFtoC method so that it uses a number.

Listing 6-15. Using a Number Argument in the main.ts File in the src Folder

```
import { Name, WeatherLocation } from "./modules/NameAndWeather";
import { Name as OtherName } from "./modules/DuplicateName";
import { TempConverter } from "./tempConverter";

let name = new Name("Adam", "Freeman");
let loc = new WeatherLocation("raining", "London");
let other = new OtherName();

let cTemp = TempConverter.convertFtoC(38);

console.log(name.nameMessage);
console.log(loc.weatherMessage);
console.log(other.message);
console.log(`The temp is ${cTemp}C`);
```

When you save the changes, you will see the following messages displayed in the browser's JavaScript console:

```
Hello Adam Freeman
It is raining in London
Other Name
The temp is 3.3C
```

Type Annotating Properties and Variables

Type annotations can also be applied to properties and variables, ensuring that all of the types used in an application can be verified by the compiler. In Listing 6-16, I have added type annotations to the classes in the NameAndWeather module.

Listing 6-16. Adding Annotations in the NameAndWeather.ts File in the src/modules Folder

```
export class Name {
    first: string;
    second: string;

    constructor(first: string, second: string) {
        this.first = first;
        this.second = second;
    }

    get nameMessage() : string {
        return `Hello ${this.first} ${this.second}`;
    }
}

export class WeatherLocation {
    weather: string;
    city: string;

    constructor(weather: string, city: string) {
        this.weather = weather;
        this.city = city;
    }

    get weatherMessage() : string {
        return `It is ${this.weather} in ${this.city}`;
    }
}
```

Properties are declared with a type annotation, following the same pattern as for parameter and result annotations. The changes in Listing 6-17 resolve the remaining errors reported by the TypeScript compiler, which was complaining because it didn't know what the types were for the properties created in the constructors.

The pattern of receiving constructor parameters and assigning their values to variables is so common that TypeScript includes an optimization, as shown in Listing 6-17.

Listing 6-17. Using Parameters in the NameAndWeather.ts File in the src/modules Folder

```
export class Name {

    constructor(private first: string, private second: string) {}

    get nameMessage() : string {
        return `Hello ${this.first} ${this.second}`;
    }
}
```

```
export class WeatherLocation {

    constructor(private weather: string, private city: string) {}

    get weatherMessage() : string {
        return `It is ${this.weather} in ${this.city}`;
    }
}
```

The keyword private is an example of an access control modifier, which I describe in the "Using Access Modifiers" section. Applying the keyword to the constructor parameter has the effect of automatically defining the class property and assigning it the parameter value. The code in Listing 6-17 is a more concise version of Listing 6-16.

Specifying Multiple Types or Any Type

TypeScript allows multiple types to be specified, separated using a bar (the | character). This can be useful when a method can accept or return multiple types or when a variable can be assigned values of different types. Listing 6-18 modifies the convertFtoC method so that it will accept number or string values.

Listing 6-18. Accepting Multiple Values in the tempConverter.ts File in the src Folder

```
export class TempConverter {

    static convertFtoC(temp: number | string): string {
        let value: number = (<number>temp).toPrecision
            ? <number>temp : parseFloat(<string>temp);
        return ((parseFloat(value.toPrecision(2)) - 32) / 1.8).toFixed(1);
    }
}
```

The type declaration for the temp parameter has changes to number | string, which means that the method can accept either value. This is called a *union type*. Within the method, a type assertion is used to work out which type has been received. This is a slightly awkward process, but the parameter value is cast to a number value to check whether there is a toPrecision method defined on the result, like this:

```
...
(<number>temp).toPrecision
...
```

The angle brackets (the < and > characters) are to declare a type assertion, which will attempt to convert an object to the specified type. You can also achieve the same result using the as keyword, as shown in Listing 6-19.

Listing 6-19. Using the as Keyword in the tempConverter.ts File in the src Folder

```
export class TempConverter {

    static convertFtoC(temp: number | string): string {
        let value: number = (temp as number).toPrecision
            ? temp as number : parseFloat(<string>temp);
```

```
        return ((parseFloat(value.toPrecision(2)) - 32) / 1.8).toFixed(1);
    }
}
```

An alternative to specifying a union type is to use the any keyword, which allows any type to be assigned to a variable, used as an argument, or returned from a method. Listing 6-20 replaces the union type in the convertFtoC method with the any keyword.

■ **Tip**   The TypeScript compiler will implicitly apply the any keyword when you omit a type annotation.

Listing 6-20. Specifying Any Type in the tempConverter.ts File in the src Folder

```
export class TempConverter {

    static convertFtoC(temp: any): string {
        let value: number;
        if ((temp as number).toPrecision) {
            value = temp;
        } else if ((temp as string).indexOf) {
            value = parseFloat(<string>temp);
        } else {
            value = 0;
        }
        return ((parseFloat(value.toPrecision(2)) - 32) / 1.8).toFixed(1);
    }
}
```

Using Tuples

Tuples are fixed-length arrays, where each item in the array is of a specified type. This is a vague-sounding description because tuples are so flexible. As an example, Listing 6-21 uses a tuple to represent a city and its current weather and temperature.

Listing 6-21. Using a Tuple in the main.ts File in the src Folder

```
import { Name, WeatherLocation } from "./modules/NameAndWeather";
import { Name as OtherName } from "./modules/DuplicateName";
import { TempConverter } from "./tempConverter";

let name = new Name("Adam", "Freeman");
let loc = new WeatherLocation("raining", "London");
let other = new OtherName();

let cTemp = TempConverter.convertFtoC("38");

let tuple: [string, string, string];
tuple = ["London", "raining", TempConverter.convertFtoC("38")]

console.log(`It is ${tuple[2]} degrees C and ${tuple[1]} in ${tuple[0]}`);
```

Tuples are defined as an array of types, and individual elements are accessed using array indexers. This example produces the following message in the browser's JavaScript console:

```
It is 3.3 degrees C and raining in London
```

Using Indexable Types

Indexable types associate a key with a value, creating a map-like collection that can be used to gather related data items together. In Listing 6-22, I have used an indexable type to collect together information about multiple cities.

Listing 6-22. Using Indexable Types in the main.ts File in the src Folder

```
import { Name, WeatherLocation } from "./modules/NameAndWeather";
import { Name as OtherName } from "./modules/DuplicateName";
import { TempConverter } from "./tempConverter";

let cities: { [index: string]: [string, string] } = {};

cities["London"] = ["raining", TempConverter.convertFtoC("38")];
cities["Paris"] = ["sunny", TempConverter.convertFtoC("52")];
cities["Berlin"] = ["snowing", TempConverter.convertFtoC("23")];

for (let key in cities) {
    console.log(`${key}: ${cities[key][0]}, ${cities[key][1]}`);
}
```

The cities variable is defined as an indexable type, with the key as a string and the data value as a [string, string] tuple. Values are assigned and read using array-style indexers, such as cities["London"]. The collection of keys in an indexable type can be accessed using a for...in loop, as shown in the example, which produces the following output in the browser's JavaScript console:

```
London: raining, 3.3
Paris: sunny, 11.1
Berlin: snowing, -5.0
```

Only number and string values can be used as the keys for indexable types, but this is a helpful feature that I use in examples in later chapters.

Using Access Modifiers

JavaScript doesn't support access protection, which means that classes, their properties, and their methods can all be accessed from any part of the application. There is a convention of prefixing the name of implementation members with an underscore (the _ character), but this is just a warning to other developers and is not enforced.

TypeScript provides three keywords that are used to manage access and that are enforced by the compiler. Table 6-2 describes the keywords.

■ **Caution** During development, these keywords have limited effect in Angular applications because a lot of functionality is delivered through properties and methods that are specified in fragments of code embedded in data binding expressions. These expressions are evaluated at runtime in the browser, where there is no enforcement of TypeScript features. They become more important when you come to deploy the application, and it is important to ensure that any property or method that is accessed in a data binding expression is marked as public or has no access modifier (which has the same effect as using the public keyword).

Table 6-2. *The TypeScript Access Modifier Keywords*

Keyword	Description
public	This keyword is used to denote a property or method that can be accessed anywhere. This is the default access protection if no keyword is used.
private	This keyword is used to denote a property or method that can be accessed only within the class that defines it.
protected	This keyword is used to denote a property or method that can be accessed only within the class that defines it or by classes that extend that class.

Listing 6-23 adds a private method to the TempConverter class.

Listing 6-23. Using an Access Modifier in the tempConverter.ts File in the src Folder

```
export class TempConverter {

    static convertFtoC(temp: any): string {
        let value: number;
        if ((temp as number).toPrecision) {
            value = temp;
        } else if ((temp as string).indexOf) {
            value = parseFloat(<string>temp);
        } else {
            value = 0;
        }
        return TempConverter.performCalculation(value).toFixed(1);
    }

    private static performCalculation(value: number): number {
        return (parseFloat(value.toPrecision(2)) - 32) / 1.8;
    }
}
```

The performCalculation method is marked as private, which means the TypeScript compiler will report an error code if any other part of the application tries to invoke the method.

Summary

In this chapter, I described the way that JavaScript supports working with objects and classes, explained how JavaScript modules work, and introduced the TypeScript features that are useful for Angular development. In the next chapter, I start the process of creating a realistic project that provides an overview of how different Angular features work together to create applications before digging into individual details in Part 2 of this book.

CHAPTER 7

■ ■ ■

SportsStore: A Real Application

In Chapter 2, I built a quick and simple Angular application. Small and focused examples allow me to demonstrate specific Angular features, but they can lack context. To help overcome this problem, I am going to create a simple but realistic e-commerce application.

My application, called SportsStore, will follow the classic approach taken by online stores everywhere. I will create an online product catalog that customers can browse by category and page, a shopping cart where users can add and remove products, and a checkout where customers can enter their shipping details and place their orders. I will also create an administration area that includes create, read, update, and delete (CRUD) facilities for managing the catalog—and I will protect it so that only logged-in administrators can make changes. Finally, I show you how to prepare and deploy an Angular application.

My goal in this chapter and those that follow is to give you a sense of what real Angular development is like by creating as realistic an example as possible. I want to focus on Angular, of course, and so I have simplified the integration with external systems, such as the data store, and omitted others entirely, such as payment processing.

The SportsStore example is one that I use in a few of my books, not least because it demonstrates the ways in which different frameworks, languages, and development styles can be used to achieve the same result. You don't need to have read any of my other books to follow this chapter, but you will find the contrasts interesting if you already own my *Pro ASP.NET Core MVC 2* book, for example.

The Angular features that I use in the SportsStore application are covered in-depth in later chapters. Rather than duplicate everything here, I tell you just enough to make sense of the example application and refer you to other chapters for in-depth information. You can either read the SportsStore chapters from end to end to get a sense of how Angular works or jump to and from the detail chapters to get into the depth. Either way, don't expect to understand everything right away—Angular has a lot of moving parts, and the SportsStore application is intended to show you how they fit together without diving too deeply into the details that I spend the rest of the book describing.

Preparing the Project

To create the SportsStore project, open a command prompt, navigate to a convenient location, and run the following command:

```
ng new SportsStore
```

The angular-cli package will create a new project for Angular development, with configuration files, placeholder content, and development tools. The project setup process can take some time since there are many NPM packages to download and install.

© Adam Freeman 2018
A. Freeman, *Pro Angular 6*, https://doi.org/10.1007/978-1-4842-3649-9_7

■ **Tip**   You can download the example project for this chapter—and for all the other chapters in this book—from `https://github.com/Apress/pro-angular-6`.

Installing the Additional NPM Packages

Additional packages are required for the SportsStore project, in addition to the core Angular packages and build tools set up by the ng new command. Run the following commands to navigate to the SportsStore folder and add the required packages:

```
cd SportsStore
npm install bootstrap@4.1.1
npm install font-awesome@4.7.0
npm install --save-dev json-server@0.12.1
npm install --save-dev jsonwebtoken@8.1.1
```

It is important to use the version numbers shown in the listing. You may see warnings about unmet peer dependencies as you add the packages, but you can ignore them. Some of the packages are installed using the --save-dev argument, which indicates they are used during development and will not be part of the SportsStore application.

Adding the CSS Style Sheets to the Application

Once the packages have been installed, add the statements shown in Listing 7-1 to the angular.json file to incorporate the CSS files from the Bootstrap CSS framework and the Font Awesome packages into the application. I will use the Bootstrap CSS styles for all the HTML content in the SportsStore application, and I use icons from the Font Awesome package to present a summary of a shopping cart to the user.

Listing 7-1. Adding CSS to the angular.json File in the SportsStore Folder

```
...
"architect": {
  "build": {
    "builder": "@angular-devkit/build-angular:browser",
    "options": {
      "outputPath": "dist/SportsStore",
      "index": "src/index.html",
      "main": "src/main.ts",
      "polyfills": "src/polyfills.ts",
      "tsConfig": "src/tsconfig.app.json",
      "assets": [
        "src/favicon.ico",
        "src/assets"
      ],
      "styles": [
        "src/styles.css",
        "node_modules/bootstrap/dist/css/bootstrap.min.css",
        "node_modules/font-awesome/css/font-awesome.min.css"
      ],
```

```
    "scripts": []
  },
...
```

Preparing the RESTful Web Service

The SportsStore application will use asynchronous HTTP requests to get model data provided by a RESTful web service. As I describe in Chapter 24, REST is an approach to designing web services that use the HTTP method or verb to specify an operation and the URL to select the data objects that the operation applies to.

I added the json-server package to the project in the previous section. This is an excellent package for creating web services from JSON data or JavaScript code. Add the statement shown in Listing 7-2 to the scripts section of the package.json file so that the json-server package can be started from the command line.

Listing 7-2. Adding a Script in the package.json File in the SportsStore Folder

```
...
"scripts": {
  "ng": "ng",
  "start": "ng serve",
  "build": "ng build",
  "test": "ng test",
  "lint": "ng lint",
  "e2e": "ng e2e",
  "json": "json-server data.js -p 3500 -m authMiddleware.js"
},
...
```

To provide the json-server package with data to work with, I added a file called data.js in the SportsStore folder and added the code shown Listing 7-3, which will ensure that the same data is available whenever the json-server package is started so that I have a fixed point of reference during development.

■ **Tip** It is important to pay attention to the file names when creating the configuration files. Some have the .json extension, which means they contain static data formatted as JSON. Other files have the .js extension, which means they contain JavaScript code. Each tool required for Angular development has expectations about its configuration file.

Listing 7-3. The Contents of the data.js File in the SportsStore Folder

```
module.exports = function () {
    return {
        products: [
            { id: 1, name: "Kayak", category: "Watersports",
                description: "A boat for one person", price: 275 },
            { id: 2, name: "Lifejacket", category: "Watersports",
                description: "Protective and fashionable", price: 48.95 },
            { id: 3, name: "Soccer Ball", category: "Soccer",
                description: "FIFA-approved size and weight", price: 19.50 },
            { id: 4, name: "Corner Flags", category: "Soccer",
```

```
                description: "Give your playing field a professional touch",
                    price: 34.95 },
                { id: 5, name: "Stadium", category: "Soccer",
                    description: "Flat-packed 35,000-seat stadium", price: 79500 },
                { id: 6, name: "Thinking Cap", category: "Chess",
                    description: "Improve brain efficiency by 75%", price: 16 },
                { id: 7, name: "Unsteady Chair", category: "Chess",
                    description: "Secretly give your opponent a disadvantage",
                    price: 29.95 },
                { id: 8, name: "Human Chess Board", category: "Chess",
                    description: "A fun game for the family", price: 75 },
                { id: 9, name: "Bling Bling King", category: "Chess",
                    description: "Gold-plated, diamond-studded King", price: 1200 }
        ],
        orders: []
    }
}
```

This code defines two data collections that will be presented by the RESTful web service. The `products` collection contains the products for sale to the customer, while the `orders` collection will contain the orders that customers have placed (but which is currently empty).

The data stored by the RESTful web service needs to be protected so that ordinary users can't modify the products or change the status of orders. The `json-server` package doesn't include any built-in authentication features, so I created a file called `authMiddleware.js` in the `SportsStore` folder and added the code shown in Listing 7-4.

Listing 7-4. The Contents of the authMiddleware.js File in the SportsStore Folder

```
const jwt = require("jsonwebtoken");

const APP_SECRET = "myappsecret";
const USERNAME = "admin";
const PASSWORD = "secret";

module.exports = function (req, res, next) {

    if ((req.url == "/api/login" || req.url == "/login")
            && req.method == "POST") {
        if (req.body != null && req.body.name == USERNAME
                && req.body.password == PASSWORD) {
            let token = jwt.sign({ data: USERNAME, expiresIn: "1h" }, APP_SECRET);
            res.json({ success: true, token: token });
        } else {
            res.json({ success: false });
        }
        res.end();
        return;
    } else if ((((req.url.startsWith("/api/products")
                || req.url.startsWith("/products"))
            || (req.url.startsWith("/api/categories")
                || req.url.startsWith("/categories"))) && req.method != "GET")
        || ((req.url.startsWith("/api/orders")
```

```
            || req.url.startsWith("/orders")) && req.method != "POST")) {
        let token = req.headers["authorization"];
        if (token != null && token.startsWith("Bearer<")) {
            token = token.substring(7, token.length - 1);
            try {
                jwt.verify(token, APP_SECRET);
                next();
                return;
            } catch (err) { }
        }
        res.statusCode = 401;
        res.end();
        return;
    }
    next();
}
```

This code inspects HTTP requests sent to the RESTful web service and implements some basic security features. This is server-side code that is not directly related to Angular development, so don't worry if its purpose isn't immediately obvious. I explain the authentication and authorization process in Chapter 9, including how to authenticate users with Angular.

■ **Caution**   Don't use the code in Listing 7-4 other than for the SportsStore application. It contains weak passwords that are hardwired into the code. This is fine for the SportsStore project because the emphasis is on the development client side with Angular, but this is not suitable for real projects.

Preparing the HTML File

Every Angular web application relies on an HTML file that is loaded by the browser and that loads and starts the application. Edit the index.html file in the SportsStore/src folder to remove the placeholder content and to add the elements shown in Listing 7-5.

Listing 7-5.   Preparing the index.html File in the src Folder

```
<!doctype html>
<html lang="en">
<head>
  <meta charset="utf-8">
  <title>SportsStore</title>
  <base href="/">
  <meta name="viewport" content="width=device-width, initial-scale=1">
  <link rel="icon" type="image/x-icon" href="favicon.ico">
</head>
<body class="m-2">
  <app>SportsStore Will Go Here</app>
</body>
</html>
```

The HTML document includes an app element, which is the placeholder for the SportsStore functionality. There is also a base element, which is required by the Angular URL routing features, which I add to the SportsStore project in Chapter 8.

Creating the Folder Structure

An important part of setting up any Angular application is to create the folder structure. The ng new command sets up a project that puts all of the application's files in the src folder, with the Angular files in the src/app folder. To add some structure to the project, create the additional folders shown in Table 7-1.

Table 7-1. *The Additional Folders Required for the SportsStore Project*

Folder	Description
SportsStore/src/app/model	This folder will contain the code for the data model.
SportsStore/src/app/store	This folder will contain the functionality for basic shopping.
SportsStore/src/app/admin	This folder will contain the functionality for administration.

Running the Example Application

Make sure that all the changes have been saved, and run the following command in the SportsStore folder:

```
ng serve --port 3000 --open
```

This command will start the development tools set up by the ng new command, which will automatically compile and package the code and content files in the src folder whenever a change is detected. A new browser window will open and show the content illustrated in Figure 7-1.

Figure 7-1. *Running the example application*

The development web server will start on port 3000, so the URL for the application will be http://localhost:3000. You don't have to include the name of the HTML document because index.html is the default file that the server responds with.

Starting the RESTful Web Service

To start the RESTful web service, open a new command prompt, navigate to the SportsStore folder, and run the following command:

```
npm run json
```

The RESTful web service is configured to run on port 3500. To test the web service request, use the browser to request the URL http://localhost:3500/products/1. The browser will display a JSON representation of one of the products defined in Listing 7-3, as follows:

```
{
  "id": 1,
  "name": "Kayak",
  "category": "Watersports",
  "description": "A boat for one person",
  "price": 275
}
```

Preparing the Angular Project Features

Every Angular project requires some basic preparation. In the sections that follow, I replace the placeholder content to build the foundation for the SportsStore application.

Updating the Root Component

The root component is the Angular building block that will manage the contents of the app element in the HTML document from Listing 7-5. An application can contain many components, but there is always a root component that takes responsibility for the top-level content presented to the user. I edited the file called app.component.ts in the SportsStore/src/app folder and replaced the existing code with the statements shown in Listing 7-6.

Listing 7-6. The Contents of the app.component.ts File in the src/app Folder

```
import { Component } from "@angular/core";

@Component({
  selector: "app",
  template: `<div class="bg-success p-2 text-center text-white">
                This is SportsStore
             </div>`
})
export class AppComponent { }
```

The @Component decorator tells Angular that the AppComponent class is a component and its properties configure how the component is applied. The complete set of component properties are described in Chapter 17, but the properties shown in the listing are the most basic and most frequently used.

The selector property tells Angular how to apply the component in the HTML document, and the template property defines the HTML content the component will display. Components can define inline templates, like this one, or they use external HTML files, which can make managing complex content easier.

There is no code in the AppComponent class because the root component in an Angular project exists just to manage the content shown to the user. Initially, I'll manage the content displayed by the root component manually, but in Chapter 8, I use a feature called *URL routing* to adapt the content automatically based on user actions.

Updating the Root Module

There are two types of Angular module: feature modules and the root module. Features modules are used to group related application functionality to make the application easier to manage. I create feature modules for each major functional area of the application, including the data model, the store interface presented to users, and the administration interface.

The root module is used to describe the application to Angular. The description includes which feature modules are required to run the application, which custom features should be loaded, and the name of the root component. The conventional name of the root component file is app.module.ts, which is created in the SportsStore/src/app folder. No changes are required to this file for the moment, and its initial content is shown in Listing 7-7.

Listing 7-7. The Contents of the app.module.ts File in the src/app Folder

```
import { BrowserModule } from '@angular/platform-browser';
import { NgModule } from '@angular/core';
import { AppComponent } from './app.component';

@NgModule({
  declarations: [AppComponent],
  imports: [BrowserModule],
  providers: [],
  bootstrap: [AppComponent]
})
export class AppModule { }
```

Similar to the root component, there is no code in the root module's class. That's because the root module only really exists to provide information through the @NgModule decorator. The imports property tells Angular that it should load the BrowserModule feature module, which contains the core Angular features required for a web application.

The declarations property tells Angular that it should load the root component, the providers property tells Angular about the shared objects used by the application, and the bootstrap property tells Angular that the root component is the AppModule class. I'll add information to this decorator's properties as I add features to the SportsStore application, but this basic configuration is enough to start the application.

Inspecting the Bootstrap File

The next piece of plumbing is the bootstrap file, which starts the application. This book is focused on using Angular to create applications that work in web browsers, but the Angular platform can be ported to different environments. The bootstrap file uses the Angular browser platform to load the root module and start the application. No changes are required for the contents of the main.ts file, which is in the SportsStore/src folder, as shown in Listing 7-8.

Listing 7-8. The Contents of the main.ts File in the src Folder

```
import { enableProdMode } from '@angular/core';
import { platformBrowserDynamic } from '@angular/platform-browser-dynamic';

import { AppModule } from './app/app.module';
import { environment } from './environments/environment';

if (environment.production) {
  enableProdMode();
}

platformBrowserDynamic().bootstrapModule(AppModule)
  .catch(err => console.log(err));
```

The development tools detect the changes to the project's file, compile the code files, and automatically reload the browser, producing the content shown in Figure 7-2.

Figure 7-2. *Starting the SportsStore application*

Starting the Data Model

The best place to start any new project is the data model. I want to get to the point where you can see some Angular features at work, so rather than define the data model from end to end, I am going to put some basic functionality in place using dummy data. I'll use this data to create user-facing features and then return to the data model to wire it up to the RESTful web service in Chapter 8.

Creating the Model Classes

Every data model needs classes that describe the types of data that will be contained in the data model. For the SportsStore application, this means classes that describe the products sold in the store and the orders that are received from customers.

Being able to describe products will be enough to get started with the SportsStore application, and I'll create other model classes to support features as I implement them. I created a file called product.model.ts in the SportsStore/src/app/model folder and added the code shown in Listing 7-9.

Listing 7-9. The Contents of the product.model.ts File in the src/app/model Folder

```
export class Product {

    constructor(
        public id?: number,
        public name?: string,
        public category?: string,
        public description?: string,
        public price?: number) { }
}
```

The Product class defines a constructor that accepts id, name, category, description, and price properties, which correspond to the structure of the data used to populate the RESTful web service in Listing 7-3. The question marks (the ? characters) that follow the parameter names indicate that these are optional parameters that can be omitted when creating new objects using the Product class, which can be useful when writing applications where model object properties will be populated using HTML forms.

Creating the Dummy Data Source

To prepare for the transition from dummy to real data, I am going to feed the application data using a data source. The rest of the application won't know where the data is coming from, which will make the switch to getting data using HTTP requests seamless.

I added a file called static.datasource.ts to the SportsStore/src/app/model folder and defined the class shown in Listing 7-10.

Listing 7-10. The Contents of the static.datasource.ts File in the src/app/model Folder

```
import { Injectable } from "@angular/core";
import { Product } from "./product.model";
import { Observable, from } from "rxjs";

@Injectable()
export class StaticDataSource {
    private products: Product[] = [
        new Product(1, "Product 1", "Category 1", "Product 1 (Category 1)", 100),
        new Product(2, "Product 2", "Category 1", "Product 2 (Category 1)", 100),
        new Product(3, "Product 3", "Category 1", "Product 3 (Category 1)", 100),
        new Product(4, "Product 4", "Category 1", "Product 4 (Category 1)", 100),
        new Product(5, "Product 5", "Category 1", "Product 5 (Category 1)", 100),
        new Product(6, "Product 6", "Category 2", "Product 6 (Category 2)", 100),
        new Product(7, "Product 7", "Category 2", "Product 7 (Category 2)", 100),
        new Product(8, "Product 8", "Category 2", "Product 8 (Category 2)", 100),
        new Product(9, "Product 9", "Category 2", "Product 9 (Category 2)", 100),
        new Product(10, "Product 10", "Category 2", "Product 10 (Category 2)", 100),
        new Product(11, "Product 11", "Category 3", "Product 11 (Category 3)", 100),
        new Product(12, "Product 12", "Category 3", "Product 12 (Category 3)", 100),
        new Product(13, "Product 13", "Category 3", "Product 13 (Category 3)", 100),
        new Product(14, "Product 14", "Category 3", "Product 14 (Category 3)", 100),
        new Product(15, "Product 15", "Category 3", "Product 15 (Category 3)", 100),
    ];
```

```
    getProducts(): Observable<Product[]> {
        return from([this.products]);
    }
}
```

The `StaticDataSource` class defines a method called `getProducts`, which returns the dummy data. The result of calling the `getProducts` method is an `Observable<Product[]>`, which is an `Observable` that produces arrays of `Product` objects.

The `Observable` class is provided by the Reactive Extensions package, which is used by Angular to handle state changes in applications. I describe the `Observable` class in Chapter 23, but for this chapter, it is enough to know that an `Observable` object represents an asynchronous task that will produce a result at some point in the future. Angular exposes its use of `Observable` objects for some features, including making HTTP requests, and this is why the `getProducts` method returns an `Observable<Product[]>` rather than simply returning the data synchronously.

The `@Injectable` decorator has been applied to the `StaticDataSource` class. This decorator is used to tell Angular that this class will be used as a service, which allows other classes to access its functionality through a feature called *dependency injection*, which is described in Chapters 19 and 20. You'll see how services work as the application takes shape.

■ **Tip**   Notice that I have to import `Injectable` from the `@angular/core` JavaScript module so that I can apply the `@Injectable` decorator. I won't highlight the all the different Angular classes that I import for the SportsStore example, but you can get full details in the chapters that describe the features they relate to.

Creating the Model Repository

The data source is responsible for providing the application with the data it requires, but access to that data is typically mediated by a *repository*, which is responsible for distributing that data to individual application building blocks so that the details of how the data has been obtained are kept hidden. I added a file called `product.repository.ts` in the `SportsStore/src/app/model` folder and defined the class shown in Listing 7-11.

Listing 7-11. The Contents of the product.repository.ts File in the src/app/model Folder

```
import { Injectable } from "@angular/core";
import { Product } from "./product.model";
import { StaticDataSource } from "./static.datasource";

@Injectable()
export class ProductRepository {
    private products: Product[] = [];
    private categories: string[] = [];

    constructor(private dataSource: StaticDataSource) {
        dataSource.getProducts().subscribe(data => {
            this.products = data;
            this.categories = data.map(p => p.category)
                .filter((c, index, array) => array.indexOf(c) == index).sort();
        });
    }
```

```
    getProducts(category: string = null): Product[] {
        return this.products
            .filter(p => category == null || category == p.category);
    }

    getProduct(id: number): Product {
        return this.products.find(p => p.id == id);
    }

    getCategories(): string[] {
        return this.categories;
    }
}
```

When Angular needs to create a new instance of the repository, it will inspect the class and see that it needs a StaticDataSource object to invoke the ProductRepository constructor and create a new object.

The repository constructor calls the data source's getProducts method and then uses the subscribe method on the Observable object that is returned to receive the product data. See Chapter 23 for details of how Observable objects work.

Creating the Feature Module

I am going to define an Angular feature model that will allow the data model functionality to be easily used elsewhere in the application. I added a file called model.module.ts in the SportsStore/src/app/model folder and defined the class shown in Listing 7-12.

■ **Tip** Don't worry if all the file names seem similar and confusing. You will get used to the way that Angular applications are structured as you work through the other chapters in the book, and you will soon be able to look at the files in an Angular project and know what they are all intended to do.

Listing 7-12. The Contents of the model.module.ts File in the src/app/model Folder

```
import { NgModule } from "@angular/core";
import { ProductRepository } from "./product.repository";
import { StaticDataSource } from "./static.datasource";

@NgModule({
    providers: [ProductRepository, StaticDataSource]
})
export class ModelModule { }
```

The @NgModule decorator is used to create feature modules, and its properties tell Angular how the module should be used. There is only one property in this module, providers, and it tells Angular which classes should be used as services for the dependency injection feature, which is described in Chapters 19 and 20. Features modules—and the @NgModule decorator—are described in Chapter 21.

Starting the Store

Now that the data model is in place, I can start to build out the store functionality, which will let the user see the products for sale and place orders for them. The basic structure of the store will be a two-column layout, with category buttons that allow the list of products to be filtered and a table that contains the list of products, as illustrated by Figure 7-3.

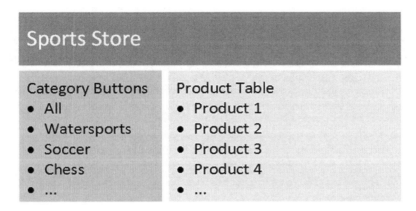

Figure 7-3. *The basic structure of the store*

In the sections that follow, I'll use Angular features and the data in the model to create the layout shown in the figure.

Creating the Store Component and Template

As you become familiar with Angular, you will learn that features can be combined to solve the same problem in different ways. I try to introduce some variety into the SportsStore project to showcase some important Angular features, but I am going to keep things simple for the moment in the interest of being able to get the project started quickly.

With this in mind, the starting point for the store functionality will be a new component, which is a class that provides data and logic to an HTML template, which contains data bindings that generate content dynamically. I created a file called `store.component.ts` in the `SportsStore/src/app/store` folder and defined the class shown in Listing 7-13.

Listing 7-13. The Contents of the store.component.ts File in the src/app/store Folder

```
import { Component } from "@angular/core";
import { Product } from "../model/product.model";
import { ProductRepository } from "../model/product.repository";

@Component({
    selector: "store",
    templateUrl: "store.component.html"
})
export class StoreComponent {
```

```
    constructor(private repository: ProductRepository) { }

    get products(): Product[] {
        return this.repository.getProducts();
    }

    get categories(): string[] {
        return this.repository.getCategories();
    }
}
```

The @Component decorator has been applied to the StoreComponent class, which tells Angular that it is a component. The decorator's properties tell Angular how to apply the component to HTML content (using an element called store) and how to find the component's template (in a file called store.component.html).

The StoreComponent class provides the logic that will support the template content. The constructor receives a ProductRepository object as an argument, provided through the dependency injection feature described in Chapters 20 and 21. The component defines products and categories properties that will be used to generate HTML content in the template, using data obtained from the repository. To provide the component with its template, I created a file called store.component.html in the SportsStore/src/app/store folder and added the HTML content shown in Listing 7-14.

Listing 7-14. The Contents of the store.component.html File in the src/app/store Folder

```
<div class="container-fluid">
  <div class="row">
    <div class="col bg-dark text-white">
      <a class="navbar-brand">SPORTS STORE</a>
    </div>
  </div>
  <div class="row text-white">
    <div class="col-3 bg-info p-2">
      {{categories.length}} Categories
    </div>
    <div class="col-9 bg-success p-2">
      {{products.length}} Products
    </div>
  </div>
</div>
```

The template is simple, just to get started. Most of the elements provide the structure for the store layout and apply some Bootstrap CSS classes. There are only two Angular data bindings at the moment, which are denoted by the {{ and }} characters. These are *string interpolation* bindings, and they tell Angular to evaluate the binding expression and insert the result into the element. The expressions in these bindings display the number of products and categories provided by the store component.

Creating the Store Feature Module

There isn't much store functionality in place at the moment, but even so, some additional work is required to wire it up to the rest of the application. To create the Angular feature module for the store functionality, I created a file called store.module.ts in the SportsStore/src/app/store folder and added the code shown in Listing 7-15.

Listing 7-15. The Contents of the store.module.ts File in the src/app/store Folder

```
import { NgModule } from "@angular/core";
import { BrowserModule } from "@angular/platform-browser";
import { FormsModule } from "@angular/forms";
import { ModelModule } from "../model/model.module";
import { StoreComponent } from "./store.component";

@NgModule({
    imports: [ModelModule, BrowserModule, FormsModule],
    declarations: [StoreComponent],
    exports: [StoreComponent]
})
export class StoreModule { }
```

The @NgModule decorator configures the module, using the imports property to tell Angular that the store module depends on the model module as well as BrowserModule and FormsModule, which contain the standard Angular features for web applications and working with HTML form elements. The decorator uses the declarations property to tell Angular about the StoreComponent class, which the exports property tells Angular can be also used in other parts of the application, which is important because it will be used by the root module.

Updating the Root Component and Root Module

Applying the basic model and store functionality requires updating the application's root module to import the two feature modules and also requires updating the root module's template to add the HTML element to which the component in the store module will be applied. Listing 7-16 shows the change to the root component's template.

Listing 7-16. Adding an Element in the app.component.ts File in the src/app Folder

```
import { Component } from "@angular/core";

@Component({
    selector: "app",
    template: "<store></store>"
})
export class AppComponent { }
```

The store element replaces the previous content in the root component's template and corresponds to the value of the selector property of the @Component decorator in Listing 7-13. Listing 7-17 shows the change required to the root module so that Angular loads the feature module that contains the store functionality.

Listing 7-17. Importing Feature Modules in the app.module.ts File in the src/app Folder

```
import { NgModule } from "@angular/core";
import { BrowserModule } from "@angular/platform-browser";
import { AppComponent } from "./app.component";
import { StoreModule } from "./store/store.module";

@NgModule({
```

```
  imports: [BrowserModule, StoreModule],
  declarations: [AppComponent],
  bootstrap: [AppComponent]
})
export class AppModule { }
```

When you save the changes to the root module, Angular will have all the details it needs to load the application and display the content from the store module, as shown in Figure 7-4.

All the building blocks created in the previous section work together to display the—admittedly simple—content, which shows how many products there are and how many categories they fit in to.

Figure 7-4. *Basic features in the SportsStore application*

Adding Store Features the Product Details

The nature of Angular development begins with a slow start as the foundation of the project is put in place and the basic building blocks are created. But once that's done, new features can be created relatively easily. In the sections that follow, I add features to the store so that the user can see the products on offer.

Displaying the Product Details

The obvious place to start is to display details for the products so that the customer can see what's on offer. Listing 7-18 adds HTML elements to the store component's template with data bindings that generate content for each product provided by the component.

Listing 7-18. Adding Elements in the store.component.html File in the src/app/store Folder

```
<div class="container-fluid">
  <div class="row">
    <div class="col bg-dark text-white">
      <a class="navbar-brand">SPORTS STORE</a>
    </div>
  </div>
  <div class="row">
    <div class="col-3 bg-info p-2 text-white">
      {{categories.length}} Categories
    </div>
```

```
<div class="col-9 p-2">
  <div *ngFor="let product of products" class="card m-1 p-1 bg-light">
    <h4>
      {{product.name}}
      <span class="badge badge-pill badge-primary float-right">
        {{ product.price | currency:"USD":"symbol":"2.2-2" }}
      </span>
    </h4>
    <div class="card-text bg-white p-1">{{product.description}}</div>
  </div>
</div>
</div>
```

Most of the elements control the layout and appearance of the content. The most important change is the addition of an Angular data binding expression.

```
...
<div *ngFor="let product of products" class="card m-1 p-1 bg-light">
...
```

This is an example of a directive, which transforms the HTML element it is applied to. This specific directive is called ngFor, and it transforms the div element by duplicating it for each object returned by the component's products property. Angular includes a range of built-in directives that perform the most commonly required tasks, as described in Chapter 13.

As it duplicates the div element, the current object is assigned to a variable called product, which allows it to be referred to in other data bindings, such as this one, which inserts the value of the current product's name description property as the content of the div element:

```
...
<div class="card-text p-1 bg-white">{{product.description}}</div>
...
```

Not all data in an application's data model can be displayed directly to the user. Angular includes a feature called *pipes*, which are classes used to transform or prepare a data value for its use in a data binding. There are several built-in pipes included with Angular, including the currency pipe, which formats number values as currencies, like this:

```
...
{{ product.price | currency:"USD":"symbol":"2.2-2" }}
...
```

The syntax for applying pipes can be a little awkward, but the expression in this binding tells Angular to format the price property of the current product using the currency pipe, with the currency conventions from the United States. Save the changes to the template, and you will see a list of the products in the data model displayed as a long list, as illustrated in Figure 7-5.

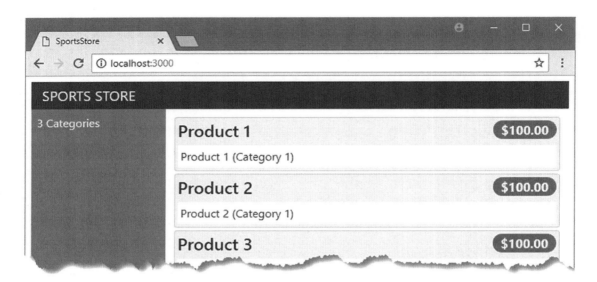

Figure 7-5. *Displaying product information*

Adding Category Selection

Adding support for filtering the list of products by category requires preparing the store component so that it keeps track of which category the user wants to display and requires changing the way that data is retrieved to use that category, as shown in Listing 7-19.

Listing 7-19. Adding Category Filtering in the store.component.ts File in the src/app/store Folder

```
import { Component } from "@angular/core";
import { Product } from "../model/product.model";
import { ProductRepository } from "../model/product.repository";

@Component({
    selector: "store",
    templateUrl: "store.component.html"
})
export class StoreComponent {
    public selectedCategory = null;

    constructor(private repository: ProductRepository) {}

    get products(): Product[] {
        return this.repository.getProducts(this.selectedCategory);
    }

    get categories(): string[] {
        return this.repository.getCategories();
    }

    changeCategory(newCategory?: string) {
```

```
        this.selectedCategory = newCategory;
    }
}
```

The changes are simple because they build on the foundation that took so long to create at the start of the chapter. The selectedCategory property is assigned the user's choice of category (where null means all categories) and is used in the updateData method as an argument to the getProducts method, delegating the filtering to the data source. The changeCategory method brings these two members together in a method that can be invoked when the user makes a category selection.

Listing 7-20 shows the corresponding changes to the component's template to provide the user with the set of buttons that change the selected category and show which category has been picked.

Listing 7-20. Adding Category Buttons in the store.component.html File in the src/app/store Folder

```html
<div class="container-fluid">
  <div class="row">
    <div class="col bg-dark text-white">
      <a class="navbar-brand">SPORTS STORE</a>
    </div>
  </div>
  <div class="row">
    <div class="col-3 p-2">
      <button class="btn btn-block btn-outline-primary" (click)="changeCategory()">
        Home
      </button>
      <button *ngFor="let cat of categories"
              class="btn btn-outline-primary btn-block"
              [class.active]="cat == selectedCategory" (click)="changeCategory(cat)">
        {{cat}}
      </button>
    </div>
    <div class="col-9 p-2">
      <div *ngFor="let product of products" class="card m-1 p-1 bg-light">
        <h4>
          {{product.name}}
          <span class="badge badge-pill badge-primary float-right">
            {{ product.price | currency:"USD":"symbol":"2.2-2" }}
          </span>
        </h4>
        <div class="card-text bg-white p-1">{{product.description}}</div>
      </div>
    </div>
  </div>
</div>
```

There are two new button elements in the template. The first is a Home button, and it has an event binding that invokes the component's changeCategory method when the button is clicked. No argument is provided to the method, which has the effect of setting the category to null and selecting all the products.

The ngFor binding has been applied to the other button element, with an expression that will repeat the element for each value in the array returned by the component's categories property. The button has a click event binding whose expression calls the changeCategory method to select the current category, which will filter the products displayed to the user. There is also a `class` binding, which adds the button element to the `active` class when the category associated with the button is the selected category. This provides the user with visual feedback when the categories are filtered, as shown in Figure 7-6.

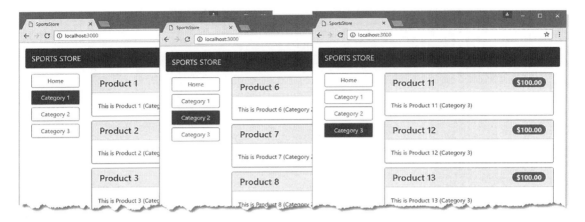

Figure 7-6. *Selecting product categories*

Adding Product Pagination

Filtering the products by category has helped make the product list more manageable, but a more typical approach is to break the list into smaller sections and present each of them as a page, along with navigation buttons that move between the pages. Listing 7-21 enhances the store component so that it keeps track of the current page and the number of items on a page.

Listing 7-21. Adding Pagination Support in the store.component.ts File in the src/app/store Folder

```
import { Component } from "@angular/core";
import { Product } from "../model/product.model";
import { ProductRepository } from "../model/product.repository";

@Component({
    selector: "store",
    templateUrl: "store.component.html"
})
export class StoreComponent {
    public selectedCategory = null;
    public productsPerPage = 4;
    public selectedPage = 1;

    constructor(private repository: ProductRepository) {}

    get products(): Product[] {
        let pageIndex = (this.selectedPage - 1) * this.productsPerPage
        return this.repository.getProducts(this.selectedCategory)
            .slice(pageIndex, pageIndex + this.productsPerPage);
    }
```

```
    get categories(): string[] {
        return this.repository.getCategories();
    }

    changeCategory(newCategory?: string) {
        this.selectedCategory = newCategory;
    }

    changePage(newPage: number) {
        this.selectedPage = newPage;
    }

    changePageSize(newSize: number) {
        this.productsPerPage = Number(newSize);
        this.changePage(1);
    }

    get pageNumbers(): number[] {
        return Array(Math.ceil(this.repository
            .getProducts(this.selectedCategory).length / this.productsPerPage))
                .fill(0).map((x, i) => i + 1);
    }
}
```

There are two new features in this listing. The first is the ability to get a page of products, and the second is to change the size of the pages, allowing the number of products that each page contains to be altered.

There is an oddity that the component has to work around. There is a limitation in the built-in ngFor directive that Angular provides, which can generate content only for the objects in an array or a collection, rather than using a counter. Since I need to generate numbered page navigation buttons, this means I need to create an array that contains the numbers I need, like this:

```
...
return Array(Math.ceil(this.repository.getProducts(this.selectedCategory).length
    / this.productsPerPage)).fill(0).map((x, i) => i + 1);
...
```

This statement creates a new array, fills it with the value 0, and then uses the map method to generate a new array with the number sequence. This works well enough to implement the pagination feature, but it feels awkward, and I demonstrate a better approach in the next section. Listing 7-22 shows the changes to the store component's template to implement the pagination feature.

Listing 7-22. Adding Pagination in the store.component.html File in the src/app/store Folder

```html
<div class="container-fluid">
  <div class="row">
    <div class="col bg-dark text-white">
      <a class="navbar-brand">SPORTS STORE</a>
    </div>
  </div>
  <div class="row">
    <div class="col-3 p-2">
      <button class="btn btn-block btn-outline-primary" (click)="changeCategory()">
```

```
      Home
    </button>
    <button *ngFor="let cat of categories"
            class="btn btn-outline-primary btn-block"
            [class.active]="cat == selectedCategory" (click)="changeCategory(cat)">
      {{cat}}
    </button>
  </div>
  <div class="col-9 p-2">
    <div *ngFor="let product of products" class="card m-1 p-1 bg-light">
      <h4>
        {{product.name}}
        <span class="badge badge-pill badge-primary float-right">
          {{ product.price | currency:"USD":"symbol":"2.2-2" }}
        </span>
      </h4>
      <div class="card-text bg-white p-1">{{product.description}}</div>
    </div>

    <div class="form-inline float-left mr-1">
      <select class="form-control" [value]="productsPerPage"
              (change)="changePageSize($event.target.value)">
        <option value="3">3 per Page</option>
        <option value="4">4 per Page</option>
        <option value="6">6 per Page</option>
        <option value="8">8 per Page</option>
      </select>
    </div>

    <div class="btn-group float-right">
      <button *ngFor="let page of pageNumbers" (click)="changePage(page)"
              class="btn btn-outline-primary"
              [class.active]="page == selectedPage">
        {{page}}
      </button>
    </div>
  </div>
 </div>
</div>
```

The new elements add a select element that allows the size of the page to be changed and a set of buttons that navigate through the product pages. The new elements have data bindings to wire them up to the properties and methods provided by the component. The result is a more manageable set of products, as shown in Figure 7-7.

■ **Tip**   The `select` element in Listing 7-22 is populated with `option` elements that are statically defined, rather than created using data from the component. One impact of this is that when the selected value is passed to the `changePageSize` method, it will be a `string` value, which is why the argument is parsed to a `number` before being used to set the page size in Listing 7-21. Care must be taken when receiving data values from HTML elements to ensure they are of the expected type. TypeScript type annotations don't help in this situation because the data binding expression is evaluated at runtime, long after the TypeScript compiler has generated JavaScript code that doesn't contain the extra type information.

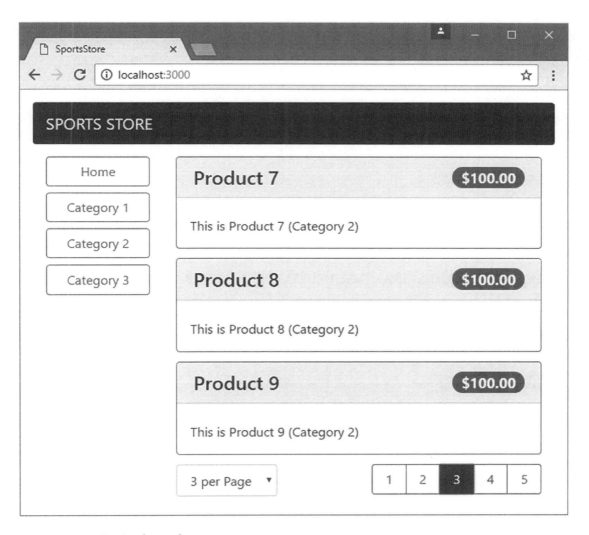

Figure 7-7. *Pagination for products*

Creating a Custom Directive

In this section, I am going to create a custom directive so that I don't have to generate an array full of numbers to create the page navigation buttons. Angular provides a good range of built-in directives, but it is a simple process to create your own directives to solve problems that are specific to your application or to support features that the built-in directives don't have. I added a file called `counter.directive.ts` in the `src/app/store` folder and used it to define the class shown in Listing 7-23.

Listing 7-23. The Contents of the counter.directive.ts File in the src/app/store Folder

```
import {
    Directive, ViewContainerRef, TemplateRef, Input, Attribute, SimpleChanges
} from "@angular/core";

@Directive({
    selector: "[counterOf]"
})
export class CounterDirective {

    constructor(private container: ViewContainerRef,
        private template: TemplateRef<Object>) {
    }

    @Input("counterOf")
    counter: number;

    ngOnChanges(changes: SimpleChanges) {
        this.container.clear();
        for (let i = 0; i < this.counter; i++) {
            this.container.createEmbeddedView(this.template,
                new CounterDirectiveContext(i + 1));
        }
    }
}

class CounterDirectiveContext {
    constructor(public $implicit: any) { }
}
```

This is an example of a structural directive, which is described in detail in Chapter 16. This directive is applied to elements through a `counter` property and relies on special features that Angular provides for creating content repeatedly, just like the built-in `ngFor` directive. In this case, rather than yield each object in a collection, the custom directive yields a series of numbers that can be used to create the page navigation buttons.

■ **Tip** This directive deletes all the content it has created and starts again when the number of pages changes. This can be an expensive process in more complex directives, and I explain how to improve performance in Chapter 16.

To use the directive, it must be added to the declarations property of its feature module, as shown in Listing 7-24.

Listing 7-24. Registering the Custom Directive in the store.module.ts File in the src/app/store Folder

```
import { NgModule } from "@angular/core";
import { BrowserModule } from "@angular/platform-browser";
import { FormsModule } from "@angular/forms";
import { ModelModule } from "../model/model.module";
import { StoreComponent } from "./store.component";
import { CounterDirective } from "./counter.directive";

@NgModule({
    imports: [ModelModule, BrowserModule, FormsModule],
    declarations: [StoreComponent, CounterDirective],
    exports: [StoreComponent]
})
export class StoreModule { }
```

Now that the directive has been registered, it can be used in the store component's template to replace the ngFor directive, as shown in Listing 7-25.

Listing 7-25. Replacing the Built-in Directive in the store.component.html File in the src/app/store Folder

```
<div class="container-fluid">
  <div class="row">
    <div class="col bg-dark text-white">
      <a class="navbar-brand">SPORTS STORE</a>
    </div>
  </div>
  <div class="row">

    <div class="col-3 p-2">
      <button class="btn btn-block btn-outline-primary" (click)="changeCategory()">
        Home
      </button>
      <button *ngFor="let cat of categories"
          class="btn btn-outline-primary btn-block"
          [class.active]="cat == selectedCategory" (click)="changeCategory(cat)">
        {{cat}}
      </button>
    </div>

    <div class="col-9 p-2">
      <div *ngFor="let product of products" class="card m-1 p-1 bg-light">
        <h4>
          {{product.name}}
          <span class="badge badge-pill badge-primary float-right">
            {{ product.price | currency:"USD":"symbol":"2.2-2" }}
          </span>
        </h4>
        <div class="card-text bg-white p-1">{{product.description}}</div>
```

```
    </div>

    <div class="form-inline float-left mr-1">
      <select class="form-control" [value]="productsPerPage"
              (change)="changePageSize($event.target.value)">
        <option value="3">3 per Page</option>
        <option value="4">4 per Page</option>
        <option value="6">6 per Page</option>
        <option value="8">8 per Page</option>
      </select>
    </div>

    <div class="btn-group float-right">
      <button *counter="let page of pageCount" (click)="changePage(page)"
          class="btn btn-outline-primary" [class.active]="page == selectedPage">
        {{page}}
      </button>
    </div>

  </div>
 </div>
</div>
```

The new data binding relies on a property called pageCount to configure the custom directive.
In Listing 7-26, I have replaced the array of numbers with a simple number that provides the expression value.

Listing 7-26. Supporting the Custom Directive in the store.component.ts File in the src/app/store Folder

```
import { Component } from "@angular/core";
import { Product } from "../model/product.model";
import { ProductRepository } from "../model/product.repository";

@Component({
    selector: "store",
    templateUrl: "store.component.html"
})
export class StoreComponent {
    public selectedCategory = null;
    public productsPerPage = 4;
    public selectedPage = 1;

    constructor(private repository: ProductRepository) {}

    get products(): Product[] {
        let pageIndex = (this.selectedPage - 1) * this.productsPerPage
        return this.repository.getProducts(this.selectedCategory)
            .slice(pageIndex, pageIndex + this.productsPerPage);
    }

    get categories(): string[] {
        return this.repository.getCategories();
    }
```

```
    changeCategory(newCategory?: string) {
        this.selectedCategory = newCategory;
    }

    changePage(newPage: number) {
        this.selectedPage = newPage;
    }

    changePageSize(newSize: number) {
        this.productsPerPage = Number(newSize);
        this.changePage(1);
    }

    get pageCount(): number {
        return Math.ceil(this.repository
            .getProducts(this.selectedCategory).length / this.productsPerPage)
    }

    //get pageNumbers(): number[] {
    //    return Array(Math.ceil(this.repository
    //        .getProducts(this.selectedCategory).length / this.productsPerPage))
    //            .fill(0).map((x, i) => i + 1);
    //}
}
```

There is no visual change to the SportsStore application, but this section has demonstrated this it is possible to supplement the built-in Angular functionality with custom code that is tailored to the needs of a specific project.

Summary

In this chapter, I started the SportsStore project. The early part of the chapter was spent creating the foundation for the project, including creating the root building blocks for the application and starting work on the feature modules. Once the foundation was in place, I was able to rapidly add features to display the dummy model data to the user, add pagination, and filter the products by category. I finished the chapter by creating a custom directive to demonstrate how the built-in features provided by Angular can be supplemented by custom code. In the next chapter, I continue to build the SportsStore application.

CHAPTER 8

SportsStore: Orders and Checkout

In this chapter, I continue adding features to the SportsStore application that I created in Chapter 7. I add support for a shopping cart and a checkout process and replace the dummy data with the data from the RESTful web service.

Preparing the Example Application

No preparation is required for this chapter, which continues using the SportsStore project from Chapter 7. To start the RESTful web service, open a command prompt and run the following command in the SportsStore folder:

```
npm run json
```

Open a second command prompt and run the following command in the SportsStore folder to start the development tools and HTTP server:

```
ng serve --port 3000 --open
```

Tip You can download the example project for this chapter—and for all the other chapters in this book—from https://github.com/Apress/pro-angular-6.

Creating the Cart

The user needs a cart into which products can be placed and used to start the checkout process. In the sections that follow, I'll add a cart to the application and integrate it into the store so that the user can select the products they want.

Creating the Cart Model

The starting point for the cart feature is a new model class that will be used to gather together the products that the user has selected. I added a file called cart.model.ts in the src/app/model folder and used it to define the class shown in Listing 8-1.

© Adam Freeman 2018

A. Freeman, *Pro Angular 6*, https://doi.org/10.1007/978-1-4842-3649-9_8

Listing 8-1. The Contents of the cart.model.ts File in the src/app/model Folder

```
import { Injectable } from "@angular/core";
import { Product } from "./product.model";

@Injectable()
export class Cart {
    public lines: CartLine[] = [];
    public itemCount: number = 0;
    public cartPrice: number = 0;

    addLine(product: Product, quantity: number = 1) {
        let line = this.lines.find(line => line.product.id == product.id);
        if (line != undefined) {
            line.quantity += quantity;
        } else {
            this.lines.push(new CartLine(product, quantity));
        }
        this.recalculate();
    }

    updateQuantity(product: Product, quantity: number) {
        let line = this.lines.find(line => line.product.id == product.id);
        if (line != undefined) {
            line.quantity = Number(quantity);
        }
        this.recalculate();
    }

    removeLine(id: number) {
        let index = this.lines.findIndex(line => line.product.id == id);
        this.lines.splice(index, 1);
        this.recalculate();
    }

    clear() {
        this.lines = [];
        this.itemCount = 0;
        this.cartPrice = 0;
    }

    private recalculate() {
        this.itemCount = 0;
        this.cartPrice = 0;
        this.lines.forEach(l => {
            this.itemCount += l.quantity;
            this.cartPrice += (l.quantity * l.product.price);
        })
    }
}
```

```
export class CartLine {

    constructor(public product: Product,
        public quantity: number) {}

    get lineTotal() {
        return this.quantity * this.product.price;
    }
}
```

Individual product selections are represented as an array of CartLine objects, each of which contains a Product object and a quantity. The Cart class keeps track of the total number of items that have been selected and their total cost.

There should be a single Cart object used throughout the entire application, ensuring that any part of the application can access the user's product selections. To achieve this, I am going to make the Cart a service, which means that Angular will take responsibility for creating an instance of the Cart class and will use it when it needs to create a component that has a Cart constructor argument. This is another use of the Angular dependency injection feature, which can be used to share objects throughout an application and which is described in detail in Chapters 19 and 20. The @Injectable decorator, which has been applied to the Cart class in the listing, indicates that this class will be used as a service.

■ **Note** Strictly speaking, the @Injectable decorator is required only when a class has its own constructor arguments to resolve, but it is a good idea to apply it anyway because it serves as a signal that the class is intended for use as a service.

Listing 8-2 registers the Cart class as a service in the providers property of the model feature module class.

Listing 8-2. Registering the Cart as a Service in the model.module.ts File in the src/app/model Folder

```
import { NgModule } from "@angular/core";
import { ProductRepository } from "./product.repository";
import { StaticDataSource } from "./static.datasource";
import { Cart } from "./cart.model";

@NgModule({
    providers: [ProductRepository, StaticDataSource, Cart]
})
export class ModelModule { }
```

Creating the Cart Summary Components

Components are the essential building blocks for Angular applications because they allow discrete units of code and content to be easily created. The SportsStore application will show users a summary of their product selections in the title area of the page, which I am going to implement by creating a component. I added a file called cartSummary.component.ts in the src/app/store folder and used it to define the component shown in Listing 8-3.

Listing 8-3. The Contents of the cartSummary.component.ts File in the src/app/store Folder

```
import { Component } from "@angular/core";
import { Cart } from "../model/cart.model";

@Component({
    selector: "cart-summary",
    templateUrl: "cartSummary.component.html"
})
export class CartSummaryComponent {

    constructor(public cart: Cart) { }
}
```

When Angular needs to create an instance of this component, it will have to provide a Cart object as a constructor argument, using the service that I configured in the previous section by adding the Cart class to the feature module's providers property. The default behavior for services means that a single Cart object will be created and shared throughout the application, although there are different service behaviors available (as described in Chapter 20).

To provide the component with a template, I created an HTML file called cartSummary.component.html in the same folder as the component class file and added the markup shown in Listing 8-4.

Listing 8-4. The Contents of the cartSummary.component.html File in the src/app/store Folder

```
<div class="float-right">
  <small>
    Your cart:
    <span *ngIf="cart.itemCount > 0">
      {{ cart.itemCount }} item(s)
      {{ cart.cartPrice | currency:"USD":"symbol":"2.2-2" }}
    </span>
    <span *ngIf="cart.itemCount == 0">
      (empty)
    </span>
  </small>
  <button class="btn btn-sm bg-dark text-white"
      [disabled]="cart.itemCount == 0">
    <i class="fa fa-shopping-cart"></i>
  </button>
</div>
```

This template uses the Cart object provided by its component to display the number of items in the cart and the total cost. There is also a button that will start the checkout process when I add it to the application later in the chapter.

■ **Tip** The button element in Listing 8-4 is styled using classes defined by Font Awesome, which is one of the packages in the package.json file from Chapter 7. This open source package provides excellent support for icons in web applications, including the shopping cart I need for the SportsStore application. See http://fontawesome.io for details.

Listing 8-5 registers the new component with the store feature module, in preparation for using it in the next section.

Listing 8-5. Registering the Component in the store.module.ts File in the src/app/store Folder

```
import { NgModule } from "@angular/core";
import { BrowserModule } from "@angular/platform-browser";
import { FormsModule } from "@angular/forms";
import { ModelModule } from "../model/model.module";
import { StoreComponent } from "./store.component";
import { CounterDirective } from "./counter.directive";
import { CartSummaryComponent } from "./cartSummary.component";

@NgModule({
    imports: [ModelModule, BrowserModule, FormsModule],
    declarations: [StoreComponent, CounterDirective, CartSummaryComponent],
    exports: [StoreComponent]
})
export class StoreModule { }
```

Integrating the Cart into the Store

The store component is the key to integrating the cart and the cart widget into the application. Listing 8-6 updates the store component so that its constructor has a Cart parameter and defines a method that will add a product to the cart.

Listing 8-6. Adding Cart Support in the store.component.ts File in the src/app/store Folder

```
import { Component } from "@angular/core";
import { Product } from "../model/product.model";
import { ProductRepository } from "../model/product.repository";
import { Cart } from "../model/cart.model";

@Component({
    selector: "store",
    templateUrl: "store.component.html"
})
export class StoreComponent {
    public selectedCategory = null;
    public productsPerPage = 4;
    public selectedPage = 1;

    constructor(private repository: ProductRepository,
                private cart: Cart) { }

    get products(): Product[] {
        let pageIndex = (this.selectedPage - 1) * this.productsPerPage
        return this.repository.getProducts(this.selectedCategory)
            .slice(pageIndex, pageIndex + this.productsPerPage);
    }
```

```
    get categories(): string[] {
        return this.repository.getCategories();
    }

    changeCategory(newCategory?: string) {
        this.selectedCategory = newCategory;
    }

    changePage(newPage: number) {
        this.selectedPage = newPage;
    }

    changePageSize(newSize: number) {
        this.productsPerPage = Number(newSize);
        this.changePage(1);
    }

    get pageCount(): number {
        return Math.ceil(this.repository
            .getProducts(this.selectedCategory).length / this.productsPerPage)
    }

    addProductToCart(product: Product) {
        this.cart.addLine(product);
    }
}
```

To complete the integration of the cart into the store component, Listing 8-7 adds the element that will apply the cart summary component to the store component's template and adds a button to each product description with the event binding that calls the addProductToCart method.

Listing 8-7. Applying the Component in the store.component.html File in the src/app/store Folder

```
<div class="container-fluid">
  <div class="row">
    <div class="col bg-dark text-white">
      <a class="navbar-brand">SPORTS STORE</a>
      <cart-summary></cart-summary>
    </div>
  </div>
  <div class="row">

    <div class="col-3 p-2">
      <button class="btn btn-block btn-outline-primary" (click)="changeCategory()">
        Home
      </button>
      <button *ngFor="let cat of categories"
          class="btn btn-outline-primary btn-block"
          [class.active]="cat == selectedCategory" (click)="changeCategory(cat)">
        {{cat}}
      </button>
    </div>
```

```
<div class="col-9 p-2">
  <div *ngFor="let product of products" class="card m-1 p-1 bg-light">
    <h4>
      {{product.name}}
      <span class="badge badge-pill badge-primary float-right">
        {{ product.price | currency:"USD":"symbol":"2.2-2" }}
      </span>
    </h4>
    <div class="card-text bg-white p-1">
      {{product.description}}
      <button class="btn btn-success btn-sm float-right"
              (click)="addProductToCart(product)">
        Add To Cart
      </button>
    </div>
  </div>

  <div class="form-inline float-left mr-1">
    <select class="form-control" [value]="productsPerPage"
            (change)="changePageSize($event.target.value)">
      <option value="3">3 per Page</option>
      <option value="4">4 per Page</option>
      <option value="6">6 per Page</option>
      <option value="8">8 per Page</option>
    </select>
  </div>

  <div class="btn-group float-right">
    <button *counter="let page of pageCount" (click)="changePage(page)"
        class="btn btn-outline-primary" [class.active]="page == selectedPage">
      {{page}}
    </button>
  </div>

    </div>
  </div>
</div>
```

The result is a button for each product that adds it to the cart, as shown in Figure 8-1. The full cart process isn't complete yet, but you can see the effect of each addition in the cart summary at the top of the page.

Figure 8-1. *Adding cart support to the SportsStore application*

Notice how clicking one of the Add To Cart buttons updates the summary component's content automatically. This happens because there is a single Cart object being shared between two components and changes made by one component are reflected when Angular evaluates the data binding expressions in the other component.

Adding URL Routing

Most applications need to show different content to the user at different times. In the case of the SportsStore application, when the user clicks one of the Add To Cart buttons, they should be shown a detailed view of their selected products and given the chance to start the checkout process.

Angular supports a feature called *URL routing*, which uses the current URL displayed by the browser to select the components that are displayed to the user. This is an approach that makes it easy to create applications whose components are loosely coupled and easy to change without needing corresponding modifications elsewhere in the applications. URL routing also makes it easy to change the path that a user follows through an application.

For the SportsStore application, I am going to add support for three different URLs, which are described in Table 8-1. This is a simple configuration, but the routing system has a lot of features, which are described in detail in Chapters 25 to 27.

Table 8-1. *The URLs Supported by the SportsStore Application*

URL	Description
/store	This URL will display the list of products.
/cart	This URL will display the user's cart in detail.
/checkout	This URL will display the checkout process.

In the sections that follow, I create placeholder components for the SportsStore cart and order checkout stages and then integrate them into the application using URL routing. Once the URLs are implemented, I will return to the components and add more useful features.

Creating the Cart Detail and Checkout Components

Before adding URL routing to the application, I need to create the components that will be displayed by the /cart and /checkout URLs. I only need some basic placeholder content to get started, just to make it obvious which component is being displayed. I started by adding a file called cartDetail.component.ts in the src/app/store folder and defined the component shown in Listing 8-8.

Listing 8-8. The Contents of the cartDetail.component.ts File in the src/app/store Folder

```
import { Component } from "@angular/core";

@Component({
    template: `<div><h3 class="bg-info p-1 text-white">Cart Detail Component</h3></div>`
})
export class CartDetailComponent {}
```

Next, I added a file called checkout.component.ts in the src/app/store folder and defined the component shown in Listing 8-9.

Listing 8-9. The Contents of the checkout.component.ts File in the src/app/store Folder

```
import { Component } from "@angular/core";

@Component({
    template: `<div><h3 class="bg-info p-1 text-white">Checkout Component</h3></div>`
})
export class CheckoutComponent { }
```

This component follows the same pattern as the cart component and displays a placeholder message. Listing 8-10 registers the components in the store feature module and adds them to the exports property, which means they can be used elsewhere in the application.

Listing 8-10. Registering Components in the store.module.ts File in the src/app/store Folder

```
import { NgModule } from "@angular/core";
import { BrowserModule } from "@angular/platform-browser";
import { FormsModule } from "@angular/forms";
import { ModelModule } from "../model/model.module";
import { StoreComponent } from "./store.component";
import { CounterDirective } from "./counter.directive";
import { CartSummaryComponent } from "./cartSummary.component";
import { CartDetailComponent } from "./cartDetail.component";
import { CheckoutComponent } from "./checkout.component";

@NgModule({
    imports: [ModelModule, BrowserModule, FormsModule],
    declarations: [StoreComponent, CounterDirective, CartSummaryComponent,
        CartDetailComponent, CheckoutComponent],
```

```
    exports: [StoreComponent, CartDetailComponent, CheckoutComponent]
})
export class StoreModule { }
```

Creating and Applying the Routing Configuration

Now that I have a range of components to display, the next step is to create the routing configuration that tells Angular how to map URLs into components. Each mapping of a URL to a component is known as a *URL route* or just a *route*. In Part 3, where I create more complex routing configurations, I define the routes in a separate file, but for this project, I am going to follow a simpler approach and define the routes within the @NgModule decorator of the application's root module, as shown in Listing 8-11.

■ **Tip** The Angular routing feature requires a base element in the HTML document, which provides the base URL against which routes are applied. This element was added to the index.html file by the ng new command when I created the SportsStore project in Chapter 7. If you omit the element, Angular will report an error and be unable to apply the routes.

Listing 8-11. Creating the Routing Configuration in the app.module.ts File in the src/app Folder

```
import { NgModule } from "@angular/core";
import { BrowserModule } from "@angular/platform-browser";
import { AppComponent } from "./app.component";
import { StoreModule } from "./store/store.module";
import { StoreComponent } from "./store/store.component";
import { CheckoutComponent } from "./store/checkout.component";
import { CartDetailComponent } from "./store/cartDetail.component";
import { RouterModule } from "@angular/router";

@NgModule({
    imports: [BrowserModule, StoreModule,
        RouterModule.forRoot([
            { path: "store", component: StoreComponent },
            { path: "cart", component: CartDetailComponent },
            { path: "checkout", component: CheckoutComponent },
            { path: "**", redirectTo: "/store" }
        ])],
    declarations: [AppComponent],
    bootstrap: [AppComponent]
})
export class AppModule { }
```

The RouterModule.forRoot method is passed a set of routes, each of which maps a URL to a component. The first three routes in the listing match the URLs from Table 8-1. The final route is a wildcard that redirects any other URL to /store, which will display StoreComponent.

When the routing feature is used, Angular looks for the router-outlet element, which defines the location in which the component that corresponds to the current URL should be displayed. Listing 8-12 replaces the store element in the root component's template with the router-outlet element.

Listing 8-12. Defining the Routing Target in the app.component.ts File in the src/app Folder

```
import { Component } from "@angular/core";

@Component({
    selector: "app",
    template: "<router-outlet></router-outlet>"
})
export class AppComponent { }
```

Angular will apply the routing configuration when you save the changes and the browser reloads the HTML document. The content displayed in the browser window hasn't changed, but if you examine the browser's URL bar, you will be able to see that the routing configuration has been applied, as shown in Figure 8-2.

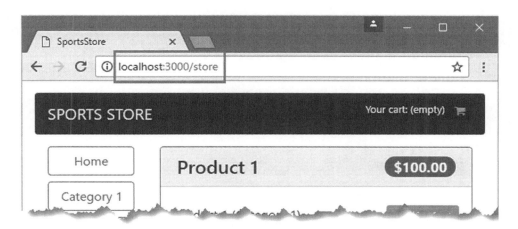

Figure 8-2. *The effect of URL routing*

Navigating Through the Application

With the routing configuration in place, it is time to add support for navigating between components by changing the browser's URL. The URL routing feature relies on a JavaScript API provided by the browser, which means the user can't simply type the target URL into the browser's URL bar. Instead, the navigation has to be performed by the application, either by using JavaScript code in a component or other building block or by adding attributes to HTML elements in the template.

When the user clicks one of the Add To Cart buttons, the cart detail component should be shown, which means that the application should navigate to the /cart URL. Listing 8-13 adds navigation to the component method that is invoked when the user clicks the button.

Listing 8-13. Navigating Using JavaScript in the store.component.ts File in the app/src/store Folder

```
import { Component } from "@angular/core";
import { Product } from "../model/product.model";
import { ProductRepository } from "../model/product.repository";
import { Cart } from "../model/cart.model";
import { Router } from "@angular/router";
```

```
@Component({
    selector: "store",
    templateUrl: "store.component.html"
})
export class StoreComponent {
    public selectedCategory = null;
    public productsPerPage = 4;
    public selectedPage = 1;

    constructor(private repository: ProductRepository,
        private cart: Cart,
        private router: Router) { }

    get products(): Product[] {
        let pageIndex = (this.selectedPage - 1) * this.productsPerPage
        return this.repository.getProducts(this.selectedCategory)
            .slice(pageIndex, pageIndex + this.productsPerPage);
    }

    get categories(): string[] {
        return this.repository.getCategories();
    }

    changeCategory(newCategory?: string) {
        this.selectedCategory = newCategory;
    }

    changePage(newPage: number) {
        this.selectedPage = newPage;
    }

    changePageSize(newSize: number) {
        this.productsPerPage = Number(newSize);
        this.changePage(1);
    }

    get pageCount(): number {
        return Math.ceil(this.repository
            .getProducts(this.selectedCategory).length / this.productsPerPage)
    }

    addProductToCart(product: Product) {
        this.cart.addLine(product);
        this.router.navigateByUrl("/cart");
    }
}
```

The constructor has a Router parameter, which is provided by Angular through the dependency injection feature when a new instance of the component is created. In the addProductToCart method, the Router.navigateByUrl method is used to navigate to the /cart URL.

Navigation can also be done by adding the routerLink attribute to elements in the template. In Listing 8-14, the routerLink attribute has been applied to the cart button in the cart summary component's template.

Listing 8-14. Adding a Navigation in the cartSummary.component.html File in the src/app/store Folder

```
<div class="float-right">
  <small>
    Your cart:
    <span *ngIf="cart.itemCount > 0">
      {{ cart.itemCount }} item(s)
      {{ cart.cartPrice | currency:"USD":"symbol":"2.2-2" }}
    </span>
    <span *ngIf="cart.itemCount == 0">
      (empty)
    </span>
  </small>
  <button class="btn btn-sm bg-dark text-white"
      [disabled]="cart.itemCount == 0" routerLink="/cart">
    <i class="fa fa-shopping-cart"></i>
  </button>
</div>
```

The value specified by the routerLink attribute is the URL that the application will navigate to when the button is clicked. This particular button is disabled when the cart is empty, so it will perform the navigation only when the user has added a product to the cart.

To add support for the routerLink attribute, the RouterModule module must be imported into the feature module, as shown in Listing 8-15.

Listing 8-15. Importing the Router Module in the store.module.ts File in the src/app/store Folder

```
import { NgModule } from "@angular/core";
import { BrowserModule } from "@angular/platform-browser";
import { FormsModule } from "@angular/forms";
import { ModelModule } from "../model/model.module";
import { StoreComponent } from "./store.component";
import { CounterDirective } from "./counter.directive";
import { CartSummaryComponent } from "./cartSummary.component";
import { CartDetailComponent } from "./cartDetail.component";
import { CheckoutComponent } from "./checkout.component";
import { RouterModule } from "@angular/router";

@NgModule({
    imports: [ModelModule, BrowserModule, FormsModule, RouterModule],
    declarations: [StoreComponent, CounterDirective, CartSummaryComponent,
        CartDetailComponent, CheckoutComponent],
    exports: [StoreComponent, CartDetailComponent, CheckoutComponent]
})
export class StoreModule { }
```

To see the effect of the navigation, save the changes of the files and, once the browser has reloaded the HTML document, click one of the Add To Cart buttons. The browser will navigate to the /cart URL, as shown in Figure 8-3.

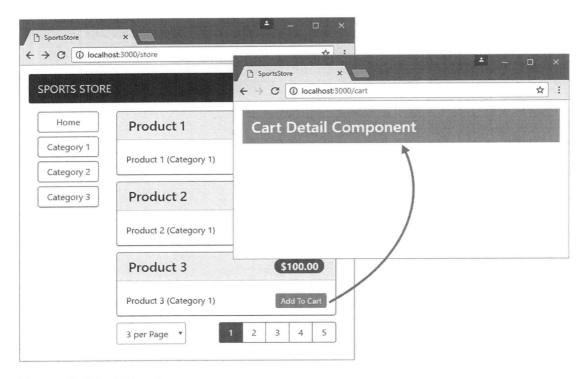

Figure 8-3. *Using URL routing*

Guarding the Routes

Remember that navigation can be performed only by the application. If you change the URL directly in the browser's URL bar, the browser will request the URL you enter from the web server. The Angular development server that is responding to HTTP requests will respond to any URL that doesn't correspond to a file by returning the contents of index.html. This is generally a useful behavior because it means you won't receive an HTTP error when the browser reload button is clicked. But it can cause problems if the application expects the user to navigate through the application following a specific path.

As an example, if you click one of the Add To Cart buttons and then click the browser's reload button, the HTTP server will return the contents of the index.html file, and Angular will immediately jump to the cart detail component, skipping over the part of the application that allows the user to select products.

For some applications, being able to start using different URLs makes sense, but if that's not the case, then Angular supports *route guards*, which are used to govern the routing system.

To prevent the application from starting with the /cart or /order URL, I added a file called storeFirst.guard.ts in the SportsStore/src/app folder and defined the class shown in Listing 8-16.

Listing 8-16. The Contents of the storeFirst.guard.ts File in the src/app Folder

```
import { Injectable } from "@angular/core";
import {
    ActivatedRouteSnapshot, RouterStateSnapshot,
    Router
} from "@angular/router";
import { StoreComponent } from "./store/store.component";
```

```
@Injectable()
export class StoreFirstGuard {
    private firstNavigation = true;

    constructor(private router: Router) { }

    canActivate(route: ActivatedRouteSnapshot,
        state: RouterStateSnapshot): boolean {
        if (this.firstNavigation) {
            this.firstNavigation = false;
            if (route.component != StoreComponent) {
                this.router.navigateByUrl("/");
                return false;
            }
        }
        return true;
    }
}
```

There are different ways to guard routes, as described in Chapter 27, and this is an example of a guard that prevents a route from being activated, which is implemented as a class that defines a canActivate method. The implementation of this method uses the context objects that Angular provides that describe the route that is about to be navigated to and checks to see whether the target component is a StoreComponent. If this is the first time that the canActivate method has been called and a different component is about to be used, then the Router.navigateByUrl method is used to navigate to the root URL.

The @Injectable decorator has been applied in the listing because route guards are services. Listing 8-17 registers the guard as a service using the root module's providers property and guards each route using the canActivate property.

Listing 8-17. Guarding Routes in the app.module.ts File in the src/app Folder

```
import { NgModule } from "@angular/core";
import { BrowserModule } from "@angular/platform-browser";
import { AppComponent } from "./app.component";
import { StoreModule } from "./store/store.module";
import { StoreComponent } from "./store/store.component";
import { CheckoutComponent } from "./store/checkout.component";
import { CartDetailComponent } from "./store/cartDetail.component";
import { RouterModule } from "@angular/router";
import { StoreFirstGuard } from "./storeFirst.guard";

@NgModule({
    imports: [BrowserModule, StoreModule,
        RouterModule.forRoot([
            {
                path: "store", component: StoreComponent,
                canActivate: [StoreFirstGuard]
            },
            {
                path: "cart", component: CartDetailComponent,
                canActivate: [StoreFirstGuard]
            },
```

```
        {
            path: "checkout", component: CheckoutComponent,
            canActivate: [StoreFirstGuard]
        },
        { path: "**", redirectTo: "/store" }
    ])],
    providers: [StoreFirstGuard],
    declarations: [AppComponent],
    bootstrap: [AppComponent]
})
export class AppModule { }
```

If you reload the browser after clicking one of the Add To Cart buttons now, then you will see the browser is automatically directed back to safety, as shown in Figure 8-4.

Figure 8-4. *Guarding routes*

Completing the Cart Detail Feature

Now that the application has navigation support, it is time to complete the view that details the contents of the user's cart. Listing 8-18 removes the inline template from the cart detail component, specifies an external template in the same directory, and adds a Cart parameter to the constructor, which will be accessible in the template through a property called cart.

Listing 8-18. Changing the Template in the cartDetail.component.ts File in the src/app/store Folder

```
import { Component } from "@angular/core";
import { Cart } from "../model/cart.model";

@Component({
```

```
    templateUrl: "cartDetail.component.html"
})
export class CartDetailComponent {

    constructor(public cart: Cart) { }
}
```

To complete the cart detail feature, I created an HTML file called cartDetail.component.html in the src/app/store folder and added the content shown in Listing 8-19.

Listing 8-19. The Contents of the cartDetail.component.html File in the src/app/store Folder

```html
<div class="container-fluid">
  <div class="row">
    <div class="col bg-dark text-white">
      <a class="navbar-brand">SPORTS STORE</a>
    </div>
  </div>
  <div class="row">
    <div class="col mt-2">
      <h2 class="text-center">Your Cart</h2>
      <table class="table table-bordered table-striped p-2">
        <thead>
          <tr>
            <th>Quantity</th>
            <th>Product</th>
            <th class="text-right">Price</th>
            <th class="text-right">Subtotal</th>
          </tr>
        </thead>
        <tbody>
          <tr *ngIf="cart.lines.length == 0">
            <td colspan="4" class="text-center">
              Your cart is empty
            </td>
          </tr>
          <tr *ngFor="let line of cart.lines">
            <td>
              <input type="number" class="form-control-sm"
                     style="width:5em"
                     [value]="line.quantity"
                     (change)="cart.updateQuantity(line.product,
                                $event.target.value)" />
            </td>
            <td>{{line.product.name}}</td>
            <td class="text-right">
              {{line.product.price | currency:"USD":true:"2.2-2"}}
            </td>
            <td class="text-right">
              {{(line.lineTotal) | currency:"USD":true:"2.2-2" }}
            </td>
            <td class="text-center">
```

```
            <button class="btn btn-sm btn-danger"
                    (click)="cart.removeLine(line.product.id)">
                Remove
            </button>
          </td>
        </tr>
      </tbody>
      <tfoot>
        <tr>
          <td colspan="3" class="text-right">Total:</td>
          <td class="text-right">
            {{cart.cartPrice | currency:"USD":"symbol":"2.2-2"}}
          </td>
        </tr>
      </tfoot>
    </table>
  </div>
</div>
<div class="row">
  <div class="col">
  <div class="text-center">
    <button class="btn btn-primary m-1" routerLink="/store">
        Continue Shopping
    </button>
    <button class="btn btn-secondary m-1" routerLink="/checkout"
            [disabled]="cart.lines.length == 0">
      Checkout
    </button>
  </div>
  </div>
</div>
```

This template displays a table showing the user's product selections. For each product, there is an input element that can be used to change the quantity and a Remove button that deletes it from the cart. There are also two navigation buttons that allow the user to return to the list of products or continue to the checkout process, as shown in Figure 8-5. The combination of the Angular data bindings and the shared Cart object means that any changes made to the cart take immediate effect, recalculating the prices; and if you click the Continue Shopping button, the changes are reflected in the cart summary component shown above the list of products.

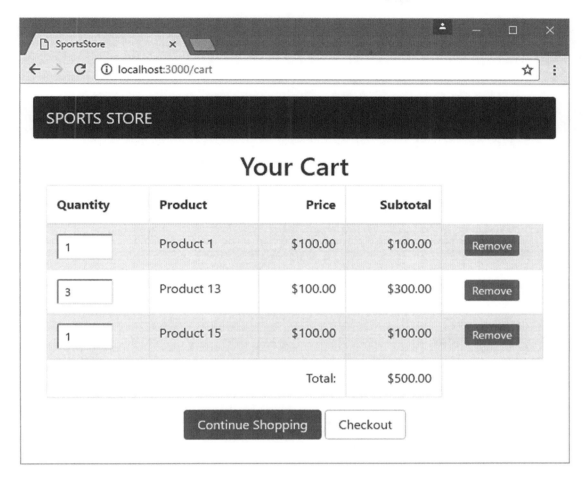

Figure 8-5. *Completing the cart detail feature*

Processing Orders

Being able to receive orders from customers is the most important aspect of an online store. In the sections that follow, I build on the application to add support for receiving the final details from the user and checking them out. To keep the process simple, I am going to avoid dealing with payment and fulfilment platforms, which are generally back-end services that are not specific to Angular applications.

Extending the Model

To describe orders placed by users, I added a file called order.model.ts in the src/app/model folder and defined the code shown in Listing 8-20.

Listing 8-20. The Contents of the order.model.ts File in the src/app/model Folder

```
import { Injectable } from "@angular/core";
import { Cart } from "./cart.model";

@Injectable()
export class Order {
    public id: number;
    public name: string;
    public address: string;
    public city: string;
    public state: string;
    public zip: string;
    public country: string;
    public shipped: boolean = false;

    constructor(public cart: Cart) { }

    clear() {
        this.id = null;
        this.name = this.address = this.city = null;
        this.state = this.zip = this.country = null;
        this.shipped = false;
        this.cart.clear();
    }
}
```

The Order class will be another service, which means there will be one instance shared throughout the application. When Angular creates the Order object, it will detect the Cart constructor parameter and provide the same Cart object that is used elsewhere in the application.

Updating the Repository and Data Source

To handle orders in the application, I need to extend the repository and the data source so they can receive Order objects. Listing 8-21 adds a method to the data source that receives an order. Since this is still the dummy data source, the method simply produces a JSON string from the order and writes it to the JavaScript console. I'll do something more useful with the objects in the next section when I create a data source that uses HTTP requests to communicate with the RESTful web service.

Listing 8-21. Handling Orders in the static.datasource.ts File in the src/app/model Folder

```
import { Injectable } from "@angular/core";
import { Product } from "./product.model";
import { Observable, from } from "rxjs";
import { Order } from "./order.model";

@Injectable()
export class StaticDataSource {
    private products: Product[] = [
        new Product(1, "Product 1", "Category 1", "Product 1 (Category 1)", 100),
        new Product(2, "Product 2", "Category 1", "Product 2 (Category 1)", 100),
        new Product(3, "Product 3", "Category 1", "Product 3 (Category 1)", 100),
```

```
        new Product(4, "Product 4", "Category 1", "Product 4 (Category 1)", 100),
        new Product(5, "Product 5", "Category 1", "Product 5 (Category 1)", 100),
        new Product(6, "Product 6", "Category 2", "Product 6 (Category 2)", 100),
        new Product(7, "Product 7", "Category 2", "Product 7 (Category 2)", 100),
        new Product(8, "Product 8", "Category 2", "Product 8 (Category 2)", 100),
        new Product(9, "Product 9", "Category 2", "Product 9 (Category 2)", 100),
        new Product(10, "Product 10", "Category 2", "Product 10 (Category 2)", 100),
        new Product(11, "Product 11", "Category 3", "Product 11 (Category 3)", 100),
        new Product(12, "Product 12", "Category 3", "Product 12 (Category 3)", 100),
        new Product(13, "Product 13", "Category 3", "Product 13 (Category 3)", 100),
        new Product(14, "Product 14", "Category 3", "Product 14 (Category 3)", 100),
        new Product(15, "Product 15", "Category 3", "Product 15 (Category 3)", 100),
    ];

    getProducts(): Observable<Product[]> {
        return from([this.products]);
    }

    saveOrder(order: Order): Observable<Order> {
        console.log(JSON.stringify(order));
        return from([order]);
    }
}
```

To manage orders, I added a file called order.repository.ts to the src/app/model folder and used it to define the class shown in Listing 8-22. There is only one method in the order repository at the moment, but I will add more functionality in Chapter 9 when I create the administration features.

■ **Tip** You don't have to use different repositories for each model type in the application, but I often do so because a single class responsible for multiple model types can become complex and difficult to maintain.

Listing 8-22. The Contents of the order.repository.ts File in the src/app/model Folder

```
import { Injectable } from "@angular/core";
import { Observable } from "rxjs";
import { Order } from "./order.model";
import { StaticDataSource } from "./static.datasource";

@Injectable()
export class OrderRepository {
    private orders: Order[] = [];

    constructor(private dataSource: StaticDataSource) {}

    getOrders(): Order[] {
        return this.orders;
    }
```

```
    saveOrder(order: Order): Observable<Order> {
        return this.dataSource.saveOrder(order);
    }
}
```

Updating the Feature Module

Listing 8-23 registers the Order class and the new repository as services using the providers property of the model feature module.

Listing 8-23. Registering Services in the model.module.ts File in the src/app/model Folder

```
import { NgModule } from "@angular/core";
import { ProductRepository } from "./product.repository";
import { StaticDataSource } from "./static.datasource";
import { Cart } from "./cart.model";
import { Order } from "./order.model";
import { OrderRepository } from "./order.repository";


@NgModule({
    providers: [ProductRepository, StaticDataSource, Cart,
                Order, OrderRepository]
})
export class ModelModule { }
```

Collecting the Order Details

The next step is to gather the details from the user required to complete the order. Angular includes built-in directives for working with HTML forms and validating their contents. Listing 8-24 prepares the checkout component, switching to an external template, receiving the Order object as a constructor parameter, and providing some additional support to help the template.

Listing 8-24. Preparing for a Form in the checkout.component.ts File in the src/app/store Folder

```
import { Component } from "@angular/core";
import { NgForm } from "@angular/forms";
import { OrderRepository } from "../model/order.repository";
import { Order } from "../model/order.model";


@Component({
    templateUrl: "checkout.component.html",
    styleUrls: ["checkout.component.css"]
})
export class CheckoutComponent {
    orderSent: boolean = false;
    submitted: boolean = false;

    constructor(public repository: OrderRepository,
                public order: Order) {}

    submitOrder(form: NgForm) {
```

```
            this.submitted = true;
            if (form.valid) {
                this.repository.saveOrder(this.order).subscribe(order => {
                    this.order.clear();
                    this.orderSent = true;
                    this.submitted = false;
                });
            }
        }
    }
}
```

The submitOrder method will be invoked when the user submits a form, which is represented by an NgForm object. If the data that the form contains is valid, then the Order object will be passed to the repository's saveOrder method, and the data in the cart and the order will be reset.

The @Component decorator's styleUrls property is used to specify one or more CSS stylesheets that should be applied to the content in the component's template. To provide validation feedback for the values that the user enters into the HTML form elements, I created a file called checkout.component.css in the src/app/store folder and defined the styles shown in Listing 8-25.

Listing 8-25. The Contents of the checkout.component.css File in the src/app/store Folder

```
input.ng-dirty.ng-invalid { border: 2px solid #ff0000 }
input.ng-dirty.ng-valid { border: 2px solid #6bc502 }
```

Angular adds elements to the ng-dirty, ng-valid, and ng-valid classes to indicate their validation status. The full set of validation classes is described in Chapter 14, but the effect of the styles in Listing 8-25 is to add a green border around input elements that are valid and a red border around those that are invalid.

The final piece of the puzzle is the template for the component, which presents the user with the form fields required to populate the properties of an Order object, as shown in Listing 8-26.

Listing 8-26. The Contents of the checkout.component.html File in the src/app/store Folder

```
<div class="container-fluid">
  <div class="row">
    <div class="col bg-dark text-white">
      <a class="navbar-brand">SPORTS STORE</a>
    </div>
  </div>
</div>

<div *ngIf="orderSent" class="m-2 text-center">
  <h2>Thanks!</h2>
  <p>Thanks for placing your order.</p>
  <p>We'll ship your goods as soon as possible.</p>
  <button class="btn btn-primary" routerLink="/store">Return to Store</button>
</div>
<form *ngIf="!orderSent" #form="ngForm" novalidate
      (ngSubmit)="submitOrder(form)" class="m-2">
  <div class="form-group">
    <label>Name</label>
    <input class="form-control" #name="ngModel" name="name"
           [(ngModel)]="order.name" required />
```

```
      <span *ngIf="submitted && name.invalid" class="text-danger">
        Please enter your name
      </span>
    </div>
    <div class="form-group">
      <label>Address</label>
      <input class="form-control" #address="ngModel" name="address"
             [(ngModel)]="order.address" required />
      <span *ngIf="submitted && address.invalid" class="text-danger">
        Please enter your address
      </span>
    </div>
    <div class="form-group">
      <label>City</label>
      <input class="form-control" #city="ngModel" name="city"
             [(ngModel)]="order.city" required />
      <span *ngIf="submitted && city.invalid" class="text-danger">
        Please enter your city
      </span>
    </div>
    <div class="form-group">
      <label>State</label>
      <input class="form-control" #state="ngModel" name="state"
             [(ngModel)]="order.state" required />
      <span *ngIf="submitted && state.invalid" class="text-danger">
        Please enter your state
      </span>
    </div>
    <div class="form-group">
      <label>Zip/Postal Code</label>
      <input class="form-control" #zip="ngModel" name="zip"
             [(ngModel)]="order.zip" required />
      <span *ngIf="submitted && zip.invalid" class="text-danger">
        Please enter your zip/postal code
      </span>
    </div>
    <div class="form-group">
      <label>Country</label>
      <input class="form-control" #country="ngModel" name="country"
             [(ngModel)]="order.country" required />
      <span *ngIf="submitted && country.invalid" class="text-danger">
        Please enter your country
      </span>
    </div>
    <div class="text-center">
      <button class="btn btn-secondary m-1" routerLink="/cart">Back</button>
      <button class="btn btn-primary m-1" type="submit">Complete Order</button>
    </div>
</form>
```

The form and input elements in this template use Angular features to ensure that the user provides values for each field, and they provide visual feedback if the user clicks the Complete Order button without completing the form. Part of this feedback comes from applying the styles that were defined in Listing 8-25, and part comes from span elements that remain hidden until the user tries to submit an invalid form.

■ **Tip** Requiring values is only one of the ways that Angular can validate form fields, and as I explained in Chapter 14, you can easily add your own custom validation as well.

To see the process, start with the list of products and click one of the Add To Cart buttons to add a product to the cart. Click the Checkout button and you will see the HTML form shown in Figure 8-6. Click the Complete Order button without entering text into any of the input elements, and you will see the validation feedback messages. Fill out the form and click the Complete Order button; you will see the confirmation message shown in the figure.

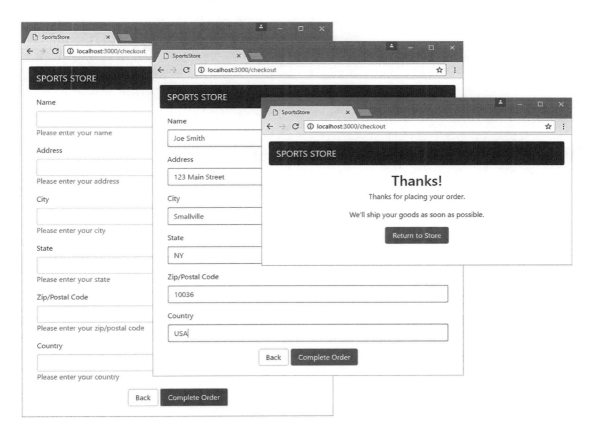

Figure 8-6. *Completing an order*

If you look at the browser's JavaScript console, you will see a JSON representation of the order like this:

```
{"cart":
    {"lines":[
        {"product":{"id":1,"name":"Product 1","category":"Category 1",
         "description":"Product 1 (Category 1)","price":100},"quantity":1}],
         "itemCount":1,"cartPrice":100},
    "shipped":false,
    "name":"Joe Smith","address":"123 Main Street",
    "city":"Smallville","state":"NY","zip":"10036","country":"USA"
}
```

Using the RESTful Web Service

Now that the basic SportsStore functionality is in place, it is time to replace the dummy data source with one that gets its data from the RESTful web service that was created during the project setup in Chapter 7.

To create the data source, I added a file called rest.datasource.ts in the src/app/model folder and added the code shown in Listing 8-27.

Listing 8-27. The Contents of the rest.datasource.ts File in the src/app/model Folder

```
import { Injectable } from "@angular/core";
import { HttpClient } from "@angular/common/http";
import { Observable } from "rxjs";
import { Product } from "./product.model";
import { Cart } from "./cart.model";
import { Order } from "./order.model";

const PROTOCOL = "http";
const PORT = 3500;

@Injectable()
export class RestDataSource {
  baseUrl: string;

  constructor(private http: HttpClient) {
    this.baseUrl = `${PROTOCOL}://${location.hostname}:${PORT}/`;
  }

  getProducts(): Observable<Product[]> {
    return this.http.get<Product[]>(this.baseUrl + "products");
  }

  saveOrder(order: Order): Observable<Order> {
    return this.http.post<Order>(this.baseUrl + "orders", order);
  }
}
```

Angular provides a built-in service called HttpClient that is used to make HTTP requests. The RestDataSource constructor receives the HttpClient service and uses the global location object provided by the browser to determine the URL that the requests will be sent to, which is port 3500 on the same host that the application has been loaded from.

The methods defined by the RestDataSource class correspond to the ones defined by the static data source but are implemented using the HttpClient service, described in Chapter 24.

■ **Tip** When obtaining data via HTTP, it is possible that network congestion or server load will delay the request and leave the user looking at an application that has no data. In Chapter 27, I explain how to configure the routing system to prevent this problem.

Applying the Data Source

To complete this chapter, I am going to apply the RESTful data source by reconfiguring the application so that the switch from the dummy data to the REST data is done with changes to a single file. Listing 8-28 changes the behavior of the data source service in the model feature module.

Listing 8-28. Changing the Service Configuration in the model.module.ts File in the src/app/model Folder

```
import { NgModule } from "@angular/core";
import { ProductRepository } from "./product.repository";
import { StaticDataSource } from "./static.datasource";
import { Cart } from "./cart.model";
import { Order } from "./order.model";
import { OrderRepository } from "./order.repository";
import { RestDataSource } from "./rest.datasource";
import { HttpClientModule } from "@angular/common/http";

@NgModule({
    imports: [HttpClientModule],
    providers: [ProductRepository, Cart, Order, OrderRepository,
        { provide: StaticDataSource, useClass: RestDataSource }]
})
export class ModelModule { }
```

The imports property is used to declare a dependency on the HttpClientModule feature module, which provides the HttpClient service used in Listing 8-27. The change to the providers property tells Angular that when it needs to create an instance of a class with a StaticDataSource constructor parameter, it should use a RestDataSource instead. Since both objects define the same methods, the dynamic JavaScript type system means that the substitution is seamless. When all the changes have been saved and the browser reloads the application, you will see the dummy data has been replaced with the data obtained via HTTP, as shown in Figure 8-7.

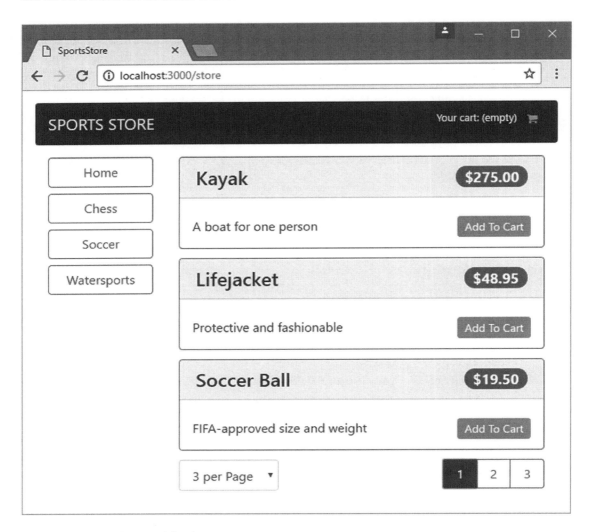

Figure 8-7. *Using the RESTful web service*

If you go through the process of selecting products and checking out, you can see that the data source has written the order to the web service by navigating to this URL:

```
http://localhost:3500/db
```

This will display the full contents of the database, including the collection of orders. You won't be able to request the /orders URL because it requires authentication, which I set up in the next chapter.

■ **Tip** Remember that the data provided by the RESTful web service is reset when you stop the server and start it again using the npm run json command.

Summary

In this chapter, I continued adding features to the SportsStore application, adding support for a shopping cart into which the user can place products and a checkout process that completes the shopping process. To complete the chapter, I replaced the dummy data source with one that sends HTTP requests to the RESTful web service. In the next chapter, I create the administration features that allow the SportsStore data to be managed.

CHAPTER 9

SportsStore: Administration

In this chapter, I continue building the SportsStore application by adding administration features. Relatively few users will need to access the administration features, so it would be wasteful to force all users to download the administration code and content when it is unlikely to be used. Instead, I am going to put the administration features in a separate module that will be loaded only when administration is required.

Preparing the Example Application

No preparation is required for this chapter, which continues using the SportsStore project from Chapter 8. To start the RESTful web service, open a command prompt and run the following command in the SportsStore folder:

```
npm run json
```

Open a second command prompt and run the following command in the SportsStore folder to start the development tools and HTTP server:

```
ng serve --port 3000 --open
```

■ **Tip** You can download the example project for this chapter—and for all the other chapters in this book—from https://github.com/Apress/pro-angular-6.

Creating the Module

The process for creating the feature module follows the same pattern you have seen in earlier chapters. The key difference is that it is important that no other part of the application has dependencies on the module or the classes it contains, which would undermine the dynamic loading of the module and cause the JavaScript module to load the administration code, even if it is not used.

The starting point for the administration features will be authentication, which will ensure that only authorized users are able to administer the application. I created a file called auth.component.ts in the src/app/admin folder and used it to define the component shown in Listing 9-1.

Listing 9-1. The Content of the auth.component.ts File in the src/app/admin Folder

```
import { Component } from "@angular/core";
import { NgForm } from "@angular/forms";
import { Router } from "@angular/router";

@Component({
    templateUrl: "auth.component.html"
})
export class AuthComponent {
    public username: string;
    public password: string;
    public errorMessage: string;

    constructor(private router: Router) {}

    authenticate(form: NgForm) {
        if (form.valid) {
            // perform authentication
            this.router.navigateByUrl("/admin/main");
        } else {
            this.errorMessage = "Form Data Invalid";
        }
    }
}
```

The component defines properties for the username and password that will be used to authenticate the user, an errorMessage property that will be used to display messages when there are problems, and an authenticate method that will perform the authentication process (but that does nothing at the moment).

To provide the component with a template, I created a file called auth.component.html in the src/app/ admin folder and added the content shown in Listing 9-2.

Listing 9-2. The Content of the auth.component.html File in the src/app/admin Folder

```
<div class="bg-info p-2 text-center text-white">
  <h3>SportsStore Admin</h3>
</div>
<div class="bg-danger mt-2 p-2 text-center text-white"
     *ngIf="errorMessage != null">
  {{errorMessage}}
</div>
<div class="p-2">
  <form novalidate #form="ngForm" (ngSubmit)="authenticate(form)">
    <div class="form-group">
      <label>Name</label>
      <input class="form-control" name="username"
             [(ngModel)]="username" required />
    </div>
    <div class="form-group">
      <label>Password</label>
      <input class="form-control" type="password" name="password"
             [(ngModel)]="password" required />
    </div>
```

```
    <div class="text-center">
      <button class="btn btn-secondary m-1" routerLink="/">Go back</button>
      <button class="btn btn-primary m-1" type="submit">Log In</button>
    </div>
  </form>
</div>
```

The template contains an HTML form that uses two-way data binding expressions for the component's properties. There is a button that will submit the form, a button that navigates back to the root URL, and a div element that is visible only when there is an error message to display.

To create a placeholder for the administration features, I added a file called admin.component.ts in the src/app/admin folder and defined the component shown in Listing 9-3.

Listing 9-3. The Contents of the admin.component.ts File in the src/app/admin Folder

```
import { Component } from "@angular/core";
@Component({
    templateUrl: "admin.component.html"
})
export class AdminComponent {}
```

The component doesn't contain any functionality at the moment. To provide a template for the component, I added a file called admin.component.html to the src/app/admin folder and the placeholder content shown in Listing 9-4.

Listing 9-4. The Contents of the admin.component.html File in the src/app/admin Folder

```
<div class="bg-info p-2 text-white">
  <h3>Placeholder for Admin Features</h3>
</div>
```

To define the feature module, I added a file called admin.module.ts in the src/app/admin folder and added the code shown in Listing 9-5.

Listing 9-5. The Contents of the admin.module.ts File in the src/app/admin Folder

```
import { NgModule } from "@angular/core";
import { CommonModule } from "@angular/common";
import { FormsModule } from "@angular/forms";
import { RouterModule } from "@angular/router";
import { AuthComponent } from "./auth.component";
import { AdminComponent } from "./admin.component";

let routing = RouterModule.forChild([
    { path: "auth", component: AuthComponent },
    { path: "main", component: AdminComponent },
    { path: "**", redirectTo: "auth" }
]);
```

```
@NgModule({
    imports: [CommonModule, FormsModule, routing],
    declarations: [AuthComponent, AdminComponent]
})
export class AdminModule { }
```

The RouterModule.forChild method is used to define the routing configuration for the feature module, which is then included in the module's imports property.

A dynamically loaded module must be self-contained and include all the information that Angular requires, including the routing URLs that are supported and the components they display. If any other part of the application depends on the module, then it will be included in the JavaScript bundle with the rest of the application code, which means that all users will have to download code and resources for features they won't use.

However, a dynamically loaded module is allowed to declare dependencies on the main part of the application. This module relies on the functionality in the data model module, which has been added to the module's imports so that components can access the model classes and the repositories.

Configuring the URL Routing System

Dynamically loaded modules are managed through the routing configuration, which triggers the loading process when the application navigates to a specific URL. Listing 9-6 extends the routing configuration of the application so that the /admin URL will load the administration feature module.

Listing 9-6. Configuring a Dynamically Loaded Module in the app.module.ts File in the src/app Folder

```
import { NgModule } from "@angular/core";
import { BrowserModule } from "@angular/platform-browser";
import { AppComponent } from "./app.component";
import { StoreModule } from "./store/store.module";
import { StoreComponent } from "./store/store.component";
import { CheckoutComponent } from "./store/checkout.component";
import { CartDetailComponent } from "./store/cartDetail.component";
import { RouterModule } from "@angular/router";
import { StoreFirstGuard } from "./storeFirst.guard";

@NgModule({
    imports: [BrowserModule, StoreModule,
        RouterModule.forRoot([
            {
                path: "store", component: StoreComponent,
                canActivate: [StoreFirstGuard]
            },
            {
                path: "cart", component: CartDetailComponent,
                canActivate: [StoreFirstGuard]
            },
            {
                path: "checkout", component: CheckoutComponent,
                canActivate: [StoreFirstGuard]
            },
```

```
        {
            path: "admin",
            loadChildren: "./admin/admin.module#AdminModule",
            canActivate: [StoreFirstGuard]
        },
        { path: "**", redirectTo: "/store" }
    ])],
    providers: [StoreFirstGuard],
    declarations: [AppComponent],
    bootstrap: [AppComponent]
})
export class AppModule { }
```

The new route tells Angular that when the application navigates to the /admin URL, it should load a feature module defined by a class called AdminModule from the admin/admin.module.ts file, whose path is specified relative to the app.module.ts file. When Angular processes the admin module, it will incorporate the routing information it contains into the overall set of routes and complete the navigation.

Navigating to the Administration URL

The final preparatory step is to provide the user with the ability to navigate to the /admin URL so that the administration feature module will be loaded and its component displayed to the user. Listing 9-7 adds a button to the store component's template that will perform the navigation.

Listing 9-7. Adding a Navigation Button in the store.component.html File in the src/app/store Folder

```
<div class="container-fluid">
  <div class="row">
    <div class="col bg-dark text-white">
      <a class="navbar-brand">SPORTS STORE</a>
      <cart-summary></cart-summary>
    </div>
  </div>
  <div class="row">

    <div class="col-3 p-2">
      <button class="btn btn-block btn-outline-primary" (click)="changeCategory()">
        Home
      </button>
      <button *ngFor="let cat of categories"
          class="btn btn-outline-primary btn-block"
          [class.active]="cat == selectedCategory" (click)="changeCategory(cat)">
        {{cat}}
      </button>
      <button class="btn btn-block btn-danger m-t-3" routerLink="/admin">
        Admin
      </button>
    </div>
```

```
    <div class="col-9 p-2">

      <!-- ...elements omitted for brevity... -->

    </div>
  </div>
</div>
```

To reflect the changes, stop the development tools and restart them by running the following command in the SportsStore folder:

```
ng serve --port 3000
```

Use the browser to navigate to http://localhost:3000 and use the browser's F12 developer tools to see the network requests made by the browser as the application is loaded. The files for the administration module will not be loaded until you click the Admin button, at which point Angular will request the files and display the login page shown in Figure 9-1.

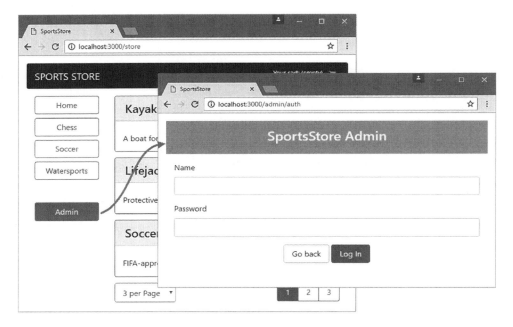

Figure 9-1. *Using a dynamically loaded module*

Enter any name and password into the form fields and click the Log In button to see the placeholder content, as shown in Figure 9-2. If you leave either of the form fields empty, a warning message will be displayed.

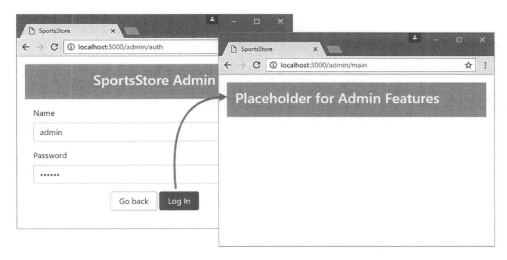

Figure 9-2. *The placeholder administration features*

Implementing Authentication

The RESTful web service has been configured so that it requires authentication for the requests that the administration feature will require. In the sections that follow, I add support for authenticating the user by sending an HTTP request to the RESTful web service.

Understanding the Authentication System

When the RESTful web service authenticates a user, it will return a JSON Web Token (JWT) that the application must include in subsequent HTTP requests to show that authentication has been successfully performed. You can read the JWT specification at `https://tools.ietf.org/html/rfc7519`, but for the purposes of the SportsStore application, it is enough to know that the Angular application can authenticate the user by sending a POST request to the `/login` URL, including a JSON-formatted object in the request body that contains name and password properties. There is only one set of valid credentials in the authentication code I added to the application in Chapter 7, which is shown in Table 9-1.

Table 9-1. *The Authentication Credentials Supported by the RESTful Web Service*

Username	Password
admin	secret

As I noted in Chapter 7, you should not hard-code credentials in real projects, but this is the username and password that you will need for the SportsStore application.

If the correct credentials are sent to the /login URL, then the response from the RESTful web service will contain a JSON object like this:

```
{
  "success": true,
  "token":"eyJhbGciOiJIUzI1NiIsInR5cCI6IkpXVCJ9.eyJkYXRhIjoiYWRtaW4iLCJleHBpcmVz
          SW4iOiIxaCIsImlhdCI6MTQ3ODk1NjI1Mn0.lJaDDrSu-bHBtdWrzO312p_DG5tKypGv6cA
          NgOyzlg8"
}
```

The success property describes the outcome of the authentication operation, and the token property contains the JWT, which should be included in subsequent requests using the Authorization HTTP header in this format:

```
Authorization: Bearer<eyJhbGciOiJIUzI1NiIsInR5cCI6IkpXVCJ9.eyJkYXRhIjoiYWRtaW4iLC
               JleHBpcmVzSW4iOiIxaCIsImlhdCI6MTQ3ODk1NjI1Mn0.lJaDDrSu-bHBtd
               WrzO312p_DG5tKypGv6cANgOyzlg8>
```

I configured the JWT tokens returned by the server so they expire after one hour.

If the wrong credentials are sent to the server, then the JSON object returned in the response will just contain a success property set to false, like this:

```
{
  "success": false
}
```

Extending the Data Source

The RESTful data source will do most of the work because it is responsible for sending the authentication request to the /login URL and including the JWT in subsequent requests. Listing 9-8 adds authentication to the RestDataSource class and defines a variable that will store the JWT once it has been obtained.

Listing 9-8. Adding Authentication in the rest.datasource.ts File in the src/app/model Folder

```
import { Injectable } from "@angular/core";
import { HttpClient } from "@angular/common/http";
import { Observable } from "rxjs";
import { Product } from "./product.model";
import { Cart } from "./cart.model";
import { Order } from "./order.model";
import { map } from "rxjs/operators";

const PROTOCOL = "http";
const PORT = 3500;
```

```
@Injectable()
export class RestDataSource {
    baseUrl: string;
    auth_token: string;

    constructor(private http: HttpClient) {
        this.baseUrl = `${PROTOCOL}://${location.hostname}:${PORT}/`;
    }

    getProducts(): Observable<Product[]> {
        return this.http.get<Product[]>(this.baseUrl + "products");
    }

    saveOrder(order: Order): Observable<Order> {
        return this.http.post<Order>(this.baseUrl + "orders", order);
    }

    authenticate(user: string, pass: string): Observable<boolean> {
        return this.http.post<any>(this.baseUrl + "login", {
            name: user, password: pass
        }).pipe(map(response => {
            this.auth_token = response.success ? response.token : null;
            return response.success;
        }));
    }

}
```

Creating the Authentication Service

Rather than expose the data source directly to the rest of the application, I am going to create a service that can be used to perform authentication and determine whether the application has been authenticated. I added a file called auth.service.ts in the src/app/model folder and added the code shown in Listing 9-9.

Listing 9-9. The Contents of the auth.service.ts File in the src/app/model Folder

```
import { Injectable } from "@angular/core";
import { Observable } from "rxjs";
import { RestDataSource } from "./rest.datasource";

@Injectable()
export class AuthService {

    constructor(private datasource: RestDataSource) {}

    authenticate(username: string, password: string): Observable<boolean> {
        return this.datasource.authenticate(username, password);
    }

    get authenticated(): boolean {
        return this.datasource.auth_token != null;
    }
```

```
    clear() {
        this.datasource.auth_token = null;
    }
}
```

The authenticate method receives the user's credentials and passes them on to the data source authenticate method, returning an Observable that will yield true if the authentication process has succeeded and false otherwise. The authenticated property is a getter-only property that returns true if the data source has obtained an authentication token. The clear method removes the token from the data source.

Listing 9-10 registers the new service with the model feature module. It also adds a providers entry for the RestDataSource class, which has been used only as a substitute for the StaticDataSource class in earlier chapters. Since the AuthService class has a RestDataSource constructor parameter, it needs its own entry in the module.

Listing 9-10. Configuring the Services in the model.module.ts File in the src/app/model Folder

```
import { NgModule } from "@angular/core";
import { ProductRepository } from "./product.repository";
import { StaticDataSource } from "./static.datasource";
import { Cart } from "./cart.model";
import { Order } from "./order.model";
import { OrderRepository } from "./order.repository";
import { RestDataSource } from "./rest.datasource";
import { HttpClientModule } from "@angular/common/http";
import { AuthService } from "./auth.service";

@NgModule({
  imports: [HttpClientModule],
  providers: [ProductRepository, Cart, Order, OrderRepository,
    { provide: StaticDataSource, useClass: RestDataSource },
    RestDataSource, AuthService]
})
export class ModelModule { }
```

Enabling Authentication

The next step is to wire up the component that obtains the credentials from the user so that it will perform authentication through the new service, as shown in Listing 9-11.

Listing 9-11. Enabling Authentication in the auth.component.ts File in the src/app/admin Folder

```
import { Component } from "@angular/core";
import { NgForm } from "@angular/forms";
import { Router } from "@angular/router";
import { AuthService } from "../model/auth.service";

@Component({
    templateUrl: "auth.component.html"
})
```

```
export class AuthComponent {
    public username: string;
    public password: string;
    public errorMessage: string;

    constructor(private router: Router,
                private auth: AuthService) { }

    authenticate(form: NgForm) {
        if (form.valid) {
            this.auth.authenticate(this.username, this.password)
                .subscribe(response => {
                    if (response) {
                        this.router.navigateByUrl("/admin/main");
                    }
                    this.errorMessage = "Authentication Failed";
                })
        } else {
            this.errorMessage = "Form Data Invalid";
        }
    }
}
```

To prevent the application from navigating directly to the administration features, which will lead to HTTP requests being sent without a token, I added a file called auth.guard.ts in the src/app/admin folder and defined the route guard shown in Listing 9-12.

Listing 9-12. The Contents of the auth.guard.ts File in the src/app/admin Folder

```
import { Injectable } from "@angular/core";
import { ActivatedRouteSnapshot, RouterStateSnapshot,
         Router } from "@angular/router";
import { AuthService } from "../model/auth.service";

@Injectable()
export class AuthGuard {

    constructor(private router: Router,
                private auth: AuthService) { }

    canActivate(route: ActivatedRouteSnapshot,
        state: RouterStateSnapshot): boolean {

        if (!this.auth.authenticated) {
            this.router.navigateByUrl("/admin/auth");
            return false;
        }
        return true;
    }
}
```

Listing 9-13 applies the route guard to one of the routes defined by the administration feature module.

Listing 9-13. Guarding a Route in the admin.module.ts File in the src/app/admin Folder

```
import { NgModule } from "@angular/core";
import { CommonModule } from "@angular/common";
import { FormsModule } from "@angular/forms";
import { RouterModule } from "@angular/router";
import { AuthComponent } from "./auth.component";
import { AdminComponent } from "./admin.component";
import { AuthGuard } from "./auth.guard";

let routing = RouterModule.forChild([
    { path: "auth", component: AuthComponent },
    { path: "main", component: AdminComponent, canActivate: [AuthGuard] },
    { path: "**", redirectTo: "auth" }
]);

@NgModule({
    imports: [CommonModule, FormsModule, routing],
    providers: [AuthGuard],
    declarations: [AuthComponent, AdminComponent]
})
export class AdminModule {}
```

To test the authentication system, click the Admin button, enter some credentials, and click the Log In button. If the credentials are the ones from Table 9-1, then you will see the placeholder for the administration features. If you enter other credentials, you will see an error message. Figure 9-3 illustrates both outcomes.

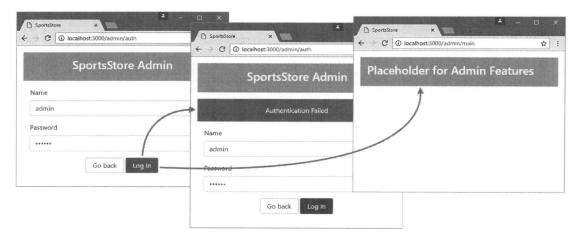

Figure 9-3. *Testing the authentication feature*

■ **Tip**   The token isn't stored persistently, so if you can, reload the application in the browser to start again and try a different set of credentials.

Extending the Data Source and Repositories

With the authentication system in place, the next step is to extend the data source so that it can send authenticated requests and to expose those features through the order and product repository classes. Listing 9-14 adds methods to the data source that include the authentication token.

Listing 9-14. Adding New Operations in the rest.datasource.ts File in the src/app/model Folder

```
import { Injectable } from "@angular/core";
import { HttpClient } from "@angular/common/http";
import { Observable } from "rxjs";
import { Product } from "./product.model";
import { Cart } from "./cart.model";
import { Order } from "./order.model";
import { map } from "rxjs/operators";
import { HttpHeaders } from '@angular/common/http';

const PROTOCOL = "http";
const PORT = 3500;

@Injectable()
export class RestDataSource {
    baseUrl: string;
    auth_token: string;

    constructor(private http: HttpClient) {
        this.baseUrl = `${PROTOCOL}://${location.hostname}:${PORT}/`;
    }

    getProducts(): Observable<Product[]> {
        return this.http.get<Product[]>(this.baseUrl + "products");
    }

    saveOrder(order: Order): Observable<Order> {
        return this.http.post<Order>(this.baseUrl + "orders", order);
    }

    authenticate(user: string, pass: string): Observable<boolean> {
        return this.http.post<any>(this.baseUrl + "login", {
            name: user, password: pass
        }).pipe(map(response => {
            this.auth_token = response.success ? response.token : null;
            return response.success;
        }));
    }
}
```

```
saveProduct(product: Product): Observable<Product> {
    return this.http.post<Product>(this.baseUrl + "products",
        product, this.getOptions());
}

updateProduct(product): Observable<Product> {
    return this.http.put<Product>(`${this.baseUrl}products/${product.id}`,
        product, this.getOptions());
}

deleteProduct(id: number): Observable<Product> {
    return this.http.delete<Product>(`${this.baseUrl}products/${id}`,
        this.getOptions());
}

getOrders(): Observable<Order[]> {
    return this.http.get<Order[]>(this.baseUrl + "orders", this.getOptions());
}

deleteOrder(id: number): Observable<Order> {
    return this.http.delete<Order>(`${this.baseUrl}orders/${id}`,
        this.getOptions());
}

updateOrder(order: Order): Observable<Order> {
    return this.http.put<Order>(`${this.baseUrl}orders/${order.id}`,
        this.getOptions());
}

private getOptions() {
    return {
        headers: new HttpHeaders({
            "Authorization": `Bearer<${this.auth_token}>`
        })
    }
}
}
```

Listing 9-15 adds new methods to the product repository class that allow products to be created, updated, or deleted. The saveProduct method is responsible for creating and updating products, which is an approach that works well when using a single object managed by a component, which you will see demonstrated later in this chapter. The listing also changes the type of the constructor argument to RestDataSource.

Listing 9-15. Adding New Operations in the product.repository.ts File in the src/app/model Folder

```
import { Injectable } from "@angular/core";
import { Product } from "./product.model";
//import { StaticDataSource } from "./static.datasource";
import { RestDataSource } from "./rest.datasource";
```

```
@Injectable()
export class ProductRepository {
    private products: Product[] = [];
    private categories: string[] = [];

    constructor(private dataSource: RestDataSource) {
        dataSource.getProducts().subscribe(data => {
            this.products = data;
            this.categories = data.map(p => p.category)
                .filter((c, index, array) => array.indexOf(c) == index).sort();
        });
    }

    getProducts(category: string = null): Product[] {
        return this.products
            .filter(p => category == null || category == p.category);
    }

    getProduct(id: number): Product {
        return this.products.find(p => p.id == id);
    }

    getCategories(): string[] {
        return this.categories;
    }

    saveProduct(product: Product) {
        if (product.id == null || product.id == 0) {
            this.dataSource.saveProduct(product)
                .subscribe(p => this.products.push(p));
        } else {
            this.dataSource.updateProduct(product)
                .subscribe(p => {
                    this.products.splice(this.products.
                        findIndex(p => p.id == product.id), 1, product);
                });
        }
    }

    deleteProduct(id: number) {
        this.dataSource.deleteProduct(id).subscribe(p => {
            this.products.splice(this.products.
                findIndex(p => p.id == id), 1);
        })
    }
}
```

Listing 9-16 makes the corresponding changes to the order repository, adding methods that allow orders to be modified and deleted.

Listing 9-16. Adding New Operations in the order.repository.ts File in the src/app/model Folder

```
import { Injectable } from "@angular/core";
import { Observable } from "rxjs";
import { Order } from "./order.model";
//import { StaticDataSource } from "./static.datasource";
import { RestDataSource } from "./rest.datasource";

@Injectable()
export class OrderRepository {
    private orders: Order[] = [];
    private loaded: boolean = false;

    constructor(private dataSource: RestDataSource) { }

    loadOrders() {
        this.loaded = true;
        this.dataSource.getOrders()
            .subscribe(orders => this.orders = orders);
    }

    getOrders(): Order[] {
        if (!this.loaded) {
            this.loadOrders();
        }
        return this.orders;
    }

    saveOrder(order: Order): Observable<Order> {
        return this.dataSource.saveOrder(order);
    }

    updateOrder(order: Order) {
        this.dataSource.updateOrder(order).subscribe(order => {
            this.orders.splice(this.orders.
                findIndex(o => o.id == order.id), 1, order);
        });
    }

    deleteOrder(id: number) {
        this.dataSource.deleteOrder(id).subscribe(order => {
            this.orders.splice(this.orders.findIndex(o => id == o.id));
        });
    }
}
```

The order repository defines a loadOrders method that gets the orders from the repository and that is used to ensure that the request isn't sent to the RESTful web service until authentication has been performed.

Creating the Administration Feature Structure

Now that the authentication system is in place and the repositories provide the full range of operations, I can create the structure that will display the administration features, which I create by building on the existing URL routing configuration. Table 9-2 lists the URLs that I am going to support and the functionality that each will present to the user.

Table 9-2. *The URLs for Administration Features*

Name	Description
/admin/main/products	Navigating to this URL will display all the products in a table, along with buttons that allow an existing product to be edited or deleted and a new product to be created.
/admin/main/products/create	Navigating to this URL will present the user with an empty editor for creating a new product.
/admin/main/products/edit/1	Navigating to this URL will present the user with a populated editor for editing an existing product.
/admin/main/orders	Navigating to this URL will present the user with all the orders in a table, along with buttons to mark an order shipped and to cancel an order by deleting it.

Creating the Placeholder Components

I find the easiest way to add features to an Angular project is to define components that have placeholder content and build the structure of the application around them. Once the structure is in place, then I return to the components and implement the features in detail. For the administration features, I started by adding a file called productTable.component.ts to the src/app/admin folder and defined the component shown in Listing 9-17. This component will be responsible for showing a list of products, along with buttons required to edit and delete them or to create a new product.

Listing 9-17. The Contents of the productTable.component.ts File in the src/app/admin Folder

```
import { Component } from "@angular/core";

@Component({
    template: `<div class="bg-info p-2 text-white">
                <h3>Product Table Placeholder</h3>
            </div>`
})
export class ProductTableComponent {}
```

I added a file called productEditor.component.ts in the src/app/admin folder and used it to define the component shown in Listing 9-18, which will be used to allow the user to enter the details required to create or edit a component.

Listing 9-18. The Contents of the productEditor.component.ts File in the src/app/admin Folder

```
import { Component } from "@angular/core";

@Component({
    template: `<div class="bg-warning p-2 text-white">
                  <h3>Product Editor Placeholder</h3>
               </div>`
})
export class ProductEditorComponent { }
```

To create the component that will be responsible for managing customer orders, I added a file called `orderTable.component.ts` to the `src/app/admin` folder and added the code shown in Listing 9-19.

Listing 9-19. The Contents of the orderTable.component.ts File in the src/app/admin Folder

```
import { Component } from "@angular/core";

@Component({
    template: `<div class="bg-primary p-2 text-white">
                  <h3>Order Table Placeholder</h3>
               </div>`
})
export class OrderTableComponent { }
```

Preparing the Common Content and the Feature Module

The components created in the previous section will be responsible for specific features. To bring those features together and allow the user to navigate between them, I need to modify the template of the placeholder component that I have been using to demonstrate the result of a successful authentication attempt. I replaced the placeholder content with the elements shown in Listing 9-20.

Listing 9-20. Replacing the Content in the admin.component.html File in the src/app/admin Folder

```
<div class="container-fluid">
    <div class="row">
        <div class="col bg-dark text-white">
            <a class="navbar-brand">SPORTS STORE</a>
        </div>
    </div>
    <div class="row mt-2">
        <div class="col-3">
            <button class="btn btn-outline-info btn-block"
                    routerLink="/admin/main/products"
                    routerLinkActive="active">
                Products
            </button>
            <button class="btn btn-outline-info btn-block"
                    routerLink="/admin/main/orders"
                    routerLinkActive="active">
                Orders
            </button>
```

```
            <button class="btn btn-outline-danger btn-block" (click)="logout()">
                Logout
            </button>
        </div>
        <div class="col-9">
            <router-outlet></router-outlet>
        </div>
    </div>
</div>
```

This template contains a `router-outlet` element that will be used to display the components from the previous section. There are also buttons that will navigate the application to the `/admin/main/products` and `/admin/main/orders` URLs, which will select the products or orders features. These buttons use the `routerLinkActive` attribute, which is used to add the element to a CSS class when the route specified by the `routerLink` attribute is active.

The template also contains a `Logout` button that has an event binding that targets a method called `logout`. Listing 9-21 adds this method to the component, which uses the authentication service to remove the bearer token and navigates the application to the default URL.

Listing 9-21. Implementing the Logout Method in the admin.component.ts File in the src/app/admin Folder

```
import { Component } from "@angular/core";
import { Router } from "@angular/router";
import { AuthService } from "../model/auth.service";

@Component({
    templateUrl: "admin.component.html"
})
export class AdminComponent {

    constructor(private auth: AuthService,
                private router: Router) { }

    logout() {
        this.auth.clear();
        this.router.navigateByUrl("/");
    }
}
```

Listing 9-22 enables the placeholder components that will be used for each administration feature and extends the URL routing configuration to implement the URLs from Table 9-2.

Listing 9-22. Configuring the Feature Module in the admin.module.ts File in the src/app/admin Folder

```
import { NgModule } from "@angular/core";
import { CommonModule } from "@angular/common";
import { FormsModule } from "@angular/forms";
import { RouterModule } from "@angular/router";
import { AuthComponent } from "./auth.component";
import { AdminComponent } from "./admin.component";
import { AuthGuard } from "./auth.guard";
import { ProductTableComponent } from "./productTable.component";
```

```
import { ProductEditorComponent } from "./productEditor.component";
import { OrderTableComponent } from "./orderTable.component";

let routing = RouterModule.forChild([
    { path: "auth", component: AuthComponent },
    {
        path: "main", component: AdminComponent, canActivate: [AuthGuard],
        children: [
            { path: "products/:mode/:id", component: ProductEditorComponent },
            { path: "products/:mode", component: ProductEditorComponent },
            { path: "products", component: ProductTableComponent },
            { path: "orders", component: OrderTableComponent },
            { path: "**", redirectTo: "products" }
        ]
    },
    { path: "**", redirectTo: "auth" }
]);

@NgModule({
    imports: [CommonModule, FormsModule, routing],
    providers: [AuthGuard],
    declarations: [AuthComponent, AdminComponent,
        ProductTableComponent, ProductEditorComponent, OrderTableComponent]
})
export class AdminModule {}
```

Individual routes can be extended using the children property, which is used to define routes that will target a nested router-outlet element, which I describe in Chapter 25. As you will see, components can get details of the active route from Angular so they can adapt their behavior. Routes can include route parameters, such as :mode or :id, that match any URL segment and that can be used to provide information to components that can be used to change their behavior.

When all the changes have been saved, click the Admin button and authenticate as admin with the password secret. You will see the new layout, as shown in Figure 9-4. Clicking the Products and Orders buttons will change the component displayed by the router-outlet element from Listing 9-20. Clicking the Logout button will exit the administration area.

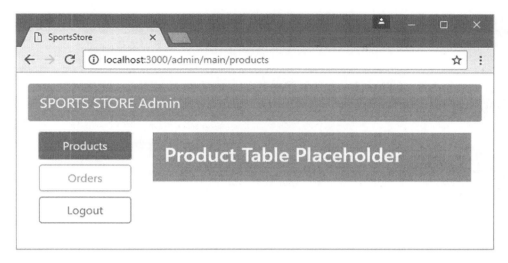

Figure 9-4. *The administration layout structure*

Implementing the Product Feature

The initial administration feature presented to the user will be a list of products, with the ability to create a new product and delete or edit an existing one. Listing 9-23 removes the placeholder content from the product table component and adds the logic required to implement this feature.

Listing 9-23. Replacing Content in the productTable.component.ts File in the src/app/admin Folder

```
import { Component } from "@angular/core";
import { Product } from "../model/product.model";
import { ProductRepository } from "../model/product.repository";

@Component({
    templateUrl: "productTable.component.html"
})
export class ProductTableComponent {

    constructor(private repository: ProductRepository) { }

    getProducts(): Product[] {
        return this.repository.getProducts();
    }

    deleteProduct(id: number) {
        this.repository.deleteProduct(id);
    }
}
```

The component methods provide access to the products in the repository and allow products to be deleted. The other operations will be handled by the editor component, which will be activated using routing URLs in the component's template. To provide the template, I added a file called productTable.component.html in the src/app/admin folder and added the markup shown in Listing 9-24.

Listing 9-24. The Contents of the productTable.component.html File in the src/app/admin Folder

```html
<table class="table table-sm table-striped">
    <thead>
        <tr>
            <th>ID</th><th>Name</th><th>Category</th><th>Price</th>
            <th></th>
        </tr>
    </thead>
    <tbody>
        <tr *ngFor="let p of getProducts()">
            <td>{{p.id}}</td>
            <td>{{p.name}}</td>
            <td>{{p.category}}</td>
            <td>{{p.price | currency:"USD":"symbol":"2.2-2"}}</td>
            <td>
                <button class="btn btn-sm btn-warning"
                        [routerLink]="['/admin/main/products/edit', p.id]">
                    Edit
                </button>
                <button class="btn btn-sm btn-danger" (click)="deleteProduct(p.id)">
                    Delete
                </button>
            </td>
        </tr>
    </tbody>
</table>
<button class="btn btn-primary" routerLink="/admin/main/products/create">
    Create New Product
</button>
```

The template contains a table that uses the ngFor directive to generate a row for each product returned by the component's getProducts method. Each row contains a Delete button that invokes the component's delete method and an Edit button that navigates to a URL that targets the editor component. The editor component is also the target of the Create New Product button, although a different URL is used.

Implementing the Product Editor

Components can receive information about the current routing URL and adapt their behavior accordingly. The editor component needs to use this feature to differentiate between requests to create a new component and edit an existing one. Listing 9-25 adds the functionality to the editor component required to create or edit products.

Listing 9-25. Adding Functionality in the productEditor.component.ts File in the src/app/admin Folder

```
import { Component } from "@angular/core";
import { Router, ActivatedRoute } from "@angular/router";
import { NgForm } from "@angular/forms";
import { Product } from "../model/product.model";
import { ProductRepository } from "../model/product.repository";

@Component({
    templateUrl: "productEditor.component.html"
})
export class ProductEditorComponent {
    editing: boolean = false;
    product: Product = new Product();

    constructor(private repository: ProductRepository,
                private router: Router,
                activeRoute: ActivatedRoute) {

        this.editing = activeRoute.snapshot.params["mode"] == "edit";
        if (this.editing) {
            Object.assign(this.product,
                repository.getProduct(activeRoute.snapshot.params["id"]));
        }
    }

    save(form: NgForm) {
        this.repository.saveProduct(this.product);
        this.router.navigateByUrl("/admin/main/products");
    }
}
```

Angular will provide an ActivatedRoute object as a constructor argument when it creates a new instance of the component class and that can be used to inspect the activated route. In this case, the component works out whether it should be editing or creating a product and, if editing, retrieves the current details from the repository. There is also a save method, which uses the repository to save changes that the user has made.

To provide the component with a template, I added a file called productEditor.component.html in the src/app/admin folder and added the markup shown in Listing 9-26.

Listing 9-26. The Contents of the productEditor.component.html File in the src/app/admin Folder

```
<div class="bg-primary p-2 text-white" [class.bg-warning]="editing"
    [class.text-dark]="editing">
    <h5>{{editing  ? "Edit" : "Create"}} Product</h5>
</div>
<form novalidate #form="ngForm" (ngSubmit)="save(form)">
    <div class="form-group">
        <label>Name</label>
        <input class="form-control" name="name" [(ngModel)]="product.name" />
    </div>
```

```
        <div class="form-group">
            <label>Category</label>
            <input class="form-control" name="category" [(ngModel)]="product.category" />
        </div>
        <div class="form-group">
            <label>Description</label>
            <textarea class="form-control" name="description"
                    [(ngModel)]="product.description">
            </textarea>
        </div>
        <div class="form-group">
            <label>Price</label>
            <input class="form-control" name="price" [(ngModel)]="product.price" />
        </div>
        <button type="submit" class="btn btn-primary" [class.btn-warning]="editing">
            {{editing ? "Save" : "Create"}}
        </button>
        <button type="reset" class="btn btn-secondary" routerLink="/admin/main/products">
            Cancel
        </button>
</form>
```

The template contains a form with fields for the properties defined by the Product model class, with the exception of the id property, which is assigned automatically by the RESTful web service.

The elements in the form adapt their appearance to differentiate between the editing and creating features. To see how the component works, authenticate to access the Admin features and click the Create New Product button that appears under the table of products. Fill out the form, click the Create button, and the new product will be sent to the RESTful web service where it will be assigned an ID property and displayed in the product table, as shown in Figure 9-5.

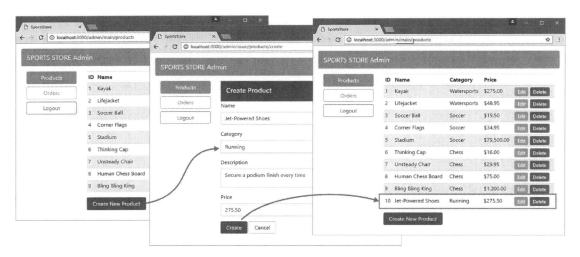

Figure 9-5. *Creating a new product*

The editing process works in a similar way. Click one of the Edit buttons to see the current details, edit them using the form fields, and click the Save button to save the changes, as shown in Figure 9-6.

Figure 9-6. *Editing an existing product*

Implementing the Orders Feature

The order management feature is nice and simple. It requires a table that lists the set of orders, along with buttons that will set the shipped property to true or delete an order entirely. Listing 9-27 replaces the placeholder content in the component with the logic required to support these operations.

Listing 9-27. Adding Operations in the orderTable.component.ts File in the src/app/admin Folder

```
import { Component } from "@angular/core";
import { Order } from "../model/order.model";
import { OrderRepository } from "../model/order.repository";

@Component({
    templateUrl: "orderTable.component.html"
})
export class OrderTableComponent {
    includeShipped = false;

    constructor(private repository: OrderRepository) {}

    getOrders(): Order[] {
        return this.repository.getOrders()
            .filter(o => this.includeShipped || !o.shipped);
    }

    markShipped(order: Order) {
        order.shipped = true;
        this.repository.updateOrder(order);
    }
```

189

```
    delete(id: number) {
        this.repository.deleteOrder(id);
    }
}
```

In addition to providing methods for marking orders as shipped and deleting orders, the component defines a getOrders method that allows shipped orders to be included or excluded based on the value of a property called includeShipped. This property is used in the template, which I created by adding a file called orderTable.component.html to the src/app/admin folder with the markup shown in Listing 9-28.

Listing 9-28. The Contents of the orderTable.component.html File in the src/app/admin Folder

```
<div class="form-check">
    <label class="form-check-label">
    <input type="checkbox" class="form-check-input" [(ngModel)]="includeShipped"/>
        Display Shipped Orders
    </label>
</div>
<table class="table table-sm">
    <thead>
        <tr><th>Name</th><th>Zip</th><th colspan="2">Cart</th><th></th></tr>
    </thead>
    <tbody>
        <tr *ngIf="getOrders().length == 0">
            <td colspan="5">There are no orders</td>
        </tr>
        <ng-template ngFor let-o [ngForOf]="getOrders()">
            <tr>
                <td>{{o.name}}</td><td>{{o.zip}}</td>
                <th>Product</th><th>Quantity</th>
                <td>
                    <button class="btn btn-warning" (click)="markShipped(o)">
                        Ship
                    </button>
                    <button class="btn btn-danger" (click)="delete(o.id)">
                        Delete
                    </button>
                </td>
            </tr>
            <tr *ngFor="let line of o.cart.lines">
                <td colspan="2"></td>
                <td>{{line.product.name}}</td>
                <td>{{line.quantity}}</td>
            </tr>
        </ng-template>
    </tbody>
</table>
```

Remember that the data presented by the RESTful web service is reset each time the process is started, which means you will have to use the shopping cart and check out to create orders. Once that's done, you can inspect and manage them using the Orders section of the administration tool, as shown in Figure 9-7.

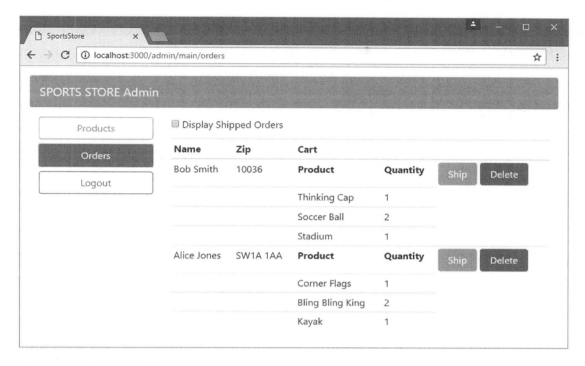

Figure 9-7. *Managing orders*

Summary

In this chapter, I created a dynamically loaded Angular feature module that contains the administration tools required to manage the catalog of products and process orders. In the next chapter, I finish the SportsStore application and prepare it for deployment into production.

CHAPTER 10

SportsStore: Progressive Features and Deployment

In this chapter, I prepare the SportsStore application for deployment by adding progressive features that will allow it to work while offline and show you how to prepare and deploy the application into a Docker container, which can be used on most hosting platforms.

Preparing the Example Application

No preparation is required for this chapter, which continues using the SportsStore project from Chapter 9.

■ **Tip** You can download the example project for this chapter—and for all the other chapters in this book—from https://github.com/Apress/pro-angular-6.

Adding Progressive Features

A *progressive web application* (PWA) is one that behaves more like a native application, which means it can continue working when there is no network connectivity, its code and content are cached so it can start immediately, and it can use features such as notifications. Progressive web application features are not specific to Angular, but in the sections that follow, I add progressive features to the SportsStore application to show you how it is done.

■ **Tip** The process for developing and testing a PWA can be laborious because it can be done only when the application is built for production, which means that the automatic build tools cannot be used.

Installing the PWA Package

The Angular team provides an NPM package that can be used to bring PWA features to Angular projects. Run the command shown in Listing 10-1 in the SportsStore folder to download and install the PWA package.

© Adam Freeman 2018
A. Freeman, *Pro Angular 6*, https://doi.org/10.1007/978-1-4842-3649-9_10

■ **Tip** Notice that this command is ng add, rather than the npm install command that I use elsewhere for adding packages. The ng add command is used specifically to install packages, such as @angular/pwa, that have been designed to enhance or reconfigure an Angular project.

Listing 10-1. Installing a Package

```
ng add @angular/pwa
```

Caching the Data URLs

The @angular/pwa package configures the application so that HTML, JavaScript, and CSS files are cached, which will allow the application to be started even when there is no network available. I also want the product catalog to be cached so that the application has data to present to the user. In Listing 10-2, I added a new section to the ngsw-config.json file, which is used to configure the PWA features for an Angular application and is added to the project by the @angular/pwa package.

Listing 10-2. Caching the Data URLs in the ngsw-config.json File in the SportsStore Folder

```
{
  "index": "/index.html",
  "assetGroups": [{
    "name": "app",
    "installMode": "prefetch",
    "resources": {
      "files": [
        "/favicon.ico",
        "/index.html",
        "/*.css",
        "/*.js"
      ]
    }
  }, {
    "name": "assets",
    "installMode": "lazy",
    "updateMode": "prefetch",
    "resources": {
      "files": [
        "/assets/**",
        "/font/*"
      ]
    }
  }],
  "dataGroups": [
    {
      "name": "api-product",
      "urls": ["/api/products"],
```

```
        "cacheConfig" : {
            "maxSize": 100,
            "maxAge": "5d"
        }
    }],
    "navigationUrls": [
        "/**"
    ]
}
```

The PWA's code and content required to run the application are cached and updated when new versions are available, ensuring that updates are applied consistently when they are available, using the configuration in the assetGroups section of the configuration file. In addition, I have added an entry so that the files required by the Font Awesome package are cached.

The application's data is cached using the dataGroups section of the configuration file, which allows data to be managed using its own cache settings. In this listing, I configured the cache so that it will contain data from 100 requests and that data will be valid for 5 days. The final configuration section is navigationUrls, which specifies the range of URLs that will be directed to the index.html file. In this example, I used a wildcard to match all URLs.

■ **Note**   I am just touching the surface of the cache features that you can use in a PWA. There are lots of choices available, including the ability to try to connect to the network and then fall back to cached data if there is no connection. See https://angular.io/guide/service-worker-intro for details.

Responding to Connectivity Changes

The SportsStore application isn't an ideal candidate for progressive features because connectivity is required to place an order. To avoid user confusion when the application is running without connectivity, I am going to disable the checkout process. The APIs that are used to add progressive features provide information about the state of connectivity and send events when the application goes offline and online. To provide the application with details of its connectivity, I added a file called connection.service.ts to the src/app/model folder and used it to define the service shown in Listing 10-3.

Listing 10-3. The Contents of the connection.service.ts File in the src/app/model Folder

```
import { Injectable } from "@angular/core";
import { Observable, Subject } from "rxjs";

@Injectable()
export class ConnectionService {
    private connEvents: Subject<boolean>;

    constructor() {
        this.connEvents = new Subject<boolean>();
        window.addEventListener("online",
            (e) => this.handleConnectionChange(e));
        window.addEventListener("offline",
            (e) => this.handleConnectionChange(e));
    }
```

```
        private handleConnectionChange(event) {
            this.connEvents.next(this.connected);
        }

        get connected() : boolean {
            return window.navigator.onLine;
        }

        get Changes(): Observable<boolean> {
            return this.connEvents;
        }
}
```

This service presets the connection status to the rest of the application, obtaining the status through the browser's `navigator.onLine` property and responding to the `online` and `offline` events, which are triggered when the connection state changes and which are accessed through the `addEventListener` method provided by the browser. In Listing 10-4, I added the new service to the module for the data model.

Listing 10-4. Adding a Service in the model.module.ts File in the src/app/model Folder

```
import { NgModule } from "@angular/core";
import { ProductRepository } from "./product.repository";
import { StaticDataSource } from "./static.datasource";
import { Cart } from "./cart.model";
import { Order } from "./order.model";
import { OrderRepository } from "./order.repository";
import { RestDataSource } from "./rest.datasource";
import { HttpClientModule } from "@angular/common/http";
import { AuthService } from "./auth.service";
import { ConnectionService } from "./connection.service";

@NgModule({
  imports: [HttpClientModule],
  providers: [ProductRepository, Cart, Order, OrderRepository,
    { provide: StaticDataSource, useClass: RestDataSource },
    RestDataSource, AuthService, ConnectionService]
})
export class ModelModule { }
```

To prevent the user from checking out when there is no connection, I updated the cart detail component so that it receives the connection service in its constructor, as shown in Listing 10-5.

Listing 10-5. Receiving a Service in the cartDetail.component.ts File in the src/app/store Folder

```
import { Component } from "@angular/core";
import { Cart } from "../model/cart.model";
import { ConnectionService } from "../model/connection.service";

@Component({
    templateUrl: "cartDetail.component.html"
})
export class CartDetailComponent {
```

```
    public connected: boolean = true;

    constructor(public cart: Cart, private connection: ConnectionService) {
        this.connected = this.connection.connected;
        connection.Changes.subscribe((state) => this.connected = state);
    }
}
```

The component defines a connected property that is set from the service and then updated when changes are received. To complete this feature, I changed the checkout button so that it is disabled when there is no connectivity, as shown in Listing 10-6.

Listing 10-6. Reflecting Connectivity in the cartDetail.component.html File in the src/app/store Folder

```
...
<div class="row">
  <div class="col">
  <div class="text-center">
    <button class="btn btn-primary m-1" routerLink="/store">
        Continue Shopping
    </button>
    <button class="btn btn-secondary m-1" routerLink="/checkout"
            [disabled]="cart.lines.length == 0 && connected">
      {{ connected ?  'Checkout' : 'Offline' }}
    </button>
  </div>
</div>
</div>
...
```

Preparing the Application for Deployment

In the sections that follow, I prepare the SportsStore application so that it can be deployed.

Creating the Data File

When I created the RESTful web service in Chapter 8, I provided the json-server package with a JavaScript file, which is executed each time the server starts and ensures that the same data is always used. That isn't helpful in production, so I added a file called serverdata.json to the SportsStore folder with the contents shown in Listing 10-7. When the json-server package is configured to use a JSON file, any changes that are made by the application will be persisted.

Listing 10-7. The Contents of the serverdata.json File in the SportsStore Folder

```
{
    "products": [
        { "id": 1, "name": "Kayak", "category": "Watersports",
            "description": "A boat for one person", "price": 275 },
        { "id": 2, "name": "Lifejacket", "category": "Watersports",
            "description": "Protective and fashionable", "price": 48.95 },
        { "id": 3, "name": "Soccer Ball", "category": "Soccer",
```

```
                    "description": "FIFA-approved size and weight", "price": 19.50 },
            { "id": 4, "name": "Corner Flags", "category": "Soccer",
                "description": "Give your playing field a professional touch",
                "price": 34.95 },
            { "id": 5, "name": "Stadium", "category": "Soccer",
                "description": "Flat-packed 35,000-seat stadium", "price": 79500 },
            { "id": 6, "name": "Thinking Cap", "category": "Chess",
                "description": "Improve brain efficiency by 75%", "price": 16 },
            { "id": 7, "name": "Unsteady Chair", "category": "Chess",
                "description": "Secretly give your opponent a disadvantage",
                "price": 29.95 },
            { "id": 8, "name": "Human Chess Board", "category": "Chess",
                "description": "A fun game for the family", "price": 75 },
            { "id": 9, "name": "Bling Bling King", "category": "Chess",
                "description": "Gold-plated, diamond-studded King", "price": 1200 }
        ],
        "orders": []
}
```

Creating the Server

When the application is deployed, I am going to use a single HTTP port to handle the requests for the application and its data, rather than the two ports that I have been using in development. Using separate ports is simpler in development because it means that I can use the Angular development HTTP server without having to integrate the RESTful web service. Angular doesn't provide an HTTP server for deployment, and since I have to provide one, I am going to configure it so that it will handle both types of request and include support for HTTP and HTTPS connections, as explained in the sidebar.

USING SECURE CONNECTIONS FOR PROGRESSIVE WEB APPLICATIONS

When you add progressive features to an application, you must deploy it so that it can be accessed over secure HTTP connections. If you do not, the progressive features will not work because the underlying technology—called *service workers*—won't be allowed by the browser over regular HTTP connections.

You can test progressive features using localhost, as I demonstrate shortly, but an SSL/TLS certificate is required when you deploy the application. If you do not have a certificate, then a good place to start is `https://letsencrypt.org`, where you can get one for free, although you should note that you also need to own the domain or hostname that you intend to deploy to generate a certificate. For the purposes of this book, I deployed the SportsStore application with its progressive features to `sportsstore.adam-freeman.com`, which is a domain that I use for development testing and receiving emails. This is not a domain that provides public HTTP services, and you won't be able to access the SportsStore application through this domain.

Run the commands shown in Listing 10-8 in the `SportsStore` folder to install the packages that are required to create the HTTP/HTTPS server.

Listing 10-8. Installing Additional Packages

```
npm install --save-dev express@4.16.3
npm install --save-dev connect-history-api-fallback@1.5.0
npm install --save-dev https@1.0.0
```

I added a file called `server.js` to the SportsStore with the content shown in Listing 10-9, which uses the newly added packages to create an HTTP and HTTPS server that includes the `json-server` functionality that will provide the RESTful web service. (The `json-server` package is specifically designed to be integrated into other applications.)

Listing 10-9. The Contents of the server.js File in the SportsStore Folder

```
const express = require("express");
const https = require("https");
const fs = require("fs");
const history = require("connect-history-api-fallback");
const jsonServer = require("json-server");
const bodyParser = require('body-parser');
const auth = require("./authMiddleware");
const router = jsonServer.router("serverdata.json");

const enableHttps = true;

const ssloptions = {}

if (enableHttps) {
    ssloptions.cert =  fs.readFileSync("./ssl/sportsstore.crt");
    ssloptions.key = fs.readFileSync("./ssl/sportsstore.pem");
}

const app = express();

app.use(bodyParser.json());
app.use(auth);
app.use("/api", router);
app.use(history());
app.use("/", express.static("./dist/SportsStore"));

app.listen(80,
    () => console.log("HTTP Server running on port 80"));

if (enableHttps) {
    https.createServer(ssloptions, app).listen(443,
        () => console.log("HTTPS Server running on port 443"));
} else {
    console.log("HTTPS disabled")
}
```

199

The server is configured to read the details of the SSL/TLS certificate from files in the ssl folder, which is where you should place the files for your certificate. If you do not have a certificate, then you can disable HTTPS by setting the enableHttps value to false. You will still be able to test the application using the local server, but you won't be able to use the progressive features in deployment.

Changing the Web Service URL in the Repository Class

Now that the RESTful data and the application's JavaScript and HTML content will be delivered by the same server, I need to change the URL that the application uses to get its data, as shown in Listing 10-10.

Listing 10-10. Changing the URL in the rest.datasource.ts File in the src/app/model Folder

```
import { Injectable } from "@angular/core";
import { HttpClient } from "@angular/common/http";
import { Observable } from "rxjs";
import { Product } from "./product.model";
import { Cart } from "./cart.model";
import { Order } from "./order.model";
import { map } from "rxjs/operators";
import { HttpHeaders } from '@angular/common/http';

const PROTOCOL = "http";
const PORT = 3500;

@Injectable()
export class RestDataSource {
    baseUrl: string;
    auth_token: string;

    constructor(private http: HttpClient) {
        //this.baseUrl = `${PROTOCOL}://${location.hostname}:${PORT}/`;
        this.baseUrl = "/api/"
    }

    // ...methods omitted for brevity...
}
```

Building and Testing the Application

To build the application for production, run the command shown in Listing 10-11 in the SportsStore folder.

Listing 10-11. Building the Application for Production

```
ng build --prod
```

This command builds an optimized version of the application without the additions that support the development tools. The output from the build process is placed in the dist/SportsStore folder. In addition to the JavaScript files, there is an index.html file that has been copied from the SportsStore/src folder and modified to use the newly built files.

■ **Note** Angular provides support for server-side rendering, where the application is run in the server, rather than the browser. This is a technique that can improve the perception of the application's startup time and can improve indexing by search engines. This is a feature that should be used with caution because it has serious limitations and can undermine the user experience. For these reasons, I have not covered server-side rendering in this book. You can learn more about this feature at `https://angular.io/guide/universal`.

The build process can take a few minutes to complete. Once the build is ready, run the command shown in Listing 10-12 in the SportsStore folder to start the HTTP server. If you have not configured the server to use a valid SSL/TLS certificate, then you should change the value of the enableHttps constant in the server.js file and then run the command in Listing 10-12.

Listing 10-12. Starting the Production HTTP Server

```
node server.js
```

Once the server has started, open a new browser window and navigate to `http://localhost`, and you will see the familiar content shown in Figure 10-1.

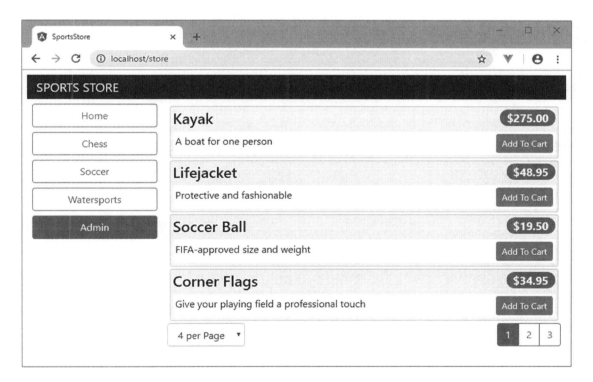

Figure 10-1. *Testing the application*

Testing the Progressive Features

Open the F12 development tools, navigate to the Network tab and check the Offline button, as shown in Figure 10-2. This simulates a device without connectivity, but since SportsStore is a progressive web application, it has been cached by the browser, along with its data.

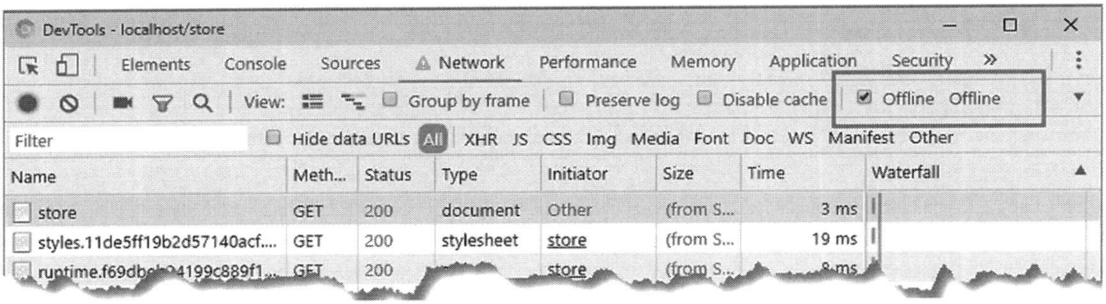

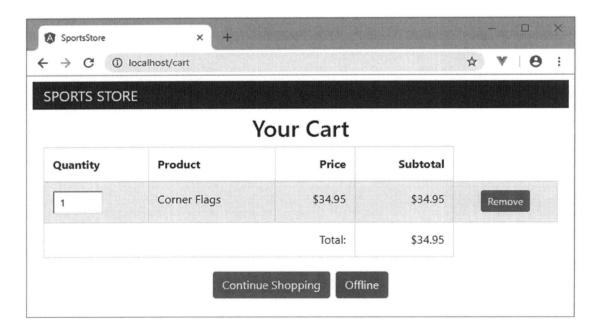

Figure 10-2. *Going offline*

Once the application is offline, click the browser reload button, and the application will be loaded from the browser's cache. If you click an Add To Cart button, you will see that the Checkout button is disabled, as shown in Figure 10-3. Uncheck the Offline checkbox, and the button's text will change so that the user can place an order.

Figure 10-3. *Reflecting the connection status in the application*

Containerizing the SportsStore Application

To complete this chapter, I am going to create a container for the SportsStore application so that it can be deployed into production. At the time of writing, Docker is the most popular way to create containers, which is a pared-down version of Linux with just enough functionality to run the application. Most cloud platforms or hosting engines have support for Docker, and its tools run on the most popular operating systems.

Installing Docker

The first step is to download and install the Docker tools on your development machine, which is available from www.docker.com/products/docker. There are versions for macOS, Windows, and Linux, and there are some specialized versions to work with the Amazon and Microsoft cloud platforms. The free Community edition is sufficient for this chapter.

■ **Caution**   One drawback of using Docker is that the company that produces the software has gained a reputation for making breaking changes. This may mean that the example that follows may not work as intended with later versions. If you have problems, check the repository for this book for updates (https://github.com/Apress/pro-angular-6) or contact me at adam@adam-freeman.com.

Preparing the Application

The first step is to create a configuration file for NPM that will be used to download the additional packages required by the application for use in the container. I created a file called deploy-package.json in the SportsStore folder with the content shown in Listing 10-13.

Listing 10-13.   The Contents of the deploy-package.json File in the SportsStore Folder

```
{
  "dependencies": {
    "bootstrap": "4.1.1",
    "font-awesome": "4.7.0"
  },

  "devDependencies": {
    "json-server": "0.12.1",
    "jsonwebtoken": "8.1.1",
    "express": "^4.16.3",
    "https": "^1.0.0",
    "connect-history-api-fallback": "^1.5.0"
  },

  "scripts": {
    "start":   "node server.js"
  }
}
```

The dependencies section omits Angular and all of the other runtime packages that were added to the package.json file when the project was created because the build process incorporates all of the JavaScript code required by the application into the files in the dist/SportsStore folder. The devDependencies section includes the tools required by the production HTTP/HTTPS server.

The scripts section of the deploy-package.json file is set up so that the npm start command will start the production server, which will provide access to the application and its data.

Creating the Docker Container

To define the container, I added a file called Dockerfile (with no extension) to the SportsStore folder and added the content shown in Listing 10-14.

Listing 10-14. The Contents of the Dockerfile File in the SportsStore Folder

```
FROM node:8.11.2

RUN mkdir -p /usr/src/sportsstore

COPY dist/SportsStore /usr/src/sportsstore/dist/SportsStore
COPY ssl /usr/src/sportsstore/ssl

COPY authMiddleware.js /usr/src/sportsstore/
COPY serverdata.json /usr/src/sportsstore/
COPY server.js /usr/src/sportsstore/server.js
COPY deploy-package.json /usr/src/sportsstore/package.json

WORKDIR /usr/src/sportsstore

RUN npm install

EXPOSE 80

CMD ["node", "server.js"]
```

The contents of the Dockerfile use a base image that has been configured with Node.js and copies the files required to run the application, including the bundle file containing the application and the package.json file that will be used to install the packages required to run the application in deployment.

To speed up the containerization process, I created a file called .dockerignore in the SportsStore folder with the content shown in Listing 10-15. This tells Docker to ignore the node_modules folder, which is not required in the container and takes a long time to process.

Listing 10-15. The Contents of the .dockerignore File in the SportsStore Folder

```
node_modules
```

Run the command shown in Listing 10-16 in the SportsStore folder to create an image that will contain the SportsStore application, along with all of the tools and packages it requires.

Listing 10-16. Building the Docker Image

```
docker build . -t sportsstore  -f  Dockerfile
```

An image is a template for containers. As Docker processes the instructions in the Docker file, the NPM packages will be downloaded and installed, and the configuration and code files will be copied into the image.

Running the Application

Once the image has been created, create and start a new container using the command shown in Listing 10-17.

■ **Tip**   Make sure you stop the test server you started in Listing 10-12 before starting the Docker container since both use the same ports to listen for requests.

Listing 10-17. Starting the Docker Container

```
docker run -p 80:80 -p 443:443 sportsstore
```

You can test the application by opening http://localhost in the browser, which will display the response provided by the web server running in the container, as shown in Figure 10-4.

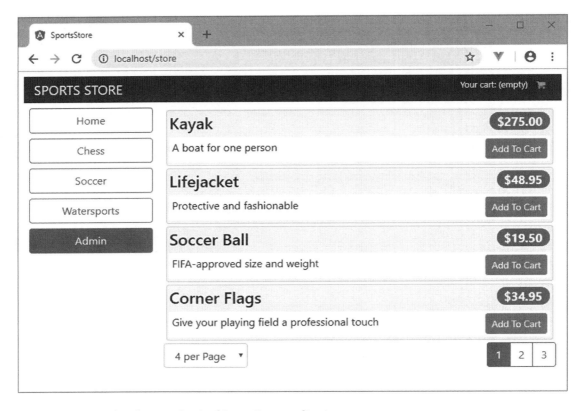

Figure 10-4. *Running the containerized SportsStore application*

To stop the container, run the command shown in Listing 10-18.

Listing 10-18. Listing the Containers

```
docker ps
```

You will see a list of running containers, like this (I have omitted some fields for brevity):

```
CONTAINER ID      IMAGE           COMMAND            CREATED
ecc84f7245d6      sportsstore     "node server.js"   33 seconds ago
```

Using the value in the Container ID column, run the command shown in Listing 10-19.

Listing 10-19. Stopping the Container

```
docker stop ecc84f7245d6
```

The application is ready to deploy to any platform that supports Docker, although the progressive features will work only if you have configured an SSL/TLS certificate for the domain to which the application is deployed.

Summary

This chapter completes the SportsStore application, showing how an Angular application can be prepared for deployment and how easy it is to put an Angular application into a container such as Docker. That's the end of this part of the book. In Part 2, I begin the process of digging into the details and show you how the features I used to create the SportsStore application work in depth.

■ ■ ■

PART II

Angular in Detail

CHAPTER 11

■ ■ ■

Creating an Angular Project

In this chapter, I explain the process of starting a new Angular project and creating an application in detail. The result is a simple Angular application that, admittedly, does little. However, by the end of the chapter, you will understand how the parts of a project fit together and have a foundation on which to apply the more advanced features that are described in the chapters that follow. Table 11-1 summarizes the chapter.

Table 11-1. *Chapter Summary*

Problem	Solution	Listing
Start Angular development	Use the ng new command to create a project and use the ng serve command to start the development tools	1, 2
Check the project source code for common errors and formatting issues	Use the ng lint command	3–5
Create a simple Angular application	Create a data model and a root component, which can then be used to update the root module	6–15

Creating a New Angular Project

The angular-cli package you installed in Chapter 2 contains all the functionality required to create a new Angular project that contains some placeholder content to jump-start development and a set of tightly integrated tools that are used to build, test, and prepare Angular applications for deployment.

To create a new Angular project, open a command prompt, navigate to a convenient location, and run the following command:

```
ng new example
```

The ng new command creates new projects, and the argument is the project name, which is example in this case. The ng new command has a set of arguments that shape the project that is created, and the most useful are described in Table 11-2.

© Adam Freeman 2018
A. Freeman, *Pro Angular 6*, https://doi.org/10.1007/978-1-4842-3649-9_11

Table 11-2. *Useful ng new Options*

Argument	Description
--directory	This option is used to specify the name of the directory for the project. It defaults to the project name.
--dry-run	This option is used to simulate the project creation process without actually performing it.
--inline-style	This option specifies that the project will be configured with styles that are defined in the component and not in a separate CSS file.
--inline-template	This option specifies that the project will be configured with templates that are defined in the component and not in a separate HTML file.
--prefix	This option applies a prefix to all of the component selectors, as described in the "Understanding How an Angular Application Works" section.
--routing	This option is used to create a routing module in the project. I explain how the routing feature works in detail in Chapters 25 and 26.
--skip-git	Using this option prevents a Git repository from being created in the project.
--skip-commit	Using this option prevents the initial commit to the Git repository that is added to the project by default.
--skip-install	This option prevents the initial npm install operation that downloads and installs the NPM packages required by Angular applications and the project's development tools.
--skip-tests	This option prevents the addition of the initial configuration for testing tools.
--verbose	This option enables additional messages during the project initialization process.

■ **Tip**   Don't worry if the purpose of these options doesn't make sense at the moment. You will understand all of these options by the time you have finished this book, and running the ng new command without any arguments provides a good starting point for most projects.

The project initialization process performed by the ng new command can take some time to complete because there are a large number of packages required by the project, both to run the Angular application and for the development and testing tools that I describe in this chapter.

■ **Tip**   You can download the example project for this chapter—and for all the other chapters in this book—from https://github.com/Apress/pro-angular-6.

Understanding the Project Structure

Use your preferred code editor to open the example folder, and you will see the files and folder structure shown in Figure 11-1. The figure shows the way that Visual Studio presents the project, and other editors may present the project contents in a different way.

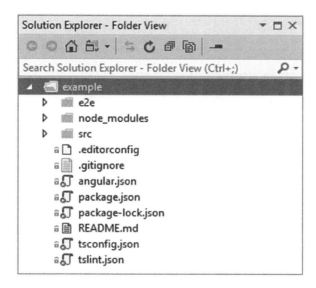

Figure 11-1. *The structure of a new Angular project*

Table 11-3 describes the files and folders that are added to a new project by the ng new command and that provide the starting point for most Angular development.

Table 11-3. *The Files and Folders in a New Angular Project*

Name	Description
e2e	This folder contains the files for end-to-end testing, which is set up to use the Protractor package. I don't describe end-to-end testing in this book because it requires additional infrastructure, but you can learn more at www.protractortest.org.
node_modules	This folder contains the NPM packages that are required for the application and for the Angular development tools, as described in the "Understanding the Packages Folder" section.
src	This folder contains the application's source code, resources, and configuration files, as described in the "Understanding the Source Code Folder" section.
.editorconfig	This file contains settings that configure text editors. Not all editors respond to this file, but it may override the preferences you have defined. You can learn more about the editor settings that can be set in this file at http://editorconfig.org.
.gitignore	This file contains a list of files and folders that are excluded from version control when using Git.
angular.json	This file contains the configuration for the Angular development tools.
package.json	This file contains details of the NPM packages required by the application and the development tools and defines the commands that run the development tools, as described in the "Understanding the Packages Folder" section.

(*continued*)

213

Table 11-3. (*continued*)

Name	Description
package-lock.json	This file contains version information for all the packages that are installed in the node_modules folder, as described in the "Understanding the Packages Folder" section.
README.md	This is a readme file that contains the list of commands for the development tools, which are described in the "Using the Development Tools" section.
tsconfig.json	This file contains the configuration settings for the TypeScript compiler.
tstlint.json	This file contains the settings for the TypeScript linter, as described in the "Using the Linter" section.

You won't always need all these files in every project, and you can remove the ones you don't require. I tend to remove the README.md, .editorconfig, and .gitignore files, for example, because I am already familiar with the tool commands, I prefer not to override my editor settings, and I don't use Git for version control, tending to create my projects with the --skip-git option described in Table 11-2.

Understanding the Source Code Folder

The src folder contains the application's files, including the source code and static assets, such as images. This folder is the focus of most development activity, and Figure 11-2 shows the contents of the src folder created using the ng new command.

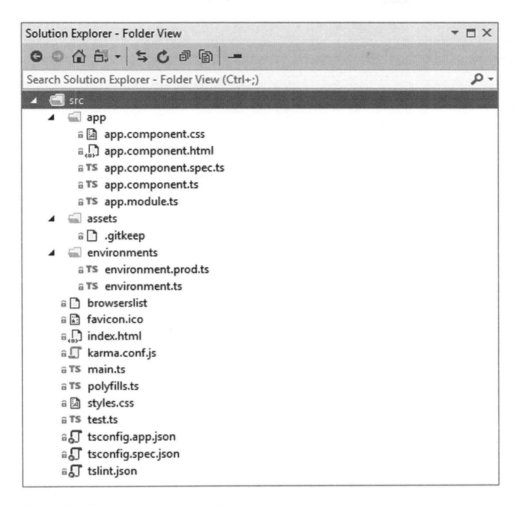

Figure 11-2. *The contents of the src folder*

The app folder is where you will add the custom code and content for your application, and its structure becomes more complex as you add features. The other files support the development process, as described in Table 11-4.

Table 11-4. *The Files and Folders in the src Folder*

Name	Description
app	This folder contains an application's source code and content. The contents of this folder are the topic of the "Understanding How an Angular Application Works" section and other chapters in this part of the book.
assets	This folder is used for the static resources required by the application, such as images.
environments	This folder contains configuration files that define settings for different environments. By default, the only configuration setting is the production flag, which is set to true when the application is built for deployment, as explained in the "Understanding the Application Bootstrap" section.
browserlist	This file is used to support the CSS processing packages that are used by the development tools.
favicon.ico	This file contains an icon that browsers will display in the tab for the application. The default image is the Angular logo.
index.html	This is the HTML file that is sent to the browser during development, as explained in the "Understanding the HTML Document" section.
karma.conf.js	This file contains the configuration for the Karma testing tool, which I describe in Chapter 29.
main.ts	This file contains the TypeScript statements that start the application when they are executed, as described in the "Understanding the Application Bootstrap" section.
polyfills.ts	This file is used to include polyfills in the project to provide support for features that are not available natively in some browsers, especially Internet Explorer.
styles.css	This file is used to define CSS styles that are applied throughout the application.
tests.ts	This is the configuration file for the Karma test package, which I describe in Chapter 29.
tsconfig.app.json	This is the configuration file for the TypeScript compiler that is used during development.
tsconfig.spec.json	This is the configuration file for the TypeScript compiler that is used during testing.

Understanding the Packages Folder

The world of JavaScript application development depends on a rich ecosystem of packages, some of which contain the Angular framework that will be sent to the browser through to small packages that are used behind the scenes during development. A lot of packages are required for an Angular project: the example project created at the start of this chapter, for example, requires almost 900 packages.

Many of these packages are just a few lines of code, but there is a complex hierarchy of dependencies between them that is too large to manage manually, so a package manager is used. The package manager is given an initial list of packages required for the project. Each of these packages is then inspected for its dependencies, and the process continues until the complete set of packages has been created. All of the required packages are downloaded and installed in the node_modules folder.

The initial set of packages is defined in the package.json file using the dependencies and devDependencies properties. The dependencies property is used to list the packages that the application will require to run. Here are the dependencies packages from the package.json file in the example application, although you may see different version numbers in your project):

```
...
"dependencies": {
    "@angular/animations": "^6.0.3",
    "@angular/common": "^6.0.3",
    "@angular/compiler": "^6.0.3",
    "@angular/core": "^6.0.3",
    "@angular/forms": "^6.0.3",
    "@angular/http": "^6.0.3",
    "@angular/platform-browser": "^6.0.3",
    "@angular/platform-browser-dynamic": "^6.0.3",
    "@angular/router": "^6.0.3",
    "core-js": "^2.5.4",
    "rxjs": "^6.0.0",
    "zone.js": "^0.8.26"
},
...
```

Most of the packages provide Angular functionality, with a handful of supporting packages that are used behind the scenes. For each package, the package.json file includes details of the version numbers that are acceptable, using the format described in Table 11-5.

Table 11-5. *The Package Version Numbering System*

Format	Description
6.0.3	Expressing a version number directly will accept only the package with the exact matching version number, e.g., 6.0.3.
*	Using an asterisk accepts any version of the package to be installed.
>6.0.3 >=6.0.3	Prefixing a version number with > or >= accepts any version of the package that is greater than or greater than or equal to a given version.
<6.0.3 <=6.0.3	Prefixing a version number with < or <= accepts any version of the package that is less than or less than or equal to a given version.
~6.0.3	Prefixing a version number with a tilde (the ~ character) accepts versions to be installed even if the patch level number (the last of the three version numbers) doesn't match. For example, specifying ~6.0.3 will accept version 6.0.4 or 6.0.5 (which would contain patches to version 6.0.3) but not version 6.1.0 (which would be a new minor release).
^6.0.3	Prefixing a version number with a caret (the ^ character) will accept versions even if the minor release number (the second of the three version numbers) or the patch number doesn't match. For example, specifying ^6.0.3 will allow versions 6.1.0, and 6.2.0, for example, but not version 7.0.0.

The version numbers specified in the dependencies section of the package.json file will accept minor updates and patches. Version flexibility is more important when it comes to the devDependencies section of the file, which contains a list of the packages that are required for development but which will not be part of the finished application. There are 19 packages listed in devDependencies section of the package.json file in the example application, each of which has its own range of acceptable versions.

```
...
"devDependencies": {
    "@angular/compiler-cli": "^6.0.3",
    "@angular-devkit/build-angular": "~0.6.8",
    "typescript": "~2.7.2",
    "@angular/cli": "~6.0.8",
    "@angular/language-service": "^6.0.3",
    "@types/jasmine": "~2.8.6",
    "@types/jasminewd2": "~2.0.3",
    "@types/node": "~8.9.4",
    "codelyzer": "~4.2.1",
    "jasmine-core": "~2.99.1",
    "jasmine-spec-reporter": "~4.2.1",
    "karma": "~1.7.1",
    "karma-chrome-launcher": "~2.2.0",
    "karma-coverage-istanbul-reporter": "~2.0.0",
    "karma-jasmine": "~1.1.1",
    "karma-jasmine-html-reporter": "^0.2.2",
    "protractor": "~5.3.0",
    "ts-node": "~5.0.1",
    "tslint": "~5.9.1"
}
...
```

Once again, you may see different details, but the key point is that the management of dependencies between packages is too complex to do manually and is delegated to a package manager. The most widely used package manager is NPM, which is installed alongside Node.js and was part of the preparations for this book in Chapter 2.

All the packages required for development are automatically downloaded and installed into the node_modules folder when you create a project, but Table 11-6 lists some commands that you may find useful during development. All of these commands should be run inside the project folder, which is the one that contains the package.json file.

Table 11-6. Useful NPM Commands

Command	Description
npm install	This command performs a local install of the packages specified in the package.json file.
npm install package@version	This command performs a local install of the specific version of a package and updates the package.json file to add the package to the dependencies section.

(continued)

Table 11-6. (*continued*)

Command	Description
`npm install package@version --save-dev`	This command performs a local install of a specific version of a package and updates the `package.json` file to add the package to the devDependencies section.
`npm install --global package@version`	This command will perform a global install of a specific version of a package.
`npm list`	This command will list all of the local packages and their dependencies.
`npm run <script name>`	This command will execute one of the scripts defined in the `package.json` file, as described next.

UNDERSTANDING GLOBAL AND LOCAL PACKAGES

NPM can install packages so they are specific to a single project (known as a *local install*) or so they can be accessed from anywhere (known as a *global install*). Few packages require global installs, but one exception is the `@angular/cli` package installed in Chapter 2 as part of the preparations for this book. The `@angular-cli` package requires a global install because it is used to create new projects. The individual packages required for the project are installed locally, into the `node_modules` folder.

The last command described in Table 11-6 is an oddity, but package managers have traditionally included support for running commands that are defined in the `scripts` section of the `package.json` file. In an Angular project, this feature is used to provide access to the tools that are used during development and that prepare the application for deployment. Here is the `scripts` section of the `package.json` file in the example project:

```
...
"scripts": {
    "ng": "ng",
    "start": "ng serve",
    "build": "ng build",
    "test": "ng test",
    "lint": "ng lint",
    "e2e": "ng e2e"
},
...
```

Table 11-7 summarizes these commands, and I demonstrate their use in later sections of this chapter or in later chapters in this part of the book.

Table 11-7. *The Commands in the Scripts Section of the package.json File*

Name	Description
ng	This command runs the ng command, which provides access to the Angular development tools.
start	This command starts the development tools, as described in the next section, and is equivalent to the ng serve command.
build	This command performs the production build process, as demonstrated in Chapter 10, and is equivalent to running the ng build command with the --prod argument.
test	This command starts the unit testing tools, which are described in Chapter 29, and is equivalent to the ng test command.
lint	This command starts the TypeScript linter, as described in the "Using the Linter" section, and is equivalent to the ng list command.
e2e	This command starts the end-to-end testing tools and is equivalent to the ng e2e command.

The commands in Table 11-7 are run by using npm run followed by the name of the command that you require, and this must be done in the folder that contains the package.json file. So, if you want to run the lint command in the example project, you would navigate to the example folder and type npm run lint. You can also get the same result by using the command ng lint.

USING YARN FOR PACKAGE MANAGEMENT

Yarn is a recent alternative to NPM. Yarn was introduced as a response to limitations in NPM, but some of the features that differentiated Yarn have since made their way into NPM, such as a file that keeps track of the exact version of all packages that are installed by the npm install command, which avoids inconsistencies when different developers work on the same project. NPM has since added many of the features that were unique to Yarn, and the choice of package manager is one of personal preference.

For Angular development, either package manager can be used, and I chose NPM because it is installed alongside Node.js. You can download Yarn from yarnpkg.com, and you can configure the angular-cli package to use Yarn by running this command:

```
ng set --global packageManager=yarn
```

Once you have configured Yarn as your package manager, it will be used to download and install the packages required by new projects created with the ng new command.

Using the Development Tools

Projects created using the ng new command include a complete set of development tools that monitor the application's files and build the project when a change is detected. You don't have to use these tools for Angular development, but they result in a pleasant development experience that suits most developers. Run the commands shown in Listing 11-1 to navigate to the example folder and start the development tools.

Listing 11-1. Starting the Development Tools

```
cd example
ng serve
```

The key package for Angular development is called *webpack*, and it is installed automatically by ng new when the project is created. Webpack is a module bundler, which means that it packages JavaScript modules for use in a browser. That's a bland description for an important function, and it is one of the key tools that you will rely on while developing an Angular application, albeit one that you won't deal with directly since it is managed for you by the Angular development tools.

When you run the commands in Listing 11-1, you will see a series of messages as webpack prepares the bundles required to run the example application. Webpack starts with the code in the main.ts file and loads all of the modules for which there are import statements to create a set of dependencies. This process is repeated for each of the modules that main.ts depends on, and webpack keeps working its way through the application until it has a complete set of dependencies for the entire application, which is then combined into a file known as a *bundle*.

During the bundling process, webpack reports on its process as it works its way through the modules and finds the ones that it needs to include in its bundle, like this:

```
...
10% building modules 4/7 modules 3 active
...
```

The bundling process can take a moment, but it only needs to be performed when you start the development tools. At the end of the process, you will see a summary of the bundles that have been created, like this:

```
...
** Angular Live Development Server is listening on localhost:4200, open your browser on
http://localhost:4200/ **

Date: 2018-07-05T07:53:12.614Z
Hash: e8e3505bb172de5054c9
Time: 6559ms
chunk {main} main.js, main.js.map (main) 10.8 kB [initial] [rendered]
chunk {polyfills} polyfills.js, polyfills.js.map (polyfills) 227 kB [initial] [rendered]
chunk {runtime} runtime.js, runtime.js.map (runtime) 5.22 kB [entry] [rendered]
chunk {styles} styles.js, styles.js.map (styles) 15.7 kB [initial] [rendered]
chunk {vendor} vendor.js, vendor.js.map (vendor) 3.07 MB [initial] [rendered]
wdm: Compiled successfully.
...
```

Understanding the Development HTTP Server

To simplify the development process, the project incorporates the webpack-dev-server package, which is an HTTP server that is tightly integrated with webpack. The summary that reports the completion of the initial bundling process also tells you that the development HTTP server is ready and tells you the port on which it is listening for requests.

```
...
** NG Live Development Server is listening on localhost:4200, open your browser on http://
localhost:4200/ **

...
```

The default port for the development HTTP server is 4200, and once you see this message, you can open a new browser window and request http://localhost:4200, which will produce the response shown in Figure 11-3.

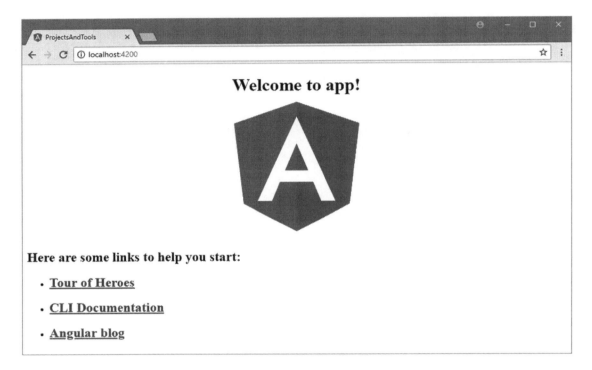

Figure 11-3. *Running the example application*

Understanding Hot Model Replacement

The bundles that webpack creates include support for a feature called *hot module replacement* (HMR). When you make a change to the application's source or content files, the altered file is compiled, put into a bundle by webpack, and sent to the browser. In most cases, only a small change is sent to the browser, and the application is updated on the fly.

As a demonstration, I replaced the contents of the app.component.html file in the src/app folder with the elements shown in Listing 11-2.

Listing 11-2. Replacing the Contents of the app.component.html File in the src/app Folder

```
<div style="text-align:center">
  <h1>Hot Module Replacement</h1>
</div>
```

As soon as the file is saved, the change is detected, and webpack creates a replacement module. The HMR feature includes code that is sent to the browser in the original bundle to open a persistent connection to the development HTTP server and listen for updates. When the new module is available, it is sent to the browser, and the application is automatically updated, as shown in Figure 11-4.

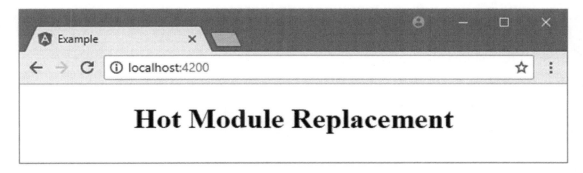

Figure 11-4. *Using the hot module replacement feature*

■ **Tip** The hot module replacement feature tries to preserve the state of the application where possible, but doesn't always get it right, in which case reloading the browser will refresh the application.

Using the Linter

A linter is a tool that inspects source code to ensure that it conforms to a set of coding conventions and rules. Projects created with the ng new command include a TypeScript linter called TSLint, and the rules it supports are described at https://github.com/palantir/tslint, covering everything from common errors that are likely to cause unexpected results through to issues of style.

You can enable and disable linting rules in the tslint.json file, and many of the rules have configuration options that fine-tune the problems they detect. To demonstrate how the linter works, I made two changes to a TypeScript file, as shown in Listing 11-3.

Listing 11-3. Making Changes in the app.component.ts File in the src/app Folder

```
import { Component } from '@angular/core';

debugger;

@Component({
  selector: 'app-root',
  templateUrl: './app.component.html',
```

223

```
  styleUrls: ['./app.component.css']
})
export class AppComponent {
  title = 'app'
}
```

I added a debugger statement and removed the semicolon from the end of the statement that sets the value for the `title` property in the `AppComponent` class. Both these changes contravene the default TSLint rules, and you can see the result by opening a new command prompt, navigating to the `example` project folder, and running the linter using the command shown in Listing 11-4.

Listing 11-4. Running the TypeScript Linter

```
ng lint
```

The linter inspects the TypeScript files in the project and reports any problems that it encounters. The changes in Listing 11-4 result in the following messages:

```
...
ERROR: /example/src/app/app.component.ts[3, 1]: Use of debugger statements is forbidden
ERROR: /example/src/app/app.component.ts[11, 16]: Missing semicolon

Lint errors found in the listed files.
...
```

Linting isn't integrated into the regular build process and can be performed only manually. The most common use for linting is to check for potential problems before committing changes to a version control system, although some project teams make broader use of the linting facility by integrating it into other processes.

You may find that there are individual statements that cause the linter to report an error but that you are not able to change. Rather than disable the rule entirely, you can add a comment to the code that tells the linter to ignore the next line, like this:

```
...
// tslint:disable-next-line
...
```

If you have a file that is full of problems but you cannot make changes—often because there are constraints applied from some other part of the application—then you can disable linting for the entire file by adding this comment at the top of the page:

```
...
/* tslint:disable */
...
```

These comments allow you to ignore code that doesn't conform to the rules but that cannot be changed, while still linting the rest of the project.

To address the linter warnings, I commented out the debugger statement and restored the semicolon in the `app.component.ts` file, as shown in Listing 11-5.

Listing 11-5. Addressing Linting Warnings in the app.component.ts File in the src/app Folder

```
import { Component } from '@angular/core';

// debugger;

@Component({
  selector: 'app-root',
  templateUrl: './app.component.html',
  styleUrls: ['./app.component.css']
})
export class AppComponent {
  title = 'app';
}
```

THE JOY AND MISERY OF LINTING

Linters can be a powerful tool for good, especially in a development team with mixed levels of skill and experience. Linters can detect common problems and subtle errors that lead to unexpected behavior or long-term maintenance issues. A good example is the difference between the JavaScript == and === operators, where a linter can warn when the wrong type of comparison has been performed. I like this kind of linting, and I like to run my code through the linting process after I have completed a major application feature or before I commit my code into version control.

But linters can also be a tool of division and strife. In addition to detecting coding errors, linters can also be used to enforce rules about indentation, brace placement, the use of semicolons and spaces, and dozens of other style issues. Most developers have style preferences—I certainly do: I like four spaces for indentation, and I like opening braces to be on the same line and the expression they relate to. I know that some programmers have different preferences, just as I know those people are plain wrong and will one day see the light and start formatting their code correctly.

Linters allow people with strong views about formatting to enforce them on others, generally under the banner of being "opinionated," which can tend toward "obnoxious." The logic is that developers waste time arguing about different coding styles and everyone is better off being forced to write in the same way, which is typically the way preferred by the person with the strong views and ignores the fact that developers will just argue about something else because arguing is fun.

I especially dislike linting of formatting, which I see as divisive and unnecessary. I often help readers when they can't get book examples working (my e-mail address is adam@adam-freeman.com if you need help), and I see all sorts of coding style every week. But rather than forcing readers to code my way, I just get my code editor to reformat the code to the format that I prefer, which is a feature that every capable editor provides.

My advice is to use linting sparingly and focus on the issues that will cause real problems. Leave formatting decisions to the individuals and rely on code editor reformatting when you need to read code written by a team member who has different preferences.

Understanding How an Angular Application Works

Angular can seem like magic when you first start using it, and it is easy to become wary of making changes to the project files for fear of breaking something. Although there are a lot of files in an Angular application, they all have a specific purpose, and they work together to do something that far from magic: display HTML content to the user. In this section, I explain how the example Angular application works and how each part works toward the end result.

Understanding the HTML Document

The HTML document that is sent to the browser by the development HTTP server is the first part of the process. When the browser requests the default URL, such as `http://localhost:4200,` the development server responds with the contents of the `index.html` file in the `src` folder, which contains the following elements:

```
<!doctype html>
<html lang="en">
<head>
  <meta charset="utf-8">
  <title>Example</title>
  <base href="/">
  <meta name="viewport" content="width=device-width, initial-scale=1">
  <link rel="icon" type="image/x-icon" href="favicon.ico">
</head>
<body>
  <app-root></app-root>
</body>
</html>
```

The body contains only an `app-root` element, whose purpose will become clear shortly. As it processes the HTML document, the development HTTP server populates the body with script elements that tell the browser to load the bundle files created during the build process, like this:

```
<!doctype html>
<html lang="en">
<head>
  <meta charset="utf-8">
  <title>Example</title>
  <base href="/">

  <meta name="viewport" content="width=device-width, initial-scale=1">
  <link rel="icon" type="image/x-icon" href="favicon.ico">
</head>
<body>
  <app-root></app-root>
  <script type="text/javascript" src="runtime.js"></script>
  <script type="text/javascript" src="polyfills.js"></script>
  <script type="text/javascript" src="styles.js"></script>
  <script type="text/javascript" src="vendor.js"></script>
  <script type="text/javascript" src="main.js"></script></body>
</html>
```

Understanding the Application Bootstrap

Browsers execute JavaScript files in the order in which their `script` elements appear, starting with the `runtime.js` file, which contains the Angular framework code. For most projects, the interesting file is `main.js`, which contains the custom application code. This is the file that contains the code defined in the `main.ts` file, which starts the application and relies on the code contained in the other JavaScript files. Here are the statements added to the `main.ts` file by the ng new command when it creates a project:

```
import { enableProdMode } from '@angular/core';
import { platformBrowserDynamic } from '@angular/platform-browser-dynamic';

import { AppModule } from './app/app.module';
import { environment } from './environments/environment';

if (environment.production) {
  enableProdMode();
}

platformBrowserDynamic().bootstrapModule(AppModule)
  .catch(err => console.log(err));
```

The `import` statements declare dependencies on other JavaScript modules, providing access to Angular features (the dependencies on @angular modules) and the custom code in the application (the AppModule dependency). The final import is for environment settings, which are used to create different configuration settings for development, test, and production platforms, such as this code:

```
...
if (environment.production) {
  enableProdMode();
}
...
```

Angular has a production mode that disables some useful checks that are performed during development and that are described in later chapters. Enabling production mode means provides a performance increase and means that the results of the checks are not reported in the browser's JavaScript console where they can be seen by the user. Production mode is enabled by calling the enableProdMode function, which is imported from the @angular/core module.

To work out whether production mode should be enabled, a check is performed to see whether `environment.production` is `true`. This check corresponds to the contents of the `enviironment.prod.ts` file in the `src/enviironments` folder, which sets this value and is applied when the application is built in preparation for deployment. The result is that production mode will be enabled if the application has been built for production but disabled the rest of the time.

The remaining statement in the `main.ts` file is responsible for starting the application.

```
...
platformBrowserDynamic().bootstrapModule(AppModule).catch(err => console.log(err));
...
```

The `platformBrowserDynamic` function initializes the Angular platform for use in a web browser and is imported from the `@angular/platform-browser-dynamic` module. Angular has been designed to run in a range of different environments, and calling the `platformBrowserDynamic` function is the first step in starting an application in a browser. The next step is to call the bootstrapModule method, which accepts the Angular root module for the application, which is AppModule by default and which is imported from the app.module.ts file in the src/app folder and described in the next section. The bootstrapModule method provides Angular with the entry point into the application and represents the bridge between the functionality provided by the @angular modules and the custom code and content in the project. The final part of this statement uses the catch keyword to handle any bootstrapping errors by writing them to the browser's JavaScript console.

■ **Tip** Notice that the argument to the bootstrapModule method is the name of the class and not a new instance of that class. Put another way, you call bootstrapModule(AppModule) and not bootstrapModule (new AppModule()) or bootstrapModule("AppModule").

Understanding the Root Angular Module

The term *module* does double duty in an Angular application and refers to both a JavaScript module and an Angular module. JavaScript modules are used to track dependencies in the application and ensure that the browser receives only the code it requires. Angular modules are used to configure a part of the Angular application.

Every application has a *root* Angular module, which is responsible for describing the application to Angular. The root module is called AppModule, and it is defined in the app.module.ts file in the src/app folder; it contains the following code:

```
import { BrowserModule } from '@angular/platform-browser';
import { NgModule } from '@angular/core';

import { AppComponent } from './app.component';

@NgModule({
  declarations: [AppComponent],
  imports: [BrowserModule],
  providers: [],
  bootstrap: [AppComponent]
})
export class AppModule { }
```

The AppModule class doesn't define any members, but it provides Angular with essential information through the configuration properties of its @NgModule decorator. I describe the different properties that are used to configure an Angular module in later chapters, but the one that is of interest now is the bootstrap property, which tells Angular that it should load a component called AppComponent as part of the application startup process. Components are the main building block in Angular applications, and the content provided by the component called AppComponent will be displayed to the user.

Understanding the Angular Component

The component called AppComponent, which is selected by the root Angular module, is defined in the app. component.ts file in the src/app folder. Here are the contents of the app.component.ts file, which I edited earlier in the chapter to demonstrate linting:

```
import { Component } from '@angular/core';

//debugger;

@Component({
  selector: 'app-root',
  templateUrl: './app.component.html',
  styleUrls: ['./app.component.css']
})
export class AppComponent {
  title = 'app';
}
```

The properties for the @Component decorator configure its behavior. The selector property tells Angular that this component will be used to replace an HTML element called app-root. The templateUrl and styleUrls properties tell Angular that the HTML content that the component wants to present to the user can be found in a file called app.component.html and that the CSS styles to apply to the HTML content are defined in a file called app.component.css (although the CSS file is empty in new projects).

Here is the content of the app.component.html file, which I edited earlier in the chapter to demonstrate hot module reloading:

```
<div style="text-align:center">
  <h1>
    Hot Module Replacement
  </h1>
</div>
```

This file contains regular HTML elements, but, as you will learn, Angular features are applied by using custom HTML elements or by adding attributes to regular HTML elements.

Understanding Content Display

When the application starts, Angular processes the index.html file, locates the element that matches the root component's selector property, and replaces it with the contents of the files specified by the root component's templateUrl and styleUrls properties. This is done using the Domain Object Model (DOM) API provided by the browser for JavaScript applications, and the changes can be seen only by right-clicking in the browser window and selecting Inspect from the pop-up menu, producing the following result:

```
<html lang="en"><head>
    <meta charset="utf-8">
    <title>Example</title>
    <base href="/">
    <meta name="viewport" content="width=device-width, initial-scale=1">
    <link rel="icon" type="image/x-icon" href="favicon.ico">
```

```
<style type="text/css">
    /* You can add global styles to this file, and also import other style files */
</style>
<style></style>
</head>
<body>
<app-root _nghost-c0="" ng-version="6.0.7">
    <div _ngcontent-c0="" style="text-align:center">
        <h1 _ngcontent-c0="">Hot Module Replacement</h1>
    </div>
</app-root>
<script type="text/javascript" src="runtime.js"></script>
<script type="text/javascript" src="polyfills.js"></script>
<script type="text/javascript" src="styles.js"></script>
<script type="text/javascript" src="vendor.js"></script>
<script type="text/javascript" src="main.js"></script>
</body></html>
```

The app-root element contains the div and h1 elements from the component's template, and the attributes are added by Angular during the initialization process. The style elements represent the contents of the styles.css file in the app folder and the app.component.css file in the src/app folder. (The CSS files do not contain any styles when the project is created, which is why the style elements do not contain any styles.) The result of the bootstrap process is the component's content is presented to the user, as shown in Figure 11-5.

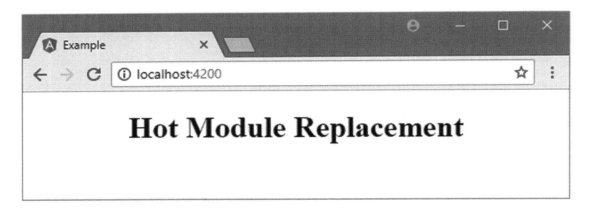

Figure 11-5. *Displaying a component's content*

Starting Development in an Angular Project

You have seen how the initial building blocks of an Angular application fit together and how the bootstrap process results in content being displayed to the user. In this section, I add a simple data model to the project, which is the typical starting point for most developers, and replace placeholder content created by the ng new command with a new component and HTML template.

Adding the Bootstrap CSS Framework

I use the Bootstrap CSS framework throughout this book because it lets me easily style HTML elements by assigning them to classes. Run the command shown in Listing 11-6 in the example folder to download the Bootstrap package and add it to the project.

Listing 11-6. Installing the Bootstrap Package

```
npm install bootstrap@4.1.1
```

In Listing 11-7, I have added the path to the file that contains the Bootstrap CSS styles to the angular.json file, which is used to configure the development tools.

Listing 11-7. Configuring a CSS File in the angular.json File in the example Folder

```
...
"styles": [
    "styles.css",
    "node_modules/bootstrap/dist/css/bootstrap.min.css"
],
...
```

This tells the Angular development tools to include the Bootstrap CSS styles in the content that is sent to the browser.

■ **Tip**   There are two `style` sections in the `angular.json` file. The Bootstrap CSS file should be added to the one closest to the top of the file.

The development tools must be restarted to reflect the configuration change. Use Ctrl+C to terminate any existing Angular processes and run the command shown in Listing 11-8 in the example folder.

Listing 11-8. Starting the Development Tools

```
ng serve
```

Creating the Data Model

Of all the building blocks in an application, the data model is the one for which Angular is the least prescriptive. Elsewhere in the application, Angular requires specific decorators to be applied or parts of the API to be used, but the only requirement for the model is that it provides access to the data that the application requires; the details of how this is done and what that data looks like is left to the developer.

This can feel a little odd, and it can be difficult to know how to begin, but, at its heart, the model can be broken into three different parts.

- A class that describes the data in the model
- A data source that loads and saves data, typically to a server
- A repository that allows the data in the model to be manipulated

In the following sections, I create a simple model, which provides the functionality that I need to describe Angular features in the chapters that follow.

Creating the Descriptive Model Class

Descriptive classes, as the name suggests, describe the data in the application. In a real project, there will usually be a lot of classes to fully describe the data that the application operates on. To get started for this chapter, I am going to create a single, simple class and add a file called `product.model.ts` to the `src/app` folder with the code shown in Listing 11-9.

Listing 11-9. The Contents of the product.model.ts File in the src/app Folder

```
export class Product {

    constructor(public id?: number,
        public name?: string,
        public category?: string,
        public price?: number) { }
}
```

The `Product` class defines properties for a product identifier, the name of the product, its category, and the price. The properties are defined as optional constructor arguments, which is a useful approach if you are creating objects using an HTML form, which I demonstrate in Chapter 14.

Creating the Data Source

The data source provides the application with the data. The most common type of data source uses HTTP to request data from a web service, which I describe in Chapter 24. For this chapter, I need something simpler that I can reset to a known state each time the application is started to ensure that you get the expected results from the examples. I added a file called `datasource.model.ts` to the `src/app` folder with the code shown in Listing 11-10.

Listing 11-10. The Contents of the datasource.model.ts File in the src/app Folder

```
import { Product } from "./product.model";

export class SimpleDataSource {
    private data: Product[];

    constructor() {
        this.data = new Array<Product>(
            new Product(1, "Kayak", "Watersports", 275),
            new Product(2, "Lifejacket", "Watersports", 48.95),
            new Product(3, "Soccer Ball", "Soccer", 19.50),
            new Product(4, "Corner Flags", "Soccer", 34.95),
            new Product(5, "Thinking Cap", "Chess", 16));
    }

    getData(): Product[] {
        return this.data;
    }
}
```

The data in this class is hardwired, which means that any changes that are made in the application will be lost when the browser is reloaded. This is far from useful in a real application, but it is ideal for book examples.

Creating the Model Repository

The final step to complete the simple model is to define a repository that will provide access to the data from the data source and allow it to be manipulated in the application. I added a file called repository.model.ts in the src/app folder and used it to defined the class shown in Listing 11-11.

Listing 11-11. The Contents of the repository.model.ts File in the src/app Folder

```
import { Product } from "./product.model";
import { SimpleDataSource } from "./datasource.model";

export class Model {
    private dataSource: SimpleDataSource;
    private products: Product[];
    private locator = (p: Product, id: number) => p.id == id;

    constructor() {
        this.dataSource = new SimpleDataSource();
        this.products = new Array<Product>();
        this.dataSource.getData().forEach(p => this.products.push(p));
    }

    getProducts(): Product[] {
        return this.products;
    }

    getProduct(id: number): Product {
        return this.products.find(p => this.locator(p, id));
    }

    saveProduct(product: Product) {
        if (product.id == 0 || product.id == null) {
            product.id = this.generateID();
            this.products.push(product);
        } else {
            let index = this.products
                .findIndex(p => this.locator(p, product.id));
            this.products.splice(index, 1, product);
        }
    }

    deleteProduct(id: number) {
        let index = this.products.findIndex(p => this.locator(p, id));
        if (index > -1) {
            this.products.splice(index, 1);
        }
    }
```

```
    private generateID(): number {
        let candidate = 100;
        while (this.getProduct(candidate) != null) {
            candidate++;
        }
        return candidate;
    }
}
```

The Model class defines a constructor that gets the initial data from the data source class and provides access to it through a set of methods. These methods are typical of those defined by a repository and are described in Table 11-8.

Table 11-8. *The Types of Web Forms Code Nuggets*

Name	Description
getProducts	This method returns an array containing all the Product objects in the model.
getProduct	This method returns a single Product object based on its ID.
saveProduct	This method updates an existing Product object or adds a new one to the model.
deleteProduct	This method removes a Product object from the model based on its ID.

The implementation of the repository may seem odd because the data objects are stored in a standard JavaScript array, but the methods defined by the Model class present the data as though it were a collection of Product objects indexed by the id property. There are two main considerations when writing a repository for model data. The first is that it should present the data that will be displayed as efficiently as possible. For the example application, this means presenting all the data in the model in a form that can be iterated, such as an array. This is important because the iteration can happen often, as I explain in Chapter 16. The other operations of the Model class are inefficient, but they will be used less often.

The second consideration is being able to present unchanged data for Angular to work with. I explain why this is important in Chapter 13, but in terms of implementing the repository, it means that the getProducts method should return the same object when it is called multiple times, unless one of the other methods or another part of the application has made a change to the data that the getProducts method provides. If a method returns a different object each time it is returned, even if they are different arrays containing the same objects, then Angular will report an error. Taking both of these points into account means that the best way to implement the repository is to store the data in an array and accept the inefficiencies.

Creating a Component and Template

Templates contain the HTML content that a component wants to present to the user. Templates can range from a single HTML element through to a complex block of content.

To create a template, I added a file called template.html to the src/app folder and added the HTML elements shown in Listing 11-12.

Listing 11-12. *The Contents of the template.html File in the src/app Folder*

```
<div class="bg-info text-white m-2 p-2">
    There are {{model.getProducts().length}} products in the model
</div>
```

Most of this template is standard HTML, but the part between the double brace characters (the {{ and }} in the div element) is an example of a data binding. When the template is displayed, Angular will process its content, discover the binding, and evaluate the expression that it contains to produce the content that will be displayed by the data binding.

The logic and data required to support the template are provided by its component, which is a TypeScript class to which the @Component decorator has been applied. To provide a component for the template in Listing 11-12, I added a file called component.ts to the src/app folder and defined the class shown in Listing 11-13.

Listing 11-13. The Contents of the component.ts File in the src/app Folder

```
import { Component } from "@angular/core";
import { Model } from "./repository.model";

@Component({
    selector: "app",
    templateUrl: "template.html"
})
export class ProductComponent {
    model: Model = new Model();
}
```

The @Component decorator configures the component. The selector property specifies the HTML element that the directive will be applied to, which is app. The templateUrl property in the @Component directive specifies the content that will be used as the contents of the app element, and, for this example, this property specifies the template.html file.

The component class, which is ProductComponent for this example, is responsible for providing the template with the data and logic that is needed for its bindings. The ProductComponent class defines a single property, called model, which provides access to a Model object.

The app element I used for the component's selector isn't the same element that the ng new command uses when it creates a project and that is expected in the index.html file. In Listing 11-14, I have modified the index.html file to introduce an app element to match the component's selector from Listing 11-13.

Listing 11-14. Changing the Custom Element in the index.html File in the app Folder

```
<!doctype html>
<html lang="en">
<head>
  <meta charset="utf-8">
  <title>Example</title>
  <base href="/">

  <meta name="viewport" content="width=device-width, initial-scale=1">
  <link rel="icon" type="image/x-icon" href="favicon.ico">
</head>
<body>
  <app></app>
</body>
</html>
```

This isn't something you need to do in a real project, but it further demonstrates that Angular applications fit together in simple and predictable ways and that you can change any part that you need to or want to.

Configuring the Root Angular Module

The component that I created in the previous section won't be part of the application until I register it with the root Angular module. In Listing 11-15, I have used the import keyword to import the component and used the @NgModule configuration properties to register the component.

Listing 11-15. Registering a Component in the app.module.ts File in the app/src Folder

```
import { BrowserModule } from '@angular/platform-browser';
import { NgModule } from '@angular/core';

//import { AppComponent } from './app.component';
import { ProductComponent } from "./component";

@NgModule({
    declarations: [ProductComponent],
    imports: [BrowserModule],
    providers: [],
    bootstrap: [ProductComponent]
})
export class AppModule { }
```

I used the name ProductComponent in the import statement, and I added this name to the declarations array, which configures the set of components and other features in the application. I also changed the value of the bootstrap property so that the new component is the one that is used when the application starts. When the change to the app.module.ts file is saved, the new configuration will take effect, and you will see the content shown in Figure 11-6.

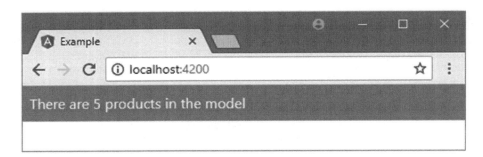

Figure 11-6. The effect of a new component and template

The standard Angular bootstrap sequence is performed, but the custom component and template that I created in the previous section are used, rather than the ones set up when the project was created.

Summary

In this chapter, I created an Angular project and used it to introduce the tools that it contains and explained how a simple Angular application works. In the next chapter, I start digging into the detail, starting with data bindings.

CHAPTER 12

■ ■ ■

Using Data Bindings

The example application in the previous chapter contains a simple template that was displayed to the user and that contained a data binding that showed how many objects were in the data model. In this chapter, I describe the basic data bindings that Angular provides and demonstrate how they can be used to produce dynamic content. In later chapters, I describe more advanced data bindings and explain how to extend the Angular binding system with custom features. Table 12-1 puts data bindings in context.

Table 12-1. *Putting Data Bindings in Context*

Question	Answer
What are they?	Data bindings are expressions embedded into templates and are evaluated to produce dynamic content in the HTML document.
Why are they useful?	Data bindings provide the link between the HTML elements in the HTML document and in template files with the data and code in the application.
How are they used?	Data bindings are applied as attributes on HTML elements or as special sequences of characters in strings.
Are there any pitfalls or limitations?	Data bindings contain simple JavaScript expressions that are evaluated to generate content. The main pitfall is including too much logic in a binding because such logic cannot be properly tested or used elsewhere in the application. Data binding expressions should be as simple as possible and rely on components (and other Angular features such pipes) to provide complex application logic.
Are there any alternatives?	No. Data bindings are an essential part of Angular development.

Table 12-2 summarizes the chapter.

Table 12-2. *Chapter Summary*

Problem	Solution	Listing
Display data dynamically in the HTML document	Define a data binding	1–4
Configure an HTML element	Use a standard property or attribute binding	5, 8
Set the contents of an element	Use a string interpolation binding	6, 7
Configure the classes to which an element is assigned	Use a class binding	9–13
Configure the individual styles applied to an element	Use a style binding	14–17
Manually trigger a data model update	Use the browser's JavaScript console	18, 19

© Adam Freeman 2018
A. Freeman, *Pro Angular 6*, https://doi.org/10.1007/978-1-4842-3649-9_12

Preparing the Example Project

For this chapter, I continue using the example project from Chapter 11. To prepare for this chapter, I added a method to the component class, as shown in Listing 12-1.

■ **Tip**   You can download the example project for this chapter—and for all the other chapters in this book—from https://github.com/Apress/pro-angular-6.

Listing 12-1. Adding a Method in the component.ts File in the src/app Folder

```
import { Component } from "@angular/core";
import { Model } from "./repository.model";

@Component({
    selector: "app",
    templateUrl: "template.html"
})
export class ProductComponent {
    model: Model = new Model();

    getClasses(): string {
        return this.model.getProducts().length == 5 ? "bg-success" : "bg-warning";
    }
}
```

Run the following command in the example folder to start the Angular development tools:

```
ng serve
```

Open a new browser and navigate to http://localhost:4200 to see the content shown in Figure 12-1 will be displayed.

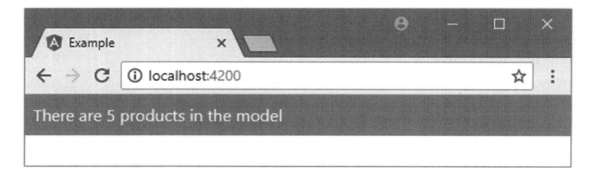

Figure 12-1. Running the example application

Understanding One-Way Data Bindings

One-way data bindings are used to generate content for the user and are the basic building block for Angular templates. The term *one-way* refers to the fact that the data flows in one direction, which means that data flows from the component to the data binding so that it can be displayed in a template.

■ **Tip** There are other types of Angular data binding, which I describe in later chapters. Event bindings flow in the other direction, from the elements in the template into the rest of the application, and allow user interaction. *Two-way bindings* allow data to flow in both directions and are most commonly used in forms. See Chapters 13 and 14 for details of other bindings.

To get started with one-way data bindings, I have replaced the content of the template, as shown in Listing 12-2.

Listing 12-2. The Contents of the template.html File in the src/app Folder

```
<div [ngClass]="getClasses()" >
    Hello, World.
</div>
```

When you save the changes to the template, the development server will trigger a browser reload and display the output shown in Figure 12-2.

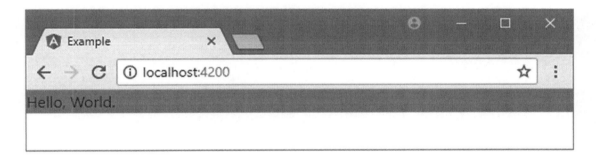

Figure 12-2. Using a one-way data binding

This is a simple example, but it shows the basic structure of a data binding, which is illustrated in Figure 12-3.

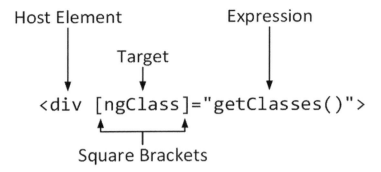

Figure 12-3. *The anatomy of a data binding*

A data binding has these four parts:

- The *host element* is the HTML element that the binding will affect, by changing its appearance, content, or behavior.

- The *square brackets* tell Angular that this is a one-way data binding. When Angular sees square brackets in a data binding, it will evaluate the expression and pass the result to the binding's *target* so that it can modify the host element.

- The *target* specifies what the binding will do. There are two different types of target: a *directive* or a *property binding*.

- The *expression* is a fragment of JavaScript that is evaluated using the template's component to provide context, meaning that the component's property and methods can be included in the expression, like the getClasses method in the example binding.

Looking at the binding in Listing 12-2, you can see that the host element is a div element, meaning that's the element that the binding is intended to modify. The expression invokes the component's getClasses method, which was defined at the start of the chapter. This method returns a string containing a Bootstrap CSS class based on the number of objects in the data model.

```
...
getClasses(): string {
    return this.model.getProducts().length == 5 ? "bg-success" : "bg-warning";
}
...
```

If there are five objects in the data model, then the method returns bg-success, which is a Bootstrap class that applies a green background. Otherwise, the method returns bg-warning, which is a Bootstrap class that applies an amber background.

The target for the data binding in Listing 12-2 is a directive, which is a class that is specifically written to support a data binding. Angular comes with some useful built-in directives, and you can create your own to provide custom functionality. The names of the built-in directives start with ng, which tells you that the ngClass target is one of the built-in directives. The target usually gives an indication of what the directive

240

does, and, as its name suggests, the ngClass directive will add or remove the host element from the class or classes whose names are returned when the expression is evaluated.

Putting it all together, the data binding in Listing 12-2 will add the div element to the bg-success or bg-warning classes based on the number of items in the data model.

Since there are five objects in the model when the application starts (because the initial data is hard-coded into the SimpleDataSource class created in Chapter 12), the getClasses method returns bg-success and produces the result shown in Figure 12-3, adding a green background to the div element.

Understanding the Binding Target

When Angular processes the target of a data binding, it starts by checking to see whether it matches a directive. Most applications will rely on a mix of the built-in directives provided by Angular and custom directives that provide application-specific features. You can usually tell when a directive is the target of a data binding because the name will be distinctive and give some indication of what the directive is for. The built-in directives can be recognized by the ng prefix. The binding in Listing 12-2 gives you a hint that the target is a built-in directive that is related to the class membership of the host element. For quick reference, Table 12-3 describes the basic built-in Angular directives and where they are described in this book. (There are other directives described in later chapters, but these are the simplest and most commonly used.)

Table 12-3. *The Basic Built-in Angular Directives*

Name	Description
ngClass	This directive is used to assign host elements to classes, as described in the "Setting Classes and Styles" section.
ngStyle	This directive is used to set individual styles, as described in the "Setting Classes and Styles" section.
ngIf	This directive is used to insert content in the HTML document when its expression evaluates as true, as described in Chapter 13.
ngFor	This directive inserts the same content into the HTML document for each item in a data source, as described in Chapter 13.
ngSwitchngSwitchCasengSwitchDefault	These directives are used to choose between blocks of content to insert into the HTML document based on the value of the expression, as described in Chapter 13.
ngTemplateOutlet	This directive is used to repeat a block of content, as described in Chapter 13.

Understanding Property Bindings

If the binding target doesn't correspond to a directive, then Angular checks to see whether the target can be used to create a property binding. There are five different types of property binding, which are listed in Table 12-4, along with the details of where they are described in detail.

Table 12-4. *The Angular Property Bindings*

Name	Description
[property]	This is the standard property binding, which is used to set a property on the JavaScript object that represents the host element in the Document Object Model (DOM), as described in the "Using the Standard Property and Attribute Bindings" section.
[attr.name]	This is the attribute binding, which is used to set the value of attributes on the host HTML element for which there are no DOM properties, as described in the "Using the Attribute Binding" section.
[class.name]	This is the special class property binding, which is used to configure class membership of the host element, as described in the "Using the Class Bindings" section.
[style.name]	This is the special style property binding, which is used to configure style settings of the host element, as described in the "Using the Style Bindings" section.

Understanding the Expression

The expression in a data binding is a fragment of JavaScript code that is evaluated to provide a value for the target. The expression has access to the properties and methods defined by the component, which is how the binding in Listing 12-2 is able to invoke the getClasses method to provide the ngClass directive with the name of the class that the host element should be added to.

Expressions are not restricted to just calling methods or reading properties from the component; they can also perform most standard JavaScript operations. As an example, Listing 12-3 shows an expression that has a literal string value being concatenated with the result of the getClasses method.

Listing 12-3. Performing an Operation in the template.html File in the src/app Folder

```
<div [ngClass]="'text-white m-2 p-2 ' + getClasses()" >
    Hello, World.
</div>
```

The expression is enclosed in double quotes, which means that the string literal has to be defined using single quotes. The JavaScript concatenation operator is the + character, and the result from the expression will be the combination of both strings, like this:

```
text-white m-2 p-2 bg-success
```

The effect is that the ngClass directive will add the host element to four classes: text-white, m-2, and p-2, which Bootstrap uses to set the text color and add margin and padding around an element's content; and bg-success, which sets the background color. Figure 12-4 shows the combination of these two classes.

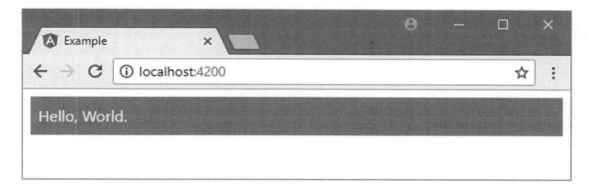

Figure 12-4. *Combining classes in a JavaScript expression*

It is easy to get carried away when writing expressions and include complex logic in the template. This can cause problems because the expressions are not checked by the TypeScript compiler nor can they be easily unit tested, which means that bugs are more likely to remain undetected until the application has been deployed. To avoid this issue, expressions should be as simple as possible and, ideally, used only to retrieve data from the component and format it for display. All the complex retrieval and processing logic should be defined in the component or the model, where it can be compiled and tested.

Understanding the Brackets

The square brackets (the [and] characters) tell Angular that this is a one-way data binding that has an expression that should be evaluated. Angular will still process the binding if you omit the brackets and the target is a directive, but the expression won't be evaluated, and the content between the quote characters will be passed to the directive as a literal value. Listing 12-4 adds an element to the template with a binding that doesn't have square brackets.

Listing 12-4. Omitting the Brackets in a Data Binding in the template.html File in the src/app Folder

```
<div [ngClass]="'text-white m-2 p-2 ' + getClasses()">
  Hello, World.
</div>
<div ngClass="'text-white m-2 p-2 ' + getClasses()">
  Hello, World.
</div>
```

If you examine the HTML element in the browser's DOM viewer (by right-clicking in the browser window and selecting Inspect or Inspect Element from the pop-up menu), you will see that its class attribute has been set to the literal string, like this:

```
class="'text-white m-2 p-2 ' + getClasses()"
```

The browser will try to process the classes to which the host element has been assigned, but the element's appearance won't be as expected since they don't correspond to the class names used by Bootstrap. This is a common mistake to make, so it is the first thing to check if a binding doesn't have the effect you expected.

243

The square brackets are not the only ones that Angular uses in data bindings. For quick reference, Table 12-5 provides the complete set of brackets, the meaning of each, and where they are described in detail.

Table 12-5. *The Angular Brackets*

Name	Description
[target]="expr"	The square brackets indicate a one-way data binding where data flows from the expression to the target. The different forms of this type of binding are the topic of this chapter.
{{expression}}	This is the string interpolation binding, which is described in the "Using the String Interpolation Binding" section.
(target) ="expr"	The round brackets indicate a one-way binding where the data flows from the target to the destination specified by the expression. This is the binding used to handle events, as described in Chapter 14.
[(target)] ="expr"	This combination of brackets—known as the ban*ana-in-a-box*—indicates a two-way binding, where data flows in both directions between the target and the destination specified by the expression, as described in Chapter 14.

Understanding the Host Element

The host element is the simplest part of a data binding. Data bindings can be applied to any HTML element in a template, and an element can have multiple bindings, each of which can manage a different aspect of the element's appearance or behavior. You will see elements with multiple bindings in later examples.

Using the Standard Property and Attribute Bindings

If the target of a binding doesn't match a directive, Angular will try to apply a property binding. The sections that follow describe the most common property bindings: the standard property binding and the attribute binding.

Using the Standard Property Binding

The browser uses the Document Object Model (DOM) to represent the HTML document. Each element in the HTML document, including the host element, is represented using a JavaScript object in the DOM. Like all JavaScript objects, the ones used to represent HTML elements have properties. These properties are used to manage the state of the element so that the value property, for example, is used to set the contents of an input element. When the browser parses an HTML document, it encounters each new HTML element, creates an object in the DOM to represent it, and uses the element's attributes to set the initial values for the object's properties.

The standard property binding lets you set the value of a property for the object that represents the host element, using the result of an expression. For example, setting the target of a binding to value will set the content of an input element, as shown in Listing 12-5.

Listing 12-5. Using the Standard Property Binding in the template.html File in the src/app Folder

```
<div [ngClass]="'text-white m-2 p-2 ' + getClasses()">
  Hello, World.
</div>
<div class="form-group m-2">
  <label>Name:</label>
  <input class="form-control" [value]="model.getProduct(1)?.name || 'None'" />
</div>
```

The new binding in this example specifies that the `value` property should be bound to the result of an expression that calls a method on the data model to retrieve a data object from the repository by specifying a key. It is possible that there is no data object with that key, in which case the repository method will return `null`.

To guard against using `null` for the host element's value property, the binding uses the template null conditional operator (the ? character) to safely navigate the result returned by the method, like this:

```
...
<input class="form-control" [value]="model.getProduct(1)?.name || 'None'" />
...
```

If the result from the `getProduct` method isn't `null`, then the expression will read the value of the name property and use it as the result. But if the result from the method is `null`, then the name property won't be read, and the null coalescing operator (the || characters) will set the result to None instead.

GETTING TO KNOW THE HTML ELEMENT PROPERTIES

Using property bindings can require some work figuring out which property you need to set. There is some inconsistency in the HTML specification. The name of most properties matches the name of the attribute that sets their initial value so that if you are used to setting the `value` attribute on an `input` element, for example, then you can achieve the same effect by setting the `value` property. Some property names don't match their attribute names, and some properties are not configured by attributes at all.

The Mozilla Foundation provides a useful reference for all the objects that are used to represent HTML elements in the DOM at `developer.mozilla.org/en-US/docs/Web/API`. For each element, Mozilla provides a summary of the properties that are available and what each is used for. Start with `HTMLElement` (`developer.mozilla.org/en-US/docs/Web/API/HTMLElement`), which provides the functionality common to all elements. You can then branch out into the objects that are for specific elements, such as `HTMLInputElement`, which is used to represent `input` elements.

When you save the changes to the template, the browser will reload and display an `input` element whose content is the name property of the data object with the key of 1 in the model repository, as shown in Figure 12-5.

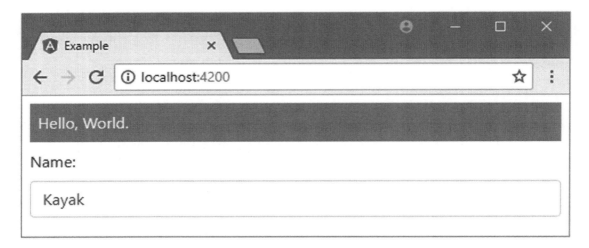

Figure 12-5. *Using the standard property binding*

Using the String Interpolation Binding

Angular provides a special version of the standard property binding, known as the *string interpolation binding*, that is used to include expression results in the text content of host elements. To understand why this special binding is useful, it helps to look at what binding is required when the standard property binding is used.

The textContent property is used to set the content of HTML elements, which means that the content of an element can be set using a data binding like the one shown in Listing 12-6.

Listing 12-6. Setting an Element's Content in the template.html File in the src/app Folder

```
<div [ngClass]="'text-white m-2 p-2 ' + getClasses()"
        [textContent]="'Name: ' + (model.getProduct(1)?.name || 'None')">
</div>
<div class="form-group m-2">
  <label>Name:</label>
  <input class="form-control" [value]="model.getProduct(1)?.name || 'None'" />
</div>
```

The expression in the new binding concatenates a literal string with the results of a method call in order to set the content of the div element.

The expression in this example is awkward to write, requiring careful attention to quotes, spaces, and brackets to ensure that the expected result is displayed in the output. The problem becomes worse for more complex bindings, where multiple dynamic values are interspersed among blocks of static content.

The string interpolation binding simplified this process by allowing fragments of expressions to be defined within the content of an element, as shown in Listing 12-7.

Listing 12-7. Using the String Interpolation Binding in the template.html File in the src/app Folder

```
<div [ngClass]="'text-white m-2 p-2 ' + getClasses()">
  Name: {{ model.getProduct(1)?.name || 'None' }}
</div>
<div class="form-group m-2">
  <label>Name:</label>
  <input class="form-control" [value]="model.getProduct(1)?.name || 'None'" />
</div>
```

The string interpolation binding is denoted using pairs of curly brackets ({{ and }}). A single element can contain multiple string interpolation bindings.

Angular combines the content of the HTML element with the contents of the brackets in order to create a binding for the textContent property. The result is the same as Listing 12-6, which is shown in Figure 12-6, but the process of writing the binding is simpler and less error-prone.

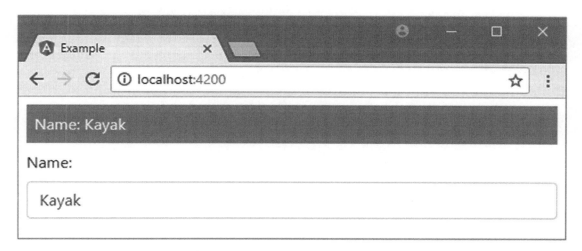

Figure 12-6. Using the string interpolation binding

Using the Attribute Binding

There are some oddities in the HTML and DOM specifications that mean that not all HTML element attributes have equivalent properties in the DOM API. For these situations, Angular provides the *attribute binding*, which is used to set an attribute on the host element rather than setting the value of the JavaScript object that represents it in the DOM.

The most commonly encountered attribute without a corresponding property is colspan, which is used to set the number of columns that a td element will occupy in a table. Listing 12-8 shows using the attribute binding to set the colspan element based on the number of objects in the data model.

Listing 12-8. Using an Attribute Binding in the template.html File in the src/app Folder

```
<div [ngClass]="'text-white m-2 p-2 ' + getClasses()">
  Name: {{model.getProduct(1)?.name || 'None'}}
</div>
<div class="form-group m-2">
```

```
  <label>Name:</label>
  <input class="form-control" [value]="model.getProduct(1)?.name || 'None'" />
</div>
<table class="table table-sm table-bordered table-striped mt-2">
    <tr>
        <th>1</th><th>2</th><th>3</th><th>4</th><th>5</th>
    </tr>
    <tr>
        <td [attr.colspan]="model.getProducts().length">
            {{model.getProduct(1)?.name || 'None'}}
        </td>
    </tr>
</table>
```

The attribute binding is applied by defining a target that prefixes the name of the attribute with `attr.` (the term `attr`, followed by a period). In the listing, I have used the attribute binding to set the value of the colspan element on one of the `td` elements in the table, like this:

```
...
<td [attr.colspan]="model.getProducts().length">
...
```

Angular will evaluate the expression and set the value of the `colspan` attribute to the result. Since the data model is hardwired to start with five data objects, the effect is that the `colspan` attribute creates a table cell that spans five columns, as shown in Figure 12-7.

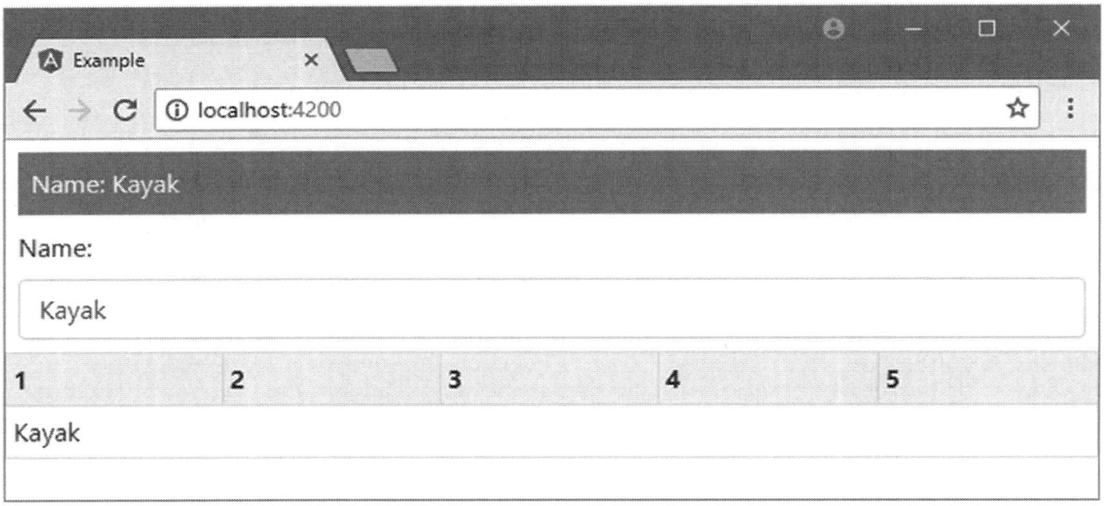

Figure 12-7. *Using an attribute binding*

Setting Classes and Styles

Angular provides special support in property bindings for assigning the host element to classes and for configuring individual style properties. I describe these bindings in the sections that follow, along with details of the ngClass and ngStyle directives, which provide closely related features.

Using the Class Bindings

There are three different ways in which you can use data bindings to manage the class memberships of an element: the standard property binding, the special class binding, and the ngClass directive. All three are described in Table 12-6, and each works in a slightly different way and is useful in different circumstances, as described in the sections that follow.

Table 12-6. *The Angular Class Bindings*

Example	Description
`<div [class]="expr"></div>`	This binding evaluates the expression and uses the result to replace any existing class memberships.
`<div [class.myClass]="expr"></div>`	This binding evaluates the expression and uses the result to set the element's membership of myClass.
`<div [ngClass]="map"></div>`	This binding sets class membership of multiple classes using the data in a map object.

Setting All of an Element's Classes with the Standard Binding

The standard property binding can be used to set all of an element's classes in a single step, which is useful when you have a method or property in the component that returns all of the classes that an element should belong to in a single string, with the names separated by spaces. Listing 12-9 shows the revision of the getClasses method in the component that returns a different string of class names based on the price property of a Product object.

Listing 12-9. Providing All Classes in a Single String in the component.ts File in the src/app Folder

```
import { Component } from "@angular/core";
import { Model } from "./repository.model";

@Component({
    selector: "app",
    templateUrl: "template.html"
})
export class ProductComponent {
    model: Model = new Model();

    getClasses(key: number): string {
        let product = this.model.getProduct(key);
        return "p-2 " + (product.price < 50 ? "bg-info" : "bg-warning");
    }
}
```

249

The result from the getClasses method will include the p-2 class, which adds padding around the host element's content, for all Product objects. If the value of the price property is less than 50, the bg-info class will be included in the result, and if the value is 50 or more, the bg-warning class will be included (these classes set different background colors).

■ **Tip**   You must ensure that the names of the classes are separated by spaces.

Listing 12-10 shows the standard property binding being used in the template to set the class property of host elements using the component's getClasses method.

Listing 12-10. Setting Class Memberships in the template.html File in the src/app Folder

```
<div class="text-white m-2">
  <div [class]="getClasses(1)">
    The first product is {{model.getProduct(1).name}}.
  </div>
  <div [class]="getClasses(2)">
    The second product is {{model.getProduct(2).name}}
  </div>
</div>
```

When the standard property binding is used to set the class property, the result of the expression replaces any previous classes that an element belonged to, which means that it can be used only when the binding expression returns all the classes that are required, as in this example, producing the result shown in Figure 12-8.

Figure 12-8. *Setting class memberships*

Setting Individual Classes Using the Special Class Binding

The special class binding provides finer-grained control than the standard property binding and allows membership of a single class to be managed using an expression. This is useful if you want to build on the existing class memberships of an element, rather than replace them entirely. Listing 12-11 shows the use of the special class binding.

Listing 12-11. Using the Special Class Binding in the template.html File in the src/app Folder

```
<div class="text-white m-2">
  <div [class]="getClasses(1)">
    The first product is {{model.getProduct(1).name}}.
  </div>
  <div class="p-2"
       [class.bg-success]="model.getProduct(2).price < 50"
       [class.bg-info]="model.getProduct(2).price >= 50">
    The second product is {{model.getProduct(2).name}}
  </div>
</div>
```

The special class binding is specified with a target that combines the term class, followed by a period, followed by the name of the class whose membership is being managed. In the listing, there are two special class bindings, which manage the membership of the bg-success and bg-info classes.

The special class binding will add the host element to the specified class if the result of the expression is *truthy* (as described in the "Understanding Truthy and Falsy" sidebar). In this case, the host element will be a member of the bg-success class if the price property is less than 50 and a member of the bg-info class if the price property is 50 or more.

These bindings act independently from one another and do not interfere with any existing classes that an element belongs to, such as the p-2 class, which Bootstrap uses to add padding around an element's content.

UNDERSTANDING TRUTHY AND FALSY

JavaScript has an odd feature, where the result of an expression can be truthy or falsy, providing a pitfall for the unwary. The following results are always falsy:

- The false (boolean) value
- The 0 (number) value
- The empty string ("")
- null
- undefined
- NaN (a special number value)

All other values are truthy, which can be confusing. For example, "false" (a string whose content is the word false) is truthy. The best way to avoid confusion is to only use expressions that evaluate to the boolean values true and false.

Setting Classes Using the ngClass Directive

The ngClass directive is a more flexible alternative to the standard and special property bindings and behaves differently based on the type of data that is returned by the expression, as described in Table 12-7.

Table 12-7. *The Expression Result Types Supported by the ngClass Directive*

Name	Description
String	The host element is added to the classes specified by the string. Multiple classes are separated by spaces.
Array	Each object in the array is the name of a class that the host element will be added to.
Object	Each property on the object is the name of one or more classes, separated by spaces. The host element will be added to the class if the value of the property is truthy.

The string and array features are useful, but it is the ability to use an object (known as a *map*) to create complex class membership policies that makes the ngClass directive especially useful. Listing 12-12 shows the addition of a component method that returns a map object.

Listing 12-12. Returning a Class Map Object in the component.ts File in the src/app Folder

```
import { Component } from "@angular/core";
import { Model } from "./repository.model";

@Component({
    selector: "app",
    templateUrl: "template.html"
})
export class ProductComponent {
    model: Model = new Model();

    getClasses(key: number): string {
        let product = this.model.getProduct(key);
        return "p-2 " + (product.price < 50 ? "bg-info" : "bg-warning");
    }

    getClassMap(key: number): Object {
        let product = this.model.getProduct(key);
        return {
            "text-center bg-danger": product.name == "Kayak",
            "bg-info": product.price < 50
        };
    }
}
```

The getClassMap method returns an object with properties whose values are one or more class names, with values based on the property values of the Product object whose key is specified as the method argument. As an example, when the key is 1, the method returns this object:

```
...
{
  "text-center bg-danger":true,
  "bg-info":false
}
...
```

The first property will assign the host element to the text-center class (which Bootstrap uses to center the text horizontally) and the bg-danger class (which sets the element's background color). The second property evaluates to false, which means that the host element will not be added to the bg-info class. It may seem odd to specify a property that doesn't result in an element being added to a class, but, as you will see shortly, the value of expressions is automatically updated to reflect changes in the application, and being able to define a map object that specifies memberships this way can be useful.

Listing 12-13 shows the getClassMap and the map objects it returns used as the expression for data bindings that target the ngClass directive.

Listing 12-13. Using the ngClass Directive in the template.html File in the src/app Folder

```html
<div class="text-white m-2">
  <div class="p-2" [ngClass]="getClassMap(1)">
    The first product is {{model.getProduct(1).name}}.
  </div>
  <div class="p-2" [ngClass]="getClassMap(2)">
    The second product is {{model.getProduct(2).name}}.
  </div>
  <div class="p-2" [ngClass]="{'bg-success': model.getProduct(3).price < 50,
                              'bg-info': model.getProduct(3).price >= 50}">
        The third product is {{model.getProduct(3).name}}
  </div>
</div>
```

The first two div elements have bindings that use the getClassMap method. The third div element shows an alternative approach, which is to define the map in the template. For this element, membership of the bg-info and bg-warning classes is tied to the value of the price property of a Product object, as shown in Figure 12-9. Care should be taken with this technique because the expression contains JavaScript logic that cannot be readily tested.

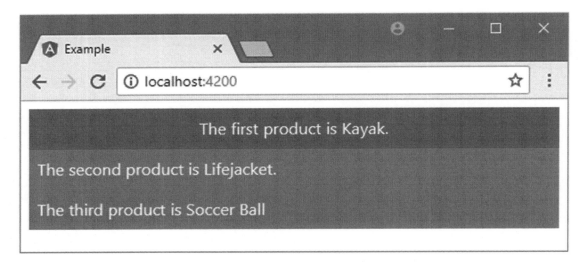

Figure 12-9. *Using the ngClass directive*

Using the Style Bindings

There are three different ways in which you can use data bindings to set style properties of the host element: the standard property binding, the special style binding, and the ngStyle directive. All three are described in Table 12-8 and demonstrated in the sections that follow.

Table 12-8. *The Angular Style Bindings*

Example	Description
`<div [style.myStyle]="expr"></div>`	This is the standard property binding, which is used to set a single style property to the result of the expression.
`<div [style.myStyle.units]="expr"></div>`	This is the special style binding, which allows the units for the style value to be specified as part of the target.
`<div [ngStyle]="map"></div>`	This binding sets multiple style properties using the data in a map object.

Setting a Single Style Property

The standard property binding and the special style bindings are used to set the value of a single style property. The difference between these bindings is that the standard property binding must include the units required for the style, while the special binding allows for the units to be included in the binding target.

To demonstrate the difference, Listing 12-14 adds two new properties to the component.

Listing 12-14. Adding Properties in the component.ts File in the src/app Folder

```
import { Component } from "@angular/core";
import { Model } from "./repository.model";

@Component({
    selector: "app",
    templateUrl: "template.html"
})
export class ProductComponent {
    model: Model = new Model();

    getClasses(key: number): string {
        let product = this.model.getProduct(key);
        return "p-2 " + (product.price < 50 ? "bg-info" : "bg-warning");
    }

    getClassMap(key: number): Object {
        let product = this.model.getProduct(key);
        return {
            "text-center bg-danger": product.name == "Kayak",
            "bg-info": product.price < 50
        };
    }

    fontSizeWithUnits: string = "30px";
    fontSizeWithoutUnits: string= "30";
}
```

The fontSizeWithUnits property returns a value that includes a quantity and the units that quantity is expressed in: 30 pixels. The fontSizeWithoutUnits property returns just the quantity, without any unit information. Listing 12-15 shows how these properties can be used with the standard and special bindings.

■ **Caution** Do not try to use the standard property binding to target the style property to set multiple style values. The object returned by the style property of the JavaScript object that represents the host element in the DOM is read-only. Some browsers will ignore this and allow changes to be made, but the results are unpredictable and cannot be relied on. If you want to set multiple style properties, then create a binding for each of them or use the ngStyle directive.

Listing 12-15. Using Style Bindings in the template.html File in the src/app Folder

```
<div class="text-white m-2">
  <div class="p-2 bg-warning">
    The <span [style.fontSize]="fontSizeWithUnits">first</span>
    product is {{model.getProduct(1).name}}.
  </div>
  <div class="p-2 bg-info">
    The <span [style.fontSize.px]="fontSizeWithoutUnits">second</span>
    product is {{model.getProduct(2).name}}
  </div>
</div>
```

The target for the binding is `style.fontSize`, which sets the size of the font used for the host element's content. The expression for this binding uses the `fontSizeWithUnits` property, whose value includes the units, px for pixels, required to set the font size.

The target for the special binding is `style.fontSize.px`, which tells Angular that the value of the expression specifies the number in pixels. This allows the binding to use the component's `fontSizeWithoutUnits` property, which doesn't include units.

■ **Tip**   You can specify style properties using the JavaScript property name format (`[style.fontSize]`) or using the CSS property name format (`[style.font-size]`).

The result of both bindings is the same, which is to set the font size of the span elements to 30 pixels, producing the result shown in Figure 12-10.

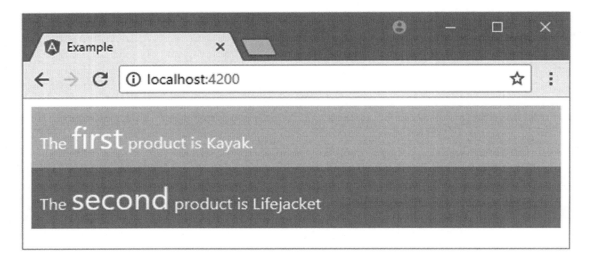

Figure 12-10. *Setting individual style properties*

Setting Styles Using the ngStyle Directive

The ngStyle directive allows multiple style properties to be set using a map object, similar to the way that the ngClass directive works. Listing 12-16 shows the addition of a component method that returns a map containing style settings.

Listing 12-16. Creating a Style Map Object in the component.ts File in the src/app Folder

```
import { Component } from "@angular/core";
import { Model } from "./repository.model";

@Component({
    selector: "app",
    templateUrl: "template.html"
})
```

```
export class ProductComponent {
    model: Model = new Model();

    getClasses(key: number): string {
        let product = this.model.getProduct(key);
        return "p-2 " + (product.price < 50 ? "bg-info" : "bg-warning");
    }

    getStyles(key: number) {
        let product = this.model.getProduct(key);
        return {
            fontSize: "30px",
            "margin.px": 100,
            color: product.price > 50 ? "red" : "green"
        };
    }
}
```

The map object returned by the getStyle method shows that the ngStyle directive is able to support both of the formats that can be used with property bindings, including either the units in the value or the property name. Here is the map object that the getStyles method produces when the value of the key argument is 1:

```
...
{
  "fontSize":"30px",
  "margin.px":100,
  "color":"red"
}
...
```

Listing 12-17 shows data bindings in the template that use the ngStyle directive and whose expressions call the getStyles method.

Listing 12-17. Using the ngStyle Directive in the template.html File in the src/app Folder

```
<div class="text-white m-2">
  <div class="p-2 bg-warning">
    The <span [ngStyle]="getStyles(1)">first</span>
    product is {{model.getProduct(1).name}}.
  </div>
  <div class="p-2 bg-info">
    The <span [ngStyle]="getStyles(2)">second</span>
    product is {{model.getProduct(2).name}}
  </div>
</div>
```

The result is that each span element receives a tailored set of styles, based on the argument passed to the getStyles method, as shown in Figure 12-11.

Figure 12-11. *Using the ngStyle directive*

Updating the Data in the Application

When you start out with Angular, it can seem like a lot of effort to deal with the data bindings, remembering which binding is required in different situations. You might be wondering if it is worth the effort.

Bindings are worth understanding because their expressions are re-evaluated when the data they depend on changes. As an example, if you are using a string interpolation binding to display the value of a property, then the binding will automatically update when the value of the property is changed.

To provide a demonstration, I am going to jump ahead and show you how to take manual control of the updating process. This is not a technique that is required in normal Angular development, but it provides a solid demonstration of why bindings are so important. Listing 12-18 shows some changes to the component that enable the demonstration.

Listing 12-18. Preparing the Component in the component.ts File in the src/app Folder

```
import { ApplicationRef, Component } from "@angular/core";
import { Model } from "./repository.model";
import { Product } from "./product.model";

@Component({
    selector: "app",
    templateUrl: "template.html"
})
export class ProductComponent {
    model: Model = new Model();

    constructor(ref: ApplicationRef) {
        (<any>window).appRef = ref;
        (<any>window).model = this.model;
    }
```

```
    getProductByPosition(position: number): Product {
        return this.model.getProducts()[position];
    }

    getClassesByPosition(position: number): string {
        let product = this.getProductByPosition(position);
        return "p-2 " + (product.price < 50 ? "bg-info" : "bg-warning");
    }
}
```

I have imported the ApplicationRef type from the @angular/core module. When Angular performs the bootstrapping process, it creates an ApplicationRef object to represent the application. Listing 12-18 adds a constructor to the component that receives an ApplicationRef object as an argument, using the Angular dependency injection feature, which I describe in Chapter 19. Without going into detail now, declaring a constructor argument like this tells Angular that the component wants to receive the ApplicationRef object when a new instance is created.

Within the constructor, there are two statements that make a demonstration possible but would undermine many of the benefits of using TypeScript and Angular if used in a real project.

```
...
(<any>window).appRef = ref;
(<any>window).model = this.model;
...
```

These statements define variables in the global namespace and assign the ApplicationRef and Model objects to them. It is good practice to keep the global namespace as clear as possible, but exposing these objects allows them to be manipulated through the browser's JavaScript console, which is important for this example.

The other methods added to the constructor allow a Product object to be retrieved from the repository based on its position, rather than by its key, and to generate a class map that differs based on the value of the price property.

Listing 12-19 shows the corresponding changes to the template, which uses the ngClass directive to set class memberships and the string interpolation binding to display the value of the Product.name property.

Listing 12-19. Preparing for Changes in the template.html File in the src/app Folder

```
<div class="text-white m-2">
  <div [ngClass]="getClassesByPosition(0)">
    The first product is {{getProductByPosition(0).name}}.
  </div>
  <div [ngClass]="getClassesByPosition(1)">
    The second product is {{getProductByPosition(1).name}}
  </div>
</div>
```

Save the changes to the component and template. Once the browser has reloaded the page, enter the following statement into the browser's JavaScript console and press Return:

```
model.products.shift()
```

This statement calls the `shift` method on the array of `Product` objects in the model, which removes the first item from the array and returns it. You won't see any changes yet because Angular doesn't know that the model has been modified. To tell Angular to check for changes, enter the following statement into the browser's JavaScript console and press Return:

```
appRef.tick()
```

The `tick` method starts the Angular change detection process, where Angular looks at the data in the application and the expressions in the data binding and processes any changes. The data bindings in the template use specific array indexes to display data, and now that an object has been removed from the model, the bindings will be updated to display new values, as shown in Figure 12-12.

Figure 12-12. Manually updating the application model

It is worth taking a moment to think about what happened when the change detection process ran. Angular reevaluated the expressions on the bindings in the template and updated their values. In turn, the `ngClass` directive and the string interpolation binding reconfigured their host elements by changing their class memberships and displaying new content.

The happens because Angular data bindings are *live*, meaning that the relationship between the expression, the target, and the host element continues to exist after the initial content is displayed to the user and dynamically reflects changes to the application state. This effect is, I admit, much more impressive when you don't have to make changes using the JavaScript console. I explain how Angular allows the user to trigger changes using events and forms in Chapter 14.

Summary

In this chapter, I described the structure of Angular data bindings and showed you how they are used to create relationships between the data in the application and the HTML elements that are displayed to the user. I introduced the property bindings and described how two of the built-in directives—`ngClass` and `ngStyle`—are used. In the next chapter, I explain how more of the built-in directives work.

CHAPTER 13

■ ■ ■

Using the Built-in Directives

In this chapter, I describe the built-in directives that are responsible for some of the most commonly required functionality for creating web applications: selectively including content, choosing between different fragments of content, and repeating content. I also describe some limitations that Angular puts on the expressions that are used for one-way data bindings and the directives that provide them. Table 13-1 puts the built-in template directives in context.

Table 13-1. *Putting the Built-in Directives in Context*

Question	Answer
What are they?	The built-in directives described in this chapter are responsible for selectively including content, selecting between fragments of content, and repeating content for each item in an array. There are also directives for setting an element's styles and class memberships, as described in Chapter 13.
Why are they useful?	The tasks that can be performed with these directives are the most common and fundamental in web application development, and they provide the foundation for adapting the content shown to the user based on the data in the application.
How are they used?	The directives are applied to HTML elements in templates. There are examples throughout this chapter (and in the rest of the book).
Are there any pitfalls or limitations?	The syntax for using the built-in template directives requires you to remember that some of them (including ngIf and ngFor) must be prefixed with an asterisk, while others (including ngClass, ngStyle, and ngSwitch) must be enclosed in square brackets. I explain why this is required in the "Understanding Micro-Template Directives" sidebar, but it is easy to forget and get an unexpected result.
Are there any alternatives?	You could write your own custom directives—a process that I described in Chapters 15 and 16—but the built-in directives are well-written and comprehensively tested. For most applications, using the built-in directives is preferable, unless they cannot provide exactly the functionality that is required.

© Adam Freeman 2018
A. Freeman, *Pro Angular 6*, https://doi.org/10.1007/978-1-4842-3649-9_13

Table 13-2 summarizes the chapter.

Table 13-2. *Chapter Summary*

Problem	Solution	Listing
Conditionally display content based on a data binding expression	Use the ngIf directive	1–3
Choose between different content based on the value of a data binding expression	Use the ngSwitch directive	4, 5
Generate a section of content for each object produced by a data binding expression	Use the ngFor directive	6–12
Repeat a block of content	Use the ngTemplateOutlet directive	13–14
Prevent template errors	Avoid modifying the application state as a side effect of a data binding expression	15–19
Avoid context errors	Ensure that data binding expressions use only the properties and methods provided by the template's component	20–22

Preparing the Example Project

This chapter relies on the example project that was created in Chapter 11 and modified in Chapter 12. To prepare for the topic of this chapter, Listing 13-1 shows changes to the component class that remove features that are no longer required and adds new methods and a property.

■ **Tip** You can download the example project for this chapter—and for all the other chapters in this book—from `https://github.com/Apress/pro-angular-6`.

Listing 13-1. Changes in the component.ts File in the src/app Folder

```
import { ApplicationRef, Component } from "@angular/core";
import { Model } from "./repository.model";
import { Product } from "./product.model";

@Component({
    selector: "app",
    templateUrl: "template.html"
})
export class ProductComponent {
    model: Model = new Model();

    constructor(ref: ApplicationRef) {
        (<any>window).appRef = ref;
        (<any>window).model = this.model;
    }
```

```
    getProductByPosition(position: number): Product {
        return this.model.getProducts()[position];
    }

    getProduct(key: number): Product {
        return this.model.getProduct(key);
    }

    getProducts(): Product[] {
        return this.model.getProducts();
    }

    getProductCount(): number {
        return this.getProducts().length;
    }

    targetName: string = "Kayak";
}
```

Listing 13-2 shows the contents of the template file, which displays the number of products in the data model by calling the component's new getProductCount method.

Listing 13-2. The Contents of the template.html File in the src/app Folder

```
<div class="text-white m-2">
  <div class="bg-info p-2">
    There are {{getProductCount()}} products.
  </div>
</div>
```

Run the following command from the command line in the example folder to start the TypeScript compiler and the development HTTP server:

```
ng serve
```

Open a new browser window and navigate to http://localhost:4200 to see the content shown in Figure 13-1.

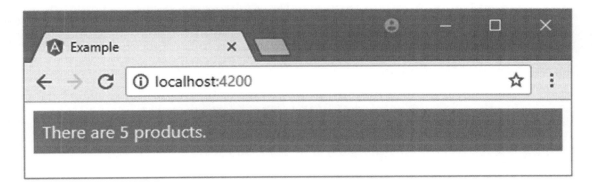

Figure 13-1. *Running the example application*

Using the Built-in Directives

Angular comes with a set of built-in directives that provide features commonly required in web applications. Table 13-3 describes the directives that are available, which I demonstrate in the sections that follow (except for the ngClass and ngStyle directives, which are covered in Chapter 12).

Table 13-3. *The Built-in Directives*

Example	Description
`<div *ngIf="expr"></div>`	The ngIf directive is used to include an element and its content in the HTML document if the expression evaluates as true. The asterisk before the directive name indicates that this is a micro-template directive, as described in the "Understanding Micro-Template Directives" sidebar.

`<div [ngSwitch]="expr">`
`<span *ngSwitchCase="expr"></span>`
`<span *ngSwitchDefault></span>`
`</div>`
	The ngSwitch directive is used to choose between multiple elements to include in the HTML document based on the result of an expression, which is then compared to the result of the individual expressions defined using ngSwitchCase directives. If none of the ngSwitchCase values matches, then the element to which the ngSwitchDefault directive has been applied will be used. The asterisks before the ngSwitchCase and ngSwitchDefault directives indicate they are micro-template directives, as described in the "Understanding Micro-Template Directives" sidebar.

`<div *ngFor="#item of expr"></div>`	The ngFor directive is used to generate the same set of elements for each object in an array. The asterisk before the directive name indicates that this is a micro-template directive, as described in the "Understanding Micro-Template Directives" sidebar.

`<ng-template`
`[ngTemplateOutlet]="myTempl">`
`</ngtemplate>`
	The ngTemplateOutlet directive is used to repeat a block of content in a template.

`<div ngClass="expr"></div>`	The ngClass directive is used to manage class membership, as described in Chapter 12.
`<div ngStyle="expr"></div>`	The ngStyle directive is used to manage styles applied directly to elements (as opposed to applying styles through classes), as described in Chapter 12.

Using the ngIf Directive

The ngIf is the simplest of the built-in directives and is used to include a fragment of HTML in the document when an expression evaluates as true, as shown in Listing 13-3.

Listing 13-3. Using the ngIf Directive in the template.html File in the src/app Folder

```
<div class="text-white m-2">
  <div class="bg-info p-2">
    There are {{getProductCount()}} products.
  </div>

  <div *ngIf="getProductCount() > 4" class="bg-info p-2 mt-1">
    There are more than 4 products in the model
  </div>

  <div *ngIf="getProductByPosition(0).name != 'Kayak'" class="bg-info p-2 mt-1">
    The first product isn't a Kayak
  </div>
</div>
```

The ngIf directive has been applied to two div elements, with expressions that check the number of Product objects in the model and whether the name of the first Product is Kayak.

The first expression evaluates as true, which means that div element and its content will be included in the HTML document; the second expression evaluates as false, which means that the second div element will be excluded. Figure 13-2 shows the result.

■ **Note** The ngIf directive adds and removes elements from the HTML document, rather than just showing or hiding them. Use the property or style bindings, described in Chapter 12, if you want to leave elements in place and control their visibility, either by setting the hidden element property to true or by setting the display style property to none.

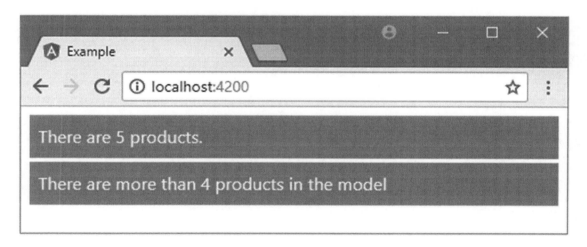

Figure 13-2. Using the ngIf directive

UNDERSTANDING MICRO-TEMPLATE DIRECTIVES

Some directives, such as ngFor, ngIf, and the nested directives used with ngSwitch are prefixed with an asterisk, as in *ngFor, *ngIf, and *ngSwitch. The asterisk is shorthand for using directives that rely on content provided as part of the template, known as a *micro-template*. Directives that use micro-templates are known as *structural directives*, a description that I revisit in Chapter 16 when I show you how to create them.

Listing 13-3 applied the ngIf directive to div elements, which tells the directive to use the div element and its content as the micro-template for each of the objects that it processes. Behind the scenes, Angular expands the micro-template and the directive like this:

```
...
<ng-template ngIf="model.getProductCount() > 4">
    <div class="bg-info p-2 mt-1">
        There are more than 4 products in the model
    </div>
</ng-template>
...
```

You can use either syntax in your templates, but if you use the compact syntax, then you must remember to use the asterisk. I explain how to create your own micro-template directives in Chapter 14.

Like all directives, the expression used for ngIf will be re-evaluated to reflect changes in the data model. Run the following statements in the browser's JavaScript console to remove the first data object and to run the change detection process:

```
model.products.shift()
appRef.tick()
```

The effect of modifying the model is to remove the first div element because there are too few Product objects now and to add the second div element because the name property of the first Product in the array is no longer Kayak. Figure 13-3 shows the change.

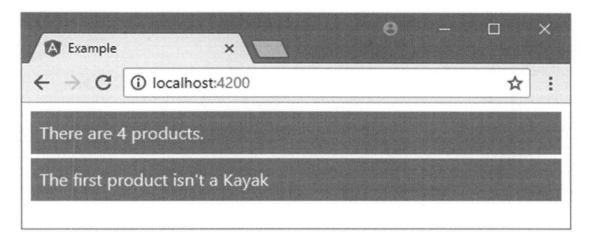

Figure 13-3. *The effect of reevaluating directive expressions*

Using the ngSwitch Directive

The ngSwitch directive selects one of several elements based on the expression result, similar to a JavaScript switch statement. Listing 13-4 shows the ngSwitch directive being used to choose an element based on the number of objects in the model.

Listing 13-4. Using the ngSwitch Directive in the template.html File in the src/app Folder

```
<div class="text-white m-2">
  <div class="bg-info p-2">
    There are {{getProductCount()}} products.
  </div>

  <div class="bg-info p-2 mt-1" [ngSwitch]="getProductCount()">
    <span *ngSwitchCase="2">There are two products</span>
    <span *ngSwitchCase="5">There are five products</span>
    <span *ngSwitchDefault>This is the default</span>
  </div>
</div>
```

The ngSwitch directive syntax can be confusing to use. The element that the ngSwitch directive is applied to is always included in the HTML document, and the directive name isn't prefixed with an asterisk. It must be specified within square brackets, like this:

```
...
<div class="bg-info p-2 mt-1" [ngSwitch]="getProductCount()">
...
```

Each of the inner elements, which are span elements in this example, is a micro-template, and the directives that specify the target expression result are prefixed with an asterisk, like this:

```
...
<span *ngSwitchCase="5">There are five products</span>
...
```

267

The ngSwitchCase directive is used to specify a particular expression result. If the ngSwitch expression evaluates to the specified result, then that element and its contents will be included in the HTML document. If the expression doesn't evaluate to the specified result, then the element and its contents will be excluded from the HTML document.

The ngSwitchDefault directive is applied to a fallback element—equivalent to the default label in a JavaScript switch statement—which is included in the HTML document if the expression result doesn't match any of the results specified by the ngSwitchCase directives.

For the initial data in the application, the directives in Listing 13-4 produce the following HTML:

```
...
<div class="bg-info p-2 mt-1" ng-reflect-ng-switch="5">
    <span>There are five products</span>
</div>
...
```

The div element, to which the ngSwitch directive has been applied, is always included in the HTML document. For the initial data in the model, the span element whose ngSwitchCase directive has a result of 5 is also included, producing the result shown on the left of Figure 13-4.

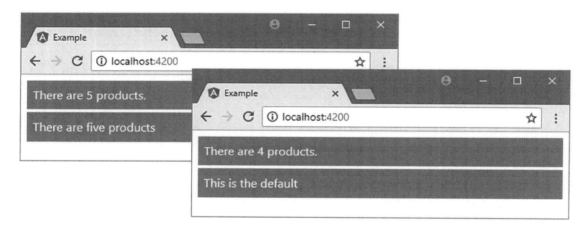

Figure 13-4. *Using the ngSwitch directive*

The ngSwitch binding responds to changes in the data model, which you can test by executing the following statements in the browser's JavaScript console:

```
model.products.shift()
appRef.tick()
```

These statements remove the first item from the model and force Angular to run the change detection process. Neither of the results for the two ngSwitchCase directives matches the result from the getProductCount expression, so the ngSwitchDefault element is included in the HTML document, as shown on the right of Figure 13-4.

Avoiding Literal Value Problems

A common problem arises when using the ngSwitchCase directive to specify literal string values, and care must be taken to get the right result, as shown in Listing 13-5.

Listing 13-5. Component and String Literal Values in the template.html File in the src/app Folder

```
<div class="text-white m-2">
  <div class="bg-info p-2">
    There are {{getProductCount()}} products.
  </div>

  <div class="bg-info p-2 mt-1" [ngSwitch]="getProduct(1).name">
    <span *ngSwitchCase="targetName">Kayak</span>
    <span *ngSwitchCase="'Lifejacket'">Lifejacket</span>
    <span *ngSwitchDefault>Other Product</span>
  </div>
</div>
```

The values assigned to the ngSwitchCase directives are also expressions, which means that you can invoke methods, perform simple inline operations, and read property values, just as you would for the basic data bindings.

As an example, this expression tells Angular to include the span element to which the directive has been applied when the result of evaluating the ngSwitch expression matches the value of the targetName property defined by the component:

```
...
<span *ngSwitchCase="targetName">Kayak</span>
...
```

If you want to compare a result to a specific string, then you must double quote it, like this:

```
...
<span *ngSwitchCase="'Lifejacket'">Lifejacket</span>
...
```

This expression tells Angular to include the span element when the value of the ngSwitch expression is equal to the literal string value Lifejacket, producing the result shown in Figure 13-5.

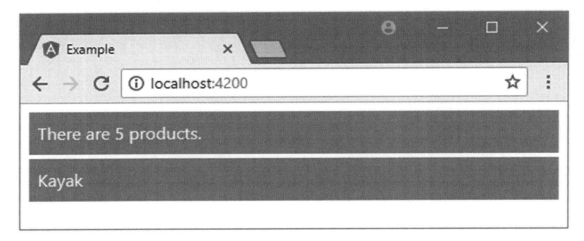

Figure 13-5. *Using expressions and literal values with the ngSwitch directive*

Using the ngFor Directive

The ngFor directive repeats a section of content for each object in an array, providing the template equivalent of a foreach loop. In Listing 13-6, I have used the ngFor directive to populate a table by generating a row for each Product object in the model.

Listing 13-6. Using the ngFor Directive in the template.html File in the src/app Folder

```
<div class="text-white m-2">
  <div class="bg-info p-2">
    There are {{getProductCount()}} products.
  </div>

  <table class="table table-sm table-bordered mt-1 text-dark">
    <tr><th>Name</th><th>Category</th><th>Price</th></tr>
    <tr *ngFor="let item of getProducts()">
      <td>{{item.name}}</td>
      <td>{{item.category}}</td>
      <td>{{item.price}}</td>
    </tr>
  </table>
</div>
```

The expression used with the ngFor directive is more complex than for the other built-in directives, but it will start to make sense when you see how the different parts fit together. Here is the directive that I used in the example:

```
...
<tr *ngFor="let item of getProducts()">
...
```

The asterisk before the name is required because the directive is using a micro-template, as described in the "Understanding Micro-Template Directives" sidebar. This will make more sense as you become familiar with Angular, but at first, you just have to remember that this directive requires an asterisk to use (or, as I often do, forget until you see an error displayed in the browser's JavaScript console and *then* remember).

For the expression itself, there are two distinct parts, joined together with the of keyword. The right-hand part of the expression provides the data source that will be enumerated.

```
...
<tr *ngFor="let item of getProducts()">
...
```

This example specifies the component's getProducts method as the source of data, which allows content to be for each of the Product objects in the model. The right-hand side is an expression in its own right, which means you can prepare data or perform simple manipulation operations within the template.

The left-hand side of the ngFor expression defines a *template variable*, denoted by the let keyword, which is how data is passed between elements within an Angular template.

```
...
<tr *ngFor="let item of getProducts()">
...
```

The ngFor directive assigns the variable to each object in the data source so that it is available for use by the nested elements. The local template variable in the example is called item, and it is used to access the Product object's properties for the td elements, like this:

```
...
<td>{{item.name}}</td>
...
```

Put together, the directive in the example tells Angular to enumerate the objects returned by the component's getProducts method, assign each of them to a variable called item, and then generate a tr element and its td children, evaluating the template expressions they contain.

For the example in Listing 13-6, the result is a table where the ngFor directive is used to generate table rows for each of the Product objects in the model and where each table row contains td elements that display the value of the Product object's name, category, and price properties, as shown in Figure 13-6.

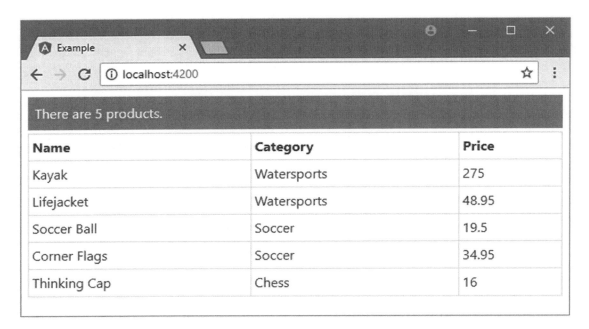

Figure 13-6. *Using the ngFor directive to create table rows*

Using Other Template Variables

The most important template variable is the one that refers to the data object being processed, which is item in the previous example. But the ngFor directive supports a range of other values that can also be assigned to variables and then referred to within the nested HTML elements, as described in Table 13-4 and demonstrated in the sections that follow.

Table 13-4. *The ngFor Local Template Values*

Name	Description
index	This number value is assigned to the position of the current object.
odd	This boolean value returns true if the current object has an odd-numbered position in the data source.
even	This boolean value returns true if the current object has an even-numbered position in the data source.
first	This boolean value returns true if the current object is the first one in the data source.
last	This boolean value returns true if the current object is the last one in the data source.

Using the Index Value

The index value is set to the position of the current data object and is incremented for each object in the data source. In Listing 13-7, I have defined a table that is populated using the ngFor directive and that assigns the index value to a local template variable called i, which is then used in a string interpolation binding.

Listing 13-7. Using the Index Value in the template.html File in the src/app Folder

```
<div class="text-white m-2">
  <div class="bg-info p-2">
    There are {{getProductCount()}} products.
  </div>

  <table class="table table-sm table-bordered mt-1 text-dark">
    <tr><th></th><th>Name</th><th>Category</th><th>Price</th></tr>
    <tr *ngFor="let item of getProducts(); let i = index">
      <td>{{i +1}}</td>
      <td>{{item.name}}</td>
      <td>{{item.category}}</td>
      <td>{{item.price}}</td>
    </tr>
  </table>
</div>
```

A new term is added to the ngFor expression, separated from the existing one using a semicolon (the ; character). The new expression uses the let keyword to assign the index value to a local template variable called i, like this:

```
...
<tr *ngFor="let item of getProducts(); let i = index">
...
```

This allows the value to be accessed within the nested elements using a binding, like this:

```
...
<td>{{i + 1}}</td>
...
```

The index value is zero-based, and adding 1 to the value creates a simple counter, producing the result shown in Figure 13-7.

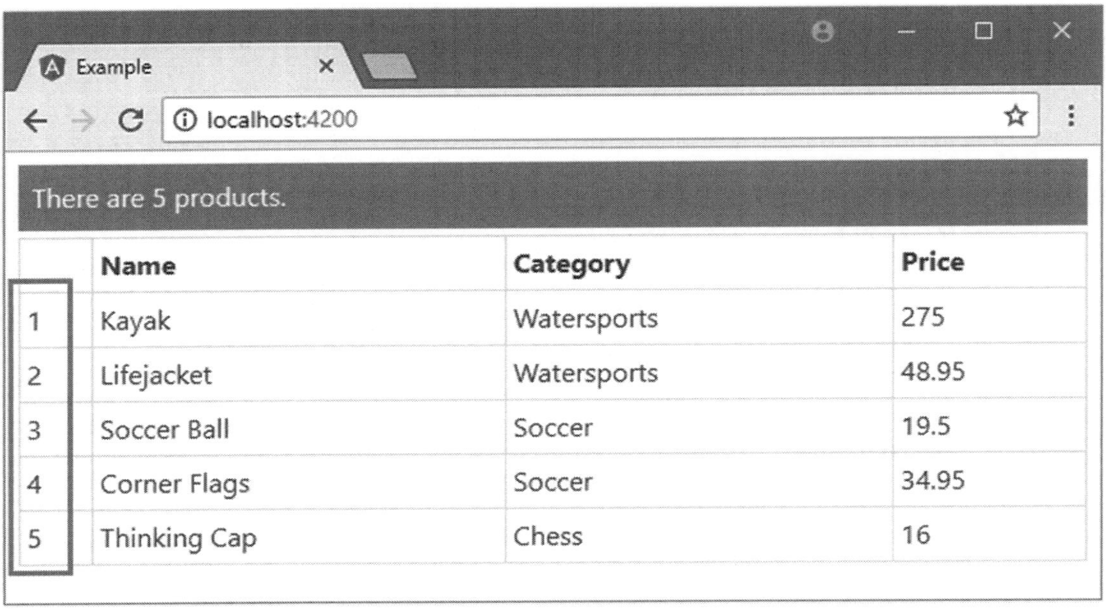

Figure 13-7. *Using the index value*

Using the Odd and Even Values

The odd value is `true` when the `index` value for a data item is odd. Conversely, the even value is `true` when the index value for a data item is even. In general, you only need to use either the odd or even value since they are boolean values where odd is `true` when even is `false`, and vice versa. In Listing 13-8, the odd value is used to manage the class membership of the `tr` elements in the table.

Listing 13-8. Using the odd Value in the template.html File in the src/app Folder

```
<div class="text-white m-2">
  <div class="bg-info p-2">
    There are {{getProductCount()}} products.
  </div>

  <table class="table table-sm table-bordered mt-1">
    <tr><th></th><th>Name</th><th>Category</th><th>Price</th></tr>
    <tr *ngFor="let item of getProducts(); let i = index; let odd = odd"
        [class.bg-primary]="odd" [class.bg-info]="!odd">
      <td>{{i + 1}}</td>
      <td>{{item.name}}</td>
      <td>{{item.category}}</td>
      <td>{{item.price}}</td>
    </tr>
  </table>
</div>
```

I have used a semicolon and added another term to the ngFor expression that assigns the odd value to a local template variable that is also called odd.

```
...
<tr *ngFor="let item of getProducts(); let i = index; let odd = odd"
    [class.bg-primary]="odd" [class.bg-info]="!odd">
...
```

This may seem redundant, but you cannot access the ngFor values directly and must use a local variable even if it has the same name. I used the class binding to assign alternate rows to the bg-primary and bg-info classes, which are Bootstrap background color classes that stripe the table rows, as shown in Figure 13-8.

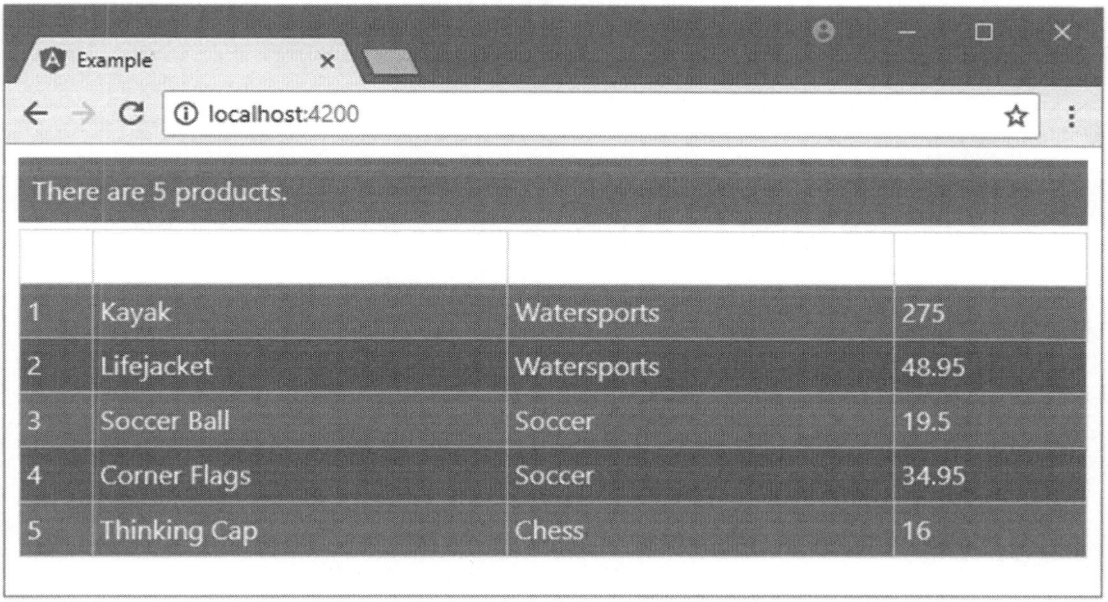

Figure 13-8. *Using the odd value*

EXPANDING THE *NGFOR DIRECTIVE

Notice that in Listing 13-8, I am able to use the template variable in expressions applied to the same tr element that defines it. This is possible because ngFor is a micro-template directive—denoted by the * that precedes the name—and so Angular expands the HTML so that it looks like this:

```
...
<table class="table table-sm table-bordered mt-1">
    <tr><th></th><th>Name</th><th>Category</th><th>Price</th></tr>
    <ng-template ngFor let-item [ngForOf]="getProducts()"
            let-i="index" let-odd="odd">
        <tr [class.bg-primary]="odd" [class.bg-info]="!odd">
            <td>{{i + 1}}</td>
```

```
            <td>{{item.name}}</td>
            <td>{{item.category}}</td>
            <td>{{item.price}}</td>
         </tr>
      </ng-template>
</table>
...
```

You can see that the ng-template element defines the variables, using the somewhat awkward let-
<name> attributes, which are then accessed by the tr and td elements within it. As with so much in
Angular, what appears to happen by magic turns out to be straightforward once you understand what is
going on behind the scenes, and I explain these features in detail in Chapter 16. A good reason to use
the *ngFor syntax is that it provides a more elegant way to express the directive expression, especially
when there are multiple template variables.

Using the First and Last Values

The first value is true only for the first object in the sequence provided by the data source and is false for
all other objects. Conversely, the last value is true only for the last object in the sequence. Listing 13-9 uses
these values to treat the first and last objects differently from the others in the sequence.

Listing 13-9. Using the first and last Values in the template.html File in the src/app Folder

```html
<div class="text-white m-2">
  <div class="bg-info p-2">
    There are {{getProductCount()}} products.
  </div>

  <table class="table table-sm table-bordered mt-1">
    <tr class="text-dark">
      <th></th><th>Name</th><th>Category</th><th>Price</th>
    </tr>
    <tr *ngFor="let item of getProducts(); let i = index; let odd = odd;
          let first = first; let last = last"
      [class.bg-primary]="odd" [class.bg-info]="!odd"
      [class.bg-warning]="first || last">
      <td>{{i + 1}}</td>
      <td>{{item.name}}</td>
      <td>{{item.category}}</td>
      <td *ngIf="!last">{{item.price}}</td>
    </tr>
  </table>
</div>
```

The new terms in the ngFor expression assign the first and last values to template variables called
first and last. These variables are then used by a class binding on the tr element, which assigns the
element to the bg-warning class when either is true, and used by the ngIf directive on one of the td
elements, which will exclude the element for the last item in the data source, producing the effect shown in
Figure 13-9.

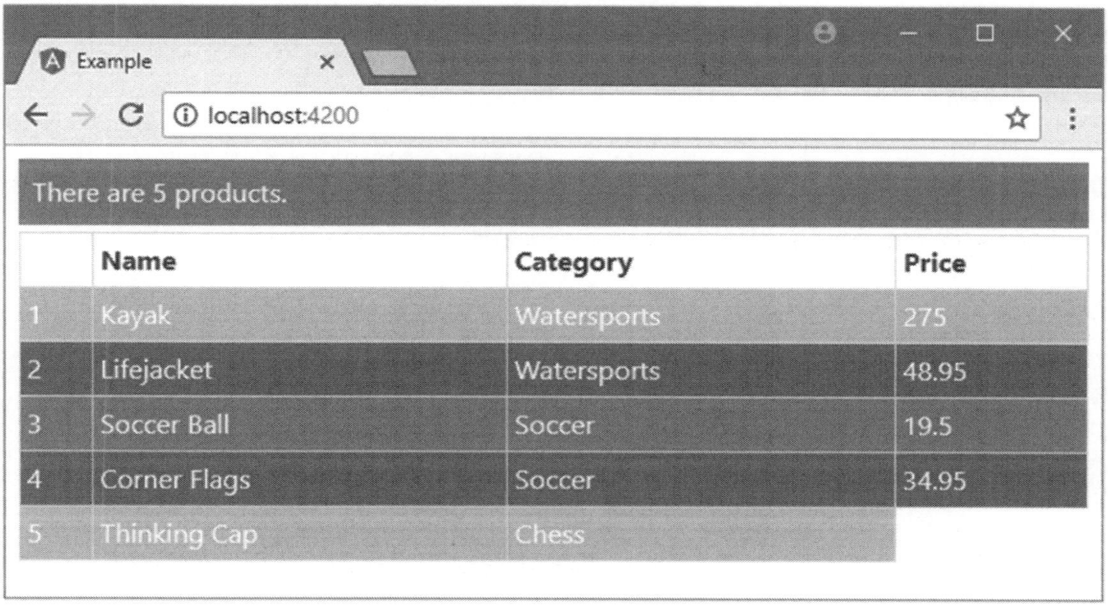

Figure 13-9. *Using the first and last values*

Minimizing Element Operations

When there is a change to the data model, the ngFor directive evaluates its expression and updates the elements that represent its data objects. The update process can be expensive, especially if the data source is replaced with one that contains different objects representing the same data. Replacing the data source may seem like an odd thing to do, but it happens often in web applications, especially when the data is retrieved from a web service, like the ones I describe in Chapter 24. The same data values are represented by new objects, which present an efficiency problem for Angular. To demonstrate the problem, I added a method to the component that replaces one of the Product objects in the data model, as shown in Listing 13-10.

Listing 13-10. Replacing an Object in the repository.model.ts File in the src/app Folder

```
import { Product } from "./product.model";
import { SimpleDataSource } from "./datasource.model";

export class Model {
    private dataSource: SimpleDataSource;
    private products: Product[];
    private locator = (p:Product, id:number) => p.id == id;

    constructor() {
        this.dataSource = new SimpleDataSource();
        this.products = new Array<Product>();
        this.dataSource.getData().forEach(p => this.products.push(p));
    }
```

```
    // ...other methods omitted for brevity...

    swapProduct() {
        let p = this.products.shift();
        this.products.push(new Product(p.id, p.name, p.category, p.price));
    }
}
```

The swapProduct method removes the first object from the array and adds a new object that has the same values for the id, name, category, and price properties. This is an example of data values being represented by a new object.

Run the following statements using the browser's JavaScript console to modify the data model and run the change-detection process:

```
model.swapProduct()
appRef.tick()
```

When the ngFor directive examines its data source, it sees it has two operations to perform to reflect the change to the data. The first operation is to destroy the HTML elements that represent the first object in the array. The second operation is to create a new set of HTML elements to represent the new object at the end of the array.

Angular has no way of knowing that the data objects it is dealing with have the same values and that it could perform its work more efficiently by simply moving the existing elements within the HTML document.

This problem affects only two elements in this example, but the problem is much more severe when the data in the application is refreshed from an external data source using Ajax, where all the data model objects can be replaced each time a response is received. Since it is not aware that there have been few real changes, the ngFor directive has to destroy all of its HTML elements and re-create them, which can be an expensive and time-consuming operation.

To improve the efficiency of an update, you can define a component method that will help Angular determine when two different objects represent the same data, as shown in Listing 13-11.

Listing 13-11. Adding the Object Comparison Method in the component.ts File in the src/app Folder

```
import { ApplicationRef, Component } from "@angular/core";
import { Model } from "./repository.model";
import { Product } from "./product.model";

@Component({
    selector: "app",
    templateUrl: "template.html"
})
export class ProductComponent {
    model: Model = new Model();

    // ...constructor and methods omitted for brevity...

    getKey(index: number, product: Product) {
        return product.id;
    }
}
```

The method has to define two parameters: the position of the object in the data source and the data object. The result of the method uniquely identifies an object, and two objects are considered to be equal if they produce the same result.

Two Product objects will be considered equal if they have the same id value. Telling the ngFor expression to use the comparison method is done by adding a trackBy term to the expression, as shown in Listing 13-12.

Listing 13-12. Providing an Equality Method in the template.html File in the src/app Folder

```
<div class="text-white m-2">
  <div class="bg-info p-2">
    There are {{getProductCount()}} products.
  </div>

  <table class="table table-sm table-bordered mt-1">
    <tr class="text-dark">
      <th></th><th>Name</th><th>Category</th><th>Price</th>
    </tr>
    <tr *ngFor="let item of getProducts(); let i = index; let odd = odd;
          let first = first; let last = last; trackBy:getKey"
        [class.bg-primary]="odd" [class.bg-info]="!odd"
        [class.bg-warning]="first || last">
      <td>{{i + 1}}</td>
      <td>{{item.name}}</td>
      <td>{{item.category}}</td>
      <td *ngIf="!last">{{item.price}}</td>
    </tr>
  </table>
</div>
```

With this change, the ngFor directive will know that the Product that is removed from the array using the swapProduct method defined in Listing 13-12 is equivalent to the one that is added to the array, even though they are different objects. Rather than delete and create elements, the existing elements can be moved, which is a much simpler and quicker task to perform.

Changes can still be made to the elements—such as by the ngIf directive, which will remove one of the td elements because the new object will be the last item in the data source, but even this is faster than treating the objects separately.

TESTING THE EQUALITY METHOD

Checking whether the equality method has an effect is a little tricky. The best way that I have found requires using the browser's F12 developer tools, in this case using the Chrome browser.

Once the application has loaded, right-click the td element that contains the word *Kayak* in the browser window and select Inspect from the pop-up menu. This will open the Developer Tools window and show the Elements panel.

Click the ellipsis button (marked ...) in the left margin and select Add Attribute from the menu. Add an id attribute with the value old. This will result in an element that looks like this:

```
<td id="old">Kayak</td>
```

Adding an id attribute makes it possible to access the object that represents the HTML element using the JavaScript console. Switch to the Console panel and enter the following statement:

```
window.old
```

When you hit Return, the browser will locate the element by its id attribute value and display the following result:

```
<td id="old">Kayak</td>
```

Now execute the following statements in the JavaScript console, hitting Return after each one:

```
model.swapProduct()
appRef.tick()
```

Once the change to the data model has been processed, executing the following statement in the JavaScript console will determine whether the td element to which the id attribute was added has been moved or destroyed:

```
window.old
```

If the element has been moved, then you will see the element shown in the console, like this:

```
<td id="old">Kayak</td>
```

If the element has been destroyed, then there won't be an element whose id attribute is old, and the browser will display the word undefined.

Using the ngTemplateOutlet Directive

The ngTemplateOutlet directive is used to repeat a block of content at a specified location, which can be useful when you need to generate the same content in different places and want to avoid duplication. Listing 13-13 shows the directive in use.

Listing 13-13. Using the ngTemplateOutlet Directive in the template.html File in the src/app Folder

```
<ng-template #titleTemplate>
  <h4 class="p-2 bg-success text-white">Repeated Content</h4>
</ng-template>

<ng-template [ngTemplateOutlet]="titleTemplate"></ng-template>

<div class="bg-info p-2 m-2 text-white">
  There are {{getProductCount()}} products.
</div>

<ng-template [ngTemplateOutlet]="titleTemplate"></ng-template>
```

The first step is to define the template that contains the content that you want to repeat using the directive. This is done using the ng-template element and assigning it a name using a *reference variable*, like this:

```
...
<ng-template #titleTemplate let-title="title">
  <h4 class="p-2 bg-success text-white">Repeated Content</h4>
</ng-template>
...
```

When Angular encounters a reference variable, it sets its value to the element to which it has been defined, which is the ng-template element in this case. The second step is to insert the content into the HTML document, using the ngTemplateOutlet directive, like this:

```
...
<ng-template [ngTemplateOutlet]="titleTemplate"></ng-template>
...
```

The expression is the name of the reference variable that was assigned to the content that should be inserted. The directive replaces the host element with the contents of the specified ng-template element. Neither the ng-template element that contains the repeated content nor the one that is the host element for the binding is included in the HTML document. Figure 13-10 shows how the directive has used the repeated content.

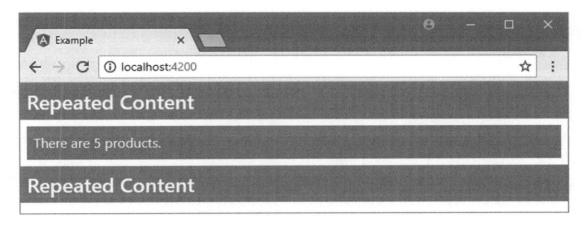

Figure 13-10. *Using the ngTemplateOutlet directive*

Providing Context Data

The ngTemplateOutlet directive can be used to provide the repeated content with a context object that can be used in data bindings defined within the ng-template element, as shown in Listing 13-14.

Listing 13-14. Providing Context Data in the template.html File in the src/app Folder

```
<ng-template #titleTemplate let-text="title">
  <h4 class="p-2 bg-success text-white">{{text}}</h4>
</ng-template>

<ng-template [ngTemplateOutlet]="titleTemplate"
             [ngTemplateOutletContext]="{title: 'Header'}">
</ng-template>

<div class="bg-info p-2 m-2 text-white">
  There are {{getProductCount()}} products.
</div>

<ng-template [ngTemplateOutlet]="titleTemplate"
             [ngTemplateOutletContext]="{title: 'Footer'}">
</ng-template>
```

To receive the context data, the `ng-template` element that contains the repeated content defines a `let-` attribute that specifies the name of a variable, similar to the expanded syntax used for the `ngFor` directive. The value of the expression assigns the `let-` variable a value, like this:

```
...
<ng-template #titleTemplate let-text="title">
...
```

The `let-` attribute in this example creates a variable called `text`, which is assigned a value by evaluating the expression `title`. To provide the data against which the expression is evaluated, the `ng-template` element to which the `ngTemplateOutletContext` directive has been applied provides a map object, like this:

```
...
<ng-template [ngTemplateOutlet]="titleTemplate"
        [ngTemplateOutletContext]="{title: 'Footer'}">
</ng-template>
...
```

The target of this new binding is `ngTemplateOutletContext`, which looks like another directive but is actually an example of an *input property*, which some directives use to receive data values and that I describe in detail in Chapter 15. The expression for the binding is a map object whose property name corresponds to the `let-` attribute on the other `ng-template` element. The result is that the repeated content can be tailored using bindings, as shown in Figure 13-11.

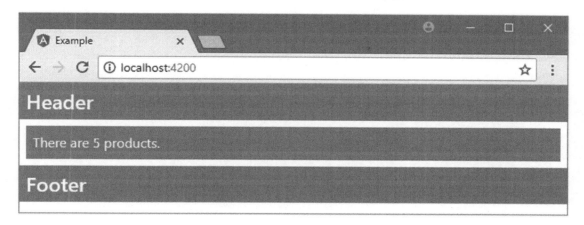

Figure 13-11. *Providing context data for repeated content*

Understanding One-Way Data Binding Restrictions

Although the expressions used in one-way data binding and directives look like JavaScript code, you can't use all the JavaScript—or TypeScript—language features. I explain the restrictions and the reasons for them in the sections that follow.

Using Idempotent Expressions

One-way data bindings must be *idempotent*, meaning that they can be evaluated repeatedly without changing the state of the application. To demonstrate why, I added a debugging statement to the component's getProductCount method, as shown in Listing 13-15.

■ **Note**   Angular *does* support modifying the application state, but it must be done using the techniques I describe in Chapter 14.

Listing 13-15. Adding a Statement in the component.ts File in the src/app Folder

```
...
getProductCount(): number {
    console.log("getProductCount invoked");
    return this.getProducts().length;
}
...
```

When the changes are saved and the browser reloads the page, you will see a long series of messages like these in the browser's JavaScript console:

```
...
getProductCount invoked
getProductCount invoked
```

```
getProductCount invoked
getProductCount invoked
...
```

As the messages show, Angular evaluates the binding expression several times before displaying the content in the browser. If an expression modifies the state of an application, such as removing an object from a queue, you won't get the results you expect by the time the template is displayed to the user. To avoid this problem, Angular restricts the way that expressions can be used. In Listing 13-16, I added a `counter` property to the component to help demonstrate.

Listing 13-16. Adding a Property in the component.ts File in the src/app Folder

```typescript
import { ApplicationRef, Component } from "@angular/core";
import { Model } from "./repository.model";
import { Product } from "./product.model";

@Component({
    selector: "app",
    templateUrl: "template.html"
})
export class ProductComponent {
    model: Model = new Model();

    // ...constructor and methods omitted for brevity...

    targetName: string = "Kayak";

    counter: number = 1;
}
```

In Listing 13-17, I added a binding whose expression increments the counter when it is evaluated.

Listing 13-17. Adding a Binding in the template.html File in the src/app Folder

```html
<ng-template #titleTemplate let-text="title">
  <h4 class="p-2 bg-success text-white">{{text}}</h4>
</ng-template>

<ng-template [ngTemplateOutlet]="titleTemplate"
             [ngTemplateOutletContext]="{title: 'Header'}">
</ng-template>

<div class="bg-info p-2 m-2 text-white">
  There are {{getProductCount()}} products.
</div>

<ng-template [ngTemplateOutlet]="titleTemplate"
             [ngTemplateOutletContext]="{title: 'Footer'}">
</ng-template>

<div class="bg-info p-2">
  Counter: {{counter = counter + 1}}
</div>
```

When the browser loads the page, you will see an error in the JavaScript console, like this:

```
...
EXCEPTION: Template parse errors:
Parser Error: Bindings cannot contain assignments at column 11 in [
        Counter: {{counter = counter + 1}}
in ng:///AppModule/ProductComponent.html@16:25 ("]
...
```

Angular will report an error if a data binding expression contains an operator that can be used to perform an assignment, such as =, +=, -+, ++, and --. In addition, when Angular is running in development mode, it performs an additional check to make sure that one-way data bindings have not been modified after their expressions are evaluated. To demonstrate, Listing 13-18 adds a property to the component that removes and returns a Product object from the model array.

Listing 13-18. Modifying Data in the component.ts File in the src/app Folder

```typescript
import { ApplicationRef, Component } from "@angular/core";
import { Model } from "./repository.model";
import { Product } from "./product.model";

@Component({
    selector: "app",
    templateUrl: "template.html"
})
export class ProductComponent {
    model: Model = new Model();

    // ...constructor and methods omitted for brevity...

    counter: number = 1;

    get nextProduct(): Product {
        return this.model.getProducts().shift();
    }
}
```

In Listing 13-19, you can see the data binding that I used to read the nextProduct property.

Listing 13-19. Binding to a Property in the template.html File in the src/app Folder

```html
<ng-template #titleTemplate let-text="title">
  <h4 class="p-2 bg-success text-white">{{text}}</h4>
</ng-template>

<ng-template [ngTemplateOutlet]="titleTemplate"
             [ngTemplateOutletContext]="{title: 'Header'}">
</ng-template>

<div class="bg-info p-2 m-2 text-white">
  There are {{getProductCount()}} products.
</div>
```

```
<ng-template [ngTemplateOutlet]="titleTemplate"
             [ngTemplateOutletContext]="{title: 'Footer'}">
</ng-template>
```

```
<div class="bg-info p-2 text-white">
  Next Product is {{nextProduct.name}}
</div>
```

When you save the changes and Angular processes the template, you will see that the attempt to change the application data in the data binding produces the following error in the JavaScript console:

```
...
Error: ExpressionChangedAfterItHasBeenCheckedError: Expression has changed after it was
checked. Previous value: 'null: 4'. Current value: 'null: 3'.
...
```

Understanding the Expression Context

When Angular evaluates an expression, it does so in the context of the template's component, which is how the template is able to access methods and properties without any kind of prefix, like this:

```
...
<div class="bg-info p-2">
    There are {{getProductCount()}} products.
</div>
...
```

When Angular processes these expressions, the component provides the getProductCount method, which Angular invokes with the specified arguments and then incorporates the result into the HTML document. The component is said to provide the template's *expression context*.

The expression context means you can't access objects defined outside of the template's component and, in particular, templates can't access the global namespace. The global namespace is used to define common utilities, such as the console object, which defines the log method I have been using to write out debugging information to the browser's JavaScript console. The global namespace also includes the Math object, which provides access to some useful arithmetical methods, such as min and max.

To demonstrate this restriction, Listing 13-20 adds a string interpolation binding to the template that relies on the Math.floor method to round down a number value to the nearest integer.

Listing 13-20. Accessing the Global Namespace in the template.html File in the src/app Folder

```
<ng-template #titleTemplate let-text="title">
  <h4 class="p-2 bg-success text-white">{{text}}</h4>
</ng-template>
```

```
<ng-template [ngTemplateOutlet]="titleTemplate"
             [ngTemplateOutletContext]="{title: 'Header'}">
</ng-template>
```

```
<div class="bg-info p-2 m-2 text-white">
  There are {{getProductCount()}} products.
</div>
```

```
<ng-template [ngTemplateOutlet]="titleTemplate"
             [ngTemplateOutletContext]="{title: 'Footer'}">
</ng-template>
```

```
<div class='bg-info p-2'>
  The rounded price is {{Math.floor(getProduct(1).price)}}
</div>
```

When Angular processes the template, it will produce the following error in the browser's JavaScript console:

```
EXCEPTION: TypeError: Cannot read property 'floor' of undefined
```

The error message doesn't specifically mention the global namespace. Instead, Angular has tried to evaluate the expression using the component as the context and failed to find a Math property.

If you want to access functionality in the global namespace, then it must be provided by the component, acting as on behalf of the template. In the case of the example, the component could just define a Math property that is assigned to the global object, but template expressions should be as clear and simple as possible, so a better approach is to define a method that provides the template with the specific functionality it requires, as shown in Listing 13-21.

Listing 13-21. Defining a Method in the component.ts File in the src/app Folder

```
import { ApplicationRef, Component } from "@angular/core";
import { Model } from "./repository.model";
import { Product } from "./product.model";

@Component({
    selector: "app",
    templateUrl: "template.html"
})
export class ProductComponent {
    model: Model = new Model();

    // ...constructor and methods omitted for brevity...

    counter: number = 1;

    get nextProduct(): Product {
        return this.model.getProducts().shift();
    }

    getProductPrice(index: number): number {
        return Math.floor(this.getProduct(index).price);
    }
}
```

In Listing 13-22, I have changed the data binding in the template to use the newly defined method.

Listing 13-22. Access Global Namespace Functionality in the template.html File in the src/app Folder

```
<ng-template #titleTemplate let-text="title">
  <h4 class="p-2 bg-success text-white">{{text}}</h4>
</ng-template>

<ng-template [ngTemplateOutlet]="titleTemplate"
             [ngTemplateOutletContext]="{title: 'Header'}">
</ng-template>

<div class="bg-info p-2 m-2 text-white">
  There are {{getProductCount()}} products.
</div>

<ng-template [ngTemplateOutlet]="titleTemplate"
             [ngTemplateOutletContext]="{title: 'Footer'}">
</ng-template>

<div class="bg-info p-2 text-white">
  The rounded price is {{getProductPrice(1)}}
</div>
```

When Angular processes the template, it will call the getProductPrice method and indirectly take advantage of the Math object in the global namespace, producing the result shown in Figure 13-12.

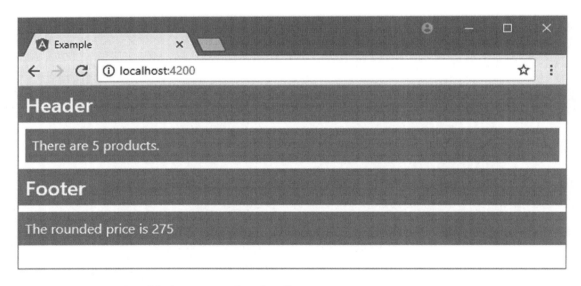

Figure 13-12. *Accessing global namespace functionality*

Summary

In this chapter, I explained how to use the built-in template directives. I showed you how to select content with the ngIf and ngSwitch directives and how to repeat content using the ngFor directive. I explained why some directive names are prefixed with an asterisk and described the limitations that are placed on template expressions used with these directives and with one-way data bindings in general. In the next chapter, I describe how data bindings are used for events and form elements.

CHAPTER 14

■ ■ ■

Using Events and Forms

In this chapter, I continue describing the basic Angular functionality, focusing on features that respond to user interaction. I explain how to create event bindings and how to use two-way bindings to manage the flow of data between the model and the template. One of the main forms of user interaction in a web application is the use of HTML forms, and I explain how event and two-way data bindings are used to support them and validate the content that the user provides. Table 14-1 puts events and forms in context.

Table 14-1. *Putting Event Bindings and Forms in Context*

Question	Answer
What are they?	Event bindings evaluate an expression when an event is triggered, such as a user pressing a key, moving the mouse, or submitting a form. The broader form-related features build on this foundation to create forms that are automatically validated to ensure that the user provides useful data.
Why are they useful?	These features allow the user to change the state of the application, changing or adding to the data in the model.
How are they used?	Each feature is used in a different way. See the examples for details.
Are there any pitfalls or limitations?	In common with all Angular bindings, the main pitfall is using the wrong kind of bracket to denote a binding. Pay close attention to the examples in this chapter and check the way you have applied bindings when you don't get the results you expect.
Are there any alternatives?	No. These features are a core part of Angular.

© Adam Freeman 2018
A. Freeman, *Pro Angular 6*, https://doi.org/10.1007/978-1-4842-3649-9_14

Table 14-2 summarizes the chapter.

Table 14-2. Chapter Summary

Problem	Solution	Listing
Enable forms support	Add the @angular/forms module to the application	1–3
Respond to an event	Use an event binding	4–6
Get details of an event	Use the $event object	7
Refer to elements in the template	Define template variables	8
Enable the flow of data in both directions between the element and the component	Use a two-way data binding	9, 10
Capture user input	Use an HTML form	11, 12
Validate the data provided by the user	Perform form validation	13–22
Define validation information using JavaScript code	Use a model-based form	23–28
Extend the built-in form validation features	Define a custom form validation class	29–30

Preparing the Example Project

For this chapter, I will continue using the example project that I created in Chapter 11 and have been modifying in the chapters since.

■ **Tip** You can download the example project for this chapter—and for all the other chapters in this book—from `https://github.com/Apress/pro-angular-6`.

Importing the Forms Module

The features demonstrated in this chapter rely on the Angular forms module, which must be imported to the Angular module, as shown in Listing 14-1.

Listing 14-1. Declaring a Dependency in the app.module.ts File in the src/app Folder

```
import { BrowserModule } from '@angular/platform-browser';
import { NgModule } from '@angular/core';
import { ProductComponent } from "./component";
import { FormsModule } from "@angular/forms";

@NgModule({
  declarations: [ProductComponent],
  imports: [BrowserModule, FormsModule],
  providers: [],
  bootstrap: [ProductComponent]
})
export class AppModule { }
```

The `imports` property of the `NgModule` decorator specifies the dependencies of the application. Adding `FormsModule` to the list of dependencies enables the form features and makes them available for use throughout the application.

Preparing the Component and Template

Listing 14-2 removes the constructor and some of the methods from the component class to keep the code as simple as possible.

Listing 14-2. Simplifying the Component in the component.ts File in the src/app Folder

```
import { ApplicationRef, Component } from "@angular/core";
import { Model } from "./repository.model";
import { Product } from "./product.model";

@Component({
    selector: "app",
    templateUrl: "template.html"
})
export class ProductComponent {
    model: Model = new Model();

    getProduct(key: number): Product {
        return this.model.getProduct(key);
    }

    getProducts(): Product[] {
        return this.model.getProducts();
    }
}
```

Listing 14-3 simplifies the component's template, leaving just a table that is populated using the `ngFor` directive.

Listing 14-3. Simplifying the Template in the template.html File in the src/app Folder

```
<div class="m-2">
  <table class="table table-sm table-bordered">
    <tr><th></th><th>Name</th><th>Category</th><th>Price</th></tr>
    <tr *ngFor="let item of getProducts(); let i = index">
      <td>{{i + 1}}</td>
      <td>{{item.name}}</td>
      <td>{{item.category}}</td>
      <td>{{item.price}}</td>
    </tr>
  </table>
</div>
```

To start the development server, open a command prompt, navigate to the example folder, and run the following command:

```
ng serve
```

Open a new browser window and navigate to http://localhost:4200 to see the table shown in Figure 14-1.

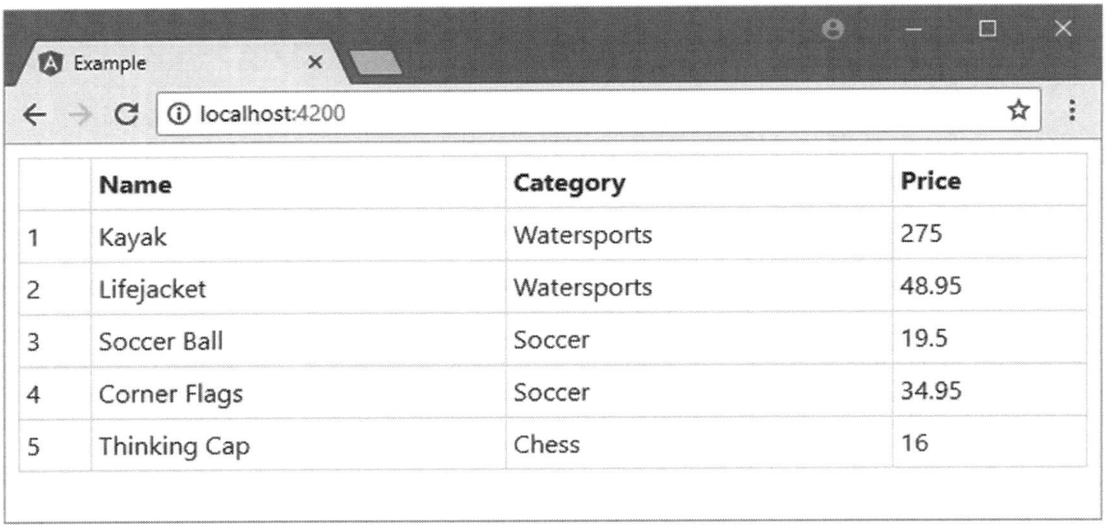

Figure 14-1. *Running the example application*

Using the Event Binding

The *event binding* is used to respond to the events sent by the host element. Listing 14-4 demonstrates the event binding, which allows a user to interact with an Angular application.

Listing 14-4. Using the Event Binding in the template.html File in the src/app Folder

```
<div class="m-2">
  <div class="bg-info text-white p-2">
    Selected Product: {{selectedProduct || '(None)'}}
  </div>
  <table class="table table-sm table-bordered m-2">
    <tr><th></th><th>Name</th><th>Category</th><th>Price</th></tr>
    <tr *ngFor="let item of getProducts(); let i = index">
      <td (mouseover)="selectedProduct=item.name">{{i + 1}}</td>
      <td>{{item.name}}</td>
      <td>{{item.category}}</td>
      <td>{{item.price}}</td>
    </tr>
  </table>
</div>
```

When you save the changes to the template, you can test the binding by moving the mouse pointer over the first column in the HTML table, which displays a series of numbers. As the mouse moves from row to row, the name of the product displayed in that row is displayed at the top of the page, as shown in Figure 14-2.

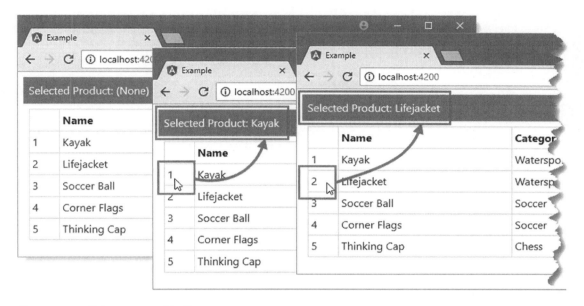

Figure 14-2. *Using an event binding*

This is a simple example, but it shows the structure of an event binding, which is illustrated in Figure 14-3.

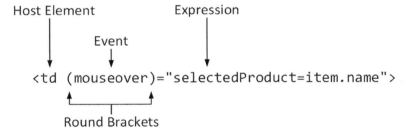

Figure 14-3. *The anatomy of an event binding*

An event binding has these four parts:

- The *host element* is the source of events for the binding.

- The *round brackets* tell Angular that this is an event binding, which is a form of one-way binding where data flows from the element to the rest of the application.

- The *event* specifies which event the binding is for.

- The *expression* is evaluated when the event is triggered.

Looking at the binding in Listing 14-4, you can see that the host element is a td element, meaning that this is the element that will be the source of events. The binding specifies the mouseover event, which is triggered when the mouse pointer moves over the part of the screen occupied by the host element.

Unlike one-way bindings, the expressions in event bindings are allowed to make changes to the state of the application and can contain assignment operators, such as =. The expression for the binding assigns a variable called selectedProduct a value of item.name. The selectedProduct variable is used in a string interpolation binding at the top of the template, like this:

```
...
<div class="bg-info text-white p-2">
    Selected Product: {{selectedProduct || '(None)'}}
</div>
...
```

The value displayed by the string interpolation binding is updated when the value of the selectedProduct variable is changed by the event binding. Manually starting the change detection process using the ApplicationRef.tick method is no longer required because the bindings and directives in this chapter take care of the process automatically.

WORKING WITH DOM EVENTS

If you are unfamiliar with the events that an HTML element can send, then there is a good summary available at developer.mozilla.org/en-US/docs/Web/Events. There are a lot of events, however, and not all of them are supported widely or consistently in all browsers. A good place to start is the "DOM Events" and "HTML DOM Events" sections of the mozilla.org page, which define the basic interactions that a user has with an element (clicking, moving the pointer, submitting forms, and so on) and that can be relied on to work in most browsers.

If you use the less common events, then you should make sure they are available and work as expected in your target browsers. The excellent http://caniuse.com provides details of which features are implemented by different browsers, but you should also perform thorough testing.

Understanding Dynamically Defined Properties

You may be wondering where the selectedProduct variable appeared from in Listing 14-4 because it is used in the template without being first defined in the component. In fact, it was created the first time the event binding was triggered because JavaScript allows properties to be added to objects dynamically.

The object, in this case, is the component, and this example is a useful reminder that while TypeScript adds structure when you are writing code, the Angular application is plain JavaScript at runtime. This means you can take advantage of JavaScript's dynamic features when it is useful to do so. It also means you can create unexpected results if you are not paying attention, so care is required.

Although you can define properties dynamically, a safer approach is to define all the properties that a template uses in the component, and this is something that you will have to do if you write other methods and properties that depend on them; otherwise, the TypeScript compiler will report errors. In Listing 14-5, the component has been updated to keep track of the selected product, which means defining the selectedProduct property that was previously created dynamically.

Listing 14-5. Enhancing the Component in the component.ts File in the src/app Folder

```
import { ApplicationRef, Component } from "@angular/core";
import { Model } from "./repository.model";
import { Product } from "./product.model";

@Component({
    selector: "app",
    templateUrl: "template.html"
})
export class ProductComponent {
    model: Model = new Model();

    getProduct(key: number): Product {
        return this.model.getProduct(key);
    }

    getProducts(): Product[] {
        return this.model.getProducts();
    }

    selectedProduct: string;

    getSelected(product: Product): boolean {
        return product.name == this.selectedProduct;
    }
}
```

In addition to the selectedProduct property, there is a new method called getSelected that accepts a
Product object and compares its name to the selectedProduct property. In Listing 14-6, the getSelected
method is used by a class binding to control membership of the bg-info class, which is a Bootstrap class that
assigns a background color to an element.

Listing 14-6. Setting Class Membership in the template.html File in the src/app Folder

```
<div class="m-2">
  <div class="bg-info text-white p-2">
    Selected Product: {{selectedProduct || '(None)'}}
  </div>
  <table class="table table-sm table-bordered m-2">
    <tr><th></th><th>Name</th><th>Category</th><th>Price</th></tr>
    <tr *ngFor="let item of getProducts(); let i = index"
        [class.bg-info]="getSelected(item)">
      <td (mouseover)="selectedProduct=item.name">{{i + 1}}</td>
      <td>{{item.name}}</td>
      <td>{{item.category}}</td>
      <td>{{item.price}}</td>
    </tr>
  </table>
</div>
```

The result is that tr elements are added to the bg-info class when the selectedProduct property value matches the name property of the Product object used to create them, which is changed by the event binding when the mouseover event is triggered, as shown in Figure 14-4.

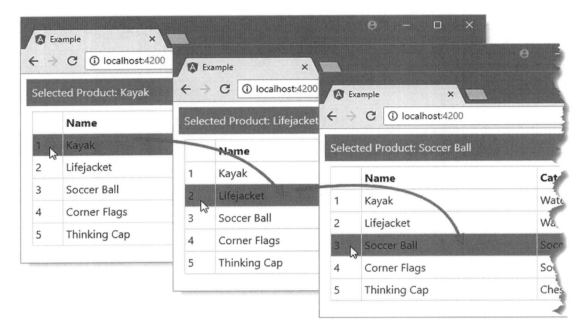

Figure 14-4. *Highlighting table rows through an event binding*

This example shows how user interaction drives new data into the application and starts the change-detection process, causing Angular to reevaluate the expressions used by the string interpolation and class bindings. This flow of data is what brings Angular applications to life: the bindings and directives described in Chapters 12 and 13 respond dynamically to changes in the application state, creating content generated and managed entirely within the browser.

Using Event Data

The previous example used the event binding to connect two pieces of data provided by the component: when the mouseevent is triggered, the binding's expression sets the selectedProduct property using a data value that was provided to the ngfor directive by the component's getProducts method.

The event binding can also be used to introduce new data into the application from the event itself, using details that are provided by the browser. Listing 14-7 adds an input element to the template and uses the event binding to listen for the input event, which is triggered when the content of the input element changes.

Listing 14-7. Using an Event Object in the template.html File in the src/app Folder

```
<div class="m-2">
  <div class="bg-info text-white p-2">
    Selected Product: {{selectedProduct || '(None)'}}
```

```
    </div>
    <table class="table table-sm table-bordered m-2">
      <tr><th></th><th>Name</th><th>Category</th><th>Price</th><th></th></tr>
      <tr *ngFor="let item of getProducts(); let i = index"
          [class.bg-info]="getSelected(item)">
        <td (mouseover)="selectedProduct=item.name">{{i + 1}}</td>
        <td>{{item.name}}</td>
        <td>{{item.category}}</td>
        <td>{{item.price}}</td>
      </tr>
    </table>
    <div class="form-group">
      <label>Product Name</label>
      <input class="form-control" (input)="selectedProduct=$event.target.value" />
    </div>
</div>
```

When the browser triggers an event, it provides an object that describes it. There are different types of event object for different categories of event (mouse events, keyboard events, form events, and so on), but all events share the three properties described in Table 14-3.

Table 14-3. *The Properties Common to All DOM Event Objects*

Name	Description
type	This property returns a string that identifies the type of event that has been triggered.
target	This property returns the object that triggered the event, which will generally be the object that represents the HTML element in the DOM.
timeStamp	This property returns a number that contains the time that the event was triggered, expressed as milliseconds since January 1, 1970.

The event object is assigned to a template variable called $event, and the binding expression in Listing 14-7 uses this variable to access the event object's target property.

The input element is represented in the DOM by an HTMLInputElement object, which defines a value property that can be used to get and set the contents of the input element. The binding expression responds to the input event by setting the value of the component's selectedProduct property to the value of the input element's value property, like this:

```
...
<input class="form-control" (input)="selectedProduct=$event.target.value" />
...
```

The input event is triggered when the user edits the contents of the input element, so the component's selectedProduct property is updated with the contents of the input element after each keystroke. As the user types into the input element, the text that has been entered is displayed at the top of the browser window using the string interpolation binding.

The ngClass binding applied to the tr elements sets the background color of the table rows when the selectedProduct property matches the name of the product they represent. And, now that the value of the selectedProduct property is driven by the contents of the input element, typing the name of a product will cause the appropriate row to be highlighted, as shown in Figure 14-5.

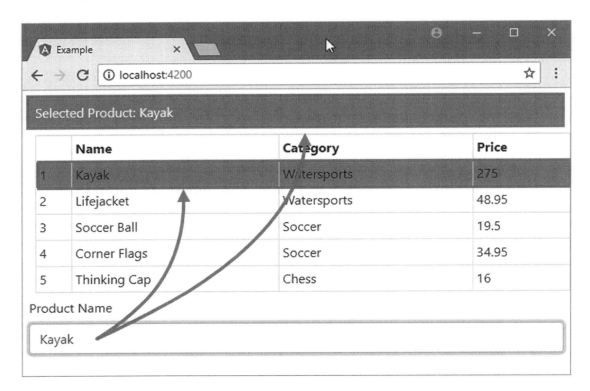

Figure 14-5. *Using event data*

Using different bindings to work together is at the heart of effective Angular development and makes it possible to create applications that respond immediately to user interaction and to changes in the data model.

Using Template Reference Variables

In Chapter 13, I explained how template variables are used to pass data around within a template, such as defining a variable for the current object when using the ngFor directive. *Template reference variables* are a form of template variable that can be used to refer to elements *within* the template, as shown in Listing 14-8.

Listing 14-8. Using a Template Variable in the template.html File in the src/app Folder

```
<div class="m-2">
  <div class="bg-info text-white p-2">
    Selected Product: {{product.value || '(None)'}}
  </div>
  <table class="table table-sm table-bordered m-2">
```

```
      <tr><th></th><th>Name</th><th>Category</th><th>Price</th></tr>
      <tr *ngFor="let item of getProducts(); let i = index"
          (mouseover)="product.value=item.name"
          [class.bg-info]="product.value==item.name">
        <td (mouseover)="selectedProduct=item.name">{{i + 1}}</td>
        <td>{{item.name}}</td>
        <td>{{item.category}}</td>
        <td>{{item.price}}</td>
      </tr>
    </table>
    <div class="form-group">
      <label>Product Name</label>
      <input #product class="form-control" (input)="false" />
    </div>
</div>
```

Reference variables are defined using the # character, followed by the variable name. In the listing, I defined a variable called product like this:

```
...
<input #product class="form-control" (input)="false" />
...
```

When Angular encounters a reference variable in a template, it sets its value to the element to which it has been applied. For this example, the product reference variable is assigned the object that represents the input element in the DOM, the HTMLInputElement object. Reference variables can be used by other bindings in the same template. This is demonstrated by the string interpolation binding, which also uses product variable, like this:

```
...
Selected Product: {{product.value || '(None)'}}
...
```

This binding displays the value property defined by the HTMLInputElement that has been assigned to the product variable or the string (None) if the value property returns null. Template variables can also be used to change the state of the element, as shown in this binding:

```
...
<tr *ngFor="let item of getProducts(); let i = index"
    (mouseover)="product.value=item.name"
    [class.bg-info]="product.value==item.name">
...
```

The event binding responds the mouseover event by setting the value property on the HTMLInputElement that has been assigned to the product variable. The result is that moving the mouse over one of the tr elements will update the contents of the input element.

There is one awkward aspect to this example, which is the binding for the input event on the input element.

```
...
<input #product class="form-control" (input)="false" />
...
```

301

Angular won't update the data bindings in the template when the user edits the contents of the input element unless there is an event binding on that element. Setting the binding to false gives Angular something to evaluate just so the update process will begin and distribute the current contents of the input element throughout the template. This is a quirk of stretching the role of a template reference variable a little too far and isn't something you will need to do in most real projects. As you will see in later examples—and later chapters—most data bindings rely on variables defined by the template's component.

FILTERING KEY EVENTS

The input event is triggered every time the content in the input element is changed. This provides an immediate and responsive set of changes, but it isn't what every application requires, especially if updating the application state involves expensive operations.

The event binding has built-in support to be more selective when binding to keyboard events, which means that updates will be performed only when a specific key is pressed. Here is a binding that responds to every keystroke:

```
...
<input #product class="form-control" (keyup)="selectedProduct=product.value" />
...
```

The keyup event is a standard DOM event, and the result is that application is updated as the user releases each key while typing in the input element. I can be more specific about which key I am interested in by specifying its name as part of the event binding, like this:

```
...
<input #product class="form-control"
    (keyup.enter)="selectedProduct=product.value" />
...
```

The key that the binding will respond to is specified by appending a period after the DOM event name, followed by the name of the key. This binding is for the enter key, and the result is that the changes in the input element won't be pushed into the rest of the application until that key is pressed.

Using Two-Way Data Bindings

Bindings can be combined to create a two-way flow of data for a single element, allowing the HTML document to respond when the application model changes and also allowing the application to respond when the element emits an event, as shown in Listing 14-9.

Listing 14-9. Creating a Two-Way Binding in the template.html File in the src/app Folder

```
<div class="m-2">
  <div class="bg-info text-white p-2">
    Selected Product: {{selectedProduct || '(None)'}}
  </div>
  <table class="table table-sm table-bordered m-2">
    <tr><th></th><th>Name</th><th>Category</th><th>Price</th></tr>
    <tr *ngFor="let item of getProducts(); let i = index"
        [class.bg-info]="getSelected(item)">
      <td (mouseover)="selectedProduct=item.name">{{i + 1}}</td>
```

```
        <td>{{item.name}}</td>
        <td>{{item.category}}</td>
        <td>{{item.price}}</td>
      </tr>
    </table>
    <div class="form-group">
      <label>Product Name</label>
      <input class="form-control" (input)="selectedProduct=$event.target.value"
          [value]="selectedProduct || "" />
    </div>
    <div class="form-group">
      <label>Product Name</label>
      <input class="form-control" (input)="selectedProduct=$event.target.value"
          [value]="selectedProduct || "" />
    </div>
</div>
```

Each of the input elements has an event binding and a property binding. The event binding responds to the input event by updating the component's selectedProduct property. The property binding ties the value of the selectedProduct property to the element's value property.

The result is that the contents of the two input elements are synchronized, and editing one causes the other to be updated as well. And, since there are other bindings in the template that depend on the selectedProduct property, editing the contents of an input element also changes the data displayed by string interpolation binding and changes the highlighted table row, as shown in Figure 14-6.

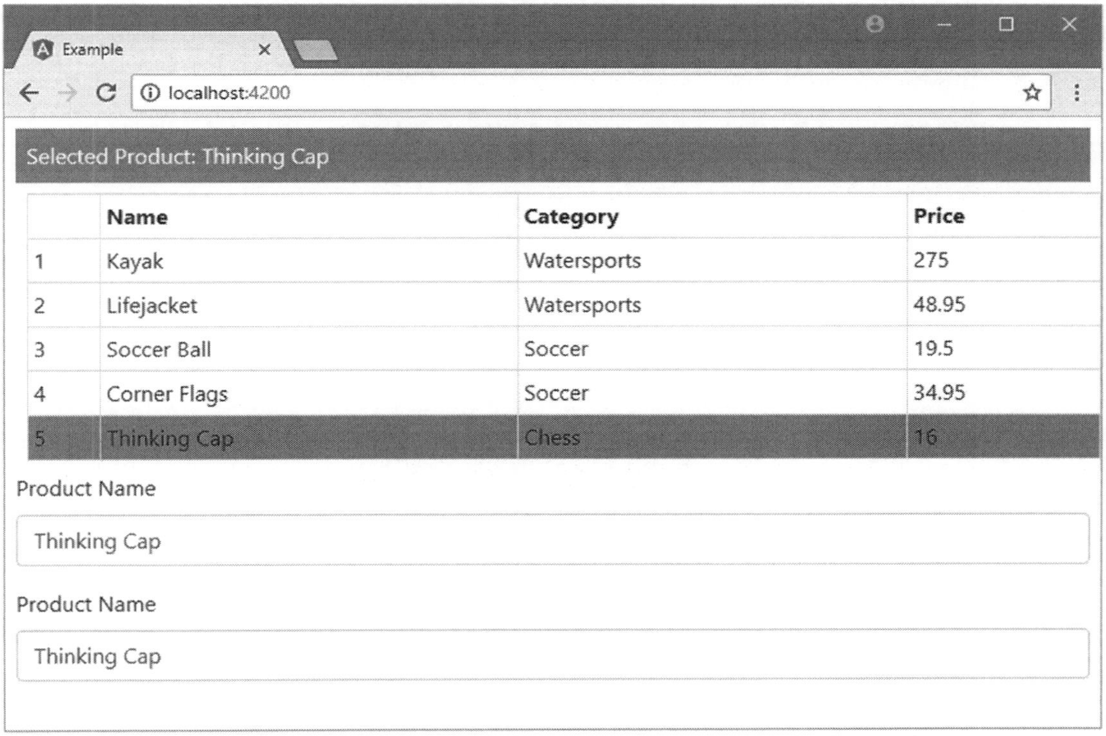

Figure 14-6. *Creating a two-way data binding*

This is an example that makes the most sense when you experiment with it in the browser. Enter some text into one of the input elements and you will see the same text displayed in the other input element and in the div element whose content is managed by the string interpolation binding. If you enter the name of a product into one of the input elements, such as Kayak or Lifejacket, then you will also see the corresponding row in the table highlighted.

The event binding for the mouseover event still takes effect, which means as you move the mouse pointer over the first row in the table, the changes to the selectedProduct value will cause the input elements to display the product name.

Using the ngModel Directive

The ngModel directive is used to simplify two-way bindings so that you don't need to apply both an event and a property binding to the same element. Listing 14-10 shows how to replace the separate bindings with the ngModel directive.

Listing 14-10. Using the ngModel Directive in the template.html File in the src/app Folder

```
<div class="m-2">
  <div class="bg-info text-white p-2">
    Selected Product: {{selectedProduct || '(None)'}}
  </div>
  <table class="table table-sm table-bordered m-2">
    <tr><th></th><th>Name</th><th>Category</th><th>Price</th></tr>
    <tr *ngFor="let item of getProducts(); let i = index"
        [class.bg-info]="getSelected(item)">
      <td (mouseover)="selectedProduct=item.name">{{i + 1}}</td>
      <td>{{item.name}}</td>
      <td>{{item.category}}</td>
      <td>{{item.price}}</td>
    </tr>
  </table>
  <div class="form-group">
    <label>Product Name</label>
    <input class="form-control" [(ngModel)]="selectedProduct" />
  </div>
  <div class="form-group">
    <label>Product Name</label>
    <input class="form-control" [(ngModel)]="selectedProduct" />
  </div>
</div>
```

Using the ngModel directive requires combining the syntax of the property and event bindings, as illustrated in Figure 14-7.

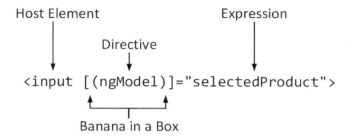

Figure 14-7. *The anatomy of a two-way data binding*

A combination of square and round brackets is used to denote a two-way data binding, with the round brackets placed inside the square ones: [(and)]. The Angular development team refers to this as the *banana-in-a-box* binding because that's what the brackets and parentheses look like when placed like this [()]. Well, sort of.

The target for the binding is the ngModel directive, which is included in Angular to simplify creating two-way data bindings on form elements, such as the input elements used in the example.

The expression for a two-way data binding is the name of a property, which is used to set up the individual bindings behind the scenes. When the contents of the input element change, the new content will be used to update the value of the selectedProduct property. Equally, when the value of the selectedProduct value changes, it will be used to update the contents of the element.

The ngModel directive knows the combination of events and properties that the standard HTML elements define. Behind the scenes, an event binding is applied to the input event, and a property binding is applied to the value property.

■ **Tip** It is important that you remember to use both brackets and parentheses with the ngModel binding. If you use just parentheses—(ngModel)—then you are setting an event binding for an event called ngModel, which doesn't exist. The result is an element that won't be updated or won't update the rest of the application. You can use the ngModel directive with just square brackets—[ngModel]—and Angular will set the initial value of the element but won't listen for events, which means that changes made by the user won't be automatically reflected in the application model.

Working with Forms

Most web applications rely on forms for receiving data from users, and the two-way ngModel binding described in the previous section provides the foundation for using forms in Angular applications. In this section, I create a form that allows new products to be created and added to the application's data model and then describe some of the more advanced form features that Angular provides.

Adding a Form to the Example Application

Listing 14-11 shows some enhancements to the component that will be used when the form is created and removes some features that are no longer required.

Listing 14-11. Enhancing the Component in the component.ts File in the src/app Folder

```
import { ApplicationRef, Component } from "@angular/core";
import { Model } from "./repository.model";
import { Product } from "./product.model";

@Component({
    selector: "app",
    templateUrl: "template.html"
})
export class ProductComponent {
    model: Model = new Model();

    getProduct(key: number): Product {
        return this.model.getProduct(key);
    }

    getProducts(): Product[] {
        return this.model.getProducts();
    }

    newProduct: Product = new Product();

    get jsonProduct() {
        return JSON.stringify(this.newProduct);
    }

    addProduct(p: Product) {
        console.log("New Product: " + this.jsonProduct);
    }
}
```

The listing adds a new property called newProduct, which will be used to store the data entered into the form by the user. There is also a jsonProduct property with a getter that returns a JSON representation of the newProduct property and that will be used in the template to show the effect of the two-way bindings. (I can't create a JSON representation of an object directly in the template because the JSON object is defined in the global namespace, which, as I explained in Chapter 13, cannot be accessed directly from template expressions.)

The final addition is an addProduct method that writes out the value of the jsonProduct method to the console; this will let me demonstrate some basic form-related features before adding support for updating the data model later in the chapter.

In Listing 14-12, the template content has been replaced with a series of input elements for each of the properties defined by the Product class.

Listing 14-12. Adding Input Elements in the template.html File in the src/app Folder

```
<div class="m-2">
  <div class="bg-info text-white mb-2 p-2">Model Data: {{jsonProduct}}</div>

  <div class="form-group">
    <label>Name</label>
    <input class="form-control" [(ngModel)]="newProduct.name" />
```

```
    </div>
    <div class="form-group">
      <label>Category</label>
      <input class="form-control" [(ngModel)]="newProduct.category" />
    </div>
    <div class="form-group">
      <label>Price</label>
      <input class="form-control" [(ngModel)]="newProduct.price" />
    </div>
    <button class="btn btn-primary" (click)="addProduct(newProduct)">Create</button>
</div>
```

Each input element is grouped together with a label and contained in a div element, which is styled using the Bootstrap form-group class. Individual input elements are assigned to the Bootstrap form-control class to manage the layout and style.

The ngModel binding has been applied to each input element to create a two-way binding with the corresponding property on the component's newProduct object, like this:

```
...
<input class="form-control" [(ngModel)]="newProduct.name" />
...
```

There is also a button element, which has a binding for the click event that calls the component's addProduct method, passing in the newProduct value as an argument.

```
...
<button class="btn btn-primary" (click)="addProduct(newProduct)">Create</button>
...
```

Finally, a string interpolation binding is used to display a JSON representation of the component's newProduct property at the top of the template, like this:

```
...
<div class="bg-info text-white mb-2 p-2">Model Data: {{jsonProduct}}</div>
...
```

The overall result, illustrated in Figure 14-8, is a set of input elements that update the properties of a Product object managed by the component, which are reflected immediately in the JSON data.

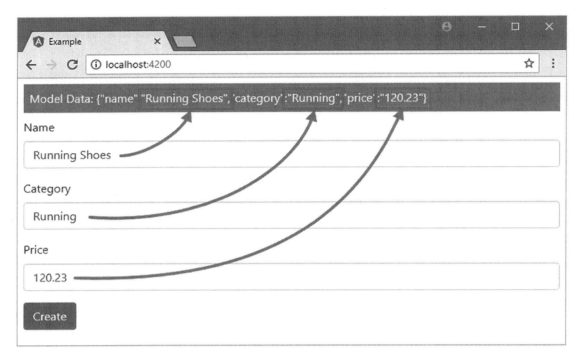

Figure 14-8. *Using the form elements to create a new object in the data model*

When the Create button is clicked, the JSON representation of the component's newProduct property is written to the browser's JavaScript console, producing a result like this:

```
New Product: {"name":"Running Shoes","category":"Running","price":"120.23"}
```

Adding Form Data Validation

At the moment, any data can be entered into the input elements in the form. Data validation is essential in web applications because users will enter a surprising range of data values, either in error or because they want to get to the end of the process as quickly as possible and enter garbage values to proceed.

Angular provides an extensible system for validating the content of form elements, based on the approach used by the HTML5 standard. There are four attributes that you can add to input elements, each of which defines a validation rule, as described in Table 14-4.

Table 14-4. *The Built-in Angular Validation Attributes*

Attribute	Description
required	This attribute is used to specify a value that must be provided.
minlength	This attribute is used to specify a minimum number of characters.
maxlength	This attribute is used to specify a maximum number of characters. This type of validation cannot be applied directly to form elements because it conflicts with the HTML5 attribute of the same name. It can be used with model-based forms, which are described later in the chapter.
pattern	This attribute is used to specify a regular expression that the value provided by the user must match.

You may be familiar with these attributes because they are part of the HTML specification, but Angular builds on these properties with some additional features. Listing 14-13 removes all but one of the input elements to demonstrate the process of adding validation to the form as simply as possible. (I restore the missing elements later in the chapter.)

Listing 14-13. Adding Form Validation in the template.html File in the src/app Folder

```
<div class="m-2">
  <div class="bg-info p-2 mb-2">Model Data: {{jsonProduct}}</div>

  <form novalidate (ngSubmit)="addProduct(newProduct)">
    <div class="form-group">
      <label>Name</label>
      <input class="form-control"
             name="name"
             [(ngModel)]="newProduct.name"
             required
             minlength="5"
             pattern="^[A-Za-z ]+$" />
    </div>
    <button class="btn btn-primary" type="submit">
      Create
    </button>
  </form>
</div>
```

Angular requires elements being validated to define the name attribute, which is used to identify the element in the validation system. Since this input element is being used to capture the value of the Product. name property, the name attribute on the element has been set to name.

This listing adds three of the four validation attributes to the input element. The required attribute specifies that the user must provide a value, the minlength attribute specifies that there should be at least three characters, and the pattern attribute specifies that only alphabetic characters and spaces are allowed.

The validation attributes that Angular uses are the same ones used by the HTML 5 specification, so I have added the novalidate attribute to the form element, which tells the browser not to use its native validation features, which are inconsistently implemented by different browsers and generally get in the way. Since Angular will be providing the validation, the browser's own implementation of these features is not required.

Finally, notice that a form element has been added to the template. Although you can use input elements independently, the Angular validation features work only when there is a form element present, and Angular will report an error if you add the ngControl directive to an element that is not contained in a form.

When using a form element, the convention is to use an event binding for a special event called ngSubmit like this:

```
...
<form novalidate (ngSubmit)="addProduct(newProduct)">
...
```

The ngSubmit binding handles the form element's submit event. You can achieve the same effect binding to the click event on individual button elements within the form if you prefer.

Styling Elements Using Validation Classes

Once you have saved the template changes in Listing 14-13 and the browser has reloaded the HTML, right-click the input element in the browser window and select Inspect or Inspect Element from the pop-up window. The browser will display the HTML representation of the element in the Developer Tools window, and you will see that the input element has been added to three classes, like this:

```
...
<input class="form-control ng-pristine ng-invalid ng-touched" minlength="5"
    name="name" pattern="^[A-Za-z ]+$" required="" ng-reflect-name="name">
...
```

The classes to which an input element is assigned provide details of its validation state. There are three pairs of validation classes, which are described in Table 14-5. Elements will always be members of one class from each pair, for a total of three classes. The same classes are applied to the form element to show the overall validation status of all the elements it contains. As the status of the input element changes, the ngControl directive switches the classes automatically for both the individual elements and the form element.

Table 14-5. *The Angular Form Validation Classes*

Name	Description
ng-untouchedng-touched	An element is assigned to the ng-untouched class if it has not been visited by the user, which is typically done by tabbing through the form fields. Once the user has visited an element, it is added to the ng-touched class.
ng-pristineng-dirty	An element is assigned to the ng-pristine class if its contents have not been changed by the user and to the ng-dirty class otherwise. Once the contents have been edited, an element remains in the ng-dirty class, even if the user then returns to the previous contents.
ng-validng-invalid	An element is assigned to the ng-valid class if its contents meet the criteria defined by the validation rules that have been applied to it and to the ng-invalid class otherwise.

These classes can be used to style form elements to provide the user with validation feedback. Listing 14-14 adds a `style` element to the template and defines styles that indicate when the user has entered invalid or valid data.

■ **Tip** In real applications, styles should be defined in separate stylesheets and included in the application through the `index.html` file or using a component's decorator settings (which I describe in Chapter 17). I have included the styles directly in the template for simplicity, but this makes real applications harder to maintain because it makes it difficult to figure out where styles are coming from when there are multiple templates in use.

Listing 14-14. Providing Validation Feedback in the template.html File in the src/app Folder

```
<style>
    input.ng-dirty.ng-invalid { border: 2px solid #ff0000 }
    input.ng-dirty.ng-valid { border: 2px solid #6bc502 }
</style>

<div class="m-2">
  <div class="bg-info p-2 mb-2">Model Data: {{jsonProduct}}</div>

  <form novalidate (ngSubmit)="addProduct(newProduct)">
    <div class="form-group">
      <label>Name</label>
      <input class="form-control"
             name="name"
             [(ngModel)]="newProduct.name"
             required
             minlength="5"
             pattern="^[A-Za-z ]+$" />
    </div>
    <button class="btn btn-primary" type="submit">
      Create
    </button>
  </form>
</div>
```

These styles set green and red borders for `input` elements whose content has been edited and is valid (and so belong to both the `ng-dirty` and `ng-valid` classes) and whose content is invalid (and so belong to the `ng-dirty` and `ng-invalid` classes). Using the `ng-dirty` class means that the appearance of the elements won't be changed until after the user has entered some content.

Angular validates the contents and changes the class memberships of the `input` elements after each keystroke or focus change. The browser detects the changes to the elements and applies the styles dynamically, which provides users with validation feedback as they enter data into the form, as shown in Figure 14-9.

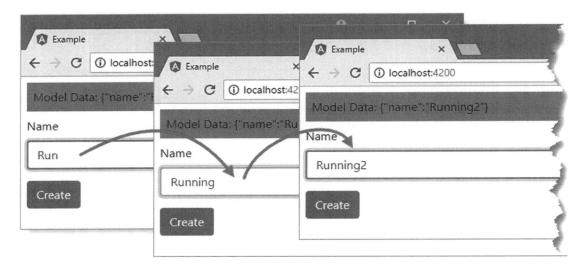

Figure 14-9. *Providing validation feedback*

As I start to type, the input element is shown as invalid because there are not enough characters to satisfy the minlength attribute. Once there are five characters, the border is green, indicating that the data is valid. When I type the character 2, the border turns red again because the pattern attribute is set to allow only letters and spaces.

■ **Tip** If you look at the JSON data at the top of the page in Figure 14-9, you will see that the data bindings are still being updated, even when the data values are not valid. Validation runs alongside data bindings, and you should not act on form data without checking that the overall form is valid, as described in the "Validating the Entire Form" section.

Displaying Field-Level Validation Messages

Using colors to provide validation feedback tells the user that something is wrong but doesn't provide any indication of what the user should do about it. The ngModel directive provides access to the validation status of the elements it is applied to, which can be used to display guidance to the user. Listing 14-15 adds validation messages for each of the attributes applied to the input element using the support provided by the ngModel directive.

Listing 14-15. Adding Validation Messages in the template.html File in the src/app Folder

```
<style>
    input.ng-dirty.ng-invalid { border: 2px solid #ff0000 }
    input.ng-dirty.ng-valid { border: 2px solid #6bc502 }
</style>

<div class="m-2">
  <div class="bg-info p-2 mb-2">Model Data: {{jsonProduct}}</div>
```

```
<form novalidate (ngSubmit)="addProduct(newProduct)">
  <div class="form-group">
    <label>Name</label>
    <input class="form-control"
           name="name"
           [(ngModel)]="newProduct.name"
           #name="ngModel"
           required
           minlength="5"
           pattern="^[A-Za-z ]+$" />
    <ul class="text-danger list-unstyled" *ngIf="name.dirty && name.invalid">
      <li *ngIf="name.errors.required">
        You must enter a product name
      </li>
      <li *ngIf="name.errors.pattern">
        Product names can only contain letters and spaces
      </li>
      <li *ngIf="name.errors.minlength">
        Product names must be at least
        {{name.errors.minlength.requiredLength}} characters
      </li>
    </ul>
  </div>
  <button class="btn btn-primary" type="submit">
    Create
  </button>
</form>
</div>
```

To get validation working, I have to create a template reference variable to access the validation state in expressions, which I do like this:

```
...
<input class="form-control" name="name" [(ngModel)]="newProduct.name"
    #name="ngModel" required minlength="5" pattern="^[A-Za-z ]+$"/>
...
```

I create a template reference variable called name and set its value to ngModel. This use of ngModel value is a little confusing: it is a feature provided by the ngModel directive to give access to the validation status. This will make more sense once you have read Chapters 15 and 16, in which I explain how to create custom directives and you see how they provide access to their features. For this chapter, it is enough to know that in order to display validation messages, you need to create a template reference variable and assign it ngModel to access the validation data for the input element. The object that is assigned to the template reference variable defines the properties that are described in Table 14-6.

313

Table 14-6. *The Validation Object Properties*

Name	Description
path	This property returns the name of the element.
valid	This property returns true if the element's contents are valid and false otherwise.
invalid	This property returns true if the element's contents are invalid and false otherwise.
pristine	This property returns true if the element's contents have not been changed.
dirty	This property returns true if the element's contents have been changed.
touched	This property returns true if the user has visited the element.
untouched	This property returns true if the user has not visited the element.
errors	This property returns an object whose properties correspond to each attribute for which there is a validation error.
value	This property returns the value of the element, which is used when defining custom validation rules, as described in the "Creating Custom Form Validators" section.

Listing 14-15 displays the validation messages in a list. The list should be shown only if there is at least one validation error, so I applied the ngIf directive to the ul element, with an expression that uses the dirty and invalid properties, like this:

```
...
<ul class="text-danger list-unstyled" *ngIf="name.dirty && name.invalid">
...
```

Within the ul element, there is an li element that corresponds to each validation error that can occur. Each li element has an ngIf directive that uses the errors property described in Table 14-6, like this:

```
...
<li *ngIf="name.errors.required">You must enter a product name</li>
...
```

The errors.required property will be defined only if the element's contents have failed the required validation check, which ties the visibility of the li element to the outcome of that particular validation check.

USING THE SAFE NAVIGATION PROPERTY WITH FORMS

The errors property is created only when there are validation errors, which is why I check the value of the invalid property in the expression on the ul element. An alternative approach is to use the safe navigation property, which is used in templates to navigate through a series of properties without generating an error if one of them returns null. Here is an alternative approach to defining the template in Listing 14-15 that doesn't check the valid property and relies on the safe navigation property instead:

```
...
<ul class="text-danger list-unstyled" *ngIf="name.dirty">
    <li *ngIf="name.errors?.required">
        You must enter a product name
```

```
    </li>
    <li *ngIf="name.errors?.pattern">
        Product names can only contain letters and spaces
    </li>
    <li *ngIf="name.errors?.minlength">
        Product names must be at least
        {{name.errors.minlength.requiredLength}} characters
    </li>
</ul>
...
```

Appending a ? character after a property name tells Angular not to try to access any subsequent properties or methods if the property is null or undefined. In this example, I have applied the ? character after the errors property, which means Angular won't try to read the required, pattern, or minlength properties if the error property hasn't been defined.

Each property defined by the errors object returns an object whose properties provide details of why the content has failed the validation check for its attribute, which can be used to make the validation messages more helpful to the user. Table 14-7 describes the error properties provided for each attribute.

Table 14-7. *The Angular Form Validation Error Description Properties*

Name	Description
required	This property returns true if the required attribute has been applied to the input element. This is not especially useful because this can be deduced from the fact that the required property exists.
minlength.requiredLength	This property returns the number of characters required to satisfy the minlength attribute.
minlength.actualLength	This property returns the number of characters entered by the user.
pattern.requiredPattern	This property returns the regular expression that has been specified using the pattern attribute.
pattern.actualValue	This property returns the contents of the element.

These properties are not displayed directly to the user, who is unlikely to understand an error message that includes a regular expression, although they can be useful during development to figure out validation problems. The exception is the minlength.requiredLength property, which can be useful for avoiding duplicating the value assigned to the minlength attribute on the element, like this:

```
...
<li *ngIf="name.errors.minlength">
  Product names must be at least {{name.errors.minlength.requiredLength}} characters
</li>
...
```

The overall result is a set of validation messages that are shown as soon as the user starts editing the input element and that change to reflect each new keystroke, as illustrated in Figure 14-10.

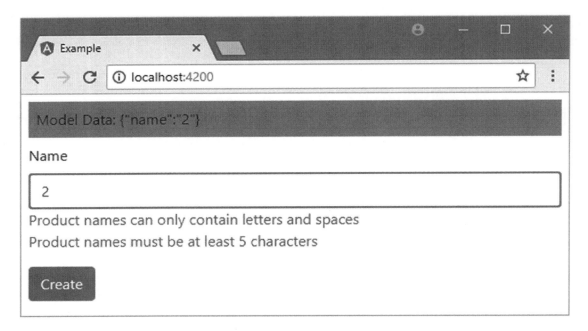

Figure 14-10. *Displaying validation messages*

Using the Component to Display Validation Messages

Including separate elements for all possible validation errors quickly becomes verbose in complex forms. A better approach is to add some logic to the component to prepare the validation messages in a method, which can then be displayed to the user through the ngFor directive in the template. Listing 14-16 shows the addition of a component method that accepts the validation state for an input element and produces an array of validation messages.

Listing 14-16. Generating Validation Messages in the component.ts File in the src/app Folder

```
import { ApplicationRef, Component } from "@angular/core";
import { Model } from "./repository.model";
import { Product } from "./product.model";

@Component({
    selector: "app",
    templateUrl: "template.html"
})
export class ProductComponent {
    model: Model = new Model();

    getProduct(key: number): Product {
        return this.model.getProduct(key);
    }

    getProducts(): Product[] {
        return this.model.getProducts();
```

```
    }

    newProduct: Product = new Product();

    get jsonProduct() {
        return JSON.stringify(this.newProduct);
    }

    addProduct(p: Product) {
        console.log("New Product: " + this.jsonProduct);
    }

    getValidationMessages(state: any, thingName?: string) {
        let thing: string = state.path || thingName;
        let messages: string[] = [];
        if (state.errors) {
            for (let errorName in state.errors) {
                switch (errorName) {
                    case "required":
                        messages.push(`You must enter a ${thing}`);
                        break;
                    case "minlength":
                        messages.push(`A ${thing} must be at least
                            ${state.errors['minlength'].requiredLength}
                            characters`);
                        break;
                    case "pattern":
                        messages.push(`The ${thing} contains
                            illegal characters`);
                        break;
                }
            }
        }
        return messages;
    }
}
```

The getValidationMessages method uses the properties described in Table 14-6 to produce validation messages for each error, returning them in a string array. To make this code as widely applicable as possible, the method accepts a value that describes the data item that an input element is intended to collect from the user, which is then used to generate error messages, like this:

```
...
messages.push(`You must enter a ${thing}`);
...
```

This is an example of the JavaScript string interpolation feature, which allows strings to be defined like templates, without having to use the + operator to include data values. Note that the template string is denoted with backtick characters (the ` character and not the regular JavaScript ' character). The getValidationMessages method defaults to using the path property as the descriptive string if an argument isn't received when the method is invoked, like this:

```
...
let thing: string = state.path || thingName;
...
```

Listing 14-17 shows how the getValidationMessages can be used in the template to generate validation error messages for the user without needing to define separate elements and bindings for each one.

Listing 14-17. Getting Validation Messages in the template.html File in the src/app Folder

```html
<style>
    input.ng-dirty.ng-invalid { border: 2px solid #ff0000 }
    input.ng-dirty.ng-valid { border: 2px solid #6bc502 }
</style>

<div class="m-2">
  <div class="bg-info p-2 mb-2">Model Data: {{jsonProduct}}</div>

  <form novalidate (ngSubmit)="addProduct(newProduct)">
    <div class="form-group">
      <label>Name</label>
      <input class="form-control"
             name="name"
             [(ngModel)]="newProduct.name"
             #name="ngModel"
             required
             minlength="5"
             pattern="^[A-Za-z ]+$" />
      <ul class="text-danger list-unstyled" *ngIf="name.dirty && name.invalid">
        <li *ngFor="let error of getValidationMessages(name)">
          {{error}}
        </li>
      </ul>
    </div>
    <button class="btn btn-primary" type="submit">
      Create
    </button>
  </form>
</div>
```

There is no visual change, but the same method can be used to produce validation messages for multiple elements, which results in a simpler template that is easier to read and maintain.

Validating the Entire Form

Displaying validation error messages for individual fields is useful because it helps emphasize where problems need to be fixed. But it can also be useful to validate the entire form. Care must be taken not to overwhelm the user with error messages until they try to submit the form, at which point a summary of any problems can be useful. In preparation, Listing 14-18 adds two new members to the component.

Listing 14-18. Enhancing the Component in the component.ts File in the src/app Folder

```
import { ApplicationRef, Component } from "@angular/core";
import { NgForm } from "@angular/forms";
import { Model } from "./repository.model";
import { Product } from "./product.model";

@Component({
    selector: "app",
    templateUrl: "template.html"
})
export class ProductComponent {
    model: Model = new Model();

    // ...other methods omitted for brevity...

    formSubmitted: boolean = false;

    submitForm(form: NgForm) {
        this.formSubmitted = true;
        if (form.valid) {
            this.addProduct(this.newProduct);
            this.newProduct = new Product();
            form.reset();
            this.formSubmitted = false;
        }
    }
}
```

The formSubmitted property will be used to indicate whether the form has been submitted and will be used to prevent validation of the entire form until the user has tried to submit.

The submitForm method will be invoked when the user submits the form and receives an NgForm object as its argument. This object represents the form and defines the set of validation properties, which are used to describe the overall validation status of the form so that, for example, the invalid property will be true if there are validation errors on any of the elements contained by the form. In addition to the validation property, NgForm provides the reset method, which resets the validation status of the form and returns it to its original and pristine state.

The effect is that the whole form will be validated when the user performs a submit, and if there are no validation errors, a new object will be added to the data model before the form is reset so that it can be used again. Listing 14-19 shows the changes required to the template to take advantage of these new features and implement form-wide validation.

Listing 14-19. Performing Form-Wide Validation in the template.html File in the src/app Folder

```
<style>
    input.ng-dirty.ng-invalid { border: 2px solid #ff0000 }
    input.ng-dirty.ng-valid { border: 2px solid #6bc502 }
</style>

<div class="m-2">

  <form novalidate #form="ngForm" (ngSubmit)="submitForm(form)">
```

```
<div class="bg-danger text-white p-2 mb-2"
    *ngIf="formSubmitted && form.invalid">
  There are problems with the form
</div>

<div class="form-group">
  <label>Name</label>
  <input class="form-control"
         name="name"
         [(ngModel)]="newProduct.name"
         #name="ngModel"
         required
         minlength="5"
         pattern="^[A-Za-z ]+$" />
  <ul class="text-danger list-unstyled"
      *ngIf="(formSubmitted || name.dirty) && name.invalid">
    <li *ngFor="let error of getValidationMessages(name)">
      {{error}}
    </li>
  </ul>
</div>
<button class="btn btn-primary" type="submit">
  Create
</button>
  </form>
</div>
```

The form element now defines a reference variable called form, which has been assigned to ngForm. This is how the ngForm directive provides access to its functionality, through a process that I describe in Chapter 15. For now, however, it is important to know that the validation information for the entire form can be accessed through the form reference variable.

The listing also changes the expression for the ngSubmit binding so that it calls the submitForm method defined by the controller, passing in the template variable, like this:

```
...
<form novalidate ngForm="productForm" #form="ngForm" (ngSubmit)="submitForm(form)">
...
```

It is this object that is received as the argument of the submitForm method and that is used to check the validation status of the form and to reset the form so that it can be used again.

Listing 14-19 also adds a div element that uses the formSubmitted property from the component along with the valid property (provided by the form template variable) to show a warning message when the form contains invalid data, but only after the form has been submitted.

In addition, the ngIf binding has been updated to display the field-level validation messages so that they will be shown when the form has been submitted, even if the element itself hasn't been edited. The result is a validation summary that is shown only when the user submits the form with invalid data, as illustrated by Figure 14-11.

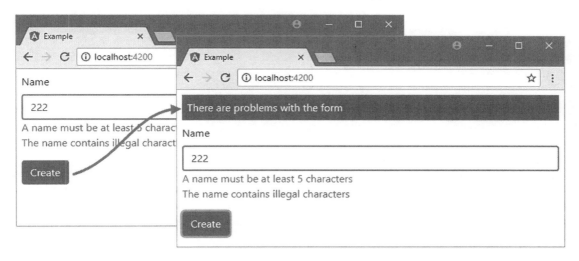

Figure 14-11. *Displaying a validation summary message*

Displaying Summary Validation Messages

In a complex form, it can be helpful to provide the user with a summary of all the validation errors that have to be resolved. The NgForm object assigned to the form template reference variable provides access to the individual elements through a property named controls. This property returns an object that has properties for each of the individual elements in the form. For example, there is a name property that represents the input element in the example, which is assigned an object that represents that element and defines the same validation properties that are available for individual elements. In Listing 14-20, I have added a method to the component that receives the object assigned to the form element's template reference variables and uses its controls property to generate a list of errors messages for the entire form.

Listing 14-20. Generating Form-Wide Validation Messages in the component.ts File in the src/app Folder

```
import { ApplicationRef, Component } from "@angular/core";
import { NgForm } from "@angular/forms";
import { Model } from "./repository.model";
import { Product } from "./product.model";

@Component({
    selector: "app",
    templateUrl: "template.html"
})
export class ProductComponent {
    model: Model = new Model();

    // ...other methods omitted for brevity...

    getFormValidationMessages(form: NgForm): string[] {
        let messages: string[] = [];
        Object.keys(form.controls).forEach(k => {
```

```
            this.getValidationMessages(form.controls[k], k)
                .forEach(m => messages.push(m));
        });
        return messages;
    }
}
```

The getFormValidationMessages method builds its list of messages by calling the getValidationMessages method defined in Listing 14-16 for each control in the form. The Object.keys method creates an array from the properties defined by the object returned by the controls property, which is enumerated using the forEach method.

In Listing 14-21, I have used this method to include the individual messages at the top of the form, which will be visible once the user clicks the Create button.

Listing 14-21. Displaying Form-Wide Validation Messages in the template.html File in the src/app Folder

```html
<style>
    input.ng-dirty.ng-invalid { border: 2px solid #ff0000 }
    input.ng-dirty.ng-valid { border: 2px solid #6bc502 }
</style>

<div class="m-2">

  <form novalidate #form="ngForm" (ngSubmit)="submitForm(form)">

    <div class="bg-danger text-white p-2 mb-2"
        *ngIf="formSubmitted && form.invalid">
      There are problems with the form
      <ul>
        <li *ngFor="let error of getFormValidationMessages(form)">
          {{error}}
        </li>
      </ul>
    </div>

    <div class="form-group">
      <label>Name</label>
      <input class="form-control"
            name="name"
            [(ngModel)]="newProduct.name"
            #name="ngModel"
            required
            minlength="5"
            pattern="^[A-Za-z ]+$" />
      <ul class="text-danger list-unstyled"
          *ngIf="(formSubmitted || name.dirty) && name.invalid">
        <li *ngFor="let error of getValidationMessages(name)">
          {{error}}
        </li>
      </ul>
    </div>
    <button class="btn btn-primary" type="submit">
```

```
        Create
      </button>
    </form>
  </div>
</div>
```

The result is that validation messages are displayed alongside the input element and collected together at the top of the form once it has been submitted, as shown in Figure 14-12.

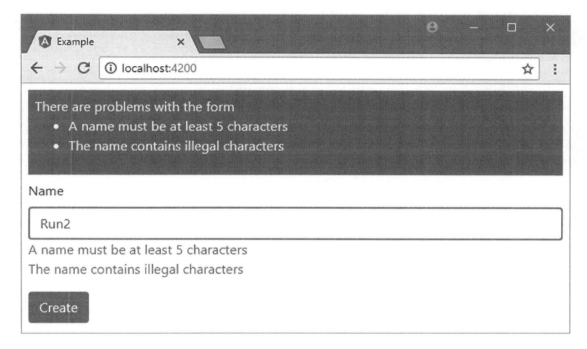

Figure 14-12. Displaying an overall validation summary

Disabling the Submit Button

The final adjustment in this section is to disable the button once the user has submitted the form, preventing the user from clicking it again until all the validation errors have been resolved. This is a commonly used technique even though it has little bearing on the application, which won't accept the data from the form while it contains invalid values but provides useful reinforcement to the user that they cannot proceed until the validation problems have been resolved.

In Listing 14-22, I have used the property binding on the button element and added an input element for the price property to show how the approach scales up with multiple elements in the form.

Listing 14-22. Disabling the Button and Adding an Input Element in the template.html File in the src/app Folder

```
<style>
    input.ng-dirty.ng-invalid { border: 2px solid #ff0000 }
    input.ng-dirty.ng-valid { border: 2px solid #6bc502 }
</style>
```

```
<div class="m-2">
    <form novalidate #form="ngForm" (ngSubmit)="submitForm(form)">

        <div class="bg-danger text-white p-2 mb-2"
                *ngIf="formSubmitted && form.invalid">
            There are problems with the form
            <ul>
                <li *ngFor="let error of getFormValidationMessages(form)">
                    {{error}}
                </li>
            </ul>
        </div>

        <div class="form-group">
            <label>Name</label>
            <input class="form-control"
                    name="name"
                    [(ngModel)]="newProduct.name"
                    #name="ngModel"
                    required
                    minlength="5"
                    pattern="^[A-Za-z ]+$" />
            <ul class="text-danger list-unstyled"
                *ngIf="(formSubmitted || name.dirty) && name.invalid">
                <li *ngFor="let error of getValidationMessages(name)">
                    {{error}}
                </li>
            </ul>
        </div>

        <div class="form-group">
            <label>Price</label>
            <input class="form-control" name="price" [(ngModel)]="newProduct.price"
                    #price="ngModel" required pattern="^[0-9\.]+$" />
            <ul class="text-danger list-unstyled"
                *ngIf="(formSubmitted || price.dirty) && price.invalid">
                <li *ngFor="let error of getValidationMessages(price)">
                    {{error}}
                </li>
            </ul>
        </div>

        <button class="btn btn-primary" type="submit"
                [disabled]="formSubmitted && form.invalid"
                [class.btn-secondary]="formSubmitted && form.invalid">
            Create
        </button>
    </form>
</div>
```

For extra emphasis, I used the class binding to add the `button` element to the `btn-secondary` class when the form has been submitted and has invalid data. This class applies a Bootstrap CSS style, as shown in Figure 14-13.

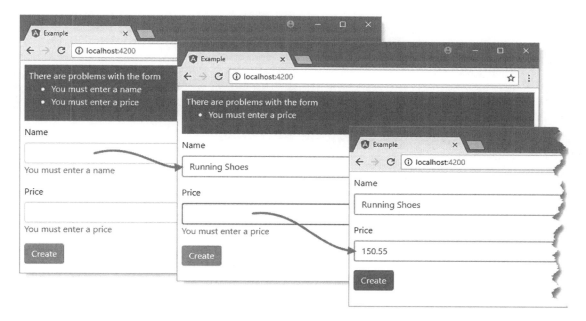

Figure 14-13. *Disabling the submit button*

Using Model-Based Forms

The form in the previous section relies on HTML elements and attributes to define the fields that make up the form and also to apply the validation constraints. The advantage of this approach is that it is familiar and simple. The disadvantage is that large forms become complex and difficult to maintain, with each field demanding its own block of content to manage its layout and its validation requirements and to display any validation messages.

Angular provides another approach, known as *model-based forms*, in which the details of the form and its validation are defined in code rather in a template. This approach scales up better, but it requires some up-front effort, and the results are not as natural as defining everything in the template. In the sections that follow, I set up and apply a model that describes the form and the validation it requires.

Enabling Model-Based Forms Feature

The support for model-based forms requires a new dependency to be declared in the application's Angular module, as shown in Listing 14-23.

Listing 14-23. Enabling Model-Based Forms in the app.module.ts File in the src/app Folder

```
import { NgModule } from "@angular/core";
import { BrowserModule } from "@angular/platform-browser";
import { ProductComponent } from "./component";
```

```
import { FormsModule, ReactiveFormsModule } from "@angular/forms";

@NgModule({
    imports: [BrowserModule, FormsModule, ReactiveFormsModule],
    declarations: [ProductComponent],
    bootstrap: [ProductComponent]
})
export class AppModule {}
```

The model-based forms feature is defined in a module called ReactiveFormsModule, which is defined in the @angular/forms JavaScript module, which was added to the project at the start of the chapter.

Defining the Form Model Classes

I am going to start by defining classes that will describe the form so that I can keep the template as simple as possible. You don't have to follow this approach completely, but if you are going to adopt model-based forms, it makes sense to handle as much of the form as possible in the model and minimize the complexity of the template. I added a file called form.model.ts to the src/app folder and added the code shown in Listing 14-24.

Listing 14-24. The Contents of the form.model.ts File in the src/app Folder

```
import { FormControl, FormGroup, Validators } from "@angular/forms";

export class ProductFormControl extends FormControl {
    label: string;
    modelProperty: string;

    constructor(label:string, property:string, value: any, validator: any) {
        super(value, validator);
        this.label = label;
        this.modelProperty = property;
    }
}

export class ProductFormGroup extends FormGroup {

    constructor() {
        super({
            name: new ProductFormControl("Name", "name", "", Validators.required),

            category: new ProductFormControl("Category", "category", "",
                Validators.compose([Validators.required,
                    Validators.pattern("^[A-Za-z ]+$"),
                    Validators.minLength(3),
                    Validators.maxLength(10)])),

            price: new ProductFormControl("Price", "price", "",
                Validators.compose([Validators.required,
                    Validators.pattern("^[0-9\.]+$")]))
        });
```

```
    }

    get productControls(): ProductFormControl[] {
        return Object.keys(this.controls)
            .map(k => this.controls[k] as ProductFormControl);
    }
}
```

The two classes defined in the listing extend the ones that Angular uses to manage forms and their contents behind the scenes. The FormControl class is used to represent a single element in a form, such as input element, and the FormGroup class is used to manage a form element and its contents.

The new subclasses add features that will make it easier to generate the HTML form programmatically. The ProductFormControl class extends the FormControl class with properties that specify the text for the label element associated with an input element and the name of the Product class property that the input element will represent. The ProductFormGroup class extends FormGroup with a property that presents an array of the ProductFormControl objects that have been defined in the form and that will be used in the template to generate content using the ngFor directive.

The important part of this class is the constructor for the ProductFormGroup class, which is responsible for setting up the model that will be used to create and validate the form. The constructor for the FormGroup class, which is the superclass for ProductFormGroup, accepts an object whose property names correspond to the names of the input elements in the template, each of which is assigned a ProductFormControl object that will represent it and that specifies the validation checks that are required. The first property in the object passed to the super constructor is the simplest:

```
...
name: new ProductFormControl("Name", "name", "", Validators.required),
...
```

The property is called name, which tells Angular that it corresponds to an input element called name in the template. The arguments for the ProductFormControl constructor specify the content for the label element that will be associated with the input element (Name), the name of the Product class property that the input element will be bound to (name), the initial value for the data binding (the empty string), and the validation checks that are required. Angular defines a class called Validators in the @angular/forms module that has properties for each of the built-in validation checks, as described in Table 14-8.

Table 14-8. *The Validator Properties*

Name	Description
Validators.required	This property corresponds to the required attribute and ensures that a value is entered.
Validators.minLength	This property corresponds to the minlength attribute and ensures a minimum number of characters.
Validators.maxLength	This property corresponds to the maxlength attribute and ensures a maximum number of characters.
Validators.pattern	This property corresponds to the pattern attribute and matches a regular expression.

Validators can be combined using the `Validators.compose` method so that several checks are performed on a single element, like this:

```
...
category: new ProductFormControl("Category", "category", "",
    Validators.compose([Validators.required,
        Validators.pattern("^[A-Za-z ]+$"),
        Validators.minLength(3),
        Validators.maxLength(10)])),
...
```

The `Validators.compose` method accepts an array of validators. The constructor arguments defined by the `pattern`, `minLength`, and `maxLength` validators correspond to the attribute values. The overall effect for this element is that values are required, must contain only alphabet characters and spaces, and must be between three and ten characters.

The next step is to move the methods that generate validation error messages from the component into the new form model classes, as shown in Listing 14-25. This keeps all the form-related code together and helps keep the component as simple as possible. (I have also added validation message support for the `maxLength` validator in the `ProductFormControl` class's `getValidationMessages` method.)

Listing 14-25. Moving the Validation Message Methods in the form.model.ts File in the src/app Folder

```
import { FormControl, FormGroup, Validators } from "@angular/forms";

export class ProductFormControl extends FormControl {
    label: string;
    modelProperty: string;

    constructor(label:string, property:string, value: any, validator: any) {
        super(value, validator);
        this.label = label;
        this.modelProperty = property;
    }

    getValidationMessages() {
        let messages: string[] = [];
        if (this.errors) {
            for (let errorName in this.errors) {
                switch (errorName) {
                    case "required":
                        messages.push(`You must enter a ${this.label}`);
                        break;
                    case "minlength":
                        messages.push(`A ${this.label} must be at least
                            ${this.errors['minlength'].requiredLength}
                            characters`);
                        break;
                    case "maxlength":
                        messages.push(`A ${this.label} must be no more than
                            ${this.errors['maxlength'].requiredLength}
                            characters`);
                        break;
```

```
                        case "pattern":
                            messages.push(`The ${this.label} contains
                                illegal characters`);
                            break;
                    }
                }
            }
            return messages;
        }
    }

export class ProductFormGroup extends FormGroup {

        constructor() {
            super({
                name: new ProductFormControl("Name", "name", "", Validators.required),

                category: new ProductFormControl("Category", "category", "",
                    Validators.compose([Validators.required,
                        Validators.pattern("^[A-Za-z ]+$"),
                        Validators.minLength(3),
                        Validators.maxLength(10)])),

                price: new ProductFormControl("Price", "price", "",
                    Validators.compose([Validators.required,
                        Validators.pattern("^[0-9\.]+$")]))
            });
        }

        get productControls(): ProductFormControl[] {
            return Object.keys(this.controls)
                .map(k => this.controls[k] as ProductFormControl);
        }

        getFormValidationMessages(form: any) : string[] {
            let messages: string[] = [];
            this.productControls.forEach(c => c.getValidationMessages()
                .forEach(m => messages.push(m)));
            return messages;
        }
    }
}
```

The validation messages are generated in the same way as they were previously, with minor adjustments to reflect the fact that the code is now part of the form model rather than the component.

Using the Model for Validation

Now that I have a form model, I can use it to validate the form. Listing 14-26 shows how the component class has been updated to enable model-based forms and to make the form model classes available to the template. It also removes the methods that generate the validation error messages, which were moved into the form model classes in Listing 14-25.

Listing 14-26. Using a Form Model in the component.ts File in the src/app Folder

```
import { ApplicationRef, Component } from "@angular/core";
import { NgForm } from "@angular/forms";
import { Model } from "./repository.model";
import { Product } from "./product.model";
import { ProductFormGroup } from "./form.model";

@Component({
    selector: "app",
    templateUrl: "template.html"
})
export class ProductComponent {
    model: Model = new Model();
    form: ProductFormGroup = new ProductFormGroup();

    getProduct(key: number): Product {
        return this.model.getProduct(key);
    }

    getProducts(): Product[] {
        return this.model.getProducts();
    }

    newProduct: Product = new Product();

    get jsonProduct() {
        return JSON.stringify(this.newProduct);
    }

    addProduct(p: Product) {
        console.log("New Product: " + this.jsonProduct);
    }

    formSubmitted: boolean = false;

    submitForm(form: NgForm) {
        this.formSubmitted = true;
        if (form.valid) {
            this.addProduct(this.newProduct);
            this.newProduct = new Product();
            form.reset();
            this.formSubmitted = false;
        }
    }
}
```

The listing imports the ProductFormGroup class from the form.model module and uses it to define a property called form, which makes the custom form model class available for use in the template.

Listing 14-27 updates the template to use the model-based features to handle validation, replacing the attribute-based validation configuration defined in the template.

Listing 14-27. Using a Form Model in the template.html File in the src/app Folder

```
<style>
    input.ng-dirty.ng-invalid { border: 2px solid #ff0000 }
    input.ng-dirty.ng-valid { border: 2px solid #6bc502 }
</style>

<form class="m-2" novalidate [formGroup]="form" (ngSubmit)="submitForm(form)">

    <div class="bg-danger text-white p-2 mb-2" *ngIf="formSubmitted && form.invalid">
        There are problems with the form
        <ul>
            <li *ngFor="let error of form.getFormValidationMessages()">
                {{error}}
            </li>
        </ul>
    </div>

    <div class="form-group">
        <label>Name</label>
        <input class="form-control" name="name" [(ngModel)]="newProduct.name"
            formControlName="name" />
        <ul class="text-danger list-unstyled"
                *ngIf="(formSubmitted || form.controls['name'].dirty) &&
                        form.controls['name'].invalid">
            <li *ngFor="let error of form.controls['name'].getValidationMessages()">
                {{error}}
            </li>
        </ul>
    </div>

    <div class="form-group">
        <label>Category</label>
        <input class="form-control" name="name" [(ngModel)]="newProduct.category"
            formControlName="category" />
        <ul class="text-danger list-unstyled"
                *ngIf="(formSubmitted || form.controls['category'].dirty) &&
                        form.controls['category'].invalid">
            <li *ngFor="let error of form.controls['category']
                    .getValidationMessages()">
                {{error}}
            </li>
        </ul>
    </div>

    <div class="form-group">
        <label>Price</label>
        <input class="form-control" name="price" [(ngModel)]="newProduct.price"
            formControlName="price" />
        <ul class="text-danger list-unstyled"
                *ngIf="(formSubmitted || form.controls['price'].dirty) &&
                  form.controls['price'].invalid">
```

```
        <li *ngFor="let error of form.controls['price'].getValidationMessages()">
            {{error}}
        </li>
    </ul>
</div>

<button class="btn btn-primary" type="submit"
    [disabled]="formSubmitted && form.invalid"
    [class.btn-secondary]="formSubmitted && form.invalid">
        Create
</button>
</form>
```

The first changes are to the form element. Using model-based validation requires the formGroup directive, like this:

```
...
<form class="m-2" novalidate [formGroup]="form" (ngSubmit)="submitForm(form)">
...
```

The value assigned to the formGroup directive is the component's form property, which returns the ProductFormGroup object, which is the source of validation information about the form.

The next changes are to the input elements. The individual validation attributes and the template variable that was assigned the special ngForm value have been removed. A new forControlName attribute has been added, which identifies the input element to the model-based form system, using the name used in the ProductFormGroup in Listing 14-24.

```
...
<input class="form-control" name="name" [(ngModel)]="newProduct.name"
    formControlName="name" />
...
```

This attribute also allows Angular to add and remove the validation classes for the input element. In this case, the formControlName attribute has been set to name, which tells Angular that this element should be validated using specific validators.

```
...
name: new ProductFormControl("Name", "name", "", Validators.required),
...
```

The component's form property provides access to the validation information for each element, like this:

```
...
<li *ngFor="let error of form.controls['name'].getValidationMessages()">
    {{error}}
</li>
...
```

The FormGroup class provides a controls property that returns a collection of the FormControl objects that it is managing, indexed by name. Individual FormControl objects can be retrieved from the collection and either inspected to get the validation state or used to generate validation messages.

As part of the changed in Listing 14-27, I have added all three input elements required to get the data to create new Product objects, each of which is checked using the validation model, as shown in Figure 14-14.

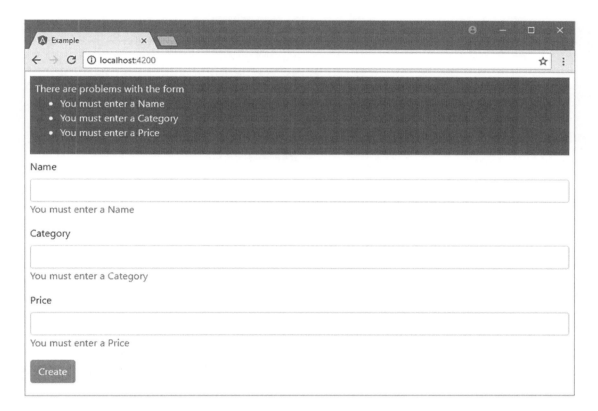

Figure 14-14. *Using model-based form validation*

Generating the Elements from the Model

There is a lot of duplication in Listing 14-27. The validation attributes have been moved into the code, but each input element still requires a supporting framework of content to handle its layout and to display its validation messages to the user.

The next step is to simplify the template by using the form model to generate the elements in the form and not just validate them. Listing 14-28 shows how the standard Angular directives can be combined with the form model to generate the form programmatically.

Listing 14-28. Using the Model to Generate the Form in the template.html File in the src/app Folder

```
<style>
    input.ng-dirty.ng-invalid { border: 2px solid #ff0000 }
    input.ng-dirty.ng-valid { border: 2px solid #6bc502 }
</style>
```

```
<form class="m-2" novalidate [formGroup]="form" (ngSubmit)="submitForm(form)">

    <div class="bg-danger text-white p-2 mb-2" *ngIf="formSubmitted && form.invalid">
        There are problems with the form
        <ul>
            <li *ngFor="let error of form.getFormValidationMessages()">
                {{error}}
            </li>
        </ul>
    </div>

    <div class="form-group" *ngFor="let control of form.productControls">
        <label>{{control.label}}</label>
        <input class="form-control"
            [(ngModel)]="newProduct[control.modelProperty]"
            name="{{control.modelProperty}}"
            formControlName="{{control.modelProperty}}" />
        <ul class="text-danger list-unstyled"
                *ngIf="(formSubmitted || control.dirty) && control.invalid">
            <li *ngFor="let error of control.getValidationMessages()">
                {{error}}
            </li>
        </ul>
    </div>

    <button class="btn btn-primary" type="submit"
        [disabled]="formSubmitted && form.invalid"
        [class.btn-secondary]="formSubmitted && form.invalid">
            Create
    </button>
</form>
```

This listing uses the ngFor directive to create form elements using the description provided by the ProductFormControl and ProductFormGroup model classes. Each element is configured with the same attributes as in Listing 14-27, but their values are taken from the model descriptions, which allows the template to be simplified and rely on the model for both the definition of the form elements and their validation.

Once you have a basic form model in place, you can expand it and extend it to reflect the needs of the application. For example, you can add new elements, extend the FormControl subclass to contain additional information (such as values for the type attribute of the input element), generate select elements for fields, and provide placeholder values to help guide the user.

Creating Custom Form Validators

Angular supports custom form validators, which can be used to enforce a validation policy that is specified to the application, rather than the general-purpose validation that the built-in validators provide. To demonstrate, I added a file called limit.formvalidator.ts to the src/app folder and used it to define the class shown in Listing 14-29.

Listing 14-29. The Contents of the limit.formvalidator.ts File in the src/app Folder

```
import { FormControl } from "@angular/forms";

export class LimitValidator {

    static Limit(limit:number) {
        return (control:FormControl) : {[key: string]: any} => {
            let val = Number(control.value);
            if (val != NaN && val > limit) {
                return {"limit": {"limit": limit, "actualValue": val}};
            } else {
                return null;
            }
        }
    }
}
```

Custom validators are factories that create functions used to perform validation. In this case, the LimitValidator class defines the Limit method, which is static and is the factory that returns the validation function. The argument to the Limit method is the largest value that should be allowed to pass validation.

When Angular invokes the validation function returned by the Limit method, it provides a FormControl method as the argument. The custom validation function in the listing uses the value property to get the value entered by the user, convert it to a number, and compare it to the allowed limit.

Validation functions return null for valid values and return an object that contains details of the error for invalid values. To describe a validation error, the object defines a property that specifies which validation rule has failed, which is limit in this case, and assigns the property another object that provides details. The limit property returns an object that has a limit property that is set to the validation limit and an actualValue property that is set to the value entered by the user.

Applying a Custom Validator

Listing 14-30 shows how the form model has been extended to support the new custom validator class and apply it to the input element for the product's price property.

Listing 14-30. Applying a Custom Validator in the form.model.ts File in the src/app Folder

```
import { FormControl, FormGroup, Validators } from "@angular/forms";
import { LimitValidator } from "./limit.formvalidator";

export class ProductFormControl extends FormControl {
    label: string;
    modelProperty: string;

    constructor(label:string, property:string, value: any, validator: any) {
        super(value, validator);
        this.label = label;
        this.modelProperty = property;
    }
```

```
    getValidationMessages() {
        let messages: string[] = [];
        if (this.errors) {
            for (let errorName in this.errors) {
                switch (errorName) {
                    case "required":
                        messages.push(`You must enter a ${this.label}`);
                        break;
                    case "minlength":
                        messages.push(`A ${this.label} must be at least
                            ${this.errors['minlength'].requiredLength}
                            characters`);
                        break;
                    case "maxlength":
                        messages.push(`A ${this.label} must be no more than
                            ${this.errors['maxlength'].requiredLength}
                            characters`);
                        break;
                    case "limit":
                        messages.push(`A ${this.label} cannot be more
                                than ${this.errors['limit'].limit}`);
                        break;
                    case "pattern":
                        messages.push(`The ${this.label} contains
                            illegal characters`);
                        break;
                }
            }
        }
        return messages;
    }
}

export class ProductFormGroup extends FormGroup {

    constructor() {
        super({
            name: new ProductFormControl("Name", "name", "", Validators.required),
            category: new ProductFormControl("Category", "category", "",
                Validators.compose([Validators.required,
                    Validators.pattern("^[A-Za-z ]+$"),
                    Validators.minLength(3),
                    Validators.maxLength(10)])),
            price: new ProductFormControl("Price", "price", "",
                Validators.compose([Validators.required,
                    LimitValidator.Limit(100),
                    Validators.pattern("^[0-9\.]+$")]))
        });
    }
```

```
get productControls(): ProductFormControl[] {
    return Object.keys(this.controls)
        .map(k => this.controls[k] as ProductFormControl);
}

getFormValidationMessages(form: any) : string[] {
    let messages: string[] = [];
    this.productControls.forEach(c => c.getValidationMessages()
        .forEach(m => messages.push(m)));
    return messages;
}
}
```

The result is that the value entered into the Price field has a limit of 100, and larger values display the validation error message shown in Figure 14-15.

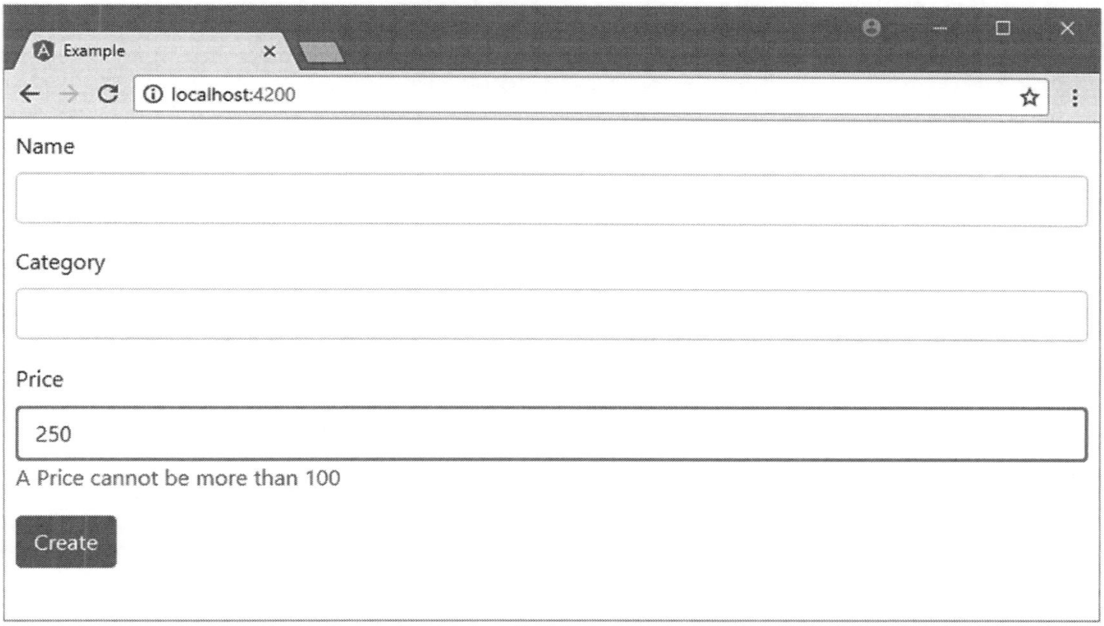

Figure 14-15. *A custom validation message*

Summary

In this chapter, I introduced the way that Angular supports user interaction using events and forms. I explained how to create event bindings, how to create two-way bindings, and how they can be simplified using the ngModel directive. I also described the support that Angular provides for managing and validating HTML forms. In the next chapter, I explain how to create custom directives.

CHAPTER 15

▓ ▓ ▓

Creating Attribute Directives

In this chapter, I describe how custom directives can be used to supplement the functionality provided by the built-in ones provided by Angular. The focus of this chapter is *attribute directives*, which are the simplest type that can be created and that change the appearance or behavior of a single element. In Chapter 16, I explain how to create *structural directives*, which are used to change the layout of the HTML document. Components are also a type of directive, and I explain how they work in Chapter 17.

    Throughout these chapters, I describe how custom directives work by re-creating the features provided by some of the built-in directives. This isn't something you would typically do in a real project, but it provides a useful baseline against which the process can be explained. Table 15-1 puts attribute directives into context.

Table 15-1. *Putting Attribute Directives in Context*

Question	Answer
What are they?	Attribute directives are classes that are able to modify the behavior or appearance of the element they are applied to. The style and class bindings described in Chapter 12 are examples of attribute directives.
Why are they useful?	The built-in directives cover the most common tasks required in web application development but don't deal with every situation. Custom directives allow application-specific features to be defined.
How are they used?	Attribute directives are classes to which the @Directive decorator has been applied. They are enabled in the directives property of the component responsible for a template and applied using a CSS selector.
Are there any pitfalls or limitations?	The main pitfall when creating a custom directive is the temptation to write code to perform tasks that can be better handled using directive features such as input and output properties and host element bindings.
Are there any alternatives?	Angular supports two other types of directive—structural directives and components—that may be more suitable for a given task. You can sometimes combine the built-in directives to create a specific effect If you prefer to avoid writing custom code, although the result can be brittle and leads to complex HTML that is hard to read and maintain.

© Adam Freeman 2018
A. Freeman, *Pro Angular 6*, https://doi.org/10.1007/978-1-4842-3649-9_15

Table 15-2 summarizes the chapter.

Table 15-2. *Chapter Summary*

Problem	Solution	Listing
Create an attribute directive	Apply the @Directive to a class	1–5
Access host element attribute values	Apply the @Attribute decorator to a constructor parameter	6–9
Create a data-bound input property	Apply the @Input decorator to a class property	10–11
Receive a notification when a data-bound input property value changes	Implement the ngOnChanges method	12
Define an event	Apply the @Output decorator	13, 14
Create a property binding or event binding on the host element	Apply the @HostBinding or @HostListener decorators	15–19
Export a directive's functionality for use in the template	Use the exportAs property of the @Directive decorator	20, 21

Preparing the Example Project

As I have been doing throughout this part of the book, I will continue using the example project from the previous chapter. To prepare for this chapter, I have added a table to the template that displays the products in the data model and removed the form-level validation messages, as shown in Listing 15-1.

■ **Tip** You can download the example project for this chapter—and for all the other chapters in this book—from https://github.com/Apress/pro-angular-6.

Listing 15-1. Preparing the Template in the template.html File in the src/app Folder

```
<style>
  input.ng-dirty.ng-invalid { border: 2px solid #ff0000 }
  input.ng-dirty.ng-valid { border: 2px solid #6bc502 }
</style>
<div class="row m-2">
  <div class="col-6">
    <form novalidate [formGroup]="form" (ngSubmit)="submitForm(form)">
      <div class="form-group" *ngFor="let control of form.productControls">
        <label>{{control.label}}</label>
        <input class="form-control"
               [(ngModel)]="newProduct[control.modelProperty]"
               name="{{control.modelProperty}}"
               formControlName="{{control.modelProperty}}" />
        <ul class="text-danger list-unstyled"
            *ngIf="(formSubmitted || control.dirty) && control.invalid">
```

```
        <li *ngFor="let error of control.getValidationMessages()">
          {{error}}
        </li>
      </ul>
    </div>
    <button class="btn btn-primary" type="submit"
            [disabled]="formSubmitted && !form.valid"
            [class.btn-secondary]="formSubmitted && form.invalid">
      Create
    </button>
  </form>
</div>

<div class="col-6">
  <table class="table table-sm table-bordered table-striped">
    <tr><th></th><th>Name</th><th>Category</th><th>Price</th></tr>
    <tr *ngFor="let item of getProducts(); let i = index">
      <td>{{i + 1}}</td>
      <td>{{item.name}}</td>
      <td>{{item.category}}</td>
      <td>{{item.price}}</td>
    </tr>
  </table>
</div>
</div>
```

This listing uses the Bootstrap grid layout to position the form and the table side by side. Listing 15-2 removes the jsonProperty property and updates the component's addProduct method so that it adds a new object to the data model.

Listing 15-2. Modifying the Data Model in the component.ts File in the src/app Folder

```
import { ApplicationRef, Component } from "@angular/core";
import { NgForm } from "@angular/forms";
import { Model } from "./repository.model";
import { Product } from "./product.model";
import { ProductFormGroup } from "./form.model";

@Component({
    selector: "app",
    templateUrl: "template.html"
})
export class ProductComponent {
    model: Model = new Model();
    form: ProductFormGroup = new ProductFormGroup();

    getProduct(key: number): Product {
        return this.model.getProduct(key);
    }

    getProducts(): Product[] {
        return this.model.getProducts();
    }
```

```
newProduct: Product = new Product();

addProduct(p: Product) {
    this.model.saveProduct(p);
}

formSubmitted: boolean = false;

submitForm(form: NgForm) {
    this.formSubmitted = true;
    if (form.valid) {
        this.addProduct(this.newProduct);
        this.newProduct = new Product();
        form.reset();
        this.formSubmitted = false;
    }
}
}
```

To start the application, navigate to the example project folder and run the following command:

```
ng serve
```

Open a new browser window and navigate to http://localhost:4200 to see the form in Figure 15-1. When you submit the form, the data will be validated, and either error messages will be displayed or a new item will be added to the data model and displayed in the table.

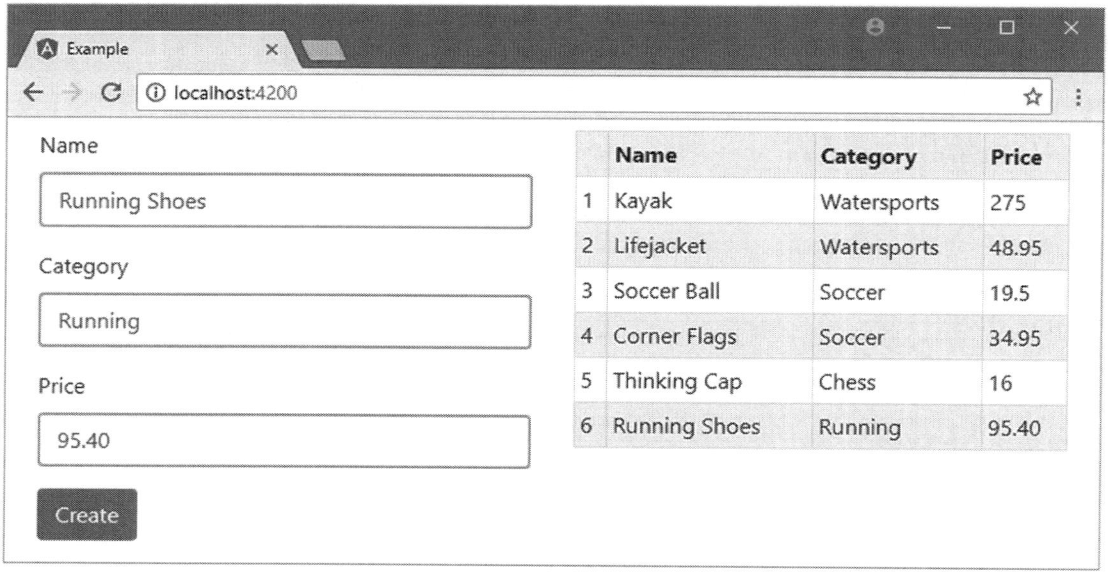

Figure 15-1. *Running the example application*

Creating a Simple Attribute Directive

The best place to start is to jump in and create a directive to see how they work. I added a file called `attr.directive.ts` to the `src/app` folder with the code shown in Listing 15-3. The name of the file indicates that it contains a directive. I set the first part of the file name to `attr` to indicate that this is an example of an attribute directive.

Listing 15-3. The Contents of the attr.directive.ts File in the src/app Folder

```
import { Directive, ElementRef } from "@angular/core";

@Directive({
    selector: "[pa-attr]",
})
export class PaAttrDirective {

    constructor(element: ElementRef) {
        element.nativeElement.classList.add("bg-success", "text-white");
    }
}
```

Directives are classes to which the `@Directive` decorator has been applied. The decorator requires the `selector` property, which is used to specify how the directive is applied to elements, expressed using a standard CSS style selector. The selector I used is `[pa-attr]`, which will match any element that has an attribute called `pa-attr`, regardless of the element type or the value assigned to the attribute.

Custom directives are given a distinctive prefix so they can be easily recognized. The prefix can be anything that is meaningful to your application. I have chosen the prefix Pa for my directive, reflecting the title of this book, and this prefix is used in the attribute specified by the `selector` decorator property and the name of the attribute class. The case of the prefix is changed to reflect its use so that an initial lowercase character is used for the selector attribute name (`pa-attr`) and an initial uppercase character is used in the name of the directive class (`PaAttrDirective`).

■ **Note** The prefix Ng/ng is reserved for use for built-in Angular features and should not be used.

The directive constructor defines a single `ElementRef` parameter, which Angular provides when it creates a new instance of the directive and which represents the host element. The `ElementRef` class defines a single property, `nativeElement`, which returns the object used by the browser to represent the element in the Domain Object Model. This object provides access to the methods and properties that manipulate the element and its contents, including the `classList` property, which can be used to manage the class membership of the element, like this:

```
...
element.nativeElement.classList.add("bg-success", "text-white");
...
```

To summarize, the `PaAttrDirective` class is a directive that is applied to elements that have a `pa-attr` attribute and adds those elements to the `bg-success` and `text-white` classes, which the Bootstrap CSS library uses to assign background and text colors to elements.

Applying a Custom Directive

There are two steps to apply a custom directive. The first is to update the template so that there are one or more elements that match the `selector` that the directive uses. In the case of the example directive, this means adding the `pa-attr` attribute to an element, as shown in Listing 15-4.

Listing 15-4. Adding a Directive Attribute in the template.html File in the src/app Folder

```
...
<table class="table table-sm table-bordered table-striped">
    <tr><th></th><th>Name</th><th>Category</th><th>Price</th></tr>
    <tr *ngFor="let item of getProducts(); let i = index" pa-attr>
        <td>{{i + 1}}</td>
        <td>{{item.name}}</td>
        <td>{{item.category}}</td>
        <td>{{item.price}}</td>
    </tr>
</table>
...
```

The directive's selector matches any element that has the attribute, regardless of whether a value has been assigned to it or what that value is. The second step to applying a directive is to change the configuration of the Angular module, as shown in Listing 15-5.

Listing 15-5. Configuring the Component in the app.module.ts File in the src/app Folder

```
import { NgModule } from "@angular/core";
import { BrowserModule } from "@angular/platform-browser";
import { ProductComponent } from "./component";
import { FormsModule, ReactiveFormsModule  } from "@angular/forms";
import { PaAttrDirective } from "./attr.directive";

@NgModule({
    imports: [BrowserModule, FormsModule, ReactiveFormsModule],
    declarations: [ProductComponent, PaAttrDirective],
    bootstrap: [ProductComponent]
})
export class AppModule { }
```

The `declarations` property of the `NgModule` decorator declares the directives and components that the application will use. Don't worry if the relationship and differences between directives and components seem muddled at the moment; it will become clear in Chapter 17.

Once both steps have been completed, the effect is that the `pa-attr` attribute applied to the `tr` element in the template will trigger the custom directive, which uses the DOM API to add the element to the `bg-success` and `text-white` classes. Since the `tr` element is part of the micro-template used by the `ngFor` directive, all the rows in the table are affected, as shown in Figure 15-2.

Figure 15-2. *Applying a custom directive*

Accessing Application Data in a Directive

The example in the previous section shows the basic structure of a directive, but it doesn't do anything that couldn't be performed just by using a class property binding on the tr element. Directives become useful when they can interact with the host element and with the rest of the application.

Reading Host Element Attributes

The simplest way to make a directive more useful is to configure it using attributes applied to the host element, which allows each instance of the directive to be provided with its own configuration information and to adapt its behavior accordingly.

As an example, Listing 15-6 applies the directive to some of the td elements in the template table and adds an attribute that specifies the class that the host element should be added to. The directive's selector means that it will match any element that has the pa-attr attribute, regardless of the tag type, and will work as well on td elements as it does on tr elements.

Listing 15-6. Adding Attributes in the template.html File in the src/app Folder

```
...
<table class="table table-sm table-bordered table-striped">
    <tr><th></th><th>Name</th><th>Category</th><th>Price</th></tr>
    <tr *ngFor="let item of getProducts(); let i = index" pa-attr>
        <td>{{i + 1}}</td>
        <td>{{item.name}}</td>
        <td pa-attr pa-attr-class="bg-warning">{{item.category}}</td>
        <td pa-attr pa-attr-class="bg-info">{{item.price}}</td>
    </tr>
</table>
...
```

345

The pa-attr attribute has been applied to two of the td elements, along with a new attribute called pa-attr-class, which has been used to specify the class to which the directive should add the host element. Listing 15-7 shows the changes required to the directive to get the value of the pa-attr-class attribute and use it to change the element.

Listing 15-7. Reading an Attribute in the attr.directive.ts File in the src/app Folder

```
import { Directive, ElementRef, Attribute } from "@angular/core";

@Directive({
  selector: "[pa-attr]",
})
export class PaAttrDirective {

  constructor(element: ElementRef, @Attribute("pa-attr-class") bgClass: string) {
    element.nativeElement.classList.add(bgClass || "bg-success", "text-white");
  }
}
```

To receive the value of the pa-attr-class attribute, I added a new constructor parameter called bgClass, to which the @Attribute decorator has been applied. This decorator is defined in the @angular/core module, and it specifies the name of the attribute that should be used to provide a value for the constructor parameter when a new instance of the directive class is created. Angular creates a new instance of the decorator for each element that matches the selector and uses that element's attributes to provide the values for the directive constructor arguments that have been decorated with @Attribute.

Within the constructor, the value of the attribute is passed to the classList.add method, with a default value that allows the directive to be applied to elements that have the pa-attr attribute but not the pa-attr-class attribute.

The result is that the class to which elements are added can now be specified using an attribute, producing the result shown in Figure 15-3.

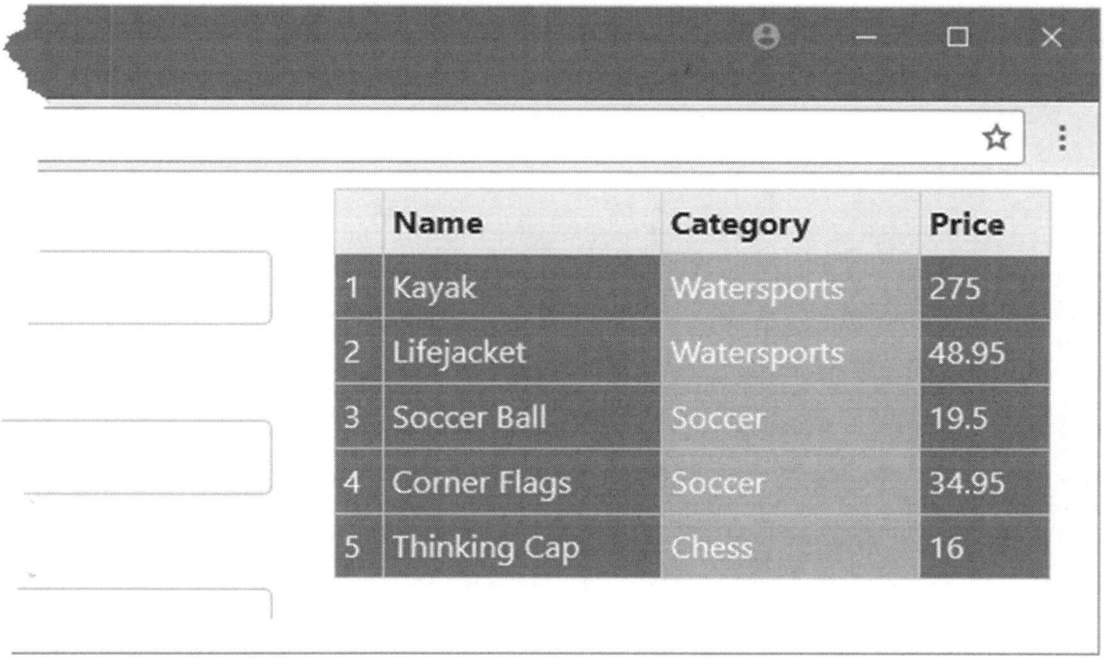

Figure 15-3. *Configuring a directive using a host element attribute*

Using a Single Host Element Attribute

Using one attribute to apply a directive and another to configure it is redundant, and it makes more sense to make a single attribute do double duty, as shown in Listing 15-8.

Listing 15-8. Reusing an Attribute in the attr.directive.ts File in the src/app Folder

```
import { Directive, ElementRef, Attribute } from "@angular/core";

@Directive({
    selector: "[pa-attr]",
})
export class PaAttrDirective {

    constructor(element: ElementRef, @Attribute("pa-attr") bgClass: string) {
        element.nativeElement.classList.add(bgClass || "bg-success", "text-white");
    }
}
```

The @Attribute decorator now specifies the pa-attr attribute as the source of the bgClass parameter value. In Listing 15-9, I have updated the template to reflect the dual-purpose attribute.

Listing 15-9. Applying a Directive in the template.html File in the src/app Folder

```
...
<table class="table table-sm table-bordered table-striped">
    <tr><th></th><th>Name</th><th>Category</th><th>Price</th></tr>
    <tr *ngFor="let item of getProducts(); let i = index" pa-attr>
        <td>{{i + 1}}</td>
        <td>{{item.name}}</td>
        <td pa-attr="bg-warning">{{item.category}}</td>
        <td pa-attr="bg-info">{{item.price}}</td>
    </tr>
</table>
...
```

There is no visual change in the result produced by this example, but it has simplified the way that the directive is applied in the HTML template.

Creating Data-Bound Input Properties

The main limitation of reading attributes with @Attribute is that values are static. The real power in Angular directives comes through support for expressions that are updated to reflect changes in the application state and that can respond by changing the host element.

Directives receive expressions using *data-bound input properties*, also known as *input properties* or, simply, *inputs*. Listing 15-10 changes the application's template so that the pa-attr attributes applied to the tr and td elements contain expressions, rather than just static class names.

Listing 15-10. Using Expressions in the template.html File in the src/app Folder

```
...
<table class="table table-sm table-bordered table-striped">
    <tr><th></th><th>Name</th><th>Category</th><th>Price</th></tr>
    <tr *ngFor="let item of getProducts(); let i = index"
        [pa-attr]="getProducts().length < 6 ? 'bg-success' : 'bg-warning'">
        <td>{{i + 1}}</td>
        <td>{{item.name}}</td>
        <td [pa-attr]="item.category == 'Soccer' ? 'bg-info' : null">
            {{item.category}}
        </td>
        <td [pa-attr]="'bg-info'">{{item.price}}</td>
    </tr>
</table>
...
```

There are three expressions in the listing. The first, which is applied to the tr element, uses the number of objects returned by the component's getProducts method to select a class.

```
...
<tr *ngFor="let item of getProducts(); let i = index"
    [pa-attr]="getProducts().length < 6 ? 'bg-success' : 'bg-warning'">
...
```

The second expression, which is applied to the td element for the Category column, specifies the bg-info class for Product objects whose Category property returns Soccer and null for all other values.

```
...
<td [pa-attr]="item.category == 'Soccer' ? 'bg-info' : null">
...
```

The third and final expression returns a fixed string value, which I have enclosed in single quotes, since this is an expression and not a static attribute value.

```
...
<td [pa-attr]="'bg-info'">{{item.price}}</td>
...
```

Notice that the attribute name is enclosed in square brackets. That's because the way to receive an expression in a directive is to create a data binding, just like the built-in directives that are described in Chapters 13 and 14.

■ **Tip** Forgetting to use the square brackets is a common mistake. Without them, Angular will just pass the raw text of the expression to the directive without evaluating it. This is the first thing to check if you encounter an error when applying a custom directive.

Implementing the other side of the data binding means creating an input property in the directive class and telling Angular how to manage its value, as shown in Listing 15-11.

Listing 15-11. Defining an Input Property in the attr.directive.ts File in the src/app Folder

```
import { Directive, ElementRef, Attribute, Input } from "@angular/core";

@Directive({
    selector: "[pa-attr]"
})
export class PaAttrDirective {

    constructor(private element: ElementRef) {}

    @Input("pa-attr")
    bgClass: string;

    ngOnInit() {
        this.element.nativeElement.classList.add(this.bgClass || "bg-success",
            "text-white");
    }
}
```

Input properties are defined by applying the @Input decorator to a property and using it to specify the name of the attribute that contains the expression. This listing defines a single input property, which tells Angular to set the value of the directive's bgClass property to the value of the expression contained in the pa-attr attribute.

■ **Tip** You don't need to provide an argument to the @Input decorator if the name of the property corresponds to the name of the attribute on the host element. So, if you apply @Input() to a property called myVal, then Angular will look for a myVal attribute on the host element.

The role of the constructor has changed in this example. When Angular creates a new instance of a directive class, the constructor is invoked to create a new directive object and only then is the value of the input property set. This means that the constructor cannot access the input property value because its value will not be set by Angular until after the constructor has completed and the new directive object has been produced. To address this, directives can implement *lifecycle hook methods*, which Angular uses to provide directives with useful information after they have been created and while the application is running, as described in Table 15-3.

Table 15-3. *The Directive Lifecycle Hook Methods*

Name	Description
ngOnInit	This method is called after Angular has set the initial value for all the input properties that the directive has declared.
ngOnChanges	This method is called when the value of an input property has changed and also just before the ngOnInit method is called.
ngDoCheck	This method is called when Angular runs its change detection process so that directives have an opportunity to update any state that isn't directly associated with an input property.
ngAfterContentInit	This method is called when the directive's content has been initialized. See the "Receiving Query Change Notifications" section in Chapter 16 for an example that uses this method.
ngAfterContentChecked	This method is called after the directive's content has been inspected as part of the change detection process.
ngOnDestroy	This method is called immediately before Angular destroys a directive.

To set the class on the host element, the directive in Listing 15-11 implements the ngOnInit method, which is called after Angular has set the value of the bgClass property. The constructor is still needed to receive the ElementRef object that provides access to the host element, which is assigned to a property called element.

The result is that Angular will create a directive object for each tr element, evaluate the expressions specified in the pa-attr attribute, use the results to set the value of the input properties, and then call the ngOnInit methods, which allows the directives to respond to the new input property values.

To see the effect, use the form to add a new product to the example application. Since there are initially five items in the model, the expression for the tr element will select the bg-success class. When you add a new item, Angular will create another instance of the directive class and evaluate the expression to set the value of the input property; since there are now six items in the model, the expression will select the bg-warning class, which provides the new row with a different background color, as shown in Figure 15-4.

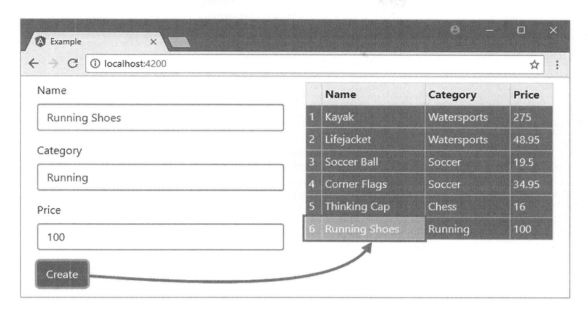

Figure 15-4. *Using an input property in a custom directive*

Responding to Input Property Changes

Something odd happened in the previous example: adding a new item affected the appearance of the new elements but not the existing elements. Behind the scenes, Angular has updated the value of the bgClass property for each of the directives that it created—one for each td element in the table column—but the directives didn't notice because changing a property value doesn't automatically cause directives to respond.

To handle changes, a directive must implement the ngOnChanges method to receive notifications when the value of an input property changes, as shown in Listing 15-12.

Listing 15-12. Receiving Change Notifications in the attr.directive.ts File in the src/app Folder

```
import { Directive, ElementRef, Attribute, Input,
        SimpleChange } from "@angular/core";

@Directive({
    selector: "[pa-attr]"
})
export class PaAttrDirective {

    constructor(private element: ElementRef) {}

    @Input("pa-attr")
    bgClass: string;

    ngOnChanges(changes: {[property: string]: SimpleChange }) {
        let change = changes["bgClass"];
        let classList = this.element.nativeElement.classList;
```

351

```
        if (!change.isFirstChange() && classList.contains(change.previousValue)) {
            classList.remove(change.previousValue);
        }
        if (!classList.contains(change.currentValue)) {
            classList.add(change.currentValue);
        }
    }
}
```

The ngOnChanges method is called once before the ngOnInit method and then called again each time there are changes to any of a directive's input properties. The ngOnChanges parameter is an object whose property names refer to each changed input property and whose values are SimpleChange objects, which are defined in the @angular/core module. TypeScript represents this data structure as follows:

```
...
ngOnChanges(changes: {[property: string]: SimpleChange }) {
...
```

The SimpleChange class defines the members shown in Table 15-4.

Table 15-4. *The Properties and Method of the SimpleChange Class*

Name	Description
previousValue	This property returns the previous value of the input property.
currentValue	This property returns the current value of the input property.
isFirstChange()	This method returns true if this is the call to the ngOnChanges method that occurs before the ngOnInit method.

The easiest way to understand the way that changes are presented to the ngOnChanges method is to serialize the object as JSON and look at it then.

```
...
{
    "target": {
        "previousValue":"bg-success",
        "currentValue":"bg-warning"
    }
}
...
```

This strips out the isFirstChange method, but it does help show the way that each property in the argument object is used to indicate a change to an input property.

When responding to changes to the input property value, a directive has to make sure to undo the effect of previous updates. In the case of the example directive, this means removing the element from the previousValue class and adding it to the currentValue class instead.

It is important to use the isFirstChange method so that you don't undo a value that hasn't actually been applied since the ngOnChanges method is called the first time a value is assigned to the input property.

The result of handling these change notifications is that the directive responds when Angular reevaluates the expressions and updates the input properties. Now when you add a new product to the application, the background colors for all the tr elements are updated, as shown in Figure 15-5.

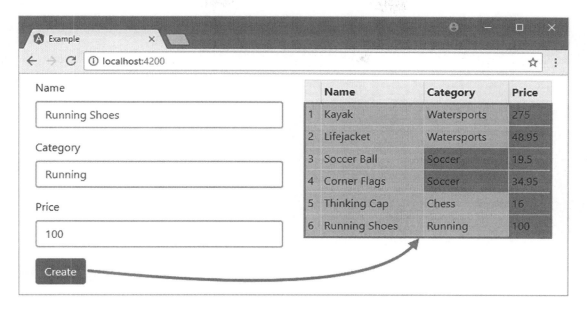

Figure 15-5. *Responding to input property changes*

Creating Custom Events

Output properties are the Angular feature that allows directives to add custom events to their host elements, through which details of important changes can be sent to the rest of the application. Output properties are defined using the @Output decorator, which is defined in the @angular/core module, as shown in Listing 15-13.

Listing 15-13. Defining an Output Property in the attr.directive.ts File in the src/app Folder

```
import { Directive, ElementRef, Attribute, Input,
        SimpleChange, Output, EventEmitter } from "@angular/core";
import { Product } from "./product.model";

@Directive({
    selector: "[pa-attr]"
})
export class PaAttrDirective {

    constructor(private element: ElementRef) {
        this.element.nativeElement.addEventListener("click", e => {
            if (this.product != null) {
                this.click.emit(this.product.category);
            }
        });
    }
```

```
@Input("pa-attr")
bgClass: string;

@Input("pa-product")
product: Product;

@Output("pa-category")
click = new EventEmitter<string>();

ngOnChanges(changes: {[property: string]: SimpleChange }) {
    let change = changes["bgClass"];
    let classList = this.element.nativeElement.classList;
    if (!change.isFirstChange() && classList.contains(change.previousValue)) {
        classList.remove(change.previousValue);
    }
    if (!classList.contains(change.currentValue)) {
        classList.add(change.currentValue);
    }
}
}
```

The EventEmitter class provides the event mechanism for Angular directives. The listing creates an EventEmitter object and assigns it to a variable called click, like this:

```
...
@Output("pa-category")
click = new EventEmitter<string>();
...
```

The string type parameter indicates that listeners to the event will receive a string when the event is triggered. Directives can provide any type of object to their event listeners, but common choices are string and number values, data model objects, and JavaScript Event objects.

The custom event in the listing is triggered when the mouse button is clicked on the host element, and the event provides its listeners with the category of the Product object that was used to create the table row using the ngFor directive. The effect is that the directive is responding to a DOM event on the host element and generating its own custom event in response. The listener for the DOM event is set up in the directive class constructor using the browser's standard addEventListener method, like this:

```
...
constructor(private element: ElementRef) {
    this.element.nativeElement.addEventListener("click", e => {
        if (this.product != null) {
            this.click.emit(this.product.category);
        }
    });
}
...
```

The directive defines an input property to receive the Product object whose category will be sent in the event. (The directive is able to refer to the value of the input property value in the constructor because Angular will have set the property value before the function assigned to handle the DOM event is invoked.)

The most important statement in the listing is the one that uses the EventEmitter object to send the event, which is done using the EventEmitter.emit method, which is described in Table 15-5 for quick reference. The argument to the emit method is the value that you want the event listeners to receive, which is the value of the category property for this example.

Table 15-5. *The EventEmitter Method*

Name	Description
emit(value)	This method triggers the custom event associated with the EventEmitter, providing the listeners with the object or value received as the method argument.

Tying everything together is the @Output decorator, which creates a mapping between the directive class EventEmitter property and the name that will be used to bind to the event in the template, like this:

```
...
@Output("pa-category")
click = new EventEmitter<string>();
...
```

The argument to the decorator specifies the attribute name that will be used in event bindings applied to the host element. You can omit the argument if the TypeScript property name is also the name you want for the custom event. I have specified pa-category in the listing, which allows me to refer to the event as click within the directive class but require a more meaningful name externally.

Binding to a Custom Event

Angular makes it easy to bind to custom events in templates by using the same binding syntax that is used for built-in events, which was described in Chapter 14. Listing 15-14 adds the pa-product attribute to the tr element in the template to provide the directive with its Product object and adds a binding for the pa-category event.

Listing 15-14. Binding to a Custom Event in the template.html File in the src/app Folder

```
...
<table class="table table-sm table-bordered table-striped">
    <tr><th></th><th>Name</th><th>Category</th><th>Price</th></tr>
    <tr *ngFor="let item of getProducts(); let i = index"
            [pa-attr]="getProducts().length < 6 ? 'bg-success' : 'bg-warning'"
            [pa-product]="item" (pa-category)="newProduct.category=$event">
        <td>{{i + 1}}</td>
        <td>{{item.name}}</td>
        <td [pa-attr]="item.category == 'Soccer' ? 'bg-info' : null">
            {{item.category}}
        </td>
        <td [pa-attr]="'bg-info'">{{item.price}}</td>
    </tr>
</table>
...
```

The term $event is used to access the value the directive passed to the EventEmitter.emit method. That means $event will be a string value containing the product category in this example. The value received from the event is assigned to the component's newProduct.category property, which causes the data binding for one of the input elements to be updated, meaning that clicking a row in the table displays the product's category in the form, as shown in Figure 15-6.

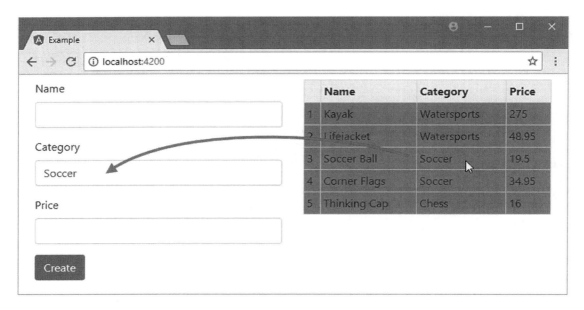

Figure 15-6. *Defining and receiving a custom event using an output property*

Creating Host Element Bindings

The example directive relies on the browser's DOM API to manipulate its host element, both to add and remove class memberships and to receive the click event. Working with the DOM API in an Angular application is a useful technique, but it does mean that your directive can be used only in applications that are run in a web browser. Angular is intended to be run in a range of different execution environments, and not all of them can be assumed to provide the DOM API.

Even if you are sure that a directive will have access to the DOM, the same results can be achieved in a more elegant way using standard Angular directive features: property and event bindings. Rather than use the DOM to add and remove classes, a class binding can be used on the host element. And rather than use the addEventListener method, an event binding can be used to deal with the mouse click.

Behind the scenes, Angular implements these features using the DOM API when the directive is used in a web browser—or some equivalent mechanism when the directive is used in a different environment.

Bindings on the host element are defined using two decorators, @HostBinding and @HostListener, both of which are defined in the @angular/core module, as shown in Listing 15-15.

Listing 15-15. Creating Host Bindings in the attr.directive.ts File in the src/app Folder

```
import { Directive, ElementRef, Attribute, Input,
         SimpleChange, Output, EventEmitter, HostListener, HostBinding }
            from "@angular/core";
 import { Product } from "./product.model";

@Directive({
    selector: "[pa-attr]"
})
export class PaAttrDirective {

    @Input("pa-attr")
    @HostBinding("class")
    bgClass: string;

    @Input("pa-product")
    product: Product;

    @Output("pa-category")
    click = new EventEmitter<string>();

    @HostListener("click")
    triggerCustomEvent() {
        if (this.product != null) {
            this.click.emit(this.product.category);
        }
    }
}
```

The @HostBinding decorator is used to set up a property binding on the host element and is applied to a directive property. The listing sets up a binding between the class property on the host element and the decorator's bgClass property.

■ **Tip**   If you want to manage the contents of an element, you can use the @HostBinding decorator to bind to the textContent property. See Chapter 19 for an example.

The @HostListener decorator is used to set up an event binding on the host element and is applied to a method. The listing creates an event binding for the click event that invokes the triggerCustomEvent method when the mouse button is pressed and released. As its name suggests, the triggerCustomEvent method uses the EventEmitter.emit method to dispatch the custom event through the output property.

Using the host element bindings means that the directive constructor can be removed since there is no longer any need to access the HTML element via the ElementRef object. Instead, Angular takes care of setting up the event listener and setting the element's class membership through the property binding.

Although the directive code is much simpler, the effect of the directive is the same: clicking a table row sets the value of one of the input elements, and adding a new item using the form triggers a change in the background color of the table cells for products that are not part of the Soccer category.

Creating a Two-Way Binding on the Host Element

Angular provides special support for creating directives that support two-way bindings so they can be used with the banana-in-a-box bracket style that ngModel uses and can bind to a model property in both directions.

The two-way binding feature relies on a naming convention. To demonstrate how it works, Listing 15-16 adds some new elements and bindings to the template.html file.

Listing 15-16. Applying a Directive in the template.html File in the src/app Folder

```
...
<div class="col-6">

    <div class="form-group bg-info text-white p-2">
        <label>Name:</label>
        <input class="bg-primary text-white" [paModel]="newProduct.name"
            (paModelChange)="newProduct.name=$event" />
    </div>

    <table class="table table-sm table-bordered table-striped">
        <tr><th></th><th>Name</th><th>Category</th><th>Price</th></tr>
        <tr *ngFor="let item of getProducts(); let i = index"
                [pa-attr]="getProducts().length < 6 ? 'bg-success' : 'bg-warning'"
                [pa-product]="item" (pa-category)="newProduct.category=$event">
            <td>{{i + 1}}</td>
            <td>{{item.name}}</td>
            <td [pa-attr]="item.category == 'Soccer' ? 'bg-info' : null">
                {{item.category}}
            </td>
            <td [pa-attr]="'bg-info'">{{item.price}}</td>
        </tr>
    </table>
</div>
...
```

I am going to create a directive that supports two one-way bindings. The binding whose target is paModel will be updated when the value of the newProduct.name property changes, which provides a flow of data from the application to the directive and will be used to update the contents of the input element. The custom event, paModelChange, will be triggered when the user changes the contents of the input element and will provide a flow of data from the directive to the rest of the application.

To implement the directive, I added a file called twoway.directive.ts to the src/app folder and used it to define the directive shown in Listing 15-17.

Listing 15-17. The Contents of the twoway.directive.ts File in the src/app Folder

```
import { Input, Output, EventEmitter, Directive,
        HostBinding, HostListener, SimpleChange } from "@angular/core";

@Directive({
    selector: "input[paModel]"
})
```

```
export class PaModel {

    @Input("paModel")
    modelProperty: string;

    @HostBinding("value")
    fieldValue: string = "";

    ngOnChanges(changes: { [property: string]: SimpleChange }) {
        let change = changes["modelProperty"];
        if (change.currentValue != this.fieldValue) {
            this.fieldValue = changes["modelProperty"].currentValue || "";
        }
    }

    @Output("paModelChange")
    update = new EventEmitter<string>();

    @HostListener("input", ["$event.target.value"])
    updateValue(newValue: string) {
        this.fieldValue = newValue;
        this.update.emit(newValue);
    }
}
```

This directive uses features that have been described previously. The selector property for this directive specifies that it will match input elements that have a paModel attribute. The built-in ngModel two-way directive has support for a range of form elements and knows which events and properties each of them uses, but I want to keep this example simple, so I am going to support just input elements, which define a value property that gets and sets the element content.

The paModel binding is implemented using an input property and the ngOnChanges method, which responds to changes in the expression value by updating the contents of the input element through a host binding on the input element's value property.

The paModelChange event is implemented using a host listener on the input event, which then sends an update through an output property. Notice that the method invoked by the event is able to receive the event object by specifying an additional argument to the @HostListener decorator, like this:

```
...
@HostListener("input", ["$event.target.value"])
updateValue(newValue: string) {
...
```

The first argument to the @HostListener decorator specifies the name of the event that will be handled by the listener. The second argument is an array that will be used to provide the decorated methods with arguments. In this example, the input event will be handled by the listener, and when the updateValue method is invoked, its newValue argument will be set to the target.value property of the Event object, which is referred to using $event.

To enable the directive, I added it to the Angular module, as shown in Listing 15-18.

Listing 15-18. Registering the Directive in the app.module.ts File in the src/app Folder

```
import { NgModule } from "@angular/core";
import { BrowserModule } from "@angular/platform-browser";
import { ProductComponent } from "./component";
import { FormsModule, ReactiveFormsModule } from "@angular/forms";
import { PaAttrDirective } from "./attr.directive";
import { PaModel } from "./twoway.directive";

@NgModule({
    imports: [BrowserModule, FormsModule, ReactiveFormsModule],
    declarations: [ProductComponent, PaAttrDirective, PaModel],
    bootstrap: [ProductComponent]
})
export class AppModule { }
```

When you save the changes and the browser has reloaded, you will see a new input element that responds to changes to a model property and updates the model property if its host element's content is changed. The expressions in the bindings specify the same model property used by the Name field in the form on the left side of the HTML document, which provides a convenient way to test the relationship between them, as shown in Figure 15-7.

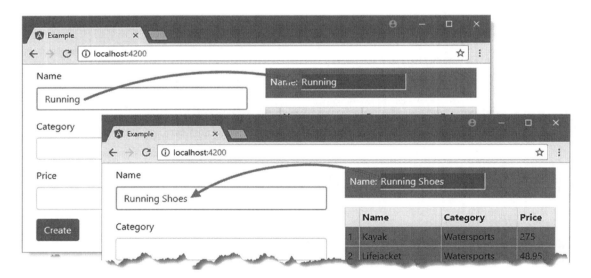

Figure 15-7. Testing the two-way flow of data

The final step is to simplify the bindings and apply the banana-in-a-box style of brackets, as shown in Listing 15-19.

Listing 15-19. Simplifying the Bindings in the template.html File in the src/app Folder

```
...
<div class="col-6">

    <div class="form-group bg-info text-white p-2">
        <label>Name:</label>
        <input class="bg-primary text-white" [(paModel)]="newProduct.name" />
    </div>

    <table class="table table-sm table-bordered table-striped">
        <tr><th></th><th>Name</th><th>Category</th><th>Price</th></tr>
        <tr *ngFor="let item of getProducts(); let i = index"
                [pa-attr]="getProducts().length < 6 ? 'bg-success' : 'bg-warning'"
                [pa-product]="item" (pa-category)="newProduct.category=$event">
            <td>{{i + 1}}</td>
            <td>{{item.name}}</td>
            <td [pa-attr]="item.category == 'Soccer' ? 'bg-info' : null">
                {{item.category}}
            </td>
            <td [pa-attr]="'bg-info'">{{item.price}}</td>
        </tr>
    </table>
</div>
...
```

When Angular encounters the [()] brackets, it expands the binding to match the format used in Listing 15-16, targeting the paModel input property and setting up the paModelChange event. As long as a directive exposes these to Angular, it can be targeted using the banana-in-a-box brackets, producing a simpler template syntax.

Exporting a Directive for Use in a Template Variable

In earlier chapters, I used template variables to access functionality provided by built-in directives, such as ngForm. As an example, here is an element from Chapter 14:

```
...
<form novalidate #form="ngForm" (ngSubmit)="submitForm(form)">
...
```

The form template variable is assigned ngForm, which is then used to access validation information for the HTML form. This is an example of how a directive can provide access to its properties and methods so they can be used in data bindings and expressions.

Listing 15-20 modifies the directive from the previous section so that it provides details of whether it has expanded the text in its host element.

Listing 15-20. Exporting a Directive in the twoway.directive.ts File in the src/app Folder

```
import { Input, Output, EventEmitter, Directive,
    HostBinding, HostListener, SimpleChange } from "@angular/core";

@Directive({
    selector: "input[paModel]",
    exportAs: "paModel"
})
export class PaModel {

    direction: string = "None";

    @Input("paModel")
    modelProperty: string;

    @HostBinding("value")
    fieldValue: string = "";

    ngOnChanges(changes: { [property: string]: SimpleChange }) {
        let change = changes["modelProperty"];
        if (change.currentValue != this.fieldValue) {
            this.fieldValue = changes["modelProperty"].currentValue || "";
            this.direction = "Model";
        }
    }

    @Output("paModelChange")
    update = new EventEmitter<string>();

    @HostListener("input", ["$event.target.value"])
    updateValue(newValue: string) {
        this.fieldValue = newValue;
        this.update.emit(newValue);
        this.direction = "Element";
    }
}
```

The exportAs property of the @Directive decorator specifies a name that will be used to refer to the directive in template variables. This example uses paModel as the value for the exportAs property, and you should try to use names that make it clear which directive is providing the functionality.

The listing adds a property called direction to the directive, which used to indicate when data is flowing from the model to the element or from the element to the model.

When you use the exportAs decorator, you are providing access to all the methods and properties defined by the directive to be used in template expressions and data bindings. Some developers prefix the names of the methods and properties that are not for use outside of the directive with an underscore (the _ character) or to apply the private keyword. This is an indication to other developers that some methods and properties should not be used but isn't enforced by Angular. Listing 15-21 creates a template variable for the directive's exported functionality and uses it in a style binding.

Listing 15-21. Using Exported Directive Functionality in the template.html File in the src/app Folder

```
...
<div class="col-6">

    <div class="form-group bg-info text-white p-2">
        <label>Name:</label>
        <input class="bg-primary text-white" [(paModel)]="newProduct.name"
            #paModel="paModel" />
        <div class="bg-primary text-white">Direction: {{paModel.direction}}</div>
    </div>

    <table class="table table-sm table-bordered table-striped">
        <tr><th></th><th>Name</th><th>Category</th><th>Price</th></tr>
        <tr *ngFor="let item of getProducts(); let i = index"
                [pa-attr]="getProducts().length < 6 ? 'bg-success' : 'bg-warning'"
                [pa-product]="item" (pa-category)="newProduct.category=$event">
            <td>{{i + 1}}</td>
            <td>{{item.name}}</td>
            <td [pa-attr]="item.category == 'Soccer' ? 'bg-info' : null">
                {{item.category}}
            </td>
            <td [pa-attr]="'bg-info'">{{item.price}}</td>
        </tr>
    </table>
</div>
...
```

The template variable is called paModel, and its value is the name used in the directive's exportAs property.

```
...
#paModel="paModel"
...
```

■ **Tip**   You don't have to use the same names for the variable and the directive, but it does help to make the source of the functionality clear.

Once the template variable has been defined, it can be used in interpolation bindings or as part of a binding expression. I opted for a string interpolation binding whose expression uses the value of the directive's direction property.

```
...
<div class="bg-primary text-white">Direction: {{paModel.direction}}</div>
...
```

The result is that you can see the effect of typing text into the two input elements that are bound to the newProduct.name model property. When you type into the one that uses the ngModel directive, then the string interpolation binding will display Model. When you type into the element that uses the paModel directive, the string interpolation binding will display Element, as shown in Figure 15-8.

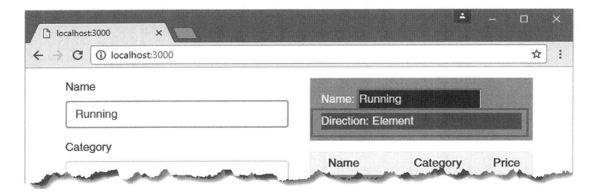

Figure 15-8. *Exporting functionality from a directive*

Summary

In this chapter, I described how to define and use attribute directives, including the use of input and output properties and host bindings. In the next chapter, I explain how structural directives work and how they can be used to change the layout or structure of the HTML document.

CHAPTER 16

■ ■ ■

Creating Structural Directives

Structural directives change the layout of the HTML document by adding and removing elements. They build on the core features available for attribute directives, described in Chapter 15, with additional support for micro-templates, which are small fragments of contents defined within the templates used by components. You can recognize when a structural directive is being used because its name will be prefixed with an asterisk, such as *ngIf and *ngFor. In this chapter, I explain how structural directives are defined and applied, how they work, and how they respond to changes in the data model. Table 16-1 puts structural directives in context.

Table 16-1. *Putting Structural Directives in Context*

Question	Answer
What are they?	Structural directives use micro-templates to add content to the HTML document.
Why are they useful?	Structural directives allow content to be added conditionally based on the result of an expression or for the same content to be repeated for each object in a data source, such as an array.
How are they used?	Structural directives are applied to an ng-template element, which contains the content and bindings that comprise its micro-template. The template class uses objects provided by Angular to control the inclusion of the content or to repeat the content.
Are there any pitfalls or limitations?	Unless care is taken, structural directives can make a lot of unnecessary changes to the HTML document, which can ruin the performance of a web application. It is important only to make changes when they are required, as explained in the "Dealing with Collection-Level Data Changes" section later in the chapter.
Are there any alternatives?	You can use the built-in directives for common tasks, but writing custom structural directives provides the ability to tailor behavior to your application.

© Adam Freeman 2018
A. Freeman, *Pro Angular 6*, https://doi.org/10.1007/978-1-4842-3649-9_16

Table 16-2 summarizes the chapter.

Table 16-2. *Chapter Summary*

Problem	Solution	Listing
Create a structural directive	Apply the @Directive decorator to a class that receives view container and template constructor parameters	1–6
Create an iterating structural directive	Define a ForOf input property in a structural directive class and iterate over its value	7–12
Handle data changes in a structural directive	Use a differ to detect changes in the ngDoCheck method	13–19
Query the content of the host element to which a structural directive has been applied	Use the @ContentChild or @ContentChildren decorators	20–25

Preparing the Example Project

In this chapter, I continue working with the example project that I created in Chapter 11 and have been using since. To prepare for this chapter, I simplified the template to remove the form, leaving only the table, as shown in Listing 16-1. (I'll add the form back in later in the chapter.)

■ **Tip** You can download the example project for this chapter—and for all the other chapters in this book—from https://github.com/Apress/pro-angular-6.

Listing 16-1. Simplifying the Template in the template.html File in the src/app Folder

```
<div class="m-2">
  <table class="table table-sm table-bordered table-striped">
    <tr><th></th><th>Name</th><th>Category</th><th>Price</th></tr>
    <tbody class="text-white">
      <tr *ngFor="let item of getProducts(); let i = index"
          [pa-attr]="getProducts().length < 6 ? 'bg-success' : 'bg-warning'"
          [pa-product]="item" (pa-category)="newProduct.category=$event">
      <td>{{i + 1}}</td>
      <td>{{item.name}}</td>
      <td [pa-attr]="item.category == 'Soccer' ? 'bg-info' : null">
        {{item.category}}
      </td>
      <td [pa-attr]="'bg-info'">{{item.price}}</td>
    </tr>
    </tbody>
  </table>
</div>
```

Run the following command in the example folder to start the development tools:

```
ng serve
```

Open a new browser window and navigate to http://localhost:4200 to see the content shown in Figure 16-1.

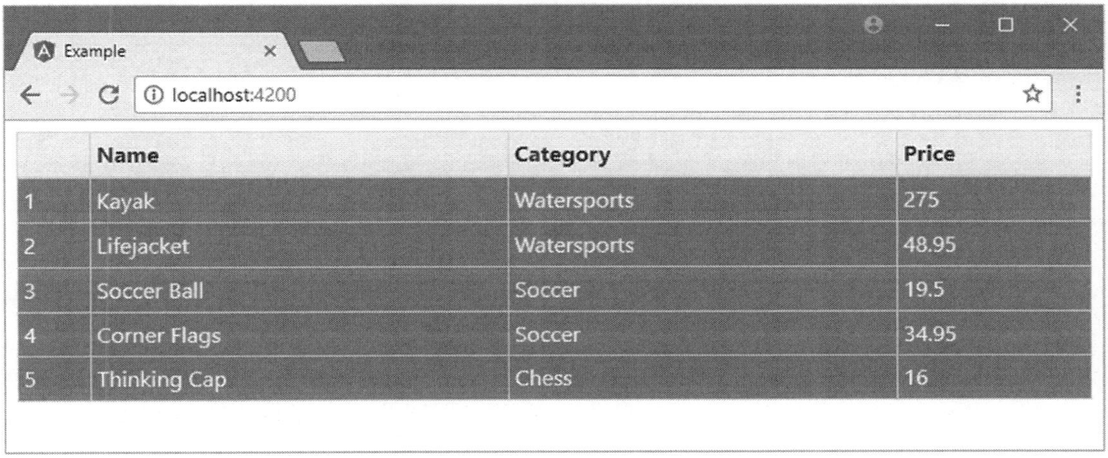

Figure 16-1. *Running the example application*

Creating a Simple Structural Directive

A good place to start with structural directives is to re-create the functionality provided by the ngIf directive, which is relatively simple, is easy to understand, and provides a good foundation for explaining how structural directives work. I start by making changes to the template and working back to write the code that supports it. Listing 16-2 shows the template changes.

Listing 16-2. Applying a Structural Directive in the template.html File in the src/app Folder

```
<div class="m-2">

    <div class="checkbox">
        <label>
            <input type="checkbox" [(ngModel)]="showTable" />
            Show Table
        </label>
    </div>

    <ng-template [paIf]="showTable">
        <table class="table table-sm table-bordered table-striped">
            <tr><th></th><th>Name</th><th>Category</th><th>Price</th></tr>
```

```
            <tr *ngFor="let item of getProducts(); let i = index"
                [pa-attr]="getProducts().length < 6 ? 'bg-success' : 'bg-warning'"
                [pa-product]="item" (pa-category)="newProduct.category=$event">
                <td>{{i + 1}}</td>
                <td>{{item.name}}</td>
                <td [pa-attr]="item.category == 'Soccer' ? 'bg-info' : null">
                    {{item.category}}
                </td>
                <td [pa-attr]="'bg-info'">{{item.price}}</td>
            </tr>
        </table>
    </ng-template>
</div>
```

This listing uses the full template syntax, in which the directive is applied to an ng-template element, which contains the content that will be used by the directive. In this case, the ng-template element contains the table element and all its contents, including bindings, directives, and expressions. (There is also a concise syntax, which I use later in the chapter.)

The ng-template element has a standard one-way data binding, which targets a directive called paIf, like this:

```
...
<ng-template [paIf]="showTable">
...
```

The expression for this binding uses the value of a property called showTable. This is the same property that is used in the other new binding in the template, which has been applied to a checkbox, as follows:

```
...
<input type="checkbox" checked="true" [(ngModel)]="showTable" />
...
```

The objectives in this section are to create a structural directive that will add the contents of the ng-template element to the HTML document when the showTable property is true, which will happen when the checkbox is checked, and to remove the contents of the ng-template element when the showTable property is false, which will happen when the checkbox is unchecked.

Implementing the Structural Directive Class

You know from the template what the directive should do. To implement the directive, I added a file called structure.directive.ts in the src/app folder and added the code shown in Listing 16-3.

Listing 16-3. The Contents of the structure.directive.ts File in the src/app Folder

```
import {
    Directive, SimpleChange, ViewContainerRef, TemplateRef, Input
} from "@angular/core";

@Directive({
    selector: "[paIf]"
})
```

```
export class PaStructureDirective {

    constructor(private container: ViewContainerRef,
        private template: TemplateRef<Object>) { }

    @Input("paIf")
    expressionResult: boolean;

    ngOnChanges(changes: { [property: string]: SimpleChange }) {
        let change = changes["expressionResult"];
        if (!change.isFirstChange() && !change.currentValue) {
            this.container.clear();
        } else if (change.currentValue) {
            this.container.createEmbeddedView(this.template);
        }
    }
}
```

The selector property of the @Directive decorator is used to match host elements that have the paIf attribute, corresponding to the template additions that I made in Listing 16-1.

There is an input property called expressionResult, which the directive uses to receive the results of the expression from the template. The directive implements the ngOnChanges method to receive change notifications so it can respond to changes in the data model.

The first indication that this is a structural directive comes from the constructor, which asks Angular to provide parameters using some new types.

```
...
constructor(private container: ViewContainerRef,
    private template: TemplateRef<Object>) {}
...
```

The ViewContainerRef object is used to manage the contents of the *view container*, which is the part of the HTML document where the ng-template element appears and for which the directive is responsible.

As its name suggests, the view container is responsible for managing a collection of *views*. A view is a region of HTML elements that contains directives, bindings, and expressions, and they are created and managed using the methods and properties provided by the ViewContainerRef class, the most useful of which are described in Table 16-3.

Table 16-3. *Useful ViewContainerRef Methods and Properties*

Name	Description
element	This property returns an ElementRef object that represents the container element.
createEmbeddedView(template)	This method uses a template to create a new view. See the text after the table for details. This method also accepts optional arguments for context data (as described in the "Creating Iterating Structural Directives" section) and an index position that specifies where the view should be inserted. The result is a ViewRef object that can be used with the other methods in this table.
clear()	This method removes all the views from the container.
length	This property returns the number of views in the container.
get(index)	This method returns the ViewRef object representing the view at the specified index.
indexOf(view)	This method returns the index of the specified ViewRef object.
insert(view, index)	This method inserts a view at the specified index.
remove(Index)	This method removes and destroys the view at the specified index.
detach(index)	This method detaches the view from the specified index without destroying it so that it can be repositioned with the insert method.

Two of the methods from Table 16-3 are required to re-create the ngIf directive's functionality: createEmbeddedView to show the ng-template element's content to the user and clear to remove it again.

The createEmbeddedView method adds a view to the view container. This method's argument is a TemplateRef object, which represents the content of the ng-template element.

The directive receives the TemplateRef object as one of its constructor arguments, for which Angular will provide a value automatically when creating a new instance of the directive class.

Putting everything together, when Angular processes the template.html file, it discovers the ng-template element and its binding and determines that it needs to create a new instance of the PaStructureDirective class. Angular examines the PaStructureDirective constructor and can see that it needs to provide it with ViewContainerRef and TemplateRef objects.

```
...
constructor(private container: ViewContainerRef,
    private template: TemplateRef<Object>) {}
...
```

The ViewContainerRef represents the place in the HTML document occupied by the ng-template element, and the TemplateRef represents the ng-template element's contents. Angular passes these objects to the constructor and creates a new instance of the directive class.

Angular then starts processing the expressions and data bindings. As described in Chapter 15, Angular invokes the ngOnChanges method during initialization (just before the ngOnInit method is invoked) and again whenever the value of the directive's expression changes.

The PaStructureDirective class's implementation of the ngOnChanges method uses the SimpleChange object that it receives to show or hide the contents of the ng-template element based on the current value of the expression. When the expression is true, the directive displays the ng-template element's content by adding them to the container view.

```
...
this.container.createEmbeddedView(this.template);
...
```

When the result of the expression is false, the directive clears the view container, which removes the elements from the HTML document.

```
...
this.container.clear();
...
```

The directive doesn't have any insight into the contents of the ng-template element and is responsible only for managing its visibility.

Enabling the Structural Directive

The directive must be enabled in the Angular module before it can be used, as shown in Listing 16-4.

Listing 16-4. Enabling the Directive in the app.module.ts File in the src/app Folder

```
import { NgModule } from "@angular/core";
import { BrowserModule } from "@angular/platform-browser";
import { ProductComponent } from "./component";
import { FormsModule, ReactiveFormsModule  } from "@angular/forms";
import { PaAttrDirective } from "./attr.directive";
import { PaModel } from "./twoway.directive";
import { PaStructureDirective } from "./structure.directive";

@NgModule({
    imports: [BrowserModule, FormsModule, ReactiveFormsModule],
    declarations: [ProductComponent, PaAttrDirective, PaModel, PaStructureDirective],
    bootstrap: [ProductComponent]
})
export class AppModule { }
```

Structural directives are enabled in the same way as attribute directives and are specified in the module's declarations array.

Once you save the changes, the browser will reload the HTML document, and you can see the effect of the new directive: the table element, which is the content of the ng-template element, will be shown only when the checkbox is checked, as shown in Figure 16-2.

▪ **Note** The contents of the ng-template element are being destroyed and re-created, not simply hidden and revealed. If you want to show or hide content without removing it from the HTML document, then you can use a style binding to set the display or visibility property.

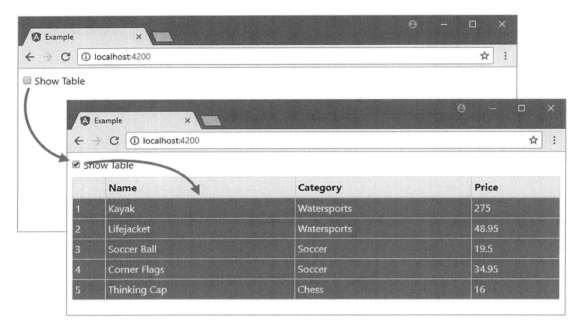

Figure 16-2. *Creating a structural directive*

Setting the Initial Expression Value

The contents of the ng-template element are not shown initially because the directive's expression relies on a variable that has not been previously defined.

```
...
<ng-template [paIf]="showTable">
...
```

The variable showTable won't be defined until the user checks the checkbox element, at which point it will be created with a value of true. This is an example of how templates can dynamically create JavaScript variables, as described in Chapter 14. I mention it again here because it is easy to get confused about where the variable is created. If you want to define an initial value for the showTable variable, then you must do so in the component, as shown in Listing 16-5, and not in the structural directive.

Listing 16-5. Defining a Variable in the component.ts File in the src/app Folder

```
import { ApplicationRef, Component } from "@angular/core";
import { Model } from "./repository.model";
import { Product } from "./product.model";
import { ProductFormGroup } from "./form.model";

@Component({
    selector: "app",
    templateUrl: "app/template.html"
})
```

```
export class ProductComponent {
    model: Model = new Model();
    form: ProductFormGroup = new ProductFormGroup();

    // ...other members omitted for brevity...

    showTable: boolean = true;
}
```

The structural directive receives the value of its expression through its input property and has no insight into what the expression is, and the component provides the context for Angular to evaluate the expression. The change in Listing 16-5 gives an initial true value to the showTable property, which means that the ng-template element's content is visible when the application first starts.

Using the Concise Structural Directive Syntax

The use of the ng-template element helps illustrate the role of the view container in structural directives. The concise syntax does away with the ng-template element and applies the directive and its expression to the outermost element that it would contain, as shown in Listing 16-6.

■ **Tip** The concise structural directive syntax is intended to be easier to use and read, but it is just a matter of preference as to which syntax you use.

Listing 16-6. Using the Concise Structural Directive Syntax in the template.html File in the src/app Folder

```
<div class="m-2">
  <div class="checkbox">
    <label>
      <input type="checkbox" [(ngModel)]="showTable" />
      Show Table
    </label>
  </div>

  <table *paIf="showTable"
         class="table table-sm table-bordered table-striped">
    <tr><th></th><th>Name</th><th>Category</th><th>Price</th></tr>
    <tbody class="text-white">
      <tr *ngFor="let item of getProducts(); let i = index"
          [pa-attr]="getProducts().length < 6 ? 'bg-success' : 'bg-warning'"
          [pa-product]="item" (pa-category)="newProduct.category=$event">
        <td>{{i + 1}}</td>
        <td>{{item.name}}</td>
        <td [pa-attr]="item.category == 'Soccer' ? 'bg-info' : null">
          {{item.category}}
        </td>
        <td [pa-attr]="'bg-info'">{{item.price}}</td>
      </tr>
    </tbody>
  </table>
</div>
```

The ng-template element has been removed, and the directive has been applied to the table element, like this:

```
...
<table *paIf="showTable" class="table table-sm table-bordered table-striped">
...
```

The directive's name is prefixed with an asterisk (the * character) to tell Angular that this is a structural directive that uses the concise syntax. When Angular parses the template.html file, it discovers the directive and the asterisk and handles the elements as though there were a ng-template element in the document. No changes are required to the directive class to support the concise syntax.

Creating Iterating Structural Directives

Angular provides special support for directives that need to iterate over a data source. The best way to demonstrate this is to re-create another of the built-in directives: ngFor.

To prepare for the new directive, I have removed the ngFor directive from the template.html file, inserted a ng-template element, and applied a new directive attribute and expression, as shown in Listing 16-7.

Listing 16-7. Preparing for a New Structural Directive in the template.html File in the src/app Folder

```
<div class="m-2">
  <div class="checkbox">
    <label>
      <input type="checkbox" [(ngModel)]="showTable" />
      Show Table
    </label>
  </div>

  <table *paIf="showTable"
         class="table table-sm table-bordered table-striped">
    <tr><th></th><th>Name</th><th>Category</th><th>Price</th></tr>
    <ng-template [paForOf]="getProducts()" let-item>
      <tr><td colspan="4">{{item.name}}</td></tr>
    </ng-template>
  </table>
</div>
```

The full syntax for iterating structural directives is a little odd. In the listing, the ng-template element has two attributes that are used to apply the directive. The first is a standard binding whose expression obtains the data required by the directive, bound to an attribute called paForOf.

```
...
<ng-template [paForOf]="getProducts()" let-item>
...
```

The name of this attribute is important. When using an ng-template element, the name of the data source attribute must end with Of to support the concise syntax, which I will introduce shortly.

The second attribute is used to define the *implicit value*, which allows the currently processed object to be referred to within the ng-template element as the directive iterates through the data source. Unlike other template variables, the implicit variable isn't assigned a value, and its purpose is only to define the variable name.

```
...
<ng-template [paForOf]="getProducts()" let-item>
...
```

In this example, I have used let-item to tell Angular that I want the implicit value to be assigned to a variable called item, which is then used within a string interpolation binding to display the name property of the current data item.

```
...
<td colspan="4">{{item.name}}</td>
...
```

Looking at the ng-template element, you can see that the purpose of the new directive is to iterate through the component's getProducts method and generate a table row for each of them that displays the name property. To implement this functionality, I created a file called iterator.directive.ts in the src/app folder and defined the directive shown in Listing 16-8.

Listing 16-8. The Contents of the iterator.directive.ts File in the src/app Folder

```
import { Directive, ViewContainerRef, TemplateRef,
            Input, SimpleChange } from "@angular/core";

@Directive({
    selector: "[paForOf]"
})
export class PaIteratorDirective {

    constructor(private container: ViewContainerRef,
        private template: TemplateRef<Object>) {}

    @Input("paForOf")
    dataSource: any;

    ngOnInit() {
        this.container.clear();
        for (let i = 0; i < this.dataSource.length; i++) {
            this.container.createEmbeddedView(this.template,
                new PaIteratorContext(this.dataSource[i]));
        }
    }
}

class PaIteratorContext {
    constructor(public $implicit: any) {}
}
```

The `selector` property in the `@Directive` decorator matches elements with the `paForOf` attribute, which is also the source of the data for the `dataSource` input property and which provides the source of objects that will be iterated.

The `ngOnInit` method will be called once the value of the input property has been set, and the directive empties the view container using the `clear` method and adds a new view for each object using the `createEmbeddedView` method.

When calling the `createEmbeddedView` method, the directive provides two arguments: the `TemplateRef` object received through the constructor and a context object. The `TemplateRef` provides the content to insert into the container, and the context object provides the data for the implicit value, which is specified using a property called `$implicit`. It is this object, with its `$implicit` property, that is assigned to the `item` template variable and that is referred to in the string interpolation binding. To provide templates with the context object in a type-safe way, I defined a class called `PaIteratorContext`, whose only property is called `$implicit`.

The `ngOnInit` method reveals some important aspects of working with view containers. First, a view container can be populated with multiple views—in this case, one view per object in the data source. The `ViewContainerRef` class provides the functionality required to manage these views once they have been created, as you will see in the sections that follow.

Second, a template can be reused to create multiple views. In this example, the contents of the `ng-template` element will be used to create identical `tr` and `td` elements for each object in the data source. The `td` element contains a data binding, which is processed by Angular when each view is created and is used to tailor the content to its data object.

Third, the directive has no special knowledge about the data it is working with and no knowledge of the content that is being generated. Angular takes care of providing the directive with the context it needs from the rest of the application, providing the data source through the input property and providing the content for each view through the `TemplateRef` object.

Enabling the directive requires an addition to the Angular module, as shown in Listing 16-9.

Listing 16-9. Adding a Custom Directive in the app.module.ts File in the src/app Folder

```
import { NgModule } from "@angular/core";
import { BrowserModule } from "@angular/platform-browser";
import { ProductComponent } from "./component";
import { FormsModule, ReactiveFormsModule  } from "@angular/forms";
import { PaAttrDirective } from "./attr.directive";
import { PaModel } from "./twoway.directive";
import { PaStructureDirective } from "./structure.directive";
import { PaIteratorDirective } from "./iterator.directive";

@NgModule({
    imports: [BrowserModule, FormsModule, ReactiveFormsModule],
    declarations: [ProductComponent, PaAttrDirective, PaModel,
        PaStructureDirective, PaIteratorDirective],
    bootstrap: [ProductComponent]
})
export class AppModule { }
```

The result is that the directive iterates through the objects in its data source and uses the `ng-template` element's content to create a view for each of them, providing rows for the table, as shown in Figure 16-3.

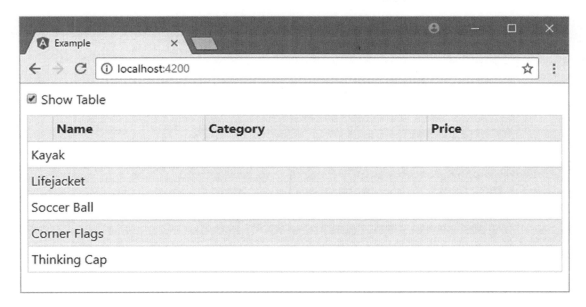

Figure 16-3. *Creating an iterating structural directive*

Providing Additional Context Data

Structural directives can provide templates with additional values to be assigned to template variables and used in bindings. For example, the ngFor directive provides odd, even, first, and last values. Context values are provided through the same object that defines the $implicit property, and in Listing 16-10, I have re-created the same set of values that ngFor provides.

Listing 16-10. Providing Context Data in the iterator.directive.ts File in the src/app Folder

```
import { Directive, ViewContainerRef, TemplateRef,
            Input, SimpleChange } from "@angular/core";

@Directive({
    selector: "[paForOf]"
})
export class PaIteratorDirective {

    constructor(private container: ViewContainerRef,
        private template: TemplateRef<Object>) {}

    @Input("paForOf")
    dataSource: any;
```

```
    ngOnInit() {
        this.container.clear();
        for (let i = 0; i < this.dataSource.length; i++) {
            this.container.createEmbeddedView(this.template,
                new PaIteratorContext(this.dataSource[i],
                    i, this.dataSource.length));
        }
    }
}

class PaIteratorContext {
    odd: boolean; even: boolean;
    first: boolean; last: boolean;

    constructor(public $implicit: any,
            public index: number, total: number ) {

        this.odd = index % 2 == 1;
        this.even = !this.odd;
        this.first = index == 0;
        this.last = index == total - 1;
    }
}
```

This listing defines additional properties in the PaIteratorContext class and expands its constructor so that it receives additional parameters, which are used to set the produce the property values.

The effect of these additions is that context object properties can be used to create template variables, which can then be referred to in binding expressions, as shown in Listing 16-11.

Listing 16-11. Using Structural Directive Context Data in the template.html File in the src/app Folder

```
<div class="m-2">
  <div class="checkbox">
    <label>
      <input type="checkbox" [(ngModel)]="showTable" />
      Show Table
    </label>
  </div>

  <table *paIf="showTable"
        class="table table-sm table-bordered table-striped">
    <tr><th></th><th>Name</th><th>Category</th><th>Price</th></tr>
    <ng-template [paForOf]="getProducts()" let-item let-i="index"
                let-odd="odd" let-even="even">
      <tr [class.bg-info]="odd" [class.bg-warning]="even">
        <td>{{i + 1}}</td>
        <td>{{item.name}}</td>
        <td>{{item.category}}</td>
        <td>{{item.price}}</td>
      </tr>
    </ng-template>
  </table>
</div>
```

Template variables are created using the `let-<name>` attribute syntax and assigned one of the context data values. In this listing, I used the odd and even context values to create template variables of the same name, which are then incorporated into class bindings on the `tr` element, resulting in striped table rows, as shown in Figure 16-4. The listing also adds additional table cells to display all the `Product` properties.

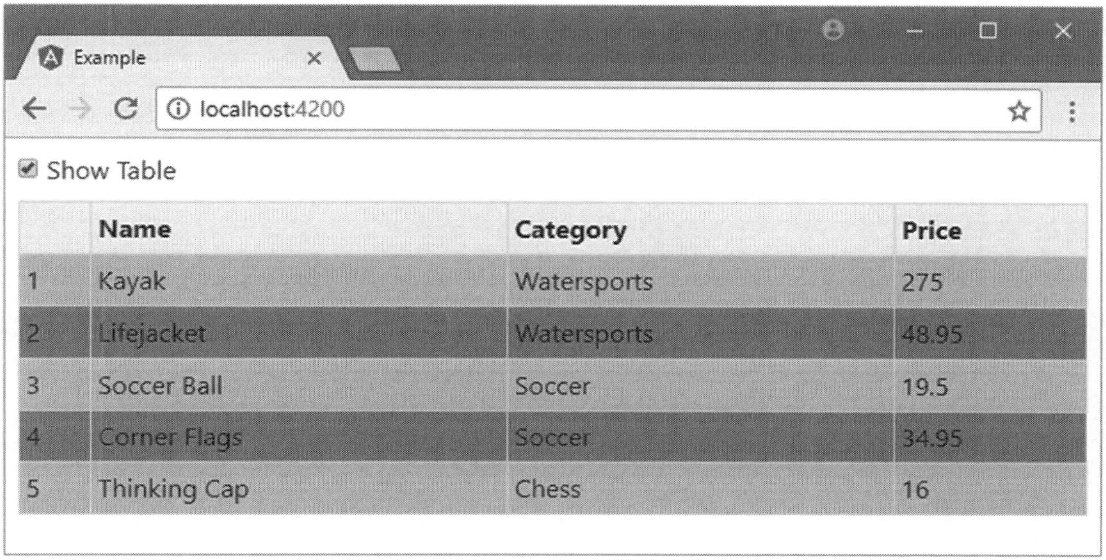

	Name	Category	Price
1	Kayak	Watersports	275
2	Lifejacket	Watersports	48.95
3	Soccer Ball	Soccer	19.5
4	Corner Flags	Soccer	34.95
5	Thinking Cap	Chess	16

Figure 16-4. *Using directive context data*

Using the Concise Structure Syntax

Iterating structural directives support the concise syntax and omit the `ng-template` element, as shown in Listing 16-12.

Listing 16-12. Using the Concise Syntax in the template.html File in the src/app Folder

```
<div class="m-2">
  <div class="checkbox">
    <label>
      <input type="checkbox" [(ngModel)]="showTable" />
      Show Table
    </label>
  </div>

  <table *paIf="showTable"
         class="table table-sm table-bordered table-striped">
    <tr><th></th><th>Name</th><th>Category</th><th>Price</th></tr>
    <tr *paFor="let item of getProducts(); let i = index; let odd = odd;
            let even = even" [class.bg-info]="odd" [class.bg-warning]="even">
      <td>{{i + 1}}</td>
      <td>{{item.name}}</td>
```

```
        <td>{{item.category}}</td>
        <td>{{item.price}}</td>
      </tr>
    </table>
</div>
```

This is a more substantial change than the one required for attribute directives. The biggest change is in the attribute used to apply the directive. When using the full syntax, the directive was applied to the ng-template element using the attribute specified by its selector, like this:

```
...
<ng-template [paForOf]="getProducts()" let-item let-i="index" let-odd="odd"
    let-even="even">
...
```

When using the concise syntax, the Of part of the attribute is omitted, the name is prefixed with an asterisk, and the brackets are omitted.

```
...
<tr *paFor="let item of getProducts(); let i = index; let odd = odd;
            let even = even" [class.bg-info]="odd" [class.bg-warning]="even">
...
```

The other change is to incorporate all the context values into the directive's expression, replacing the individual let- attributes. The main data value becomes part of the initial expression, with additional context values separated by semicolons.

No changes are required to the directive to support the concise syntax, whose selector and input property still specify an attribute called paForOf. Angular takes care of expanding the concise syntax, and the directive doesn't know or care whether an ng-template element has been used.

Dealing with Property-Level Data Changes

There are two kinds of changes that can occur in the data sources used by iterating structural directives. The first kind happens when the properties of an individual object change. This has a knock-on effect on the data bindings contained within the ng-template element, either directly through a change in the implicit value or indirectly through the additional context values provided by the directive. Angular takes care of these changes automatically, reflecting any changes in the context data in the bindings that depend on them.

To demonstrate, in Listing 16-13 I have added a call to the standard JavaScript setInterval function in the constructor of the context class. The function passed to setInterval alters the odd and even properties and changes the value of the price property of the Product object that is used as the implicit value.

Listing 16-13. Modifying Individual Objects in the iterator.directive.ts File in the src/app Folder

```
...
class PaIteratorContext {
    odd: boolean; even: boolean;
    first: boolean; last: boolean;

    constructor(public $implicit: any,
            public index: number, total: number ) {
```

```
        this.odd = index % 2 == 1;
        this.even = !this.odd;
        this.first = index == 0;
        this.last = index == total - 1;

        setInterval(() => {
            this.odd = !this.odd; this.even = !this.even;
            this.$implicit.price++;
        }, 2000);
    }
}
...
```

Once every two seconds, the values of the odd and even properties are inverted, and the price value is incremented. When you save the changes, you will see that the colors of the table rows change and the prices slowly increase, as illustrated in Figure 16-5.

Figure 16-5. *Automatic change detection for individual data source objects*

Dealing with Collection-Level Data Changes

The second type of change occurs when the objects within the collection are added, removed, or replaced. Angular doesn't detect this kind of change automatically, which means the iterating directive's ngOnChanges method won't be invoked.

Receiving notifications about collection-level changes is done by implementing the ngDoCheck method, which is called whenever a data change is detected in the application, regardless of where that change occurs or what kind of change it is. The ngDoCheck method allows a directive to respond to changes even when they are not automatically detected by Angular. Implementing the ngDoCheck method requires caution, however, because it represents a pitfall that can destroy the performance of a web application. To demonstrate the problem, Listing 16-14 implements the ngDoCheck method so that the directive updates the content it displays when there is a change.

Listing 16-14. Implementing the ngDoCheck Methods in the iterator.directive.ts File in the src/app Folder

```
import { Directive, ViewContainerRef, TemplateRef,
            Input, SimpleChange } from "@angular/core";

@Directive({
    selector: "[paForOf]"
})
export class PaIteratorDirective {

    constructor(private container: ViewContainerRef,
        private template: TemplateRef<Object>) {}

    @Input("paForOf")
    dataSource: any;

    ngOnInit() {
        this.updateContent();
    }

    ngDoCheck() {
        console.log("ngDoCheck Called");
        this.updateContent();
    }

    private updateContent() {
        this.container.clear();
        for (let i = 0; i < this.dataSource.length; i++) {
            this.container.createEmbeddedView(this.template,
                new PaIteratorContext(this.dataSource[i],
                    i, this.dataSource.length));
        }
    }
}

class PaIteratorContext {
    odd: boolean; even: boolean;
    first: boolean; last: boolean;

    constructor(public $implicit: any,
            public index: number, total: number ) {

        this.odd = index % 2 == 1;
        this.even = !this.odd;
        this.first = index == 0;
        this.last = index == total - 1;

        // setInterval(() => {
        //      this.odd = !this.odd; this.even = !this.even;
        //      this.$implicit.price++;
        // }, 2000);
    }
}
```

The ngOnInit and ngDoCheck methods both call a new updateContent method that clears the contents of the view container and generates new template content for each object in the data source. I have also commented out the call to the setInterval function in the PaIteratorContext class.

To understand the problem with collection-level changes and the ngDoCheck method, I need to restore the form to the component's template, as shown in Listing 16-15.

Listing 16-15. Restoring the HTML Form in the template.html File in the src/app Folder

```
<style>
  input.ng-dirty.ng-invalid { border: 2px solid #ff0000 }
  input.ng-dirty.ng-valid { border: 2px solid #6bc502 }
</style>

<div class="row m-2">
  <div class="col-4">
    <form novalidate [formGroup]="form" (ngSubmit)="submitForm(form)">
      <div class="form-group" *ngFor="let control of form.productControls">
        <label>{{control.label}}</label>
        <input class="form-control"
               [(ngModel)]="newProduct[control.modelProperty]"
               name="{{control.modelProperty}}"
               formControlName="{{control.modelProperty}}" />
        <ul class="text-danger list-unstyled"
            *ngIf="(formSubmitted || control.dirty) && !control.valid">
          <li *ngFor="let error of control.getValidationMessages()">
            {{error}}
          </li>
        </ul>
      </div>
      <button class="btn btn-primary" type="submit"
              [disabled]="formSubmitted && !form.valid"
              [class.btn-secondary]="formSubmitted && !form.valid">
        Create
      </button>
    </form>
  </div>
  <div class="col-8">
    <div class="checkbox">
      <label>
        <input type="checkbox" [(ngModel)]="showTable" />
        Show Table
      </label>
    </div>

    <table *paIf="showTable"
           class="table table-sm table-bordered table-striped">
      <tr><th></th><th>Name</th><th>Category</th><th>Price</th></tr>
      <tr *paFor="let item of getProducts(); let i = index; let odd = odd;
              let even = even" [class.bg-info]="odd" [class.bg-warning]="even">
        <td>{{i + 1}}</td>
        <td>{{item.name}}</td>
```

```
      <td>{{item.category}}</td>
      <td>{{item.price}}</td>
    </tr>
  </table>
</div>
</div>
```

When you save the changes to the template, the HTML form will be displayed alongside the table of products, as shown in Figure 16-6.

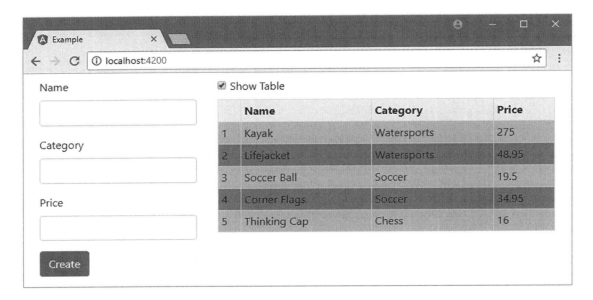

Figure 16-6. *Restoring the table in the template*

The problem with the ngDoCheck method is that it is invoked every time Angular detects a change anywhere in the application—and those changes happen more often than you might expect.

To demonstrate how often changes occur, I added a call to the console.log method within the directive's ngDoCheck method in Listing 16-14 so that a message will be displayed in the browser's JavaScript console each time the ngDoCheck method is called. Use the HTML form to create a new product and see how many messages are written out to the browser's JavaScript console, each of which represents a change detected by Angular and which results in a call to the ngDoCheck method.

A new message is displayed each time an input element gets the focus, each time a key event is triggered, each time a validation check is performed, and so on. A quick test adding a Running Shoes product in the Running category with a price of 100 generates 27 messages on my system, although the exact number will vary based on how you navigate between elements, whether you need to correct typos, and so on.

For each of those 27 times, the structural directive destroys and re-creates its content, which means producing new tr and td elements, with new directive and binding objects.

There are only a few rows of data in the example application, but these are expensive operations and a real application can grind to a halt as the content is repeatedly destroyed and re-created. The worst part of this problem is that all the changes except one were unnecessary because the content in the table didn't need to be updated until the new Product object was added to the data model. For all the other changes, the directive destroyed its content and created an identical replacement.

Fortunately, Angular provides some tools for managing updates more efficiently and updating content only when it is required. The ngDoCheck method will still be called for all changes in the application, but the directive can inspect its data to see whether any changes that require new content have occurred, as shown in Listing 16-16.

Listing 16-16. Minimizing Content Changes in the iterator.directive.ts File in the src/app Folder

```
import { Directive, ViewContainerRef, TemplateRef,
            Input, SimpleChange, IterableDiffer, IterableDiffers,
            ChangeDetectorRef, CollectionChangeRecord, DefaultIterableDiffer
} from "@angular/core";

@Directive({
    selector: "[paForOf]"
})
export class PaIteratorDirective {
    private differ: DefaultIterableDiffer<any>;

    constructor(private container: ViewContainerRef,
        private template: TemplateRef<Object>,
        private differs: IterableDiffers,
        private changeDetector: ChangeDetectorRef) {
    }

    @Input("paForOf")
    dataSource: any;

    ngOnInit() {
        this.differ =
            <DefaultIterableDiffer<any>> this.differs.find(this.dataSource).create();
    }

    ngDoCheck() {
        let changes = this.differ.diff(this.dataSource);
        if (changes != null) {
            console.log("ngDoCheck called, changes detected");
            changes.forEachAddedItem(addition => {
                this.container.createEmbeddedView(this.template,
                    new PaIteratorContext(addition.item,
                        addition.currentIndex, changes.length));
            });
        }
    }
}

class PaIteratorContext {
    odd: boolean; even: boolean;
    first: boolean; last: boolean;
```

```
    constructor(public $implicit: any,
            public index: number, total: number ) {

        this.odd = index % 2 == 1;
        this.even = !this.odd;
        this.first = index == 0;
        this.last = index == total - 1;
    }
}
```

The idea is to work out whether there have been objects added, removed, or moved from the collection. This means the directive has to do some work every time the ngDoCheck method is called to avoid unnecessary and expensive DOM operations when there are no collection changes to process.

The process starts in the constructor, which receives two new arguments whose values will be provided by Angular when a new instance of the directive class is created. The IterableDiffers and ChangeDetectorRef objects are used to set up change detection on the data source collection in the ngOnInit method, like this:

```
...
ngOnInit() {
    this.differ =
        <DefaultIterableDiffer<any>> this.differs.find(this.dataSource).create();
}
...
```

Angular includes built-in classes, known as *differs*, that can detect changes in different types of objects. The IterableDiffers.find method accepts an object and returns an IterableDifferFactory object that is capable of creating a differ class for that object. The IterableDifferFactory class defines a create method that returns an DefaultIterableDiffer object that will perform the actual change detection, using the ChangeDetectorRef object that was received in the constructor.

The important part of this incantation is the DefaultIterableDiffer object, which was assigned to a property called differ so that it can be used when the ngDoCheck method is called.

```
...
ngDoCheck() {
    let changes = this.differ.diff(this.dataSource);
    if (changes != null) {
        console.log("ngDoCheck called, changes detected");
        changes.forEachAddedItem(addition => {
            this.container.createEmbeddedView(this.template,
                new PaIteratorContext(addition.item,
                    addition.currentIndex, changes.length));
        });
    }
}
...
```

The DefaultIterableDiffer.diff method accepts an object for comparison and returns a list of the changes or null if there have been no changes. Checking for the null result allows the directive to avoid unnecessary work when the ngDoCheck method is called for changes elsewhere in the application. The object returned by the diff method provides the properties and methods described in Table 16-4 for processing changes.

Table 16-4. *The DefaultIterableDiffer.Diff Results Methods and Properties*

Name	Description
collection	This property returns the collection of objects that has been inspected for changes.
length	This property returns the number of objects in the collection.
forEachItem(func)	This method invokes the specified function for each object in the collection.
forEachPreviousItem(func)	This method invokes the specified function for each object in the previous version of the collection.
forEachAddedItem(func)	This method invokes the specified function for each new object in the collection.
forEachMovedItem(func)	This method invokes the specified function for each object whose position has changed.
forEachRemovedItem(func)	This method invokes the specified function for each object that was removed from the collection.
forEachIdentityChange(func)	This method invokes the specified function for each object whose identity has changed.

The functions that are passed to the methods described in Table 16-4 will receive a CollectionChangeRecord object that describes an item and how it has changed, using the properties shown in Table 16-5.

Table 16-5. *The CollectionChangeRecord Properties*

Name	Description
item	This property returns the data item.
trackById	This property returns the identity value if a trackBy function is used.
currentIndex	This property returns the current index of the item in the collection.
previousIndex	This property returns the previous index of the item in the collection.

The code in Listing 16-16 only needs to deal with new objects in the data source since that is the only change that the rest of the application can perform. If the result of the diff method isn't null, then I use the forEachAddedItem method to invoke a fat arrow function for each new object that has been detected. The function is called once for each new object and uses the properties in Table 16-5 to create new views in the view container.

The changes in Listing 16-16 included a new console message that is written to the browser's JavaScript console only when there has been a data change detected by the directive. If you repeat the process of adding a new product, you will see that the message is displayed only when the application first starts and when the Create button is clicked. The ngDoCheck method is still being called, and the directive has to check for data changes every time, so there is still unnecessary work going on. But these operations are much less expensive and time-consuming than destroying and then re-creating HTML elements.

Keeping Track of Views

Handling change detection is simple when you are handling the creation of new data items. Other operations—such as dealing with deletions or modifications—are more complex and require the directive to keep track of which view is associated with which data object.

To demonstrate, I am going to add support for deleting a `Product` object from the data model. First, Listing 16-17 adds a method to the component to delete a product using its key. This isn't a requirement because the template could access the repository through the component's `model` property, but it can help make applications easier to understand when all of the data is accessed and used in the same way.

Listing 16-17. Adding a Delete Method in the component.ts File in the src/app Folder

```
import { ApplicationRef, Component } from "@angular/core";
import { NgForm } from "@angular/forms";
import { Model } from "./repository.model";
import { Product } from "./product.model";
import { ProductFormGroup } from "./form.model";

@Component({
    selector: "app",
    templateUrl: "template.html"
})
export class ProductComponent {
    model: Model = new Model();
    form: ProductFormGroup = new ProductFormGroup();

    getProduct(key: number): Product {
        return this.model.getProduct(key);
    }

    getProducts(): Product[] {
        return this.model.getProducts();
    }

    newProduct: Product = new Product();

    addProduct(p: Product) {
        this.model.saveProduct(p);
    }

    deleteProduct(key: number) {
        this.model.deleteProduct(key);
    }

    formSubmitted: boolean = false;

    submitForm(form: NgForm) {
        this.formSubmitted = true;
        if (form.valid) {
            this.addProduct(this.newProduct);
            this.newProduct = new Product();
```

```
                form.reset();
                this.formSubmitted = false;
            }
        }

        showTable: boolean = true;
    }
```

Listing 16-18 updates the template so that the content generated by the structural directive contains a column of button elements that will delete the data object associated with the row that contains it.

Listing 16-18. Adding a Delete Button in the template.html File in the src/app Folder

```
...
<table *paIf="showTable"
    class="table table-sm table-bordered table-striped">
    <tr><th></th><th>Name</th><th>Category</th><th>Price</th><th></th></tr>
    <tr *paFor="let item of getProducts(); let i = index; let odd = odd;
            let even = even" [class.bg-info]="odd" [class.bg-warning]="even">
        <td style="vertical-align:middle">{{i + 1}}</td>
        <td style="vertical-align:middle">{{item.name}}</td>
        <td style="vertical-align:middle">{{item.category}}</td>
        <td style="vertical-align:middle">{{item.price}}</td>
        <td class="text-center">
            <button class="btn btn-danger btn-sm" (click)="deleteProduct(item.id)">
                Delete
            </button>
        </td>
    </tr>
</table>
...
```

The button elements have click event bindings that call the component's deleteProduct method. I also set the value of the CSS style property vertical-align on the existing td elements so the text in the table is aligned with the button text. The final step is to process the data changes in the structural directive so that it responds when an object is removed from the data source, as shown in Listing 16-19.

Listing 16-19. Responding to a Removed Item in the iterator.directive.ts File in the src/app Folder

```
import {
    Directive, ViewContainerRef, TemplateRef,
    Input, SimpleChange, IterableDiffer, IterableDiffers,
    ChangeDetectorRef, CollectionChangeRecord, DefaultIterableDiffer, ViewRef
} from "@angular/core";

@Directive({
    selector: "[paForOf]"
})
export class PaIteratorDirective {
    private differ: DefaultIterableDiffer<any>;
    private views: Map<any, PaIteratorContext> = new Map<any, PaIteratorContext>();
```

```
    constructor(private container: ViewContainerRef,
        private template: TemplateRef<Object>,
        private differs: IterableDiffers,
        private changeDetector: ChangeDetectorRef) {
    }

    @Input("paForOf")
    dataSource: any;

    ngOnInit() {
        this.differ =
            <DefaultIterableDiffer<any>>this.differs.find(this.dataSource).create();
    }

    ngDoCheck() {
        let changes = this.differ.diff(this.dataSource);
        if (changes != null) {
            changes.forEachAddedItem(addition => {
                let context = new PaIteratorContext(addition.item,
                    addition.currentIndex, changes.length);
                context.view = this.container.createEmbeddedView(this.template,
                    context);
                this.views.set(addition.trackById, context);
            });
            let removals = false;
            changes.forEachRemovedItem(removal => {
                removals = true;
                let context = this.views.get(removal.trackById);
                if (context != null) {
                    this.container.remove(this.container.indexOf(context.view));
                    this.views.delete(removal.trackById);
                }
            });
            if (removals) {
                let index = 0;
                this.views.forEach(context =>
                    context.setData(index++, this.views.size));
            }
        }
    }
}

class PaIteratorContext {
    index: number;
    odd: boolean; even: boolean;
    first: boolean; last: boolean;
    view: ViewRef;

    constructor(public $implicit: any,
            public position: number, total: number ) {
        this.setData(position, total);
    }
```

```
setData(index: number, total: number) {
    this.index = index;
    this.odd = index % 2 == 1;
    this.even = !this.odd;
    this.first = index == 0;
    this.last = index == total - 1;
}
}
```

Two tasks are required to handle removed objects. The first task is updating the set of views by removing the ones that correspond to the items provided by the forEachRemovedItem method. This means keeping track of the mapping between the data objects and the views that represent them, which I have done by adding a ViewRef property to the PaIteratorContext class and using a Map to collect them, indexed by the value of the CollectionChangeRecord.trackById property.

When processing the collection changes, the directive handles each removed object by retrieving the corresponding PaIteratorContext object from the Map, getting its ViewRef object, and passing it to the ViewContainerRef.remove element to remove the content associated with the object from the view container.

The second task is to update the context data for those objects that remain so that the bindings that rely on a view's position in the view container are updated correctly. The directive calls the PaIteratorContext.setData method for each context object left in the Map to update the view's position in the container and update the total number of views that are in use. Without these changes, the properties provided by the context object wouldn't accurately reflect the data model, which means the background colors for the rows wouldn't be striped and the Delete buttons wouldn't target the right objects.

The effect of these changes is that each table row contains a Delete button that removes the corresponding object from the data model, which in turn triggers an update of the table, as shown in Figure 16-7.

Figure 16-7. *Removing objects from the data model*

Querying the Host Element Content

Directives can query the contents of their host element to access the directives it contains, known as the *content children*, which allows directives to coordinate themselves to work together.

■ **Tip** Directives can also work together by sharing services, which I describe in Chapter 19.

To demonstrate how content can be queried, I added a file called `cellColor.directive.ts` to the `src/app` folder and used it to define the directive shown in Listing 16-20.

Listing 16-20. The Contents of the cellColor.directive.ts File in the src/app Folder

```
import { Directive, HostBinding } from "@angular/core";

@Directive({
    selector: "td"
})
export class PaCellColor {

    @HostBinding("class")
    bgClass: string = "";

    setColor(dark: Boolean) {
        this.bgClass = dark ? "bg-dark" : "";
    }
}
```

The PaCellColor class defines a simple attribute directive that operates on `td` elements and that binds to the `class` property of the host element. The `setColor` method accepts a Boolean parameter that, when the value is true, sets the `class` property to `bg-dark`, which is the Bootstrap class for a dark background.

The PaCellColor class will be the directive that is embedded in the host element's content in this example. The goal is to write another directive that will query its host element to locate the embedded directive and invoke its `setColor` method. To that end, I added a file called `cellColorSwitcher.directive.ts` to the `src/app` folder and used it to define the directive shown in Listing 16-21.

Listing 16-21. The Contents of the cellColorSwitcher.directive.ts File in the src/app Folder

```
import { Directive, Input, Output, EventEmitter,
        SimpleChange, ContentChild } from "@angular/core";
import { PaCellColor } from "./cellColor.directive";

@Directive({
    selector: "table"
})
export class PaCellColorSwitcher {

    @Input("paCellDarkColor")
    modelProperty: Boolean;
```

```
    @ContentChild(PaCellColor)
    contentChild: PaCellColor;

    ngOnChanges(changes: { [property: string]: SimpleChange }) {
        if (this.contentChild != null) {
            this.contentChild.setColor(changes["modelProperty"].currentValue);
        }
    }
}
```

The PaCellColorSwitcher class defines a directive that operates on table elements and that defines an input property called paCellDarkColor. The important part of this directive is the contentChild property.

```
...
@ContentChild(PaCellColor)
contentChild: PaCellColor;
...
```

The @ContentChild decorator tells Angular that the directive needs to query the host element's content and assign the first result of the query to the property. The argument to the @ContentChild director is one or more directive classes. In this case, the argument to the @ContentChild decorator is PaCellColor, which tells Angular to locate the first PaCellColor object contained within the host element's content and assign it to the decorated property.

■ **Tip** You can also query using template variable names, such that @ContentChild("myVariable") will find the first directive that has been assigned to myVariable.

The query result provides the PaCellColorSwitcher directive with access to the child component and allows it to call the setColor method in response to changes to the input property.

■ **Tip** If you want to include the descendants of children in the results, then you can configure the query, like this: @ContentChild(PaCellColor, { descendants: true}).

In Listing 16-22, I added a checkbox to the template that uses the ngModel directive to set a variable that is bound to the PaCellColorSwitcher directive's input property.

Listing 16-22. Applying the Directives in the template.html File in the src/app Folder

```
...
<div class="col-8">
    <div class="checkbox">
        <label>
            <input type="checkbox" [(ngModel)]="showTable" />
            Show Table
        </label>
    </div>
```

```
<div class="checkbox">
    <label>
        <input type="checkbox" [(ngModel)]="darkColor" />
        Dark Cell Color
    </label>
</div>

<table *paIf="showTable" [paCellDarkColor]="darkColor"
        class="table table-sm table-bordered table-striped">
    <tr><th></th><th>Name</th><th>Category</th><th>Price</th><th></th></tr>
    <tr *paFor="let item of getProducts(); let i = index; let odd = odd;
            let even = even" [class.bg-info]="odd" [class.bg-warning]="even">
    <td style="vertical-align:middle">{{i + 1}}</td>
    <td style="vertical-align:middle">{{item.name}}</td>
    <td style="vertical-align:middle">{{item.category}}</td>
    <td style="vertical-align:middle">{{item.price}}</td>
    <td class="text-xs-center">
        <button class="btn btn-danger btn-sm" (click)="deleteProduct(i)">
            Delete
        </button>
    </td>
    </tr>
</table>
</div>
...
```

The final step is to register the new directives with the Angular module's declarations property, as shown in Listing 16-23.

Listing 16-23. Registering New Directives in the app.module.ts File in the src/app Folder

```
import { NgModule } from "@angular/core";
import { BrowserModule } from "@angular/platform-browser";
import { ProductComponent } from "./component";
import { FormsModule, ReactiveFormsModule  } from "@angular/forms";
import { PaAttrDirective } from "./attr.directive";
import { PaModel } from "./twoway.directive";
import { PaStructureDirective } from "./structure.directive";
import { PaIteratorDirective } from "./iterator.directive";
import { PaCellColor } from "./cellColor.directive";
import { PaCellColorSwitcher } from "./cellColorSwitcher.directive";

@NgModule({
    imports: [BrowserModule, FormsModule, ReactiveFormsModule],
    declarations: [ProductComponent, PaAttrDirective, PaModel,
        PaStructureDirective, PaIteratorDirective,
        PaCellColor, PaCellColorSwitcher],
    bootstrap: [ProductComponent]
})
export class AppModule { }
```

When you save the changes, you will see a new checkbox above the table. When you check the box, the ngModel directive will cause the PaCellColorSwitcher directive's input property to be updated, which will call the setColor method of the PaCellColor directive object that was found using the @ContentChild decorator. The visual effect is small because only the first PaCellColor directive is affected, which is the cell that displays the number 1, at the top-left corner of the table, as shown in Figure 16-8.

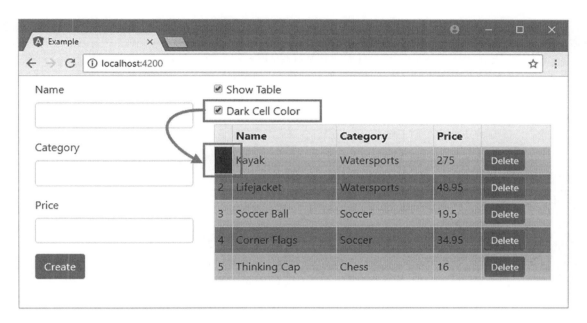

Figure 16-8. *Operating on a content child*

Querying Multiple Content Children

The @ContentChild decorator finds the first directive object that matches the argument and assigns it to the decorated property. If you want to receive all the directive objects that match the argument, then you can use the @ContentChildren decorator instead, as shown in Listing 16-24.

Listing 16-24. Querying Multiple Children in the cellColorSwitcher.directive.ts File in the src/app Folder

```
import { Directive, Input, Output, EventEmitter,
        SimpleChange, ContentChildren, QueryList } from "@angular/core";
import { PaCellColor } from "./cellColor.directive";

@Directive({
    selector: "table"
})
export class PaCellColorSwitcher {

    @Input("paCellDarkColor")
    modelProperty: Boolean;
```

```
@ContentChildren(PaCellColor)
contentChildren: QueryList<PaCellColor>;

ngOnChanges(changes: { [property: string]: SimpleChange }) {
    this.updateContentChildren(changes["modelProperty"].currentValue);
}

private updateContentChildren(dark: Boolean) {
    if (this.contentChildren != null && dark != undefined) {
        this.contentChildren.forEach((child, index) => {
            child.setColor(index % 2 ? dark : !dark);
        });
    }
}
}
```

When you use the @ContentChildren decorator, the results of the query are provided through a QueryList, which provides access to the directive objects using the methods and properties described in Table 16-6.

Table 16-6. The QueryList Members

Name	Description
length	This property returns the number of matched directive objects.
first	This property returns the first matched directive object.
last	This property returns the last matched directive object.
map(function)	This method calls a function for each matched directive object to create a new array, equivalent to the Array.map method.
filter(function)	This method calls a function for each matched directive object to create an array containing the objects for which the function returns true, equivalent to the Array.filter method.
reduce(function)	This method calls a function for each matched directive object to create a single value, equivalent to the Array.reduce method.
forEach(function)	This method calls a function for each matched directive object, equivalent to the Array.forEach method.
some(function)	This method calls a function for each matched directive object and returns true if the function returns true at least once, equivalent to the Array.some method.
changes	This property is used to monitor the results for changes, as described in the upcoming "Receiving Query Change Notifications" section.

In the listing, the directive responds to changes in the input property value by calling the updateContentChildren method, which in turns uses the forEach method on the QueryList and invokes the setColor method on every second directive that has matched the query. Figure 16-9 shows the effect when the checkbox is selected.

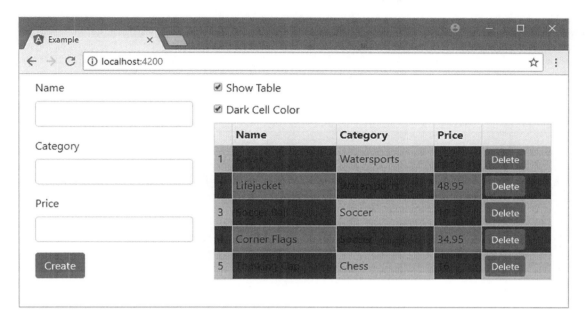

Figure 16-9. *Operating on multiple content children*

Receiving Query Change Notifications

The results of content queries are live, meaning that they are automatically updated to reflect additions, changes, or deletions in the host element's content. Receiving a notification when there is a change in the query results requires using the Observable interface, which is provided by the Reactive Extensions package added to the project in Chapter 11. The Reactive Extensions package provides features for distributing change events through a JavaScript application. I explain how Observable objects work in more detail in Chapter 23, but for now, it is enough to know that they are used internally by Angular to manage changes.

In Listing 16-25, I have updated the PaCellColorSwitcher directive so that it receives notifications when the set of content children in the QueryList changes.

Listing 16-25. Receiving Notifications in the cellColorSwitcher.directive.ts File in the src/app Folder

```
import { Directive, Input, Output, EventEmitter,
        SimpleChange, ContentChildren, QueryList } from "@angular/core";
import { PaCellColor } from "./cellColor.directive";

@Directive({
    selector: "table"
})
export class PaCellColorSwitcher {

    @Input("paCellDarkColor")
    modelProperty: Boolean;

    @ContentChildren(PaCellColor)
    contentChildren: QueryList<PaCellColor>;
```

397

```
    ngOnChanges(changes: { [property: string]: SimpleChange }) {
        this.updateContentChildren(changes["modelProperty"].currentValue);
    }

    ngAfterContentInit() {
        this.contentChildren.changes.subscribe(() => {
            setTimeout(() => this.updateContentChildren(this.modelProperty), 0);
        });
    }

    private updateContentChildren(dark: Boolean) {
        if (this.contentChildren != null && dark != undefined) {
            this.contentChildren.forEach((child, index) => {
                child.setColor(index % 2 ? dark : !dark);
            });
        }
    }
}
```

The value of a content child query property isn't set until the ngAfterContentInit lifecycle method is invoked, so I use this method to set up the change notification. The QueryList class defines a changes method that returns a Reactive Extensions Observable object, which defines a subscribe method. This method accepts a function that is called when the contents of the QueryList change, meaning that there is some change in the set of directives matched by the argument to the @ContentChildren decorator. The function that I passed to the subscribe method calls the updateContentChildren method to set the colors, but it does so within a call to the setTimeout function, which delays the execution of the method call until after the subscribe callback function has completed. Without the call to setTimeout, Angular will report an error because the directive tries to start a new content update before the existing one has been fully processed. The result of these changes is that the dark coloring is automatically applied to new table cells that are created when the HTML form is used, as shown in Figure 16-10.

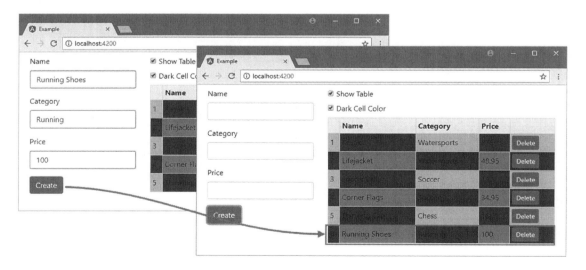

Figure 16-10. *Acting on content query change notifications*

Summary

In this chapter, I explained how structural directives work by re-creating the functionality of the built-in `ngIf` and `ngFor` directives. I explained the use of view containers and templates, described the full and concise syntax for applying structural directives, and showed you how to create a directive that iterates over a collection of data objects and how directives can query the content of their host element. In the next chapter, I introduce components and explain how they differ from directives.

CHAPTER 17

■ ■ ■

Understanding Components

Components are directives that have their own templates, rather than relying on content provided from elsewhere. Components have access to all the directive features described in earlier chapters and still have a host element, can still define input and output properties, and so on. But they also define their own content.

It can be easy to underestimate the importance of the template, but attribute and structural directives have limitations. Directives can do useful and powerful work, but they don't have much insight into the elements they are applied to. Directives are most useful when they are general-purpose tools, such as the ngModel directive, which can be applied to any data model property and any form element, without regard to what the data or the element is being used for.

Components, by contrast, are closely tied to the contents of their templates. Components provide the data and logic that will be used by the data bindings that are applied to the HTML elements in the template, which provide the context used to evaluate data binding expressions and act as the glue between the directives and the rest of the application. Components are also a useful tool in allowing large Angular projects to be broken up into manageable chunks.

In this chapter, I explain how components work and explain how to restructure an application by introducing some additional components. Table 17-1 puts components in context.

Table 17-1. *Putting Components in Context*

Question	Answer
What are they?	Components are directives that define their own HTML content and, optionally, CSS styles.
Why are they useful?	Components make it possible to define self-contained blocks of functionality, which makes projects more manageable and allows for functionality to be more readily reused.
How are they used?	The @Component decorator is applied to a class, which is registered in the application's Angular module.
Are there any pitfalls or limitations?	No. Components provide all the functionality of directives, with the addition of providing their own templates.
Are there any alternatives?	An Angular application must contain at least one component, which is used in the bootstrap process. Aside from this, you don't have to add additional components, although the resulting application becomes unwieldy and difficult to manage.

© Adam Freeman 2018
A. Freeman, *Pro Angular 6*, https://doi.org/10.1007/978-1-4842-3649-9_17

Table 17-2 summarizes the chapter.

Table 17-2. *Chapter Summary*

Problem	Solution	Listing
Create a component	Apply the @Component directive to a class	1–5
Define the content displayed by a component	Create an inline or external template	6–8
Include data in a template	Use a data binding in the component's template	9
Coordinate between components	Use input or output properties	10–16
Display content in an element to which a component has been applied	Project the host element's content	17–21
Style component content	Create component styles	22–30
Query the content in the component's template	Use the @ViewChildren decorator	31

Preparing the Example Project

In this chapter, I continue using the example project that I created in Chapter 11 and have been modifying since. No changes are required to prepare for this chapter.

■ **Tip**   You can download the example project for this chapter—and for all the other chapters in this book—from `https://github.com/Apress/pro-angular-6`.

Run the following command in the `example` folder to start the Angular development tools:

```
ng serve
```

Open a new browser and navigate to `http://localhost:4200` to see the content in Figure 17-1.

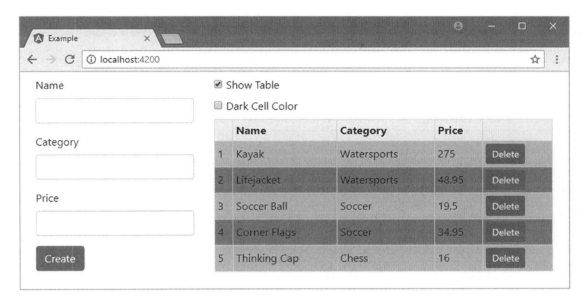

Figure 17-1. *Running the example project*

Structuring an Application with Components

At the moment, the example project contains only one component and one template. Angular applications require at least one component, known as the *root component*, which is the entry point specified in the Angular module.

The problem with having only one component is that it ends up containing the logic required for all the application's features, with its template containing all the markup required to expose those features to the user. The result is that a single component and its template are responsible for handling a lot of tasks. The component in the example application is responsible for the following:

- Providing Angular with an entry point into the application, as the root component

- Providing access to the application's data model so that it can be used in data bindings

- Defining the HTML form used to create new products

- Defining the HTML table used to display products

- Defining the layout that contains the form and the table

- Checking that the form data is valid when a new product is created

- Maintaining state information used to prevent invalid data being used to create data

- Maintaining state information about whether the table should be displayed

There is a lot going on for such a simple application, and not all of these tasks are related. This effect tends to creep up gradually as development proceeds, but it means that the application is harder to test because individual features can't be isolated effectively and is harder to enhance and maintain because the code and markup become increasingly complex.

403

Adding components to the application allows features to be separated into building blocks that can be used repeatedly in different parts of the application and tested in isolation. In the sections that follow, I create components that break up the functionality contained in the example application into manageable, reusable, and self-contained units. Along the way, I'll explain the different features that components provide beyond those available to directives. To prepare for these changes, I have simplified the existing component's template, as shown in Listing 17-1.

Listing 17-1. Simplifying the Content of the template.html File in the src/app Folder

```
<div class="row text-white m-2">
  <div class="col-4 p-2 bg-success">
    Form will go here
  </div>
  <div class="col-8 p-2 bg-primary">
    Table will go here
  </div>
</div>
```

When you save the changes to the template, you will see the content in Figure 17-2. The placeholders will be replaced with application functionality as I develop the new components and add them to the application.

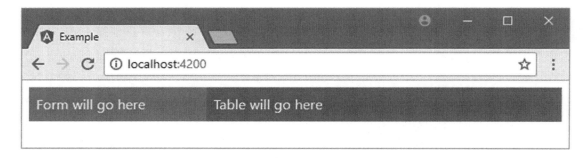

Figure 17-2. Simplifying the existing template

Creating New Components

To create a new component, I added a file called productTable.component.ts to the src/app folder and used it to define the component shown in Listing 17-2.

Listing 17-2. The Contents of the productTable.component.ts File in the src/app Folder

```
import { Component } from "@angular/core";

@Component({
    selector: "paProductTable",
    template: "<div>This is the table component</div>"
})
export class ProductTableComponent {

}
```

A component is a class to which the @Component decorator has been applied. This is as simple as a component can get, and it provides just enough functionality to count as a component without yet doing anything useful.

The naming convention for the files that define components is to use a descriptive name that suggests the purpose of the component, followed by a period and then component.ts. For this component, which will be used to generate the table of products, the file name is productTable.component.ts. The name of the class should be equally descriptive. This component's class is named ProductTableComponent.

The @Component decorator describes and configures the component. The most useful decorator properties are described in Table 17-3, which also includes details of where they are described (not all of them are covered in this chapter).

Table 17-3. *The Component Decorator Properties*

Name	Description
animations	This property is used to configuration animations, as described in Chapter 28.
encapsulation	This property is used to change the view encapsulation settings, which control how component styles are isolated from the rest of the HTML document. See the "Setting View Encapsulation" section for details.
selector	This property is used to specify the CSS selector used to match host elements, as described after the table.
styles	This property is used to define CSS styles that are applied only to the component's template. The styles are defined inline, as part of the TypeScript file. See the "Using Component Styles" section for details.
styleUrls	This property is used to define CSS styles that are applied only to the component's template. The styles are defined in separate CSS files. See the "Using Component Styles" section for details.
template	This property is used to specify an inline template, as described in the "Defining Templates" section.
templateUrl	This property is used to specify an external template, as described in the "Defining Templates" section.
providers	This property is used to create local providers for services, as described in Chapter 19.
viewProviders	This property is used to create local providers for services that are available only to view children, as described in Chapter 20.

For the second component, I created a file called productForm.component.ts in the src/app folder and added the code shown in Listing 17-3.

Listing 17-3. The Contents of the productForm.component.ts File in the src/app Folder

```
import { Component } from "@angular/core";

@Component({
    selector: "paProductForm",
    template: "<div>This is the form component</div>"
})
export class ProductFormComponent {

}
```

This component is equally simple and is just a placeholder for the moment. Later in the chapter, I'll add some more useful features. To enable the components, they must be declared in the application's Angular module, as shown in Listing 17-4.

Listing 17-4. Enabling New Components in the app.module.ts File in the src/app Folder

```
import { NgModule } from "@angular/core";
import { BrowserModule } from "@angular/platform-browser";
import { ProductComponent } from "./component";
import { FormsModule, ReactiveFormsModule  } from "@angular/forms";
import { PaAttrDirective } from "./attr.directive";
import { PaModel } from "./twoway.directive";
import { PaStructureDirective } from "./structure.directive";
import { PaIteratorDirective } from "./iterator.directive";
import { PaCellColor } from "./cellColor.directive";
import { PaCellColorSwitcher } from "./cellColorSwitcher.directive";
import { ProductTableComponent } from "./productTable.component";
import { ProductFormComponent } from "./productForm.component";

@NgModule({
    imports: [BrowserModule, FormsModule, ReactiveFormsModule],
    declarations: [ProductComponent, PaAttrDirective, PaModel,
        PaStructureDirective, PaIteratorDirective,
        PaCellColor, PaCellColorSwitcher, ProductTableComponent,
        ProductFormComponent],
    bootstrap: [ProductComponent]
})
export class AppModule { }
```

The component class is brought into scope using an import statement and added to the NgModule decorator's declarations array. The final step is to add an HTML element that matches the component's selector property, as shown in Listing 17-5, which will provide the component with its host element.

Listing 17-5. Adding a Host Element in the template.html File in the src/app Folder

```
<div class="row text-white m-2">
  <div class="col-4 p-2 bg-success">
    <paProductForm></paProductForm>
  </div>
  <div class="col-8 p-2 bg-primary">
    <paProductTable></paProductTable>
  </div>
</div>
```

When all the changes have been saved, the browser will display the content shown in Figure 17-3, which shows that parts of the HTML document are now under the management of the new components.

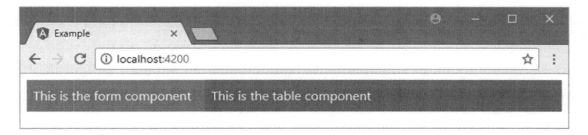

Figure 17-3. Adding new components

Understanding the New Application Structure

The new components have changed the structure of the application. Previously, the root component was responsible for all the HTML content displayed by the application. Now, however, there are three components, and responsibility for some of the HTML content has been delegated to the new additions, as illustrated in Figure 17-4.

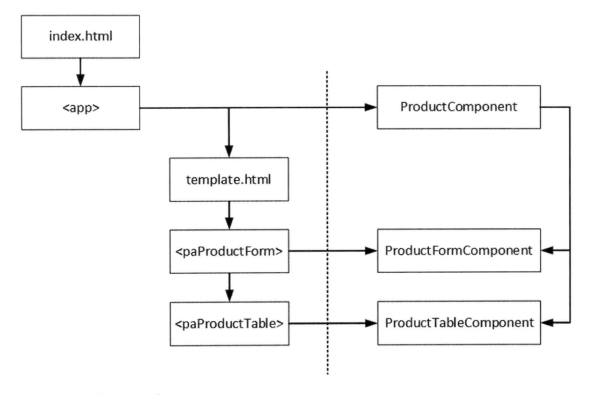

Figure 17-4. The new application structure

When the browser loads the index.html file, the Angular bootstrap process starts and Angular processes the application's module, which provides a list of the components that the application requires. Angular inspects the decorator for each component in its configuration, including the value of the selector property, which is used to identify which elements will be hosts.

Angular then begins processing the body of the index.html file and finds the app element, which is specified by the selector property of the ProductComponent component. Angular populates the app element with the component's template, which is contained in the template.html file. Angular inspects the contents of the template.html file and finds the paProductForm and paProductTable elements, which match the selector properties of the newly added components. Angular populates these elements with each component's template, producing the placeholder content shown in Figure 17-3.

There are some important new relationships to understand. First, the HTML content that is displayed in the browser window is now composed of several templates, each of which is managed by a component. Second, the ProductComponent is now the parent component to the ProductFormComponent and ProductTableComponent objects, a relationship that is formed by the fact that the host elements for the new components are defined in the template.html file, which is the ProductComponent template. Equally, the new components are children of the ProductComponent. The parent-child relationship is an important one when it comes to Angular components, as you will see as I describe how components work in later sections.

Defining Templates

Although there are new components in the application, they don't have much impact at the moment because they display only placeholder content. Each component has its own template, which defines the content that will be used to replace its host element in the HTML document. There are two different ways to define templates: inline within the @Component decorator or externally in an HTML file.

The new components that I added use templates, where a fragment of HTML is assigned to the template property of the @Component decorator, like this:

```
...
template: "<div>This is the form component</div>"
...
```

The advantage of this approach is simplicity: the component and the template are defined in a single file, and there is no way that the relationship between them can be confused. The drawback of inline templates is that they can get out of control and be hard to read if they contain more than a few HTML elements.

■ **Note** Another problem is that editors that highlight syntax errors as you type usually rely on the file extension to figure out what type of checking should be performed and won't realize that the value of the template property is HTML and will simply treat it as a string.

If you are using TypeScript, then you can use multiline strings to make inline templates more readable. Multiline strings are denoted with the backtick character (the ` character, which is also known as the *grave accent*), and they allow strings to spread over multiple lines, as shown in Listing 17-6.

Listing 17-6. Using a Multiline String in the productTable.component.ts File in the src/app Folder

```
import { Component } from "@angular/core";

@Component({
    selector: "paProductTable",
    template: `<div class='bg-info p-2'>
                    This is a multiline template
                </div>`
})
export class ProductTableComponent {

}
```

Multiline strings allow the structure of the HTML elements in a template to be preserved, which make it easier to read and increase the size of template that can be practically included inline before it becomes too unwieldy to manage. Figure 17-5 shows the effect of the template in Listing 17-6.

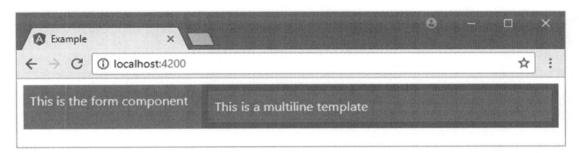

Figure 17-5. *Using a multiline inline template*

■ **Tip** My advice is to use external templates (explained in the next section) for any template that contains more than two or three simple elements, largely to take advantage of the HTML editing and syntax highlighting features that modern editors provide, which can go a long way to reduce the number of errors you discover when running the application.

Defining External Templates

External templates are defined in a different file from the rest of the component. The advantage of this approach is that the code and HTML are not mixed together, which makes both easier to read and unit test, and it also means that code editors will know they are working with HTML content when you are working on a template file, which can help reduce coding-time errors by highlighting errors.

The drawback of external templates is that you have to manage more files in the project and ensure that each component is associated with the correct template file. The best way to do this is to follow a consistent file naming strategy so that it is immediately obvious that a file contains a template for a given component. The convention for Angular is to create pairs of files using the convention <componentname>. component.<type> so that when you see a file called productTable.component.ts, you know it contains a component called Products written in TypeScript, and when you see a file called productTable.component. html, you know that it contains an external template for the Products component.

409

■ **Tip** The syntax and features for both types of template are the same, and the only difference is where the content is stored, either in the same file as the component code or in a separate file.

To define an external template using the naming convention, I created a file called productTable.component.html in the src/app folder and added the markup shown in Listing 17-7.

Listing 17-7. The Contents of the productTable.component.html File in the src/app Folder

```
<div class="bg-info p-2">
    This is an external template
</div>
```

This is the kind of template that I have been using for the root component since Chapter 11.
To specify an external template, the templateURL property is used in the @Component decorator, as shown in Listing 17-8.

Listing 17-8. Using an External Template in the productTable.component.html File in the src/app Folder

```
import { Component } from "@angular/core";

@Component({
    selector: "paProductTable",
    templateUrl: "productTable.component.html"
})
export class ProductTableComponent {

}
```

Notice that different properties are used: template is for inline templates, and templateUrl is for external templates. Figure 17-6 shows the effect of using an external template.

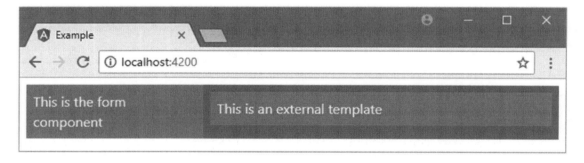

Figure 17-6. Using an external template

Using Data Bindings in Component Templates

A component's template can contain the full range of data bindings and target any of the built-in directives or custom directives that have been registered in the application's Angular module. Each component class provides the context for evaluating the data binding expressions in its template, and, by default, each component is isolated from the others. This means that the component doesn't have to worry about using the same property and method names that other components use and can rely on Angular to keep everything separate. As an example, Listing 17-9 shows the addition of a property called model to the form child component, which would conflict with the property of the same name in the root component were they not kept separate.

Listing 17-9. Adding a Property in the productForm.component.ts File in the src/app Folder

```
import { Component } from "@angular/core";

@Component({
    selector: "paProductForm",
    template: "<div>{{model}}</div>"
})
export class ProductFormComponent {

    model: string = "This is the model";
}
```

The component class uses the model property to store a message that is displayed in the template using a string interpolation binding. Figure 17-7 shows the result.

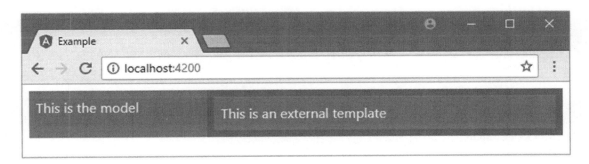

Figure 17-7. Using a data binding in a child component

Using Input Properties to Coordinate Between Components

Few components exist in isolation and need to share data with other parts of the application. Components can define input properties to receive the value of data binding expressions on their host elements. The expression will be evaluated in the context of the parent component, but the result will be passed to the child component's property.

To demonstrate, Listing 17-10 adds an input property to the table component, which it will use to receive the model data that it should display.

Listing 17-10. Defining an Input Property in the productTable.component.ts File in the src/app Folder

```
import { Component, Input } from "@angular/core";
import { Model } from "./repository.model";
import { Product } from "./product.model";

@Component({
    selector: "paProductTable",
    templateUrl: "productTable.component.html"
})
export class ProductTableComponent {

    @Input("model")
    dataModel: Model;

    getProduct(key: number): Product {
        return this.dataModel.getProduct(key);
    }

    getProducts(): Product[] {
        return this.dataModel.getProducts();
    }

    deleteProduct(key: number) {
        this.dataModel.deleteProduct(key);
    }

    showTable: boolean = true;
}
```

The component now defines an input property that will be assigned the value expression assigned to the model attribute on the host element. The getProduct, getProducts, and deleteProduct methods use the input property to provide access to the data model to bindings in the component's template, which is modified in Listing 17-11. The showTable property is used when I enhance the template in Listing 17-14 later in the chapter.

Listing 17-11. Adding a Data Binding in the productTable.component.html File

```
There are {{getProducts().length}} items in the model
```

To provide the child component with the data that it requires means adding a binding to its host element, which is defined in the template of the parent component, as shown in Listing 17-12.

Listing 17-12. Adding a Data Binding in the template.html File in the src/app Folder

```
<div class="row text-white m-2">
  <div class="col-4 p-2 bg-success">
    <paProductForm></paProductForm>
  </div>
  <div class="col-8 p-2 bg-primary">
    <paProductTable [model]="model"></paProductTable>
  </div>
</div>
```

The effect of this binding is to provide the child component with access to the parent component's
model property. This can be a confusing feature because it relies on the fact that the host element is defined
in the parent component's template but that the input property is defined by the child component, as
illustrated by Figure 17-8.

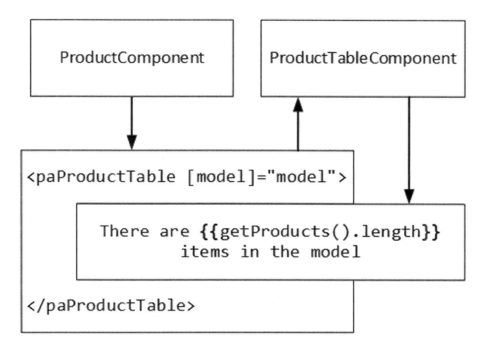

Figure 17-8. *Sharing data between parent and child components*

The child component's host element acts as the bridge between the parent and child components, and
the input property allows the component to provide the child with the data it needs, producing the result
shown in Figure 17-9.

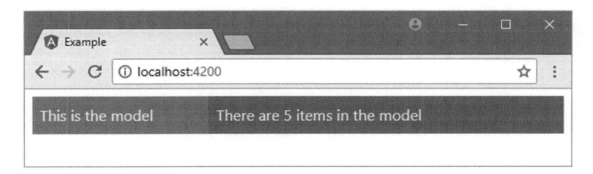

Figure 17-9. *Sharing data from a parent to a child component*

Using Directives in a Child Component Template

Once the input property has been defined, the child component can use the full range of data bindings and directives, either by using the data provided through the parent component or by defining its own. In Listing 17-13, I have restored the original table functionality from earlier chapters that displays a list of the Product objects in the data model, along with a checkbox that determines whether the table is displayed. This was functionality that was previously managed by the root component and its template.

Listing 17-13. Restoring the Table in the productTable.component.html File in the src/app Folder

```
<table class="table table-sm table-bordered table-striped">
    <tr><th></th><th>Name</th><th>Category</th><th>Price</th><th></th></tr>
    <tr *paFor="let item of getProducts(); let i = index; let odd = odd;
            let even = even" [class.bg-info]="odd" [class.bg-warning]="even">
        <td style="vertical-align:middle">{{i + 1}}</td>
        <td style="vertical-align:middle">{{item.name}}</td>
        <td style="vertical-align:middle">{{item.category}}</td>
        <td style="vertical-align:middle">{{item.price}}</td>
        <td class="text-xs-center">
            <button class="btn btn-danger btn-sm" (click)="deleteProduct(item.id)">
                Delete
            </button>
        </td>
    </tr>
</table>
```

The same HTML elements, data bindings, and directives (including custom directives like paIf and paFor) are used, producing the result shown in Figure 17-10. The key difference is not in the appearance of the table but in the way that it is now managed by a dedicated component.

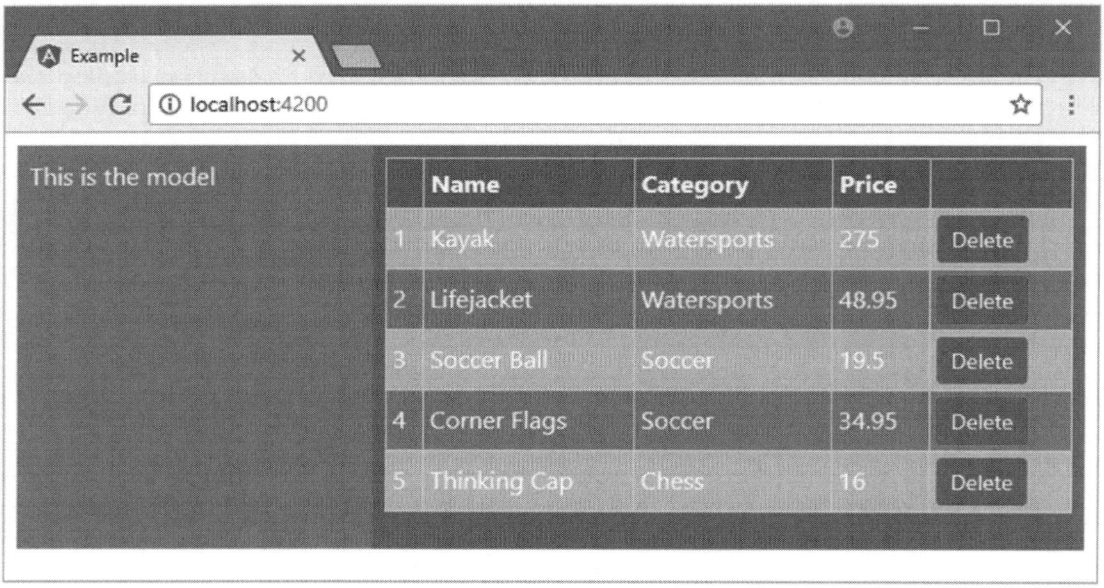

Figure 17-10. *Restoring the table display*

Using Output Properties to Coordinate Between Components

Child components can use output properties that define custom events that signal important changes and that allow the parent component to respond when they occur. Listing 17-14 shows the addition of an output property to the form component, which will be triggered when the user creates a new Product object.

Listing 17-14. Defining an Output Property in the productForm.component.ts File in the src/app Folder

```
import { Component, Output, EventEmitter } from "@angular/core";
import { Product } from "./product.model";
import { ProductFormGroup } from "./form.model";

@Component({
    selector: "paProductForm",
    templateUrl: "productForm.component.html"
})
export class ProductFormComponent {
    form: ProductFormGroup = new ProductFormGroup();
    newProduct: Product = new Product();
    formSubmitted: boolean = false;

    @Output("paNewProduct")
    newProductEvent = new EventEmitter<Product>();

    submitForm(form: any) {
        this.formSubmitted = true;
        if (form.valid) {
            this.newProductEvent.emit(this.newProduct);
            this.newProduct = new Product();
            this.form.reset();
            this.formSubmitted = false;
        }
    }
}
```

The output property is called newProductEvent, and the component triggers it when the submitForm method is called. Aside from the output property, the additions in the listing are based on the logic in the root controller, which previously managed the form. I also removed the inline template and created a file called productForm.component.html in the src/app folder, with the content shown in Listing 17-15.

Listing 17-15. The Contents of the productForm.component.html File in the src/app Folder

```
<form novalidate [formGroup]="form" (ngSubmit)="submitForm(form)">
    <div class="form-group" *ngFor="let control of form.productControls">
        <label>{{control.label}}</label>
        <input class="form-control"
            [(ngModel)]="newProduct[control.modelProperty]"
            name="{{control.modelProperty}}"
            formControlName="{{control.modelProperty}}" />
```

```
        <ul class="text-danger list-unstyled"
                *ngIf="(formSubmitted || control.dirty) && !control.valid">
            <li *ngFor="let error of control.getValidationMessages()">
                {{error}}
            </li>
        </ul>
    </div>
    <button class="btn btn-primary" type="submit"
        [disabled]="formSubmitted && !form.valid"
        [class.btn-secondary]="formSubmitted && !form.valid">
            Create
    </button>
</form>
```

As with the input property, the child component's host element acts as the bridge to the parent component, which can register interest in the custom event, as shown in Listing 17-16.

Listing 17-16. Registering for the Custom Event in the template.html File in the src/app Folder

```
<div class="row text-white m-2">
  <div class="col-4 p-2 text-dark">
    <paProductForm (paNewProduct)="addProduct($event)"></paProductForm>
  </div>
  <div class="col-8 p-2">
    <paProductTable [model]="model"></paProductTable>
  </div>
</div>
```

The new binding handles the custom event by passing the event object to the addProduct method. The child component is responsible for managing the form elements and validating their contents. When the data passes validation, the custom event is triggered, and the data binding expression is evaluated in the context of the parent component, whose addProduct method adds the new object to the model. Since the model has been shared with the table child component through its input property, the new data is displayed to the user, as shown in Figure 17-11.

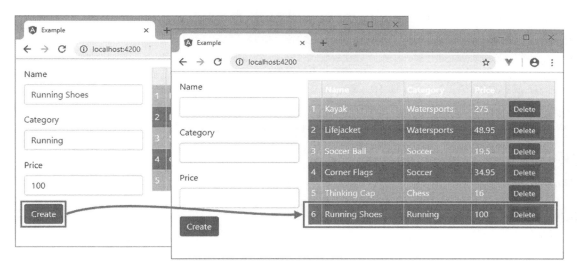

Figure 17-11. *Using a custom event in a child component*

Projecting Host Element Content

If the host element for a component contains content, it can be included in the template using the special ng-content element. This is known as *content projection*, and it allows components to be created that combine the content in their template with the content in the host element. To demonstrate, I added a file called toggleView.component.ts to the src/app folder and used it to define the component shown in Listing 17-17.

Listing 17-17. The Contents of the toggleView.component.ts File in the src/app Folder

```
import { Component } from "@angular/core";

@Component({
    selector: "paToggleView",
    templateUrl: "toggleView.component.html"
})
export class PaToggleView {

    showContent: boolean = true;
}
```

This component defines a showContent property that will be used to determine whether the host element's content will be displayed within the template. To provide the template, I added a file called toggleView.component.html to the src/app folder and added the elements shown in Listing 17-18.

417

Listing 17-18. The Contents of the toggleView.component.html File in the src/app Folder

```
<div class="checkbox">
    <label>
        <input type="checkbox" [(ngModel)]="showContent" />
        Show Content
    </label>
</div>
<ng-content *ngIf="showContent"></ng-content>
```

The important element is ng-content, which Angular will replace with the content of the host element. The ngIf directive has been applied to the ng-content element so that it will be visible only if the checkbox in the template is checked. Listing 17-19 registers the component with the Angular module.

Listing 17-19. Registering the Component in the app.module.ts File in the src/app Folder

```
import { NgModule } from "@angular/core";
import { BrowserModule } from "@angular/platform-browser";
import { ProductComponent } from "./component";
import { FormsModule, ReactiveFormsModule } from "@angular/forms";
import { PaAttrDirective } from "./attr.directive";
import { PaModel } from "./twoway.directive";
import { PaStructureDirective } from "./structure.directive";
import { PaIteratorDirective } from "./iterator.directive";
import { PaCellColor } from "./cellColor.directive";
import { PaCellColorSwitcher } from "./cellColorSwitcher.directive";
import { ProductTableComponent } from "./productTable.component";
import { ProductFormComponent } from "./productForm.component";
import { PaToggleView } from "./toggleView.component";

@NgModule({
    imports: [BrowserModule, FormsModule, ReactiveFormsModule],
    declarations: [ProductComponent, PaAttrDirective, PaModel,
        PaStructureDirective, PaIteratorDirective,
        PaCellColor, PaCellColorSwitcher, ProductTableComponent,
        ProductFormComponent, PaToggleView],
    bootstrap: [ProductComponent]
})
export class AppModule { }
```

The final step is to apply the new component to a host element that contains content, as shown in Listing 17-20.

Listing 17-20. Adding a Host Element with Content in the template.html File in the src/app Folder

```
<div class="row m-2">
  <div class="col-4 p-2">
    <paProductForm (paNewProduct)="addProduct($event)"></paProductForm>
  </div>
```

```
<div class="col-8 p-2">
  <paToggleView>
    <paProductTable [model]="model"></paProductTable>
  </paToggleView>
</div>
</div>
```

The paToggleView element is the host for the new component, and it contains the paProductTable element, which applies the component that creates the product table. The result is that there is a checkbox that controls the visibility of the table, as shown in Figure 17-12. The new component has no knowledge of the content of its host element, and its inclusion in the template is possible only through the ng-content element.

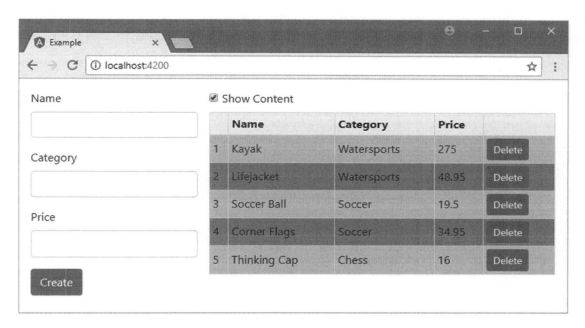

Figure 17-12. *Including host element content in the template*

Completing the Component Restructure

The functionality that was previously contained in the root component has been distributed to the new child components. All that remains is to tidy up the root component to remove the code that is no longer required, as shown in Listing 17-21.

Listing 17-21. Removing Obsolete Code in the component.ts File in the src/app Folder

```
import { ApplicationRef, Component } from "@angular/core";
import { Model } from "./repository.model";
import { Product } from "./product.model";
import { ProductFormGroup } from "./form.model";
```

419

```
@Component({
    selector: "app",
    templateUrl: "template.html"
})
export class ProductComponent {
    model: Model = new Model();

    addProduct(p: Product) {
        this.model.saveProduct(p);
    }
}
```

Many of the responsibilities of the root component have been moved elsewhere in the application. Of the original list from the start of the chapter, only the following remain the responsibility of the root component:

- Providing Angular with an entry point into the application, as the root component

- Providing access to the application's data model so that it can be used in data bindings

The child components have assumed the rest of the responsibilities, providing self-contained blocks of functionality that are simpler, easier to develop, and easier to maintain and that can be reused as required.

Using Component Styles

Components can define styles that apply only to the content in their templates, which allows content to be styled by a component without it being affected by the styles defined by its parents or other antecedents and without affecting the content in its child and other descendant components. Styles can be defined inline using the styles property of the @Component decorator, as shown in Listing 17-22.

Listing 17-22. Defining Inline Styles in the productForm.component.ts File in the src/app Folder

```
import { Component, Output, EventEmitter } from "@angular/core";
import { Product } from "./product.model";
import { ProductFormGroup } from "./form.model";

@Component({
    selector: "paProductForm",
    templateUrl: "productForm.component.html",
    styles: ["div { background-color: lightgreen }"]
})
export class ProductFormComponent {
    form: ProductFormGroup = new ProductFormGroup();
    newProduct: Product = new Product();
    formSubmitted: boolean = false;

    @Output("paNewProduct")
    newProductEvent = new EventEmitter<Product>();
```

```
submitForm(form: any) {
    this.formSubmitted = true;
    if (form.valid) {
        this.newProductEvent.emit(this.newProduct);
        this.newProduct = new Product();
        this.form.reset();
        this.formSubmitted = false;
    }
  }
}
```

The `styles` property is set to an array, where each item contains a CSS selector and one or more properties. In the listing, I have specified styles that set the background color of `div` elements to `lightgreen`. Even though there are `div` elements throughout the combined HTML document, this style will affect only the elements in the template of the component that defines them, which is the form component in this case, as shown in Figure 17-13.

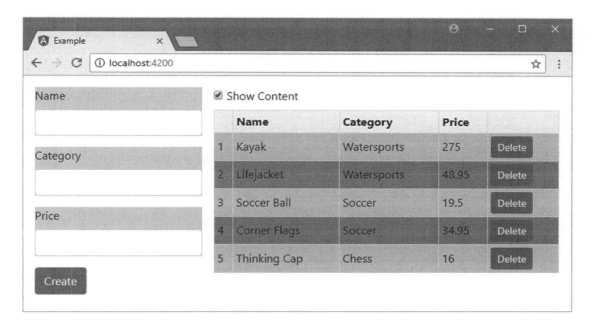

Figure 17-13. *Defining inline component styles*

■ **Tip** The styles included in the bundles created by the development tools are still applied, which is why the elements are still styled using Bootstrap.

Defining External Component Styles

Inline styles offer the same benefits and drawbacks as inline templates: they are simple and keep everything in one file, but they can be hard to read, can be hard to manage, and can confuse code editors.

The alternative is to define styles in a separate file and associate them with a component using the styleUrls property in its decorator. External style files follow the same naming convention as templates and code files. I added a file called productForm.component.css to the src/app folder and used it to define the styles shown in Listing 17-23.

Listing 17-23. The Contents of the productForm.component.css File in the src/app Folder

```
div {
    background-color: lightcoral;
}
```

This is the same style that was defined inline but with a different color value to confirm that this is the CSS being used by the component. In Listing 17-24, the component's decorator has been updated to specify the styles file.

Listing 17-24. Using External Styles in the productForm.component.ts File in the src/app Folder

```
import { Component, Output, EventEmitter } from "@angular/core";
import { Product } from "./product.model";
import { ProductFormGroup } from "./form.model";

@Component({
  selector: "paProductForm",
  templateUrl: "productForm.component.html",
  styleUrls: ["productForm.component.css"]
})
export class ProductFormComponent {
  form: ProductFormGroup = new ProductFormGroup();
  newProduct: Product = new Product();
  formSubmitted: boolean = false;

  @Output("paNewProduct")
  newProductEvent = new EventEmitter<Product>();

  submitForm(form: any) {
    this.formSubmitted = true;
    if (form.valid) {
      this.newProductEvent.emit(this.newProduct);
      this.newProduct = new Product();
      this.form.reset();
      this.formSubmitted = false;
    }
  }
}
```

The styleUrls property is set to an array of strings, each of which specifies a CSS file. Figure 17-14 shows the effect of adding the external styles file.

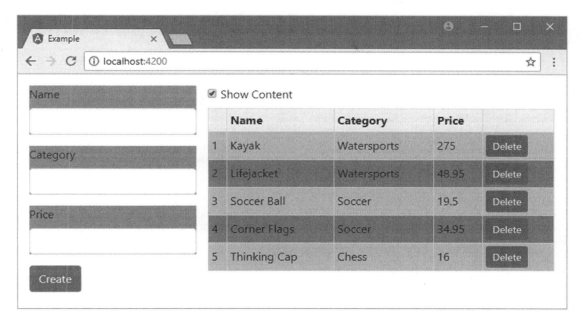

Figure 17-14. Defining external component styles

Using Advanced Style Features

Defining styles in components is a useful feature, but you won't always get the results you expect. Some advanced features allow you to take control of how component styles work.

Setting View Encapsulation

By default, component-specific styles are implemented by writing the CSS that has been applied to the component so that it targets special attributes, which Angular then adds to all of the top-level elements contained in the component's template. If you inspect the DOM using the browser's F12 developer tools, you will see that the contents of the external CSS file in Listing 17-23 have been rewritten like this:

```
...
<style>
div[_ngcontent-c0] {
    background-color: lightcoral;
}
</style>
...
```

The selector has been modified so that it matches div elements with an attribute called _ngcontent-c0 although you may see a different name in your browser since the name of the attribute is generated dynamically by Angular.

To ensure that the CSS in the `style` element affects only the HTML elements managed by the component, the elements in the template are modified so they have the same dynamically generated attribute, like this:

```
...
<div _ngcontent-c0="" class="form-group">
        <label _ngcontent-c0="">Name</label>
        <input _ngcontent-c0="" class="form-control ng-untouched ng-pristine
                ng-invalid" ng-reflect-name="name" name="name">
</div>
...
```

This is known as the component's *view encapsulation* behavior, and what Angular is doing is emulating a feature known as the *shadow DOM*, which allows sections of the Domain Object Model to be isolated so they have their own scope, meaning that JavaScript, styles, and templates can be applied to part of the HTML document. The reason that Angular emulates this behavior is that it is implemented by only a small number of browsers (at the time of writing, only Google Chrome and the latest versions of Safari and Opera support the shadow DOM feature), but there are two other encapsulation options, which are set using the `encapsulation` property in the `@Component` decorator.

■ **Tip** You can learn more about the shadow DOM at `http://developer.mozilla.org/en-US/docs/Web/Web_Components/Shadow_DOM`. You can see which browsers support the shadow DOM feature at `http://caniuse.com/#feat=shadowdom`.

The `encapsulation` property is assigned a value from the `ViewEncapsulation` enumeration, which is defined in the `@angular/core` module, and it defines the values described in Table 17-4.

Table 17-4. *The ViewEncapsulation Values*

Name	Description
Emulated	When this value is specified, Angular emulates the shadow DOM by writing content and styles to add attributes, as described earlier. This is the default behavior if no `encapsulation` value is specified in the `@Component` decorator.
Native	When this value is specified, Angular uses the browser's shadow DOM feature. This will work only if the browser implements the shadow DOM or if you are using a polyfill.
None	When this value is specified, Angular simply adds the unmodified CSS styles to the head section of the HTML document and lets the browser figure out how to apply the styles using the normal CSS precedence rules.

The `Native` and `None` values should be used with caution. Browser support for the shadow DOM feature is so limited that using the `Native` option is sensible only if you are using a polyfill library that provides compatibility for other browsers.

The `None` option adds all the styles defined by components to the head section of the HTML document and lets the browser figure out how to apply them. This has the benefit of working in all browsers, but the results are unpredictable, and there is no isolation between the styles defined by different components.

For completeness, Listing 17-25 shows the `encapsulation` property being set to `Emulated`, which is the default value and which works in all the browsers that Angular supports, without the need for polyfills.

Listing 17-25. Setting View Encapsulation in the productForm.component.ts File in the src/app Folder

```
import { Component, Output, EventEmitter, ViewEncapsulation } from "@angular/core";
import { Product } from "./product.model";
import { ProductFormGroup } from "./form.model";

@Component({
    selector: "paProductForm",
    templateUrl: "productForm.component.html",
    styleUrls: ["productForm.component.css"],
    encapsulation: ViewEncapsulation.Emulated
})
export class ProductFormComponent {
    form: ProductFormGroup = new ProductFormGroup();
    newProduct: Product = new Product();
    formSubmitted: boolean = false;

    @Output("paNewProduct")
    newProductEvent = new EventEmitter<Product>();

    submitForm(form: any) {
        this.formSubmitted = true;
        if (form.valid) {
            this.newProductEvent.emit(this.newProduct);
            this.newProduct = new Product();
            this.form.reset();
            this.formSubmitted = false;
        }
    }
}
```

Using the Shadow DOM CSS Selectors

Using the shadow DOM means that there are boundaries that regular CSS selectors do not operate across. To help address this, there are a number of special CSS selectors that are useful when using styles that rely on the shadow DOM (even when it is being emulated), as described in Table 17-5 and demonstrated in the sections that follow.

Table 17-5. *The Shadow DOM CSS Selectors*

Name	Description
:host	This selector is used to match the component's host element.
:host-context(classSelector)	This selector is used to match the ancestors of the host element that are members of a specific class.
/deep/ or >>>	This selector is used by a parent component to define styles that affect the elements in child component templates. This selector should be used only when the @Component decorator's encapsulation property is set to emulated, as described in the "Setting View Encapsulation" section.

Selecting the Host Element

A component's host element appears outside of its template, which means that the selectors in its styles apply only to elements that the host element contains and not the element itself. This can be addressed by using the :host selector, which matches the host element. Listing 17-26 defines a style that is applied only when the mouse pointer is hovering over the host element, which is specified by combining the :host and :hover selectors.

Listing 17-26. Matching the Host Element in the productForm.component.css File in the src/app Folder

```
div {
    background-color: lightcoral;
}
:host:hover {
    font-size: 25px;
}
```

When the mouse pointer is over the host element, its font-size property will be set to 25px, which increases the text size to 25 points for all the elements in the form, as shown in Figure 17-15.

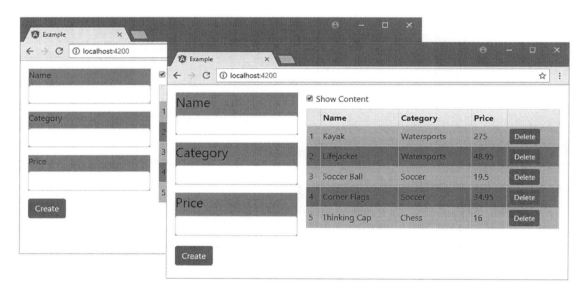

Figure 17-15. *Selecting the host element in a component style*

Selecting the Host Element's Ancestors

The :host-context selector is used to style elements within the component's template based on the class membership of the host element's ancestors (which are outside the template). This is a more limited selector than :host and cannot be used to specify anything other than a class selector, without support for matching tag types, attributes, or any other selector. Listing 17-27 shows the use of the :host-context selector.

Listing 17-27. Selecting Ancestors in the productForm.component.css File in the src/app Folder

```
div {
    background-color: lightcoral;
}
:host:hover {
    font-size: 25px;
}
:host-context(.angularApp) input {
    background-color: lightgray;
}
```

The selector in the listing sets the background-color property of input elements within the component's template to lightgrey only if one of the host element's ancestor elements is a member of a class called angularApp. In Listing 17-28, I have added the app element in the index.html file, which is the host element for the root component, to the angularApp class.

Listing 17-28. Adding the Host Element to a Class in the index.html File in the src/app Folder

```
<!doctype html>
<html lang="en">
<head>
  <meta charset="utf-8">
  <title>Example</title>
  <base href="/">
  <meta name="viewport" content="width=device-width, initial-scale=1">
  <link rel="icon" type="image/x-icon" href="favicon.ico">
</head>
<body>
  <app class="angularApp"></app>
</body>
</html>
```

Figure 17-16 shows the effect of the selector before and after the changes in Listing 17-28.

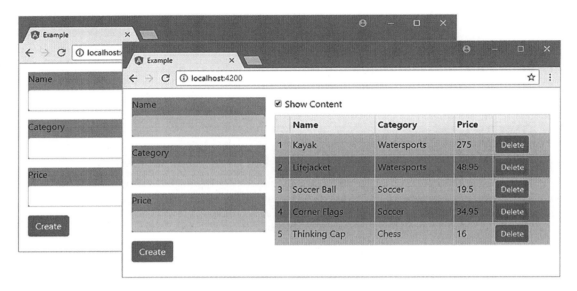

Figure 17-16. *Selecting the host element's ancestors*

Pushing a Style into the Child Component's Template

Styles defined by a component are not automatically applied to the elements in the child component's templates. As a demonstration, Listing 17-29 adds a style to the @Component decorator of the root component.

Listing 17-29. Defining Styles in the component.ts File in the src/app Folder

```
import { ApplicationRef, Component } from "@angular/core";
import { Model } from "./repository.model";
import { Product } from "./product.model";
import { ProductFormGroup } from "./form.model";

@Component({
    selector: "app",
    templateUrl: "template.html",
    styles: ["div { border: 2px black solid;  font-style:italic }"]
})
export class ProductComponent {
    model: Model = new Model();

    addProduct(p: Product) {
        this.model.saveProduct(p);
    }
}
```

The selector matches all div elements and applies a border and changes the font style. Figure 17-17 shows the result.

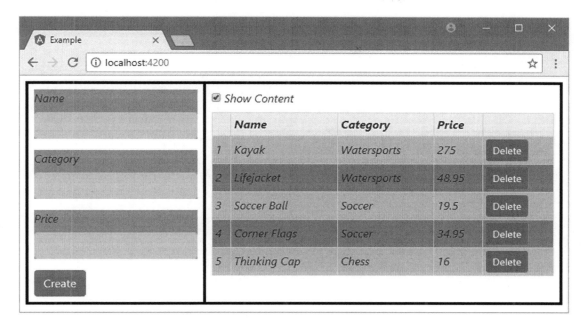

Figure 17-17. Applying regular CSS styles

Some CSS style properties, such as font-style, are inherited by default, which means that setting such a property in a parent component will affect the elements in child component templates because the browser automatically applies the style.

Other properties, such as border, are not inherited by default, and setting such a property in a parent component has no effect on child component templates, unless the /deep/ or >>> selectors are used, as shown in Listing 17-30. (These selectors are aliases of one another and have the same effect.)

Listing 17-30. Pushing a Style into Child Templates in the component.ts File in the src/app Folder

```
import { ApplicationRef, Component } from "@angular/core";
import { Model } from "./repository.model";
import { Product } from "./product.model";
import { ProductFormGroup } from "./form.model";

@Component({
    selector: "app",
    templateUrl: "template.html",
    styles: ["/deep/ div { border: 2px black solid;  font-style:italic }"]
})
export class ProductComponent {
    model: Model = new Model();

    addProduct(p: Product) {
        this.model.saveProduct(p);
    }
}
```

The selector for the style uses /deep/ to push the styles into the child components' templates, which means that all the div elements are given a border, as shown in Figure 17-18.

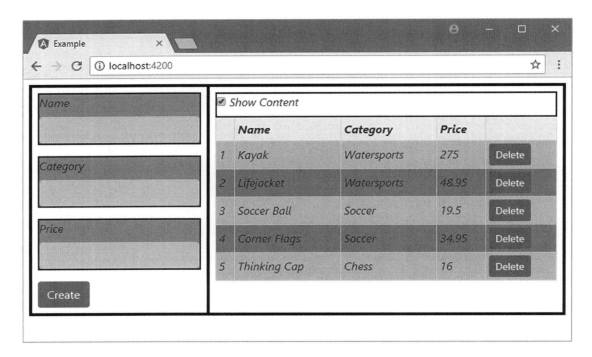

Figure 17-18. *Pushing a style into child component templates*

Querying Template Content

Components can query the content of their templates to locate instances of directives or components, which are known as *view children*. These are similar to the directive content children queries that were described in Chapter 16 but with some important differences.

In Listing 17-31, I have added some code to the component that manages the table that queries for the PaCellColor directive that was created to demonstrate directive content queries. This directive is still registered in the Angular module and selects td elements, so Angular will have applied it to the cells in the table component's content.

Listing 17-31. Selecting View Children in the productTable.component.ts File in the src/app Folder

```
import { Component, Input, ViewChildren, QueryList } from "@angular/core";
import { Model } from "./repository.model";
import { Product } from "./product.model";
import { PaCellColor } from "./cellColor.directive";

@Component({
    selector: "paProductTable",
    templateUrl: "productTable.component.html"
})
```

```
export class ProductTableComponent {

    @Input("model")
    dataModel: Model;

    getProduct(key: number): Product {
        return this.dataModel.getProduct(key);
    }

    getProducts(): Product[] {
        return this.dataModel.getProducts();
    }

    deleteProduct(key: number) {
        this.dataModel.deleteProduct(key);
    }

    showTable: boolean = true;

    @ViewChildren(PaCellColor)
    viewChildren: QueryList<PaCellColor>;

    ngAfterViewInit() {
        this.viewChildren.changes.subscribe(() => {
            this.updateViewChildren();
        });
        this.updateViewChildren();
    }

    private updateViewChildren() {
        setTimeout(() => {
            this.viewChildren.forEach((child, index) => {
                child.setColor(index % 2 ? true : false);
            })
        }, 0);
    }
}
```

There are two property decorators that are used to query for directives or components defined in the template, as described in Table 17-6.

Table 17-6. *The View Children Query Property Decorators*

Name	Description
@ViewChild(class)	This decorator tells Angular to query for the first directive or component object of the specified type and assign it to the property. The class name can be replaced with a template variable. Multiple classes or templates can be separated by commas.
@ViewChildren(class)	This decorator assigns all the directive and component objects of the specified type to the property. Template variables can be used instead of classes, and multiple values can be separated by commas. The results are provided in a QueryList object, described in Chapter 16.

In the listing, I used the @ViewChildren decorator to select all the PaCellColor objects from the component's template. Aside from the different property decorators, components have two different lifecycle methods that are used to provide information about how the template has been processed, as described in Table 17-7.

Table 17-7. *The Additional Component Lifecycle Methods*

Name	Description
ngAfterViewInit	This method is called when the component's view has been initialized. The results of the view queries are set before this method is invoked.
ngAfterViewChecked	This method is called after the component's view has been checked as part of the change detection process.

In the listing, I implement the ngAfterViewInit method to ensure that Angular has processed the component's template and set the result of the query. Within the method I perform the initial call to the updateViewChildren method, which operates on the PaCellColor objects, and set up the function that will be called when the query results change, using the QueryList.changes property, as described in Chapter 16. The view children are updated within a call to the setTimeout function, as explained in Chapter 16. The result is that the color of every second table cell is changed, as shown in Figure 17-19.

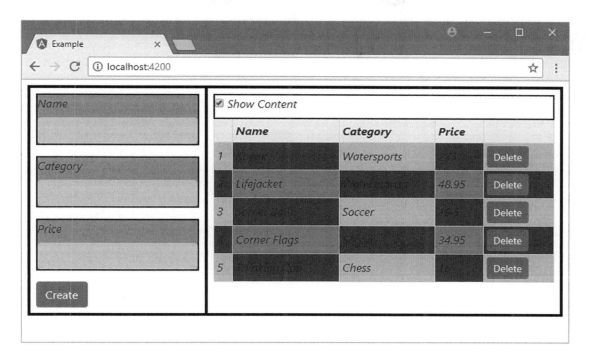

Figure 17-19. *Querying for view children*

■ **Tip** You may need to combine view child and content child queries if you have used the ng-content element. The content defined in the template is queried using the technique shown in Listing 17-31, but the project content—which replaces the ng-content element—is queried using the child queries described in Chapter 16.

Summary

In this chapter, I revisited the topic of components and explained how to combine all of the features of directives with the ability to provide their own templates. I explained how to structure an application to create small module components and how components can coordinate between themselves using input and output properties. I also showed you how components can define CSS styles that are applied only to their templates and no other parts of the application. In the next chapter, I introduce pipes, which are used to prepare data for display in templates.

CHAPTER 18

███

Using and Creating Pipes

Pipes are small fragments of code that transform data values so they can be displayed to the user in templates. Pipes allow transformation logic to be defined in self-contained classes so that it can be applied consistently throughout an application. Table 18-1 puts pipes in context.

Table 18-1. *Putting Pipes in Context*

Question	Answer
What are they?	Pipes are classes that are used to prepare data for display to the user.
Why are they useful?	Pipes allow preparation logic to be defined in a single class that can be used throughout an application, ensuing that data is presented consistently.
How are they used?	The @Pipe decorator is applied to a class and used to specify a name by which the pipe can be used in a template.
Are there any pitfalls or limitations?	Pipes should be simple and focused on preparing data. It can be tempting to let the functionality creep into areas that are the responsibility of other building blocks, such as directives or components.
Are there any alternatives?	You can implement data preparation code in components or directives, but that makes it harder to reuse in other parts of the application.

Table 18-2 summarizes the chapter.

© Adam Freeman 2018
A. Freeman, *Pro Angular 6*, https://doi.org/10.1007/978-1-4842-3649-9_18

Table 18-2. *Chapter Summary*

Problem	Solution	Listing
Format a data value for inclusion in a template	Use a pipe in a data binding expression	1–6
Create a custom pipe	Apply the @Pipe decorator to a class	7–9
Format a data value using multiple pipes	Chain the pipe names together using the bar character	10
Specify when Angular should reevaluate the output from a pipe	Use the pure property of the @Pipe decorator	11–14
Format numerical values	Use the number pipe	15, 16
Format currency values	Use the currency pipe	17, 18
Format percentage values	Use the percent pipe	19–22
Change the case of strings	Use the uppercase or lowercase pipes	23
Serialize objects into the JSON format	Use the json pipe	24
Select elements from an array	Use the slice pipe	25

Preparing the Example Project

I am going to continue working with the example project that was first created in Chapter 11 and that has been expanded and modified in the chapters since. In the final examples in the previous chapter, component styles and view children queries left the application with a strikingly garish appearance that I am going to tone down for this chapter. In Listing 18-1, I have disabled the inline component styles applied to the form elements.

■ **Tip** You can download the example project for this chapter—and for all the other chapters in this book—from https://github.com/Apress/pro-angular-6.

Listing 18-1. Disabling CSS Styles in the productForm.component.ts File in the src/app Folder

```
import { Component, Output, EventEmitter, ViewEncapsulation } from "@angular/core";
import { Product } from "./product.model";
import { ProductFormGroup } from "./form.model";

@Component({
    selector: "paProductForm",
    templateUrl: "productForm.component.html",
    // styleUrls: ["app/productForm.component.css"],
    // encapsulation: ViewEncapsulation.Emulated
})
export class ProductFormComponent {
    form: ProductFormGroup = new ProductFormGroup();
    newProduct: Product = new Product();
    formSubmitted: boolean = false;
```

```
    @Output("paNewProduct")
    newProductEvent = new EventEmitter<Product>();

    submitForm(form: any) {
        this.formSubmitted = true;
        if (form.valid) {
            this.newProductEvent.emit(this.newProduct);
            this.newProduct = new Product();
            this.form.reset();
            this.formSubmitted = false;
        }
    }
}
```

To disable the checkerboard coloring of the table cells, I changed the selector for the `PaCellColor` directive so that it matches an attribute that is not currently applied to the HTML elements, as shown in Listing 18-2.

Listing 18-2. Changing the Selector in the cellColor.directive.ts File in the src/app Folder

```
import { Directive, HostBinding } from "@angular/core";

@Directive({
    selector: "td[paApplyColor]"
})
export class PaCellColor {

    @HostBinding("class")
    bgClass: string = "";

    setColor(dark: Boolean) {
        this.bgClass = dark ? "bg-dark" : "";
    }
}
```

Listing 18-3 disables the deep styles defined by the root component.

Listing 18-3. Disabling CSS Styles in the component.ts File in the src/app Folder

```
import { ApplicationRef, Component } from "@angular/core";
import { Model } from "./repository.model";
import { Product } from "./product.model";
import { ProductFormGroup } from "./form.model";

@Component({
    selector: "app",
    templateUrl: "template.html",
    //styles: ["/deep/ div { border: 2px black solid;  font-style:italic }"]
})
```

```
export class ProductComponent {
    model: Model = new Model();

    addProduct(p: Product) {
        this.model.saveProduct(p);
    }
}
```

The next change for the existing code in the example application is to simplify the ProductTableComponent class to remove methods and properties that are no longer required, as shown in Listing 18-4.

Listing 18-4. Simplifying the Code in the productTable.component.ts File in the src/app Folder

```
import { Component, Input, ViewChildren, QueryList } from "@angular/core";
import { Model } from "./repository.model";
import { Product } from "./product.model";

@Component({
    selector: "paProductTable",
    templateUrl: "productTable.component.html"
})
export class ProductTableComponent {

    @Input("model")
    dataModel: Model;

    getProduct(key: number): Product {
        return this.dataModel.getProduct(key);
    }

    getProducts(): Product[] {
        return this.dataModel.getProducts();
    }

    deleteProduct(key: number) {
        this.dataModel.deleteProduct(key);
    }
}
```

Finally, I have removed one of the component elements from the root component's template to disable the checkbox that shows and hides the table, as shown in Listing 18-5.

Listing 18-5. Simplifying the Elements in the template.html File in the src/app Folder

```
<div class="row m-2">
  <div class="col-4 p-2">
    <paProductForm (paNewProduct)="addProduct($event)"></paProductForm>
  </div>
  <div class="col-8 p-2">
    <paProductTable [model]="model"></paProductTable>
  </div>
</div>
```

Run the following command in the example folder to start the Angular development tools:

```
ng serve
```

Open a new browser tab and navigate to http://localhost:4200 to see the content shown in Figure 18-1.

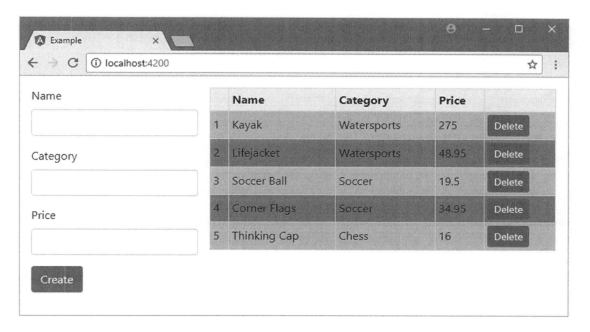

Figure 18-1. *Running the example application*

Understanding Pipes

Pipes are classes that transform data before it is received by a directive or component. That may not sound like an important job, but pipes can be used to perform some of the most commonly required development tasks easily and consistently.

As a quick example to demonstrate how pipes are used, Listing 18-6 applies one of the built-in pipes to transform the values displayed in the Price column of the table displayed by the application.

Listing 18-6. Using a Pipe in the productTable.component.html File in the src/app Folder

```
<table class="table table-sm table-bordered table-striped">
    <tr><th></th><th>Name</th><th>Category</th><th>Price</th><th></th></tr>
    <tr *paFor="let item of getProducts(); let i = index; let odd = odd;
            let even = even" [class.bg-info]="odd" [class.bg-warning]="even">
        <td style="vertical-align:middle">{{i + 1}}</td>
        <td style="vertical-align:middle">{{item.name}}</td>
        <td style="vertical-align:middle">{{item.category}}</td>
```

```
<td style="vertical-align:middle">
    {{item.price | currency:"USD":"symbol" }}
</td>
<td class="text-center">
    <button class="btn btn-danger btn-sm" (click)="deleteProduct(item.id)">
        Delete
    </button>
</td>
    </tr>
</table>
```

The syntax for applying a pipe is similar to the style used by command prompts, where a value is "piped" for transformation using the vertical bar symbol (the | character). Figure 18-2 shows the structure of the data binding that contains the pipe.

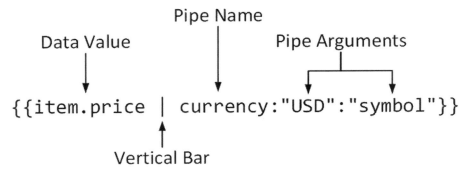

Figure 18-2. *The anatomy of data binding with a pipe*

The name of the pipe used in Listing 18-6 is currency, and it formats numbers into currency values. Arguments to the pipe are separated by colons (the : character). The first pipe argument specifies the currency code that should be used, which is USD in this case, representing U.S. dollars. The second pipe argument, which is symbol, specifies whether the currency symbol, rather than its code, should be displayed.

When Angular processes the expression, it obtains the data value and passes it to the pipe for transformation. The result produced by the pipe is then used as the expression result for the data binding. In the example, the bindings are string interpolations, and the results can be seen in Figure 18-3.

440

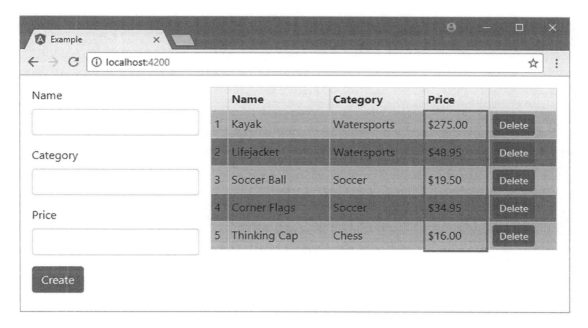

Figure 18-3. *The effect of using the currency pipe*

Creating a Custom Pipe

I will return to the built-in pipes that Angular provides later in the chapter, but the best way to understand how pipes work and what they are capable of is to create a custom pipe. I added a file called addTax.pipe.ts in the src/app folder and defined the class shown in Listing 18-7.

Listing 18-7. The Contents of the addTax.pipe.ts File in the src/app Folder

```
import { Pipe } from "@angular/core";

@Pipe({
    name: "addTax"
})
export class PaAddTaxPipe {

    defaultRate: number = 10;

    transform(value: any, rate?: any): number {
        let valueNumber = Number.parseFloat(value);
        let rateNumber = rate == undefined ?
            this.defaultRate : Number.parseInt(rate);
        return valueNumber + (valueNumber * (rateNumber / 100));
    }
}
```

Pipes are classes to which the @Pipe decorator has been applied and that implement a method called transform. The @Pipe decorator defines two properties, which are used to configure pipes, as described in Table 18-3.

Table 18-3. *The @Pipe Decorator Properties*

Name	Description
name	This property specifies the name by which the pipe is applied in templates.
pure	When true, this pipe is reevaluated only when its input value or its arguments are changed. This is the default value. See the "Creating Impure Pipes" section for details.

The example pipe is defined in a class called PaAddTaxPipe, and its decorator name property specifies that the pipe will be applied using addTax in templates. The transform method must accept at least one argument, which Angular uses to provide the data value that the pipe formats. The pipe does its work in the transform method and its result is used by Angular in the binding expression. In this example, the transform method accepts a number value and its result is the received value plus sales tax.

The transform method can also define additional arguments that are used to configure the pipe. In the example, the optional rate argument can be used to specify the sales tax rate, which defaults to 10 percent.

■ **Caution**   Be careful when dealing with the arguments received by the transform method and make sure that you parse or convert them to the types you need. The TypeScript type annotations are not enforced at runtime, and Angular will pass you whatever data values it is working with.

Registering a Custom Pipe

Pipes are registered using the declarations property of the Angular module, as shown in Listing 18-8.

Listing 18-8. Registering a Custom Pipe in the app.module.ts File in the src/app Folder

```
import { NgModule } from "@angular/core";
import { BrowserModule } from "@angular/platform-browser";
import { ProductComponent } from "./component";
import { FormsModule, ReactiveFormsModule } from "@angular/forms";
import { PaAttrDirective } from "./attr.directive";
import { PaModel } from "./twoway.directive";
import { PaStructureDirective } from "./structure.directive";
import { PaIteratorDirective } from "./iterator.directive";
import { PaCellColor } from "./cellColor.directive";
import { PaCellColorSwitcher } from "./cellColorSwitcher.directive";
import { ProductTableComponent } from "./productTable.component";
import { ProductFormComponent } from "./productForm.component";
import { PaToggleView } from "./toggleView.component";
import { PaAddTaxPipe } from "./addTax.pipe";
```

```
@NgModule({
    imports: [BrowserModule, FormsModule, ReactiveFormsModule],
    declarations: [ProductComponent, PaAttrDirective, PaModel,
        PaStructureDirective, PaIteratorDirective,
        PaCellColor, PaCellColorSwitcher, ProductTableComponent,
        ProductFormComponent, PaToggleView, PaAddTaxPipe],
    bootstrap: [ProductComponent]
})
export class AppModule { }
```

Applying a Custom Pipe

Once a custom pipe has been registered, it can be used in data binding expressions. In Listing 18-9, I have applied the pipe to the `price` value in the tables and added a `select` element that allows the tax rate to be specified.

Listing 18-9. Applying the Custom Pipe in the productTable.component.html File in the src/app Folder

```html
<div>
    <label>Tax Rate:</label>
    <select [value]="taxRate || 0" (change)="taxRate=$event.target.value">
        <option value="0">None</option>
        <option value="10">10%</option>
        <option value="20">20%</option>
        <option value="50">50%</option>
    </select>
</div>

<table class="table table-sm table-bordered table-striped">
    <tr><th></th><th>Name</th><th>Category</th><th>Price</th><th></th></tr>
    <tr *paFor="let item of getProducts(); let i = index; let odd = odd;
            let even = even" [class.bg-info]="odd" [class.bg-warning]="even">
        <td style="vertical-align:middle">{{i + 1}}</td>
        <td style="vertical-align:middle">{{item.name}}</td>
        <td style="vertical-align:middle">{{item.category}}</td>
        <td style="vertical-align:middle">
            {{item.price | addTax:(taxRate || 0) }}
        </td>
        <td class="text-center">
            <button class="btn btn-danger btn-sm" (click)="deleteProduct(item.id)">
                Delete
            </button>
        </td>
    </tr>
</table>
```

Just for variety, I defined the tax rate entirely within the template. The `select` element has a binding that sets its `value` property to a component variable called `taxRate` or defaults to 0 if the property has not been defined. The event binding handles the `change` event and sets the value of the `taxRate` property. You cannot specify a fallback value when using the `ngModel` directive, which is why I have split up the bindings.

In applying the custom pipe, I have used the vertical bar character, followed by the value specified by the name property in the pipe's decorator. The name of the pipe is followed by a colon, which is followed by an expression that is evaluated to provide the pipe with its argument. In this case, the taxRate property will be used if it has been defined, with a fallback value of zero.

Pipes are part of the dynamic nature of Angular data bindings, and the pipe's transform method will be called to get an updated value if the underlying data value changes or if the expression used for the arguments changes. The dynamic nature of pipes can be seen by changing the value displayed by the select element, which will define or change the taxRate property, which will, in turn, update the amount added to the price property by the custom pipe, as shown in Figure 18-4.

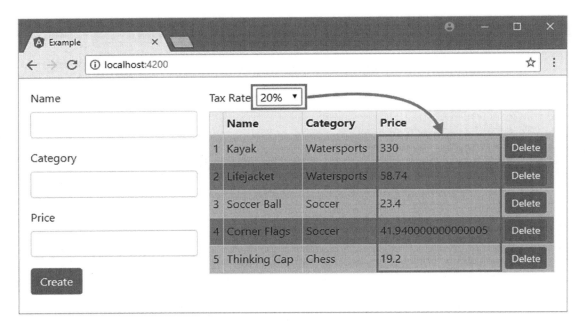

Figure 18-4. *Using a custom pipe*

Combining Pipes

The addTax pipe is applying the tax rate, but the fractional amounts that are produced by the calculation are unsightly—and unhelpful since few tax authorities insist on accuracy to 15 fractional digits.

I could fix this by adding support to the custom pipe to format the number values as currencies, but that would require duplicating the functionality of the built-in currency pipe that I used earlier in the chapter. A better approach is to combine the functionality of both pipes so that the output from the custom addTax pipe is fed into the built-in currency pipe, which is then used to produce the value displayed to the user.

Pipes are chained together in this way using the vertical bar character, and the names of the pipes are specified in the order that data should flow, as shown in Listing 18-10.

Listing 18-10. Combining Pipes in the productTable.component.html File in the src/app Folder

```
...
<td style="vertical-align:middle">
    {{item.price | addTax:(taxRate || 0) | currency:"USD":"symbol"  }}
</td>
...
```

The value of the item.price property is passed to the addTax pipe, which adds the sales tax, and then to the currency pipe, which formats the number value into a currency amount, as shown in Figure 18-5.

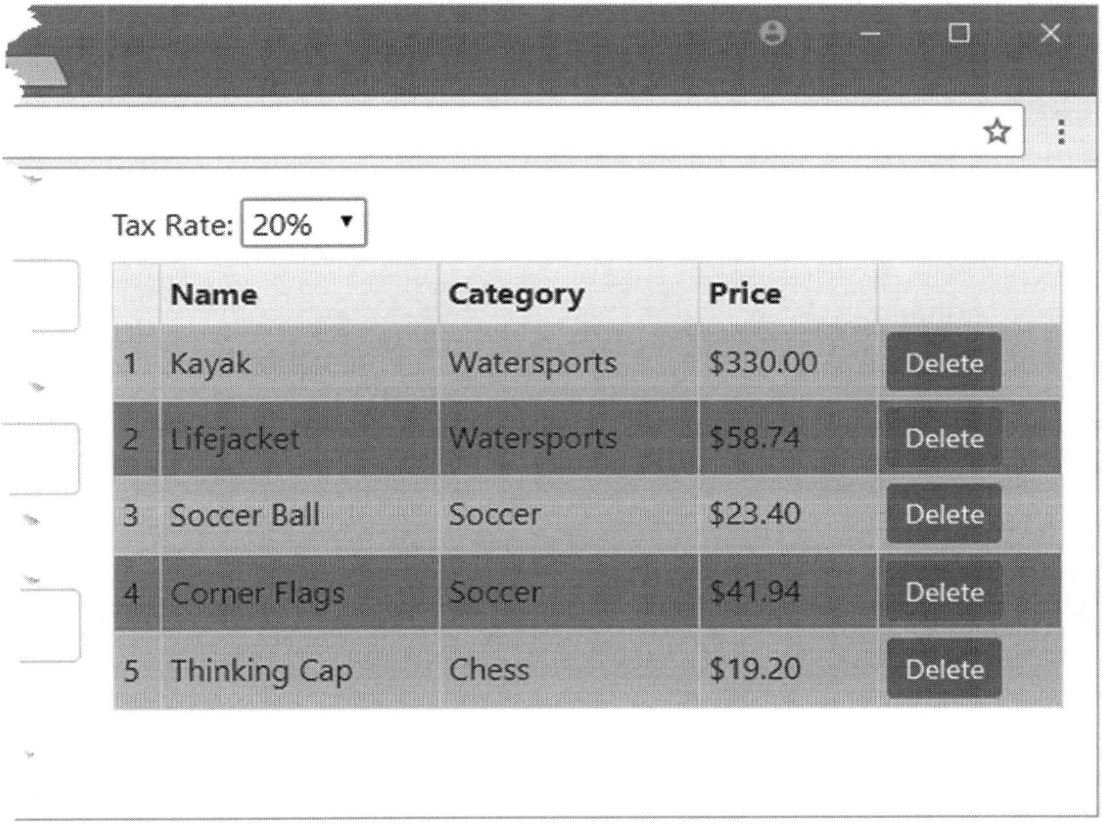

Figure 18-5. *Combining the functionality of pipes*

Creating Impure Pipes

The pure decorator property is used to tell Angular when to call the pipe's transform method. The default value for the pure property is true, which tells Angular that the pipe's transform method will generate a new value only if the input data value—the data value before the vertical bar character in the template—changes or when one or more of its arguments is modified. This is known as a *pure* pipe because it has no independent internal state and all its dependencies can be managed using the Angular change detection process.

445

Setting the pure decorator property to `false` creates an *impure pipe* and tells Angular that the pipe has its own state data or that it depends on data that may not be picked up in the change detection process when there is a new value.

When Angular performs its change detection process, it treats impure pipes as sources of data values in their own right and invokes the `transform` methods even when there has been no data value or argument changes.

The most common need for impure pipes is when they process the contents of arrays and the elements in the array change. As you saw in Chapter 16, Angular doesn't automatically detect changes that occur within arrays and won't invoke a pure pipe's transform method when an array element is added, edited, or deleted because it just sees the same array object being used as the input data value.

■ **Caution**   Impure pipes should be used sparingly because Angular has to call the `transform` method whenever there is any data change or user interaction in the application, just in case it might result in a different result from the `pipe`. If you do create an impure pipe, then keep it as simple as possible. Performing complex operations, such as sorting an array, can devastate the performance of an Angular application.

As a demonstration, I added a file called `categoryFilter.pipe.ts` in the `src/app` folder and used it to define the pipe shown in Listing 18-11.

Listing 18-11. The Contents of the categoryFilter.pipe.ts File in the src/app Folder

```
import { Pipe } from "@angular/core";
import { Product } from "./product.model";

@Pipe({
    name: "filter",
    pure: true
})
export class PaCategoryFilterPipe {

    transform(products: Product[], category: string): Product[] {
        return category == undefined ?
            products : products.filter(p => p.category == category);
    }
}
```

This is a pure filter that receives an array of `Product` objects and returns only the ones whose `category` property matches the `category` argument. Listing 18-12 shows the new pipe registered in the Angular module.

Listing 18-12. Registering a Pipe in the app.module.ts File in the src/app Folder

```
import { NgModule } from "@angular/core";
import { BrowserModule } from "@angular/platform-browser";
import { ProductComponent } from "./component";
import { FormsModule, ReactiveFormsModule } from "@angular/forms";
import { PaAttrDirective } from "./attr.directive";
import { PaModel } from "./twoway.directive";
import { PaStructureDirective } from "./structure.directive";
```

```
import { PaIteratorDirective } from "./iterator.directive";
import { PaCellColor } from "./cellColor.directive";
import { PaCellColorSwitcher } from "./cellColorSwitcher.directive";
import { ProductTableComponent } from "./productTable.component";
import { ProductFormComponent } from "./productForm.component";
import { PaToggleView } from "./toggleView.component";
import { PaAddTaxPipe } from "./addTax.pipe";
import { PaCategoryFilterPipe } from "./categoryFilter.pipe";

@NgModule({
    imports: [BrowserModule, FormsModule, ReactiveFormsModule],
    declarations: [ProductComponent, PaAttrDirective, PaModel,
        PaStructureDirective, PaIteratorDirective,
        PaCellColor, PaCellColorSwitcher, ProductTableComponent,
        ProductFormComponent, PaToggleView, PaAddTaxPipe,
        PaCategoryFilterPipe],
    bootstrap: [ProductComponent]
})
export class AppModule { }
```

Listing 18-13 shows the application of the new pipe to the binding expression that targets the ngFor directive as well as a new select element that allows the filter category to be selected.

Listing 18-13. Applying a Pipe in the productTable.component.html File in the src/app Folder

```
<div>
    <label>Tax Rate:</label>
    <select [value]="taxRate || 0" (change)="taxRate=$event.target.value">
        <option value="0">None</option>
        <option value="10">10%</option>
        <option value="20">20%</option>
        <option value="50">50%</option>
    </select>
</div>

<div>
    <label>Category Filter:</label>
    <select [(ngModel)]="categoryFilter">
        <option>Watersports</option>
        <option>Soccer</option>
        <option>Chess</option>
    </select>
</div>

<table class="table table-sm table-bordered table-striped">
    <tr><th></th><th>Name</th><th>Category</th><th>Price</th><th></th></tr>
    <tr *paFor="let item of getProducts() | filter:categoryFilter;
            let i = index; let odd = odd; let even = even"
            [class.bg-info]="odd" [class.bg-warning]="even">
        <td style="vertical-align:middle">{{i + 1}}</td>
        <td style="vertical-align:middle">{{item.name}}</td>
        <td style="vertical-align:middle">{{item.category}}</td>
```

```
    <td style="vertical-align:middle">
        {{item.price | addTax:(taxRate || 0) | currency:"USD":"symbol" }}
    </td>
    <td class="text-center">
        <button class="btn btn-danger btn-sm" (click)="deleteProduct(item.id)">
            Delete
        </button>
    </td>
</tr>
</table>
```

To see the problem, use the select element to filter the products in the table so that only those in the Soccer category are shown. Then use the form elements to create a new product in that category. Clicking the Create button will add the product to the data model, but the new product won't be shown in the table, as illustrated in Figure 18-6.

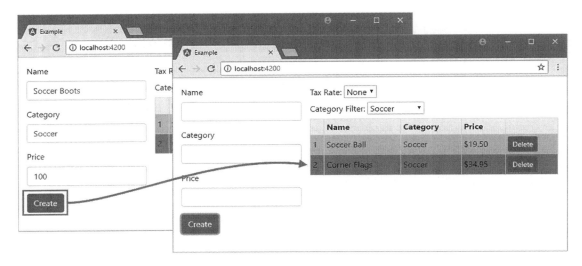

Figure 18-6. *A problem caused by a pure pipe*

The table isn't updated because, as far as Angular is concerned, none of the inputs to the filter pipe has changed. The component's getProducts method returns the same array object, and the categoryFilter property is still set to Soccer. The fact that there is a new object inside the array returned by the getProducts method isn't recognized by Angular.

The solution is to set the pipe's pure property to false, as shown in Listing 18-14.

Listing 18-14. Marking a Pipe as Impure in the categoryFilter.pipe.ts File in the src/app Folder

```
import { Pipe } from "@angular/core";
import { Product } from "./product.model";

@Pipe({
    name: "filter",
    pure: false
})
```

```
export class PaCategoryFilterPipe {

    transform(products: Product[], category: string): Product[] {
        return category == undefined ?
            products : products.filter(p => p.category == category);
    }
}
```

If you repeat the test, you will see that the new product is now correctly displayed in the table, as shown in Figure 18-7.

Figure 18-7. *Using an impure pipe*

Using the Built-in Pipes

Angular includes a set of built-in pipes that perform commonly required tasks. These pipes are described in Table 18-4 and demonstrated in the sections that follow.

Table 18-4. *The Built-in Pipes*

Name	Description
number	This pipe performs location-sensitive formatting of number values. See the "Formatting Numbers" section for details.
currency	This pipe performs location-sensitive formatting of currency amounts. See the "Formatting Currency Values" section for details.
percent	This pipe performs location-sensitive formatting of percentage values. See the "Formatting Percentages" section for details.
date	This pipe performs location-sensitive formatting of dates. See the "Formatting Dates" section for details.

(continued)

449

Table 18-4. (*continued*)

Name	Description
uppercase	This pipe transforms all the characters in a string to uppercase. See the "Changing String Case" section for details.
lowercase	This pipe transforms all the characters in a string to lowercase. See the "Changing String Case" section for details.
json	This pipe transforms an object into a JSON string. See the "Serializing Data as JSON" section for details.
slice	This pipe selects items from an array or characters from a string, as described in the "Slicing Data Arrays" section.
async	This pipe subscribes to an observable or a promise and displays the most recent value it produces. This pipe is demonstrated in Chapter 23.

Formatting Numbers

The number pipe formats number values using locale-sensitive rules. Listing 18-15 shows the use of the number pipe, along with the argument that specifies the formatting that will be used. I have removed the custom pipes and the associated select elements from the template.

Listing 18-15. Using the number Pipe in the productTable.component.html File in the src/app Folder

```
<table class="table table-sm table-bordered table-striped">
    <tr><th></th><th>Name</th><th>Category</th><th>Price</th><th></th></tr>
    <tr *paFor="let item of getProducts(); let i = index; let odd = odd;
            let even = even" [class.bg-info]="odd" [class.bg-warning]="even">
        <td style="vertical-align:middle">{{i + 1}}</td>
        <td style="vertical-align:middle">{{item.name}}</td>
        <td style="vertical-align:middle">{{item.category}}</td>
        <td style="vertical-align:middle">{{item.price | number:"3.2-2" }}</td>
        <td class="text-center">
            <button class="btn btn-danger btn-sm" (click)="deleteProduct(item.id)">
                Delete
            </button>
        </td>
    </tr>
</table>
```

The number pipe accepts a single argument that specifies the number of digits that are included in the formatted result. The argument is in the following format (note the period and hyphen that separate the values and that the entire argument is quoted as a string):

```
"<minIntegerDigits>.<minFactionDigits>-<maxFractionDigits>"
```

Each element of the formatting argument is described in Table 18-5.

Table 18-5. *The Elements of the number Pipe Argument*

Name	Description
minIntegerDigits	This value specifies the minimum number of digits. The default value is 1.
minFractionDigits	This value specifies the minimum number of fractional digits. The default value is 0.
maxFractionDigits	This value specifies the maximum number of fractional digits. The default value is 3.

The argument used in the listing is `"3.2-2"`, which specifies that at least three digits should be used to display the integer portion of the number and that two fractional digits should always be used. This produces the result shown in Figure 18-8.

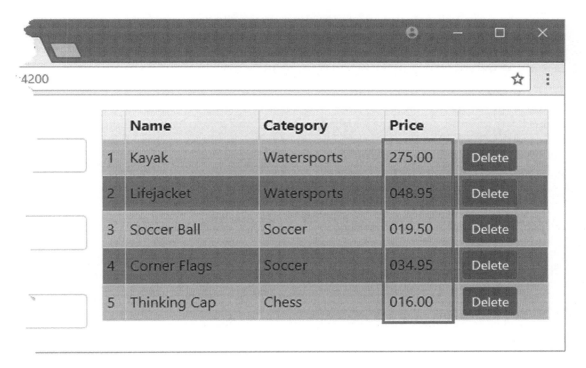

Figure 18-8. *Formatting number values*

The number pipe is location sensitive, which means that the same format argument will produce differently formatted results based on the user's locale setting. Angular applications default to the en-US locale by default and require other locales to be loaded explicitly, as shown in Listing 18-16.

Listing 18-16. Setting the Locale in the app.module.ts File in the src/app Folder

```
import { NgModule } from "@angular/core";
import { BrowserModule } from "@angular/platform-browser";
import { ProductComponent } from "./component";
import { FormsModule, ReactiveFormsModule } from "@angular/forms";
import { PaAttrDirective } from "./attr.directive";
import { PaModel } from "./twoway.directive";
import { PaStructureDirective } from "./structure.directive";
import { PaIteratorDirective } from "./iterator.directive";
import { PaCellColor } from "./cellColor.directive";
import { PaCellColorSwitcher } from "./cellColorSwitcher.directive";
import { ProductTableComponent } from "./productTable.component";
import { ProductFormComponent } from "./productForm.component";
import { PaToggleView } from "./toggleView.component";
import { PaAddTaxPipe } from "./addTax.pipe";
import { PaCategoryFilterPipe } from "./categoryFilter.pipe";
import { LOCALE_ID } from "@angular/core";
import localeFr from '@angular/common/locales/fr';
import { registerLocaleData } from '@angular/common';

registerLocaleData(localeFr);

@NgModule({
    imports: [BrowserModule, FormsModule, ReactiveFormsModule],
    declarations: [ProductComponent, PaAttrDirective, PaModel,
        PaStructureDirective, PaIteratorDirective,
        PaCellColor, PaCellColorSwitcher, ProductTableComponent,
        ProductFormComponent, PaToggleView, PaAddTaxPipe,
        PaCategoryFilterPipe],
    providers: [{ provide: LOCALE_ID, useValue: "fr-FR" }],
    bootstrap: [ProductComponent]
})
export class AppModule { }
```

Setting the locale requires importing the locale you require from the modules that contain each region's data and registering it by calling the registerLocaleData function, which is imported from the @angular/ common module. In the listing, I have imported the fr-FR locale, which is for French as it is spoken in France. The final step is to configure the providers property, which I describe in Chapter 20, but the effect of the configuration in Listing 18-16 is to enable the fr-FR locale, which changes the formatting of the numerical values, as shown in Figure 18-9.

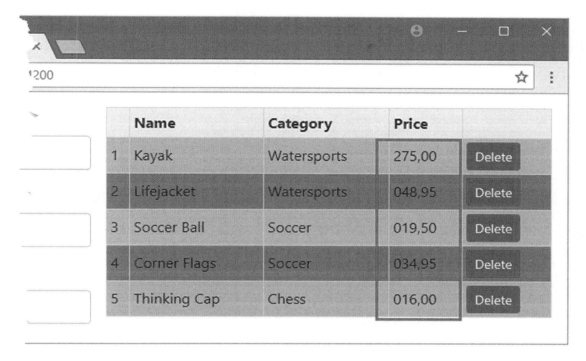

Figure 18-9. *Locale-sensitive formatting*

Formatting Currency Values

The currency pipe formats number values that represent monetary amounts. Listing 18-6 used this pipe to introduce the topic, and Listing 18-17 shows another application of the same pipe but with the addition of number format specifiers.

Listing 18-17. Using the currency Pipe in the productTable.component.html File in the src/app Folder

```
<table class="table table-sm table-bordered table-striped">
    <tr><th></th><th>Name</th><th>Category</th><th>Price</th><th></th></tr>
    <tr *paFor="let item of getProducts(); let i = index; let odd = odd;
            let even = even" [class.bg-info]="odd" [class.bg-warning]="even">
        <td style="vertical-align:middle">{{i + 1}}</td>
        <td style="vertical-align:middle">{{item.name}}</td>
        <td style="vertical-align:middle">{{item.category}}</td>
        <td style="vertical-align:middle">
            {{item.price | currency:"USD":"symbol":"2.2-2" }}
        </td>
        <td class="text-center">
            <button class="btn btn-danger btn-sm" (click)="deleteProduct(item.id)">
                Delete
            </button>
        </td>
    </tr>
</table>
```

453

The currency pipe can be configured using four arguments, which are described in Table 18-6.

Table 18-6. *The Types of Web Forms Code Nuggets*

Name	Description
currencyCode	This string argument specifies the currency using an ISO 4217 code. The default value is USD if this argument is omitted. You can see a list of currency codes at http://en.wikipedia.org/wiki/ISO_4217.
display	This string indicates whether the currency symbol or code should be displayed. The supported values are code (use the currency code), symbol (use the currency symbol), and symbol-narrow (which shows the concise form when a currency has narrow and wide symbols). The default value is symbol.
digitInfo	This string argument specifies the formatting for the number, using the same formatting instructions supported by the number pipe, as described in the "Formatting Numbers" section.
locale	This string argument specifies the locale for the currency. This defaults to the LOCALE_ID value, the configuration of which is shown in Listing 18-16.

The arguments specified in Listing 18-17 tell the pipe to use the U.S. dollar as the currency (which has the ISO code USD), to display the symbol rather than the code in the output, and to format the number so that it has at least two integer digits and exactly two fraction digits.

This pipe relies on the Internationalization API to get details of the currency—especially its symbol— but doesn't select the currency automatically to reflect the user's locale setting.

This means that the formatting of the number and the position of the currency symbol are affected by the application's locale setting, regardless of the currency that has been specified by the pipe. The example application is still configured to use the fr-FR locale, which produces the results shown in Figure 18-10.

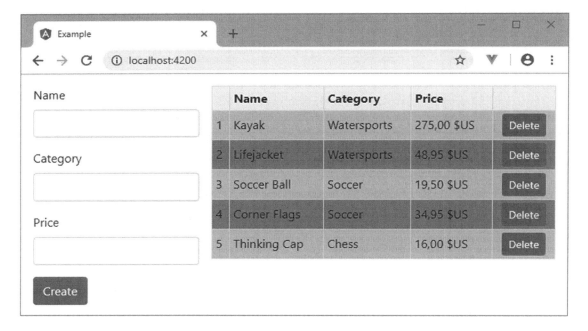

Figure 18-10. *Location-sensitive currency formatting*

To revert to the default locale, Listing 18-18 removes the `fr-FR` setting from the application's root module.

Listing 18-18. Removing the locale Setting in the app.module.ts File in the src/app Folder

```
import { NgModule } from "@angular/core";
import { BrowserModule } from "@angular/platform-browser";
import { ProductComponent } from "./component";
import { FormsModule, ReactiveFormsModule } from "@angular/forms";
import { PaAttrDirective } from "./attr.directive";
import { PaModel } from "./twoway.directive";
import { PaStructureDirective } from "./structure.directive";
import { PaIteratorDirective } from "./iterator.directive";
import { PaCellColor } from "./cellColor.directive";
import { PaCellColorSwitcher } from "./cellColorSwitcher.directive";
import { ProductTableComponent } from "./productTable.component";
import { ProductFormComponent } from "./productForm.component";
import { PaToggleView } from "./toggleView.component";
import { PaAddTaxPipe } from "./addTax.pipe";
import { PaCategoryFilterPipe } from "./categoryFilter.pipe";

import { LOCALE_ID } from "@angular/core";
import localeFr from '@angular/common/locales/fr';
import { registerLocaleData } from '@angular/common';

registerLocaleData(localeFr);

@NgModule({
  imports: [BrowserModule, FormsModule, ReactiveFormsModule],
  declarations: [ProductComponent, PaAttrDirective, PaModel,
    PaStructureDirective, PaIteratorDirective,
    PaCellColor, PaCellColorSwitcher, ProductTableComponent,
    ProductFormComponent, PaToggleView, PaAddTaxPipe,
    PaCategoryFilterPipe],
  //providers: [{ provide: LOCALE_ID, useValue: "fr-FR" }],
  bootstrap: [ProductComponent]
})
export class AppModule { }
```

Figure 18-11 shows the result.

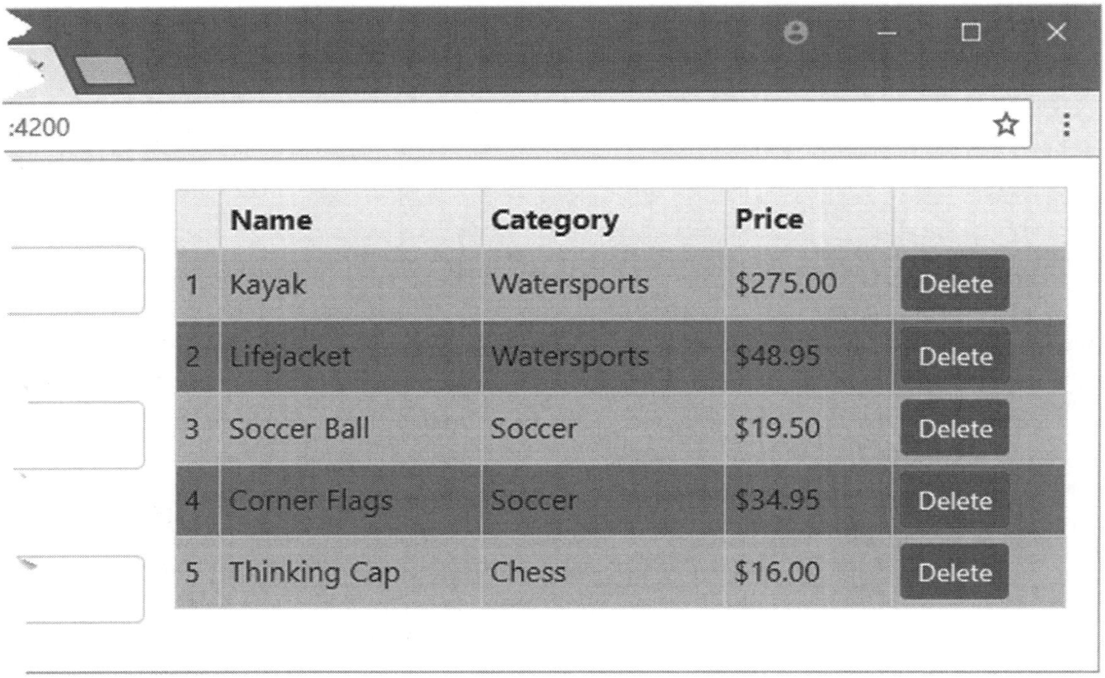

Figure 18-11. *Formatting currency values*

Formatting Percentages

The percent pipe formats number values as percentages, where values between 0 and 1 are formatted to represent 0 to 100 percent. This pipe has optional arguments that are used to specify the number formatting options, using the same format as the number pipe, and override the default locale. Listing 18-19 re-introduces the custom sales tax filter and populates the associated select element with option elements whose content is formatted with the percent filter.

Listing 18-19. Formatting Percentages in the productTable.component.html File in the src/app Folder

```
<div>
    <label>Tax Rate:</label>
    <select [value]="taxRate || 0" (change)="taxRate=$event.target.value">
        <option value="0">None</option>
        <option value="10">{{ 0.1 | percent }}</option>
        <option value="20">{{ 0.2 | percent }}</option>
        <option value="50">{{ 0.5 | percent }}</option>
        <option value="150">{{ 1.5 | percent }}</option>
    </select>
</div>

<table class="table table-sm table-bordered table-striped">
    <tr><th></th><th>Name</th><th>Category</th><th>Price</th><th></th></tr>
    <tr *paFor="let item of getProducts(); let i = index; let odd = odd;
            let even = even" [class.bg-info]="odd" [class.bg-warning]="even">
```

```
        <td style="vertical-align:middle">{{i + 1}}</td>
        <td style="vertical-align:middle">{{item.name}}</td>
        <td style="vertical-align:middle">{{item.category}}</td>
        <td style="vertical-align:middle">
            {{item.price | addTax:(taxRate || 0) | currency:"USD":"symbol":"2.2-2" }}
        </td>
        <td class="text-center">
            <button class="btn btn-danger btn-sm" (click)="deleteProduct(item.id)">
                Delete
            </button>
        </td>
    </tr>
</table>
```

Values that are greater than 1 are formatted into percentages greater than 100 percent. You can see this in the last item shown in Figure 18-12, where the value 1.5 produces a formatted value of 150 percent.

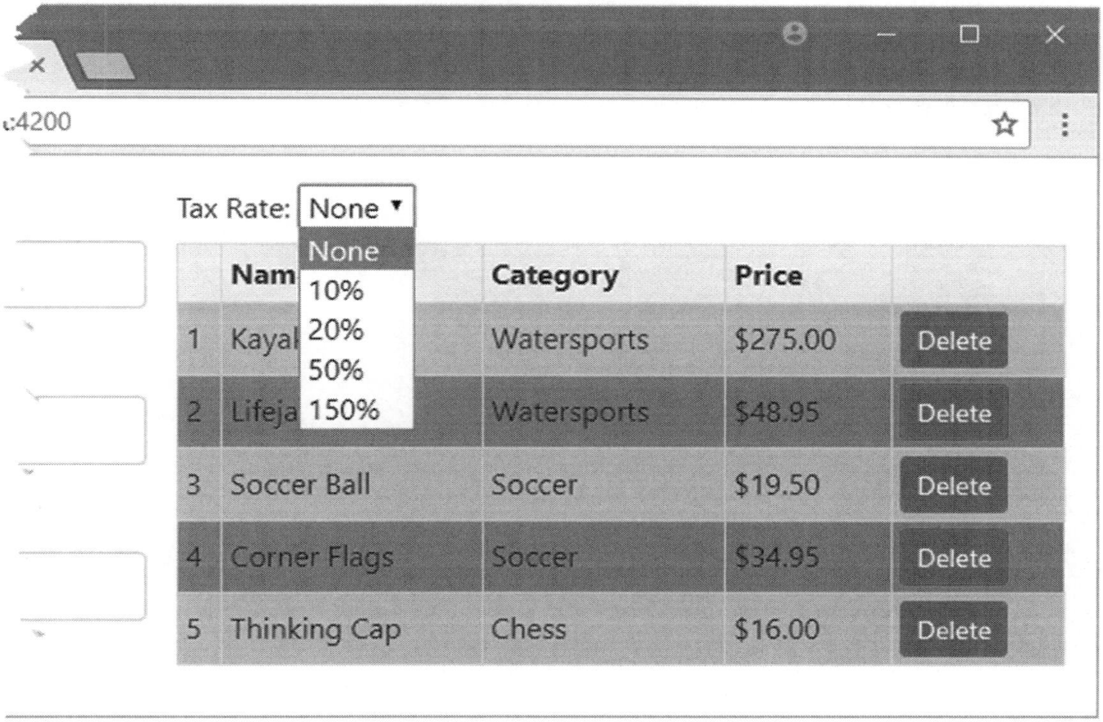

Figure 18-12. *Formatting percentage values*

The formatting of percentage values is location-sensitive, although the differences between locales can be subtle. As an example, while the en-US locale produces a result such as 10 percent, with the numerals and the percent sign next to one another, many locales, including fr-FR, will produce a result such as 10 %, with a space between the numerals and the percent sign.

Formatting Dates

The date pipe performs location-sensitive formatting of dates. Dates can be expressed using JavaScript Date objects, as a number value representing milliseconds since the beginning of 1970 or as a well-formatted string. Listing 18-20 adds three properties to the `ProductTableComponent` class, each of which encodes a date in one of the formats supported by the date pipe.

Listing 18-20. Defining Dates in the productTable.component.ts File in the src/app Folder

```
import { Component, Input, ViewChildren, QueryList } from "@angular/core";
import { Model } from "./repository.model";
import { Product } from "./product.model";

@Component({
    selector: "paProductTable",
    templateUrl: "productTable.component.html"
})
export class ProductTableComponent {

    @Input("model")
    dataModel: Model;

    getProduct(key: number): Product {
        return this.dataModel.getProduct(key);
    }

    getProducts(): Product[] {
        return this.dataModel.getProducts();
    }

    deleteProduct(key: number) {
        this.dataModel.deleteProduct(key);
    }

    dateObject: Date = new Date(2020, 1, 20);
    dateString: string = "2020-02-20T00:00:00.000Z";
    dateNumber: number = 1582156800000;
}
```

All three properties describe the same date, which is February 20, 2020, with no time specified. In Listing 18-21, I have used the date pipe to format all three properties.

Listing 18-21. Formatting Dates in the productTable.component.html File in the src/app Folder

```
<div class="bg-info p-2 text-white">
    <div>Date formatted from object: {{ dateObject | date }}</div>
    <div>Date formatted from string: {{ dateString | date }}</div>
    <div>Date formatted from number: {{ dateNumber | date }}</div>
</div>
```

```
<table class="table table-sm table-bordered table-striped">
    <tr><th></th><th>Name</th><th>Category</th><th>Price</th><th></th></tr>
    <tr *paFor="let item of getProducts(); let i = index; let odd = odd;
         let even = even" [class.bg-info]="odd" [class.bg-warning]="even">
        <td style="vertical-align:middle">{{i + 1}}</td>
        <td style="vertical-align:middle">{{item.name}}</td>
        <td style="vertical-align:middle">{{item.category}}</td>
        <td style="vertical-align:middle">
            {{item.price | addTax:(taxRate || 0) | currency:"USD":"symbol":"2.2-2" }}
        </td>
        <td class="text-center">
            <button class="btn btn-danger btn-sm" (click)="deleteProduct(item.id)">
                Delete
            </button>
        </td>
    </tr>
</table>
```

The pipe works out which data type it is working with, parses the value to get a date, and then formats it, as shown in Figure 18-13.

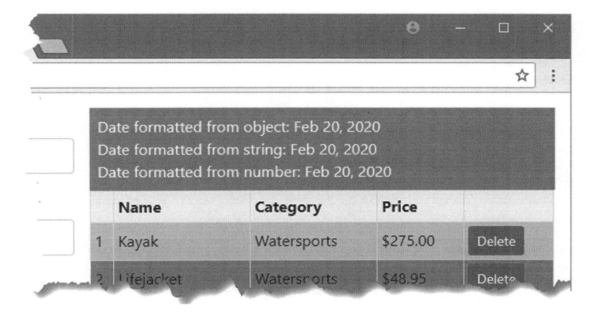

Figure 18-13. *Formatting dates*

The date pipe accepts an argument that specifies the date format that should be used. Individual date components can be selected for the output using the symbols described in Table 18-7.

Table 18-7. *The Date Pipe Format Symbols*

Name	Description
y, yy	These symbols select the year.
M, MMM, MMMM	These symbols select the month.
d, dd	These symbols select the day (as a number).
E, EE, EEEE	These symbols select the day (as a name).
j, jj	These symbols select the hour.
h, hh, H, HH	These symbols select the hour in 12- and 24-hour forms.
m, mm	These symbols select the minutes.
s, ss	These symbols select the seconds.
Z	This symbol selects the time zone.

The symbols in Table 18-7 provide access to the date components in differing levels of brevity so that M will return 2 if the month is February, MM will return 02, MMM will return Feb, and MMMM will return February, assuming that you are using the en-US locale. The date pipe also supports predefined date formats for commonly used combinations, as described in Table 18-8.

Table 18-8. *The Predefined date Pipe Formats*

Name	Description
short	This format is equivalent to the component string yMdjm. It presents the date in a concise format, including the time component.
medium	This format is equivalent to the component string yMMMdjms. It presents the date as a more expansive format, including the time component.
shortDate	This format is equivalent to the component string yMd. It presents the date in a concise format and excludes the time component.
mediumDate	This format is equivalent to the component string yMMMd. It presents the date in a more expansive format and excludes the time component.
longDate	This format is equivalent to the component string yMMMMd. It presents the date and excludes the time component.
fullDate	This format is equivalent to the component string yMMMMEEEEd. It presents the date fully and excludes the date format.
shortTime	This format is equivalent to the component string jm.
mediumTime	This format is equivalent to the component string jms.

The date pipe also accepts an argument that specifies a time zone and an argument that can be used to override the locale. Listing 18-22 shows the use of the predefined formats as arguments to the date pipe, rendering the same date in different ways.

Listing 18-22. Formatting Dates in the productTable.component.html File in the src/app Folder

```
...
<div class="bg-info p-2 text-white">
  <div>Date formatted as shortDate: {{ dateObject | date:"shortDate" }}</div>
  <div>Date formatted as mediumDate: {{ dateObject | date:"mediumDate" }}</div>
  <div>Date formatted as longDate: {{ dateObject | date:"longDate" }}</div>
</div>
...
```

Formatting arguments are specified as literal strings. Take care to capitalize the format string correctly because shortDate will be interpreted as one of the predefined formats from Table 18-8, but shortdate (with a lowercase letter d) will be interpreted a series of characters from Table 18-7 and produce nonsensical output.

■ **Caution** Date parsing and formatting is a complex and time-consuming process. As a consequence, the pure property for the date pipe is true; as a result, changes to individual components of a Date object won't trigger an update. If you need to reflect changes in the way that a date is displayed, then you must change the reference to the Date object that the binding containing the date pipe refers to.

Date formatting is location-sensitive, which means you will receive different components for different locales. Do not assume that a date format that makes sense in one locale will have any meaning in another. Figure 18-14 shows the formatted dates, in the en-US and fr-FR locales.

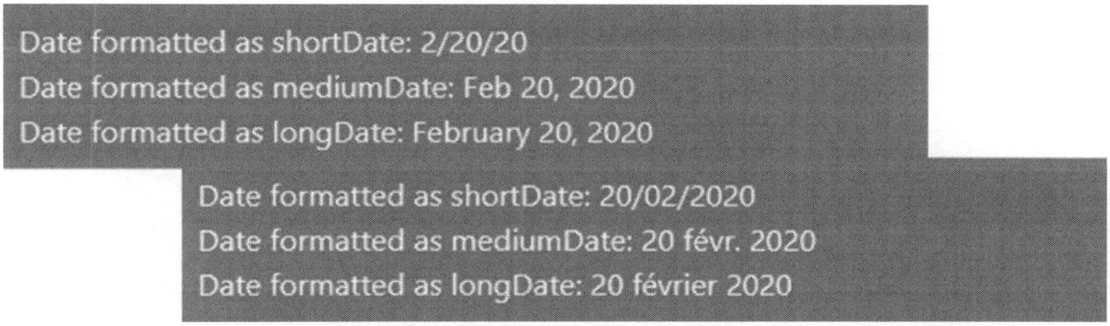

Figure 18-14. Location-sensitive date formatting

Changing String Case

The uppercase and lowercase pipes convert all the characters in a string to uppercase or lowercase, respectively. Listing 18-23 shows both pipes applied to cells in the product table.

Listing 18-23. Changing Character Case in the productTable.component.html File in the src/app Folder

```
<table class="table table-sm table-bordered table-striped">
    <tr><th></th><th>Name</th><th>Category</th><th>Price</th><th></th></tr>
    <tr *paFor="let item of getProducts(); let i = index; let odd = odd;
            let even = even" [class.bg-info]="odd" [class.bg-warning]="even">
        <td style="vertical-align:middle">{{i + 1}}</td>
        <td style="vertical-align:middle">{{item.name | uppercase }}</td>
        <td style="vertical-align:middle">{{item.category | lowercase }}</td>
        <td style="vertical-align:middle">
            {{item.price | addTax:(taxRate || 0) | currency:"USD":"symbol":"2.2-2" }}
        </td>
        <td class="text-center">
            <button class="btn btn-danger btn-sm" (click)="deleteProduct(item.id)">
                Delete
            </button>
        </td>
    </tr>
</table>
```

These pipes use the standard JavaScript string methods toUpperCase and toLowerCase, which are not sensitive to locale settings, as shown in Figure 18-15.

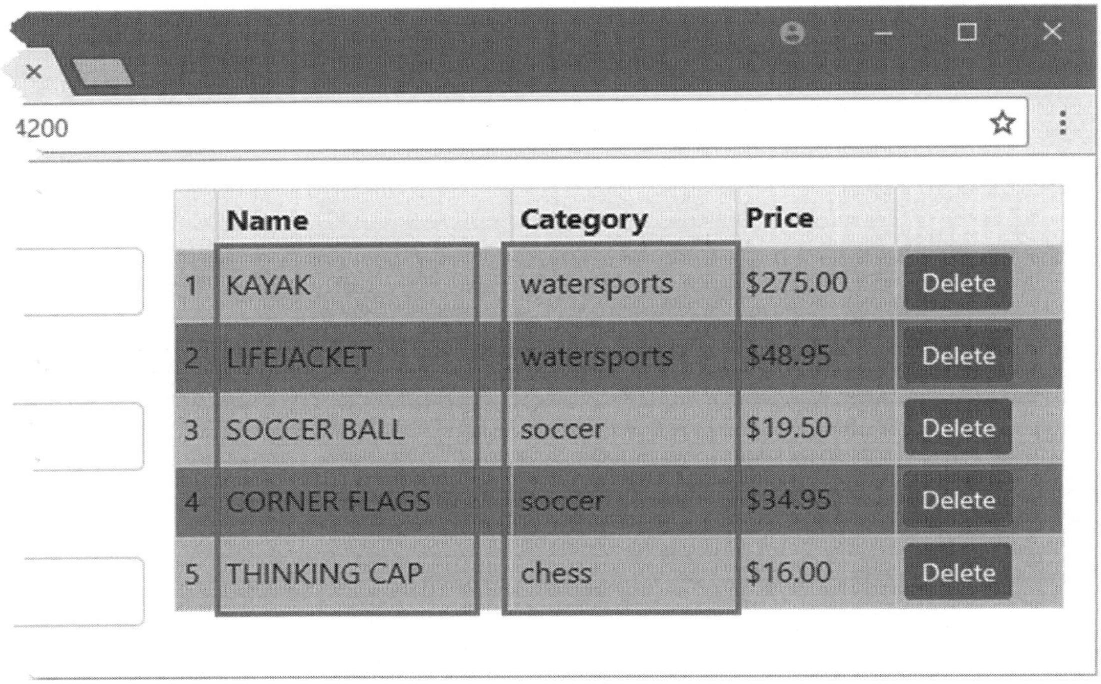

Figure 18-15. Changing character case

Serializing Data as JSON

The json pipe creates a JSON representation of a data value. No arguments are accepted by this pipe, which uses the browser's JSON.stringify method to create the JSON string. Listing 18-24 applies this pipe to create a JSON representation of the objects in the data model.

Listing 18-24. Creating a JSON String in the productTable.component.html File in the src/app Folder

```
<div class="bg-info p-2 text-white">
    <div>{{ getProducts() | json }}</div>
</div>

<table class="table table-sm table-bordered table-striped">
    <tr><th></th><th>Name</th><th>Category</th><th>Price</th><th></th></tr>
    <tr *paFor="let item of getProducts(); let i = index; let odd = odd;
            let even = even" [class.bg-info]="odd" [class.bg-warning]="even">
        <td style="vertical-align:middle">{{i + 1}}</td>
        <td style="vertical-align:middle">{{item.name | uppercase }}</td>
        <td style="vertical-align:middle">{{item.category | lowercase }}</td>
        <td style="vertical-align:middle">
            {{item.price | addTax:(taxRate || 0) | currency:"USD":"symbol":"2.2-2" }}
        </td>
        <td class="text-center">
            <button class="btn btn-danger btn-sm" (click)="deleteProduct(item.id)">
                Delete
            </button>
        </td>
    </tr>
</table>
```

This pipe is useful during debugging, and its decorator's pure property is false so that any change in the application will cause the pipe's transform method to be invoked, ensuring that even collection-level changes are shown. Figure 18-16 shows the JSON generated from the objects in the example application's data model.

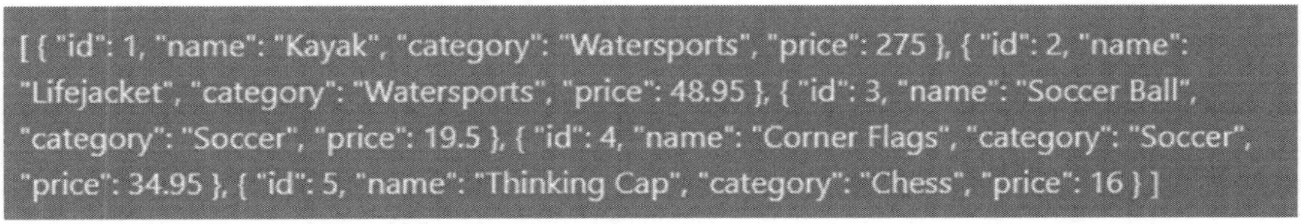

```
[ { "id": 1, "name": "Kayak", "category": "Watersports", "price": 275 }, { "id": 2, "name":
"Lifejacket", "category": "Watersports", "price": 48.95 }, { "id": 3, "name": "Soccer Ball",
"category": "Soccer", "price": 19.5 }, { "id": 4, "name": "Corner Flags", "category": "Soccer",
"price": 34.95 }, { "id": 5, "name": "Thinking Cap", "category": "Chess", "price": 16 } ]
```

Figure 18-16. *Generating JSON strings for debugging*

Slicing Data Arrays

The slice pipe operates on an array or string and returns a subset of the elements or characters it contains. This is an impure pipe, which means it will reflect any changes that occur within the data object it is operating on but also means that the slice operation will be performed after any change in the application, even if that change was not related to the source data.

The objects or characters selected by the slice pipe are specified using two arguments, which are described in Table 18-9.

Table 18-9. *The Slice Pipe Arguments*

Name	Description
start	This argument must be specified. If the value is positive, the start index for items to be included in the result counts from the first position in the array. If the value is negative, then the pipe counts back from the end of the array.
end	This optional argument is used to specify how many items from the start index should be included in the result. If this value is omitted, all the items after the start index (or before in the case of negative values) will be included.

Listing 18-25 demonstrates the use of the slice pipe in combination with a select element that specifies how many items should be displayed in the product table.

Listing 18-25. Using the slice Pipe in the productTable.component.html File in the src/app Folder

```
<div>
    <label>Number of items:</label>
    <select [value]="itemCount || 1" (change)="itemCount=$event.target.value">
        <option *ngFor="let item of getProducts(); let i = index" [value]="i + 1">
            {{i + 1}}
        </option>
    </select>
</div>

<table class="table table-sm table-bordered table-striped">
    <tr><th></th><th>Name</th><th>Category</th><th>Price</th><th></th></tr>
    <tr *paFor="let item of getProducts() | slice:0:(itemCount || 1);
            let i = index; let odd = odd; let even = even"
            [class.bg-info]="odd" [class.bg-warning]="even">
        <td style="vertical-align:middle">{{i + 1}}</td>
        <td style="vertical-align:middle">{{item.name | uppercase }}</td>
        <td style="vertical-align:middle">{{item.category | lowercase }}</td>
        <td style="vertical-align:middle">
            {{item.price | addTax:(taxRate || 0) | currency:"USD":"symbol":"2.2-2" }}
        </td>
        <td class="text-center">
            <button class="btn btn-danger btn-sm" (click)="deleteProduct(item.id)">
                Delete
            </button>
        </td>
    </tr>
</table>
```

The select element is populated with option elements created with the ngFor directive. This directive doesn't directly support iterating a specific number of times, so I have used the index variable to generate the values that are required. The select element sets a variable called itemCount, which is used as the second argument of the slice pipe, like this:

```
...
<tr *paFor="let item of getProducts() | slice:0:(itemCount || 1);
    let i = index; let odd = odd; let even = even"
    [class.bg-info]="odd" [class.bg-warning]="even">
...
```

The effect is that changing the value displayed by the select element changes the number of items displayed in the product table, as shown in Figure 18-17.

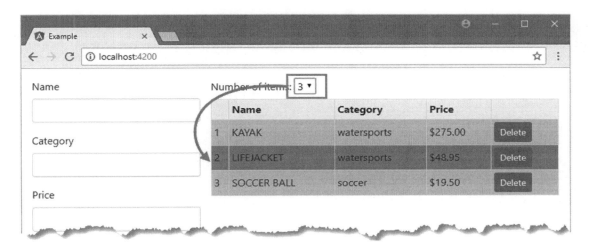

Figure 18-17. *Using the slice pipe*

Summary

In this chapter, I introduced pipes and explained how they are used to transform data values so they can be presented to the user in the template. I demonstrated the process for creating custom pipes, explained how some pipes are pure and others are not, and demonstrated the built-in pipes that Angular provides for handling common tasks. In the next chapter, I introduce services, which can be used to simplify the design of Angular applications and allow building blocks to easily collaborate.

CHAPTER 19

■ ■ ■

Using Services

Services are objects that provide common functionality to support other building blocks in an application, such as directives, components, and pipes. What's important about services is the way that they are used, which is through a process called *dependency injection*. Using services can increase the flexibility and scalability of an Angular application, but dependency injection can be a difficult topic to understand. To that end, I start this chapter slowly and explain the problems that services and dependency injection can be used to solve, how dependency injection works, and why you should consider using services in your own projects. In Chapter 20, I introduce some more advanced features that Angular provides for service. Table 19-1 puts services in context.

Table 19-1. *Putting Services in Context*

Question	Answer
What are they?	Services are objects that define functionality required by other building blocks such as components or directives. What separates services from regular objects is that they are provided to building blocks by an external provider, rather than being created directly using the new keyword or received by an input property.
Why are they useful?	Services simplify the structure of applications, make it easier to move or reuse functionality, and make it easier to isolate building blocks for effective unit testing.
How are they used?	Classes declare dependencies on services using constructor parameters, which are then resolved using the set of services for which the application has been configured. Services are classes to which the @Injectable decorator has been applied.
Are there any pitfalls or limitations?	Dependency injection is a contentious topic, and not all developers like using it. If you don't perform unit tests or if your applications are relatively simple, the extra work required to implement dependency injection is unlikely to pay any long-term dividends.
Are there any alternatives?	Services and dependency injection are hard to avoid because Angular uses them to provide access to built-in functionality. But you are not required to define services for your own custom functionality if that is your preference.

© Adam Freeman 2018

A. Freeman, *Pro Angular 6*, https://doi.org/10.1007/978-1-4842-3649-9_19

Table 19-2 summarizes the chapter.

Table 19-2. *Chapter Summary*

Problem	Solution	Listing
Avoid the need to distribute shared objects manually	Use services	1–14, 21–28
Declare a dependency on a service	Add a constructor argument with the type of the service you require	15–20

Preparing the Example Project

I continue using the example project in this chapter that I have been working with since Chapter 11. To prepare for this chapter, I have removed most of the pipes from the data binding expressions in the table of products and also removed the select element that was used to choose how many products were displayed, as shown in Listing 19-1.

■ **Tip** You can download the example project for this chapter—and for all the other chapters in this book—from https://github.com/Apress/pro-angular-6.

Listing 19-1. Removing the Pipe from the productTable.component.html File in the src/app Folder

```
<table class="table table-sm table-bordered table-striped">
    <tr><th></th><th>Name</th><th>Category</th><th>Price</th><th></th></tr>
    <tr *paFor="let item of getProducts(); let i = index;
            let odd = odd; let even = even" [class.bg-info]="odd"
            [class.bg-warning]="even">
        <td style="vertical-align:middle">{{i + 1}}</td>
        <td style="vertical-align:middle">{{item.name}}</td>
        <td style="vertical-align:middle">{{item.category}}</td>
        <td style="vertical-align:middle">
            {{item.price | currency:"USD":"symbol" }}
        </td>
        <td class="text-center">
            <button class="btn btn-danger btn-sm" (click)="deleteProduct(item.id)">
                Delete
            </button>
        </td>
    </tr>
</table>
```

Run the following command in the example folder to start the TypeScript compiler and the development HTTP server:

```
ng serve
```

Open a new browser window and navigate to http://localhost:4200 to see the content shown in Figure 19-1.

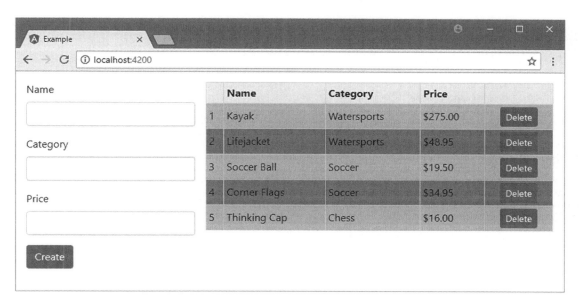

Figure 19-1. *Running the example application*

Understanding the Object Distribution Problem

In Chapter 17, I added components to the project to help break up the monolithic structure of the application. In doing this, I used input and output properties to connect components together, using host elements to bridge the isolation that Angular enforces between a parent component and its children. I also showed you how to query the contents of the template for view children, which complements the content children feature described in Chapter 16.

These techniques for coordinating between directives and components can be powerful and useful if applied carefully. But they can also end up as a general tool for distributing shared objects throughout an application, where the result is to increase the complexity of the application and to tightly bind components together.

Demonstrating the Problem

To help demonstrate the problem, I am going to add a shared object to the project and two components that rely on it. I created a file called discount.service.ts to the src/app folder and defined the class shown in Listing 19-2. I'll explain the significance of the service part of the file name later in the chapter.

Listing 19-2. The Contents of the discount.service.ts File in the src/app Folder

```
export class DiscountService {
    private discountValue: number = 10;

    public get discount(): number {
        return this.discountValue;
    }

    public set discount(newValue: number) {
        this.discountValue = newValue || 0;
    }

    public applyDiscount(price: number) {
        return Math.max(price - this.discountValue, 5);
    }
}
```

The DiscountService class defines a private property called discountValue that is used to store a number that will be used to reduce the product prices in the data model. This value is exposed through getters and setters called discount, and there is a convenience method called applyDiscount that reduces a price while ensuring that a price is never less than $5.

For the first component that makes use of the DiscountService class, I added a file called discountDisplay.component.ts to the src/app folder and added the code shown in Listing 19-3.

Listing 19-3. The Contents of the discountDisplay.component.ts File in the src/app Folder

```
import { Component, Input } from "@angular/core";
import { DiscountService } from "./discount.service";

@Component({
    selector: "paDiscountDisplay",
    template: `<div class="bg-info text-white p-2">
                The discount is {{discounter.discount}}
              </div>`
})
export class PaDiscountDisplayComponent {

    @Input("discounter")
    discounter: DiscountService;
}
```

The DiscountDisplayComponent uses an inline template to display the discount amount, which is obtained from a DiscountService object received through an input property.

For the second component that makes use of the DiscountService class, I added a file called discountEditor.component.ts to the src/app folder and added the code shown in Listing 19-4.

Listing 19-4. The Contents of the discountEditor.component.ts File in the src/app Folder

```
import { Component, Input } from "@angular/core";
import { DiscountService } from "./discount.service";

@Component({
    selector: "paDiscountEditor",
    template: `<div class="form-group">
                    <label>Discount</label>
                    <input [(ngModel)]="discounter.discount"
                        class="form-control" type="number" />
                </div>`
})
export class PaDiscountEditorComponent {

    @Input("discounter")
    discounter: DiscountService;
}
```

The DiscountEditorComponent uses an inline template with an input element that allows the discount amount to be edited. The input element has a two-way binding on the DiscountService.discount property that targets the ngModel directive. Listing 19-5 shows the new components being enabled in the Angular module.

Listing 19-5. Enabling the Components in the app.module.ts File in the src/app Folder

```
import { NgModule } from "@angular/core";
import { BrowserModule } from "@angular/platform-browser";
import { ProductComponent } from "./component";
import { FormsModule, ReactiveFormsModule } from "@angular/forms";
import { PaAttrDirective } from "./attr.directive";
import { PaModel } from "./twoway.directive";
import { PaStructureDirective } from "./structure.directive";
import { PaIteratorDirective } from "./iterator.directive";
import { PaCellColor } from "./cellColor.directive";
import { PaCellColorSwitcher } from "./cellColorSwitcher.directive";
import { ProductTableComponent } from "./productTable.component";
import { ProductFormComponent } from "./productForm.component";
import { PaToggleView } from "./toggleView.component";
import { PaAddTaxPipe } from "./addTax.pipe";
import { PaCategoryFilterPipe } from "./categoryFilter.pipe";
import { LOCALE_ID } from "@angular/core";
import localeFr from '@angular/common/locales/fr';
import { registerLocaleData } from '@angular/common';
import { PaDiscountDisplayComponent } from "./discountDisplay.component";
import { PaDiscountEditorComponent } from "./discountEditor.component";

registerLocaleData(localeFr);

@NgModule({
  imports: [BrowserModule, FormsModule, ReactiveFormsModule],
  declarations: [ProductComponent, PaAttrDirective, PaModel,
    PaStructureDirective, PaIteratorDirective,
```

```
    PaCellColor, PaCellColorSwitcher, ProductTableComponent,
    ProductFormComponent, PaAddTaxPipe, PaCategoryFilterPipe,
    PaDiscountDisplayComponent, PaDiscountEditorComponent],
  bootstrap: [ProductComponent]
})
export class AppModule { }
```

To get the new components working, I added them to parent component's template, positioning the new content underneath the table that lists the products, which means that I need to edit the productTable. component.html file, as shown in Listing 19-6.

Listing 19-6. Adding Component Elements in the productTable.component.html File in the src/app Folder

```html
<table class="table table-sm table-bordered table-striped">
    <tr><th></th><th>Name</th><th>Category</th><th>Price</th><th></th></tr>
    <tr *paFor="let item of getProducts(); let i = index;
            let odd = odd; let even = even" [class.bg-info]="odd"
            [class.bg-warning]="even">
        <td style="vertical-align:middle">{{i + 1}}</td>
        <td style="vertical-align:middle">{{item.name}}</td>
        <td style="vertical-align:middle">{{item.category}}</td>
        <td style="vertical-align:middle">
            {{item.price | currency:"USD":"symbol" }}
        </td>
        <td class="text-center">
            <button class="btn btn-danger btn-sm" (click)="deleteProduct(item.id)">
                Delete
            </button>
        </td>
    </tr>
</table>


<paDiscountEditor [discounter]="discounter"></paDiscountEditor>
<paDiscountDisplay [discounter]="discounter"></paDiscountDisplay>
```

These elements correspond to the components' selector properties in Listing 19-3 and Listing 19-4 and use data bindings to set the value of the input properties. The final step is to create an object in the parent component that will provide the value for the data binding expressions, as shown in Listing 19-7.

Listing 19-7. Creating the Shared Object in the productTable.component.ts File in the src/app Folder

```typescript
import { Component, Input, ViewChildren, QueryList } from "@angular/core";
import { Model } from "./repository.model";
import { Product } from "./product.model";
import { DiscountService } from "./discount.service";

@Component({
    selector: "paProductTable",
    templateUrl: "productTable.component.html"
})
```

472

```
export class ProductTableComponent {
    discounter: DiscountService = new DiscountService();

    @Input("model")
    dataModel: Model;

    getProduct(key: number): Product {
        return this.dataModel.getProduct(key);
    }

    getProducts(): Product[] {
        return this.dataModel.getProducts();
    }

    deleteProduct(key: number) {
        this.dataModel.deleteProduct(key);
    }

    dateObject: Date = new Date(2020, 1, 20);
    dateString: string = "2020-02-20T00:00:00.000Z";
    dateNumber: number = 1582156800000;
}
```

Figure 19-2 shows the content from the new components. Changes to the value in the input element provided by one of the components will be reflected in the content presented by the other component, reflecting the use of the shared DiscountService object and its discount property.

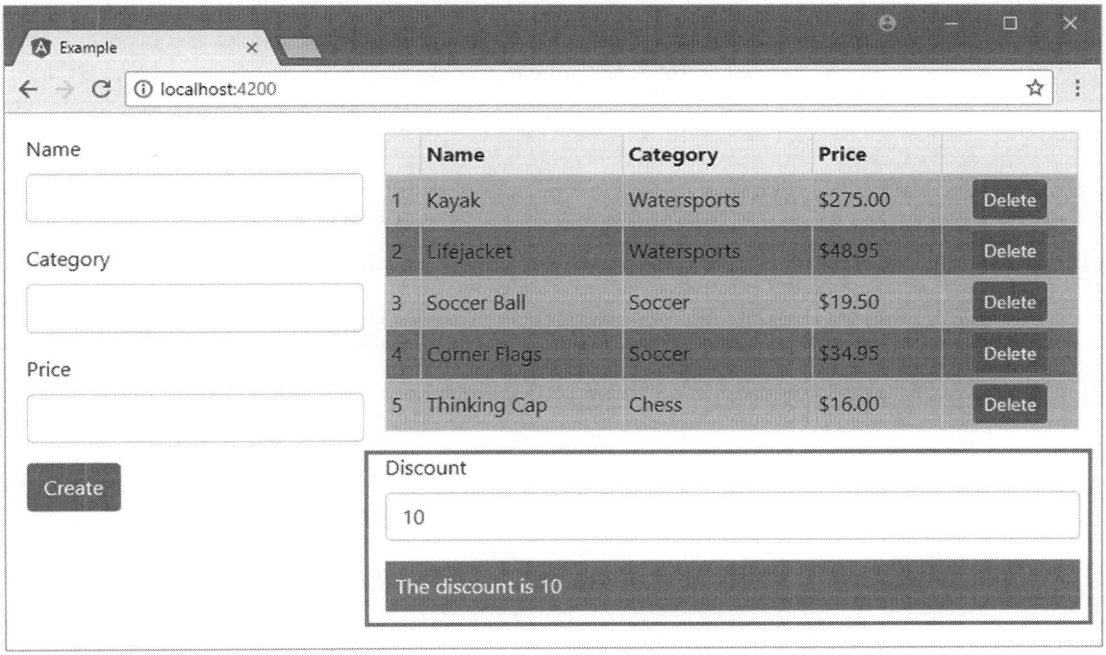

Figure 19-2. *Adding components to the example application*

The process for adding the new components and the shared object was straightforward and logical, until the final stage. The problem arises in the way that I had to create and distribute the shared object: the instance of the DiscountService class.

Because Angular isolates components from one another, I had no way to share the DiscountService object directly between the DiscountEditorComponent and DiscountDisplayComponent. Each component could have created its own DiscountService object, but that means changes from the editor component wouldn't be shown in the display component.

That is what led me to create the DiscountService object in the product table component, which is the first shared ancestor of the discount editor and display components. This allowed me to distribute the DiscountService object through the product table component's template, ensuring that a single object was shared with both of the components that need it.

But there are a couple of problems. The first is that the ProductTableComponent class doesn't actually need or use a DiscountService object to deliver its own functionality. It just happens to be the first common ancestor of the components that do need the object. And creating the shared object in the ProductTableComponent class makes that class slightly more complex and slightly more difficult to test effectively. This is a modest increment of complexity, but it will occur for every shared object that the application requires—and a complex application can depend on a lot of shared objects, each of which ends up being created by components that just happen to be the first common ancestor of the classes that depend on them.

The second problem is hinted at by the term *first common ancestor*. The ProductTableComponent class happens to be the parent of both of the classes that depend on the DiscountService object, but think about what would happen if I wanted to move the DiscountEditorComponent so that it was displayed under the form rather than the table. In this situation, I have to work my way up the tree of components until I find a common ancestor, which would end up being the root component. And then I would have to work my way down the component tree adding input properties and modifying templates so that each intermediate component could receive the DiscountService object from its parent and pass it on to any children who have descendants that need it. And the same applies to any directives that depend on receiving a DiscountService object, where any component whose template contains data bindings that target that directive must make sure they are part of the distribution chain, too.

The result is that the components and directives in the application become tightly bound together. A major refactoring is required if you need to move or reuse a component in a different part of the application and the management of the input properties and data bindings become unmanageable.

Distributing Objects as Services Using Dependency Injection

There is a better way to distribute objects to the classes that depend on them, which is to use *dependency injection*, where objects are provided to classes from an external source. Angular includes a built-in dependency injection system and supplies the external source of objects, known as *providers*. In the sections that follow, I rework the example application to provide the DiscountService object without needing to use the component hierarchy as a distribution mechanism.

Preparing the Service

Any object that is managed and distributed through dependency injection is called a *service*, which is why I selected the name DiscountService for the class that defines the shared object and why that class is defined in a file called discount.service.ts. Angular denotes service classes using the @Injectable decorator, as shown in Listing 19-8. The @Injectable decorator doesn't define any configuration properties.

Listing 19-8. Preparing a Class as a Service in the discount.service.ts File in the src/app Folder

```
import { Injectable } from "@angular/core";

@Injectable()
export class DiscountService {
    private discountValue: number = 10;

    public get discount(): number {
        return this.discountValue;
    }

    public set discount(newValue: number) {
        this.discountValue = newValue || 0;
    }

    public applyDiscount(price: number) {
        return Math.max(price - this.discountValue, 5);
    }
}
```

■ **Tip** Strictly speaking, the `@Injectable` decorator is required only when a class has its own constructor arguments to resolve, but it is a good idea to apply it anyway because it serves as a signal that the class is intended for use as a service.

Preparing the Dependent Components

A class declares dependencies using its constructor. When Angular needs to create an instance of the class—such as when it finds an element that matches the `selector` property defined by a component—its constructor is inspected, and the type of each argument is examined. Angular then uses the services that have been defined to try to satisfy the dependencies. The term *dependency injection* arises because each dependency is *injected* into the constructor to create the new instance.

For the example application, it means that the components that depend on a `DiscountService` object no longer require input properties and can declare a constructor dependency instead. Listing 19-9 shows the changes to the `DiscountDisplayComponent` class.

Listing 19-9. Declaring a Dependency in the discountDisplay.component.ts File in the src/app Folder

```
import { Component, Input } from "@angular/core";
import { DiscountService } from "./discount.service";

@Component({
  selector: "paDiscountDisplay",
  template: `<div class="bg-info text-white p-2">
                The discount is {{discounter.discount}}
             </div>`
})
export class PaDiscountDisplayComponent {

  constructor(private discounter: DiscountService) { }
}
```

The same change can be applied to the DiscountEditorComponent class, replacing the input property with a dependency declared through the constructor, as shown in Listing 19-10.

Listing 19-10. Declaring a Dependency in the discountEditor.component.ts File in the src/app Folder

```
import { Component, Input } from "@angular/core";
import { DiscountService } from "./discount.service";

@Component({
    selector: "paDiscountEditor",
    template: `<div class="form-group">
                    <label>Discount</label>
                    <input [(ngModel)]="discounter.discount"
                        class="form-control" type="number" />
                </div>`
})
export class PaDiscountEditorComponent {

    constructor(private discounter: DiscountService) { }
}
```

These are small changes, but they avoid the need to distribute objects using templates and input properties and produce a more flexible application. I can now remove the DiscountService object from the product table component, as shown in Listing 19-11.

Listing 19-11. Removing the Shared Object in the productTable.component.ts File in the src/app Folder

```
import { Component, Input, ViewChildren, QueryList } from "@angular/core";
import { Model } from "./repository.model";
import { Product } from "./product.model";
import { DiscountService } from "./discount.service";

@Component({
  selector: "paProductTable",
  templateUrl: "productTable.component.html"
})
export class ProductTableComponent {
  // discounter: DiscountService = new DiscountService();

  @Input("model")
  dataModel: Model;

  getProduct(key: number): Product {
    return this.dataModel.getProduct(key);
  }

  getProducts(): Product[] {
    return this.dataModel.getProducts();
  }
```

```
deleteProduct(key: number) {
  this.dataModel.deleteProduct(key);
}

dateObject: Date = new Date(2020, 1, 20);
dateString: string = "2020-02-20T00:00:00.000Z";
dateNumber: number = 1582156800000;
}
```

And since the parent component is no longer providing the shared object through data bindings, I can remove them from the template, as shown in Listing 19-12.

Listing 19-12. Removing the Data Bindings in the productTable.component.html File in the src/app Folder

```
<table class="table table-sm table-bordered table-striped">
  <tr><th></th><th>Name</th><th>Category</th><th>Price</th><th></th></tr>
  <tr *paFor="let item of getProducts(); let i = index;
          let odd = odd; let even = even" [class.bg-info]="odd"
      [class.bg-warning]="even">
    <td style="vertical-align:middle">{{i + 1}}</td>
    <td style="vertical-align:middle">{{item.name}}</td>
    <td style="vertical-align:middle">{{item.category}}</td>
    <td style="vertical-align:middle">
      {{item.price | currency:"USD":"symbol" }}
    </td>
    <td class="text-center">
      <button class="btn btn-danger btn-sm" (click)="deleteProduct(item.id)">
        Delete
      </button>
    </td>
  </tr>
</table>

<paDiscountEditor></paDiscountEditor>
<paDiscountDisplay></paDiscountDisplay>
```

Registering the Service

The final change is to configure the dependency injection feature so that it can provide DiscountService objects to the components that require them. To make the service available throughout the application, it is registered in the Angular module, as shown in Listing 19-13.

Listing 19-13. Registering a Service in the app.module.ts File in the src/app Folder

```
import { NgModule } from "@angular/core";
import { BrowserModule } from "@angular/platform-browser";
import { ProductComponent } from "./component";
import { FormsModule, ReactiveFormsModule } from "@angular/forms";
import { PaAttrDirective } from "./attr.directive";
import { PaModel } from "./twoway.directive";
import { PaStructureDirective } from "./structure.directive";
```

```
import { PaIteratorDirective } from "./iterator.directive";
import { PaCellColor } from "./cellColor.directive";
import { PaCellColorSwitcher } from "./cellColorSwitcher.directive";
import { ProductTableComponent } from "./productTable.component";
import { ProductFormComponent } from "./productForm.component";
import { PaToggleView } from "./toggleView.component";
import { PaAddTaxPipe } from "./addTax.pipe";
import { PaCategoryFilterPipe } from "./categoryFilter.pipe";
import { LOCALE_ID } from "@angular/core";
import localeFr from '@angular/common/locales/fr';
import { registerLocaleData } from '@angular/common';
import { PaDiscountDisplayComponent } from "./discountDisplay.component";
import { PaDiscountEditorComponent } from "./discountEditor.component";
import { DiscountService } from "./discount.service";

registerLocaleData(localeFr);

@NgModule({
  imports: [BrowserModule, FormsModule, ReactiveFormsModule],
  declarations: [ProductComponent, PaAttrDirective, PaModel,
    PaStructureDirective, PaIteratorDirective,
    PaCellColor, PaCellColorSwitcher, ProductTableComponent,
    ProductFormComponent, PaAddTaxPipe, PaCategoryFilterPipe,
    PaDiscountDisplayComponent, PaDiscountEditorComponent],
  providers: [DiscountService],
  bootstrap: [ProductComponent]
})
export class AppModule { }
```

The NgModule decorator's providers property is set to an array of the classes that will be used as services. There is only one service at the moment, which is provided by the DiscountService class.

When you save the changes to the application, there won't be any visual changes, but the dependency injection feature will be used to provide the components with the DiscountService object they require.

Reviewing the Dependency Injection Changes

Angular seamlessly integrates dependency injection into its feature set. Each time that Angular encounters an element that requires a new building block, such as a component or a pipe, it examines the class constructor to check what dependencies have been declared and uses its services to try to resolve them. The set of services used to resolve dependencies includes the custom services defined by the application, such as the DiscountService service that has been registered in Listing 19-13, and a set of built-in services provided by Angular that are described in later chapters.

The changes to introduce dependency injection in the previous section didn't result in a big-bang change in the way that the application works—or any visible change at all. But there is a profound difference in the way that the application is put together that makes it more flexible and fluid. The best demonstration of this is to add the components that require the DiscountService to a different part of the application, as shown in Listing 19-14.

Listing 19-14. Adding Components in the productForm.component.html File in the src/app Folder

```
<form novalidate [formGroup]="form" (ngSubmit)="submitForm(form)">
  <div class="form-group" *ngFor="let control of form.productControls">
    <label>{{control.label}}</label>
    <input class="form-control"
           [(ngModel)]="newProduct[control.modelProperty]"
           name="{{control.modelProperty}}"
           formControlName="{{control.modelProperty}}" />
    <ul class="text-danger list-unstyled"
        *ngIf="(formSubmitted || control.dirty) && !control.valid">
      <li *ngFor="let error of control.getValidationMessages()">
        {{error}}
      </li>
    </ul>
  </div>
  <button class="btn btn-primary" type="submit"
          [disabled]="formSubmitted && !form.valid"
          [class.btn-secondary]="formSubmitted && !form.valid">
    Create
  </button>
</form>
<paDiscountEditor></paDiscountEditor>
<paDiscountDisplay></paDiscountDisplay>
```

These new elements duplicate the discount display and editor components so they appear below the form used to create new products, as shown in Figure 19-3.

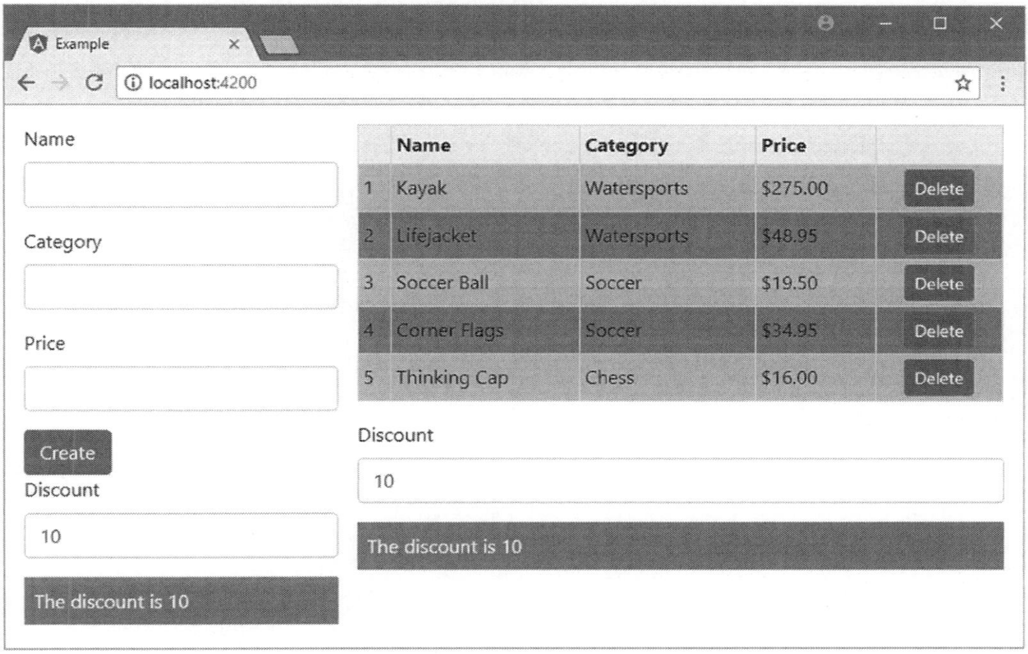

Figure 19-3. *Duplicating components with dependencies*

479

There are two points of note. First, using dependency injection made this a simple process of adding elements to a template, without needing to modify the ancestor components to provide a DiscountService object using input properties.

The second point of note is that all the components in the application that have declared a dependency on DiscountService have received the same object. If you edit the value in either of the input elements, the changes will be reflected in the other input element and in the string interpolation bindings, as shown in Figure 19-4.

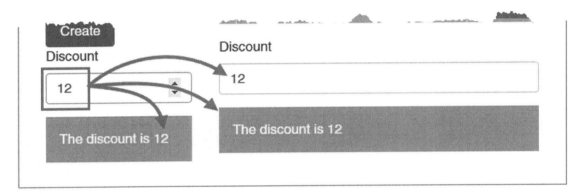

Figure 19-4. *Checking that the dependency is resolved using a shared object*

Declaring Dependencies in Other Building Blocks

It isn't just components that can declare constructor dependencies. Once you have defined a service, you can use it more widely, including in other building blocks in the application, such as pipes and directives, as demonstrated in the sections that follow.

Declaring a Dependency in a Pipe

Pipes can declare dependencies on services by defining a constructor with arguments for each required service. To demonstrate, I added a file called discount.pipe.ts to the src/app folder and used it to define the pipe shown in Listing 19-15.

Listing 19-15. The Contents of the discount.pipe.ts File in the src/app Folder

```
import { Pipe, Injectable } from "@angular/core";
import { DiscountService } from "./discount.service";

@Pipe({
    name: "discount",
    pure: false
})
```

```
export class PaDiscountPipe {

    constructor(private discount: DiscountService) { }

    transform(price: number): number {
        return this.discount.applyDiscount(price);
    }
}
```

The PaDiscountPipe class is a pipe that receives a price and generates a result by calling the DiscountService.applyDiscount method, where the service is received through the constructor. The pure property in the @Pipe decorator is false, which means that the pipe will be asked to update its result when the value stored by the DiscountService changes, which won't be recognized by the Angular change-detection process.

■ **Tip** As explained in Chapter 18, this feature should be used with caution because it means that the transform method will be called after every change in the application, not just when the service is changed.

Listing 19-16 shows the new pipe being registered in the application's Angular module.

Listing 19-16. Registering a Pipe in the app.module.ts File in the src/app Folder

```
import { NgModule } from "@angular/core";
import { BrowserModule } from "@angular/platform-browser";
import { ProductComponent } from "./component";
import { FormsModule, ReactiveFormsModule } from "@angular/forms";
import { PaAttrDirective } from "./attr.directive";
import { PaModel } from "./twoway.directive";
import { PaStructureDirective } from "./structure.directive";
import { PaIteratorDirective } from "./iterator.directive";
import { PaCellColor } from "./cellColor.directive";
import { PaCellColorSwitcher } from "./cellColorSwitcher.directive";
import { ProductTableComponent } from "./productTable.component";
import { ProductFormComponent } from "./productForm.component";
import { PaToggleView } from "./toggleView.component";
import { PaAddTaxPipe } from "./addTax.pipe";
import { PaCategoryFilterPipe } from "./categoryFilter.pipe";
import { LOCALE_ID } from "@angular/core";
import localeFr from '@angular/common/locales/fr';
import { registerLocaleData } from '@angular/common';
import { PaDiscountDisplayComponent } from "./discountDisplay.component";
import { PaDiscountEditorComponent } from "./discountEditor.component";
import { DiscountService } from "./discount.service";
import { PaDiscountPipe } from "./discount.pipe";

registerLocaleData(localeFr);
```

```
@NgModule({
  imports: [BrowserModule, FormsModule, ReactiveFormsModule],
  declarations: [ProductComponent, PaAttrDirective, PaModel,
    PaStructureDirective, PaIteratorDirective,
    PaCellColor, PaCellColorSwitcher, ProductTableComponent,
    ProductFormComponent, PaAddTaxPipe, PaCategoryFilterPipe,
    PaDiscountDisplayComponent, PaDiscountEditorComponent,
    PaDiscountPipe],
  providers: [DiscountService],
  bootstrap: [ProductComponent]
})
export class AppModule { }
```

Listing 19-17 shows the new pipe applied to the Price column in the product table.

Listing 19-17. Applying a Pipe in the productTable.component.html File in the src/app Folder

```
<table class="table table-sm table-bordered table-striped">
    <tr><th></th><th>Name</th><th>Category</th><th>Price</th><th></th></tr>
    <tr *paFor="let item of getProducts(); let i = index;
            let odd = odd; let even = even" [class.bg-info]="odd"
            [class.bg-warning]="even">
        <td style="vertical-align:middle">{{i + 1}}</td>
        <td style="vertical-align:middle">{{item.name}}</td>
        <td style="vertical-align:middle">{{item.category}}</td>
        <td style="vertical-align:middle">
            {{item.price | discount | currency:"USD":"symbol" }}
        </td>
        <td class="text-center">
            <button class="btn btn-danger btn-sm" (click)="deleteProduct(item.id)">
                Delete
            </button>
        </td>
    </tr>
</table>

<paDiscountEditor></paDiscountEditor>
<paDiscountDisplay></paDiscountDisplay>
```

The discount pipe processes the price to apply the discount and then passes on the value to the currency pipe for formatting. You can see the effect of using the service in the pipe by changing the value in one of the discount input elements, as shown in Figure 19-5.

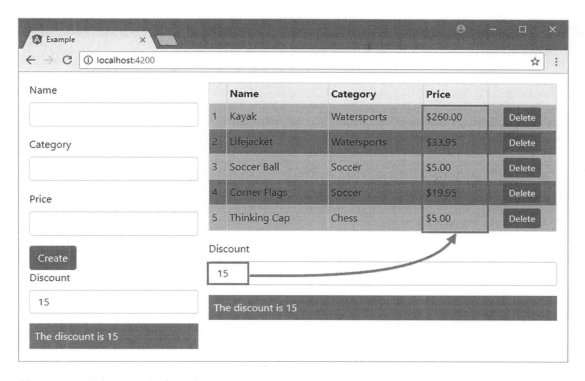

Figure 19-5. *Using a service in a pipe*

Declaring Dependencies in Directives

Directives can also use services. As I explained in Chapter 17, components are just directives with templates, so anything that works in a component will also work in a directive.

To demonstrate using a service in a directive, I added a file called `discountAmount.directive.ts` to the src/app folder and used it to define the directive shown in Listing 19-18.

Listing 19-18. The Contents of the discountAmount.directive.ts File in the src/app Folder

```
import { Directive, HostBinding, Input,
    SimpleChange, KeyValueDiffer, KeyValueDiffers,
    ChangeDetectorRef } from "@angular/core";
import { DiscountService } from "./discount.service";

@Directive({
    selector: "td[pa-price]",
    exportAs: "discount"
})
export class PaDiscountAmountDirective {
    private differ: KeyValueDiffer<any, any>;

    constructor(private keyValueDiffers: KeyValueDiffers,
        private changeDetector: ChangeDetectorRef,
        private discount: DiscountService) { }
```

483

```
    @Input("pa-price")
    originalPrice: number;

    discountAmount: number;

    ngOnInit() {
        this.differ =
            this.keyValueDiffers.find(this.discount).create();
    }

    ngOnChanges(changes: { [property: string]: SimpleChange }) {
        if (changes["originalPrice"] != null) {
            this.updateValue();
        }
    }

    ngDoCheck() {
        if (this.differ.diff(this.discount) != null) {
            this.updateValue();
        }
    }

    private updateValue() {
        this.discountAmount = this.originalPrice
            - this.discount.applyDiscount(this.originalPrice);
    }
}
```

Directives don't have an equivalent to the pure property used by pipes and must take direct responsibility for responding to changes propagated through services. This directive displays the discounted amount for a product. The selector property matches td elements that have a pa-price attribute, which is also used as an input property to receive the price that will be discounted. The directive exports its functionality using the exportAs property and provides a property called discountAmount whose value is set to the discount that has been applied to the product.

There are two other points to note about this directive. The first is that the DiscountService object isn't the only constructor parameters in the directive's class.

```
...
constructor(private keyValueDiffers: KeyValueDiffers,
            private changeDetector: ChangeDetectorRef,
            private discount: DiscountService) { }
...
```

The KeyValueDiffers and ChangeDetectorRef parameters are also dependencies that Angular will have to resolve when it creates a new instance of the directive class. These are examples of the built-in services that Angular provides that deliver commonly required functionality.

The second point of note is what the directive does with the services it receives. The components and the pipe that use the DiscountService service don't have to worry about tracking updates, either because Angular automatically evaluates the expressions of the data bindings and updates them when the discount rate changed (for the components) or because any change in the application triggers an update (for the impure pipe). The data binding for this directive is on the price property, which will trigger a change if is altered. But there is also a dependency on the discount property defined by the DiscountService class.

Changes in the discount property are detected using the services received through the constructor, which are similar to the ones used to track changes in iterable sequences described in Chapter 16 but which operate on key-value pair objects, such as Map objects or regular objects that define properties, such as DiscountService. When Angular invokes the ngDoCheck method, the directive uses the key-value pair differ to see whether there has been a change. (This change direction could also have been handled by keeping track of the previous update in the directive class, but I wanted to provide an example of using the key-value differ feature.)

The directive also implements the ngOnChanges method so that it can respond to changes in the value of the input property. For both types of update, the updateValue method is called, which calculates the discounted price and assigns it to the discountAmount property.

Listing 19-19 registers the new directive in the application's Angular module.

Listing 19-19. Registering a Directive in the app.module.ts File in the src/app Folder

```
import { NgModule } from "@angular/core";
import { BrowserModule } from "@angular/platform-browser";
import { ProductComponent } from "./component";
import { FormsModule, ReactiveFormsModule } from "@angular/forms";
import { PaAttrDirective } from "./attr.directive";
import { PaModel } from "./twoway.directive";
import { PaStructureDirective } from "./structure.directive";
import { PaIteratorDirective } from "./iterator.directive";
import { PaCellColor } from "./cellColor.directive";
import { PaCellColorSwitcher } from "./cellColorSwitcher.directive";
import { ProductTableComponent } from "./productTable.component";
import { ProductFormComponent } from "./productForm.component";
import { PaToggleView } from "./toggleView.component";
import { PaAddTaxPipe } from "./addTax.pipe";
import { PaCategoryFilterPipe } from "./categoryFilter.pipe";
import { LOCALE_ID } from "@angular/core";
import localeFr from '@angular/common/locales/fr';
import { registerLocaleData } from '@angular/common';
import { PaDiscountDisplayComponent } from "./discountDisplay.component";
import { PaDiscountEditorComponent } from "./discountEditor.component";
import { DiscountService } from "./discount.service";
import { PaDiscountPipe } from "./discount.pipe";
import { PaDiscountAmountDirective } from "./discountAmount.directive";

registerLocaleData(localeFr);

@NgModule({
  imports: [BrowserModule, FormsModule, ReactiveFormsModule],
  declarations: [ProductComponent, PaAttrDirective, PaModel,
    PaStructureDirective, PaIteratorDirective,
    PaCellColor, PaCellColorSwitcher, ProductTableComponent,
    ProductFormComponent, PaAddTaxPipe, PaCategoryFilterPipe,
    PaDiscountDisplayComponent, PaDiscountEditorComponent,
    PaDiscountPipe, PaDiscountAmountDirective],
  providers: [DiscountService],
  bootstrap: [ProductComponent]
})
export class AppModule { }
```

To apply the new directive, Listing 19-20 adds a new column to the table, using a string interpolation binding to access the property provided by the directive and pass it to the currency pipe.

Listing 19-20. Creating a New Column in the productTable.component.html File in the src/app Folder

```
<table class="table table-sm table-bordered table-striped">
    <tr>
        <th></th><th>Name</th><th>Category</th><th>Price</th>
        <th>Discount</th><th></th>
    </tr>
    <tr *paFor="let item of getProducts(); let i = index;
            let odd = odd; let even = even" [class.bg-info]="odd"
            [class.bg-warning]="even">
        <td style="vertical-align:middle">{{i + 1}}</td>
        <td style="vertical-align:middle">{{item.name}}</td>
        <td style="vertical-align:middle">{{item.category}}</td>
        <td style="vertical-align:middle">
            {{item.price | discount | currency:"USD":"symbol" }}
        </td>
        <td style="vertical-align:middle" [pa-price]="item.price"
                #discount="discount">
            {{ discount.discountAmount | currency:"USD":"symbol"}}
        </td>
        <td class="text-center">
            <button class="btn btn-danger btn-sm" (click)="deleteProduct(item.id)">
                Delete
            </button>
        </td>
    </tr>
</table>

<paDiscountEditor></paDiscountEditor>
<paDiscountDisplay></paDiscountDisplay>
```

The directive could have created a host binding on the textContent property to set the contents of its host element, but that would have prevented the currency pipe from being used. Instead, the directive is assigned to the discount template variable, which is then used in the string interpolation binding to access and then format the discountAmount value. Figure 19-6 shows the results. Changes to the discount amount in either of the discount editor input elements will be reflected in the new table column.

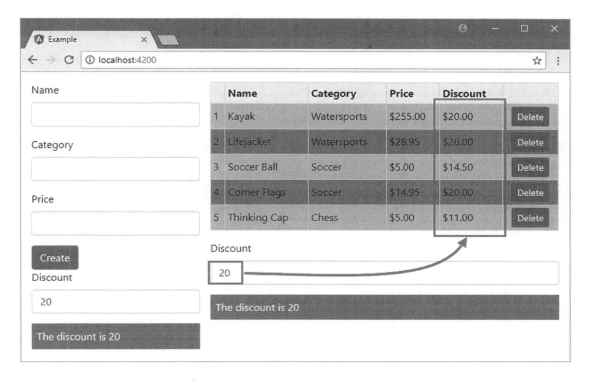

Figure 19-6. *Using a service in a directive*

Understanding the Test Isolation Problem

The example application contains a related problem that services and dependency injection can be used to solve. Consider how the Model class is created in the root component:

```
import { ApplicationRef, Component } from "@angular/core";
import { Model } from "./repository.model";
import { Product } from "./product.model";
import { ProductFormGroup } from "./form.model";

@Component({
    selector: "app",
    templateUrl: "app/template.html"
})
export class ProductComponent {
    model: Model = new Model();

    addProduct(p: Product) {
        this.model.saveProduct(p);
    }
}
```

The root component is defined as the ProductComponent class, and it sets up a value for its model property by creating a new instance of the Model class. This works—and is a perfectly legitimate way to create an object—but it makes it harder to perform unit testing effectively.

Unit testing works best when you can isolate one small part of the application and focus on it to perform tests. But when you create an instance of the ProductComponent class, you are implicitly creating an instance of the Model class as well. If you were to run tests on the root component's addProduct method and you found a problem, you would have no indication of whether the problem was in the ProductComponent or Model class.

Isolating Components Using Services and Dependency Injection

The underlying problem is that the ProductComponent class is tightly bound to the Model class, which is, in turn, tightly bound to the SimpleDataSource class. Dependency injection can be used to tease apart the building blocks in an application so that each class can be isolated and tested on its own. In the sections that follow, I walk through the process of breaking up these tightly coupled classes, following essentially the same process as in the previous section but delving deeper into the example application.

Preparing the Services

The @Injectable decorator is used to denote services, just as in the previous example. Listing 19-21 shows the decorator applied to the SimpleDataSource class.

Listing 19-21. Denoting a Service in the datasource.model.ts File in the src/app Folder

```
import { Injectable } from "@angular/core";
import { Product } from "./product.model";


@Injectable()
export class SimpleDataSource {
    private data:Product[];

    constructor() {
        this.data = new Array<Product>(
        new Product(1, "Kayak", "Watersports", 275),
        new Product(2, "Lifejacket", "Watersports", 48.95),
        new Product(3, "Soccer Ball", "Soccer", 19.50),
        new Product(4, "Corner Flags", "Soccer", 34.95),
        new Product(5, "Thinking Cap", "Chess", 16));
    }

    getData(): Product[] {
        return this.data;
    }
}
```

No other changes are required. Listing 19-22 shows the same decorator being applied to the data repository, and since this class has a dependency on the SimpleDataSource class, it declares it as a constructor dependency rather than creating an instance directly.

Listing 19-22. Denoting a Service and Dependency in the repository.model.ts File in the src/app Folder

```
import { Injectable } from "@angular/core";
import { Product } from "./product.model";
import { SimpleDataSource } from "./datasource.model";

@Injectable()
export class Model {
    //private dataSource: SimpleDataSource;
    private products: Product[];
    private locator = (p:Product, id:number) => p.id == id;

    constructor(private dataSource: SimpleDataSource) {
        //this.dataSource = new SimpleDataSource();
        this.products = new Array<Product>();
        this.dataSource.getData().forEach(p => this.products.push(p));
    }

    // ...other members omitted for brevity...
}
```

The important point to note in this listing is that services can declare dependencies on other services. When Angular comes to create a new instance of a service class, it inspects the constructor and tries to resolve the services in the same way as when dealing with a component or directive.

Registering the Services

These services must be registered so that Angular knows how to resolve dependencies on them, as shown in Listing 19-23.

Listing 19-23. Registering the Services in the app.module.ts File in the src/app Folder

```
import { NgModule } from "@angular/core";
import { BrowserModule } from "@angular/platform-browser";
import { ProductComponent } from "./component";
import { FormsModule, ReactiveFormsModule } from "@angular/forms";
import { PaAttrDirective } from "./attr.directive";
import { PaModel } from "./twoway.directive";
import { PaStructureDirective } from "./structure.directive";
import { PaIteratorDirective } from "./iterator.directive";
import { PaCellColor } from "./cellColor.directive";
import { PaCellColorSwitcher } from "./cellColorSwitcher.directive";
import { ProductTableComponent } from "./productTable.component";
import { ProductFormComponent } from "./productForm.component";
import { PaToggleView } from "./toggleView.component";
import { PaAddTaxPipe } from "./addTax.pipe";
import { PaCategoryFilterPipe } from "./categoryFilter.pipe";
import { LOCALE_ID } from "@angular/core";
import localeFr from '@angular/common/locales/fr';
import { registerLocaleData } from '@angular/common';
import { PaDiscountDisplayComponent } from "./discountDisplay.component";
```

489

```
import { PaDiscountEditorComponent } from "./discountEditor.component";
import { DiscountService } from "./discount.service";
import { PaDiscountPipe } from "./discount.pipe";
import { PaDiscountAmountDirective } from "./discountAmount.directive";
import { SimpleDataSource } from "./datasource.model";
import { Model } from "./repository.model";

registerLocaleData(localeFr);

@NgModule({
  imports: [BrowserModule, FormsModule, ReactiveFormsModule],
  declarations: [ProductComponent, PaAttrDirective, PaModel,
    PaStructureDirective, PaIteratorDirective,
    PaCellColor, PaCellColorSwitcher, ProductTableComponent,
    ProductFormComponent, PaAddTaxPipe, PaCategoryFilterPipe,
    PaDiscountDisplayComponent, PaDiscountEditorComponent,
    PaDiscountPipe, PaDiscountAmountDirective],
  providers: [DiscountService, SimpleDataSource, Model],
  bootstrap: [ProductComponent]
})
export class AppModule { }
```

Preparing the Dependent Component

Rather than create a Model object directly, the root component can declare a constructor dependency that Angular will resolve using dependency injection when the application starts, as shown in Listing 19-24.

Listing 19-24. Declaring a Service Dependency in the component.ts File in the src/app Folder

```
import { ApplicationRef, Component } from "@angular/core";
import { Model } from "./repository.model";
import { Product } from "./product.model";
import { ProductFormGroup } from "./form.model";

@Component({
    selector: "app",
    templateUrl: "template.html"
})
export class ProductComponent {
    //model: Model = new Model();

    constructor(private model: Model) { }

    addProduct(p: Product) {
        this.model.saveProduct(p);
    }
}
```

There is now a chain of dependencies that Angular has to resolve. When the application starts, the Angular module specifies that the ProductComponent class needs a Model object. Angular inspects the Model class and finds that it needs a SimpleDataSource object. Angular inspects the SimpleDataSource object and finds that there are no declared dependencies and therefore knows that this is the end of the chain. It creates a SimpleDataSource object and passes it as an argument to the Model constructor in order to create a Model object, which can then be passed to the ProductComponent class constructor to create the object that will be used as the root component. All of this happens automatically, based on the constructors defined by each class and the use of the @Injectable decorator.

These changes don't create any visible changes in the way that the application works, but they do allow a completely different way of performing unit tests. The ProductComponent class requires that a Model object is provided as a constructor argument, which allows for a mock object to be used.

Breaking up the direct dependencies between the classes in the application means that each of them can be isolated for the purposes of unit testing and provided with mock objects through their constructor, allowing the effect of a method or some other feature to be consistently and independently assessed.

Completing the Adoption of Services

Once you start using services in an application, the process generally takes on a life of its own, and you start to examine the relationships between the building blocks you have created. The extent to which you introduce services is—at least in part—a matter of personal preference.

A good example is the use of the Model class in the root component. Although the component does implement a method that uses the Model object, it does so because it needs to handle a custom event from one of its child components. The only other reason that the root component has for needing a Model object is to pass it on via its template to the other child component using an input property.

This situation isn't an enormous problem, and your preference may be to have these kinds of relationships in a project. After all, each of the components can be isolated for unit testing, and there is some purpose, however limited, to the relationships between them. This kind of relationship between components can help make sense of the functionality that an application provides.

On the other hand, the more you use services, the more the building blocks in your project become self-contained and reusable blocks of functionality, which can ease the process of adding or changing functionality as the project matures.

There is no absolute right or wrong, and you must find the balance that suits you, your team, and, ultimately, your users and customers. Not everyone likes using dependency injection, and not everyone performs unit testing.

My preference is to use dependency injection as widely as possible. I find that the final structure of my applications can differ significantly from what I expect when I start a new project and that the flexibility offered by dependency injection helps me avoid repeated periods of refactoring. So, to complete this chapter, I am going to push the use of the Model service into the rest of the application, breaking the coupling between the root component and its immediate children.

Updating the Root Component and Template

The first changes I will make are to remove the Model object from the root component, along with the method that uses it and the input property in the template that distributes the model to one of the child components. Listing 19-25 shows the changes to the component class.

Listing 19-25. Removing the Model Object from the component.ts File in the src/app Folder

```
import { Component } from "@angular/core";
//import { Model } from "./repository.model";
//import { Product } from "./product.model";
//import { ProductFormGroup } from "./form.model";
```

```
@Component({
    selector: "app",
    templateUrl: "template.html"
})
export class ProductComponent {
    //model: Model = new Model();

    //constructor(private model: Model) { }

    //addProduct(p: Product) {
    //    this.model.saveProduct(p);
    //}
}
```

The revised root component class doesn't define any functionality and now exists only to provide the top-level application content in its template. Listing 19-26 shows the corresponding changes in the root template to remove the custom event binding and the input property.

Listing 19-26. Removing the Data Bindings in the template.html File in the src/app Folder

```
<div class="row m-2">
  <div class="col-4 p-2">
    <paProductForm></paProductForm>
  </div>
  <div class="col-8 p-2">
    <paProductTable></paProductTable>
  </div>
</div>
```

Updating the Child Components

The component that provides the form for creating new Product objects relied on the root component to handle its custom event and update the model. Without this support, the component must now declare a Model dependency and perform the update itself, as shown in Listing 19-27.

Listing 19-27. Working with the Model in the productForm.component.ts File in the src/app Folder

```
import { Component, Output, EventEmitter, ViewEncapsulation } from "@angular/core";
import { Product } from "./product.model";
import { ProductFormGroup } from "./form.model";
import { Model } from "./repository.model";

@Component({
    selector: "paProductForm",
    templateUrl: "productForm.component.html",
    //styleUrls: ["productForm.component.css"],
    //encapsulation: ViewEncapsulation.Emulated
})
export class ProductFormComponent {
    form: ProductFormGroup = new ProductFormGroup();
    newProduct: Product = new Product();
    formSubmitted: boolean = false;
```

```
constructor(private model: Model) { }

//@Output("paNewProduct")
//newProductEvent = new EventEmitter<Product>();

submitForm(form: any) {
    this.formSubmitted = true;
    if (form.valid) {
        //this.newProductEvent.emit(this.newProduct);
        this.model.saveProduct(this.newProduct);
        this.newProduct = new Product();
        this.form.reset();
        this.formSubmitted = false;
    }
}
}
```

The component that manages the table of product objects used an input property to receive a Model object from its parent but must now obtain it directly by declaring a constructor dependency, as shown in Listing 19-28.

Listing 19-28. Declaring a Model Dependency in the productTable.component.ts File in the src/app Folder

```
import { Component, Input } from "@angular/core";
import { Model } from "./repository.model";
import { Product } from "./product.model";
import { DiscountService } from "./discount.service";

@Component({
    selector: "paProductTable",
    templateUrl: "productTable.component.html"
})
export class ProductTableComponent {
    //discounter: DiscountService = new DiscountService();

    constructor(private dataModel: Model) { }

    //@Input("model")
    //dataModel: Model;

    getProduct(key: number): Product {
        return this.dataModel.getProduct(key);
    }

    getProducts(): Product[] {
        return this.dataModel.getProducts();
    }

    deleteProduct(key: number) {
        this.dataModel.deleteProduct(key);
    }
```

```
    dateObject: Date = new Date(2020, 1, 20);
    dateString: string = "2020-02-20T00:00:00.000Z";
    dateNumber: number = 1582156800000;
}
```

You will see the same functionality displayed in the browser window when all of the changes have been saved and the browser reloads the Angular application—but the way that the functionality is wired up has changed substantially, with each component obtaining the share objects it needs through the dependency injection feature, rather than relying on its parent component to provide it.

Summary

In this chapter, I explained the problems that dependency injection can be used to address and demonstrated the process of defining and consuming services. I described how services can be used to increase the flexibility in the structure of an application and how dependency injection makes it possible to isolate building blocks so they can be unit tested effectively. In the next chapter, I describe the advanced features that Angular provides for working with services.

CHAPTER 20

■ ■ ■

Using Service Providers

In the previous chapter, I introduced services and explained how they are distributed using dependency injection. When using dependency injection, the objects that are used to resolve dependencies are created by *service providers*, known more commonly as *providers*. In this chapter, I explain how providers work, describe the different types of provider available, and demonstrate how providers can be created in different parts of the application to change the way that services behave. Table 20-1 puts providers in context.

WHY YOU SHOULD CONSIDER SKIPPING THIS CHAPTER

Dependency injection provokes strong reactions in developers and polarizes opinion. If you are new to dependency injection and have yet to form your own opinion, then you might want to skip this chapter and just use the features that I described in Chapter 19. That's because features like the ones I describe in this chapter are exactly why many developers dread using dependency injection and form a strong preference against its use.

The basic Angular dependency injection features are easy to understand and have an immediate and obvious benefit in making applications easier to write and maintain. The features described in this chapter provide fine-grained control over how dependency injection works, but they also make it possible to sharply increase the complexity of an Angular application and, ultimately, undermine many of the benefits that the basic features offer.

If you decide that you want all of the gritty detail, then read on. But if you are new to the world of dependency injection, you may prefer to skip this chapter until you find that the basic features from Chapter 19 don't deliver the functionality you require.

© Adam Freeman 2018
A. Freeman, *Pro Angular 6*, https://doi.org/10.1007/978-1-4842-3649-9_20

Table 20-1. *Putting Service Providers in Context*

Question	Answer
What are they?	Providers are classes that create service objects the first time that Angular needs to resolve a dependency.
Why are they useful?	Providers allow the creation of service objects to be tailored to the needs of the application. The simplest provider just creates an instance of a specified class, but there are other providers that can be used to tailor the way that service objects are created and configured.
How are they used?	Providers are defined in the providers property of the Angular module's decorator. They can also be defined by components and directives to provide services to their children, as described in the "Using Local Providers" section.
Are there any pitfalls or limitations?	It is easy to create unexpected behavior, especially when working with local providers. If you encounter problems, check the scope of the local providers you have created and make sure that your dependencies and providers are using the same tokens.
Are there any alternatives?	Many applications will require only the basic dependency injection features described in Chapter 19. You should use the features in this chapter only if you cannot build your application using the basic features and only if you have a solid understanding of dependency injection.

Table 20-2 summarizes the chapter.

Table 20-2. *Chapter Summary*

Problem	Solution	Listing
Change the way that services are created	Use a service provider	1–3
Specify a service using a class	Use the class provider	4–6, 10–13
Define arbitrary tokens for services	Use the `InjectionToken` class	7–9
Specify a service using an object	Use the value provider	14–15
Specify a service using a function	Use the factory provider	16–18
Specify one service using another	Use the existing service provider	19
Change the scope of a service	Use a local service provider	20–28
Control the resolution of dependencies	Use the `@Host`, `@Optional`, or `@SkipSelf` decorator	29–30

Preparing the Example Project

As with the other chapters in this part of the book, I am going to continue working with the project created in Chapter 11 and most recently modified in Chapter 19. To prepare for this chapter, I added a file called `log.service.ts` to the `src/app` folder and used it to define the service shown in Listing 20-1.

■ **Tip** You can download the example project for this chapter—and for all the other chapters in this book—from `https://github.com/Apress/pro-angular-6`.

Listing 20-1. The Contents of the log.service.ts File in the src/app Folder

```
import { Injectable } from "@angular/core";

export enum LogLevel {
    DEBUG, INFO, ERROR
}

@Injectable()
export class LogService {
    minimumLevel: LogLevel = LogLevel.INFO;

    logInfoMessage(message: string) {
        this.logMessage(LogLevel.INFO, message);
    }

    logDebugMessage(message: string) {
        this.logMessage(LogLevel.DEBUG, message);
    }

    logErrorMessage(message: string) {
        this.logMessage(LogLevel.ERROR, message);
    }

    logMessage(level: LogLevel, message: string) {
        if (level >= this.minimumLevel) {
            console.log(`Message (${LogLevel[level]}): ${message}`);
        }
    }
}
```

This service writes out log messages, with differing levels of severity, to the browser's JavaScript console. I will register and use this service later in the chapter.

When you have created the service and saved the changes, run the following command in the example folder to start the Angular development tools:

```
ng serve
```

Open a new browser window and navigate to `http://localhost:4200` to see the application, as shown in Figure 20-1.

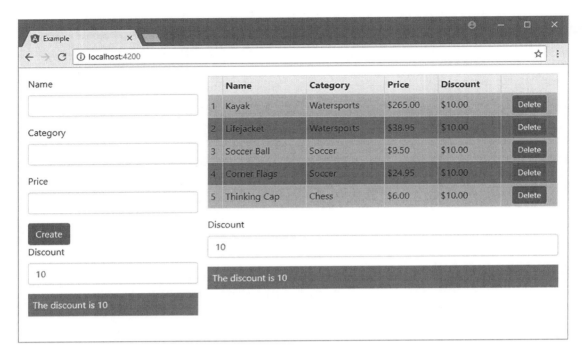

Figure 20-1. *Running the example application*

Using Service Providers

As I explained in the previous chapters, classes declare dependencies on services using their constructor arguments. When Angular needs to create a new instance of the class, it inspects the constructor and uses a combination of built-in and custom services to resolve each argument. Listing 20-2 updates the DiscountService class so that it depends on the LogService class created in the previous section.

Listing 20-2. Creating a Dependency in the discount.service.ts File in the src/app Folder

```
import { Injectable } from "@angular/core";
import { LogService } from "./log.service";

@Injectable()
export class DiscountService {
    private discountValue: number = 10;

    constructor(private logger: LogService) { }

    public get discount(): number {
        return this.discountValue;
    }

    public set discount(newValue: number) {
        this.discountValue = newValue || 0;
    }
```

```
    public applyDiscount(price: number) {
        this.logger.logInfoMessage(`Discount ${this.discount}`
            + ` applied to price: ${price}`);
        return Math.max(price - this.discountValue, 5);
    }
}
```

The changes in Listing 20-2 prevent the application from running. Angular processes the HTML document and starts creating the hierarchy of components, each with their templates that require directives and data bindings, and it encounters the classes that depend on the DiscountService class. But it can't create an instance of DiscountService because its constructor requires a LogService object and it doesn't know how to handle this class.

When you save the changes in Listing 20-2, you will see an error like this one in the browser's JavaScript console:

```
NullInjectorError: No provider for LogService!
```

Angular delegates responsibility for creating the objects needed for dependency injection to *providers*, each of which managed a single type of dependency. When it needs to create an instance of the DiscountService class, it looks for a suitable provider to resolve the LogService dependency. Since there is no such provider, Angular can't create the objects it needs to start the application and reports the error.

The simplest way to create a provider is to add the service class to the array assigned to the Angular module's providers property, as shown in Listing 20-3. (I have taken the opportunity to remove some of the statements that are no longer required in the module.)

Listing 20-3. Creating a Provider in the app.module.ts File in the src/app Folder

```
import { NgModule } from "@angular/core";
import { BrowserModule } from "@angular/platform-browser";
import { ProductComponent } from "./component";
import { FormsModule, ReactiveFormsModule } from "@angular/forms";
import { PaAttrDirective } from "./attr.directive";
import { PaModel } from "./twoway.directive";
import { PaStructureDirective } from "./structure.directive";
import { PaIteratorDirective } from "./iterator.directive";
import { PaCellColor } from "./cellColor.directive";
import { PaCellColorSwitcher } from "./cellColorSwitcher.directive";
import { ProductTableComponent } from "./productTable.component";
import { ProductFormComponent } from "./productForm.component";
import { PaAddTaxPipe } from "./addTax.pipe";
import { PaCategoryFilterPipe } from "./categoryFilter.pipe";
import { PaDiscountDisplayComponent } from "./discountDisplay.component";
import { PaDiscountEditorComponent } from "./discountEditor.component";
import { DiscountService } from "./discount.service";
import { PaDiscountPipe } from "./discount.pipe";
import { PaDiscountAmountDirective } from "./discountAmount.directive";
import { SimpleDataSource } from "./datasource.model";
import { Model } from "./repository.model";
import { LogService } from "./log.service";
```

```
@NgModule({
    imports: [BrowserModule, FormsModule, ReactiveFormsModule],
    declarations: [ProductComponent, PaAttrDirective, PaModel,
        PaStructureDirective, PaIteratorDirective,
        PaCellColor, PaCellColorSwitcher, ProductTableComponent,
        ProductFormComponent, PaAddTaxPipe, PaCategoryFilterPipe,
        PaDiscountDisplayComponent, PaDiscountEditorComponent,
        PaDiscountPipe, PaDiscountAmountDirective],
    providers: [DiscountService, SimpleDataSource, Model, LogService],
    bootstrap: [ProductComponent]
})
export class AppModule { }
```

When you save the changes, you will have defined the provider that Angular requires to handle the
LogService dependency, and you will see messages like this one shown in the browser's JavaScript console:

```
Message (INFO): Discount 10 applied to price: 16
```

You might wonder why the configuration step in Listing 20-3 is required. After all, Angular could just
assume that it should create a new LogService object the first time it needs one.

In fact, Angular provides a range of different providers, each of which creates objects in a different
way to let you take control of the service creation process. Table 20-3 describes the set of providers that are
available, which are described in the sections that follow.

Table 20-3. *The Angular Providers*

Name	Description
Class provider	This provider is configured using a class. Dependencies on the service are resolved by an instance of the class, which Angular creates.
Value provider	This provider is configured using an object, which is used to resolve dependencies on the service.
Factory provider	This provider is configured using a function. Dependencies on the service are resolved using an object that is created by invoking the function.
Existing service provider	This provider is configured using the name of another service and allows aliases for services to be created.

Using the Class Provider

This provider is the most commonly used and is the one I applied by adding the class names to the module's
providers property in Listing 20-3. This listing shows the shorthand syntax, and there is also a literal syntax
that achieves the same result, as shown in Listing 20-4.

Listing 20-4. Using the Class Provider Literal Syntax in the app.module.ts File in the src/app Folder

```
...
@NgModule({
    imports: [BrowserModule, FormsModule, ReactiveFormsModule],
    declarations: [ProductComponent, PaAttrDirective, PaModel,
        PaStructureDirective, PaIteratorDirective,
```

```
        PaCellColor, PaCellColorSwitcher, ProductTableComponent,
        ProductFormComponent, PaAddTaxPipe, PaCategoryFilterPipe,
        PaDiscountDisplayComponent, PaDiscountEditorComponent,
        PaDiscountPipe, PaDiscountAmountDirective],
    providers: [DiscountService, SimpleDataSource, Model,
                { provide: LogService, useClass: LogService }],
    bootstrap: [ProductComponent]
})
...
```

Providers are defined as classes, but they can be specified and configured using the JavaScript object literal format, like this:

```
...
{
    provide: LogService,
    useClass: LogService
}
...
```

The class provider supports three properties, which are described in Table 20-4 and explained in the sections that follow.

Table 20-4. *The Class Provider's Properties*

Name	Description
provide	This property is used to specify the token, which is used to identify the provider and the dependency that will be resolved. See the "Understanding the Token" section.
useClass	This property is used to specify the class that will be instantiated to resolve the dependency by the provider. See the "Understanding the useClass Property" section.
multi	This property can be used to deliver an array of service objects to resolve dependencies. See the "Resolving a Dependency with Multiple Objects" section.

Understanding the Token

All providers rely on a token, which Angular uses to identify the dependency that the provider can resolve. The simplest approach is to use a class as the token, which is what I did in Listing 20-4. However, you can use any object as the token, which allows the dependency and the type of the object to be separated. This has the effect of increasing the flexibility of the dependency injection configuration because it allows a provider to supply objects of different types, which can be useful with some of the more advanced providers described later in the chapter. As a simple example, Listing 20-5 uses the class provider to register the log service created at the start of the chapter using a string as a token, rather than a class.

Listing 20-5. Registering a Service with a Token in the app.module.ts File in the src/app Folder

```
...
@NgModule({
    imports: [BrowserModule, FormsModule, ReactiveFormsModule],
    declarations: [ProductComponent, PaAttrDirective, PaModel,
        PaStructureDirective, PaIteratorDirective,
        PaCellColor, PaCellColorSwitcher, ProductTableComponent,
        ProductFormComponent, PaAddTaxPipe, PaCategoryFilterPipe,
        PaDiscountDisplayComponent, PaDiscountEditorComponent,
        PaDiscountPipe, PaDiscountAmountDirective],
    providers: [DiscountService, SimpleDataSource, Model,
                { provide: "logger", useClass: LogService }],
    bootstrap: [ProductComponent]
})
...
```

In the listing the provide property of the new provider is set to logger. Angular will automatically match providers whose token is a class but needs some additional help for other token types. Listing 20-6 shows the DiscountService class updated with a dependency on the logging service, accessed using the logger token.

Listing 20-6. Using a String Provider Token in the discount.service.ts File in the src/app Folder

```
import { Injectable, Inject } from "@angular/core";
import { LogService } from "./log.service";

@Injectable()
export class DiscountService {
    private discountValue: number = 10;

    constructor(@Inject("logger") private logger: LogService) { }

    public get discount(): number {
        return this.discountValue;
    }

    public set discount(newValue: number) {
        this.discountValue = newValue || 0;
    }

    public applyDiscount(price: number) {
        this.logger.logInfoMessage(`Discount ${this.discount}`
            + ` applied to price: ${price}`);
        return Math.max(price - this.discountValue, 5);
    }
}
```

The @Inject decorator is applied to the constructor argument and used to specify the token that should be used to resolve the dependency. When Angular needs to create an instance of the DiscountService class, it will inspect the constructor and use the @Inject decorator argument to select the provider that will be used to resolve the dependency, resolving the dependency on the LogService class.

Using Opaque Tokens

When using simple types as provider tokens, there is a chance that two different parts of the application will try to use the same token to identify different services, which means that the wrong type of object may be used to resolve dependencies and cause errors.

To help work around this, Angular provides the InjectionToken class, which provides an object wrapper around a string value and can be used to create unique token values. In Listing 20-7, I have used the InjectionToken class to create a token that will be used to identify dependencies on the LogService class.

Listing 20-7. Using the InjectionToken Class in the log.service.ts File in the src/app Folder

```
import { Injectable, InjectionToken } from "@angular/core";

export const LOG_SERVICE = new InjectionToken("logger");

export enum LogLevel {
    DEBUG, INFO, ERROR
}

@Injectable()
export class LogService {
    minimumLevel: LogLevel = LogLevel.INFO;

    // ...methods omitted for brevity...
}
```

The constructor for the InjectionToken class accepts a string value that describes the service, but it is the InjectionToken object that will be the token. Dependencies must be declared on the same InjectionToken that is used to create the provider in the module, which is why the token has been created using the const keyword, which prevents the object from being modified. Listing 20-8 shows the provider configuration using the new token.

Listing 20-8. Creating a Provider Using an InjectionToken in the app.module.ts File in the src/app Folder

```
import { NgModule } from "@angular/core";
import { BrowserModule } from "@angular/platform-browser";
import { ProductComponent } from "./component";
import { FormsModule, ReactiveFormsModule  } from "@angular/forms";
import { PaAttrDirective } from "./attr.directive";
import { PaModel } from "./twoway.directive";
import { PaStructureDirective } from "./structure.directive";
import { PaIteratorDirective } from "./iterator.directive";
import { PaCellColor } from "./cellColor.directive";
import { PaCellColorSwitcher } from "./cellColorSwitcher.directive";
import { ProductTableComponent } from "./productTable.component";
import { ProductFormComponent } from "./productForm.component";
import { PaAddTaxPipe } from "./addTax.pipe";
import { PaCategoryFilterPipe } from "./categoryFilter.pipe";
import { PaDiscountDisplayComponent } from "./discountDisplay.component";
import { PaDiscountEditorComponent } from "./discountEditor.component";
import { DiscountService } from "./discount.service";
```

```
import { PaDiscountPipe } from "./discount.pipe";
import { PaDiscountAmountDirective } from "./discountAmount.directive";
import { SimpleDataSource } from "./datasource.model";
import { Model } from "./repository.model";
import { LogService, LOG_SERVICE } from "./log.service";

@NgModule({
    imports: [BrowserModule, FormsModule, ReactiveFormsModule],
    declarations: [ProductComponent, PaAttrDirective, PaModel,
        PaStructureDirective, PaIteratorDirective,
        PaCellColor, PaCellColorSwitcher, ProductTableComponent,
        ProductFormComponent, PaAddTaxPipe, PaCategoryFilterPipe,
        PaDiscountDisplayComponent, PaDiscountEditorComponent,
        PaDiscountPipe, PaDiscountAmountDirective],
    providers: [DiscountService, SimpleDataSource, Model,
        { provide: LOG_SERVICE, useClass: LogService }],
    bootstrap: [ProductComponent]
})
export class AppModule { }
```

Finally, Listing 20-9 shows the DiscountService class updated to declare a dependency using the InjectionToken instead of a string.

Listing 20-9. Declaring a Dependency in the discount.service.ts File in the src/app Folder

```
import { Injectable, Inject } from "@angular/core";
import { LogService, LOG_SERVICE } from "./log.service";

@Injectable()
export class DiscountService {
    private discountValue: number = 10;

    constructor( @Inject(LOG_SERVICE) private logger: LogService) { }

    public get discount(): number {
        return this.discountValue;
    }

    public set discount(newValue: number) {
        this.discountValue = newValue || 0;
    }

    public applyDiscount(price: number) {
        this.logger.logInfoMessage(`Discount ${this.discount}`
            + ` applied to price: ${price}`);
        return Math.max(price - this.discountValue, 5);
    }
}
```

There is no difference in the functionality offered by the application, but using the InjectionToken means that there will be no confusion between services.

Understanding the useClass Property

The class provider's useClass property specifies the class that will be instantiated to resolve dependencies. The provider can be configured with any class, which means you can change the implementation of a service by changing the provider configuration. This feature should be used with caution because the recipients of the service object will be expecting a specific type and a mismatch won't result in an error until the application is running in the browser. (TypeScript type enforcement has no effect on dependency injection because it occurs at runtime after the type annotations have been processed by the TypeScript compiler.)

The most common way to change classes is to use different subclasses. In Listing 20-10, I extended the LogService class to create a service that writes a different format of message in the browser's JavaScript console.

Listing 20-10. Creating a Subclassed Service in the log.service.ts File in the src/app Folder

```
import { Injectable, InjectionToken } from "@angular/core";

export const LOG_SERVICE = new InjectionToken("logger");

export enum LogLevel {
    DEBUG, INFO, ERROR
}

@Injectable()
export class LogService {
    minimumLevel: LogLevel = LogLevel.INFO;

    logInfoMessage(message: string) {
        this.logMessage(LogLevel.INFO, message);
    }

    logDebugMessage(message: string) {
        this.logMessage(LogLevel.DEBUG, message);
    }

    logErrorMessage(message: string) {
        this.logMessage(LogLevel.ERROR, message);
    }

    logMessage(level: LogLevel, message: string) {
        if (level >= this.minimumLevel) {
            console.log(`Message (${LogLevel[level]}): ${message}`);
        }
    }
}

@Injectable()
export class SpecialLogService extends LogService {

    constructor() {
        super()
        this.minimumLevel = LogLevel.DEBUG;
    }
```

```
        logMessage(level: LogLevel, message: string) {
            if (level >= this.minimumLevel) {
                console.log(`Special Message (${LogLevel[level]}): ${message}`);
            }
        }
    }
}
```

The SpecialLogService class extends LogService and provides its own implementation of the logMessage method. Listing 20-11 updates the provider configuration so that the useClass property specifies the new service.

Listing 20-11. Configuring the Provider in the app.module.ts File in the src/app Folder

```
import { NgModule } from "@angular/core";
import { BrowserModule } from "@angular/platform-browser";
import { ProductComponent } from "./component";
import { FormsModule, ReactiveFormsModule } from "@angular/forms";
import { PaAttrDirective } from "./attr.directive";
import { PaModel } from "./twoway.directive";
import { PaStructureDirective } from "./structure.directive";
import { PaIteratorDirective } from "./iterator.directive";
import { PaCellColor } from "./cellColor.directive";
import { PaCellColorSwitcher } from "./cellColorSwitcher.directive";
import { ProductTableComponent } from "./productTable.component";
import { ProductFormComponent } from "./productForm.component";
import { PaAddTaxPipe } from "./addTax.pipe";
import { PaCategoryFilterPipe } from "./categoryFilter.pipe";
import { PaDiscountDisplayComponent } from "./discountDisplay.component";
import { PaDiscountEditorComponent } from "./discountEditor.component";
import { DiscountService } from "./discount.service";
import { PaDiscountPipe } from "./discount.pipe";
import { PaDiscountAmountDirective } from "./discountAmount.directive";
import { SimpleDataSource } from "./datasource.model";
import { Model } from "./repository.model";
import { LogService, LOG_SERVICE, SpecialLogService } from "./log.service";

@NgModule({
    imports: [BrowserModule, FormsModule, ReactiveFormsModule],
    declarations: [ProductComponent, PaAttrDirective, PaModel,
        PaStructureDirective, PaIteratorDirective,
        PaCellColor, PaCellColorSwitcher, ProductTableComponent,
        ProductFormComponent, PaAddTaxPipe, PaCategoryFilterPipe,
        PaDiscountDisplayComponent, PaDiscountEditorComponent,
        PaDiscountPipe, PaDiscountAmountDirective],
    providers: [DiscountService, SimpleDataSource, Model,
        { provide: LOG_SERVICE, useClass: SpecialLogService }],
    bootstrap: [ProductComponent]
})
export class AppModule { }
```

The combination of token and class means that dependencies on the LOG_SERVICE opaque token will be resolved using a SpecialLogService object. When you save the changes, you will see messages like this one displayed in the browser's JavaScript console, indicating that the derived service has been used:

```
Special Message (INFO): Discount 10 applied to price: 275
```

Care must be taken when setting the useClass property to specify a type that the dependent classes are expecting. Specifying a subclass is the safest option because the functionality of the base class is guaranteed to be available.

Resolving a Dependency with Multiple Objects

The class provider can be configured to deliver an array of objects to resolve a dependency, which can be useful if you want to provide a set of related services that differ in how they are configured. To provide an array, multiple class providers are configured using the same token and with the multi property set to true, as shown in Listing 20-12.

Listing 20-12. Configuring Multiple Service Objects in the app.module.ts File in the src/app Folder

```
...
@NgModule({
    imports: [BrowserModule, FormsModule, ReactiveFormsModule],
    declarations: [ProductComponent, PaAttrDirective, PaModel,
        PaStructureDirective, PaIteratorDirective,
        PaCellColor, PaCellColorSwitcher, ProductTableComponent,
        ProductFormComponent, PaAddTaxPipe, PaCategoryFilterPipe,
        PaDiscountDisplayComponent, PaDiscountEditorComponent,
        PaDiscountPipe, PaDiscountAmountDirective],
    providers: [DiscountService, SimpleDataSource, Model,
        { provide: LOG_SERVICE, useClass: LogService, multi: true },
        { provide: LOG_SERVICE, useClass: SpecialLogService, multi: true }],
    bootstrap: [ProductComponent]
})
...
```

The Angular dependency injection system will resolve dependencies on the LOG_SERVICE token by creating LogService and SpecialLogService objects, placing them in an array, and passing them to the dependent class's constructor. The class that receives the services must be expecting an array, as shown in Listing 20-13.

Listing 20-13. Receiving Multiple Services in the discount.service.ts File in the src/app Folder

```
import { Injectable, Inject } from "@angular/core";
import { LogService, LOG_SERVICE, LogLevel } from "./log.service";

@Injectable()
export class DiscountService {
    private discountValue: number = 10;
    private logger: LogService;

    constructor( @Inject(LOG_SERVICE) loggers: LogService[]) {
        this.logger = loggers.find(l => l.minimumLevel == LogLevel.DEBUG);
    }
```

507

```
    public get discount(): number {
        return this.discountValue;
    }

    public set discount(newValue: number) {
        this.discountValue = newValue || 0;
    }

    public applyDiscount(price: number) {
        this.logger.logInfoMessage(`Discount ${this.discount}`
            + ` applied to price: ${price}`);
        return Math.max(price - this.discountValue, 5);
    }
}
}
```

The services are received as an array by the constructor, which uses the array `find` method to locate the first logger whose `minimumLevel` property is `LogLevel.Debug` and assign it to the `logger` property. The `applyDiscount` method calls the service's `logDebugMessage` method, which results in messages like this one displayed in the browser's JavaScript console:

```
Special Message (INFO): Discount 10 applied to price: 275
```

Using the Value Provider

The value provider is used when you want to take responsibility for creating the service objects yourself, rather than leaving it to the class provider. This can also be useful when services are simple types, such as `string` or `number` values, which can be a useful way of providing access to common configuration settings. The value provider can be applied using a literal object and supports the properties described in Table 20-5.

Table 20-5. The Value Provider Properties

Name	Description
provide	This property defines the service token, as described in the "Understanding the Token" section earlier in the chapter.
useValue	This property specifies the object that will be used to resolve the dependency.
multi	This property is used to allow multiple providers to be combined to provide an array of objects that will be used to resolve a dependency on the token. See the "Resolving a Dependency with Multiple Objects" section earlier in the chapter for an example.

The value provider works in the same way as the class provider except that it is configured with an object rather than a type. Listing 20-14 shows the use of the value provider to create an instance of the `LogService` class that is configured with a specific property value.

Listing 20-14. Using the Value Provider in the app.module.ts File in the src/app Folder

```
import { NgModule } from "@angular/core";
import { BrowserModule } from "@angular/platform-browser";
import { ProductComponent } from "./component";
import { FormsModule, ReactiveFormsModule  } from "@angular/forms";
```

```
import { PaAttrDirective } from "./attr.directive";
import { PaModel } from "./twoway.directive";
import { PaStructureDirective } from "./structure.directive";
import { PaIteratorDirective } from "./iterator.directive";
import { PaCellColor } from "./cellColor.directive";
import { PaCellColorSwitcher } from "./cellColorSwitcher.directive";
import { ProductTableComponent } from "./productTable.component";
import { ProductFormComponent } from "./productForm.component";
import { PaAddTaxPipe } from "./addTax.pipe";
import { PaCategoryFilterPipe } from "./categoryFilter.pipe";
import { PaDiscountDisplayComponent } from "./discountDisplay.component";
import { PaDiscountEditorComponent } from "./discountEditor.component";
import { DiscountService } from "./discount.service";
import { PaDiscountPipe } from "./discount.pipe";
import { PaDiscountAmountDirective } from "./discountAmount.directive";
import { SimpleDataSource } from "./datasource.model";
import { Model } from "./repository.model";
import { LogService, LOG_SERVICE, SpecialLogService, LogLevel } from "./log.service";

let logger = new LogService();
logger.minimumLevel = LogLevel.DEBUG;

@NgModule({
    imports: [BrowserModule, FormsModule, ReactiveFormsModule],
    declarations: [ProductComponent, PaAttrDirective, PaModel,
        PaStructureDirective, PaIteratorDirective,
        PaCellColor, PaCellColorSwitcher, ProductTableComponent,
        ProductFormComponent, PaAddTaxPipe, PaCategoryFilterPipe,
        PaDiscountDisplayComponent, PaDiscountEditorComponent,
        PaDiscountPipe, PaDiscountAmountDirective],
    providers: [DiscountService, SimpleDataSource, Model,
        { provide: LogService, useValue: logger }],
    bootstrap: [ProductComponent]
})
export class AppModule { }
```

This value provider is configured to resolve dependencies on the LogService token with a specific object that has been created and configured outside of the module class.

The value provider—and, in fact, all of the providers—can use any object as the token, as described in the previous section, but I have returned to using types as tokens because it is the most commonly used technique and because it works so nicely with TypeScript constructor parameter typing. Listing 20-15 shows the corresponding change to the DiscountService, which declares a dependency using a typed constructor argument.

Listing 20-15. Declaring a Dependency Using a Type in the discount.service.ts File in the src/app Folder

```
import { Injectable, Inject } from "@angular/core";
import { LogService, LOG_SERVICE, LogLevel } from "./log.service";

@Injectable()
export class DiscountService {
    private discountValue: number = 10;
```

```
constructor(private logger: LogService) { }

    public get discount(): number {
        return this.discountValue;
    }

    public set discount(newValue: number) {
        this.discountValue = newValue || 0;
    }

    public applyDiscount(price: number) {
        this.logger.logInfoMessage(`Discount ${this.discount}`
            + ` applied to price: ${price}`);
        return Math.max(price - this.discountValue, 5);
    }
}
}
```

Using the Factory Provider

The factory provider uses a function to create the object required to resolve a dependency. This provider supports the properties described in Table 20-6.

Table 20-6. *The Factory Provider Properties*

Name	Description
provide	This property defines the service token, as described in the "Understanding the Token" section earlier in the chapter.
deps	This property specifies an array of provider tokens that will be resolved and passed to the function specified by the useFactory property.
useFactory	This property specifies the function that will create the service object. The objects produced by resolving the tokens specified by the deps property will be passed to the function as arguments. The result returned by the function will be used as the service object.
multi	This property is used to allow multiple providers to be combined to provide an array of objects that will be used to resolve a dependency on the token. See the "Resolving a Dependency with Multiple Objects" section earlier in the chapter for an example.

This is the provider that gives the most flexibility in how service objects are created because you can define functions that are tailored to your application's requirements. Listing 20-16 shows a factory function that creates LogService objects.

Listing 20-16. Using the Factory Provider in the app.module.ts File in the src/app Folder

```
...
@NgModule({
    imports: [BrowserModule, FormsModule, ReactiveFormsModule],
    declarations: [ProductComponent, PaAttrDirective, PaModel,
```

```
        PaStructureDirective, PaIteratorDirective,
        PaCellColor, PaCellColorSwitcher, ProductTableComponent,
        ProductFormComponent, PaAddTaxPipe, PaCategoryFilterPipe,
        PaDiscountDisplayComponent, PaDiscountEditorComponent,
        PaDiscountPipe, PaDiscountAmountDirective],
    providers: [DiscountService, SimpleDataSource, Model,
        {
            provide: LogService, useFactory: () => {
                let logger = new LogService();
                logger.minimumLevel = LogLevel.DEBUG;
                return logger;
            }
        }],

    bootstrap: [ProductComponent]
})
...
```

The function in this example is simple: it receives no arguments and just creates a new LogService object. The real flexibility of this provider comes when the deps property is used, which allows for dependencies to be created on other services. In Listing 20-17, I have defined a token that specifies a debugging level.

Listing 20-17. Defining a Logging Level Service in the log.service.ts File in the src/app Folder

```
import { Injectable, InjectionToken } from "@angular/core";

export const LOG_SERVICE = new InjectionToken("logger");
export const LOG_LEVEL = new InjectionToken("log_level");

export enum LogLevel {
    DEBUG, INFO, ERROR
}

@Injectable()
export class LogService {
    minimumLevel: LogLevel = LogLevel.INFO;

    // ...methods omitted for brevity...
}

@Injectable()
export class SpecialLogService extends LogService {

    // ...methods omitted for brevity...
}
```

In Listing 20-18, I have defined a value provider that creates a service using the LOG_LEVEL token and used that service in the factory function that creates the LogService object.

Listing 20-18. Using Factory Dependencies in the app.module.ts File in the src/app Folder

```
import { NgModule } from "@angular/core";
import { BrowserModule } from "@angular/platform-browser";
import { ProductComponent } from "./component";
import { FormsModule, ReactiveFormsModule  } from "@angular/forms";
import { PaAttrDirective } from "./attr.directive";
import { PaModel } from "./twoway.directive";
import { PaStructureDirective } from "./structure.directive";
import { PaIteratorDirective } from "./iterator.directive";
import { PaCellColor } from "./cellColor.directive";
import { PaCellColorSwitcher } from "./cellColorSwitcher.directive";
import { ProductTableComponent } from "./productTable.component";
import { ProductFormComponent } from "./productForm.component";
import { PaAddTaxPipe } from "./addTax.pipe";
import { PaCategoryFilterPipe } from "./categoryFilter.pipe";
import { PaDiscountDisplayComponent } from "./discountDisplay.component";
import { PaDiscountEditorComponent } from "./discountEditor.component";
import { DiscountService } from "./discount.service";
import { PaDiscountPipe } from "./discount.pipe";
import { PaDiscountAmountDirective } from "./discountAmount.directive";
import { SimpleDataSource } from "./datasource.model";
import { Model } from "./repository.model";
import { LogService, LOG_SERVICE, SpecialLogService,
         LogLevel, LOG_LEVEL} from "./log.service";

@NgModule({
    imports: [BrowserModule, FormsModule, ReactiveFormsModule],
    declarations: [ProductComponent, PaAttrDirective, PaModel,
        PaStructureDirective, PaIteratorDirective,
        PaCellColor, PaCellColorSwitcher, ProductTableComponent,
        ProductFormComponent, PaAddTaxPipe, PaCategoryFilterPipe,
        PaDiscountDisplayComponent, PaDiscountEditorComponent,
        PaDiscountPipe, PaDiscountAmountDirective],
    providers: [DiscountService, SimpleDataSource, Model,
        { provide: LOG_LEVEL, useValue: LogLevel.DEBUG },
        { provide: LogService,
          deps: [LOG_LEVEL],
          useFactory: (level) => {
            let logger = new LogService();
            logger.minimumLevel = level;
            return logger;
          }
        }],
    bootstrap: [ProductComponent]
})
export class AppModule { }
```

The LOG_LEVEL token is used by a value provider to define a simple value as a service. The factory provider specifies this token in its deps array, which the dependency injection system resolves and provides as an argument to the factory function, which uses it to set the minimumLevel property of a new LogService object.

Using the Existing Service Provider

This provider is used to create aliases for services so they can be targeted using more than one token, using the properties described in Table 20-7.

Table 20-7. *The Existing Provider Properties*

Name	Description
provide	This property defines the service token, as described in the "Understanding the Token" section earlier in the chapter.
useExisting	This property is used to specify the token of another provider, whose service object will be used to resolve dependencies on this service.
multi	This property is used to allow multiple providers to be combined to provide an array of objects that will be used to resolve a dependency on the token. See the "Resolving a Dependency with Multiple Objects" section earlier in the chapter for an example.

This provider can be useful when you want to refactor the set of providers but don't want to eliminate all the obsolete tokens in order to avoid refactoring the rest of the application. Listing 20-19 shows the use of this provider.

Listing 20-19. Creating a Service Alias in the app.module.ts File in the src/app Folder

```
...
@NgModule({
    imports: [BrowserModule, FormsModule, ReactiveFormsModule],
    declarations: [ProductComponent, PaAttrDirective, PaModel,
        PaStructureDirective, PaIteratorDirective,
        PaCellColor, PaCellColorSwitcher, ProductTableComponent,
        ProductFormComponent, PaAddTaxPipe, PaCategoryFilterPipe,
        PaDiscountDisplayComponent, PaDiscountEditorComponent,
        PaDiscountPipe, PaDiscountAmountDirective],
    providers: [DiscountService, SimpleDataSource, Model,
        { provide: LOG_LEVEL, useValue: LogLevel.DEBUG },
        { provide: "debugLevel", useExisting: LOG_LEVEL },
        { provide: LogService,
          deps: ["debugLevel"],
          useFactory: (level) => {
            let logger = new LogService();
            logger.minimumLevel = level;
            return logger;
        }
        }],
    bootstrap: [ProductComponent]
})
...
```

The token for the new service is the string debugLevel, and it is aliased to the provider with the LOG_LEVEL token. Using either token will result in the dependency being resolved with the same value.

Using Local Providers

When Angular creates a new instance of a class, it resolves any dependencies using an *injector*. It is an injector that is responsible for inspecting the constructors of classes to determine what dependencies have been declared and resolving them using the available providers.

So far, all of the dependency injection examples have relied on providers configured in the application's Angular module. But the Angular dependency injection system is more complex: there is a hierarchy of injectors that corresponds to the application's tree of components and directives. Each component and directive can have its own injector, and each injector can be configured with its own set of providers, known as *local providers*.

When there is a dependency to resolve, Angular uses the injector for the nearest component or directive. The injector first tries to resolve the dependency using its own set of local providers. If no local providers have been set up or there are no providers that can be used to resolve this specific dependency, then the injector consults the parent component's injector. The process is repeated—the parent component's injector tries to resolve the dependency using its own set of local providers. If a suitable provider is available, then it is used to provide the service object required to resolve the dependency. If there is no suitable provider, then the request is passed up to the next level in the hierarchy, to the grandparent of the original injector. At the top of the hierarchy is the root Angular module, whose providers are the last resort before reporting an error.

Defining providers in the Angular module means that all dependencies for a token within the application will be resolved using the same object. As I explain in the following sections, registering providers further down the injector hierarchy can change this behavior and alter the way that services are created and used.

Understanding the Limitations of Single Service Objects

Using a single service object can be a powerful tool, allowing building blocks in different parts of the application to share data and respond to user interactions. But some services don't lend themselves to being shared so widely. As a simple example, Listing 20-20 adds a dependency on LogService to one of the pipes created in Chapter 18.

Listing 20-20. Adding a Service Dependency in the discount.pipe.ts File in the src/app Folder

```
import { Pipe, Injectable } from "@angular/core";
import { DiscountService } from "./discount.service";
import { LogService } from "./log.service";

@Pipe({
    name: "discount",
    pure: false
})
export class PaDiscountPipe {

    constructor(private discount: DiscountService,
                private logger: LogService) { }

    transform(price: number): number {
        if (price > 100) {
            this.logger.logInfoMessage(`Large price discounted: ${price}`);
        }
        return this.discount.applyDiscount(price);
    }
}
```

The pipe's transform method uses the LogService object, which is received as a constructor argument, to generate logging messages when the price it transforms is greater than 100.

The problem is that these log messages are drowned out by the messages generated by the DiscountService object, which creates a message every time a discount is applied. The obvious thing to do is to change the minimum level in the LogService object when it is created by the module provider's factory function, as shown in Listing 20-21.

Listing 20-21. Changing the Logging Level in the app.module.ts File in the src/app Folder

```
...
@NgModule({
    imports: [BrowserModule, FormsModule, ReactiveFormsModule],
    declarations: [ProductComponent, PaAttrDirective, PaModel,
        PaStructureDirective, PaIteratorDirective,
        PaCellColor, PaCellColorSwitcher, ProductTableComponent,
        ProductFormComponent, PaAddTaxPipe, PaCategoryFilterPipe,
        PaDiscountDisplayComponent, PaDiscountEditorComponent,
        PaDiscountPipe, PaDiscountAmountDirective],
    providers: [DiscountService, SimpleDataSource, Model,
        { provide: LOG_LEVEL, useValue: LogLevel.ERROR },
        { provide: "debugLevel", useExisting: LOG_LEVEL },
        {
            provide: LogService,
            deps: ["debugLevel"],
            useFactory: (level) => {
                let logger = new LogService();
                logger.minimumLevel = level;
                return logger;
            }
        }],
    bootstrap: [ProductComponent]
})
...
```

Of course, this doesn't have the desired effect because the same LogService object is used throughout the application and filtering the DiscountService messages means that the pipe messages are filtered too.

I could enhance the LogService class so there are different filters for each source of logging messages, but that gets complicated pretty quickly. Instead, I am going to solve the problem by creating a local provider so that there are multiple LogService objects in the application, each of which can then be configured separately.

Creating Local Providers in a Component

Components can define local providers, which allow separate servers to be created and used by part of the application. Components support two decorator properties for creating local providers, as described in Table 20-8.

Table 20-8. *The Component Decorator Properties for Local Providers*

Name	Description
providers	This property is used to create a provider used to resolve dependencies of view and content children.
viewProviders	This property is used to create a provider used to resolve dependencies of view children.

The simplest way to address my LogService issue is to use the providers property to set up a local provider, as shown in Listing 20-22.

Listing 20-22. Creating a Local Provider in the productTable.component.ts File in the src/app Folder

```
import { Component, Input } from "@angular/core";
import { Model } from "./repository.model";
import { Product } from "./product.model";
import { DiscountService } from "./discount.service";
import { LogService } from "./log.service";

@Component({
  selector: "paProductTable",
  templateUrl: "productTable.component.html",
  providers:[LogService]
})
export class ProductTableComponent {

  constructor(private dataModel: Model) { }

  getProduct(key: number): Product {
    return this.dataModel.getProduct(key);
  }

  getProducts(): Product[] {
    return this.dataModel.getProducts();
  }

  deleteProduct(key: number) {
    this.dataModel.deleteProduct(key);
  }

  dateObject: Date = new Date(2020, 1, 20);
  dateString: string = "2020-02-20T00:00:00.000Z";
  dateNumber: number = 1582156800000;
}
```

When Angular needs to create a new pipe object, it detects the dependency on LogService and starts working its way up the application hierarchy, examining each component it finds to determine whether they have a provider that can be used to resolve the dependency. The ProductTableComponent does have a LogService provider, which is used to create the service used to resolve the pipe's dependency. This means there are now two LogService objects in the application, each of which can be configured separately, as shown in Figure 20-2.

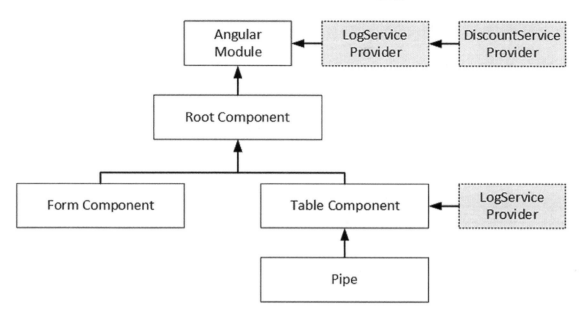

Figure 20-2. *Creating a local provider*

The LogService object created by the component's provider uses the default value for its minimumLevel property and will display LogLevel.INFO messages. The LogService object created by the module, which will be used to resolve all other dependencies in the application, including the one declared by the DiscountService class, is configured so that it will display only LogLevel.ERROR messages. When you save the changes, you will see the logging messages from the pipe (which receives the service from the component) but not from DiscountService (which receives the service from the module).

Understanding the Provider Alternatives

As described in Table 20-8, there are two properties that can be used to create local providers. To demonstrate how these properties differ, I added a file called valueDisplay.directive.ts to the src/app folder and used it to define the directive shown in Listing 20-23.

Listing 20-23. The Contents of the valueDisplay.directive.ts File in the src/app Folder

```
import { Directive, InjectionToken, Inject, HostBinding} from "@angular/core";

export const VALUE_SERVICE = new InjectionToken("value_service");

@Directive({
    selector: "[paDisplayValue]"
})
export class PaDisplayValueDirective {

    constructor( @Inject(VALUE_SERVICE) serviceValue: string) {
        this.elementContent = serviceValue;
    }
```

```
@HostBinding("textContent")
elementContent: string;
}
```

The VALUE_SERVICE opaque token will be used to define a value-based service, on which the directive in this listing declares a dependency so that it can be displayed in the host element's content. Listing 20-24 shows the service being defined and the directive being registered in the Angular module. I have also simplified the LogService provider in the module for brevity.

Listing 20-24. Registering the Directive and Service in the app.module.ts File in the src/app Folder

```
import { NgModule } from "@angular/core";
import { BrowserModule } from "@angular/platform-browser";
import { ProductComponent } from "./component";
import { FormsModule, ReactiveFormsModule  } from "@angular/forms";
import { PaAttrDirective } from "./attr.directive";
import { PaModel } from "./twoway.directive";
import { PaStructureDirective } from "./structure.directive";
import { PaIteratorDirective } from "./iterator.directive";
import { PaCellColor } from "./cellColor.directive";
import { PaCellColorSwitcher } from "./cellColorSwitcher.directive";
import { ProductTableComponent } from "./productTable.component";
import { ProductFormComponent } from "./productForm.component";
import { PaAddTaxPipe } from "./addTax.pipe";
import { PaCategoryFilterPipe } from "./categoryFilter.pipe";
import { PaDiscountDisplayComponent } from "./discountDisplay.component";
import { PaDiscountEditorComponent } from "./discountEditor.component";
import { DiscountService } from "./discount.service";
import { PaDiscountPipe } from "./discount.pipe";
import { PaDiscountAmountDirective } from "./discountAmount.directive";
import { SimpleDataSource } from "./datasource.model";
import { Model } from "./repository.model";
import { LogService, LOG_SERVICE, SpecialLogService,
    LogLevel, LOG_LEVEL} from "./log.service";
import { VALUE_SERVICE, PaDisplayValueDirective} from "./valueDisplay.directive";

@NgModule({
    imports: [BrowserModule, FormsModule, ReactiveFormsModule],
    declarations: [ProductComponent, PaAttrDirective, PaModel,
        PaStructureDirective, PaIteratorDirective,
        PaCellColor, PaCellColorSwitcher, ProductTableComponent,
        ProductFormComponent, PaAddTaxPipe, PaCategoryFilterPipe,
        PaDiscountDisplayComponent, PaDiscountEditorComponent,
        PaDiscountPipe, PaDiscountAmountDirective, PaDisplayValueDirective],
    providers: [DiscountService, SimpleDataSource, Model, LogService,
                { provide: VALUE_SERVICE, useValue: "Apples" }],
    bootstrap: [ProductComponent]
})
export class AppModule { }
```

The provider sets up a value of Apples for the VALUE_SERVICE service. The next step is to apply the new directive so there is an instance that is a view child of a component and another that is a content child. Listing 20-25 sets up the content child instance.

Listing 20-25. Applying a Content Child Directive in the template.html File in the src/app Folder

```
<div class="row m-2">
  <div class="col-4 p-2">
    <paProductForm>
      <span paDisplayValue></span>
    </paProductForm>
  </div>
  <div class="col-8 p-2">
    <paProductTable></paProductTable>
  </div>
</div>
```

Listing 20-26 projects the host element's content and adds a view child instance of the new directive.

Listing 20-26. Adding Directives in the productForm.component.html File in the src/app Folder

```
<form novalidate [formGroup]="form" (ngSubmit)="submitForm(form)">
    <div class="form-group" *ngFor="let control of form.productControls">
        <label>{{control.label}}</label>
        <input class="form-control"
            [(ngModel)]="newProduct[control.modelProperty]"
            name="{{control.modelProperty}}"
            formControlName="{{control.modelProperty}}" />
        <ul class="text-danger list-unstyled"
                *ngIf="(formSubmitted || control.dirty) && !control.valid">
            <li *ngFor="let error of control.getValidationMessages()">
                {{error}}
            </li>
        </ul>
    </div>
    <button class="btn btn-primary" type="submit"
        [disabled]="formSubmitted && !form.valid"
        [class.btn-secondary]="formSubmitted && !form.valid">
            Create
    </button>
</form>
<div class="bg-info text-white m-2 p-2">
    View Child Value: <span paDisplayValue></span>
</div>
<div class="bg-info text-white m-2 p-2">
    Content Child Value: <ng-content></ng-content>
</div>
```

When you save the changes, you will see the new elements, as shown in Figure 20-3, both of which show the same value because the only provider for VALUE_SERVICE is defined in the module.

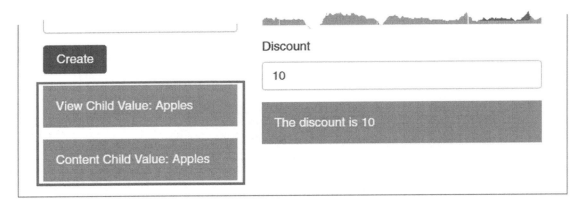

Figure 20-3. *View and content child directives*

Creating a Local Provider for All Children

The @Component decorator's providers property is used to define providers that will be used to resolve service dependencies for all children, regardless of whether they are defined in the template (view children) or projected from the host element (content children). Listing 20-27 defines a VALUE_SERVICE provider in the parent component for two new directive instances.

Listing 20-27. Defining a Provider in the productForm.component.ts File in the src/app Folder

```
import { Component, Output, EventEmitter, ViewEncapsulation } from "@angular/core";
import { Product } from "./product.model";
import { ProductFormGroup } from "./form.model";
import { Model } from "./repository.model";
import { VALUE_SERVICE } from "./valueDisplay.directive";

@Component({
    selector: "paProductForm",
    templateUrl: "productForm.component.html",
    providers: [{ provide: VALUE_SERVICE, useValue: "Oranges" }]
})
export class ProductFormComponent {
    form: ProductFormGroup = new ProductFormGroup();
    newProduct: Product = new Product();
    formSubmitted: boolean = false;

    constructor(private model: Model) { }

    submitForm(form: any) {
        this.formSubmitted = true;
        if (form.valid) {
            this.model.saveProduct(this.newProduct);
            this.newProduct = new Product();
```

```
            this.form.reset();
            this.formSubmitted = false;
        }
    }
}
```

The new provider changes the service value. When Angular comes to create the instances of the new directive, it begins its search for providers by working its way up the application hierarchy and finds the VALUE_SERVICE provider defined in Listing 20-27. The service value is used by both instances of the directive, as shown in Figure 20-4.

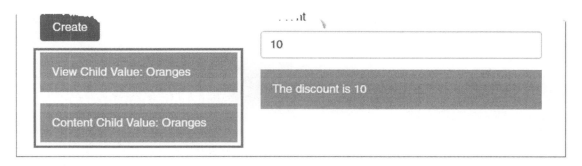

Figure 20-4. *Defining a provider for all children in a component*

Creating a Provider for View Children

The viewProviders property defines providers that are used to resolve dependencies for view children but not content children. Listing 20-28 uses the viewProviders property to define a provider for VALUE_SERVICE.

Listing 20-28. Defining a View Child Provider in the productForm.component.ts File in the src/app Folder

```
import { Component, Output, EventEmitter, ViewEncapsulation } from "@angular/core";
import { Product } from "./product.model";
import { ProductFormGroup } from "./form.model";
import { Model } from "./repository.model";
import { VALUE_SERVICE } from "./valueDisplay.directive";

@Component({
    selector: "paProductForm",
    templateUrl: "productForm.component.html",
    viewProviders: [{ provide: VALUE_SERVICE, useValue: "Oranges" }]
})
export class ProductFormComponent {

    // ...methods and properties omitted for brevity...
}
```

Angular uses the provider when resolving dependencies for view children but not for content children. This means dependencies for content children are referred up the application's hierarchy as though the component had not defined a provider. In the example, this means that the view child will receive the service created by the component's provider, and the content child will receive the service created by the module's provider, as shown in Figure 20-5.

■ **Caution** Defining providers for the same service using both the `providers` and `viewProviders` properties is not supported. If you do this, the view and content children both will receive the service created by the `viewProviders` provider.

Figure 20-5. *Defining a provider for view children*

Controlling Dependency Resolution

Angular provides three decorators that can be used to provide instructions about how a dependency is resolved. These decorators are described in Table 20-9 and demonstrated in the following sections.

Table 20-9. *The Dependency Resolution Decorators*

Name	Description
@Host	This decorator restricts the search for a provider to the nearest component.
@Optional	This decorator stops Angular from reporting an error if the dependency cannot be resolved.
@SkipSelf	This decorator excludes the providers defined by the component/directive whose dependency is being resolved.

Restricting the Provider Search

The `@Host` decorator restricts the search for a suitable provider so that it stops once the closest component has been reached. The decorator is typically combined with `@Optional`, which prevents Angular from throwing an exception if a service dependency cannot be resolved. Listing 20-29 shows the addition of both decorators to the directive in the example.

Listing 20-29. Adding Dependency Decorators in the valueDisplay.directive.ts File in the src/app Folder

```
import { Directive, InjectionToken, Inject,
        HostBinding, Host, Optional} from "@angular/core";

export const VALUE_SERVICE = new InjectionToken("value_service");

@Directive({
    selector: "[paDisplayValue]"
})
export class PaDisplayValueDirective {

    constructor( @Inject(VALUE_SERVICE) @Host() @Optional() serviceValue: string) {
        this.elementContent = serviceValue || "No Value";
    }

    @HostBinding("textContent")
    elementContent: string;
}
```

When using the @Optional decorator, you must ensure that the class is able to function if the service cannot be resolved, in which case the constructor argument for the service is undefined. The nearest component defines a service for its view children but not content children, which means that one instance of the directive will receive a service object and the other will not, as illustrated in Figure 20-6.

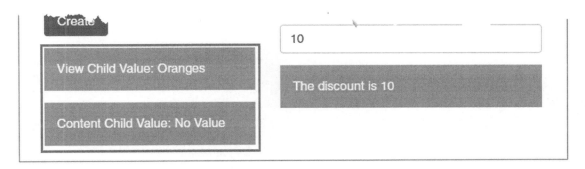

Figure 20-6. *Controlling how a dependency is resolved*

Skipping Self-Defined Providers

By default, the providers defined by a component are used to resolve its dependencies. The @SkipSelf decorator can be applied to constructor arguments to tell Angular to ignore the local providers and start the search at the next level in the application hierarchy, which means that the local providers will be used only to resolve dependencies for children. In Listing 20-30, I have added a dependency on the VALUE_SERVICE provider that is decorated with @SkipSelf.

Listing 20-30. Skipping Local Providers in the productForm.component.ts File in the src/app Folder

```
import { Component, Output, EventEmitter, ViewEncapsulation,
         Inject, SkipSelf } from "@angular/core";
import { Product } from "./product.model";
import { ProductFormGroup } from "./form.model";
import { Model } from "./repository.model";
import { VALUE_SERVICE } from "./valueDisplay.directive";

@Component({
    selector: "paProductForm",
    templateUrl: "productForm.component.html",
    viewProviders: [{ provide: VALUE_SERVICE, useValue: "Oranges" }]
})
export class ProductFormComponent {
    form: ProductFormGroup = new ProductFormGroup();
    newProduct: Product = new Product();
    formSubmitted: boolean = false;

    constructor(private model: Model,
            @Inject(VALUE_SERVICE) @SkipSelf() private serviceValue: string) {
        console.log("Service Value: " + serviceValue);
    }

    submitForm(form: any) {
        this.formSubmitted = true;
        if (form.valid) {
            this.model.saveProduct(this.newProduct);
            this.newProduct = new Product();
            this.form.reset();
            this.formSubmitted = false;
        }
    }
}
```

When you save the changes and the browser reloads the page, you will see the following message in the browser's JavaScript console, showing that the service value defined locally (Oranges) has been skipped and allowing the dependency to be resolved by the Angular module:

```
Service Value: Apples
```

Summary

In this chapter, I explained the role that providers play in dependency injection and explained how they can be used to change how services are used to resolve dependencies. I described the different types of provider that can be used to create service objects and demonstrated how directives and components can define their own providers to resolve their own dependencies and those of their children. In the next chapter, I describe modules, which are the final building block for Angular applications.

CHAPTER 21

■ ■ ■

Using and Creating Modules

In this chapter, I describe the last of the Angular building blocks: modules. In the first part of the chapter, I describe the root module, which every Angular application uses to describe the configuration of the application to Angular. In the second part of the chapter, I describe feature modules, which are used to add structure to an application so that related features can be grouped as a single unit. Table 21-1 puts modules in context.

Table 21-1. *Putting Modules in Context*

Question	Answer
What are they?	Modules provide configuration information to Angular.
Why are they useful?	The root module describes the application to Angular, setting up essential features such as components and services. Feature modules are useful for adding structure to complex projects, making them easier to manage and maintain.
How are they used?	Modules are classes to which the @NgModule decorator has been applied. The properties used by the decorator have different meanings for root and feature modules.
Are there any pitfalls or limitations?	There is no module-wide scope for providers, which means that the providers defined by a feature module will be available as though they had been defined by the root module.
Are there any alternatives?	Every application must have a root module, but the use of feature modules is entirely optional. However, if you don't use feature modules, then the files in an application can become difficult to manage.

Table 21-2 summarizes the chapter.

Table 21-2. *Chapter Summary*

Problem	Solution	Listing
Describe an application and the building blocks it contains	Use the root module	1–7
Group related features together	Create a feature module	8–28

© Adam Freeman 2018

A. Freeman, *Pro Angular 6*, https://doi.org/10.1007/978-1-4842-3649-9_21

Preparing the Example Project

As with the other chapters in this part of the book, I am going to use the example project that was created in Chapter 11 and has been expanded and extended in each chapter since.

■ **Tip** You can download the example project for this chapter—and for all the other chapters in this book—from `https://github.com/Apress/pro-angular-6`.

To prepare for this chapter, I have removed some functionality from the component templates. Listing 21-1 shows the template for the product table, in which I have commented out the elements for the discount editor and display components.

Listing 21-1. The Contents of the productTable.component.html File in the src/app Folder

```
<table class="table table-sm table-bordered table-striped">
  <tr>
    <th></th>
    <th>Name</th>
    <th>Category</th>
    <th>Price</th>
    <th>Discount</th>
    <th></th>
  </tr>
  <tr *paFor="let item of getProducts(); let i = index;
          let odd = odd; let even = even" [class.bg-info]="odd"
      [class.bg-warning]="even">
    <td style="vertical-align:middle">{{i + 1}}</td>
    <td style="vertical-align:middle">{{item.name}}</td>
    <td style="vertical-align:middle">{{item.category}}</td>
    <td style="vertical-align:middle">
      {{item.price | discount | currency:"USD":"symbol" }}
    </td>
    <td style="vertical-align:middle" [pa-price]="item.price"
        #discount="discount">
      {{ discount.discountAmount | currency:"USD":"symbol"}}
    </td>
    <td class="text-center">
      <button class="btn btn-danger btn-sm" (click)="deleteProduct(item.id)">
        Delete
      </button>
    </td>
  </tr>
</table>


<!--<paDiscountEditor></paDiscountEditor>-->
<!--<paDiscountDisplay></paDiscountDisplay>-->
```

Listing 21-2 shows the template from the product form component, in which I have commented out the elements that I used to demonstrate the difference between providers for view children and content children in Chapter 20.

Listing 21-2. The Contents of the productForm.component.html File in the src/app Folder

```
<form novalidate [formGroup]="form" (ngSubmit)="submitForm(form)">
  <div class="form-group" *ngFor="let control of form.productControls">
    <label>{{control.label}}</label>
    <input class="form-control"
           [(ngModel)]="newProduct[control.modelProperty]"
           name="{{control.modelProperty}}"
           formControlName="{{control.modelProperty}}" />
    <ul class="text-danger list-unstyled"
        *ngIf="(formSubmitted || control.dirty) && !control.valid">
      <li *ngFor="let error of control.getValidationMessages()">
        {{error}}
      </li>
    </ul>
  </div>
  <button class="btn btn-primary" type="submit"
          [disabled]="formSubmitted && !form.valid"
          [class.btn-secondary]="formSubmitted && !form.valid">
    Create
  </button>
</form>
<!--<div class="bg-info text-white m-2 p-2">
  View Child Value: <span paDisplayValue></span>
</div>
<div class="bg-info text-white m-2 p-2">
  Content Child Value: <ng-content></ng-content>
</div>-->
```

Run the following command in the example folder to start the Angular development tools:

```
ng serve
```

Open a new browser window and navigate to http://localhost:4200 to see the content shown in Figure 21-1.

Figure 21-1. *Running the example application*

Understanding the Root Module

Every Angular has at least one module, known as the *root module*. The root module is conventionally defined in a file called app.module.ts in the src/app folder, and it contains a class to which the @NgModule decorator has been applied. Listing 21-3 shows the root module from the example application.

Listing 21-3. The Root Module in the app.module.ts File in the src/app Folder

```
import { NgModule } from "@angular/core";
import { BrowserModule } from "@angular/platform-browser";
import { ProductComponent } from "./component";
import { FormsModule, ReactiveFormsModule } from "@angular/forms";
import { PaAttrDirective } from "./attr.directive";
import { PaModel } from "./twoway.directive";
import { PaStructureDirective } from "./structure.directive";
import { PaIteratorDirective } from "./iterator.directive";
import { PaCellColor } from "./cellColor.directive";
import { PaCellColorSwitcher } from "./cellColorSwitcher.directive";
import { ProductTableComponent } from "./productTable.component";
import { ProductFormComponent } from "./productForm.component";
import { PaAddTaxPipe } from "./addTax.pipe";
import { PaCategoryFilterPipe } from "./categoryFilter.pipe";
import { PaDiscountDisplayComponent } from "./discountDisplay.component";
import { PaDiscountEditorComponent } from "./discountEditor.component";
import { DiscountService } from "./discount.service";
import { PaDiscountPipe } from "./discount.pipe";
import { PaDiscountAmountDirective } from "./discountAmount.directive";
import { SimpleDataSource } from "./datasource.model";
import { Model } from "./repository.model";
```

```
import {
  LogService, LOG_SERVICE, SpecialLogService,
  LogLevel, LOG_LEVEL
} from "./log.service";
import { VALUE_SERVICE, PaDisplayValueDirective } from "./valueDisplay.directive";

@NgModule({
  imports: [BrowserModule, FormsModule, ReactiveFormsModule],
  declarations: [ProductComponent, PaAttrDirective, PaModel,
    PaStructureDirective, PaIteratorDirective,
    PaCellColor, PaCellColorSwitcher, ProductTableComponent,
    ProductFormComponent, PaAddTaxPipe, PaCategoryFilterPipe,
    PaDiscountDisplayComponent, PaDiscountEditorComponent,
    PaDiscountPipe, PaDiscountAmountDirective, PaDisplayValueDirective],
  providers: [DiscountService, SimpleDataSource, Model, LogService,
    { provide: VALUE_SERVICE, useValue: "Apples" }],
  bootstrap: [ProductComponent]
})
export class AppModule { }
```

There can be multiple modules in a project, but the root module is the one used in the bootstrap file, which is conventionally called main.ts and is defined in the src folder. Listing 21-4 shows the main.ts file for the example project.

Listing 21-4. The Angular Bootstrap in the main.ts File in the src Folder

```
import { enableProdMode } from '@angular/core';
import { platformBrowserDynamic } from '@angular/platform-browser-dynamic';

import { AppModule } from './app/app.module';
import { environment } from './environments/environment';

if (environment.production) {
  enableProdMode();
}

platformBrowserDynamic().bootstrapModule(AppModule)
  .catch(err => console.log(err));
```

Angular applications can be run in different environments, such as web browsers and native application containers. The job of the bootstrap file is to select the platform and identify the root module. The platformBrowserDynamic method creates the browser runtime, and the bootstrapModule method is used to specify the module, which is the AppModule class from Listing 21-3.

When defining the root module, the @NgModule decorator properties described in Table 21-3 are used. (There are additional decorator properties, which are described later in the chapter.)

Table 21-3. *The @NgModule Decorator Root Module Properties*

Name	Description
imports	This property specifies the Angular modules that are required to support the directives, components, and pipes in the application.
declarations	This property is used to specify the directives, components, and pipes that are used in the application.
providers	This property defines the service providers that will be used by the module's injector. These are the providers that will be available throughout the application and used when no local provider for a service is available, as described in Chapter 20.
bootstrap	This property specifies the root components for the application.

Understanding the imports Property

The `imports` property is used to list the other modules that the application requires. In the example application, these are all modules provided by the Angular framework.

```
...
imports: [BrowserModule, FormsModule, ReactiveFormsModule],
...
```

The `BrowserModule` provides the functionality required to run Angular applications in web browsers. The other two modules provide support for working with HTML forms and model-based forms, as described in Chapter 14. There are other Angular modules, which are introduced in later chapters.

The `imports` property is also used to declare dependencies on custom modules, which are used to manage complex Angular applications and to create units of reusable functionality. I explain how custom modules are defined in the "Creating Feature Modules" section.

Understanding the declarations Property

The `declarations` property is used to provide Angular with a list of the directives, components, and pipes that the application requires, known collectively as the *declarable classes*. The `declarations` property in the example project root module contains a long list of classes, each of which is available for use elsewhere in the application only because it is listed here.

```
...
declarations: [ProductComponent, PaAttrDirective, PaModel,
    PaStructureDirective, PaIteratorDirective,
    PaCellColor, PaCellColorSwitcher, ProductTableComponent,
    ProductFormComponent, PaAddTaxPipe, PaCategoryFilterPipe,
    PaDiscountDisplayComponent, PaDiscountEditorComponent,
    PaDiscountPipe, PaDiscountAmountDirective, PaDisplayValueDirective],
...
```

Notice that the built-in declarable classes, such as the directives described in Chapter 13 and the pipes described in Chapter 18, are not included in the `declarations` property for the root module. This is because they are part of the `BrowserModule` module, and when you add a module to the `imports` property, its declarable classes are automatically available for use in the application.

Understanding the providers Property

The providers property is used to define the service providers that will be used to resolve dependencies when there are no suitable local providers available. The use of providers for services is described in detail in Chapters 19 and 20.

Understanding the bootstrap Property

The bootstrap property specifies the root component or components for the application. When Angular process the main HTML document, which is conventionally called index.html, it inspects the root components and applies them using the value of the selector property in the @Component decorators.

■ **Tip** The components listed in the bootstrap property must also be included in the declarations list.

Here is the bootstrap property from the example project's root module:

```
...
bootstrap: [ProductComponent]
...
```

The ProductComponent class provides the root component, and its selector property specifies the app element, as shown in Listing 21-5.

Listing 21-5. The Root Component in the component.ts File in the src/app Folder

```
import { Component } from "@angular/core";

@Component({
  selector: "app",
  templateUrl: "template.html"
})
export class ProductComponent {

}
```

When I started the example project in Chapter 11, the root component had a lot of functionality. But since the introduction of additional components, the role of this component has been reduced, and it is now essentially a placeholder that tells Angular to project the contents of the app/template.html file into the app element in the HTML document, which allows the components that do the real work in the application to be loaded.

There is nothing wrong with this approach, but it does mean the root component in the application doesn't have a great deal to do. If this kind of redundancy feels untidy, then you can specify multiple root components in the root module, and all of them will be used to target elements in the HTML document. To demonstrate, I have removed the existing root component from the root module's bootstrap property and replaced it with the component classes that are responsible for the product form and the product table, as shown in Listing 21-6.

Listing 21-6. Specifying Multiple Root Components in the app.module.ts File in the src/app Folder

```
...
@NgModule({
  imports: [BrowserModule, FormsModule, ReactiveFormsModule],
  declarations: [ProductComponent, PaAttrDirective, PaModel,
    PaStructureDirective, PaIteratorDirective,
    PaCellColor, PaCellColorSwitcher, ProductTableComponent,
    ProductFormComponent, PaAddTaxPipe, PaCategoryFilterPipe,
    PaDiscountDisplayComponent, PaDiscountEditorComponent,
    PaDiscountPipe, PaDiscountAmountDirective, PaDisplayValueDirective],
  providers: [DiscountService, SimpleDataSource, Model, LogService,
    { provide: VALUE_SERVICE, useValue: "Apples" }],
  bootstrap: [ProductFormComponent, ProductTableComponent]
})
export class AppModule { }
...
```

Listing 21-7 reflects the change in the root components in the main HTML document.

Listing 21-7. Changing the Root Component Elements in the index.html File in the src Folder

```
<!doctype html>
<html lang="en">
<head>
  <meta charset="utf-8">
  <title>Example</title>
  <base href="/">
  <meta name="viewport" content="width=device-width, initial-scale=1">
  <link rel="icon" type="image/x-icon" href="favicon.ico">
</head>
<body class="m-2 row">
    <div class="col-8 p-2">
        <paProductTable></paProductTable>
    </div>
    <div class="col-4 p-2">
        <paProductForm></paProductForm>
    </div>
</body>
</html>
```

I have reversed the order in which these components appear compared to previous examples, just to create a detectable change in the application's layout. When all the changes are saved and the browser has reloaded the page, you will see the new root components displayed, as illustrated by Figure 21-2.

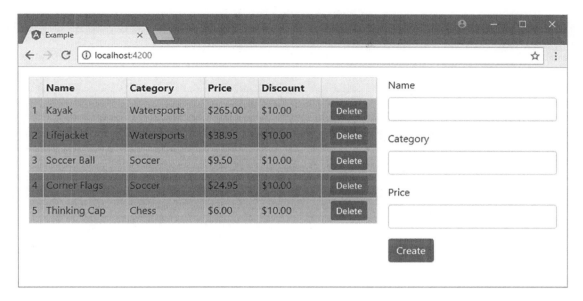

Figure 21-2. *Using multiple root components*

The module's service providers are used to resolve dependencies for all root components. In the case of the example application, this means there is a single Model service object that is shared throughout the application and that allows products created with the HTML form to be displayed automatically in the table, even though these components have been promoted to be root components.

Creating Feature Modules

The root module has become increasingly complex as I added features in earlier chapters, with a long list of import statements to load JavaScript modules and a set of classes in the declararations property of the @NgModule decorator that spans several lines, as shown in Listing 21-8.

Listing 21-8. The Contents of the app.module.ts File in the src/app Folder

```
import { NgModule } from "@angular/core";
import { BrowserModule } from "@angular/platform-browser";
import { ProductComponent } from "./component";
import { FormsModule, ReactiveFormsModule } from "@angular/forms";
import { PaAttrDirective } from "./attr.directive";
import { PaModel } from "./twoway.directive";
import { PaStructureDirective } from "./structure.directive";
import { PaIteratorDirective } from "./iterator.directive";
import { PaCellColor } from "./cellColor.directive";
import { PaCellColorSwitcher } from "./cellColorSwitcher.directive";
import { ProductTableComponent } from "./productTable.component";
```

```
import { ProductFormComponent } from "./productForm.component";
import { PaAddTaxPipe } from "./addTax.pipe";
import { PaCategoryFilterPipe } from "./categoryFilter.pipe";
import { PaDiscountDisplayComponent } from "./discountDisplay.component";
import { PaDiscountEditorComponent } from "./discountEditor.component";
import { DiscountService } from "./discount.service";
import { PaDiscountPipe } from "./discount.pipe";
import { PaDiscountAmountDirective } from "./discountAmount.directive";
import { SimpleDataSource } from "./datasource.model";
import { Model } from "./repository.model";
import {
  LogService, LOG_SERVICE, SpecialLogService,
  LogLevel, LOG_LEVEL
} from "./log.service";
import { VALUE_SERVICE, PaDisplayValueDirective } from "./valueDisplay.directive";

@NgModule({
  imports: [BrowserModule, FormsModule, ReactiveFormsModule],
  declarations: [ProductComponent, PaAttrDirective, PaModel,
    PaStructureDirective, PaIteratorDirective,
    PaCellColor, PaCellColorSwitcher, ProductTableComponent,
    ProductFormComponent, PaAddTaxPipe, PaCategoryFilterPipe,
    PaDiscountDisplayComponent, PaDiscountEditorComponent,
    PaDiscountPipe, PaDiscountAmountDirective, PaDisplayValueDirective],
  providers: [DiscountService, SimpleDataSource, Model, LogService,
    { provide: VALUE_SERVICE, useValue: "Apples" }],
  bootstrap: [ProductFormComponent, ProductTableComponent]
})
export class AppModule { }
```

Feature modules are used to group related functionality so that it can be used as a single entity, just like the Angular modules such as BrowserModule. When I need to use the features for working with forms, for example, I don't have to add import statements and declarations entries for each individual directive, component, or pipe. Instead, I just add BrowserModule to the decorator's imports property, and all of the functionality it contains is available throughout the application.

When you create a feature module, you can choose to focus on an application function or elect to group a set of related building blocks that provide your application's infrastructure. I'll do both in the sections that follow because they work in slightly different ways and have different considerations. Feature modules use the same @NgModule decorator but with an overlapping set of configuration properties, some of which are new and some of which are used in common with the root module but have a different effect. I explain how these properties are used in the following sections, but Table 21-4 provides a summary for quick reference.

Table 21-4. *The @NgModule Decorator Properties for Feature Modules*

Name	Description
imports	This property is used to import the modules that are required by the classes in the modules.
providers	This property is used to define the module's providers. When the feature module is loaded, the set of providers are combined with those in the root module, which means that the feature module's services are available throughout the application (and not just within the module).
declarations	This property is used to specify the directives, components, and pipes in the module. This property must contain the classes that are used within the module and those that are exposed by the module to the rest of the application.
exports	This property is used to define the public exports from the module. It contains some or all of the directives, components, and pipes from the declarations property and some or all of the modules from the imports property.

Creating a Model Module

The term *model module* might be a tongue twister, but it is generally a good place to start when refactoring an application using feature modules because just about every other building block in the application depends on the model.

The first step is to create the folder that will contain the module. Module folders are defined within the src/app folder and are given a meaningful name. For this module, I created an src/app/model folder.

The naming conventions used for Angular files makes it easy to move and delete multiple files. Run the following commands in the example folder to move the files (they will work in Windows PowerShell, Linux, and macOS):

```
mv src/app/*.model.ts src/app/model/
mv src/app/limit.formvalidator.ts src/app/model/
```

The result is that the files listed in Table 21-5 are moved to the model folder.

Table 21-5. *The File Moves Required for the Module*

File	New Location
src/app/datasource.model.ts	src/app/model/datasource.model.ts
src/app/form.model.ts	src/app/model/form.model.ts
src/app/limit.formvalidator.ts	src/app/model/limit.formvalidator.ts
src/app/product.model.ts	src/app/model/product.model.ts
src/app/repository.model.ts	src/app/model/repository.model.ts

If you try to build the project once you have moved the files, the TypeScript compiler will list a series of compiler errors because some of the key declarable classes are unavailable. I'll deal with these problems shortly.

Creating the Module Definition

The next step is to define a module that brings together the functionality in the files that have been moved to the new folder. I added a file called `model.module.ts` in the `src/app/model` folder and defined the module shown in Listing 21-9.

Listing 21-9. The Contents of the model.module.ts File in the src/app/model Folder

```
import { NgModule } from "@angular/core";
import { SimpleDataSource } from "./datasource.model";
import { Model } from "./repository.model";

@NgModule({
    providers: [Model, SimpleDataSource]
})
export class ModelModule { }
```

This purpose of a feature module is to selectively expose the contents of the module folder to the rest of the application. The `@NgModule` decorator for this module uses only the `providers` property to define class providers for the `Model` and `SimpleDataSource` services. When you use providers in a feature module, they are registered with the root module's injector, which means they are available throughout the application, which is exactly what is required for the data model in the example application.

■ **Tip** A common mistake is to assume that services defined in a module are accessible only to the classes within that module. There is no module scope in Angular. Providers defined by a feature module are used as though they were defined by the root module. Local providers defined by directives and components in the feature module are available to their view and content children even if they are defined in other modules.

Updating the Other Classes in the Application

Moving classes into the `model` folder has broken `import` statements in other parts of the application, which depend on either the `Product` or `ProductFormGroup` class. The next step is to update those `import` statements to point to the new module. There are four affected files: `attr.directive.ts`, `categoryFilter.pipe.ts`, `productForm.component.ts`, and `productTable.component.ts`. Listing 21-10 shows the changes required to the `attr.directive.ts` file.

Listing 21-10. Updating the Import Reference in the attr.directive.ts File in the src/app Folder

```
import { Directive, ElementRef, Attribute, Input,
    SimpleChange, Output, EventEmitter, HostListener, HostBinding }
from "@angular/core";
import { Product } from "./model/product.model";

@Directive({
    selector: "[pa-attr]"
})
export class PaAttrDirective {

    // ...statements omitted for brevity...
}
```

The only change that is required is to update the path used in the `import` statement to reflect the new location of the code file. Listing 21-11 shows the same change applied to the `categoryFilter.pipe.ts` file.

Listing 21-11. Updating the Import Reference in the categoryFilter.pipe.ts File in the src/app Folder

```
import { Pipe } from "@angular/core";
import { Product } from "./model/product.model";

@Pipe({
    name: "filter",
    pure: false
})
export class PaCategoryFilterPipe {

    transform(products: Product[], category: string): Product[] {
        return category == undefined ?
            products : products.filter(p => p.category == category);
    }
}
```

Listing 21-12 updates the `import` statements in the `productForm.component.ts` file.

Listing 21-12. Updating Import Paths in the productForm.component.ts File in the src/app Folder

```
import { Component, Output, EventEmitter, ViewEncapsulation,
    Inject, SkipSelf } from "@angular/core";
import { Product } from "./model/product.model";
import { ProductFormGroup } from "./model/form.model";
import { Model } from "./model/repository.model";
import { VALUE_SERVICE } from "./valueDisplay.directive";

@Component({
    selector: "paProductForm",
    templateUrl: "productForm.component.html",
    viewProviders: [{ provide: VALUE_SERVICE, useValue: "Oranges" }]
})
export class ProductFormComponent {

    // ...statements omitted for brevity...
}
```

Listing 21-13 updates the paths in the final file, `productTable.component.ts`.

Listing 21-13. Updating Import Paths in the productTable.component.ts File in the src/app Folder

```
import { Component, Input, ViewChildren, QueryList } from "@angular/core";
import { Model } from "./model/repository.model";
import { Product } from "./model/product.model";
import { DiscountService } from "./discount.service";

@Component({
    selector: "paProductTable",
    templateUrl: "productTable.component.html"
```

```
})
export class ProductTableComponent {

    // ...statements omitted for brevity...
}
```

USING A JAVASCRIPT MODULE WITH AN ANGULAR MODULE

Creating an Angular module allows related application features to be grouped together but still requires that each one is imported from its own file when it is needed elsewhere in the application, as you have seen in the listings in this section.

You can also define a JavaScript module that exports the public-facing features of the Angular module so they can be accessed with the same kind of import statement that is used for the @angular/core module, for example. To use a JavaScript module, add a file called index.ts in the module folder alongside the TypeScript file that defines the Angular module, which is the src/app/model folder for the examples in this section. For each of the application features that you want to use outside of the application, add an export...from statement, like this:

```
export { ModelModule } from "./model.module";
export { Product } from "./product.model";
export { ProductFormGroup, ProductFormControl } from "./form.model";
export { SimpleDataSource } from "./datasource.model";
export { LimitValidator } from "./limit.formvalidator";
export { Model } from "./repository.model";
```

These statements export the contents of the individual TypeScript files. You can then import the features you require without having to specify individual files, like this:

```
...
import { Component, Output, EventEmitter, ViewEncapsulation,
    Inject, SkipSelf } from "@angular/core";
import { Product, ProductFormGroup, Model } from "./model";
import { VALUE_SERVICE } from "./valueDisplay.directive";
...
```

Using the file name index.ts means that you only have to specify the name of the folder in the import statement, producing a result that is neater and more consistent with the Angular core packages.

That said, I don't use this technique in my own projects. Using an index.ts file means that you have to remember to add every feature to both the Angular and JavaScript modules, which is an extra step that I often forget to do. Instead, I use the approach shown in this chapter and import directly from the files that contain the application's features.

Updating the Root Module

The final step is to update the root module so that the services defined in the feature module are made available throughout the application. Listing 21-14 shows the required changes.

Listing 21-14. Updating the Root Module in the app.module.ts File in the src/app Folder

```
import { NgModule } from "@angular/core";
import { BrowserModule } from "@angular/platform-browser";
import { ProductComponent } from "./component";
import { FormsModule, ReactiveFormsModule } from "@angular/forms";
import { PaAttrDirective } from "./attr.directive";
import { PaModel } from "./twoway.directive";
import { PaStructureDirective } from "./structure.directive";
import { PaIteratorDirective } from "./iterator.directive";
import { PaCellColor } from "./cellColor.directive";
import { PaCellColorSwitcher } from "./cellColorSwitcher.directive";
import { ProductTableComponent } from "./productTable.component";
import { ProductFormComponent } from "./productForm.component";
import { PaAddTaxPipe } from "./addTax.pipe";
import { PaCategoryFilterPipe } from "./categoryFilter.pipe";
import { PaDiscountDisplayComponent } from "./discountDisplay.component";
import { PaDiscountEditorComponent } from "./discountEditor.component";
import { DiscountService } from "./discount.service";
import { PaDiscountPipe } from "./discount.pipe";
import { PaDiscountAmountDirective } from "./discountAmount.directive";
import { ModelModule } from "./model/model.module";
import {
    LogService, LOG_SERVICE, SpecialLogService,
    LogLevel, LOG_LEVEL
} from "./log.service";
import { VALUE_SERVICE, PaDisplayValueDirective } from "./valueDisplay.directive";

@NgModule({
    imports: [BrowserModule, FormsModule, ReactiveFormsModule, ModelModule],
    declarations: [ProductComponent, PaAttrDirective, PaModel,
        PaStructureDirective, PaIteratorDirective,
        PaCellColor, PaCellColorSwitcher, ProductTableComponent,
        ProductFormComponent, PaAddTaxPipe, PaCategoryFilterPipe,
        PaDiscountDisplayComponent, PaDiscountEditorComponent,
        PaDiscountPipe, PaDiscountAmountDirective, PaDisplayValueDirective],
    providers: [DiscountService, LogService,
        { provide: VALUE_SERVICE, useValue: "Apples" }],
    bootstrap: [ProductFormComponent, ProductTableComponent]
})
export class AppModule { }
```

I imported the feature module and added it to the root module's imports list. Since the feature module defines providers for Model and SimpleDataSource, I removed the entries from the root module's providers list and removed the associated import statements.

Once you have saved the changes, you can run ng serve to start the Angular development tools. The application will compile, and the revised root module will provide access to the model service. There are no visible changes to the content displayed in the browser, and the changes are limited to the structure of the project.

Creating a Utility Feature Module

A model module is a good place to start because it demonstrates the basic structure of a feature module and how it relates to the root module. The impact on the application was slight, however, and not a great deal of simplification was achieved.

The next step up in complexity is a utility feature module, which groups together all of the common functionality in the application, such as pipes and directives. In a real project, you might be more selective about how you group these types of building block together so that there are several modules, each containing similar functionality. For the example application, I am going to move all of the pipes, directives, and services into a single module.

Creating the Module Folder and Moving the Files

As with the previous module, the first step is to create the folder. For this module, I created a folder called `src/app/common`. Run the following commands in the `example` folder to move the TypeScript files for the pipes and directives:

```
mv src/app/*.pipe.ts src/app/common/
mv src/app/*.directive.ts src/app/common/
```

These commands should work in Windows PowerShell, Linux, and macOS. Some of the directives and pipes in the application rely on the `DiscountService` and `LogServices` classes, which is provided to them through dependency injection. Run the following command in the `example` folder to move the TypeScript file for the service into the module folder:

```
mv src/app/*.service.ts src/app/common/
```

The result is that the files listed in Table 21-6 are moved to the `common` module folder.

Table 21-6. *The File Moves Required for the Module*

File	New Location
app/addTax.pipe.ts	app/common/addTax.pipe.ts
app/attr.directive.ts	app/common/attr.directive.ts
app/categoryFilter.pipe.ts	app/common/categoryFilter.pipe.ts
app/cellColor.directive.ts	app/common/cellColor.directive.ts
app/cellColorSwitcher.directive.ts	app/common/cellColorSwitcher.directive.ts
app/discount.pipe.ts	app/common/discount.pipe.ts
app/discountAmount.directive.ts	app/common/discountAmount.directive.ts
app/iterator.directive.ts	app/common/iterator.directive.ts
app/structure.directive.ts	app/common/structure.directive.ts
app/twoway.directive.ts	app/common/twoway.directive.ts
app/valueDisplay.directive.ts	app/common/valueDisplay.directive.ts
app/discount.service.ts	app/common/discount.service.ts
app/log.service.ts	app/common/log.service.ts

Updating the Classes in the New Module

Some of the classes that have been moved into the new folder have import statements that have to be updated to reflect the new path to the model module. Listing 21-15 shows the change required to the attr.directive.ts file.

Listing 21-15. Updating the Imports in the attr.directive.ts File in the src/app/common Folder

```
import {
    Directive, ElementRef, Attribute, Input,
    SimpleChange, Output, EventEmitter, HostListener, HostBinding
}
    from "@angular/core";
import { Product } from "../model/product.model";

@Directive({
    selector: "[pa-attr]"
})
export class PaAttrDirective {

    // ...statements omitted for brevity...
}
```

Listing 21-16 shows the corresponding change to the categoryFilter.pipe.ts file.

Listing 21-16. Updating the Imports in the categoryFilter.pipe.ts File in the src/app/common Folder

```
import { Pipe } from "@angular/core";
import { Product } from "../model/product.model";

@Pipe({
    name: "filter",
    pure: false
})
export class PaCategoryFilterPipe {

    transform(products: Product[], category: string): Product[] {
        return category == undefined ?
            products : products.filter(p => p.category == category);
    }
}
```

Creating the Module Definition

The next step is to define a module that brings together the functionality in the files that have been moved to the new folder. I added a file called common.module.ts in the src/app/common folder and defined the module shown in Listing 21-17.

Listing 21-17. The Contents of the common.module.ts File in the src/app/common Folder

```
import { NgModule } from "@angular/core";
import { PaAddTaxPipe } from "./addTax.pipe";
import { PaAttrDirective } from "./attr.directive";
import { PaCategoryFilterPipe } from "./categoryFilter.pipe";
import { PaCellColor } from "./cellColor.directive";
import { PaCellColorSwitcher } from "./cellColorSwitcher.directive";
import { PaDiscountPipe } from "./discount.pipe";
import { PaDiscountAmountDirective } from "./discountAmount.directive";
import { PaIteratorDirective } from "./iterator.directive";
import { PaStructureDirective } from "./structure.directive";
import { PaModel } from "./twoway.directive";
import { VALUE_SERVICE, PaDisplayValueDirective} from "./valueDisplay.directive";
import { DiscountService } from "./discount.service";
import { LogService } from "./log.service";
import { ModelModule } from "../model/model.module";

@NgModule({
    imports: [ModelModule],
    providers: [LogService, DiscountService,
        { provide: VALUE_SERVICE, useValue: "Apples" }],
    declarations: [PaAddTaxPipe, PaAttrDirective, PaCategoryFilterPipe,
        PaCellColor, PaCellColorSwitcher, PaDiscountPipe,
        PaDiscountAmountDirective, PaIteratorDirective, PaStructureDirective,
        PaModel, PaDisplayValueDirective],
    exports: [PaAddTaxPipe, PaAttrDirective, PaCategoryFilterPipe,
        PaCellColor, PaCellColorSwitcher, PaDiscountPipe,
        PaDiscountAmountDirective, PaIteratorDirective, PaStructureDirective,
        PaModel, PaDisplayValueDirective]
})
export class CommonModule { }
```

This is a more complex module than the one required for the data model. In the sections that follow, I describe the values that are used for each of the decorator's properties.

Understanding the Imports

Some of the directives and pipes in the module depend on the services defined in the model module, created earlier in this chapter. To ensure that the features in that module are available, I have added to the common module's imports property.

Understanding the Providers

The providers property ensures that the services that the directives and pipes in the feature module have access to the services they require. This means adding class providers to create LogService and DiscountService services, which will be added to the root module's providers when the module is loaded. Not only will the services be available to the directives and pipes in the common module; they will also be available throughout the application.

Understanding the Declarations

The declarations property is used to provide Angular with a list of the directives and pipes (and components, if there are any) in the module. In a feature module, this property has two purposes: it enables the declarable classes for use in any templates contained within the module, and it allows a module to make those declarable classes available outside of the module. I create a module that contains template content later in this chapter, but for this module, the value of the declarations property is that it must be used in order to prepare for the exports property, described in the next section.

Understanding the Exports

For a module that contains directives and pipes intended for use elsewhere in the application, the exports property is the most important in the @NgModule decorator because it defines the set of directives, components, and pipes that the module provides for use when it is imported elsewhere in the application. The exports property can contain individual classes and module types, although both must already be listed in the declarations or imports property. When the module is imported, the types listed behave as though they had been added to the importing module's declarations property.

Updating the Other Classes in the Application

Now that the module has been defined, I can update the other files in the application that contain import statements for the types that are now part of the common module. Listing 21-18 shows the changes required to the discountDisplay.component.ts file.

Listing 21-18. Updating the Import in the discountDisplay.component.ts File in the src/app Folder

```
import { Component, Input } from "@angular/core";
import { DiscountService } from "./common/discount.service";

@Component({
    selector: "paDiscountDisplay",
    template: `<div class="bg-info p-2">
                The discount is {{discounter.discount}}
            </div>`
})
export class PaDiscountDisplayComponent {

    constructor(private discounter: DiscountService) { }
}
```

Listing 21-19 shows the changes to the discountEditor.component.ts file.

Listing 21-19. Updating the Import Reference in the discountEditor.component.ts File in the src/app Folder

```
import { Component, Input } from "@angular/core";
import { DiscountService } from "./common/discount.service";

@Component({
    selector: "paDiscountEditor",
    template: `<div class="form-group">
                    <label>Discount</label>
```

```
                    <input [(ngModel)]="discounter.discount"
                        class="form-control" type="number" />
                </div>`
})
export class PaDiscountEditorComponent {

    constructor(private discounter: DiscountService) { }
}
```

Listing 21-20 shows the changes to the productForm.component.ts file.

Listing 21-20. Updating the Import Reference in the productForm.component.ts File in the src/app Folder

```
import { Component, Output, EventEmitter, ViewEncapsulation,
    Inject, SkipSelf } from "@angular/core";
import { Product } from "./model/product.model";
import { ProductFormGroup } from "./model/form.model";
import { Model } from "./model/repository.model";
import { VALUE_SERVICE } from "./common/valueDisplay.directive";

@Component({
    selector: "paProductForm",
    templateUrl: "app/productForm.component.html",
    viewProviders: [{ provide: VALUE_SERVICE, useValue: "Oranges" }]
})
export class ProductFormComponent {

    // ...statements omitted for brevity...
}
```

The final change is to the productTable.component.ts file, as shown in Listing 21-21.

Listing 21-21. Updating the Import Reference in the productTable.component.ts File in the src/app Folder

```
import { Component, Input, ViewChildren, QueryList } from "@angular/core";
import { Model } from "./model/repository.model";
import { Product } from "./model/product.model";
import { DiscountService } from "./common/discount.service";
import { LogService } from "./common/log.service";

@Component({
    selector: "paProductTable",
    templateUrl: "app/productTable.component.html",
    providers:[LogService]
})
export class ProductTableComponent {

    // ...statements omitted for brevity...
}
```

Updating the Root Module

The final step is to update the root module so that it loads the common module to provide access to the directives and pipes it contains, as shown in Listing 21-22.

Listing 21-22. Importing a Feature Module in the app.module.ts File in the src/app Folder

```
import { NgModule } from "@angular/core";
import { BrowserModule } from "@angular/platform-browser";
import { ProductComponent } from "./component";
import { FormsModule, ReactiveFormsModule } from "@angular/forms";
import { ProductTableComponent } from "./productTable.component";
import { ProductFormComponent } from "./productForm.component";
import { PaDiscountDisplayComponent } from "./discountDisplay.component";
import { PaDiscountEditorComponent } from "./discountEditor.component";
import { ModelModule } from "./model/model.module";
import { CommonModule } from "./common/common.module";

@NgModule({
    imports: [BrowserModule, FormsModule, ReactiveFormsModule,
        ModelModule, CommonModule],
    declarations: [ProductComponent, ProductTableComponent,
        ProductFormComponent, PaDiscountDisplayComponent, PaDiscountEditorComponent],
    bootstrap: [ProductFormComponent, ProductTableComponent]
})
export class AppModule { }
```

The root module has been substantially simplified with the creation of the common module, which has been added to the imports list. All of the individual classes for directives and pipes have been removed from the declarations list, and their associated import statements have been removed from the file. When common module is imported, all of the types listed in its exports property will be added to the root module's declarations property.

Once you have saved the changes in this section, you can run the ng serve command to start the Angular development tools. Once again, there is no visible change in the content presented to the user, and the differences are all in the structure of the application.

Creating a Feature Module with Components

The final module that I am going to create will contain the application's components. The process for creating the module is the same as in the previous examples, as described in the sections that follow.

Creating the Module Folder and Moving the Files

The module will be called components, and I created a src/app/components to contain the files. Run the following commands in the example folder to move the directive TypeScript, HTML, and CSS files into the new folder and to delete the corresponding JavaScript files:

```
mv src/app/*.component.ts src/app/components/
mv src/app/*.component.html src/app/components/
mv src/app/*.component.css src/app/components/
```

The result of these commands is that the component code files, templates, and style sheets are moved into the new folder, as listed in Table 21-7.

Table 21-7. *The File Moves Required for the Component Module*

File	New Location
src/app/app.component.ts	src/app/component/app.component.ts
src/app/app.component.html	src/app/component/app.component.html
src/app/app.component.css	src/app/component/app.component.css
src/app /discountDisplay.component.ts	src/app/component /discountDisplay.component.ts
src/app/discountEditor.component.ts	src/app/component/discountEditor.component.ts
src/app/productForm.component.ts	src/app/component/productForm.component.ts
src/app/productForm.component.html	src/app/component/productForm.component.html
src/app/productForm.component.css	src/app/component/productForm.component.css
src/app/productTable.component.ts	src/app/component/productTable.component.ts
src/app/productTable.component.html	src/app/component/productTable.component.html
src/app/productTable.component.css	src/app/component/productTable.component.css
src/app/toggleView.component.ts	src/app/component/toggleView.component.ts
src/app/toggleView.component.html	src/app/component/toggleView.component.ts

Creating the Module Definition

To create the module, I added a file called components.module.ts to the src/app/components folder and added the statements shown in Listing 21-23.

Listing 21-23. The Contents of the components.module.ts File in the src/app/components Folder

```
import { NgModule } from "@angular/core";
import { BrowserModule } from "@angular/platform-browser";
import { CommonModule } from "../common/common.module";
import { FormsModule, ReactiveFormsModule } from "@angular/forms"
import { PaDiscountDisplayComponent } from "./discountDisplay.component";
import { PaDiscountEditorComponent } from "./discountEditor.component";
import { ProductFormComponent } from "./productForm.component";
import { ProductTableComponent } from "./productTable.component";

@NgModule({
    imports: [BrowserModule, FormsModule, ReactiveFormsModule, CommonModule],
    declarations: [PaDiscountDisplayComponent, PaDiscountEditorComponent,
        ProductFormComponent, ProductTableComponent],
    exports: [ProductFormComponent, ProductTableComponent]
})
export class ComponentsModule { }
```

This module imports BrowserModule and CommonModule to ensure that the directives have access to the services and the declarable classes they require. It exports the ProductFormComponent and ProductTableComponent, which are the two components used in the root component's bootstrap property. The other components are private to the module.

Updating the Other Classes

Moving the TypeScript files into the components folder requires some changes to the paths in the import statements. Listing 21-24 shows the change required for the discountDisplay.component.ts file.

Listing 21-24. Updating a Path in the discountDisplay.component.ts File in the src/app/component Folder

```
import { Component, Input } from "@angular/core";
import { DiscountService } from "../common/discount.service";

@Component({
  selector: "paDiscountDisplay",
  template: `<div class="bg-info text-white p-2">
                The discount is {{discounter.discount}}
             </div>`
})
export class PaDiscountDisplayComponent {

  constructor(private discounter: DiscountService) { }
}
```

Listing 21-25 shows the change required to the discountEditor.component.ts file.

Listing 21-25. Updating a Path in the discountEditor.component.ts File in the src/app/component Folder

```
import { Component, Input } from "@angular/core";
import { DiscountService } from "../common/discount.service";

@Component({
  selector: "paDiscountEditor",
  template: `<div class="form-group">
                <label>Discount</label>
                <input [(ngModel)]="discounter.discount"
                    class="form-control" type="number" />
             </div>`
})
export class PaDiscountEditorComponent {

  constructor(private discounter: DiscountService) { }
}
```

Listing 21-26 shows the changes required for the `productForm.component.ts` file.

Listing 21-26. Updating a Path in the productForm.component.ts File in the src/app/component Folder

```
import {
  Component, Output, EventEmitter, ViewEncapsulation,
  Inject, SkipSelf
} from "@angular/core";
import { Product } from "../model/product.model";
import { ProductFormGroup } from "../model/form.model";
import { Model } from "../model/repository.model";
import { VALUE_SERVICE } from "../common/valueDisplay.directive";

@Component({
  selector: "paProductForm",
  templateUrl: "productForm.component.html",
  viewProviders: [{ provide: VALUE_SERVICE, useValue: "Oranges" }]
})
export class ProductFormComponent {
  form: ProductFormGroup = new ProductFormGroup();
  newProduct: Product = new Product();
  formSubmitted: boolean = false;

  constructor(private model: Model,
    @Inject(VALUE_SERVICE) @SkipSelf() private serviceValue: string) {
    console.log("Service Value: " + serviceValue);
  }

  submitForm(form: any) {
    this.formSubmitted = true;
    if (form.valid) {
      this.model.saveProduct(this.newProduct);
      this.newProduct = new Product();
      this.form.reset();
      this.formSubmitted = false;
    }
  }
}
```

Listing 21-27 shows the changes required to the `productTable.component.ts` file.

Listing 21-27. Updating a Path in the productTable.component.ts File in the src/app/component Folder

```
import { Component, Input } from "@angular/core";
import { Model } from "../model/repository.model";
import { Product } from "../model/product.model";
import { DiscountService } from "../common/discount.service";
import { LogService } from "../common/log.service";

@Component({
  selector: "paProductTable",
  templateUrl: "productTable.component.html",
  providers:[LogService]
})
```

548

```
export class ProductTableComponent {

  constructor(private dataModel: Model) { }

  getProduct(key: number): Product {
    return this.dataModel.getProduct(key);
  }

  getProducts(): Product[] {
    return this.dataModel.getProducts();
  }

  deleteProduct(key: number) {
    this.dataModel.deleteProduct(key);
  }

  dateObject: Date = new Date(2020, 1, 20);
  dateString: string = "2020-02-20T00:00:00.000Z";
  dateNumber: number = 1582156800000;
}
```

Updating the Root Module

The final step is to update the root module to remove the outdated references to the individual files and to import the new module, as shown in Listing 21-28.

Listing 21-28. Importing a Feature Module in the app.module.ts File in the src/app Folder

```
import { NgModule } from "@angular/core";
import { BrowserModule } from "@angular/platform-browser";
import { ProductComponent } from "./component";
import { FormsModule, ReactiveFormsModule } from "@angular/forms";
import { ProductTableComponent } from "./components/productTable.component";
import { ProductFormComponent } from "./components/productForm.component";
import { ModelModule } from "./model/model.module";
import { CommonModule } from "./common/common.module";
import { ComponentsModule } from "./components/components.module";

@NgModule({
    imports: [BrowserModule, FormsModule, ReactiveFormsModule,
        ModelModule, CommonModule, ComponentsModule],
    bootstrap: [ProductFormComponent, ProductTableComponent]
})
export class AppModule { }
```

Adding modules to the application has radically simplified the root module and allows related features to be defined in self-contained blocks, which can be extended or modified in relative isolation from the rest of the application.

Summary

In this chapter, I described in the last of the Angular building blocks: modules. I explained the role of the root module and demonstrated how to create feature modules in order to add structure to an application. In the next part of the book, I describe the features that Angular provides to shape the building blocks into complex and responsive applications.

PART III

Advanced Angular Features

CHAPTER 22

Creating the Example Project

Throughout the chapters in the previous part of the book, I added classes and content to the example project to demonstrate different Angular features and then, in Chapter 21, introduced feature modules to add some structure to the project. The result is a project with a lot of redundant and unused functionality, and for this part of the book, I am going to start a new project that takes some of the core features from earlier chapters and provides a clean foundation on which to build in the chapters that follow.

■ **Tip** You can download the example project for this chapter—and for all the other chapters in this book—from https://github.com/Apress/pro-angular-6.

Starting the Example Project

To create the project and populate it with tools and placeholder content, open a new command prompt, navigate to a convenient location, and run the following command:

```
ng new exampleApp
```

To distinguish the project used in this part of the book from earlier examples, I created a project called exampleApp. The project initialization process will take a while to complete as all of the required packages are downloaded.

Adding and Configuring the Bootstrap CSS Package

I continue to use the Bootstrap CSS framework to style the HTML elements in this chapter and the rest of the book. Run the following commands to navigate to the exampleApp folder and add the Bootstrap package to the project:

```
cd exampleApp
npm install bootstrap@4.1.1
```

Add the line shown in Listing 22-1 to the angular.json file to include the Bootstrap CSS styles in the bundles that are prepared by the Angular development tools.

© Adam Freeman 2018

A. Freeman, *Pro Angular 6*, https://doi.org/10.1007/978-1-4842-3649-9_22

Listing 22-1. Configuring a CSS File in the angular.json File in the exampleApp Folder

```
...
"styles": [
    "styles.css",
    "node_modules/bootstrap/dist/css/bootstrap.min.css"
],
...
```

Creating the Project Structure

To prepare for the contents of the example application, I added a series of subfolders that will be used to contain the application code and some feature modules, as listed in Table 22-1.

Table 22-1. *The Folders Created for the Example Application*

Name	Description
src/app/model	This folder will contain a feature module containing the data model.
src/app/core	This folder will contain a feature module containing components that provide the core features of the application.
src/app/messages	This folder will contain a feature module that is used to display messages and errors to the user.

Creating the Model Module

The first feature module will contain the project's data model, which is similar to the one used in Part 2, although it won't contain the form validation logic, which will be handled elsewhere.

Creating the Product Data Type

To define the basic data type around which the application is based, I added a file called `product.model.ts` to the `src/app/model` folder and defined the class shown in Listing 22-2.

Listing 22-2. The product.model.ts File in the src/app/model Folder

```
export class Product {

    constructor(public id?: number,
                public name?: string,
                public category?: string,
                public price?: number) {}
}
```

Creating the Data Source and Repository

To provide the application with some initial data, I created a file called `static.datasource.ts` in the `src/app/model` folder and defined the service shown in Listing 22-3. This class will be used as the data source until Chapter 24, where I explain how to use asynchronous HTTP requests to request data from web services.

■ **Tip**   I am more relaxed about following the name conventions for Angular files when creating files within a feature module, especially if the purpose of the module is obvious from its name.

Listing 22-3. The static.datasource.ts File in the src/app/model Folder

```
import { Injectable } from "@angular/core";
import { Product } from "./product.model";

@Injectable()
export class StaticDataSource {
    private data: Product[];

    constructor() {
        this.data = new Array<Product>(
            new Product(1, "Kayak", "Watersports", 275),
            new Product(2, "Lifejacket", "Watersports", 48.95),
            new Product(3, "Soccer Ball", "Soccer", 19.50),
            new Product(4, "Corner Flags", "Soccer", 34.95),
            new Product(5, "Thinking Cap", "Chess", 16));
    }

    getData(): Product[] {
        return this.data;
    }
}
```

The next step is to define the repository, through which the rest of the application will access the model data. I created a file called `repository.model.ts` in the `src/app/model` folder and used it to define the class shown in Listing 22-4.

Listing 22-4. The repository.model.ts File in the src/app/model Folder

```
import { Injectable } from "@angular/core";
import { Product } from "./product.model";
import { StaticDataSource } from "./static.datasource";

@Injectable()
export class Model {
    private products: Product[];
    private locator = (p: Product, id: number) => p.id == id;

    constructor(private dataSource: StaticDataSource) {
        this.products = new Array<Product>();
        this.dataSource.getData().forEach(p => this.products.push(p));
    }

    getProducts(): Product[] {
        return this.products;
    }
```

```
    getProduct(id: number): Product {
        return this.products.find(p => this.locator(p, id));
    }

    saveProduct(product: Product) {
        if (product.id == 0 || product.id == null) {
            product.id = this.generateID();
            this.products.push(product);
        } else {
            let index = this.products
                .findIndex(p => this.locator(p, product.id));
            this.products.splice(index, 1, product);
        }
    }

    deleteProduct(id: number) {
        let index = this.products.findIndex(p => this.locator(p, id));
        if (index > -1) {
            this.products.splice(index, 1);
        }
    }

    private generateID(): number {
        let candidate = 100;
        while (this.getProduct(candidate) != null) {
            candidate++;
        }
        return candidate;
    }
}
```

Completing the Model Module

To complete the data model, I need to define the module. I created a file called model.module.ts in the src/app/model folder and used it to define the Angular module shown in Listing 22-5.

Listing 22-5. The Contents of the model.module.ts File in the src/app/model Folder

```
import { NgModule } from "@angular/core";
import { StaticDataSource } from "./static.datasource";
import { Model } from "./repository.model";

@NgModule({
    providers: [Model, StaticDataSource]
})
export class ModelModule { }
```

Creating the Core Module

The core module will contain the central functionality of the application, built on features that were described in Part 2, presenting the user with a list of the products in the model and the ability to create and edit them.

Creating the Shared State Service

To help the components in this module to collaborate, I am going to add a service that records the current mode, noting whether the user is editing or creating a product. I added a file called `sharedState.model.ts` to the `src/app/core` folder and defined the enum and class shown in Listing 22-6.

■ **Tip** I used the `model.ts` file name, rather than `service.ts`, because the role of this class will change in a later chapter. Bear with me for the moment, even though I am breaking the naming convention.

Listing 22-6. The Contents of the sharedState.model.ts File in the src/app/core Folder

```
export enum MODES {
    CREATE, EDIT
}

export class SharedState {
    mode: MODES = MODES.EDIT;
    id: number;
}
```

The `SharedState` class contains two properties that reflect the current mode and the ID of the data model object that is being operated on.

Creating the Table Component

This component will present the user with the table that lists all the products in the application and that will be the main focal point in the application, providing access to other areas of functionality through buttons that allow objects to be created, edited, or deleted. Listing 22-7 shows the contents of the `table.component.ts` file, which I created in the `src/app/core` folder.

Listing 22-7. The Contents of the table.component.ts File in the src/app/core Folder

```
import { Component } from "@angular/core";
import { Product } from "../model/product.model";
import { Model } from "../model/repository.model";
import { MODES, SharedState } from "./sharedState.model";

@Component({
    selector: "paTable",
    templateUrl: "table.component.html"
})
```

```
export class TableComponent {

    constructor(private model: Model, private state: SharedState) { }

    getProduct(key: number): Product {
        return this.model.getProduct(key);
    }

    getProducts(): Product[] {
        return this.model.getProducts();
    }

    deleteProduct(key: number) {
        this.model.deleteProduct(key);
    }

    editProduct(key: number) {
        this.state.id = key;
        this.state.mode = MODES.EDIT;
    }

    createProduct() {
        this.state.id = undefined;
        this.state.mode = MODES.CREATE;
    }
}
```

This component provides the same basic functionality used in Part 2, with the addition of the editProduct and createProduct methods. These methods update the shared state service when the user wants to edit or create a product.

Creating the Table Component Template

To provide the table component with a template, I added an HTML file called table.component.html to the src/app/core folder and added the markup shown in Listing 22-8.

Listing 22-8. The table.component.html File in the src/app/core Folder

```
<table class="table table-sm table-bordered table-striped">
    <tr>
        <th>ID</th><th>Name</th><th>Category</th><th>Price</th><th></th>
    </tr>
    <tr *ngFor="let item of getProducts()">
        <td style="vertical-align:middle">{{item.id}}</td>
        <td style="vertical-align:middle">{{item.name}}</td>
        <td style="vertical-align:middle">{{item.category}}</td>
        <td style="vertical-align:middle">
            {{item.price | currency:"USD" }}
        </td>
        <td class="text-center">
```

```
            <button class="btn btn-danger btn-sm" (click)="deleteProduct(item.id)">
                Delete
            </button>
            <button class="btn btn-warning btn-sm" (click)="editProduct(item.id)">
                Edit
            </button>
        </td>
    </tr>
</table>
<button class="btn btn-primary m-1" (click)="createProduct()">
    Create New Product
</button>
```

This template uses the ngFor directive to create rows in a table for each product in the data model, including buttons that call the deleteProduct and editProduct methods. There is also a button element outside of the table that calls the component's createProduct method when it is clicked.

Creating the Form Component

For this project, I am going to create a form component that will manage an HTML form that will allow new products to be created and allow existing products to be modified. To define the component, I added a file called form.component.ts to the src/app/core folder and added the code shown in Listing 22-9.

Listing 22-9. The Contents of the form.component.ts File in the src/app/core Folder

```
import { Component } from "@angular/core";
import { NgForm } from "@angular/forms";
import { Product } from "../model/product.model";
import { Model } from "../model/repository.model"
import { MODES, SharedState } from "./sharedState.model";

@Component({
    selector: "paForm",
    templateUrl: "form.component.html",
    styleUrls: ["form.component.css"]
})
export class FormComponent {
    product: Product = new Product();

    constructor(private model: Model,
            private state: SharedState) { }

    get editing(): boolean {
        return this.state.mode == MODES.EDIT;
    }

    submitForm(form: NgForm) {
        if (form.valid) {
            this.model.saveProduct(this.product);
            this.product = new Product();
            form.reset();
```

```
        }
    }

    resetForm() {
        this.product = new Product();
    }
}
```

The same component and form will be used to create new products and edit existing ones, so there is some additional functionality compared with the equivalent component from Part 2. The editing property will be used in the view to signal the current setting of the shared state service. The resetForm method is the other new addition and resets the object used to provide data values to the form. The submitForm method hasn't changed and relies on the data model to determine whether the object passed to the saveProduct method is a new addition to the model or a replacement for an existing object.

Creating the Form Component Template

To provide the component with a template, I added an HTML file called form.component.html to the src/app/core folder and added the markup shown in Listing 22-10.

Listing 22-10. The form.component.html File in the src/app/core Folder

```html
<div class="bg-primary text-white p-2" [class.bg-warning]="editing">
    <h5>{{editing  ? "Edit" : "Create"}} Product</h5>
</div>

<form novalidate #form="ngForm" (ngSubmit)="submitForm(form)" (reset)="resetForm()" >

    <div class="form-group">
        <label>Name</label>
        <input class="form-control" name="name"
            [(ngModel)]="product.name" required />
    </div>

    <div class="form-group">
        <label>Category</label>
        <input class="form-control" name="category"
            [(ngModel)]="product.category" required />
    </div>

    <div class="form-group">
        <label>Price</label>
        <input class="form-control" name="price"
            [(ngModel)]="product.price"
            required pattern="^[0-9\.]+$" />
    </div>

    <button type="submit" class="btn btn-primary m-1"
            [class.btn-warning]="editing" [disabled]="form.invalid">
        {{editing ? "Save" : "Create"}}
```

```
    </button>
    <button type="reset" class="btn btn-secondary m-1">Cancel</button>
</form>
```

The most important part of this template is the form element, which contains input elements for the name, category, and price properties required to create or edit a product. The header at the top of the template and the submit button for the form change their content and appearance based on the editing mode to distinguish between different operations.

Creating the Form Component Styles

To keep the example simple, I have used the basic form validation without any error messages. Instead, I rely on CSS styles that are applied using the Angular validation classes. I added a file called form.component.css to the src/app/core folder and defined the styles shown in Listing 22-11.

Listing 22-11. The form.component.css File in the src/app/core Folder

```
input.ng-dirty.ng-invalid { border: 2px solid #ff0000 }
input.ng-dirty.ng-valid { border: 2px solid #6bc502 }
```

Completing the Core Module

To define the module that contains the components, I added a file called core.module.ts to the src/app/core folder and created the Angular module shown in Listing 22-12.

Listing 22-12. The core.module.ts File in the src/app/core Folder

```
import { NgModule } from "@angular/core";
import { BrowserModule } from "@angular/platform-browser";
import { FormsModule } from "@angular/forms";
import { ModelModule } from "../model/model.module";
import { TableComponent } from "./table.component";
import { FormComponent } from "./form.component";
import { SharedState } from "./sharedState.model";

@NgModule({
    imports: [BrowserModule, FormsModule, ModelModule],
    declarations: [TableComponent, FormComponent],
    exports: [ModelModule, TableComponent, FormComponent],
    providers: [SharedState]
})
export class CoreModule { }
```

This module imports the core Angular functionality, the Angular forms features, and the application's data model, created earlier in the chapter. It also sets up a provider for the SharedState service.

Creating the Messages Module

The messages module will contain a service that is used to report messages or errors that should be displayed to the user and a component that presents them. This is functionality that will be required throughout the application and doesn't really belong in either of the other two modules.

Creating the Message Model and Service

To represent messages that should be displayed to the user, I added a file called message.model.ts to the src/app/messages folder and added the code shown in Listing 22-13.

Listing 22-13. The Contents of the message.model.ts File in the src/app/messages Folder

```
export class Message {

    constructor(private text: string,
        private error: boolean = false) { }
}
```

The Message class defines properties that present the text that will be displayed to the user and whether the message represents an error. Next, I created a file called message.service.ts in the src/app/messages folder and used it to define the service shown in Listing 22-14, which will be used to register messages that should be displayed to the user.

Listing 22-14. The Contents of the message.service.ts File in the src/app/messages Folder

```
import { Injectable } from "@angular/core";
import { Message } from "./message.model";

@Injectable()
export class MessageService {
    private handler: (m: Message) => void;

    reportMessage(msg: Message) {
        if (this.handler != null) {
            this.handler(msg);
        }
    }

    registerMessageHandler(handler: (m: Message) => void) {
        this.handler = handler;
    }
}
```

This service acts as a broker between the parts of the application that generate error messages and those that need to receive them. I'll improve the way that this service works in Chapter 23 when I introduce features from the Reactive Extensions package.

Creating the Component and Template

Now that I have a source of messages, I can create a component that will display them to the user. I added a file called message.component.ts to the src/app/messages folder and defined the component shown in Listing 22-15.

Listing 22-15. The message.component.ts File in the src/app/messages Folder

```
import { Component } from "@angular/core";
import { MessageService } from "./message.service";
import { Message } from "./message.model";

@Component({
    selector: "paMessages",
    templateUrl: "message.component.html",
})
export class MessageComponent {
    lastMessage: Message;

    constructor(messageService: MessageService) {
        messageService.registerMessageHandler(m => this.lastMessage = m);
    }
}
```

The component receives a MessageService object as its constructor argument and uses it to register a handler function that will be invoked when a message is received by the service, assigning the most recent message to a property called lastMessage. To provide a template for the component, I created a file called message.component.html in the src/app/messages folder and added the markup shown in Listing 22-16, which displays the message to the user.

Listing 22-16. The message.component.html File in the src/app/messages Folder

```
<div *ngIf="lastMessage"
    class="bg-info text-white p-2 text-center"
    [class.bg-danger]="lastMessage.error">
        <h4>{{lastMessage.text}}</h4>
</div>
```

Completing the Message Module

I added a file called message.module.ts in the src/app/messages folder and defined the module shown in Listing 22-17.

Listing 22-17. The message.module.ts File in the src/app/messages Folder

```
import { NgModule } from "@angular/core";
import { BrowserModule } from "@angular/platform-browser";
import { MessageComponent } from "./message.component";
import { MessageService } from "./message.service";
```

```
@NgModule({
    imports: [BrowserModule],
    declarations: [MessageComponent],
    exports: [MessageComponent],
    providers: [MessageService]
})
export class MessageModule { }
```

Completing the Project

To bring all of the different modules together, I made the changes shown in Listing 22-18 to the root module.

Listing 22-18. Configuring the Application in the app.module.ts File in the src/app Folder

```
import { BrowserModule } from '@angular/platform-browser';
import { NgModule } from '@angular/core';
//import { AppComponent } from './app.component';
import { ModelModule } from "./model/model.module";
import { CoreModule } from "./core/core.module";
import { TableComponent } from "./core/table.component";
import { FormComponent } from "./core/form.component";
import { MessageModule } from "./messages/message.module";
import { MessageComponent } from "./messages/message.component";

@NgModule({
  imports: [BrowserModule, ModelModule, CoreModule, MessageModule],
  bootstrap: [TableComponent, FormComponent, MessageComponent]
})
export class AppModule { }
```

The module imports the feature modules created in this chapter and specifies three bootstrap components, two of which were defined in CoreModule and one from MessageModule. These will display the product table and form and any messages or errors.

The final step is to update the HTML file so that it contains elements that will be matched by the selector properties of the bootstrap components, as shown in Listing 22-19.

Listing 22-19. Adding Custom Elements in the index.html File in the src Folder

```
<!doctype html>
<html lang="en">
<head>
  <meta charset="utf-8">
  <title>ExampleApp</title>
  <base href="/">
  <meta name="viewport" content="width=device-width, initial-scale=1">
  <link rel="icon" type="image/x-icon" href="favicon.ico">
</head>
```

```
<body class="m-2">
  <paMessages></paMessages>
  <div class="row m-2">
    <div class="col-8 p-2">
      <paTable></paTable>
    </div>
    <div class="col-4 p-2">
      <paForm></paForm>
    </div>
  </div>
</body>
</html>
```

Run the following command in the exampleApp to start the Angular development tools and build the project:

```
ng serve
```

Once the initial build process has completed, open a new browser window and navigate to http://localhost:4200 to see the content shown in Figure 22-1.

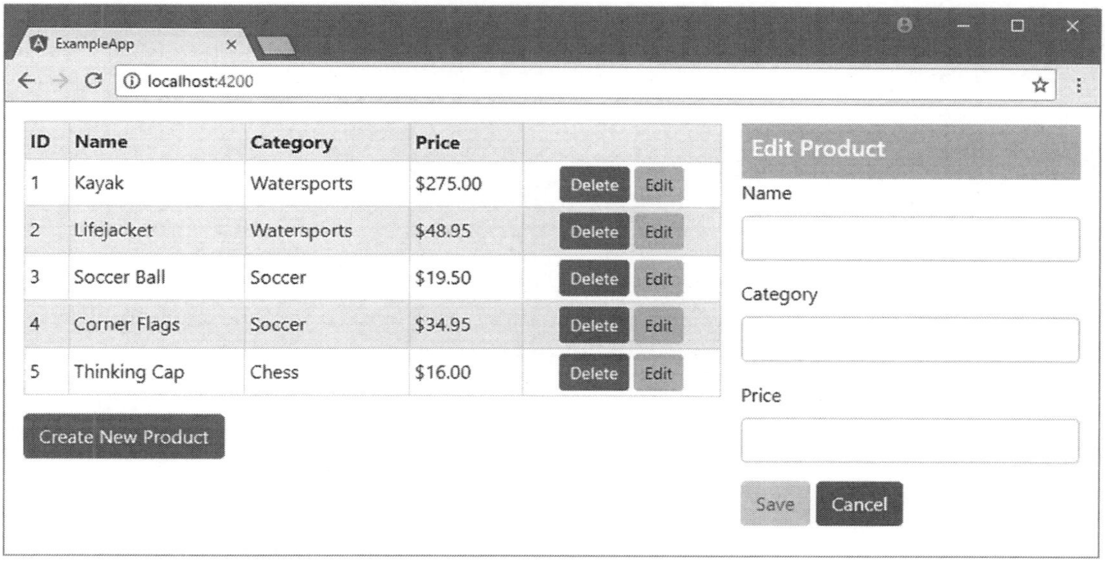

Figure 22-1. *Running the example application*

Not everything in the example application works at the moment. You can toggle between the two modes of operation by clicking the Create New Product and Edit buttons, but the editing function doesn't work. I complete the core functionality and add new features in the chapters that follow.

Summary

In this chapter, I created the example project that I will use in this part of the book. The basic structure is the same as the example used in earlier chapters but without the redundant code and markup that I used to demonstrate earlier features. In the next chapter, I introduce the Reactive Extensions package, which is used to handle updates in Angular applications.

CHAPTER 23

■ ■ ■

Using Reactive Extensions

Angular has a lot of features, but the one that grabs the most attention is the way that changes propagate through the application so that filling in a form field or clicking a button causes immediate updates to the application state. But there are limitations to the changes that Angular can detect, and some features require working directly with the library that Angular uses to distribute updates throughout an application. This library is called *Reactive Extensions*, also known as RxJS.

In this chapter, I explain why working with Reactive Extensions is required for advanced projects, introduce the core Reactive Extensions features (known as Observers and Observables), and use them to enhance the application so that users can edit existing objects in the model, as well as create new ones. Table 23-1 puts Reactive Extensions into context.

■ **Note** The focus of this chapter is on the RxJS features that are most useful in Angular projects. The RxJS package has a lot of features, and if you want more information, you should consult the project home page at https://github.com/reactivex/rxjs.

Table 23-1. *Putting the Reactive Extensions Library in Context*

Question	Answer
What is it?	The Reactive Extensions library provides an asynchronous event distribution mechanism that is used extensively inside Angular for change detection and event propagation.
Why is it useful?	RxJS allows for the parts of an application that are not addressed by the standard Angular change detection process to receive notifications of important events and respond appropriately. Since RxJS is required in order to use Angular, its functionality is readily available for use.
How is it used?	An Observer is created that collects the events and distributes them to subscribers through an Observable. The simplest way to achieve this is to create a Subject, which provides both Observer and Observable functionality. The flow of events to a subscriber can be managed using a set of operators.
Are there any pitfalls or limitations?	Once you have mastered the basics, the RxJS package is easy to use, although there are so many features that it can take some experimentation to find the combination that efficiently achieves a specific outcome.
Are there any alternatives?	RxJS is required to access some Angular features, such as updates to child and view children queries and making asynchronous HTTP requests.

© Adam Freeman 2018
A. Freeman, *Pro Angular 6*, https://doi.org/10.1007/978-1-4842-3649-9_23

Table 23-2 summarizes the chapter.

Table 23-2. *Chapter Summary*

Problem	Solution	Listing
Distribute events in an application	Use Reactive Extensions	1–5
Wait for asynchronous results in a template	Use the async pipe	6–9
Use events to enable collaboration between components	Use `Observable`	10–12
Manage the flow of events	Use operators such as `filter` or `map`	13–18

Preparing the Example Project

This chapter uses the exampleApp project created in Chapter 22. No changes are required for this chapter. Run the following command in the `exampleApp` folder to start the Angular development tools:

```
ng serve
```

Open a new browser tab and navigate to `http://localhost:4200` and show the content illustrated in Figure 23-1.

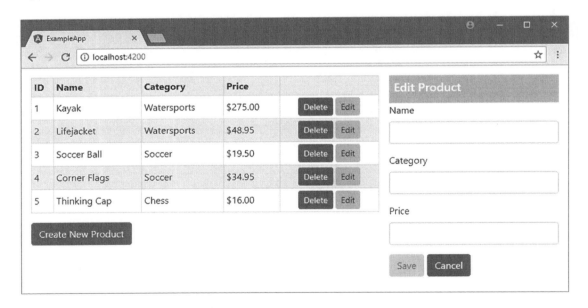

Figure 23-1. *Running the example application*

■ **Tip** You can download the example project for this chapter—and for all the other chapters in this book—from `https://github.com/Apress/pro-angular-6`.

Understanding the Problem

Angular excels at detecting changes in the expressions used for data bindings. It does this seamlessly and efficiently, and the result is a framework that makes it easy to create dynamic applications. You can see the change detection at work in the example application by clicking the Create New Product button. The service that provides the shared state information is updated by the table component, which is then reflected in the data bindings that control the appearance of the elements managed by the form component, as shown in Figure 23-2. When you click the Create New Product button, the color of the title and buttons in the form changes immediately.

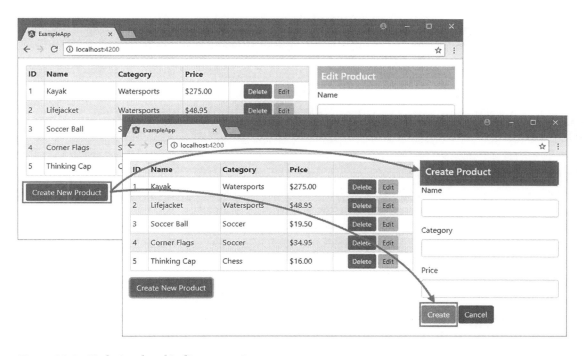

Figure 23-2. *Updating data binding expressions*

As the number of objects in an application increases, change detection can spiral out of control and put an enormous drain on an application's performance, especially on less capable devices such as phones and tablets. Rather than keep track of all the objects in the application, Angular focuses on data bindings and, specifically, on working out when property values change.

That presents a problem because Angular manages the bindings for the HTML elements automatically, but it doesn't provide any support for responding to service changes within the component itself.

You can see an immediate consequence of the lack of change in the component by clicking one of the Edit buttons in the table. Although the data bindings will update immediately, the component doesn't get a notification when the button is clicked and doesn't know it needs to update the property that will populate the form elements for editing.

The lack of updates means that the form component needs to fall back on the ngDoCheck method, originally described in Chapter 15, to determine when an important change occurs, as shown in Listing 23-1.

Listing 23-1. Monitoring Service Changes in the form.component.ts File in the src/app/core Folder

```
import { Component } from "@angular/core";
import { NgForm } from "@angular/forms";
import { Product } from "../model/product.model";
import { Model } from "../model/repository.model"
import { MODES, SharedState } from "./sharedState.model";

@Component({
    selector: "paForm",
    templateUrl: "form.component.html",
    styleUrls: ["form.component.css"]
})
export class FormComponent {
    product: Product = new Product();
    lastId: number;

    constructor(private model: Model,
        private state: SharedState) { }

    get editing(): boolean {
        return this.state.mode == MODES.EDIT;
    }

    submitForm(form: NgForm) {
        if (form.valid) {
            this.model.saveProduct(this.product);
            this.product = new Product();
            form.reset();
        }
    }

    resetForm() {
        this.product = new Product();
    }

    ngDoCheck() {
        if (this.lastId != this.state.id) {
            this.product = new Product();
            if (this.state.mode == MODES.EDIT) {
                Object.assign(this.product, this.model.getProduct(this.state.id));
            }
            this.lastId = this.state.id;
        }
    }
}
```

To see the effect of this change, click one of the Edit buttons in the table, and the form will be populated with the details for editing. When you have finished editing the values in the form, click the Save button, and the data model will be updated, reflecting your changes in the table, as shown in Figure 23-3.

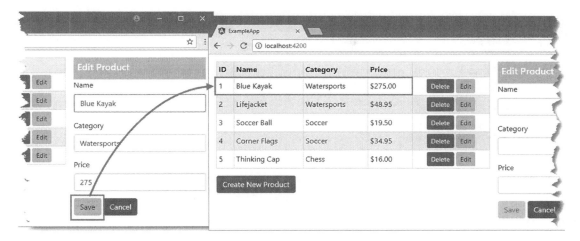

Figure 23-3. *Updating a product*

The problem with this code is that the ngDoCheck method will be called whenever Angular detects any kind of change in the application. It doesn't matter what happens or where it happens: Angular is going to have to call the ngDoCheck method to give the component a chance to update itself. You can minimize the amount of work that is done in the ngDoCheck method, but as the number of directives and components in the application increases, the number of change events and the number of calls to the ngDoCheck method will increase, which can drag down the performance of the application.

It is also harder than you might think to handle change detection correctly. As an example, try editing a product using the example application, clicking the Save button to store the changes in the model, and then clicking the Edit button again for the same product: nothing will happen. This is a common mistake in implementing the ngDoCheck method, which is called even when a change is triggered by the component itself, confusing the checks in the ngDoCheck method that are trying to avoid doing unnecessary work. Overall, this approach is unreliable, is expensive, and doesn't scale well.

Solving the Problem with Reactive Extensions

The reason that the Reactive Extensions library is useful in Angular applications is because it provides a simple and unambiguous system for sending and receiving notifications. It doesn't sound like a huge achievement, but it underpins most of the built-in Angular functionality, and it can be used directly by applications to avoid the problems that come from trying to implement change detection using ngDoCheck. To prepare for the direct use of Reactive Extensions, Listing 23-2 defines an opaque token that will be used to provide a service that uses Reactive Extensions to distribute updates and changes the SharedState class so that it defines a constructor. These changes will temporarily break the application because Angular will not be able to provide values for the SharedState constructor when it tries to instantiate an instance to use as a service. The application will start working again once the changes required for Reactive Extensions are complete.

Listing 23-2. Defining a Provider Token in the sharedState.model.ts File in the src/app/core Folder

```
import { InjectionToken } from "@angular/core";
export enum MODES {
    CREATE, EDIT
}

export class SharedState {

    constructor(public mode: MODES, public id?: number) { }
}

export const SHARED_STATE = new InjectionToken("shared_state");
```

Understanding Observables

The key Reactive Extensions building block is Observable, which represents an observable sequence of events. An object such as a component can subscribe to an Observable and receive a notification each time an event occurs, allowing it to respond only when the event has been observed instead of every time there is a change anywhere in the application.

The basic method provided by an Observable is subscribe, which accepts three functions as arguments, as described in Table 23-3.

Table 23-3. *The Types of Web Forms Code Nuggets*

Name	Description
onNext	This function is invoked when a new event occurs.
onError	This function is invoked when an error occurs.
onCompleted	This function is invoked when the sequence of events ends.

Only the onNext function is required to subscribe to an Observable, although it is generally good practice to implement the others to provide error handling and to respond if you expect the sequence of events to come to an end. There won't be an end to the events for this example, but for other uses of Observable, such as for handling HTTP responses, knowing when the event sequence has ended can be more useful. Listing 23-3 revises the form component so that it declares a dependency on an Observable service.

Listing 23-3. Using an Observable in the form.component.ts File in the src/app/core Folder

```
import { Component, Inject } from "@angular/core";
import { NgForm } from "@angular/forms";
import { Product } from "../model/product.model";
import { Model } from "../model/repository.model"
import { MODES, SharedState, SHARED_STATE } from "./sharedState.model";
import { Observable } from "rxjs";

@Component({
  selector: "paForm",
  templateUrl: "form.component.html",
  styleUrls: ["form.component.css"]
})
```

```
export class FormComponent {
  product: Product = new Product();
  // lastId: number;

  constructor(private model: Model,
    @Inject(SHARED_STATE) private stateEvents: Observable<SharedState>) {

    stateEvents.subscribe((update) => {
      this.product = new Product();
      if (update.id != undefined) {
        Object.assign(this.product, this.model.getProduct(update.id));
      }
      this.editing = update.mode == MODES.EDIT;
    });
  }

  editing: boolean = false;

  submitForm(form: NgForm) {
    if (form.valid) {
      this.model.saveProduct(this.product);
      this.product = new Product();
      form.reset();
    }
  }

  resetForm() {
    this.product = new Product();
  }

  //ngDoCheck() {
  //  if (this.lastId != this.state.id) {
  //    this.product = new Product();
  //    if (this.state.mode == MODES.EDIT) {
  //      Object.assign(this.product, this.model.getProduct(this.state.id));
  //    }
  //    this.lastId = this.state.id;
  //  }
  //}
}
```

The Reactive Extensions NPM package includes individual JavaScript modules for each of the types that it provides so that you can import the Observable type from the rxjs module.

To receive notifications, the component declares a dependency on the SHARED_STATE service, which is received as an Observable<SharedState> object. This object is an Observerable whose notifications will be SharedState objects, which will represent an edit or create operation started by the user. The component calls the Observable.subscribe method, providing a function that receives each SharedState object and uses it to update its state.

┌───┐
│   **WHAT ABOUT PROMISES?**   │
└───┘

You may be used to representing asynchronous activities using `Promise` objects. Observables perform the same basic role but are more flexible and have more features. Angular does provide support for working with Promises, which can be useful as you transition to Angular and when working with libraries that rely on Promises.

Reactive Extensions provides an `Observable.fromPromise` method that will create an `Observable` using a `Promise` as the source of events. There is also an `Observable.toPromise` method if you have an `Observable` and need a `Promise` for some reason.

In addition, there are some Angular features that let you choose which you use, such as the guards feature described in Chapter 27, which supports both.

But the Reactive Extensions library is an important part of working with Angular, and you will encounter it often in the chapters in this part of the book. I recommend you work with `Observable` when you encounter it and minimize the conversions to and from `Promise` objects.

Understanding Observers

The Reactive Extensions `Observer` provides the mechanism by which updates are created, using the methods described in Table 23-4.

Table 23-4. *The Observer Methods*

Name	Description
next(value)	This method creates a new event using the specified value.
error(errorObject)	This method reports an error, described using the argument, which can be any object.
complete()	This method ends the sequence, indicating that no further events will be sent.

Listing 23-4 updates the table component so that it uses an `Observer` to send out events when the user has clicked the Create New Product button or one of the Edit buttons.

Listing 23-4. Using an Observer in the table.component.ts File in the src/app/core Folder

```
import { Component, Inject } from "@angular/core";
import { Product } from "../model/product.model";
import { Model } from "../model/repository.model";
import { MODES, SharedState, SHARED_STATE } from "./sharedState.model";
import { Observer } from "rxjs";

@Component({
    selector: "paTable",
    templateUrl: "table.component.html"
})
export class TableComponent {
```

```
constructor(private model: Model,
    @Inject(SHARED_STATE) private observer: Observer<SharedState>) { }

getProduct(key: number): Product {
    return this.model.getProduct(key);
}

getProducts(): Product[] {
    return this.model.getProducts();
}

deleteProduct(key: number) {
    this.model.deleteProduct(key);
}

editProduct(key: number) {
    this.observer.next(new SharedState(MODES.EDIT, key));
}

createProduct() {
    this.observer.next(new SharedState(MODES.CREATE));
}
}
```

The component declares a dependency on the SHARED_STATE service, which is received as an Observer<SharedState> object, meaning an Observer will send events that are described using SharedState objects. The editProduct and createProduct methods have been updated so they call the next method on the observer to signal a change in state.

Understanding Subjects

Both of the components have declared dependencies on services using the SHARED_STATE token, but each expects to get a different type: the table component wants to receive an Observer<SharedState> object, while the form component wants an Observable<SharedState> object.

The Reactive Extensions library provides the Subject class, which implements both the Observer and Observable functionality. This makes it easy to create a service that allows events to be produced and consumed with a single object. In Listing 23-5, I have changed the service declared in the @NgModule decorator's providers property to use a Subject object.

Listing 23-5. Changing the Service in the core.module.ts File in the src/app/core Folder

```
import { NgModule } from "@angular/core";
import { BrowserModule } from "@angular/platform-browser";
import { FormsModule } from "@angular/forms";
import { ModelModule } from "../model/model.module";
import { TableComponent } from "./table.component";
import { FormComponent } from "./form.component";
import { SharedState, SHARED_STATE } from "./sharedState.model";
import { Subject } from "rxjs";
```

```
@NgModule({
    imports: [BrowserModule, FormsModule, ModelModule],
    declarations: [TableComponent, FormComponent],
    exports: [ModelModule, TableComponent, FormComponent],
    providers: [{ provide: SHARED_STATE, useValue: new Subject<SharedState>() }]
})
export class CoreModule { }
```

The value-based provider tells Angular to use a Subject<SharedState> object to resolve dependencies on the SHARED_STATE token, which will provide the components with the functionality they need to collaborate.

The result is that changing the shared service so that it is a Subject allows the table component to emit distinct events that are received by the form component and that are used to update its state without needing to rely on the awkward and expensive ngDoCheck method. There is also no need to try to work out which changes have been generated by the local component and which come from elsewhere since a component that subscribes to an Observable knows that all the events it receives must have originated from the Observer. This means that niggly problems like not being able to edit the same product twice simply go away, as shown in Figure 23-4.

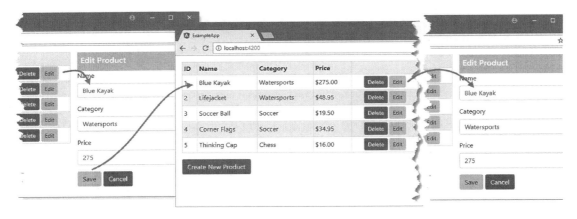

Figure 23-4. *The effect of using Reactive Extensions*

THE DIFFERENT TYPES OF SUBJECT

Listing 23-5 uses the Subject class, which is the simplest way to create an object that is both an Observer and an Observable. Its main limitation is that when a new subscriber is created using the subscribe method, it won't receive an event until the next time the next method is called. This can be unhelpful if you are creating instances of components or directives dynamically and you want them to have some context data as soon as they are created.

The Reactive Extensions library includes some specialized implementations of the Subject class that can be used to work around this problem. The BehaviorSubject class keeps track of the last event it processed and sends it to new subscribers as soon as they call the subscribe method. The ReplaySubject class does something similar, except that it keeps track of all of its events and sends them all to new subscribers, allowing them to catch up with any events that were sent before they subscribed.

Using the Async Pipe

Angular includes the `async` pipe, which can be used to consume `Observable` objects directly in a view, selecting the last object received from the event sequence. This is an impure pipe, as described in Chapter 18, because its changes are driven from outside of the view in which it is used, meaning that its `transform` method will be called often, even if a new event has not been received from the `Observable`. Listing 23-6 shows the addition of the `async` pipe to the view managed by the form component.

Listing 23-6. Using the Async Pipe in the form.component.html File in the src/app/core Folder

```
<div class="bg-primary text-white p-2" [class.bg-warning]="editing">
  <h5>{{editing  ? "Edit" : "Create"}} Product</h5>
  Last Event: {{ stateEvents | async | json }}
</div>

<form novalidate #form="ngForm" (ngSubmit)="submitForm(form)" (reset)="resetForm()">

    ...elements omitted for brevity...

</form>
```

The string interpolation binding expression gets the `stateEvents` property from the component, which is the `Observable<SharedState>` object, and passes it to the `async` pipe, which keeps track of the most recent event that has been received. The `async` filter then passes on the event to the `json` pipe, which creates a JSON representation of the event object. The result is that you can keep track of the events that are received by the form component, as shown in Figure 23-5.

Figure 23-5. *Displaying observable events*

This isn't the most useful display of data, but it does give some useful debugging insight. In this case, the most recent event has a mode value of 1, which corresponds to the Edit mode, and an id value of 4, which is the ID of the Corner Flags product.

Using the Async Pipe with Custom Pipes

The async pipe can be used with custom pipes to present the event data in a more user-friendly manner. To demonstrate, I added a file called state.pipe.ts to the src/app/core folder and used it to define the pipe shown in Listing 23-7.

Listing 23-7. The Contents of the state.pipe.ts File in the src/app/core Folder

```
import { Pipe } from "@angular/core";
import { SharedState, MODES } from "./sharedState.model";
import { Model } from "../model/repository.model";

@Pipe({
    name: "formatState",
    pure: true
})
export class StatePipe {

    constructor(private model: Model) { }

    transform(value: any): string {
        if (value instanceof SharedState) {
            let state = value as SharedState;
            return MODES[state.mode] + (state.id != undefined
                ? ` ${this.model.getProduct(state.id).name}` : "");
        } else {
            return "<No Data>"
        }
    }
}
```

In Listing 23-8, I have added the pipe to the set of declarations made by the core module.

■ **Tip** TypeScript enumerations have a useful feature through which the name of a value can be obtained. So, the expression MODES[1], for example, will return EDIT since that is the name of the MODES enumeration value at index 1. The pipe in Listing 23-7 uses this feature to present the state update to the user.

Listing 23-8. Registering the Pipe in the core.module.ts File in the src/app/core Folder

```
import { NgModule } from "@angular/core";
import { BrowserModule } from "@angular/platform-browser";
import { FormsModule } from "@angular/forms";
import { ModelModule } from "../model/model.module";
import { TableComponent } from "./table.component";
```

```
import { FormComponent } from "./form.component";
import { SharedState, SHARED_STATE } from "./sharedState.model";
import { Subject } from "rxjs";
import { StatePipe } from "./state.pipe";

@NgModule({
    imports: [BrowserModule, FormsModule, ModelModule],
    declarations: [TableComponent, FormComponent, StatePipe],
    exports: [ModelModule, TableComponent, FormComponent],
    providers: [{ provide: SHARED_STATE, useValue: new Subject<SharedState>() }]
})
export class CoreModule { }
```

Listing 23-9 shows the new pipe used to replace the built-in json pipe in the template managed by the form component.

Listing 23-9. Applying a Custom Pipe in the form.component.html File in the src/app/core Folder

```
<div class="bg-primary text-white p-2" [class.bg-warning]="editing">
  <h5>{{editing  ? "Edit" : "Create"}} Product</h5>
  Last Event: {{ stateEvents | async | formatState }}
</div>

<form novalidate #form="ngForm" (ngSubmit)="submitForm(form)" (reset)="resetForm()">

    ...elements omitted for brevity...

</form>
```

This example demonstrates that events received from Observable objects can be processed and transformed just like any other objects, as shown in Figure 23-6, which illustrates how a custom pipe can build on the core functionality provided by the async pipe.

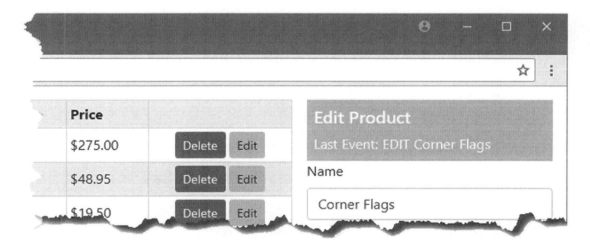

Figure 23-6. Formatting values received through an observable sequence

Scaling Up Application Feature Modules

The same Reactive Extensions building blocks can be used anywhere in the application and make it easy to allow building blocks to collaborate, even if the use of Reactive Extensions isn't exposed to all the collaborating parts of the application. As a demonstration, Listing 23-10 shows the addition of a Subject to the MessageService class to distribute the messages that should be displayed to the user.

Listing 23-10. Using a Subject in the message.service.ts File in the src/app/messages Folder

```
import { Injectable } from "@angular/core";
import { Message } from "./message.model";
import { Observable } from "rxjs";
import { Subject } from "rxjs";

@Injectable()
export class MessageService {
    private subject = new Subject<Message>();

    reportMessage(msg: Message) {
        this.subject.next(msg);
    }

    get messages(): Observable<Message> {
        return this.subject;
    }
}
```

The previous implementation of the message service supported only a single recipient of the messages that should be displayed to the user. I could have added code that managed multiple recipients, but given that the application already uses Reactive Extensions, it is much simpler to delegate that work to the Subject class, which scales up well and won't require any additional code or testing if there are multiple subscribers in the application.

Listing 23-11 shows the corresponding changes in the message component that will display the most recent message to the user.

Listing 23-11. Observing Messages in the message.component.ts File in the src/app/messages Folder

```
import { Component } from "@angular/core";
import { MessageService } from "./message.service";
import { Message } from "./message.model";
import { Observable } from "rxjs";

@Component({
    selector: "paMessages",
    templateUrl: "message.component.html",
})
export class MessageComponent {
    lastMessage: Message;

    constructor(messageService: MessageService) {
        messageService.messages.subscribe(m => this.lastMessage = m);
    }
}
```

The final step is to generate some messages to display. In Listing 23-12, I have modified the configuration of the core feature module so that the SHARED_STATE provider uses a factory function to create the Subject that is used to distribute state change events and adds a subscription that feeds the events into the message service.

Listing 23-12. Feeding the Message Service in the core.module.ts File in the src/app/core Folder

```
import { NgModule } from "@angular/core";
import { BrowserModule } from "@angular/platform-browser";
import { FormsModule } from "@angular/forms";
import { ModelModule } from "../model/model.module";
import { TableComponent } from "./table.component";
import { FormComponent } from "./form.component";
import { SharedState, SHARED_STATE } from "./sharedState.model";
import { Subject } from "rxjs";
import { StatePipe } from "./state.pipe";
import { MessageModule } from "../messages/message.module";
import { MessageService } from "../messages/message.service";
import { Message } from "../messages/message.model";
import { Model } from "../model/repository.model";
import { MODES } from "./sharedState.model";

@NgModule({
    imports: [BrowserModule, FormsModule, ModelModule, MessageModule],
    declarations: [TableComponent, FormComponent, StatePipe],
    exports: [ModelModule, TableComponent, FormComponent],
    providers: [{
        provide: SHARED_STATE,
        deps: [MessageService, Model],
        useFactory: (messageService, model) => {
            let subject = new Subject<SharedState>();
            subject.subscribe(m => messageService.reportMessage(
                    new Message(MODES[m.mode] + (m.id != undefined
                        ? ` ${model.getProduct(m.id).name}` : ""))))
                );
            return subject;
        }
    }]
})
export class CoreModule { }
```

The code is a little messy, but the result is that every state change event sent by the table component is displayed by the message component, as shown in Figure 23-7. Reactive Extensions makes it easy to wire up parts of the application, and the reason that the code in the listing is so dense is that it is also using the Model service to look up names from the data model to make the events easier to read.

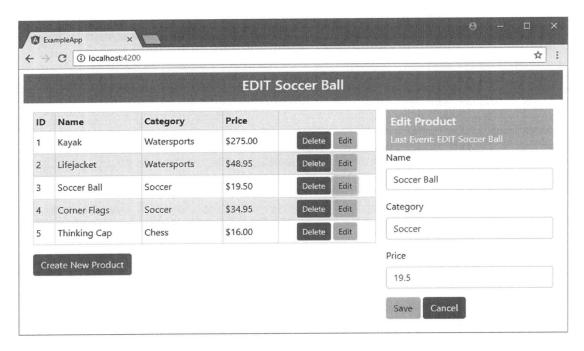

Figure 23-7. *Using Reactive Extensions in the Message service*

Going Beyond the Basics

The examples in the previous sections cover the basic use of Observable, Observer, and Subject. There is, however, a lot more functionality available when working with Reactive Extensions that can be used in advanced or complex applications. The full set of operations is described at https://github.com/reactivex/rxjs, but in this chapter, I demonstrate a small number of the features that you are most likely to require in an Angular application, as described in Table 23-5. The methods described in the table are used to control the way that events are received from an Observable object.

Table 23-5. *Useful Reactive Extensions Methods for Selecting Events*

Name	Description
filter	This method invokes a function to evaluate each event received from the Observable and discards those for which the function returns false.
map	This method invokes a function to transform each event received from the Observable and passes on the object that the function returns.
distinctUntilChanged	This method suppresses events until the event object changes.
skipWhile	This method filters events until a specified condition is satisfied, after which they are forwarded to the subscriber.
takeWhile	This method passes on events to the subscriber until a specified condition is satisfied, after which events are filtered.

Filtering Events

The filter method accepts a method that is used to inspect each object that is received from the Observable and selects only those that are required. Listing 23-13 demonstrates the use of the filter method to filter out the events that relate to a specific product.

Listing 23-13. Filtering Events in the form.component.ts File in the src/app/core Folder

```
import { Component, Inject } from "@angular/core";
import { NgForm } from "@angular/forms";
import { Product } from "../model/product.model";
import { Model } from "../model/repository.model";
import { MODES, SharedState, SHARED_STATE } from "./sharedState.model";
import { Observable } from "rxjs";
import { filter } from "rxjs/operators";

@Component({
    selector: "paForm",
    templateUrl: "form.component.html",
    styleUrls: ["form.component.css"]
})
export class FormComponent {
    product: Product = new Product();

    constructor(private model: Model,
        @Inject(SHARED_STATE) private stateEvents: Observable<SharedState>) {

            stateEvents.pipe(filter(state => state.id != 3))
            .subscribe((update) => {
                this.product = new Product();
                if (update.id != undefined) {
                    Object.assign(this.product, this.model.getProduct(update.id));
                }
                this.editing = update.mode == MODES.EDIT;
            });
    }

    editing: boolean = false;

    submitForm(form: NgForm) {
        if (form.valid) {
            this.model.saveProduct(this.product);
            this.product = new Product();
            form.reset();
        }
    }

    resetForm() {
        this.product = new Product();
    }
}
```

To use the methods described in Table 23-5, an `import` statement for the `rxjs/operators` package is required, like this:

```
...
import { filter } from "rxjs/operators";
...
```

The `filter` method is applied to an `Observable` using its `pipe` method, like this:

```
...
stateEvents.pipe(filter(state => state.id != 3)).subscribe((update) => {
...
```

The argument to the `filter` method is a statement selects the events that are required, which are passed on to the function provided using the `subscribe` method.

You can see the effect by clicking the Edit button for the Soccer Ball product, which has the ID that the filter function is checking for. The `async` pipe shows that an EDIT event has been sent through the shared service, but the `filter` method prevents it from being received by the component's `subscribe` function. The result is that the form doesn't reflect the change in state and isn't populated with the selected product information, as shown in Figure 23-8.

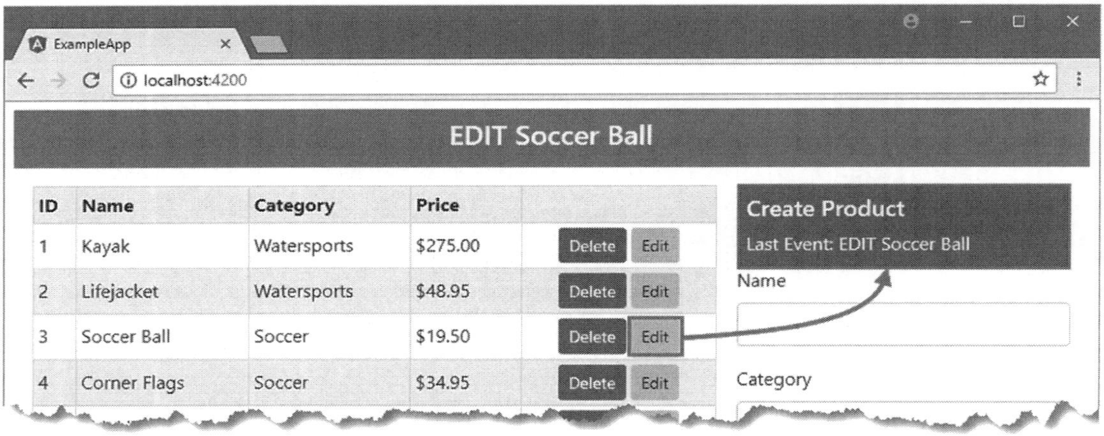

Figure 23-8. *Filtering events*

Transforming Events

The `map` method is used to transform the objects received from an `Observable`. You can use this method to transform event objects in any way, and the result from the method replaces the event object. Listing 23-14 uses the `map` method to change the value of an event object property.

Listing 23-14. Transforming Events in the form.component.ts File in the src/app/core Folder

```
import { Component, Inject } from "@angular/core";
import { NgForm } from "@angular/forms";
import { Product } from "../model/product.model";
```

```
import { Model } from "../model/repository.model";
import { MODES, SharedState, SHARED_STATE } from "./sharedState.model";
import { Observable } from "rxjs";
import { filter, map } from "rxjs/operators";

@Component({
    selector: "paForm",
    templateUrl: "form.component.html",
    styleUrls: ["form.component.css"]
})
export class FormComponent {
    product: Product = new Product();

    constructor(private model: Model,
        @Inject(SHARED_STATE) private stateEvents: Observable<SharedState>) {

            stateEvents
            .pipe(map(state => new SharedState(state.mode, state.id == 5
                ? 1 : state.id)))
            .pipe(filter(state => state.id != 3))
            .subscribe((update) => {
                this.product = new Product();
                if (update.id != undefined) {
                    Object.assign(this.product, this.model.getProduct(update.id));
                }
                this.editing = update.mode == MODES.EDIT;
            });
    }

    editing: boolean = false;

    submitForm(form: NgForm) {
        if (form.valid) {
            this.model.saveProduct(this.product);
            this.product = new Product();
            form.reset();
        }
    }

    resetForm() {
        this.product = new Product();
    }
}
```

The function passed to the map method in this example looks for SharedState objects that have an id value of 5 and, when found, changes the value to 1. The result is that clicking the Edit button for the Thinking Cap product selects the Kayak product for editing, as shown in Figure 23-9.

■ **Caution**   When using the map method, do not modify the object that is received as the argument to the function. This object is passed to all the subscribers in turn, and any changes you make will affect subsequent subscribers. This means that some subscribers will receive the unmodified object, and some will receive the object returned by the map method. Instead, create a new object, as shown in Listing 23-14.

Notice that the methods used to prepare and create a subscription on an Observable object can be chained together. In the example, the result from the map method is piped to the filter method, whose results are then passed to the subscribe method's function. Chaining methods together in this way allows complex rules to be created for the way that events are processed and received.

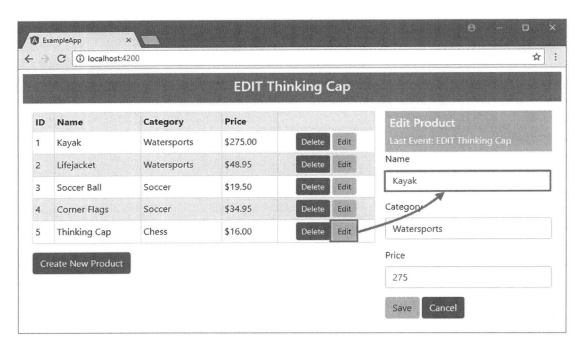

Figure 23-9. *Transforming events*

Using Different Event Objects

The map method can be used to produce any object and is not limited to changing property values on the object it receives. In Listing 23-15, I have used the map method to produce a number whose value encodes the operation and the object to which it applies.

Listing 23-15. Projecting a Different Type in the form.component.ts File in the src/app/core Folder

```
...
constructor(private model: Model,
    @Inject(SHARED_STATE) private stateEvents: Observable<SharedState>) {
        stateEvents
        .pipe(map(state => state.mode == MODES.EDIT ? state.id : -1))
```

```
    .pipe(filter(id => id != 3))
    .subscribe((id) => {
        this.editing = id != -1;
        this.product = new Product();
        if (id != -1) {
            Object.assign(this.product, this.model.getProduct(id))
        }
    });
}
...
```

There is no advantage in making a simple data type represent an operation and specify its target. In fact, it generally causes problems because it means that the component assumes that there will never be an object in the model whose id property is -1. But as a simple example, it demonstrates how the map method can project different types and how those types are then passed along the chain of Reactive Extensions methods, meaning that the number values produced by the map method are received as the values to be processed by the filter method and, in turn, the subscribe method, the functions for which have both been updated to work with the new data values.

Receiving Only Distinct Events

The distinctUntilChanged method filters the sequence of events so that only distinct values are passed along to the subscriber. To see the kind of problem that this can be used to solve, click the Edit button for the Kayak product and change the value of the Category field. Without clicking the Save button, click the Kayak's Edit button again, and you will see your edits discarded. In Listing 23-16, I have added the distinctUntilChanged method to the chain of methods so that it applies to the number values produced by the map method. Only different values will be forwarded to the filter and subscribe methods.

Listing 23-16. Preventing Duplicate Events in the form.component.ts File in the src/app/core Folder

```
import { Component, Inject } from "@angular/core";
import { NgForm } from "@angular/forms";
import { Product } from "../model/product.model";
import { Model } from "../model/repository.model";
import { MODES, SharedState, SHARED_STATE } from "./sharedState.model";
import { Observable } from "rxjs";
import { filter, map, distinctUntilChanged } from "rxjs/operators";

@Component({
    selector: "paForm",
    templateUrl: "form.component.html",
    styleUrls: ["form.component.css"]
})
export class FormComponent {
    product: Product = new Product();

    constructor(private model: Model,
        @Inject(SHARED_STATE) private stateEvents: Observable<SharedState>) {
            stateEvents
            .pipe(map(state => state.mode == MODES.EDIT ? state.id : -1))
            .pipe(distinctUntilChanged())
```

```
        .pipe(filter(id => id != 3))
        .subscribe((id) => {
            this.editing = id != -1;
            this.product = new Product();
            if (id != -1) {
                Object.assign(this.product, this.model.getProduct(id))
            }
        });
}

editing: boolean = false;

submitForm(form: NgForm) {
    if (form.valid) {
        this.model.saveProduct(this.product);
        this.product = new Product();
        form.reset();
    }
}

resetForm() {
    this.product = new Product();
}
}
```

If you repeat the Kayak editing process, you will see that the changes are no longer discarded when you click the Edit button for the product that is being edited since this will produce the same value as the previous event. Editing a different product will cause the map method to emit a different number value, which will be passed on by the distinctUntilChanged method.

Using a Custom Equality Checker

The distinctUntilChanged method can make easy comparisons between simple datatypes like number, but it doesn't know how to compare objects and will assume that any two objects are different. To address this, you can specify a comparison function that will be used to check whether events are distinct, as shown in Listing 23-17.

Listing 23-17. Using a Equality Checker in the form.component.ts File in the src/app/core Folder

```
import { Component, Inject } from "@angular/core";
import { NgForm } from "@angular/forms";
import { Product } from "../model/product.model";
import { Model } from "../model/repository.model";
import { MODES, SharedState, SHARED_STATE } from "./sharedState.model";
import { Observable } from "rxjs";
import { filter, map, distinctUntilChanged } from "rxjs/operators";
```

```
@Component({
    selector: "paForm",
    templateUrl: "form.component.html",
    styleUrls: ["form.component.css"]
})
export class FormComponent {
    product: Product = new Product();

    constructor(private model: Model,
        @Inject(SHARED_STATE) private stateEvents: Observable<SharedState>) {
            stateEvents
            .pipe(distinctUntilChanged((firstState, secondState) =>
                firstState.mode == secondState.mode
                    && firstState.id == secondState.id))
            .subscribe(update => {
                this.product = new Product();
                if (update.id != undefined) {
                    Object.assign(this.product, this.model.getProduct(update.id));
                }
                this.editing = update.mode == MODES.EDIT;
            });
    }

    editing: boolean = false;

    submitForm(form: NgForm) {
        if (form.valid) {
            this.model.saveProduct(this.product);
            this.product = new Product();
            form.reset();
        }
    }

    resetForm() {
        this.product = new Product();
    }
}
```

This listing removes the map and filter methods and provides the distinctUntilChanged method with a function that compares SharedState objects by comparing their mode and id properties. Distinct objects are passed onto the function provided to the subscribe method.

Taking and Skipping Events

The skipWhile and takeWhile methods are used to specify conditions that will cause events to be filtered or passed on to the subscriber. These methods must be used carefully because it is easy to specify conditions that will permanently filter events from the subscriber. In Listing 23-18, I have used the skipWhile method to filter events until the user clicks the Create New Product button, after which events will be passed on.

Listing 23-18. Skipping Events in the form.component.ts File in the src/app/core Folder

```
import { Component, Inject } from "@angular/core";
import { NgForm } from "@angular/forms";
import { Product } from "../model/product.model";
import { Model } from "../model/repository.model";
import { MODES, SharedState, SHARED_STATE } from "./sharedState.model";
import { Observable } from "rxjs";
import { filter, map, distinctUntilChanged, skipWhile } from "rxjs/operators";

@Component({
    selector: "paForm",
    templateUrl: "form.component.html",
    styleUrls: ["form.component.css"]
})
export class FormComponent {
    product: Product = new Product();

    constructor(private model: Model,
        @Inject(SHARED_STATE) private stateEvents: Observable<SharedState>) {
            stateEvents
            .pipe(skipWhile(state => state.mode == MODES.EDIT))
            .pipe(distinctUntilChanged((firstState, secondState) =>
                firstState.mode == secondState.mode
                    && firstState.id == secondState.id))
            .subscribe(update => {
                this.product = new Product();
                if (update.id != undefined) {
                    Object.assign(this.product, this.model.getProduct(update.id));
                }
                this.editing = update.mode == MODES.EDIT;
            });
    }

    editing: boolean = false;

    submitForm(form: NgForm) {
        if (form.valid) {
            this.model.saveProduct(this.product);
            this.product = new Product();
            form.reset();
        }
    }

    resetForm() {
        this.product = new Product();
    }
}
```

Clicking the Edit buttons in the table will still generate events, which will be displayed by the async pipe, which is subscribed to the Subject without any filtering or skipping. But the form component doesn't receive those events, as shown in Figure 23-10, since its subscription is filtered by the skipWhile method until an event whose mode property isn't MODES.EDIT is received. Clicking the Create New Product button generates an event that ends the skipping, after which the component will receive all events.

Figure 23-10. *Skipping events*

Summary

In this chapter, I introduced the Reactive Extensions package and explained how it can be used to handle changes in the parts of the application that are not managed by the Angular change-detection process. I demonstrated the use of Observable, Observer, and Subject objects to distribute events in an application, showed you how the built-in async pipe works, and introduced some of the most useful operators that the Reactive Extensions library provides for controlling the flow of events to a subscriber. In the next chapter, I explain how to make asynchronous HTTP requests in Angular applications and how to consume RESTful web services.

CHAPTER 24

■ ■ ■

Making Asynchronous HTTP Requests

All the examples since Chapter 11 have relied on static data that has been hardwired into the application. In this chapter, I demonstrate how to use asynchronous HTTP requests, often called Ajax requests, to interact with a web service to get real data into an application. Table 24-1 puts HTTP requests in context.

Table 24-1. *Putting Asynchronous HTTP Requests in Context*

Question	Answer
What are they?	Asynchronous HTTP requests are HTTP requests sent by the browser on behalf of the application. The term *asynchronous* refers to the fact that the application continues to operate while the browser is waiting for the server to respond.
Why are they useful?	Asynchronous HTTP requests allow Angular applications to interact with web services so that persistent data can be loaded into the application and changes can be sent to the server and saved.
How are they used?	Requests are made using the HttpClient class, which is delivered as a service through dependency injection. This class provides an Angular-friendly wrapper around the browser's XMLHttpRequest feature.
Are there any pitfalls or limitations?	Using the Angular HTTP feature requires the use of Reactive Extensions Observable objects, as described in Chapter 23.
Are there any alternatives?	You can work directly with the browser's XMLHttpRequest object if you prefer, and some applications—those that don't need to deal with persistent data—can be written without making HTTP requests at all.

© Adam Freeman 2018

A. Freeman, *Pro Angular 6*, https://doi.org/10.1007/978-1-4842-3649-9_24

Table 24-2 summarizes the chapter.

Table 24-2. *Chapter Summary*

Problem	Solution	Listing
Send HTTP requests in an Angular application	Use the Http service	1–8
Perform REST operations	Use the HTTP method and URL to specify an operation and a target for that operation	9–11
Make cross-origin requests	Use the HttpClient service to support CORS automatically (JSONP requests are also supported)	12–13
Include headers in a request	Set the headers property in the Request object	14–15
Respond to an HTTP error	Create an error handler class	16–19

Preparing the Example Project

This chapter uses the exampleApp project created in Chapter 22. For this chapter, I rely on a server that responds to HTTP requests with JSON data. Run the command shown in Listing 24-1 in the exampleApp folder to add the json-server package to the project.

■ **Tip** You can download the example project for this chapter—and for all the other chapters in this book—from https://github.com/Apress/pro-angular-6.

Listing 24-1. Adding a Package to the Project

```
npm install json-server@0.12.1
```

I added an entry in the scripts section of the package.json file to run the json-server package, as shown in Listing 24-2.

Listing 24-2. Adding a Script Entry in the package.json File in the exampleApp Folder

```
...
"scripts": {
    "ng": "ng",
    "start": "ng serve",
    "build": "ng build",
    "test": "ng test",
    "lint": "ng lint",
    "e2e": "ng e2e",
    "json": "json-server --p 3500 restData.js"
},
...
```

Configuring the Model Feature Module

The @angular/common/http JavaScript module contains an Angular module called HttpClientModule, which must be imported into the application in either the root module or one of the feature modules before HTTP requests can be created. In Listing 24-3, I imported the module to the model module, which is the natural place in the example application because I will be using HTTP requests to populate the model with data.

Listing 24-3. Importing a Module in the model.module.ts File in the src/app/model Folder

```
import { NgModule } from "@angular/core";
import { StaticDataSource } from "./static.datasource";
import { Model } from "./repository.model";
import { HttpClientModule } from "@angular/common/http";

@NgModule({
  imports: [HttpClientModule],
  providers: [Model, StaticDataSource]
})
export class ModelModule { }
```

Creating the Data File

To provide the json-server package with some data, I added a file called restData.js to the exampleApp folder and added the code shown in Listing 24-4.

Listing 24-4. The Contents of the restData.js File in the exampleApp Folder

```
module.exports = function () {
    var data = {
        products: [
            { id: 1, name: "Kayak", category: "Watersports", price: 275 },
            { id: 2, name: "Lifejacket", category: "Watersports", price: 48.95 },
            { id: 3, name: "Soccer Ball", category: "Soccer", price: 19.50 },
            { id: 4, name: "Corner Flags", category: "Soccer", price: 34.95 },
            { id: 5, name: "Stadium", category: "Soccer", price: 79500 },
            { id: 6, name: "Thinking Cap", category: "Chess", price: 16 },
            { id: 7, name: "Unsteady Chair", category: "Chess", price: 29.95 },
            { id: 8, name: "Human Chess Board", category: "Chess", price: 75 },
            { id: 9, name: "Bling Bling King", category: "Chess", price: 1200 }
        ]
    }
    return data
}
```

The json-server package can work with JSON or JavaScript files. If you use a JSON file, then its contents will be modified to reflect changes requests made by clients. I have chosen the JavaScript option, which allows data to be generated programmatically and means that restarting the process will return to the original data.

Updating the Form Component

In Chapter 23, I configured the component that manages the HTML form to ignore events generated by the table component until the first time that the Create New Product button is clicked. To avoid confusing results, Listing 24-5 disables the skipWhile and distinctUntilChanged methods that were applied to the Observable.

Listing 24-5. Disabling Event Skipping in the form.component.ts File in the src/app/core Folder

```
...
constructor(private model: Model,
    @Inject(SHARED_STATE) private stateEvents: Observable<SharedState>) {
        stateEvents
        // .pipe(skipWhile(state => state.mode == MODES.EDIT))
        // .pipe(distinctUntilChanged((firstState, secondState) =>
        //     firstState.mode == secondState.mode
        //         && firstState.id == secondState.id))
        .subscribe(update => {
            this.product = new Product();
            if (update.id != undefined) {
                Object.assign(this.product, this.model.getProduct(update.id));
            }
            this.editing = update.mode == MODES.EDIT;
        });
}
...
```

Running the Example Project

Open a new command prompt, navigate to the exampleApp folder, and run the following command to start the data server:

```
npm run json
```

This command will start the json-server, which will listen for HTTP requests on port 3500. Open a new browser window and navigate to http://localhost:3500/products/2. The server will respond with the following data:

```
{ "id": 2, "name": "Lifejacket", "category": "Watersports", "price": 48.95 }
```

Leave the json-server running and use a separate command prompt to start the Angular development tools by running the following command in the exampleApp folder:

```
ng serve
```

Use the browser to navigate to http://localhost:4200 to see the content illustrated in Figure 24-1.

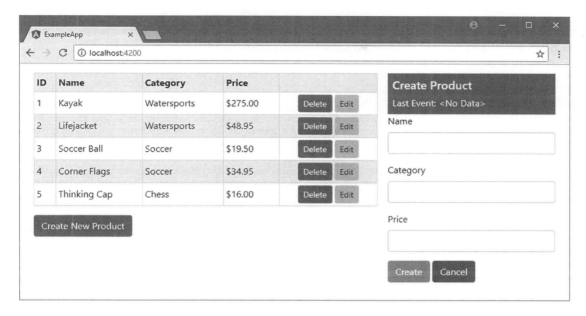

Figure 24-1. *Running the example application*

Understanding RESTful Web Services

The most common approach for delivering data to an application is to use the *Representational State Transfer* pattern, known as REST, to create a data web service. There is no detailed specification for REST, which leads to a lot of different approaches that fall under the RESTful banner. There are, however, some unifying ideas that are useful in web application development.

The core premise of a RESTful web service is to embrace the characteristics of HTTP so that request methods—also known as *verbs*—specify an operation for the server to perform, and the request URL specifies one or more data objects to which the operation will be applied.

As an example, here is a URL that might refer to a specific product in the example application:

```
http://localhost:3500/products/2
```

The first segment of the URL—products—is used to indicate the collection of objects that will be operated on and allows a single server to provide multiple services, each of which with its own data. The second segment—2—selects an individual object within the products collection. In the example, it is the value of the id property that uniquely identifies an object and that would be used in the URL, in this case, specifying the Lifejacket object.

The HTTP verb or method used to make the request tells the RESTful server what operation should be performed on the specified object. When you tested the RESTful server in the previous section, the browser sent an HTTP GET request, which the server interprets as an instruction to retrieve the specified object and send it to the client. It is for this reason that the browser displayed a JSON representation of the Lifejacket object.

Table 24-3 shows the most common combination of HTTP methods and URLs and explains what each of them does when sent to a RESTful server.

Table 24-3. *Common HTTP Verbs and Their Effect in a RESTful Web Service*

Verb	URL	Description
GET	/products	This combination retrieves all the objects in the products collection.
GET	/products/2	This combination retrieves the object whose id is 2 from the products collection.
POST	/products	This combination is used to add a new object to the products collection. The request body contains a JSON representation of the new object.
PUT	/products/2	This combination is used to replace the object in the products collection whose id is 2. The request body contains a JSON representation of the replacement object.
PATCH	/products/2	This combination is used to update a subset of the properties of the object in the products collection whose id is 2. The request body contains a JSON representation of the properties to update and the new values.
DELETE	/products/2	This combination is used to delete the product whose id is 2 from the products collection.

Caution is required because there can be considerable differences in the way that some RESTful web services work, caused by differences in the frameworks used to create them and the preferences of the development team. It is important to confirm how a web service uses verbs and what is required in the URL and request body to perform operations.

Some common variations include web services that won't accept any request bodies that contain id values (to ensure they are generated uniquely by the server's data store) and web services that don't support all of the verbs (it is common to ignore PATCH requests and only accept updates using the PUT verb).

Replacing the Static Data Source

The best place to start with HTTP requests is to replace the static data source in the example application with one that retrieves data from the RESTful web service. This will provide a foundation for describing how Angular supports HTTP requests and how they can be integrated into an application.

Creating the New Data Source Service

To create a new data source, I added a file called rest.datasource.ts in the src/app/model folder and added the statements shown in Listing 24-6.

Listing 24-6. The Contents of the rest.datasource.ts File in the src/app/model Folder

```
import { Injectable, Inject, InjectionToken } from "@angular/core";
import { HttpClient } from "@angular/common/http";
import { Observable } from "rxjs";
import { Product } from "./product.model";
```

```
export const REST_URL = new InjectionToken("rest_url");

@Injectable()
export class RestDataSource {

  constructor(private http: HttpClient,
    @Inject(REST_URL) private url: string) { }

  getData(): Observable<Product[]> {
    return this.http.get<Product[]>(this.url);
  }
}
```

This is a simple-looking class, but there are some important features at work, which I described in the sections that follow.

Setting Up the HTTP Request

Angular provides the ability to make asynchronous HTTP requests through the HttpClient class, which is defined in the @angular/common/http JavaScript module and is provided as a service in the HttpClientModule feature module. The data source declared a dependency on the HttpClient class using its constructor, like this:

```
...
constructor(private http: HttpClient, @Inject(REST_URL) private url: string) { }
...
```

The other constructor argument is used so that the URL that requests are sent to doesn't have to be hardwired into the data source. I'll create a provider using the REST_URL opaque token when I configure the feature module. The HttpClient object received through the constructor is used to make an HTTP GET request in the data source's getData method, like this:

```
...
getData(): Observable<Product[]> {
    return this.http.get<Product[]>(this.url);
}
...
```

The HttpClient class defines a set of methods for making HTTP requests, each of which uses a different HTTP verb, as described in Table 24-4.

■ **Tip** The methods in Table 24-4 accept an optional configuration object, as demonstrated in the "Configuring Request Headers" section.

Table 24-4. *The Http Methods*

Name	Description
get(url)	This method sends a GET request to the specified URL.
post(url, body)	This method sends a POST request using the specified object as the body.
put(url, body)	This method sends a PUT request using the specified object as the body.
patch(url, body)	This method sends a PATCH request using the specified object as the body.
delete(url)	This method sends a DELETE request to the specified URL.
head(url)	This method sends a HEAD request, which has the same effect as a GET request except that the server will return only the headers and not the request body.
options(url)	This method sends an OPTIONS request to the specified URL.
request(method, url, options)	This method can be used to send a request with any verb, as described in the "Consolidating HTTP Requests" section.

Processing the Response

The methods described in Table 24-4 accept a type parameter, which the HttpClient classes uses to parse the response received from the server. The RESTful web server returns JSON data, which has become the de facto standard used by web services, and the HttpClient object will automatically convert the response into an Observable that yields an instance of the type parameter when it completes. This means that if you call the get method, for example, with a Product[] type parameter, then the response from the get method will be an Observable<Product[]> that represents the eventual response from the HTTP request:

```
...
getData(): Observable<Product[]> {
  return this.http.get<Product[]>(this.url);
}
...
```

■ **Caution**   The methods in Table 24-4 prepare an HTTP request, but it isn't sent to the server until the Observer object's subscribe method is invoked. Be careful, though, because the request will be sent once per call to the subscribe method, which makes it easy to inadvertently send the same request multiple times.

Configuring the Data Source

The next step is to configure a provider for the new data source and to create a value-based provider to configure it with a URL to which requests will be sent. Listing 24-7 shows the changes to the model.module.ts file.

Listing 24-7. Configuring the Data Source in the model.module.ts File in the src/app/model Folder

```
import { NgModule } from "@angular/core";
// import { StaticDataSource } from "./static.datasource";
import { Model } from "./repository.model";
import { HttpClientModule } from "@angular/common/http";
import { RestDataSource, REST_URL } from "./rest.datasource";

@NgModule({
  imports: [HttpClientModule],
  providers: [Model, RestDataSource,
    { provide: REST_URL, useValue: `http://${location.hostname}:3500/products` }]
})
export class ModelModule { }
```

The two new providers enable the RestDataSource class as a service and use the REST_URL opaque token to configure the URL for the web service. I removed the provider for the StaticDataSource class, which is no longer required.

Using the REST Data Source

The final step is to update the repository class so that it declares a dependency on the new data source and uses it to get the application data, as shown in Listing 24-8.

Listing 24-8. Using the New Data Source in the repository.model.ts File in the src/app/model Folder

```
import { Injectable } from "@angular/core";
import { Product } from "./product.model";
//import { StaticDataSource } from "./static.datasource";
import { Observable } from "rxjs";
import { RestDataSource } from "./rest.datasource";

@Injectable()
export class Model {
    private products: Product[] = new Array<Product>();
    private locator = (p: Product, id: number) => p.id == id;

    constructor(private dataSource: RestDataSource) {
        //this.products = new Array<Product>();
        //this.dataSource.getData().forEach(p => this.products.push(p));
        this.dataSource.getData().subscribe(data => this.products = data);
    }

    getProducts(): Product[] {
        return this.products;
    }

    getProduct(id: number): Product {
        return this.products.find(p => this.locator(p, id));
    }
```

```
saveProduct(product: Product) {
    if (product.id == 0 || product.id == null) {
        product.id = this.generateID();
        this.products.push(product);
    } else {
        let index = this.products
            .findIndex(p => this.locator(p, product.id));
        this.products.splice(index, 1, product);
    }
}

deleteProduct(id: number) {
    let index = this.products.findIndex(p => this.locator(p, id));
    if (index > -1) {
        this.products.splice(index, 1);
    }
}

private generateID(): number {
    let candidate = 100;
    while (this.getProduct(candidate) != null) {
        candidate++;
    }
    return candidate;
}
}
```

The constructor dependency has changed so that the repository will receive a RestDataSource object when it is created. Within the constructor, the data source's getData method is called, and the subscribe method is used to receive the data objects that are returned from the server and process them.

When you save the changes, the browser will reload the application, and the new data source will be used. An asynchronous HTTP request will be sent to the RESTful web service, which will return the larger set of data objects shown in Figure 24-2.

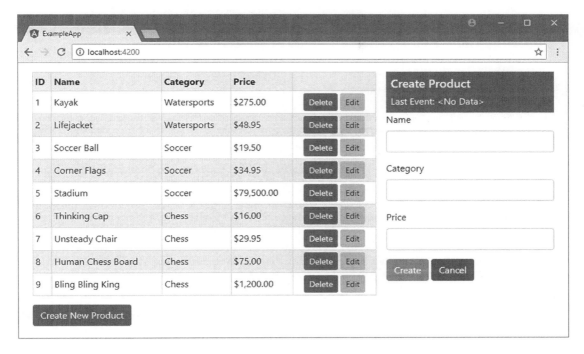

Figure 24-2. *Getting the application data*

Saving and Deleting Data

The data source is able to get data from the server, but it also needs to send data the other way, persisting changes that the user makes to objects in the model and storing new objects that are created. Listing 24-9 adds methods to the data source class to send HTTP requests to save or update objects using the Angular HttpClient class.

Listing 24-9. Sending Data in the rest.datasource.ts File in the src/app/model Folder

```
import { Injectable, Inject, InjectionToken } from "@angular/core";
import { HttpClient } from "@angular/common/http";
import { Observable } from "rxjs";
import { Product } from "./product.model";

export const REST_URL = new InjectionToken("rest_url");

@Injectable()
export class RestDataSource {
    constructor(private http: HttpClient,
        @Inject(REST_URL) private url: string) { }

    getData(): Observable<Product[]> {
        return this.http.get<Product[]>(this.url);
    }
}
```

```
    saveProduct(product: Product): Observable<Product> {
        return this.http.post<Product>(this.url, product);
    }

    updateProduct(product: Product): Observable<Product> {
        return this.http.put<Product>(`${this.url}/${product.id}`, product);
    }

    deleteProduct(id: number): Observable<Product> {
        return this.http.delete<Product>(`${this.url}/${id}`);
    }
}
```

The saveProduct, updateProduct, and deleteProduct methods follow the same pattern: they call one of the HttpClient class methods and return an Observable<Product> as the result.

When saving a new object, the ID of the object is generated by the server so that it is unique and clients don't inadvertently use the same ID for different objects. In this situation, the POST method is used, and the request is sent to the /products URL. When updating or deleting an existing object, the ID is already known, and a PUT request is sent to a URL that includes the ID. So, a request to update the object whose ID is 2, for example, is sent to the /products/2 URL. Similarly, to remove that object, a DELETE request would be sent to the same URL.

What these methods have in common is that the server is the authoritative data store and the response from the server contains the official version of the object that has been saved by the server. It is this object that is returned as the results from these methods, provided through the Observable<Product>.

Listing 24-10 shows the corresponding changes in the repository class that take advantage of the new data source features.

Listing 24-10. Using the Data Source Features in the repository.model.ts File in the src/app/model Folder

```
import { Injectable } from "@angular/core";
import { Product } from "./product.model";
import { Observable } from "rxjs";
import { RestDataSource } from "./rest.datasource";

@Injectable()
export class Model {
    private products: Product[] = new Array<Product>();
    private locator = (p: Product, id: number) => p.id == id;

    constructor(private dataSource: RestDataSource) {
        this.dataSource.getData().subscribe(data => this.products = data);
    }

    getProducts(): Product[] {
        return this.products;
    }

    getProduct(id: number): Product {
        return this.products.find(p => this.locator(p, id));
    }
```

```
saveProduct(product: Product) {
    if (product.id == 0 || product.id == null) {
        this.dataSource.saveProduct(product)
            .subscribe(p => this.products.push(p));
    } else {
        this.dataSource.updateProduct(product).subscribe(p => {
            let index = this.products
                .findIndex(item => this.locator(item, p.id));
            this.products.splice(index, 1, p);
        });
    }
}

deleteProduct(id: number) {
    this.dataSource.deleteProduct(id).subscribe(() => {
        let index = this.products.findIndex(p => this.locator(p, id));
        if (index > -1) {
            this.products.splice(index, 1);
        }
    });
}
}
```

The changes use the data source to send updates to the server and use the results to update the locally stored data so that it is displayed by the rest of the application. To test the changes, click the Edit button for the Kayak product and change its name to Green Kayak. Click the Save button, and the browser will send an HTTP PUT request to the server, which will return a modified object that is added to the repository's products array and is displayed in the table, as shown in Figure 24-3.

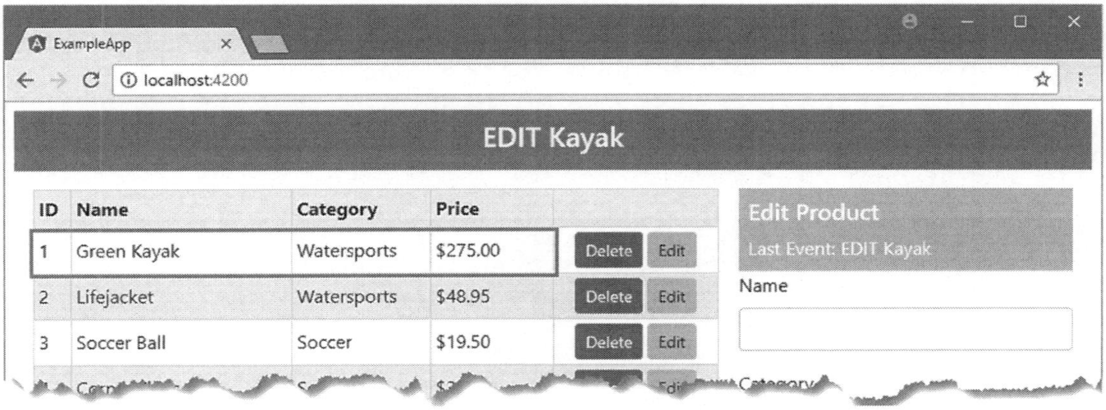

Figure 24-3. *Sending a PUT request to the server*

You can check that the server has stored the changes by using the browser to request `http://localhost:3500/products/1`, which will produce the following representation of the object:

```
{
  "id": 1,
  "name": "Green Kayak",
  "category": "Watersports",
  "price": 275
}
```

Consolidating HTTP Requests

Each of the methods in the data source class duplicates the same basic pattern of sending an HTTP request using a verb-specific `HttpClient` method. This means that any change to the way that HTTP requests are made has to be repeated in four different places, ensuring that the requests that use the GET, POST, PUT, and DELETE verbs are all correctly updated and performed consistently.

The `HttpClient` class defines the `request` method, which allows the HTTP verb to be specified as an argument. Listing 24-11 uses the `request` method to consolidate the HTTP requests in the data source class.

Listing 24-11. Consolidating HTTP Requests in the rest.datasource.ts File in the src/app/model Folder

```
import { Injectable, Inject, InjectionToken } from "@angular/core";
import { HttpClient } from "@angular/common/http";
import { Observable } from "rxjs";
import { Product } from "./product.model";

export const REST_URL = new InjectionToken("rest_url");

@Injectable()
export class RestDataSource {
    constructor(private http: HttpClient,
        @Inject(REST_URL) private url: string) { }

    getData(): Observable<Product[]> {
        return this.sendRequest<Product[]>("GET", this.url);
    }

    saveProduct(product: Product): Observable<Product> {
        return this.sendRequest<Product>("POST", this.url, product);
    }

    updateProduct(product: Product): Observable<Product> {
        return this.sendRequest<Product>("PUT",
            `${this.url}/${product.id}`, product);
    }

    deleteProduct(id: number): Observable<Product> {
        return this.sendRequest<Product>("DELETE", `${this.url}/${id}`);
    }
```

```
    private sendRequest<T>(verb: string, url: string, body?: Product)
          : Observable<T> {
      return this.http.request<T>(verb, url, {
          body: body
      });
    }
}
```

The request method accepts the HTTP verb, the URL for the request, and an optional object that is used to configure the request. The configuration object is used to set the request body using the body property, and the HttpClient will automatically take care of encoding the body object and including a serialized representation of it in the request.

Table 24-5 describes the most useful properties that can be specified to configure an HTTP request made using the request method.

Table 24-5. *Useful Request Method Configuration Object Properties*

Name	Description
headers	This property returns an HttpHeaders object that allows the request headers to be specified, as described in the "Configuring Request Headers" section.
body	This property is used to set the request body. The object assigned to this property will be serialized as JSON when the request is sent.
withCredentials	When true, this property is used to include authentication cookies when making cross-site requests. This setting must be used only with servers that include the Access-Control-Allow-Credentials header in responses, as part of the Cross-Origin Resource Sharing (CORS) specification. See the "Making Cross-Origin Requests" section for details.
responseType	This property is used to specify the type of the response expected from the server. The default value is json, indicating the JSON data format.

Making Cross-Origin Requests

By default, browsers enforce a security policy that only allows JavaScript code to make asynchronous HTTP requests within the same *origin* as the document that contains them. This policy is intended to reduce the risk of cross-site scripting (CSS) attacks, where the browser is tricked into executing malicious code. The details of this attack are beyond the scope of this book, but there is a nice article available at http://en.wikipedia.org/wiki/Cross-site_scripting that provides a good introduction to the topic.

For Angular developers, the same-origin policy can be a problem when using web services because they are typically outside of the origin that contains the application's JavaScript code. Two URLs are considered to be in the same origin if they have the same protocol, host, and port and have different origins if this is not the case. The URL for the HTML file that contains the example application's JavaScript code is http://localhost:3000/index.html. Table 24-6 summarizes how similar URLs have the same or different origins, compared with the application's URL.

Table 24-6. *URLs and Their Origins*

URL	Origin Comparison
`http://localhost:3000/otherfile.html`	Same origin
`http://localhost:3000/app/main.js`	Same origin
`https://localhost:3000/index.html`	Different origin; protocol differs
`http://localhost:3500/products`	Different origin; port differs
`http://angular.io/index.html`	Different origin; host differs

As the table shows, the URL for the RESTful web service, `http://localhost:3500/products`, has a different origin because it uses a different port from the main application.

HTTP requests made using the Angular `HttpClient` class will automatically use Cross-Origin Resource Sharing to send requests to different origins. With CORS, the browser includes headers in the asynchronous HTTP request that provide the server with the origin of the JavaScript code. The response from the server includes headers that tell the browser whether it is willing to accept the request. The details of CORS are outside the scope of this book, but there is an introduction to the topic at `https://en.wikipedia.org/wiki/Cross-origin_resource_sharing`, and the CORS specification is available at `www.w3.org/TR/cors`.

For the Angular developer, CORS is something that is taken care of automatically, just as long as the server that receives asynchronous HTTP requests supports the specification. The `json-server` package that has been providing the RESTful web service for the examples supports CORS and will accept requests from any origin, which is why the examples have been working. If you want to see CORS in action, use the browser's F12 developer tools to watch the network requests that are made when you edit or create a product. You may see a request made using the `OPTIONS` verb, known as the preflight request, which the browser uses to check that it is allowed to make the POST or PUT request to the server. This request and the subsequent request that sends the data to the server will contain an `Origin` header, and the response will contain one or more `Access-Control-Allow` headers, through which the server sets out what it is willing to accept from the client.

All of this happens automatically, and the only configuration option is the `withCredentials` property that was described in Table 24-5. When this property is `true`, the browser will include authentication cookies, and headers from the origin will be included in the request to the server.

Using JSONP Requests

CORS is available only if the server to which the HTTP requests are sent supports it. For servers that don't implement CORS, Angular also provides support for *JSONP*, which allows a more limited form of cross-origin requests.

JSONP works by adding a `script` element to the Document Object Model that specifies the cross-origin server in its `src` attribute. The browser sends a GET request to the server, which returns JavaScript code that, when executed, provides the application with the data it requires. JSONP is, essentially, a hack that works around the browser's same-origin security policy. JSONP can be used only to make GET requests, and it presents greater security risks than CORS. As a consequence, JSONP should be used only when CORS isn't available.

The Angular support for JSONP is defined in a feature module called `HttpClientJsonpModule`, which is defined in the `@angular/common/http` JavaScript module. To enable JSONP, Listing 24-12 adds `HttpClientJsonpModule` to the set of imports for the model module.

Listing 24-12. Enabling JSONP in the model.module.ts File in the src/app/model Folder

```
import { NgModule } from "@angular/core";
//import { StaticDataSource } from "./static.datasource";
import { Model } from "./repository.model";
import { HttpClientModule, HttpClientJsonpModule } from "@angular/common/http";
import { RestDataSource, REST_URL } from "./rest.datasource";

@NgModule({
    imports: [HttpClientModule, HttpClientJsonpModule],
    providers: [Model, RestDataSource,
        { provide: REST_URL, useValue: `http://${location.hostname}:3500/products` }]
})
export class ModelModule { }
```

Angular provides support for JSONP through the HttpClient service, which takes care of managing the JSONP HTTP request and processing the response, which can otherwise be a tedious and error-prone process. Listing 24-13 shows the data source using JSONP to request the initial data for the application.

Listing 24-13. Making a JSONP Request in the rest.datasource.ts File in the src/app/model Folder

```
import { Injectable, Inject, InjectionToken } from "@angular/core";
import { HttpClient } from "@angular/common/http";
import { Observable } from "rxjs";
import { Product } from "./product.model";

export const REST_URL = new InjectionToken("rest_url");

@Injectable()
export class RestDataSource {
    constructor(private http: HttpClient,
        @Inject(REST_URL) private url: string) { }

    getData(): Observable<Product[]> {
        return this.http.jsonp<Product[]>(this.url, "callback");
    }

    saveProduct(product: Product): Observable<Product> {
        return this.sendRequest<Product>("POST", this.url, product);
    }

    updateProduct(product: Product): Observable<Product> {
        return this.sendRequest<Product>("PUT",
            `${this.url}/${product.id}`, product);
    }

    deleteProduct(id: number): Observable<Product> {
        return this.sendRequest<Product>("DELETE", `${this.url}/${id}`);
    }
```

```
    private sendRequest<T>(verb: string, url: string, body?: Product)
            : Observable<T> {
        return this.http.request<T>(verb, url, {
            body: body
        });
    }
}
```

JSONP can be used only for get requests, which are sent using the `HttpClient.jsonp` method. When you call this method, you must provide the URL for the request and the name for the callback parameter, which must be set to `callback`, like this:

```
...
return this.http.jsonp<Product[]>(this.url, "callback");
...
```

When Angular makes the HTTP request, it creates a URL with the name of a dynamically generated function. If you look at the network requests that the browser makes, you will see that the initial request is sent to a URL like this one:

```
http://localhost:3500/products?callback=ng_jsonp_callback_0
```

The server JavaScript function that matches the name used in the URL and passes it the data received from the request. JSONP is a more limited way to make cross-origin requests, and, unlike CORS, it skirts around the browser's security policy, but it can be a useful fallback in a pinch.

Configuring Request Headers

If you are using a commercial RESTful web service, you will often have to set a request header to provide an API key so that the server can associate the request with your application for the purposes of access control and billing. You can set this kind of header—or any other header—by configuring the configuration object that is passed to the `request` method, as shown in Listing 24-14. (This listing also returns to using the request method for all requests, rather than JSONP.)

Listing 24-14. Setting a Request Header in the rest.datasource.ts File in the src/app/model Folder

```
import { Injectable, Inject, InjectionToken } from "@angular/core";
import { HttpClient, HttpHeaders } from "@angular/common/http";
import { Observable } from "rxjs";
import { Product } from "./product.model";

export const REST_URL = new InjectionToken("rest_url");

@Injectable()
export class RestDataSource {
    constructor(private http: HttpClient,
        @Inject(REST_URL) private url: string) { }
```

```
getData(): Observable<Product[]> {
    return this.sendRequest<Product[]>("GET", this.url);
}

saveProduct(product: Product): Observable<Product> {
    return this.sendRequest<Product>("POST", this.url, product);
}

updateProduct(product: Product): Observable<Product> {
    return this.sendRequest<Product>("PUT",
        `${this.url}/${product.id}`, product);
}

deleteProduct(id: number): Observable<Product> {
    return this.sendRequest<Product>("DELETE", `${this.url}/${id}`);
}

private sendRequest<T>(verb: string, url: string, body?: Product)
        : Observable<T> {
    return this.http.request<T>(verb, url, {
        body: body,
        headers: new HttpHeaders({
            "Access-Key": "<secret>",
            "Application-Name": "exampleApp"
        })
    });
}
}
```

The headers property is set to an HttpHeaders object, which can be created using a map object of properties that correspond to header names and the values that should be used for them. If you use the browser's F12 developer tools to inspect the asynchronous HTTP requests, you will see that the two headers specified in the listing are sent to the server along with the standard headers that the browser creates, like this:

```
...
Accept:*/*
Accept-Encoding:gzip, deflate, sdch, br
Accept-Language:en-US,en;q=0.8
access-key:<secret>
application-name:exampleApp
Connection:keep-alive
...
```

If you have more complex demands for request headers, then you can use the methods defined by the HttpHeaders class, as described in Table 24-7.

Table 24-7. *The HttpHeaders Methods*

Name	Description
keys()	Returns all the header names in the collection
get(name)	Returns the first value for the specified header
getAll(name)	Returns all the values for the specified header
has(name)	Returns true if the collection contains the specified header
set(header, value)	Returns a new HttpHeaders object that replaces all existing values for the specified header with a single value
set(header, values)	Returns a new HttpHeaders object that replaces all existing values for the specified header with an array of values
append(name, value)	Appends a value to the list of values for the specified header
delete(name)	Removes the specified header from the collection

HTTP headers can have multiple values, which is why there are methods that append values for headers or replace all the values in the collection. Listing 24-15 creates an empty HttpHeaders object and populates it with headers that have multiple values.

Listing 24-15. Setting Multiple Header Values in the rest.datasource.ts File in the src/app/model Folder

```
...
private sendRequest<T>(verb: string, url: string, body?: Product)
    : Observable<T> {

    let myHeaders = new HttpHeaders();
    myHeaders = myHeaders.set("Access-Key", "<secret>");
    myHeaders = myHeaders.set("Application-Names", ["exampleApp", "proAngular"]);

    return this.http.request<T>(verb, url, {
        body: body,
        headers: myHeaders
    });
}
...
```

When the browser sends requests to the server, they will include the following headers:

```
...
Accept:*/*
Accept-Encoding:gzip, deflate, sdch, br
Accept-Language:en-US,en;q=0.8
access-key:<secret>
application-names:exampleApp,proAngular
Connection:keep-alive
...
```

Handling Errors

At the moment, there is no error handling in the application, which means that Angular doesn't know what to do if there is a problem with an HTTP request. To make it easy to generate an error, I have added a button to the product table that will lead to an HTTP request to delete an object that doesn't exist at the server, as shown in Listing 24-16.

Listing 24-16. Adding an Error Button in the table.component.html File in the src/app/core Folder

```
<table class="table table-sm table-bordered table-striped">
  <tr>
    <th>ID</th><th>Name</th><th>Category</th><th>Price</th><th></th>
  </tr>
  <tr *ngFor="let item of getProducts()">
    <td style="vertical-align:middle">{{item.id}}</td>
    <td style="vertical-align:middle">{{item.name}}</td>
    <td style="vertical-align:middle">{{item.category}}</td>
    <td style="vertical-align:middle">
      {{item.price | currency:"USD" }}
    </td>
    <td class="text-center">
      <button class="btn btn-danger btn-sm" (click)="deleteProduct(item.id)">
        Delete
      </button>
      <button class="btn btn-warning btn-sm" (click)="editProduct(item.id)">
        Edit
      </button>
    </td>
  </tr>
</table>
<button class="btn btn-primary" (click)="createProduct()">
  Create New Product
</button>
<button class="btn btn-danger" (click)="deleteProduct(-1)">
    Generate HTTP Error
</button>
```

The button element invokes the component's deleteProduct method with an argument of -1. The component will ask the repository to delete this object, which will lead to an HTTP DELETE request being sent to /products/-1, which does not exist. If you open the browser's JavaScript console and click the new button, you will see the response from the server displayed, like this:

```
DELETE http://localhost:3500/products/-1 404 (Not Found)
```

Improving this situation means detecting this kind of error when one occurs and notifying the user, who won't typically be looking at the JavaScript console. A real application might also respond to errors by logging them so they can be analyzed later, but I am going to keep things simple and just display an error message.

Generating User-Ready Messages

The first step in handling errors is to convert the HTTP exception into something that can be displayed to the user. The default error message, which is the one written to the JavaScript console, contains too much information to display to the user. Users don't need to know the URL that the request was sent to; just having a sense of the kind of problem that has occurred will be enough.

The best way to transform error messages is to use the `catchError` and `throwError` methods. The `catchError` method is used with the `pipe` method to receive any errors that occur within an `Observable` sequence, and the `throwError` method is used to create a new `Observable` that just contains the error. Listing 24-17 applies both methods to the data source.

Listing 24-17. Transforming Errors in the rest.datasource.ts File in the src/app/model Folder

```
import { Injectable, Inject, InjectionToken } from "@angular/core";
import { HttpClient, HttpHeaders } from "@angular/common/http";
import { Observable, throwError } from "rxjs";
import { Product } from "./product.model";
import { catchError } from "rxjs/operators";

export const REST_URL = new InjectionToken("rest_url");

@Injectable()
export class RestDataSource {
    constructor(private http: HttpClient,
        @Inject(REST_URL) private url: string) { }

    getData(): Observable<Product[]> {
        return this.sendRequest<Product[]>("GET", this.url);
    }

    saveProduct(product: Product): Observable<Product> {
        return this.sendRequest<Product>("POST", this.url, product);
    }

    updateProduct(product: Product): Observable<Product> {
        return this.sendRequest<Product>("PUT",
            `${this.url}/${product.id}`, product);
    }

    deleteProduct(id: number): Observable<Product> {
        return this.sendRequest<Product>("DELETE", `${this.url}/${id}`);
    }

    private sendRequest<T>(verb: string, url: string, body?: Product)
        : Observable<T> {

        let myHeaders = new HttpHeaders();
        myHeaders = myHeaders.set("Access-Key", "<secret>");
        myHeaders = myHeaders.set("Application-Names", ["exampleApp", "proAngular"]);
```

```
    return this.http.request<T>(verb, url, {
        body: body,
        headers: myHeaders
    }).pipe(catchError((error: Response) =>
        throwError(`Network Error: ${error.statusText} (${error.status})`)));
}

}
```

The function passed to the `catchError` method is invoked when there is an error and receives the `Response` object that describes the outcome. The `throwError` function creates a new observable that contains just an error object, which in this case is used to generate an error message that contains the HTTP status code and status text from the response.

If you save the changes and then click the Generate HTTP Error button again, the error message will still be written to the browser's JavaScript console but will have changed to the format produced by the `catchError`/`throwError` methods.

```
EXCEPTION: Network Error: Not Found (404)
```

Handling the Errors

The errors have been transformed but not handled, which is why they are still being reported as exceptions in the browser's JavaScript console. There are two ways in which the errors can be handled. The first is to provide an error-handling function to the `subscribe` method for the `Observable` objects created by the `HttpClient` object. This is a useful way to localize the error and provide the repository with the opportunity to retry the operation or try to recover in some other way.

The second approach is to replace the built-in Angular error-handling feature, which responds to any unhandled errors in the application and, by default, writes them to the console. It is this feature that writes out the messages shown in the previous sections.

For the example application, I want to override the default error handler with one that uses the message service. I created a file called `errorHandler.ts` in the `src/app/messages` folder and used it to define the class shown in Listing 24-18.

Listing 24-18. The Contents of the errorHandler.ts File in the src/app/messages Folder

```
import { ErrorHandler, Injectable, NgZone } from "@angular/core";
import { MessageService } from "./message.service";
import { Message } from "./message.model";

@Injectable()
export class MessageErrorHandler implements ErrorHandler {

    constructor(private messageService: MessageService, private ngZone: NgZone) {
    }

    handleError(error) {
        let msg = error instanceof Error ? error.message : error.toString();
        this.ngZone.run(() => this.messageService
            .reportMessage(new Message(msg, true)), 0);
    }
}
```

The ErrorHandler class is defined in the @angular/core module and responds to errors through a handleError method. The class shown in the Listing replaces the default implementation of this method with one that uses the MessageService to report an error.

The constructor receives an ngZone object, which is part of the Angular support for asynchronous operations and is an essential part of the change detection feature. In this listing, the ngZone object's run method is used to report an error message so that the operation will trigger the change detection process and display the error to the user.

To replace the default ErrorHandler, I used a class provider in the message module, as shown in Listing 24-19.

Listing 24-19. Configuring an Error Handler in the message.module.ts File in the src/app/messages Folder

```
import { NgModule, ErrorHandler } from "@angular/core";
import { BrowserModule } from "@angular/platform-browser";
import { MessageComponent } from "./message.component";
import { MessageService } from "./message.service";
import { MessageErrorHandler } from "./errorHandler";

@NgModule({
    imports: [BrowserModule],
    declarations: [MessageComponent],
    exports: [MessageComponent],
    providers: [MessageService,
        { provide: ErrorHandler, useClass: MessageErrorHandler }]
})
export class MessageModule { }
```

The error handling function uses the MessageService to report an error message to the user. Once these changes have been saved, clicking the Generate HTTP Error button produces an error that the user can see, as shown in Figure 24-4.

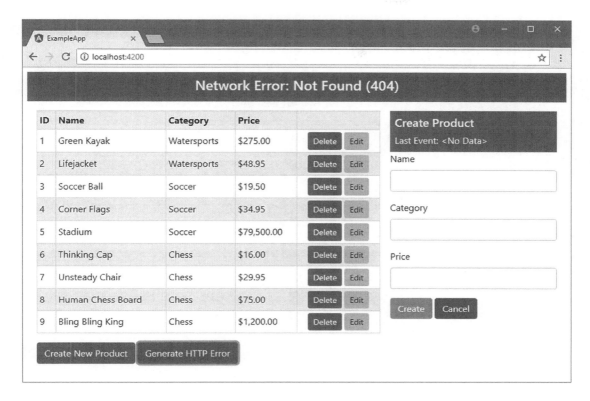

Figure 24-4. *Handling an HTTP error*

Summary

In this chapter, I explained how to make asynchronous HTTP requests in Angular applications. I introduced RESTful web services and the methods provided by the Angular HttpClient class that can be used to interact with them. I explained how the browser restricts requests to different origins and how Angular supports CORS and JSONP to make requests outside of the application's origin. In the next chapter, I introduce the URL routing feature, which allows for navigation around complex applications.

CHAPTER 25

■ ■ ■

Routing and Navigation: Part 1

The Angular routing feature allows applications to change the components and templates that are displayed to the user by responding to changes to the browser's URL. This allows complex applications to be created that adapt the content they present in an open and flexible way, with minimal coding. To support this feature, there are data bindings and services that can be used to change the browser's URL, allowing the user to navigate around the application.

Routing is useful as the complexity of a project increases because it allows the structure of an application to be defined separately from the components and directives, meaning that changes to the structure can be made in the routing configuration and do not have to be applied to the individual components.

In this chapter, I demonstrate how the basic routing system works and apply it to the example application. In Chapters 26 and 27, I explain the more advanced routing features. Table 25-1 puts routing in context.

Table 25-1. *Putting Routing and Navigation in Context*

Question	Answer
What is it?	Routing uses the browser's URL to manage the content displayed to the user.
Why is it useful?	Routing allows the structure of an application to be kept apart from the components and templates in the application. Changes to the structure of the application are made in the routing configuration rather than in individual components and directives.
How is it used?	The routing configuration is defined as a set of fragments that are used to match the browser's URL and select a component whose template is displayed as the content of an HTML element called `router-outlet`.
Are there any pitfalls or limitations?	The routing configuration can become unmanageable, especially if the URL schema is being defined gradually, on an ad hoc basis.
Are there any alternatives?	You don't have to use the routing feature. You could achieve similar results by creating a component whose view selects the content to display to the user with the `ngIf` or `ngSwitch` directive, although this approach becomes more difficult than using routing as the size and complexity of an application increases.

© Adam Freeman 2018
A. Freeman, *Pro Angular 6*, https://doi.org/10.1007/978-1-4842-3649-9_25

Table 25-2 summarizes the chapter.

Table 25-2. *Chapter Summary*

Problem	Solution	Listing
Use URL navigation to select the content shown to users	Use URL routing	1–7
Navigate using an HTML element	Apply the `routerLink` attribute	8–10
Respond to route changes	Use the routing services to receive notifications	11
Include information in URLs	Use route parameters	12–18
Navigate using code	Use the `Router` service	19
Receive notifications of routing activity	Handle the routing events	20–21

Preparing the Example Project

This chapter uses the exampleApp project created in Chapter 22. Some changes are required to prepare the project for this chapter. The application is configured to display the state change events sent from the table component to the product component in two places: through the message service and in the form component's template. These messages are no longer required, and Listing 25-1 removes the event display from the component's template.

■ **Tip**   You can download the example project for this chapter—and for all the other chapters in this book—from `https://github.com/Apress/pro-angular-6`.

Listing 25-1. Removing the Event Display in the form.component.html File in the src/app/core Folder

```
<div class="bg-primary text-white p-2" [class.bg-warning]="editing">
  <h5>{{editing  ? "Edit" : "Create"}} Product</h5>
  <!--Last Event: {{ stateEvents | async | formatState }}-->
</div>

<form novalidate #form="ngForm" (ngSubmit)="submitForm(form)" (reset)="resetForm()">

  <div class="form-group">
    <label>Name</label>
    <input class="form-control" name="name"
          [(ngModel)]="product.name" required />
  </div>

  <div class="form-group">
    <label>Category</label>
    <input class="form-control" name="category"
          [(ngModel)]="product.category" required />
  </div>
```

```
<div class="form-group">
  <label>Price</label>
  <input class="form-control" name="price"
         [(ngModel)]="product.price"
         required pattern="^[0-9\.]+$" />
</div>

<button type="submit" class="btn btn-primary"
        [class.btn-warning]="editing" [disabled]="form.invalid">
  {{editing ? "Save" : "Create"}}
</button>
<button type="reset" class="btn btn-secondary">Cancel</button>
</form>
```

Listing 25-2 disables the code that pushes the state change events into the message service.

Listing 25-2. Disabling State Change Events in the core.module.ts File in the src/app/core Folder

```
import { NgModule } from "@angular/core";
import { BrowserModule } from "@angular/platform-browser";
import { FormsModule } from "@angular/forms";
import { ModelModule } from "../model/model.module";
import { TableComponent } from "./table.component";
import { FormComponent } from "./form.component";
import { SharedState, SHARED_STATE } from "./sharedState.model";
import { Subject } from "rxjs";
import { StatePipe } from "./state.pipe";
import { MessageModule } from "../messages/message.module";
import { MessageService } from "../messages/message.service";
import { Message } from "../messages/message.model";
import { Model } from "../model/repository.model";
import { MODES } from "./sharedState.model";

@NgModule({
  imports: [BrowserModule, FormsModule, ModelModule, MessageModule],
  declarations: [TableComponent, FormComponent, StatePipe],
  exports: [ModelModule, TableComponent, FormComponent],
  providers: [{
    provide: SHARED_STATE,
    deps: [MessageService, Model],
    useFactory: (messageService, model) => {
      return new Subject<SharedState>();
      //let subject = new Subject<SharedState>();
      //subject.subscribe(m => messageService.reportMessage(
      //  new Message(MODES[m.mode] + (m.id != undefined
      //    ? ` ${model.getProduct(m.id).name}` : "")))
      //);
      //return subject;
    }
  }]
})
export class CoreModule { }
```

Open a new command prompt, navigate to the exampleApp folder, and run the following command to start the server that provides the RESTful web server:

```
npm run json
```

Open a separate command prompt, navigate to the exampleApp folder, and run the following command to start the Angular development tools:

```
ng serve
```

Open a new browser window and navigate to http://localhost:4200 to see the content shown in Figure 25-1.

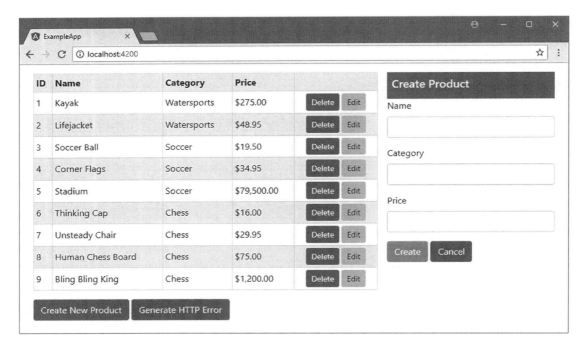

Figure 25-1. *Running the example application*

Getting Started with Routing

At the moment, all the content in the application is visible to the user all of the time. For the example application, this means that both the table and the form are always visible and it is up to the user to keep track of which part of the application they are using for the task at hand.

That's fine for a simple application, but it becomes unmanageable in a complex project, which can have many areas of functionality that would be overwhelming if they were all displayed at once.

URL routing adds structure to an application using a natural and well-understood aspect of web applications: the URL. In this section, I am going to introduce URL routing by applying it to the example application so that either the table or the form is visible, with the active component being chosen based on the user's actions. This will provide a good basis for explaining how routing works and set the foundation for more advanced features.

Creating a Routing Configuration

The first step when applying routing is to define the *routes*, which are mappings between URLs and the components that will be displayed to the user. Routing configurations are conventionally defined in a file called app.routing.ts, defined in the src/app folder. I created this file and added the statements shown in Listing 25-3.

Listing 25-3. The Contents of the app.routing.ts File in the src/app Folder

```
import { Routes, RouterModule } from "@angular/router";
import { TableComponent } from "./core/table.component";
import { FormComponent } from "./core/form.component";

const routes: Routes = [
    { path: "form/edit", component: FormComponent },
    { path: "form/create", component: FormComponent },
    { path: "", component: TableComponent }]

export const routing = RouterModule.forRoot(routes);
```

The Routes class defines a collection of routes, each of which tells Angular how to handle a specific URL. This example uses the most basic properties, where the path specifies the URL and the component property specifies the component that will be displayed to the user.

The path property is specified relative to the rest of the application, which means that the configuration in Listing 25-3 sets up the routes shown in Table 25-3.

Table 25-3. The Routes Created in the Example

URL	Displayed Component
http://localhost:4200/form/edit	FormComponent
http://localhost:4200/form/create	FormComponent
http://localhost:4200/	TableComponent

The routes are packaged into a module using the RouterModule.forRoot method. The forRoot method produces a module that includes the routing service. There is also a forChild method that doesn't include the service, and that is demonstrated in Chapter 26, where I explain how to create routes for feature modules.

Although the path and component properties are the most commonly used when defining routes, there is a range of additional properties that can be used to define routes with advanced features. These properties are described in Table 25-4, along with details of where they are described.

Table 25-4. *The Routes Properties Used to Define Routes*

Name	Description
path	This property specifies the path for the route.
component	This property specifies the component that will be selected when the active URL matches the path.
pathMatch	This property tells Angular how to match the current URL to the path property. There are two allowed values: full, which requires the path value to completely match the URL, and prefix, which allows the path value to match the URL, even if the URL contains additional segments that are not part of the path value. This property is required when using the redirectTo property, as demonstrated in Chapter 26.
redirectTo	This property is used to create a route that redirects the browser to a different URL when activated. See Chapter 26 for details.
children	This property is used to specify child routes, which display additional components in nested router-outlet elements contained in the template of the active component, as demonstrated in Chapter 26.
outlet	This property is used to support multiple outlet elements, as described in Chapter 27.
resolve	This property is used to define work that must be completed before a route can be activated, as described in Chapter 27.
canActivate	This property is used to control when a route can be activated, as described in Chapter 27.
canActivateChild	This property is used to control when a child route can be activated, as described in Chapter 27.
canDeactivate	This property is used to control when a route can be deactivated so that a new route can be activated, as described in Chapter 27.
loadChildren	This property is used to configure a module that is loaded only when it is needed, as described in Chapter 27.
canLoad	This property is used to control when an on-demand module can be loaded.

UNDERSTANDING ROUTE ORDERING

The order in which routes are defined is significant. Angular compares the URL to which the browser has navigated with the path property of each route in turn until it finds a match. This means that the most specific routes should be defined first, with the routes that follow decreasing in specificity. This isn't a big deal for the routes in Listing 25-3, but it becomes significant when using route parameters (described in the "Using Route Parameters" section of this chapter) or adding child routes (described in Chapter 26).

If you find that your routing configuration doesn't result in the behavior you expect, then the order in which the routes have been defined is the first thing to check.

Creating the Routing Component

When using routing, the root component is dedicated to managing the navigation between different parts of the application. This is the typical purpose of the app.component.ts file that was added to the project by the ng new command when it was created, and in Listing 25-4, I have updated its content for this use.

Listing 25-4. Replacing the Contents of the app.component.ts File in the src/app Folder

```
import { Component } from "@angular/core";

@Component({
    selector: "app",
    templateUrl: "./app.component.html"
})
export class AppComponent { }
```

This component is a vehicle for its template, which is the app.component.html file in the src/app folder. In Listing 25-5, I have replaced the default contents.

Listing 25-5. Replacing the Contents of the app.component.html File in the src/app File

```
<paMessages></paMessages>
<router-outlet></router-outlet>
```

The paMessages element displays any messages and errors in the application. For the purposes of routing, it is the router-outlet element—known as the *outlet*—that is important because it tells Angular that this is where the component matched by the routing configuration should be displayed.

Updating the Root Module

The next step is to update the root module so that the new root component is used to bootstrap the application, as shown in Listing 25-6, which also imports the module that contains the routing configuration.

Listing 25-6. Enabling Routing in the app.module.ts File in the src/app Folder

```
import { BrowserModule } from '@angular/platform-browser';
import { NgModule } from '@angular/core';
import { ModelModule } from "./model/model.module";
import { CoreModule } from "./core/core.module";
import { TableComponent } from "./core/table.component";
import { FormComponent } from "./core/form.component";
import { MessageModule } from "./messages/message.module";
import { MessageComponent } from "./messages/message.component";
import { AppComponent } from './app.component';
import { routing } from "./app.routing";

@NgModule({
    imports: [BrowserModule, ModelModule, CoreModule, MessageModule, routing],
    declarations: [AppComponent],
    bootstrap: [AppComponent]
})
export class AppModule { }
```

Completing the Configuration

The final step is to update the index.html file, as shown in Listing 25-7.

Listing 25-7. Configuring Routing in the index.html File in the src Folder

```
<!doctype html>
<html lang="en">
<head>
  <meta charset="utf-8">
  <title>ExampleApp</title>
  <base href="/">

  <meta name="viewport" content="width=device-width, initial-scale=1">
  <link rel="icon" type="image/x-icon" href="favicon.ico">
</head>
<body class="m-2">
  <app></app>
</body>
</html>
```

The app element applies the new root component, whose template contains the router-outlet element. When you save the changes and the browser reloads the application, you will see just the product table, as illustrated by Figure 25-2. The default URL for the application corresponds to the route that shows the product table.

■ **Tip** You may need to stop the Angular development tools and start them again using the ng serve command for this example.

Figure 25-2. *Using routing to display components to the user*

Adding Navigation Links

The basic routing configuration is in place, but there is no way to navigate around the application: nothing happens when you click the Create New Product or Edit button.

The next step is to add links to the application that will change the browser's URL and, in doing so, trigger a routing change that will display a different component to the user. Listing 25-8 adds these links to the table component's template.

Listing 25-8. Adding Navigation Links in the table.component.html File in the src/app/core Folder

```
<table class="table table-sm table-bordered table-striped">
    <tr>
        <th>ID</th><th>Name</th><th>Category</th><th>Price</th><th></th>
    </tr>
    <tr *ngFor="let item of getProducts()">
        <td style="vertical-align:middle">{{item.id}}</td>
        <td style="vertical-align:middle">{{item.name}}</td>
        <td style="vertical-align:middle">{{item.category}}</td>
        <td style="vertical-align:middle">
            {{item.price | currency:"USD" }}
        </td>
        <td class="text-center">
            <button class="btn btn-danger btn-sm" (click)="deleteProduct(item.id)">
                Delete
            </button>
```

```
                <button class="btn btn-warning btn-sm" (click)="editProduct(item.id)"
                        routerLink="/form/edit">
                    Edit
                </button>
            </td>
        </tr>
    </table>
<button class="btn btn-primary" (click)="createProduct()" routerLink="/form/create">
    Create New Product
</button>
<button class="btn btn-danger" (click)="deleteProduct(-1)">
    Generate HTTP Error
</button>
```

The routerLink attribute applies a directive from the routing package that performs the navigation change. This directive can be applied to any element, although it is typically applied to button and anchor (a) elements. The expression for the routerLink directive applied to the Edit buttons tells Angular to target the /form/edit route.

```
...
<button class="btn btn-warning btn-sm" (click)="editProduct(item.id)"
        routerLink="/form/edit">
    Edit
</button>
...
```

The same directive applied to the Create New Product button tells Angular to target the /create route.

```
...
<button class="btn btn-primary" (click)="createProduct()" routerLink="/form/create">
    Create New Product
</button>
...
```

The routing links added to the table component's template will allow the user to navigate to the form. The addition to the form component's template shown in Listing 25-9 will allow the user to navigate back again using the Cancel button.

Listing 25-9. Adding a Navigation Link in the form.component.html File in the src/app/core Folder

```
<div class="bg-primary text-white p-2" [class.bg-warning]="editing">
  <h5>{{editing  ? "Edit" : "Create"}} Product</h5>
  <!--Last Event: {{ stateEvents | async | formatState }}-->
</div>

<form novalidate #form="ngForm" (ngSubmit)="submitForm(form)" (reset)="resetForm()">

    <div class="form-group">
        <label>Name</label>
        <input class="form-control" name="name"
               [(ngModel)]="product.name" required />
    </div>
```

```html
<div class="form-group">
    <label>Category</label>
    <input class="form-control" name="category"
            [(ngModel)]="product.category" required />
</div>

<div class="form-group">
    <label>Price</label>
    <input class="form-control" name="price"
            [(ngModel)]="product.price"
            required pattern="^[0-9\.]+$" />
</div>

<button type="submit" class="btn btn-primary"
        [class.btn-warning]="editing" [disabled]="form.invalid">
    {{editing ? "Save" : "Create"}}
</button>
<button type="reset" class="btn btn-secondary" routerLink="/">Cancel</button>
</form>
```

The value assigned to the routerLink attribute targets the route that displays the product table. Listing 25-10 updates the feature module that contains the template so that it imports the RouterModule, which is the Angular module that contains the directive that selects the routerLink attribute.

Listing 25-10. Enabling the Routing Directive in the core.module.ts File in the src/app/core Folder

```typescript
import { NgModule } from "@angular/core";
import { BrowserModule } from "@angular/platform-browser";
import { FormsModule } from "@angular/forms";
import { ModelModule } from "../model/model.module";
import { TableComponent } from "./table.component";
import { FormComponent } from "./form.component";
import { SharedState, SHARED_STATE } from "./sharedState.model";
import { Subject } from "rxjs";
import { StatePipe } from "./state.pipe";
import { MessageModule } from "../messages/message.module";
import { MessageService } from "../messages/message.service";
import { Message } from "../messages/message.model";
import { Model } from "../model/repository.model";
import { MODES } from "./sharedState.model";
import { RouterModule } from "@angular/router";

@NgModule({
    imports: [BrowserModule, FormsModule, ModelModule, MessageModule, RouterModule],
    declarations: [TableComponent, FormComponent, StatePipe],
    exports: [ModelModule, TableComponent, FormComponent],
    providers: [{
        provide: SHARED_STATE,
        deps: [MessageService, Model],
```

```
        useFactory: (messageService, model) => {
            return new Subject<SharedState>();
        }
    }]
})
export class CoreModule { }
```

Understanding the Effect of Routing

When all the changes have been saved, you will be able to navigate around the application using the Edit, Create New Product, and Cancel buttons, as shown in Figure 25-3.

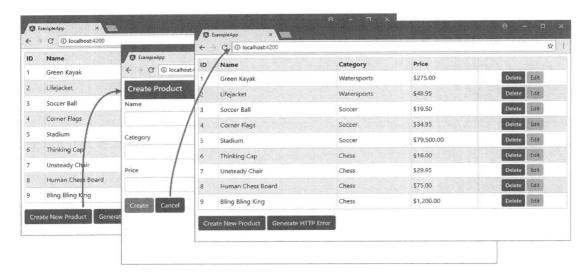

Figure 25-3. *Using routes to navigate around the application*

Not all the features in the application work yet, but this is a good time to explore the effect of adding routing to the application. Enter the root URL for the application (`http://localhost:4200`) and then click the Create New Product button. When you clicked the button, the Angular routing system changed the URL that the browser displays to this:

```
http://localhost:4200/form/create
```

If you watch the output from the development HTTP server during the transition, you will notice that no requests are received by the server for new content. This change is done entirely within the Angular application and does not produce any new HTTP requests.

The new URL is processed by the Angular routing system, which is able to match the new URL to this route from the `app.routing.ts` file.

```
...
{ path: "form/create", component: FormComponent },
...
```

The routing system takes into account the base element in the index.html file when it matches the URL to a route. The base element is configured with an href value of / that is combined with the path in the route to make a match when the URL is /form/create.

The component property tells the Angular routing system that it should display the FormComponent to the user. A new instance of the FormComponent class is created, and its template content is used as the content for the router-outlet element in the root component's template.

If you click the Cancel button below the form, then the process is repeated, but this time, the browser returns to the root URL for the application, which is matched by the route whose path component is the empty string.

```
{ path: "", component: TableComponent }
```

This route tells Angular to display the TableComponent to the user. A new instance of the TableComponent class is created, and its template is used as the content of the router-outlet element, displaying the model data to the user.

This is the essence of routing: the browser's URL changes, which causes the routing system to consult its configuration to determine which component should be displayed to the user. There are lots of options and features available, but this is the core purpose of routing, and you won't go too far wrong if you keep this in mind.

THE PERILS OF CHANGING THE URL MANUALLY

The routerLink directive sets the URL using a JavaScript API that tells the browser that this is a change relative to the current document and not a change that requires an HTTP request to the server.

If you enter a URL that matches the routing system into the browser window, you will see an effect that looks like the expected change but is actually something else entirely. Keep an eye on the output from the development HTTP server while manually entering the following URL into the browser:

http://localhost:4200/form/create

Rather than handling the change within the Angular application, the browser sends an HTTP request to the server, which reloads the application. Once the application is loaded, the routing system inspects the browser's URL, matches one of the routes in the configuration, and then displays the FormComponent.

The reason this works is that the development HTTP server will return the contents of the index.html file for URLs that don't correspond to files on the disk. As an example, request this URL:

http://localhost:4200/this/does/not/exist

The browser will display an error because the request has provided the browser with the contents of the index.html file, which it has used to load and start the example Angular application. When the routing system inspects the URL, it finds no matching route and creates an error.

There are two important points to note. The first is that when you test your application's routing configuration, you should check the HTTP requests that the browser is making because you will sometimes see the right result for the wrong reasons. On a fast machine, you may not even realize that the application has been reloaded and restarted by the browser.

Second, you must remember that the URL must be changed using the `routerLink` directive (or one of the similar features provided by the router module) and not manually, using the browser's URL bar.

Finally, since users won't know about the difference between programmatic and manual URL changes, your routing configuration should be able to deal with URLs that don't correspond to routes, as described in Chapter 26.

Completing the Routing Implementation

Adding routing to the application is a good start, but a lot of the application features just don't work. For example, clicking an Edit button displays the form, but it isn't populated, and it doesn't show the color cue that indicates editing. In the sections that follow, I use features provided by the routing system to finish wiring up the application so that everything works as expected.

Handling Route Changes in Components

The form component isn't working properly because it isn't being notified that the user has clicked a button to edit a product. This problem occurs because the routing system creates new instances of component classes only when it needs them, which means the FormComponent object is created only after the Edit button is clicked. If you click the Cancel button under the form and then click an Edit button in this table again, a second instance of the FormComponent will be created.

This leads to a timing issue in the way that the product component and the table component communicate, via a Reactive Extensions Subject. A Subject only passes on events to subscribers that arrive after the subscribe method has been called. The introduction of routing means that the FormComponent object is created after the event describing the edit operation has already been sent.

This problem could be solved by replacing the Subject with a BehaviorSubject, which sends the most recent event to subscribers when they call the subscribe method. But a more elegant approach—especially since this is a chapter on the routing system—is to use the URL to collaborate between components.

Angular provides a service that components can receive to get details of the current route. The relationship between the service and the types that it provides access to may seem complicated at first, but it will make sense as you see how the examples unfold and some of the different ways that routing can be used.

The class on which components declare a dependency is called ActivatedRoute. For the purposes of this section, it defines one important property, which is described in Table 25-5. There are other properties, too, which are described later in the chapter but which you can ignore for the moment.

Table 25-5. *The ActivatedRoute Property*

Name	Description
snapshot	This property returns an ActivatedRouteSnapshot object that describes the current route.

The snapshot property returns an instance of the ActivatedRouteSnapshot class, which provides information about the route that led to the current component being displayed to the user using the properties described in Table 25-6.

Table 25-6. *The Basic ActivatedRouteSnapshot Properties*

Name	Description
url	This property returns an array of UrlSegment objects, each of which describes a single segment in the URL that matched the current route.
params	This property returns a Params object, which describes the URL parameters, indexed by name.
queryParams	This property returns a Params object, which describes the URL query parameters, indexed by name.
fragment	This property returns a string containing the URL fragment.

The url property is the one that is most important for this example because it allows the component to inspect the segments of the current URL and extract the information from them required to perform an operation. The url property returns an array of UrlSegment objects, which provide the properties described in Table 25-7.

Table 25-7. *The URLSegment Properties*

Name	Description
path	This property returns a string that contains the segment value.
parameters	This property returns an indexed collection of parameters, as described in the "Using Route Parameters" section.

To determine what route has been activated by the user, the form component can declare a dependency on ActivatedRoute and then use the object it receives to inspect the segments of the URL, as shown in Listing 25-11.

Listing 25-11. Inspecting the Active Route in the form.component.ts File in the src/app/core Folder

```
import { Component, Inject } from "@angular/core";
import { NgForm } from "@angular/forms";
import { Product } from "../model/product.model";
import { Model } from "../model/repository.model";
import { MODES, SharedState, SHARED_STATE } from "./sharedState.model";
import { Observable } from "rxjs";
//import { filter, map, distinctUntilChanged, skipWhile } from "rxjs/operators";
import { ActivatedRoute } from "@angular/router";

@Component({
    selector: "paForm",
    templateUrl: "form.component.html",
    styleUrls: ["form.component.css"]
})
export class FormComponent {
    product: Product = new Product();
```

```
constructor(private model: Model, activeRoute: ActivatedRoute) {
    this.editing = activeRoute.snapshot.url[1].path == "edit";
}

editing: boolean = false;

submitForm(form: NgForm) {
    if (form.valid) {
        this.model.saveProduct(this.product);
        this.product = new Product();
        form.reset();
    }
}

resetForm() {
    this.product = new Product();
}
}
```

The component no longer uses Reactive Extensions to receive events. Instead, it inspects the second segment of the active route's URL to set the value of the editing property, which determines whether it should display its create or edit mode. If you click an Edit button in the table, you will now see the correct coloring displayed, as shown in Figure 25-4.

Figure 25-4. *Using the active route in a component*

Using Route Parameters

When I set up the routing configuration for the application, I defined two routes that targeted the form component, like this:

```
...
{ path: "form/edit", component: FormComponent },
{ path: "form/create", component: FormComponent },
...
```

When Angular is trying to match a route to a URL, it looks at each segment in turn and checks to see that it matches the URL that is being navigated to. Both of these URLs are made up of *static segments*, which means they have to match the navigated URL exactly before Angular will activate the route.

Angular routes can be more flexible and include route *parameters*, which allow any value for a segment to match the corresponding segment in the navigated URL. This means routes that target the same component with similar URLs can be consolidated into a single route, as shown in Listing 25-12.

Listing 25-12. Consolidating Routes in the app.routing.ts File in the src/app Folder

```
import { Routes, RouterModule } from "@angular/router";
import { TableComponent } from "./core/table.component";
import { FormComponent } from "./core/form.component";

const routes: Routes = [
    { path: "form/:mode", component: FormComponent },
    { path: "", component: TableComponent }
]

export const routing = RouterModule.forRoot(routes);
```

The second segment of the modified URL defines a route parameter, denoted by the colon (the : character) followed by a name. In this case, the route parameter is called mode. This route will match any URL that has two segments where the first segment is form, as summarized in Table 25-8. The content of the second segment will be assigned to a parameter called mode.

Table 25-8. *URL Matching with the Route Parameter*

URL	Result
http://localhost:4200/form	No match—too few segments
http://localhost:4200/form/create	Matches, with create assigned to the mode parameter
http://localhost:4200/form/london	Matches, with london assigned to the mode parameter
http://localhost:4200/product/edit	No match—the first segment is not form
http://localhost:4200/form/edit/1	No match—too many segments

Using route parameters make it simpler to handle routes programmatically because the value of the parameter can be obtained using its name, as shown in Listing 25-13.

Listing 25-13. Reading a Route Parameter in the form.component.ts File in the src/app/core Folder

```
import { Component, Inject } from "@angular/core";
import { NgForm } from "@angular/forms";
import { Product } from "../model/product.model";
import { Model } from "../model/repository.model";
import { ActivatedRoute } from "@angular/router";

@Component({
    selector: "paForm",
    templateUrl: "form.component.html",
    styleUrls: ["form.component.css"]
})
export class FormComponent {
    product: Product = new Product();

    constructor(private model: Model, activeRoute: ActivatedRoute) {
        this.editing = activeRoute.snapshot.params["mode"] == "edit";
    }

    // ...methods and property omitted for brevity...
}
```

The component doesn't need to know the structure of the URL to get the information it needs. Instead, it can use the params property provided by the ActivatedRouteSnapshot class to get a collection of the parameter values, indexed by name. The component gets the value of the mode parameter and uses it to set the editing property.

Using Multiple Route Parameters

To tell the form component which product has been selected when the user clicks an Edit button, I need to use a second route parameter. Since Angular matches URLs based on the number of segments they contain, this means I need to split up the routes that target the form component again, as shown in Listing 25-14. This cycle of consolidating and then expanding routes is typical of most development projects as you increase the amount of information that is included in routed URLs to add functionality to the application.

Listing 25-14. Adding a Route in the app.routing.ts File in the src/app Folder

```
import { Routes, RouterModule } from "@angular/router";
import { TableComponent } from "./core/table.component";
import { FormComponent } from "./core/form.component";

const routes: Routes = [
    { path: "form/:mode/:id", component: FormComponent },
    { path: "form/:mode", component: FormComponent },
    { path: "", component: TableComponent }]

export const routing = RouterModule.forRoot(routes);
```

The new route will match any URL that has three segments where the first segment is form. To create URLs that target this route, I need to use a different approach for the routerLink expressions in the template because I need to generate the third segment dynamically for each Edit button in the product table, as shown in Listing 25-15.

Listing 25-15. Generating Dynamic URLs in the table.component.html File in the src/app/core Folder

```
<table class="table table-sm table-bordered table-striped">
    <tr>
        <th>ID</th><th>Name</th><th>Category</th><th>Price</th><th></th>
    </tr>
    <tr *ngFor="let item of getProducts()">
        <td style="vertical-align:middle">{{item.id}}</td>
        <td style="vertical-align:middle">{{item.name}}</td>
        <td style="vertical-align:middle">{{item.category}}</td>
        <td style="vertical-align:middle">
            {{item.price | currency:"USD" }}
        </td>
        <td class="text-center">
            <button class="btn btn-danger btn-sm" (click)="deleteProduct(item.id)">
                Delete
            </button>
            <button class="btn btn-warning btn-sm" (click)="editProduct(item.id)"
                    [routerLink]="['/form', 'edit', item.id]">
                Edit
            </button>
        </td>
    </tr>
</table>
<button class="btn btn-primary" (click)="createProduct()" routerLink="/form/create">
    Create New Product
</button>
<button class="btn btn-danger" (click)="deleteProduct(-1)">
    Generate HTTP Error
</button>
```

The routerLink attribute is now enclosed in square brackets, telling Angular that it should treat the attribute value as a data binding expression. The expression is set out as an array, with each element containing the value for one segment. The first two segments are literal strings and will be included in the target URL without modification. The third segment will be evaluated to include the id property value for the current Product object being processed by the ngIf directive, just like the other expressions in the template. The routerLink directive will combine the individual segments to create a URL such as /form/edit/2.

Listing 25-16 shows how the form component gets the value of the new route parameter and uses it to select the product that is to be edited.

Listing 25-16. Using the New Route Parameter in the form.component.ts File in the src/app/core Folder

```
import { Component, Inject } from "@angular/core";
import { NgForm } from "@angular/forms";
import { Product } from "../model/product.model";
import { Model } from "../model/repository.model";
import { ActivatedRoute } from "@angular/router";
```

```
@Component({
    selector: "paForm",
    templateUrl: "form.component.html",
    styleUrls: ["form.component.css"]
})
export class FormComponent {
    product: Product = new Product();

    constructor(private model: Model, activeRoute: ActivatedRoute) {
        this.editing = activeRoute.snapshot.params["mode"] == "edit";
        let id = activeRoute.snapshot.params["id"];
        if (id != null) {
            Object.assign(this.product, model.getProduct(id) || new Product());
        }
    }

    editing: boolean = false;

    submitForm(form: NgForm) {
        if (form.valid) {
            this.model.saveProduct(this.product);
            this.product = new Product();
            form.reset();
        }
    }

    resetForm() {
        this.product = new Product();
    }
}
```

When the user clicks an Edit button, the routing URL that is activated tells the form component that an edit operation is required and which product is to be modified, allowing the form to be populated correctly, as shown in Figure 25-5.

■ **Tip** Notice that I check to confirm that I have been able to retrieve a Product object from the data model in Listing 25-16 and create a new object if that isn't the case. This is important because the data in the model is obtained asynchronously and may not have arrived by the time that the form component is displayed if the user requests the URL directly. This can also be a problem in development, where a change to the code in the application triggers a recompilation followed by a reload of whatever URL you navigated to before making the change. The result is an error as Angular tries to navigate directly to a route that you expected would not be required until after the data model had been populated. In Chapter 27, I explain how you can stop routes from being activated until a specific condition is true, such as the arrival of the data.

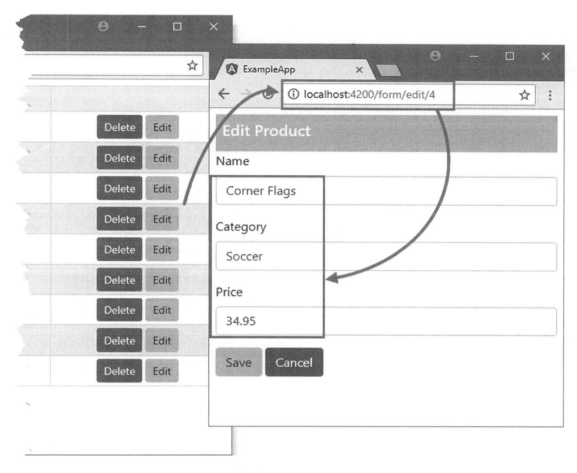

Figure 25-5. Using URLs segments to provide information

Using Optional Route Parameters

Optional route parameters allow URLs to include information to provide hints or guidance to the rest of the application, but this is not essential for the application to work.

This type of route parameter is expressed using URL matrix notation, which isn't part of the specification for URLs but which browsers support nonetheless. Here is an example of a URL that has optional route parameters:

```
http://localhost:4200/form/edit/2;name=Lifejacket;price=48.95
```

The optional route parameters are separated by semicolons (the ; character), and this URL includes optional parameters called name and price.

As a demonstration of how to use optional parameters, Listing 25-17 shows the addition of an optional route parameter that includes the object to be edited as part of the URL. This information isn't essential because the form component can get data from the model, but receiving the data via the routing URL would avoid some work.

Listing 25-17. An Optional Route Parameter in the table.component.html File in the src/app/core Folder

```
<table class="table table-sm table-bordered table-striped">
    <tr>
        <th>ID</th><th>Name</th><th>Category</th><th>Price</th><th></th>
    </tr>
    <tr *ngFor="let item of getProducts()">
        <td style="vertical-align:middle">{{item.id}}</td>
        <td style="vertical-align:middle">{{item.name}}</td>
        <td style="vertical-align:middle">{{item.category}}</td>
        <td style="vertical-align:middle">
            {{item.price | currency:"USD" }}
        </td>
        <td class="text-center">
            <button class="btn btn-danger btn-sm" (click)="deleteProduct(item.id)">
                Delete
            </button>
            <button class="btn btn-warning btn-sm" (click)="editProduct(item.id)"
                    [routerLink]="['/form', 'edit', item.id,
                    {name: item.name, category: item.category, price: item.price}]">
                Edit
            </button>
        </td>
    </tr>
</table>
<button class="btn btn-primary" (click)="createProduct()" routerLink="/form/create">
    Create New Product
</button>
<button class="btn btn-danger" (click)="deleteProduct(-1)">
    Generate HTTP Error
</button>
```

The optional values are expressed as literal objects, where property names identify the optional parameter. In this example, there are name, category, and price properties, and their values are set using the object being processed by the ngIf directive. The optional parameters will produce a URL like this one:

```
http://localhost:4200/form/edit/5;name=Stadium;category=Soccer;price=79500
```

Listing 25-18 shows how the form component checks to see whether the optional parameters are present. If they have been included in the URL, then the parameter values are used to avoid a request to the data model.

Listing 25-18. Receiving Optional Parameters in the form.component.ts File in the src/app/core Folder

```
...
constructor(private model: Model, activeRoute: ActivatedRoute) {
    this.editing = activeRoute.snapshot.params["mode"] == "edit";
    let id = activeRoute.snapshot.params["id"];
    if (id != null) {
        let name = activeRoute.snapshot.params["name"];
        let category = activeRoute.snapshot.params["category"];
```

```
    let price = activeRoute.snapshot.params["price"];

    if (name != null && category != null && price != null) {
        this.product.id = id;
        this.product.name = name;
        this.product.category = category;
        this.product.price = Number.parseFloat(price);
    } else {
        Object.assign(this.product, model.getProduct(id) || new Product());
    }
  }
}
...
```

Optional route parameters are accessed in the same way as required parameters, and it is the responsibility of the component to check to see whether they are present and to proceed anyway if they are not part of the URL. In this case, the component is able to fall back to querying the data model if the URL does not contain the optional parameters it looks for.

Navigating in Code

Using the routerLink attribute makes it easy to set up navigation in templates, but applications will often need to initiate navigation on behalf of the user within a component or directive.

To give access to the routing system to building blocks such as directives and components, Angular provides the Router class, which is available as a service through dependency injection and whose most useful methods and properties are described in Table 25-9.

Table 25-9. *Selected Router Methods and Properties*

Name	Description
navigated	This boolean property returns true if there has been at least one navigation event and false otherwise.
url	This property returns the active URL.
isActive(url, exact)	This method returns true if the specified URL is the URL defined by the active route. The exact argument specified whether all the segments in the specified URL must match the current URL for the method to return true.
events	This property returns an Observable<Event> that can be used to monitor navigation changes. See the "Receiving Navigation Events" section for details.
navigateByUrl(url, extras)	This method navigates to the specified URL. The result of the method is a Promise, which resolves with true when the navigation is successful and false when it is not and which is rejected when there is an error.
navigate(commands, extras)	This method navigates using an array of segments. The extras object can be used to specify whether the change of URL is relative to the current route. The result of the method is a Promise, which resolves with true when the navigation is successful and false when it is not and which is rejected when there is an error.

The navigate and navigateByUrl methods make it easy to perform navigation inside a building block such as a component. Listing 25-19 shows the use of the Router in the form component to redirect the application back to the table after a product has been created or updated.

Listing 25-19. Navigating Programmatically in the form.component.ts File in the src/app/core Folder

```
import { Component, Inject } from "@angular/core";
import { NgForm } from "@angular/forms";
import { Product } from "../model/product.model";
import { Model } from "../model/repository.model";
import { ActivatedRoute, Router } from "@angular/router";

@Component({
    selector: "paForm",
    templateUrl: "form.component.html",
    styleUrls: ["form.component.css"]
})
export class FormComponent {
    product: Product = new Product();

    constructor(private model: Model, activeRoute: ActivatedRoute,
                private router: Router) {

        this.editing = activeRoute.snapshot.params["mode"] == "edit";

        let id = activeRoute.snapshot.params["id"];
        if (id != null) {
            let name = activeRoute.snapshot.params["name"];
            let category = activeRoute.snapshot.params["category"];
            let price = activeRoute.snapshot.params["price"];

            if (name != null && category != null && price != null) {
                this.product.id = id;
                this.product.name = name;
                this.product.category = category;
                this.product.price = Number.parseFloat(price);
            } else {
                Object.assign(this.product, model.getProduct(id) || new Product());
            }
        }
    }

    editing: boolean = false;

    submitForm(form: NgForm) {
        if (form.valid) {
            this.model.saveProduct(this.product);
            //this.product = new Product();
            //form.reset();
            this.router.navigateByUrl("/");
        }
    }
}
```

```
    resetForm() {
        this.product = new Product();
    }
}
```

The component receives the Router object as a constructor argument and uses it in the submitForm method to navigate back to the application's root URL. The two statements that have been commented out in the submitForm method are no longer required because the routing system will destroy the form component once it is no longer on display, which means that resetting the form's state is not required.

The result is that clicking the Save or Create button in the form will cause the application to display the product table, as shown in Figure 25-6.

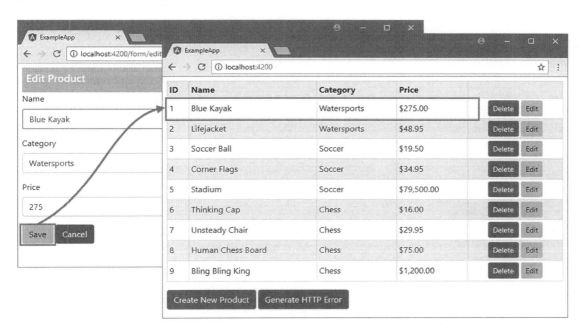

Figure 25-6. *Navigating programmatically*

Receiving Navigation Events

In many applications, there will be components or directives that are not directly involved in the application's navigation but that still need to know when navigation occurs. The example application contains an example in the message component, which displays notifications and errors to the user. This component always displays the most recent message, even when that information is stale and unlikely to be helpful to the user. To see the problem, click the Generate HTTP Error button and then click the Create New Product button or one of the Edit buttons; the error message remains on display even though you have navigated elsewhere in the application.

The events property defined by the Router class returns an Observable<Event>, which emits a sequence of Event objects that describe changes from the routing system. There are five types of event provided through the observer, as described in Table 25-10.

Table 25-10. *The Types of Event Provided by the Router.events Observer*

Name	Description
NavigationStart	This event is sent when the navigation process starts.
RoutesRecognized	This event is sent when the routing system matches the URL to a route.
NavigationEnd	This event is sent when the navigation process completes successfully.
NavigationError	This event is sent when the navigation process produces an error.
NavigationCancel	This event is sent when the navigation process is canceled.

All the event classes define an id property, which returns a number that is incremented each for each navigation, and a url property, which returns the target URL. The RoutesRecognized and NavigationEnd events also define a urlAfterRedirects property, which returns the URL that has been navigated to.

To address the issue with the messaging system, Listing 25-20 subscribes to the observer provided by the Router.events property and clears the message displayed to the user when the NavigationEnd or NavigationCancel event is received.

Listing 25-20. Responding to Events in the message.component.ts File in the src/app/messages Folder

```
import { Component } from "@angular/core";
import { MessageService } from "./message.service";
import { Message } from "./message.model";
import { Observable } from "rxjs";
import { Router, NavigationEnd, NavigationCancel } from "@angular/router";
import { filter } from "rxjs/operators";

@Component({
    selector: "paMessages",
    templateUrl: "message.component.html",
})
export class MessageComponent {
    lastMessage: Message;

    constructor(messageService: MessageService, router: Router) {
        messageService.messages.subscribe(m => this.lastMessage = m);
        router.events
            .pipe(filter(e => e instanceof NavigationEnd
                || e instanceof NavigationCancel))
            .subscribe(e => { this.lastMessage = null; });
    }
}
```

The filter method is used to select one type of event from the observer, and the subscribe method updates the lastMessage property, which will clear the message displayed by the component. Listing 25-21 imports the routing functionality into the message module. (This isn't required to make the application work since the root module already imports the routing feature, but it is good practice to have each module import all the features it requires.)

Listing 25-21. Importing the Routing Module in the message.module.ts File in the src/app/messages Folder

```
import { NgModule, ErrorHandler } from "@angular/core";
import { BrowserModule } from "@angular/platform-browser";
import { MessageComponent } from "./message.component";
import { MessageService } from "./message.service";
import { MessageErrorHandler } from "./errorHandler";
import { RouterModule } from "@angular/router";

@NgModule({
    imports: [BrowserModule, RouterModule],
    declarations: [MessageComponent],
    exports: [MessageComponent],
    providers: [MessageService,
        { provide: ErrorHandler, useClass: MessageErrorHandler }]
})
export class MessageModule { }
```

The result of these changes is that messages are shown to the user only until the next navigation event, as shown in Figure 25-7.

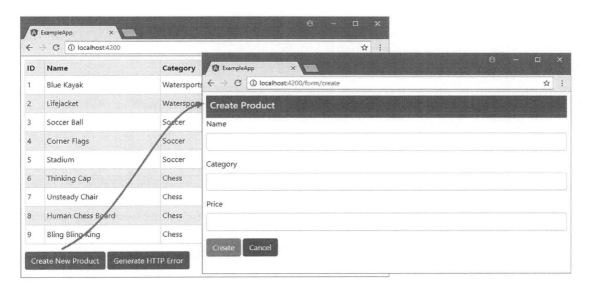

Figure 25-7. *Responding to navigation events*

Removing the Event Bindings and Supporting Code

One of the benefits of using the routing system is that it can simplify applications, replacing event bindings and the methods they invoke with navigation changes. The final change to complete the routing implementation is to remove the last traces of the previous mechanism that was used to coordinate between components. Listing 25-22 comments out the event bindings from the table component's template, which were used to respond when the user clicked the Create New Product or Edit button. (The event binding for the Delete buttons is still required.)

Listing 25-22. Removing Event Bindings in the table.component.html File in the src/app/core Folder

```html
<table class="table table-sm table-bordered table-striped">
    <tr>
        <th>ID</th><th>Name</th><th>Category</th><th>Price</th><th></th>
    </tr>
    <tr *ngFor="let item of getProducts()">
        <td style="vertical-align:middle">{{item.id}}</td>
        <td style="vertical-align:middle">{{item.name}}</td>
        <td style="vertical-align:middle">{{item.category}}</td>
        <td style="vertical-align:middle">
            {{item.price | currency:"USD" }}
        </td>
        <td class="text-center">
            <button class="btn btn-danger btn-sm" (click)="deleteProduct(item.id)">
                Delete
            </button>
            <button class="btn btn-warning btn-sm"
                [routerLink]="['/form', 'edit', item.id,
                    {name: item.name, category: item.category, price: item.price}]">
                Edit
            </button>
        </td>
    </tr>
</table>
<button class="btn btn-primary" routerLink="/form/create">
    Create New Product
</button>
<button class="btn btn-danger" (click)="deleteProduct(-1)">
    Generate HTTP Error
</button>
```

Listing 25-23 shows the corresponding changes in the component, which remove the methods that the event bindings invoked and the dependency on the service that was used to signal when a product should be edited or created.

Listing 25-23. Removing Event Handling Code in the table.component.ts File in the src/app/core Folder

```typescript
import { Component, Inject } from "@angular/core";
import { Product } from "../model/product.model";
import { Model } from "../model/repository.model";
//import { MODES, SharedState, SHARED_STATE } from "./sharedState.model";
//import { Observer } from "rxjs";

@Component({
    selector: "paTable",
    templateUrl: "table.component.html"
})
export class TableComponent {

    constructor(private model: Model,
        /*@Inject(SHARED_STATE) private observer: Observer<SharedState>*/) { }
```

```
    getProduct(key: number): Product {
        return this.model.getProduct(key);
    }

    getProducts(): Product[] {
        return this.model.getProducts();
    }

    deleteProduct(key: number) {
        this.model.deleteProduct(key);
    }

    //editProduct(key: number) {
    //    this.observer.next(new SharedState(MODES.EDIT, key));
    //}

    //createProduct() {
    //    this.observer.next(new SharedState(MODES.CREATE));
    //}
}
```

The service used for coordination by the components is no longer required, and Listing 25-24 disables it from the core module.

Listing 25-24. Removing the Shared State Service in the core.module.ts File in the src/app/core Folder

```
import { NgModule } from "@angular/core";
import { BrowserModule } from "@angular/platform-browser";
import { FormsModule } from "@angular/forms";
import { ModelModule } from "../model/model.module";
import { TableComponent } from "./table.component";
import { FormComponent } from "./form.component";
//import { SharedState, SHARED_STATE } from "./sharedState.model";
import { Subject } from "rxjs";
import { StatePipe } from "./state.pipe";
import { MessageModule } from "../messages/message.module";
import { MessageService } from "../messages/message.service";
import { Message } from "../messages/message.model";
import { Model } from "../model/repository.model";
//import { MODES } from "./sharedState.model";
import { RouterModule } from "@angular/router";

@NgModule({
    imports: [BrowserModule, FormsModule, ModelModule, MessageModule, RouterModule],
    declarations: [TableComponent, FormComponent, StatePipe],
    exports: [ModelModule, TableComponent, FormComponent],
    //providers: [{
    //    provide: SHARED_STATE,
    //    deps: [MessageService, Model],
```

```
//    useFactory: (messageService, model) => {
//        return new Subject<SharedState>();
//    }
//}]
})
export class CoreModule { }
```

The result is that the coordination between the table and form components is handled entirely through the routing system, which is now responsible for displaying the components and managing the navigation between them.

Summary

In this chapter, I introduced the Angular routing feature and demonstrated how to navigate to a URL in an application in order to select the content that is displayed to the user. I showed you how to create navigation links in templates, how to perform navigation in a component or directive, and how to respond to navigation changes programmatically. In the next chapter, I continue describing the Angular routing system.

CHAPTER 26

■ ■ ■

Routing and Navigation: Part 2

In the previous chapter, I introduced the Angular URL routing system and explained how it can be used to control the components that are displayed to the user. The routing system has a lot of features, which I continue to describe in this chapter and in Chapter 27. This emphasis on this chapter is about creating more complex routes, including routes that will match any URL, routes that redirect the browser to other URLs, routes that navigate within a component, and routes that select multiple components. Table 26-1 summarizes the chapter.

Table 26-1. *Chapter Summary*

Problem	Solution	Listing
Match multiple URLs with a single route	Use routing wildcards	1–10
Redirect one URL to another	Use a redirection route	11
Navigate within a component	Use a relative URL	12
Receive notifications when the activated URL changes	Use the Observable objects provided by the ActivatedRoute class	13
Style an element when a specific route is active	Use the routerLinkActive attribute	14–17
Use the routing system to displayed nested components	Define child routes and use the router-outlet element	18–22

Preparing the Example Project

For this chapter, I will continue using the exampleApp that was created in Chapter 22 and has been modified in each subsequent chapter. To prepare for this chapter, I have added two methods to the repository class, as shown in Listing 26-1.

■ **Tip** You can download the example project for this chapter—and for all the other chapters in this book—from https://github.com/Apress/pro-angular-6.

Listing 26-1. Adding Methods in the repository.model.ts File in the src/app/model Folder

```
import { Injectable } from "@angular/core";
import { Product } from "./product.model";
import { Observable } from "rxjs";
import { RestDataSource } from "./rest.datasource";

@Injectable()
export class Model {
    private products: Product[] = new Array<Product>();
    private locator = (p: Product, id: number) => p.id == id;

    constructor(private dataSource: RestDataSource) {
        this.dataSource.getData().subscribe(data => this.products = data);
    }

    getProducts(): Product[] {
        return this.products;
    }

    getProduct(id: number): Product {
        return this.products.find(p => this.locator(p, id));
    }

    getNextProductId(id: number): number {
        let index = this.products.findIndex(p => this.locator(p, id));
        if (index > -1) {
            return this.products[this.products.length > index + 2
                ? index + 1 : 0].id;
        } else {
            return id || 0;
        }
    }

    getPreviousProductid(id: number): number {
        let index = this.products.findIndex(p => this.locator(p, id));
        if (index > -1) {
            return this.products[index > 0
                ? index - 1 : this.products.length - 1].id;
        } else {
            return id || 0;
        }
    }

    saveProduct(product: Product) {
        if (product.id == 0 || product.id == null) {
            this.dataSource.saveProduct(product)
                .subscribe(p => this.products.push(p));
        } else {
```

```
        this.dataSource.updateProduct(product).subscribe(p => {
            let index = this.products
                .findIndex(item => this.locator(item, p.id));
            this.products.splice(index, 1, p);
        });
    }
}

deleteProduct(id: number) {
    this.dataSource.deleteProduct(id).subscribe(() => {
        let index = this.products.findIndex(p => this.locator(p, id));
        if (index > -1) {
            this.products.splice(index, 1);
        }
    });
}
}
```

The new methods accept an ID value, locate the corresponding product, and then return the IDs of the next and previous objects in the array that the repository uses to collect the data model objects. I will use this feature later in the chapter to allow the user to page through the set of objects in the data model.

To simplify the example, Listing 26-2 removes the statements in the form component that receive the details of the product to edit using optional route parameters.

Listing 26-2. Removing Optional Parameters in the form.component.ts File in the src/app/core Folder

```
import { Component, Inject } from "@angular/core";
import { NgForm } from "@angular/forms";
import { Product } from "../model/product.model";
import { Model } from "../model/repository.model";
import { ActivatedRoute, Router } from "@angular/router";

@Component({
    selector: "paForm",
    templateUrl: "form.component.html",
    styleUrls: ["form.component.css"]
})
export class FormComponent {
    product: Product = new Product();

    constructor(private model: Model, activeRoute: ActivatedRoute,
        private router: Router) {

        this.editing = activeRoute.snapshot.params["mode"] == "edit";
        let id = activeRoute.snapshot.params["id"];
        if (id != null) {
            Object.assign(this.product, model.getProduct(id) || new Product());
        }
    }
```

```
    editing: boolean = false;

    submitForm(form: NgForm) {
        if (form.valid) {
            this.model.saveProduct(this.product);
            this.router.navigateByUrl("/");
        }
    }

    resetForm() {
        this.product = new Product();
    }
}
```

Listing 26-3 removes the optional parameters from the table component's template so they are not included in the navigation URLs for the Edit buttons.

Listing 26-3. Removing Route Parameters in the table.component.html File in the src/app/core Folder

```
<table class="table table-sm table-bordered table-striped">
    <tr>
        <th>ID</th><th>Name</th><th>Category</th><th>Price</th><th></th>
    </tr>
    <tr *ngFor="let item of getProducts()">
        <td style="vertical-align:middle">{{item.id}}</td>
        <td style="vertical-align:middle">{{item.name}}</td>
        <td style="vertical-align:middle">{{item.category}}</td>
        <td style="vertical-align:middle">
            {{item.price | currency:"USD" }}
        </td>
        <td class="text-center">
            <button class="btn btn-danger btn-sm" (click)="deleteProduct(item.id)">
                Delete
            </button>
            <button class="btn btn-warning btn-sm"
                [routerLink]="['/form', 'edit', item.id]">
                Edit
            </button>
        </td>
    </tr>
</table>
<button class="btn btn-primary" routerLink="/form/create">
    Create New Product
</button>
<button class="btn btn-danger" (click)="deleteProduct(-1)">
    Generate HTTP Error
</button>
```

Adding Components to the Project

I need to add some components to the application to demonstrate some of the features covered in this chapter. These components are simple because I am focusing on the routing system, rather than adding useful features to the application. I created a file called productCount.component.ts to the src/app/core folder and used it to define the component shown in Listing 26-4.

■ **Tip**   You can omit the `selector` attribute from the `@Component` decorator if a component is only going to be displayed through the routing system. I tend to add it anyway so that I can apply the component using an HTML element as well.

Listing 26-4. The Contents of the productCount.component.ts File in the src/app/core Folder

```
import {
    Component, KeyValueDiffer, KeyValueDiffers, ChangeDetectorRef
} from "@angular/core";
import { Model } from "../model/repository.model";

@Component({
    selector: "paProductCount",
    template: `<div class="bg-info text-white p-2">There are
                    {{count}} products
                </div>`
})
export class ProductCountComponent {
    private differ: KeyValueDiffer<any, any>;
    count: number = 0;

    constructor(private model: Model,
        private keyValueDiffers: KeyValueDiffers,
        private changeDetector: ChangeDetectorRef) { }

    ngOnInit() {
        this.differ = this.keyValueDiffers
            .find(this.model.getProducts())
            .create();
    }

    ngDoCheck() {
        if (this.differ.diff(this.model.getProducts()) != null) {
            this.updateCount();
        }
    }

    private updateCount() {
        this.count = this.model.getProducts().length;
    }
}
```

This component uses an inline template to display the number of products in the data model, which is updated when the data model changes. Next, I added a file called categoryCount.component.ts in the src/app/core folder and defined the component shown in Listing 26-5.

Listing 26-5. The Contents of the categoryCount.component.ts File in the src/app/core Folder

```
import {
    Component, KeyValueDiffer, KeyValueDiffers, ChangeDetectorRef
} from "@angular/core";
import { Model } from "../model/repository.model";

@Component({
    selector: "paCategoryCount",
    template: `<div class="bg-primary p-2 text-white">
                    There are {{count}} categories
               </div>`
})
export class CategoryCountComponent {
    private differ: KeyValueDiffer<any, any>;
    count: number = 0;

    constructor(private model: Model,
        private keyValueDiffers: KeyValueDiffers,
        private changeDetector: ChangeDetectorRef) { }

    ngOnInit() {
        this.differ = this.keyValueDiffers
            .find(this.model.getProducts())
            .create();
    }

    ngDoCheck() {
        if (this.differ.diff(this.model.getProducts()) != null) {
            this.count = this.model.getProducts()
                .map(p => p.category)
                .filter((category, index, array) => array.indexOf(category) == index)
                .length;
        }
    }
}
```

This component uses a differ to track changes in the data model and count the number of unique categories, which is displayed using a simple inline template. For the final component, I added a file called notFound.component.ts in the src/app/core folder and used it to define the component shown in Listing 26-6.

Listing 26-6. The notFound.component.ts File in the src/app/core Folder

```
import { Component } from "@angular/core";

@Component({
    selector: "paNotFound",
    template: `<h3 class="bg-danger text-white p-2">Sorry, something went wrong</h3>
               <button class="btn btn-primary" routerLink="/">Start Over</button>`
})
export class NotFoundComponent {}
```

This component displays a static message that will be shown when something goes wrong with the routing system. Listing 26-7 adds the new components to the core module.

Listing 26-7. Declaring Components in the core.module.ts File in the src/app/core Folder

```
import { NgModule } from "@angular/core";
import { BrowserModule } from "@angular/platform-browser";
import { FormsModule } from "@angular/forms";
import { ModelModule } from "../model/model.module";
import { TableComponent } from "./table.component";
import { FormComponent } from "./form.component";
import { Subject } from "rxjs";
import { StatePipe } from "./state.pipe";
import { MessageModule } from "../messages/message.module";
import { MessageService } from "../messages/message.service";
import { Message } from "../messages/message.model";
import { Model } from "../model/repository.model";
import { RouterModule } from "@angular/router";
import { ProductCountComponent } from "./productCount.component";
import { CategoryCountComponent } from "./categoryCount.component";
import { NotFoundComponent } from "./notFound.component";

@NgModule({
    imports: [BrowserModule, FormsModule, ModelModule, MessageModule, RouterModule],
    declarations: [TableComponent, FormComponent, StatePipe,
        ProductCountComponent, CategoryCountComponent, NotFoundComponent],
    exports: [ModelModule, TableComponent, FormComponent]
})
export class CoreModule { }
```

Open a new command prompt, navigate to the exampleApp folder, and run the following command to start the server that provides the RESTful web server:

```
npm run json
```

Open a separate command prompt, navigate to the exampleApp folder, and run the following command to start the Angular development tools:

```
ng serve
```

655

Open a new browser window and navigate to `http://localhost:4200` to see the content shown in Figure 26-1.

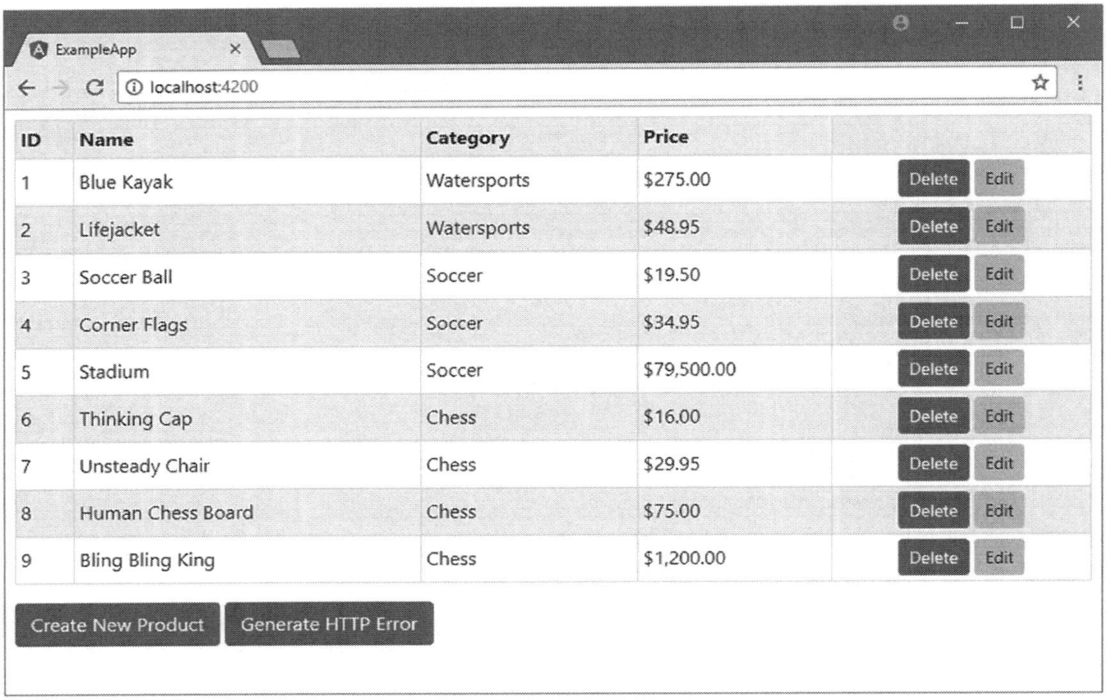

Figure 26-1. *Running the example application*

Using Wildcards and Redirections

The routing configuration in an application can quickly become complex and contain redundancies and oddities to cater for the structure of an application. Angular provides two useful tools that can help simplify routes and also deal with problems when they arise, as described in the following sections.

Using Wildcards in Routes

The Angular routing system supports a special path, denoted by two asterisks (the ** characters), that allows routes to match any URL. The basic use for the wildcard path is to deal with navigation that would otherwise create a routing error. Listing 26-8 adds a button to the table component's template that navigates to a route that hasn't been defined by the application's routing configuration.

Listing 26-8. Adding a Button in the table.component.html File in the src/app/core Folder

```
<table class="table table-sm table-bordered table-striped">
    <tr>
        <th>ID</th><th>Name</th><th>Category</th><th>Price</th><th></th>
    </tr>
    <tr *ngFor="let item of getProducts()">
        <td style="vertical-align:middle">{{item.id}}</td>
        <td style="vertical-align:middle">{{item.name}}</td>
        <td style="vertical-align:middle">{{item.category}}</td>
        <td style="vertical-align:middle">
            {{item.price | currency:"USD" }}
        </td>
        <td class="text-center">
            <button class="btn btn-danger btn-sm" (click)="deleteProduct(item.id)">
                Delete
            </button>
            <button class="btn btn-warning btn-sm"
                [routerLink]="['/form', 'edit', item.id]">
                Edit
            </button>
        </td>
    </tr>
</table>
<button class="btn btn-primary" routerLink="/form/create">
    Create New Product
</button>
<button class="btn btn-danger" (click)="deleteProduct(-1)">
    Generate HTTP Error
</button>
<button class="btn btn-danger" routerLink="/does/not/exist">
    Generate Routing Error
</button>
```

Clicking the button will ask the application to navigate to the URL /does/not/exist, for which there is no route configured. When a URL doesn't match a URL, an error is thrown, which is then picked up and processed by the error handling class, which leads to a warning being displayed by the message component, as shown in Figure 26-2.

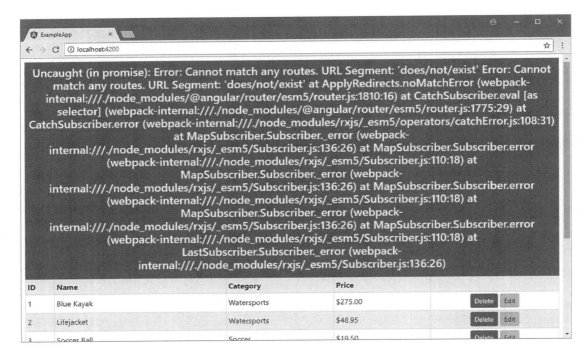

Figure 26-2. *The default navigation error*

This isn't a useful way to deal with an unknown route because the user won't know what routes are and may not realize that the application was trying to navigate to the problem URL.

A better approach is to use the wildcard route to handle navigation for URLs that have not been defined and select a component that will present a more useful message to the user, as illustrated in Listing 26-9.

Listing 26-9. Adding a Wildcard Route in the app.routing.ts File in the src/app Folder

```
import { Routes, RouterModule } from "@angular/router";
import { TableComponent } from "./core/table.component";
import { FormComponent } from "./core/form.component";
import { NotFoundComponent } from "./core/notFound.component";

const routes: Routes = [
    { path: "form/:mode/:id", component: FormComponent },
    { path: "form/:mode", component: FormComponent },
    { path: "", component: TableComponent },
    { path: "**", component: NotFoundComponent }
]

export const routing = RouterModule.forRoot(routes);
```

The new route in the listing uses the wildcard to select the NotFoundComponent, which displays the message shown in Figure 26-3 when the Generate Routing Error button is clicked.

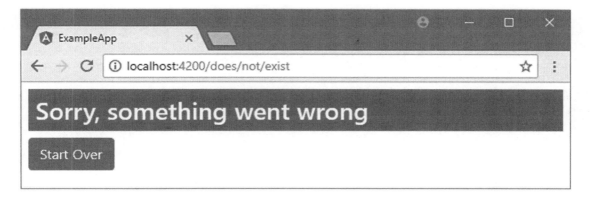

Figure 26-3. *Using a wildcard route*

Clicking the Start Over button navigates to the / URL, which will select the table component for display.

Using Redirections in Routes

Routes do not have to select components; they can also be used as aliases that redirect the browser to a different URL. Redirections are defined using the redirectTo property in a route, as shown in Listing 26-10.

Listing 26-10. Using Route Redirection in the app.routing.ts File in the src/app Folder

```
import { Routes, RouterModule } from "@angular/router";
import { TableComponent } from "./core/table.component";
import { FormComponent } from "./core/form.component";
import { NotFoundComponent } from "./core/notFound.component";

const routes: Routes = [
    { path: "form/:mode/:id", component: FormComponent },
    { path: "form/:mode", component: FormComponent },
    { path: "does", redirectTo: "/form/create", pathMatch: "prefix" },
    { path: "table", component: TableComponent },
    { path: "", redirectTo: "/table", pathMatch: "full" },
    { path: "**", component: NotFoundComponent }
]

export const routing = RouterModule.forRoot(routes);
```

The redirectTo property is used to specify the URL that the browser will be redirected to. When defining redirections, the pathMatch property must also be specified, using one of the values described in Table 26-2.

Table 26-2. *The pathMatch Values*

Name	Description
prefix	This value configures the route so that it matches URLs that start with the specified path, ignoring any subsequent segments.
full	This value configures the route so that it matches only the URL specified by the path property.

The first route added in Listing 26-10 specifies a pathMatch value of prefix and a path of does, which means it will match any URL whose first segment is does, such as the /does/not/exist URL that is navigated to by the Generate Routing Error button. When the browser navigates to a URL that has this prefix, the routing system will redirect it to the /form/create URL, as shown in Figure 26-4.

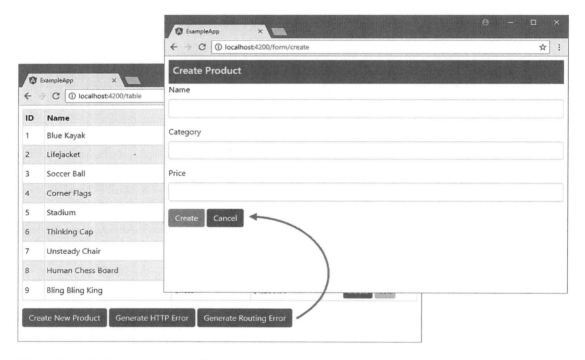

Figure 26-4. *Performing a route redirection*

The other routes in Listing 26-10 redirect the empty path to the /table URL, which displays the table component. This is a common technique that makes the URL schema more obvious because it matches the default URL (http://localhost:4200/) and redirects it to something more meaningful and memorable to the user (http://localhost:4200/table). In this case, the pathMatch property value is full, although this has no effect since it has been applied to the empty path.

Navigating Within a Component

The examples in the previous chapter navigated between different components so that clicking a button in the table component navigates to the form component and vice versa.

This isn't the only kind of navigation that's possible: you can also navigate within a component. To demonstrate, Listing 26-11 adds buttons to the form component that allow the user to edit the previous or next data objects.

Listing 26-11. Adding Buttons to the form.component.html File in the src/app/core Folder

```
<div class="bg-primary text-white p-2" [class.bg-warning]="editing">
    <h5>{{editing  ? "Edit" : "Create"}} Product</h5>
    <!--Last Event: {{ stateEvents | async | formatState }}-->
</div>
<div *ngIf="editing" class="p-2">
    <button class="btn btn-secondary"
            [routerLink]="['/form', 'edit', model.getPreviousProductid(product.id)]">
        Previous
    </button>
    <button class="btn btn-secondary"
            [routerLink]="['/form', 'edit', model.getNextProductId(product.id)]">
        Next
    </button>
</div>
<form novalidate #form="ngForm" (ngSubmit)="submitForm(form)" (reset)="resetForm()">

    <div class="form-group">
        <label>Name</label>
        <input class="form-control" name="name"
               [(ngModel)]="product.name" required />
    </div>

    <div class="form-group">
        <label>Category</label>
        <input class="form-control" name="category"
               [(ngModel)]="product.category" required />
    </div>

    <div class="form-group">
        <label>Price</label>
        <input class="form-control" name="price"
               [(ngModel)]="product.price"
               required pattern="^[0-9\.]+$" />
    </div>

    <button type="submit" class="btn btn-primary"
            [class.btn-warning]="editing" [disabled]="form.invalid">
        {{editing ? "Save" : "Create"}}
    </button>
    <button type="reset" class="btn btn-secondary" routerLink="/">Cancel</button>
</form>
```

These buttons have bindings for the routerLink directive with expressions that target the previous and next objects in the data model. This means that if you click the Edit button in the table for the Lifejacket product, for example, the Next button will navigate to the URL that edits the soccer ball, and the Previous button will navigate to the URL for the kayak.

Responding to Ongoing Routing Changes

Clicking the new buttons has no effect at the moment. Angular tries to be efficient during navigation, and it knows that the URLs that the Previous and Next buttons navigate to are handled by the same component that is currently displayed to the user. Rather than create a new instance of the component, it simply tells the component that the selected route has changed.

This is a problem because the form component isn't set up to receive change notifications. Its constructor receives the ActivatedRoute object that Angular uses to provide details of the current route, but only its snapshot property is used. The component's constructor has long been executed by the time that Angular updates the values in the ActivatedRoute, which means that it misses the notification. This worked when the configuration of the application meant that a new form component would be created each time the user wanted to create or edit a product, but it is no longer sufficient.

Fortunately, the ActivatedRoute class defines a set of properties that allow interested parties to receive notifications through Reactive Extensions Observable objects. These properties correspond to the ones provided by the ActivatedRouteSnapshot object returned by the snapshot property (described in Chapter 25) but send new events when there are any subsequent changes, as described in Table 26-3.

Table 26-3. *The Observable Properties of the ActivatedRoute Class*

Name	Description
url	This property returns an Observable<UrlSegment[]>, which provides the set of URL segments each time the route changes.
params	This property returns an Observable<Params>, which provides the URL parameters each time the route changes.
queryParams	This property returns an Observable<Params>, which provides the URL query parameters each time the route changes.
fragment	This property returns an Observable<string>, which provides the URL fragment each time the route changes.

These properties can be used by components that need to handle navigation changes that don't result in a different component being displayed to the user, as shown in Listing 26-12.

■ **Tip** If you need to combine different data elements from the route, such as using both segments and parameters, then subscribe to the Observer for one data element and use the snapshot property to get the rest of the data you require.

Listing 26-12. Observing Route Changes in the form.component.ts File

```
import { Component, Inject } from "@angular/core";
import { NgForm } from "@angular/forms";
import { Product } from "../model/product.model";
import { Model } from "../model/repository.model";
import { ActivatedRoute, Router } from "@angular/router";

@Component({
    selector: "paForm",
    templateUrl: "form.component.html",
    styleUrls: ["form.component.css"]
})
export class FormComponent {
    product: Product = new Product();

    constructor(private model: Model, activeRoute: ActivatedRoute,
        private router: Router) {

        activeRoute.params.subscribe(params => {
            this.editing = params["mode"] == "edit";
            let id = params["id"];
            if (id != null) {
                Object.assign(this.product, model.getProduct(id) || new Product());
            }
        })
    }

    editing: boolean = false;

    submitForm(form: NgForm) {
        if (form.valid) {
            this.model.saveProduct(this.product);
            this.router.navigateByUrl("/");
        }
    }

    resetForm() {
        this.product = new Product();
    }
}
```

The component subscribes to the Observer<Params> that sends a new Params object to subscribers each time the active route changes. The Observer objects returned by the ActivatedRoute properties send details of the most recent route change when the subscribe method is called, ensuring that the component's constructor doesn't miss the initial navigation that led to it being called.

The result is that the component can react to route changes that don't cause Angular to create a new component, meaning that clicking the Next or Previous button changes the product that has been selected for editing, as shown in Figure 26-5.

■ **Tip** The effect of navigation is obvious when the activated route changes the component that is displayed to the user. It may not be so obvious when just the data changes. To help emphasize changes, Angular can apply animations that can draw attention to the effects of navigation. See Chapter 28 for details.

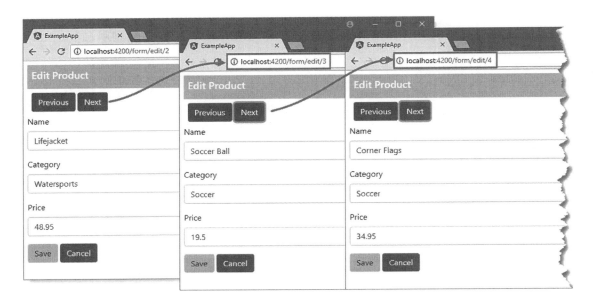

Figure 26-5. *Responding to route changes*

Styling Links for Active Routes

A common use for the routing system is to display multiple navigation elements alongside the content that they select. To demonstrate, Listing 26-13 adds a new route to the application that will allow the table component to be targeted with a URL that contains a category filter.

Listing 26-13. Defining a Route in the app.routing.ts File in the src/app Folder

```
import { Routes, RouterModule } from "@angular/router";
import { TableComponent } from "./core/table.component";
import { FormComponent } from "./core/form.component";
import { NotFoundComponent } from "./core/notFound.component";

const routes: Routes = [
    { path: "form/:mode/:id", component: FormComponent },
    { path: "form/:mode", component: FormComponent },
    { path: "does", redirectTo: "/form/create", pathMatch: "prefix" },
    { path: "table/:category", component: TableComponent },
    { path: "table", component: TableComponent },
```

```
    { path: "", redirectTo: "/table", pathMatch: "full" },
    { path: "**", component: NotFoundComponent }
]

export const routing = RouterModule.forRoot(routes);
```

Listing 26-14 updates the TableComponent class so that it uses the routing system to get details of the active route and assigns the value of the category route parameter to a category property that can be accessed in the template. The category property is used in the getProducts method to filter the objects in the data model.

Listing 26-14. Adding Category Filter Support in the table.component.ts File in the src/app/core Folder

```
import { Component, Inject } from "@angular/core";
import { Product } from "../model/product.model";
import { Model } from "../model/repository.model";
import { ActivatedRoute } from "@angular/router";

@Component({
    selector: "paTable",
    templateUrl: "table.component.html"
})
export class TableComponent {
    category: string = null;

    constructor(private model: Model, activeRoute: ActivatedRoute) {
        activeRoute.params.subscribe(params => {
            this.category = params["category"] || null;
        })
    }

    getProduct(key: number): Product {
        return this.model.getProduct(key);
    }

    getProducts(): Product[] {
        return this.model.getProducts()
            .filter(p => this.category == null || p.category == this.category);
    }

    get categories(): string[] {
        return this.model.getProducts()
            .map(p => p.category)
            .filter((category, index, array) => array.indexOf(category) == index);
    }

    deleteProduct(key: number) {
        this.model.deleteProduct(key);
    }
}
```

There is also a new categories property that will be used in the template to generate the set of categories for filtering. The final step is to add the HTML elements to the template that will allow the user to apply a filter, as shown in Listing 26-15.

Listing 26-15. Adding Filter Elements in the table.component.html File in the src/app/core Folder

```
<div class="container-fluid">
    <div class="row">
        <div class="col-3">
            <button class="btn btn-secondary btn-block"
                    routerLink="/" routerLinkActive="bg-primary">
                All
            </button>
            <button *ngFor="let category of categories"
                    class="btn btn-secondary btn-block"
                    [routerLink]="['/table', category]"
                    routerLinkActive="bg-primary">
                {{category}}
            </button>
        </div>
        <div class="col-9">
            <table class="table table-sm table-bordered table-striped">
                <tr>
                    <th>ID</th>
                    <th>Name</th>
                    <th>Category</th>
                    <th>Price</th>
                    <th></th>
                </tr>
                <tr *ngFor="let item of getProducts()">
                    <td style="vertical-align:middle">{{item.id}}</td>
                    <td style="vertical-align:middle">{{item.name}}</td>
                    <td style="vertical-align:middle">{{item.category}}</td>
                    <td style="vertical-align:middle">
                        {{item.price | currency:"USD" }}
                    </td>
                    <td class="text-center">
                        <button class="btn btn-danger btn-sm"
                                (click)="deleteProduct(item.id)">
                            Delete
                        </button>
                        <button class="btn btn-warning btn-sm"
                                [routerLink]="['/form', 'edit', item.id]">
                            Edit
                        </button>
                    </td>
                </tr>
            </table>
        </div>
```

```
<div class="col-12 p-2 text-center">
    <button class="btn btn-primary" routerLink="/form/create">
        Create New Product
    </button>
    <button class="btn btn-danger" (click)="deleteProduct(-1)">
        Generate HTTP Error
    </button>
    <button class="btn btn-danger" routerLink="/does/not/exist">
        Generate Routing Error
    </button>
</div>
    </div>
</div>
```

The important part of this example is the use of the routerLinkActive attribute, which is used to specify a CSS class that the element will be assigned to when the URL specified by the routerLink attribute matches the active route.

The listing specifies a class called bg-primary, which changes the appearance of the button and makes the selected category more obvious. When combined with the functionality added to the component in Listing 26-14, the result is a set of buttons that allow the user to view products in a single category, as shown in Figure 26-6.

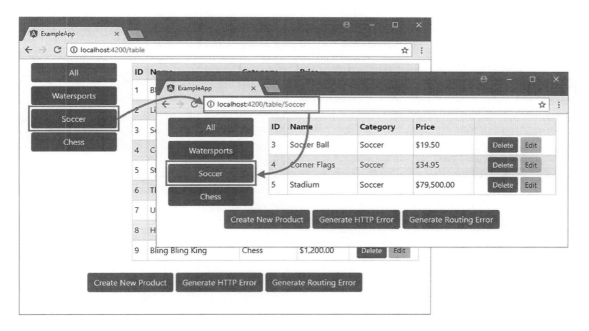

Figure 26-6. *Filtering products*

If you click the Soccer button, the application will navigate to the /table/Soccer URL, and the table will display only those products in the Soccer category. The Soccer button will also be highlighted since the routerLinkActive attribute means that Angular will add the button element to the Bootstrap bg-primary class.

Fixing the All Button

The navigation buttons reveal a common problem, which is that the All button is always added to the active class, even when the user has filtered the table to show a specific category.

This happens because the routerLinkActive attribute performs partial matches on the active URL by default. In the case of the example, the / URL will always cause the All button to be activated because it is at the start of all URLs. This problem can be fixed by configuring the routerLinkActive directive, as shown in Listing 26-16.

Listing 26-16. Configuring the Directive in the table.component.html File in the src/app/core Folder

```
...
<div class="col-3">
    <button class="btn btn-secondary btn-block"
            routerLink="/table" routerLinkActive="bg-primary"
            [routerLinkActiveOptions]="{exact: true}">
        All
    </button>
    <button *ngFor="let category of categories" class="btn btn-secondary btn-block"
            [routerLink]="['/table', category]" routerLinkActive="bg-primary">
        {{category}}
    </button>
</div>
...
```

The configuration is performed using a binding on the routerLinkActiveOptions attribute, which accepts a literal object. The exact property is the only available configuration setting and is used to control matching the active route URL. Setting this property true will add the element to the class specified by the routerLinkActive attribute only when there is an exact match with the active route's URL. With this change, the All button will be highlighted only when all of the products are shown, as illustrated by Figure 26-7.

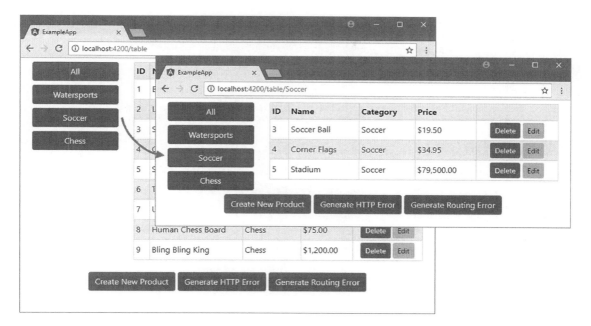

Figure 26-7. *Fixing the All button problem*

Creating Child Routes

Child routes allow components to respond to part of the URL by embedding router-outlet elements in their templates, creating more complex arrangements of content. I am going to use the simple components I created at the start of the chapter to demonstrate how child routes work. These components will be displayed above the product table, and the component that is shown will be specified in the URLs shown in Table 26-4.

Table 26-4. *The URLs and the Components They Will Select*

URL	Component
/table/products	The ProductCountComponent will be displayed.
/table/categories	The CategoryCountComponent will be displayed.
/table	Neither component will be displayed.

Listing 26-17 shows the changes to the application's routing configuration to implement the routing strategy in the table.

Listing 26-17. Configuring Routes in the app.routing.ts File in the src/app Folder

```
import { Routes, RouterModule } from "@angular/router";
import { TableComponent } from "./core/table.component";
import { FormComponent } from "./core/form.component";
```

669

```
import { NotFoundComponent } from "./core/notFound.component";
import { ProductCountComponent } from "./core/productCount.component";
import { CategoryCountComponent } from "./core/categoryCount.component";

const routes: Routes = [
    { path: "form/:mode/:id", component: FormComponent },
    { path: "form/:mode", component: FormComponent },
    { path: "does", redirectTo: "/form/create", pathMatch: "prefix" },
    {
        path: "table",
        component: TableComponent,
        children: [
            { path: "products", component: ProductCountComponent },
            { path: "categories", component: CategoryCountComponent }
        ]
    },
    { path: "table/:category", component: TableComponent },
    { path: "table", component: TableComponent },
    { path: "", redirectTo: "/table", pathMatch: "full" },
    { path: "**", component: NotFoundComponent }
]

export const routing = RouterModule.forRoot(routes);
```

Child routes are defined using the `children` property, which is set to an array of routes defined in the same way as the top-level routes. When Angular uses the entire URL to match a route that has children, there will be a match only if the URL to which the browser navigates contains segments that match both the top-level segment and the segments specified by one of the child routes.

■ **Tip**   Notice that I have added the new route before the one whose path is `table/:category`. Angular tries to match routes in the order in which they are defined. The `table/:category` path would match both the `/table/products` and `/table/categories` URLs and lead the table component to filter the products for nonexistent categories. By placing the more specific route first, the `/table/products` and `/table/categories` URLs will be matched before the `table/:category` path is considered.

Creating the Child Route Outlet

The components selected by child routes are displayed in a `router-outlet` element defined in the template of the component selected by the parent route. In the case of the example, this means the child routes will target an element in the table component's template, as shown in Listing 26-18, which also adds elements that will navigate to the new routes.

Listing 26-18. Adding an Outlet in the table.component.html File in the src/app/core Folder

```html
<div class="container-fluid">
    <div class="row">
        <div class="col-3">
            <button class="btn btn-secondary btn-block"
                    routerLink="/table" routerLinkActive="bg-primary"
                    [routerLinkActiveOptions]="{exact: true}">
                All
            </button>
            <button *ngFor="let category of categories"
                    class="btn btn-secondary btn-block"
                    [routerLink]="['/table', category]"
                    routerLinkActive="bg-primary">
                {{category}}
            </button>
        </div>
        <div class="col-9">
            <button class="btn btn-info" routerLink="/table/products">
                Count Products
            </button>
            <button class="btn btn-primary" routerLink="/table/categories">
                Count Categories
            </button>
            <button class="btn btn-secondary" routerLink="/table">
                Count Neither
            </button>
            <div class="my-2">
                <router-outlet></router-outlet>
            </div>
            <table class="table table-sm table-bordered table-striped">
                <tr>
                    <th>ID</th>
                    <th>Name</th>
                    <th>Category</th>
                    <th>Price</th>
                    <th></th>
                </tr>
                <tr *ngFor="let item of getProducts()">
                    <td style="vertical-align:middle">{{item.id}}</td>
                    <td style="vertical-align:middle">{{item.name}}</td>
                    <td style="vertical-align:middle">{{item.category}}</td>
                    <td style="vertical-align:middle">
                        {{item.price | currency:"USD" }}
                    </td>
                    <td class="text-center">
                        <button class="btn btn-danger btn-sm"
                                (click)="deleteProduct(item.id)">
                            Delete
                        </button>
```

671

```
                        <button class="btn btn-warning btn-sm"
                                [routerLink]="['/form', 'edit', item.id]">
                            Edit
                        </button>
                    </td>
                </tr>
            </table>
        </div>
        <div class="col-12 p-2 text-center">
            <button class="btn btn-primary" routerLink="/form/create">
                Create New Product
            </button>
            <button class="btn btn-danger" (click)="deleteProduct(-1)">
                Generate HTTP Error
            </button>
            <button class="btn btn-danger" routerLink="/does/not/exist">
                Generate Routing Error
            </button>
        </div>
    </div>
</div>
```

The button elements have routerLink attributes that specify the URLs listed in Table 26-4, and there is also a router-outlet element, which will be used to display the selected component, as shown in Figure 26-8, or no component if the browser navigates to the /table URL.

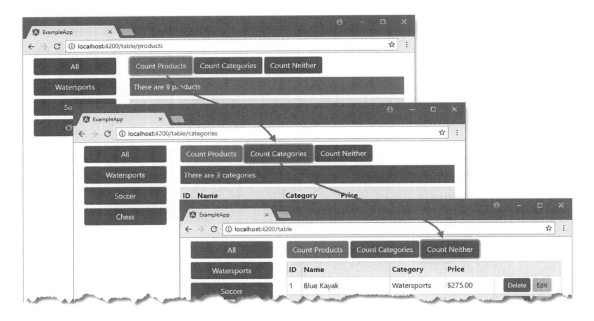

Figure 26-8. Using child routes

Accessing Parameters from Child Routes

Child routes can use all the features available to the top-level routes, including defining route parameters and even having their own child routes. Route parameters are worth special attention in child routes because of the way that Angular isolates children from their parents. For this section, I am going to add support for the URLs described in Table 26-5.

Table 26-5. *The New URLs Supported by the Example Application*

Name	Description
/table/:category/products	This route will filter the contents of the table and select the ProductCountComponent.
/table/:category/categories	This route will filter the contents of the table and select the CategoryCountComponent.

Listing 26-19 defines the routes that support the URLs shown in the table.

Listing 26-19. Adding Routes in the app.routing.ts File in the src/app Folder

```
import { Routes, RouterModule } from "@angular/router";
import { TableComponent } from "./core/table.component";
import { FormComponent } from "./core/form.component";
import { NotFoundComponent } from "./core/notFound.component";
import { ProductCountComponent } from "./core/productCount.component";
import { CategoryCountComponent } from "./core/categoryCount.component";

const childRoutes: Routes = [
    { path: "products", component: ProductCountComponent },
    { path: "categories", component: CategoryCountComponent },
    { path: "", component: ProductCountComponent }
];

const routes: Routes = [
    { path: "form/:mode/:id", component: FormComponent },
    { path: "form/:mode", component: FormComponent },
    { path: "does", redirectTo: "/form/create", pathMatch: "prefix" },
    { path: "table", component: TableComponent, children: childRoutes },
    { path: "table/:category", component: TableComponent, children: childRoutes },
    { path: "", redirectTo: "/table", pathMatch: "full" },
    { path: "**", component: NotFoundComponent }
]

export const routing = RouterModule.forRoot(routes);
```

The type of the children property is a Routes object, which makes it easy to minimize duplication in the route configuration when you need to apply the same set of child routes in different parts of the URL schema. In the listing, I have defined the child routes in a Routes object called childRoutes and used it as the value for the children property in two different top-level routes.

To make it possible to target these new routes, Listing 26-20 changes the targets of the buttons that appear above the table so they navigate relative to the current URL. I have removed the Count Neither button since the ProductCountComponent will be shown when the empty path child route matches the URL.

Listing 26-20. Using Relative URLs in the table.component.html File in the src/app/core Folder

```
...
<div class="col-9">
    <button class="btn btn-info" routerLink="products">Count Products</button>
    <button class="btn btn-primary" routerLink="categories">Count Categories</button>
    <div class="my-2">
        <router-outlet></router-outlet>
    </div>
    <table class="table table-sm table-bordered table-striped">
...
```

When Angular matches routes, the information it provides to the components that are selected through the ActivatedRoute object is segregated so that each component only receives details of the part of the route that selected it.

In the case of the routes added in Listing 26-20, this means the ProductCountComponent and CategoryCountComponent receive an ActivatedRoute object that only describes the child route that selected them, with the single segment of /products or /categories. Equally, the TableComponent component receives an ActivatedRoute object that doesn't contain the segment that was used to match the child route.

Fortunately, the ActivatedRoute class provides some properties that provide access to the rest of the route, allowing parents and children to access the rest of the routing information, as described in Table 26-6.

Table 26-6. The ActivatedRoute Properties for Child/Parent Route Information

Name	Description
pathFromRoot	This property returns an array of ActivatedRoute objects representing all the routes used to match the current URL.
parent	This property returns an ActivatedRoute representing the parent of the route that selected the component.
firstChild	This property returns an ActivatedRoute representing the first child route used to match the current URL.
children	This property returns an array of ActivatedRoute objects representing all the children routes used to match the current URL.

Listing 26-21 shows how the ProductCountComponent component can access the wider set of routes used to match the current URL to get a value for the category route parameter and adapt its output when the contents of the table are filtered for a single category.

Listing 26-21. Ancestor Routes in the productCount.component.ts File in the src/app/core Folder

```
import {
    Component, KeyValueDiffer, KeyValueDiffers, ChangeDetectorRef
} from "@angular/core";
import { Model } from "../model/repository.model";
import { ActivatedRoute } from "@angular/router";
```

```
@Component({
    selector: "paProductCount",
    template: `<div class="bg-info p-2">There are {{count}} products</div>`
})
export class ProductCountComponent {
    private differ: KeyValueDiffer<any, any>;
    count: number = 0;
    private category: string;

    constructor(private model: Model,
            private keyValueDiffers: KeyValueDiffers,
            private changeDetector: ChangeDetectorRef,
            activeRoute: ActivatedRoute) {

        activeRoute.pathFromRoot.forEach(route => route.params.subscribe(params => {
            if (params["category"] != null) {
                this.category = params["category"];
                this.updateCount();
            }
        }))
    }

    ngOnInit() {
        this.differ = this.keyValueDiffers
            .find(this.model.getProducts())
            .create();
    }

    ngDoCheck() {
        if (this.differ.diff(this.model.getProducts()) != null) {
            this.updateCount();
        }
    }

    private updateCount() {
        this.count = this.model.getProducts()
            .filter(p => this.category == null || p.category == this.category)
            .length;
    }
}
```

The pathFromRoot property is especially useful because it allows a component to inspect all the routes that have been used to match the URL. Angular minimizes the routing updates required to handle navigation, which means that a component that has been selected by a child route won't receive a change notification through its ActivatedRoute object if only its parent has changed. It is for this reason that I have subscribed to updates from all the ActivatedRoute objects returned by the pathFromRoot property, ensuring that the component will always detect changes in the value of the category route parameter.

To see the result, save the changes, click the Watersports button to filter the contents of the table, and then click the Count Products button, which selects the ProductCountComponent. This number of products reported by the component will correspond to the number of rows in the table, as shown in Figure 26-9.

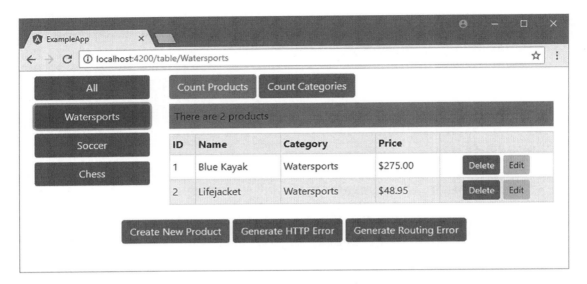

Figure 26-9. *Accessing the other routes used to match a URL*

Summary

In this chapter, I continued to describe the features provided by the Angular URL routing system, going beyond the basic features described in the previous chapter. I explained how to create wildcard and redirection routes, how to create routes that navigate relative to the current URL, and how to create child routes to display nested components. In the next chapter, I finish describing the URL routing system, focusing on the most advanced features.

CHAPTER 27

■ ■ ■

Routing and Navigation: Part 3

In this chapter, I continue to describe the Angular URL routing system, focusing on the most advanced features. I explain how to control route activation, how to load feature modules dynamically, and how to use multiple outlet elements in a template. Table 27-1 summarizes the chapter.

Table 27-1. *Chapter Summary*

Problem	Solution	Listing
Delay navigation until a task is complete	Use a route resolver	1–7
Prevent route activation	Use an activation guard	8–14
Prevent the user from navigating away from the current content	Use a deactivation guard	15–19
Defer loading a feature module until it is required	Create a dynamically loaded module	20–25
Control when a dynamically loaded module is used	Use a loading guard	26–28
Use routing to manage multiple router outlets	Use named outlets in the same template	29–34

Preparing the Example Project

For this chapter, I will continue using the exampleApp that was created in Chapter 22 and has been modified in each subsequent chapter. To prepare for this chapter, I have simplified the routing configuration, as shown in Listing 27-1.

■ **Tip** You can download the example project for this chapter—and for all the other chapters in this book—from https://github.com/Apress/pro-angular-6.

Listing 27-1. Simplifying the Routes in the app.routing.ts File in the src/app Folder

```
import { Routes, RouterModule } from "@angular/router";
import { TableComponent } from "./core/table.component";
import { FormComponent } from "./core/form.component";
import { NotFoundComponent } from "./core/notFound.component";
```

```
import { ProductCountComponent } from "./core/productCount.component";
import { CategoryCountComponent } from "./core/categoryCount.component";

const childRoutes: Routes = [
    { path: "products", component: ProductCountComponent },
    { path: "categories", component: CategoryCountComponent },
    { path: "", component: ProductCountComponent }
];

const routes: Routes = [
    { path: "form/:mode/:id", component: FormComponent },
    { path: "form/:mode", component: FormComponent },
    { path: "table", component: TableComponent, children: childRoutes },
    { path: "table/:category", component: TableComponent, children: childRoutes },
    { path: "", redirectTo: "/table", pathMatch: "full" },
    { path: "**", component: NotFoundComponent }
]

export const routing = RouterModule.forRoot(routes);
```

Open a new command prompt, navigate to the exampleApp folder, and run the following command to start the server that provides the RESTful web server:

```
npm run json
```

Open a separate command prompt, navigate to the exampleApp folder, and run the following command to start the Angular development tools:

```
ng serve
```

Open a new browser window and navigate to http://localhost:4200 to see the content shown in Figure 27-1.

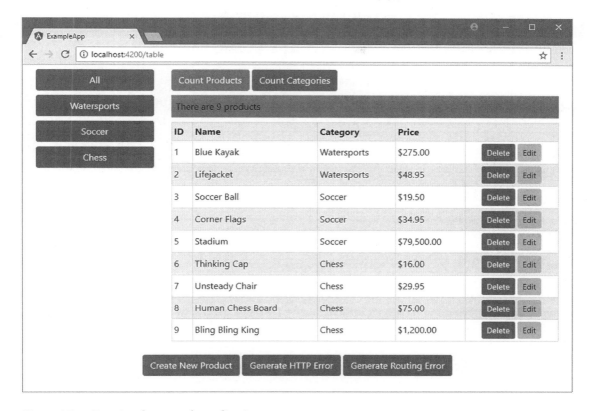

Figure 27-1. *Running the example application*

Guarding Routes

At the moment, the user can navigate to anywhere in the application at any time. This isn't always a good idea, either because some parts of the application may not always be ready or because some parts of the application are restricted until specific actions are performed. To control the use of navigation, Angular supports *guards*, which are specified as part of the route configuration using the properties defined by the Routes class, described in Table 27-2.

Table 27-2. *The Routes Properties for Guards*

Name	Description
resolve	This property is used to specify guards that will delay route activation until some operation has been completed, such as loading data from a server.
canActivate	This property is used to specify the guards that will be used to determine whether a route can be activated.
canActivateChild	This property is used to specify the guards that will be used to determine whether a child route can be activated.
canDeactivate	This property is used to specify the guards that will be used to determine whether a route can be deactivated.
canLoad	This property is used to guard routes that load feature modules dynamically, as described in the "Loading Feature Modules Dynamically" section.

Delaying Navigation with a Resolver

A common reason for guarding routes is to ensure that the application has received the data that it requires before a route is activated. The example application loads data from the RESTful web service asynchronously, which means there can be a delay between the moment at which the browser is asked to send the HTTP request and the moment at which the response is received and the data is processed. You may not have noticed this delay as you have followed the examples because the browser and the web service are running on the same machine. In a deployed application, there is a much greater prospect of there being a delay, caused by network congestion, high server load, and a dozen other factors.

To simulate network congestion, Listing 27-2 modifies the RESTful data source class to introduce a delay after the response is received from the web service.

Listing 27-2. Adding a Delay in the rest.datasource.ts File in the src/app/model Folder

```
import { Injectable, Inject, InjectionToken } from "@angular/core";
import { HttpClient, HttpHeaders } from "@angular/common/http";
import { Observable, throwError } from "rxjs";
import { Product } from "./product.model";
import { catchError, delay } from "rxjs/operators";

export const REST_URL = new InjectionToken("rest_url");

@Injectable()
export class RestDataSource {
    constructor(private http: HttpClient,
        @Inject(REST_URL) private url: string) { }

    getData(): Observable<Product[]> {
        return this.sendRequest<Product[]>("GET", this.url);
    }

    saveProduct(product: Product): Observable<Product> {
        return this.sendRequest<Product>("POST", this.url, product);
    }
```

```
updateProduct(product: Product): Observable<Product> {
    return this.sendRequest<Product>("PUT",
        `${this.url}/${product.id}`, product);
}

deleteProduct(id: number): Observable<Product> {
    return this.sendRequest<Product>("DELETE", `${this.url}/${id}`);
}

private sendRequest<T>(verb: string, url: string, body?: Product)
    : Observable<T> {

    let myHeaders = new HttpHeaders();
    myHeaders = myHeaders.set("Access-Key", "<secret>");
    myHeaders = myHeaders.set("Application-Names", ["exampleApp", "proAngular"]);

    return this.http.request<T>(verb, url, {
        body: body,
        headers: myHeaders
    })
    .pipe(delay(5000))
    .pipe(catchError((error: Response) =>
        throwError(`Network Error: ${error.statusText} (${error.status})`)));
}
}
```

The delay is added using the Reactive Extensions delay method and is applied to create a five-second delay, which is long enough to create a noticeable pause without being too painful to wait for every time the application is reloaded. To change the delay, increase or decrease the argument for the delay method, which is expressed in milliseconds.

The effect of the delay is that the user is presented with an incomplete and confusing layout while the application is waiting for the data to load, as shown in Figure 27-2.

■ **Note** The delay is applied to all HTTP requests, which means that if you create, edit, or delete a product, the change you have made will not be reflected in the product table for five seconds.

Figure 27-2. Waiting for data

Creating a Resolver Service

A *resolver* is used to ensure that a task is performed before a route can be activated. To create a resolver, I added a file called model.resolver.ts in the src/app/model folder and defined the class shown in Listing 27-3.

Listing 27-3. The Contents of the model.resolver.ts File in the src/app/model Folder

```
import { Injectable } from "@angular/core";
import { ActivatedRouteSnapshot, RouterStateSnapshot } from "@angular/router";
import { Observable } from "rxjs";
import { Model } from "./repository.model"
import { RestDataSource } from "./rest.datasource";
import { Product } from "./product.model";

@Injectable()
export class ModelResolver {

    constructor(
        private model: Model,
        private dataSource: RestDataSource) { }

    resolve(route: ActivatedRouteSnapshot,
            state: RouterStateSnapshot): Observable<Product[]> {

        return this.model.getProducts().length == 0
            ? this.dataSource.getData() : null;
    }
}
```

Resolvers are classes that define a resolve method that accepts two arguments. The first argument is an ActivatedRouteSnapshot object, which describes the route that is being navigated to using the properties described in Chapter 25. The second argument is a RouterStateSnapshot object, which describes the current route through a single property called url. These arguments can be used to adapt the resolver to the navigation that is about to be performed, although neither is required by the resolver in the listing, which uses the same behavior regardless of the routes that are being navigated to and from.

■ **Note**   All of the guards described in this chapter can implement interfaces defined in the @angular/router module. For example, resolvers can implement an interface called Resolve. These interfaces are optional, and I have not used them in this chapter.

The resolve method can return three different types of result, as described in Table 27-3.

Table 27-3. *The Result Types Allowed by the resolve Method*

Result Type	Description
Observable<any>	The browser will activate the new route when the Observer emits an event.
Promise<any>	The browser will activate the new route when the Promise resolves.
Any other result	The browser will activate the new route as soon as the method produces a result.

The Observable and Promise results are useful when dealing with asynchronous operations, such as requesting data using an HTTP request. Angular waits until the asynchronous operation is complete before activating the new route. Any other result is interpreted as the result from a synchronous operation, and Angular will activate the new route immediately.

The resolver in Listing 27-3 uses its constructor to receive Model and RestDataSource objects via dependency injection. When the resolve method is called, it checks the number of objects in the data model to determine whether the HTTP request to the RESTful web service has completed. If there are no objects in the data model, the resolve method returns the Observable from the RestDataSource. getData method, which will emit an event when the HTTP request completes. Angular will subscribe to the Observable and delay activating the new route until it emits an event. The resolve method returns null if there are objects in the model, and since this is neither an Observable nor a Promise, Angular will activate the new route immediately.

■ **Tip** Combining asynchronous and synchronous results means that the resolver will delay navigation only until the HTTP request completed and the data model has been populated. This is important because the resolve method will be called every time that the application tries to navigate to a route to which the resolver has been applied.

Registering the Resolver Service

The next step is to register the resolver as a service in its feature module, as shown in Listing 27-4.

Listing 27-4. Registering the Resolver in the model.module.ts File in the src/app/model Folder

```
import { NgModule } from "@angular/core";
import { Model } from "./repository.model";
import { HttpClientModule, HttpClientJsonpModule } from "@angular/common/http";
import { RestDataSource, REST_URL } from "./rest.datasource";
import { ModelResolver } from "./model.resolver";

@NgModule({
    imports: [HttpClientModule, HttpClientJsonpModule],
    providers: [Model, RestDataSource, ModelResolver,
        { provide: REST_URL, useValue: "http://localhost:3500/products" }]
})
export class ModelModule { }
```

Applying the Resolver

The resolver is applied to routes using the `resolve` property, as shown in Listing 27-5.

Listing 27-5. Applying a Resolver in the app.routing.ts File in the src/app Folder

```
import { Routes, RouterModule } from "@angular/router";
import { TableComponent } from "./core/table.component";
import { FormComponent } from "./core/form.component";
import { NotFoundComponent } from "./core/notFound.component";
import { ProductCountComponent } from "./core/productCount.component";
import { CategoryCountComponent } from "./core/categoryCount.component";
import { ModelResolver } from "./model/model.resolver";

const childRoutes: Routes = [
    {   path: "",
        children: [{ path: "products", component: ProductCountComponent },
                   { path: "categories", component: CategoryCountComponent },
                   { path: "", component: ProductCountComponent }],
        resolve: { model: ModelResolver }
    }
];

const routes: Routes = [
    { path: "form/:mode/:id", component: FormComponent },
    { path: "form/:mode", component: FormComponent },
    { path: "table", component: TableComponent, children: childRoutes },
    { path: "table/:category", component: TableComponent, children: childRoutes },
    { path: "", redirectTo: "/table", pathMatch: "full" },
    { path: "**", component: NotFoundComponent }
]

export const routing = RouterModule.forRoot(routes);
```

The `resolve` property accepts a map object whose property values are the resolver classes that will be applied to the route. (The property names do not matter.) I want to apply the resolver to all the views that display the product table, so to avoid duplication, I created a route with the `resolve` property and used it as the parent for the existing child routes.

Displaying Placeholder Content

Angular uses the resolver before activating any of the routes to which it has been applied, which prevents the user from seeing the product table until the model has been populated with the data from the RESTful web service. Sadly, that just means the user sees an empty window while the browser is waiting for the server to respond. To address this, Listing 27-6 enhances the resolver to use the message service to tell the user what is happening when the data is being loaded.

Listing 27-6. Displaying a Message in the model.resolver.ts File in the src/app/model Folder

```
import { Injectable } from "@angular/core";
import { ActivatedRouteSnapshot, RouterStateSnapshot } from "@angular/router";
import { Observable } from "rxjs";
import { Model } from "./repository.model"
import { RestDataSource } from "./rest.datasource";
import { Product } from "./product.model";
import { MessageService } from "../messages/message.service";
import { Message } from "../messages/message.model";

@Injectable()
export class ModelResolver {

    constructor(
        private model: Model,
        private dataSource: RestDataSource,
        private messages: MessageService) { }

    resolve(route: ActivatedRouteSnapshot,
        state: RouterStateSnapshot): Observable<Product[]> {

        if (this.model.getProducts().length == 0) {
            this.messages.reportMessage(new Message("Loading data..."));
            return this.dataSource.getData();
        }
    }
}
```

The component that displays the messages from the service clears its contents when it receives the NavigationEnd event, which means that the placeholder will be removed when the data has been loaded, as shown in Figure 27-3.

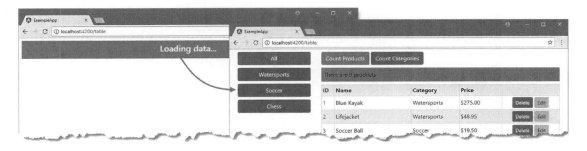

Figure 27-3. *Using a resolver to ensure data is loaded*

Using a Resolver to Prevent URL Entry Problems

As I explained in Chapter 25, the development HTTP server will return the contents of the index.html file when it receives a request for a URL for which there is no corresponding file. Combined with the automatic browser reload functionality, it is easy to make a change in the project and have the browser reload a URL that causes the application to jump to a specific URL without going through the navigation steps that the application expects and that sets up the required state data.

To see an example of the problem, click one of the Edit buttons in the product table and then reload the browser page. The browser will request a URL like http://localhost:3500/form/edit/1, but this doesn't have the expected effect because the component for the activated route attempts to retrieve an object from the model before the HTTP response from the RESTful server has been received. As a consequence, the form is empty, as shown in Figure 27-4.

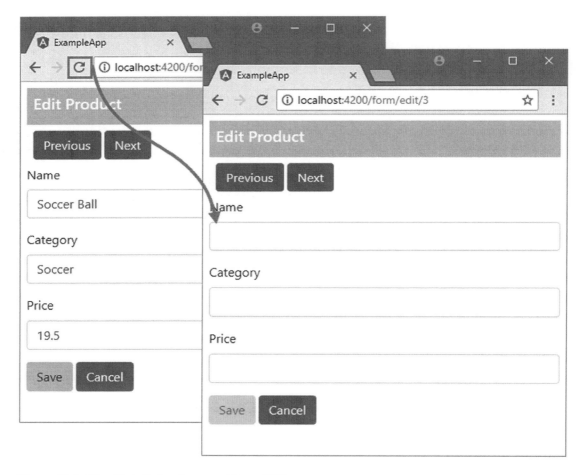

Figure 27-4. *The effect of reloading an arbitrary URL*

To avoid this problem, the resolver can be applied more broadly so that it protects other routes, as shown in Listing 27-7.

Listing 27-7. Applying the Resolver to Other Routes in the app.routing.ts File in the src/app Folder

```
import { Routes, RouterModule } from "@angular/router";
import { TableComponent } from "./core/table.component";
import { FormComponent } from "./core/form.component";
import { NotFoundComponent } from "./core/notFound.component";
import { ProductCountComponent } from "./core/productCount.component";
import { CategoryCountComponent } from "./core/categoryCount.component";
import { ModelResolver } from "./model/model.resolver";

const childRoutes: Routes = [
    {
        path: "",
        children: [{ path: "products", component: ProductCountComponent },
                   { path: "categories", component: CategoryCountComponent },
                   { path: "", component: ProductCountComponent }],
        resolve: { model: ModelResolver }
    }
];

const routes: Routes = [
    {
        path: "form/:mode/:id", component: FormComponent,
        resolve: { model: ModelResolver }
    },
    {
        path: "form/:mode", component: FormComponent,
        resolve: { model: ModelResolver }
    },
    { path: "table", component: TableComponent, children: childRoutes },
    { path: "table/:category", component: TableComponent, children: childRoutes },
    { path: "", redirectTo: "/table", pathMatch: "full" },
    { path: "**", component: NotFoundComponent }
]

export const routing = RouterModule.forRoot(routes);
```

Applying the ModelResolver class to the routes that target FormComponent prevents the problem shown in Figure 27-4. There are other ways to solve this problem, including the approach that I used in Chapter 8 for the SportsStore application, which uses the route guard feature described in the "Preventing Route Activation" section of this chapter.

Preventing Navigation with Guards

Resolvers are used to delay navigation while the application performs some prerequisite work, such as loading data. The other guards that Angular provides are used to control whether navigation can occur at all, which can be useful when you want to alert the user to prevent potentially unwanted operations (such as abandoning data edits) or limit access to parts of the application unless the application is in a specific state (such as when a user has been authenticated).

687

Many uses for route guards introduce an additional interaction with the user, either to gain explicit approval to perform an operation or to obtain additional data, such as authentication credentials. For this chapter, I am going to handle this kind of interaction by extending the message service so that messages can require user input. In Listing 27-8, I have added an optional `responses` constructor argument/property to the `Message` model class, which will allow messages to contain prompts to the user and callbacks that will be invoked when they are selected. The `responses` property is an array of TypeScript tuples, where the first value is the name of the response, which will be presented to the user, and the second value is the callback function, which will be passed the name as its argument.

Listing 27-8. Adding Responses in the message.model.ts File in the src/app/messages Folder

```
export class Message {

    constructor(private text: string,
        private error: boolean = false,
        private responses?: [string, (string) => void][]) { }
}
```

The only other change required to implement this feature is to present the response options to the user. Listing 27-9 adds `button` elements below the message text for each `response`. Clicking the buttons will invoke the callback function.

Listing 27-9. Presenting Responses in the message.component.html File in the src/app/core Folder

```
<div *ngIf="lastMessage"
    class="bg-info text-white p-2 text-center"
    [class.bg-danger]="lastMessage.error">
    <h4>{{lastMessage.text}}</h4>
</div>
<div class="text-center my-2">
    <button *ngFor="let resp of lastMessage?.responses; let i = index"
            (click)="resp[1](resp[0])"
            class="btn btn-primary m-2" [class.btn-secondary]="i > 0">
        {{resp[0]}}
    </button>
</div>
```

Preventing Route Activation

Guards can be used to prevent a route from being activated, helping to protect the application from entering an unwanted state or warning the user about the impact of performing an operation. To demonstrate, I am going to guard the /form/create URL to prevent the user from starting the process of creating a new product unless the user agrees to the application's terms and conditions.

Guards for route activation are classes that define a method called `canActivate`, which receives the same `ActivatedRouteSnapshot` and `RouterStateSnapshot` arguments as resolvers. The `canActivate` method can be implemented to return three different result types, as described in Table 27-4.

Table 27-4. *The Result Types Allowed by the canActivate Method*

Result Type	Description
boolean	This type of result is useful when performing synchronous checks to see whether the route can be activated. A true result will activate the route, and a result of false will not, effectively ignoring the navigation request.
Observable<boolean>	This type of result is useful when performing asynchronous checks to see whether the route can be activated. Angular will wait until the Observable emits a value, which will be used to determine whether the route is activated. When using this kind of result, it is important to terminate the Observable by calling the complete method; otherwise, Angular will just keep waiting.
Promise<boolean>	This type of result is useful when performing asynchronous checks to see whether the route can be activated. Angular will wait until the Promise is resolved and activate the route if it yields true. If the Promise yields false, then the route will not be activated, effectively ignoring the navigation request.

To get started, I added a file called terms.guard.ts to the src/app folder and defined the class shown in Listing 27-10.

Listing 27-10. The Contents of the terms.guard.ts File in the src/app Folder

```
import { Injectable } from "@angular/core";
import {
    ActivatedRouteSnapshot, RouterStateSnapshot,
    Router
} from "@angular/router";
import { MessageService } from "./messages/message.service";
import { Message } from "./messages/message.model";

@Injectable()
export class TermsGuard {

    constructor(private messages: MessageService,
                private router: Router) { }

    canActivate(route: ActivatedRouteSnapshot, state: RouterStateSnapshot):
        Promise<boolean> | boolean {

        if (route.params["mode"] == "create") {

            return new Promise<boolean>((resolve) => {
                let responses: [string, () => void][]
                    = [["Yes", () => resolve(true)], ["No",  () => resolve(false)]];
                this.messages.reportMessage(
                    new Message("Do you accept the terms & conditions?",
                        false, responses));
            });
        } else {
```

```
                return true;
        }
    }
}
```

The canActivate method can return two different types of result. The first type is a boolean, which allows the guard to respond immediately for routes that it doesn't need to protect, which in this case is any that lacks a parameter called mode whose value is create. If the URL matched by the route doesn't contain this parameter, the canActivate method returns true, which tells Angular to activate the route. This is important because the edit and create features both rely on the same routes, and the guard should not interfere with edit operations.

The other type of result is a Promise<boolean>, which I have used instead of Observable<true> for variety. The Promise uses the modifications to the message service to solicit a response from the user, confirming they accept the (unspecified) terms and conditions. There are two possible responses from the user. If the user clicks the Yes button, then the Promise will resolve and yield true, which tells Angular to activate the route, displaying the form that is used to create a new product. The Promise will resolve and yield false if the user clicks the No button, which tells Angular to ignore the navigation request.

Listing 27-11 registers the TermsGuard as a service so that it can be used in the application's routing configuration.

Listing 27-11. Registering the Guard as a Service in the app.module.ts File in the src/app Folder

```
import { BrowserModule } from '@angular/platform-browser';
import { NgModule } from '@angular/core';
import { ModelModule } from "./model/model.module";
import { CoreModule } from "./core/core.module";
import { TableComponent } from "./core/table.component";
import { FormComponent } from "./core/form.component";
import { MessageModule } from "./messages/message.module";
import { MessageComponent } from "./messages/message.component";
import { AppComponent } from './app.component';
import { routing } from "./app.routing";
import { TermsGuard } from "./terms.guard"

@NgModule({
    imports: [BrowserModule, ModelModule, CoreModule, MessageModule, routing],
    declarations: [AppComponent],
    providers: [TermsGuard],
    bootstrap: [AppComponent]
})
export class AppModule { }
```

Finally, Listing 27-12 applies the guard to the routing configuration. Activation guards are applied to a route using the canActivate property, which is assigned an array of guard services. The canActivate method of all the guards must return true (or return an Observable or Promise that eventually yields true) before Angular will activate the route.

Listing 27-12. Applying the Guard to a Route in the app.routing.ts File in the src/app Folder

```
import { Routes, RouterModule } from "@angular/router";
import { TableComponent } from "./core/table.component";
import { FormComponent } from "./core/form.component";
```

```
import { NotFoundComponent } from "./core/notFound.component";
import { ProductCountComponent } from "./core/productCount.component";
import { CategoryCountComponent } from "./core/categoryCount.component";
import { ModelResolver } from "./model/model.resolver";
import { TermsGuard } from "./terms.guard";

const childRoutes: Routes = [
    {
        path: "",
        children: [{ path: "products", component: ProductCountComponent },
                   { path: "categories", component: CategoryCountComponent },
                   { path: "", component: ProductCountComponent }],
        resolve: { model: ModelResolver }
    }
];

const routes: Routes = [
    {
        path: "form/:mode/:id", component: FormComponent,
        resolve: { model: ModelResolver }
    },
    {
        path: "form/:mode", component: FormComponent,
        resolve: { model: ModelResolver },
        canActivate: [TermsGuard]
    },
    { path: "table", component: TableComponent, children: childRoutes },
    { path: "table/:category", component: TableComponent, children: childRoutes },
    { path: "", redirectTo: "/table", pathMatch: "full" },
    { path: "**", component: NotFoundComponent }
]

export const routing = RouterModule.forRoot(routes);
```

The effect of creating and applying the activation guard is that the user is prompted when clicking the Create New Product button, as shown in Figure 27-5. If they respond by clicking the Yes button, then the navigation request will be completed, and Angular will activate the route that selects the form component, which will allow a new product to be created. If the user clicks the No button, then the navigation request will be canceled. In both cases, the routing system emits an event that is received by the component that displays the messages to the user, which clears its display and ensures that the user doesn't see stale messages.

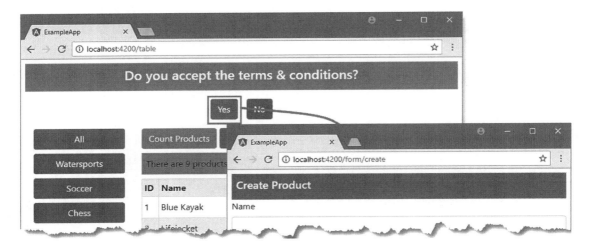

Figure 27-5. *Guarding route activation*

Consolidating Child Route Guards

If you have a set of child routes, you can guard against their activation using a child route guard, which is a class that defines a method called canActivateChild. The guard is applied to the parent route in the application's configuration, and the canActivateChild method is called whenever any of the child routes are about to be activated. The method receives the same ActivatedRouteSnapshot and RouterStateSnapshot objects as the other guards and can return the set of result types described in Table 27-4.

This guard in this example is more readily dealt with by changing the configuration before implementing the canActivateChild method, as shown in Listing 27-13.

Listing 27-13. Guarding Child Routes in the app.routing.ts File in the src/app Folder

```
import { Routes, RouterModule } from "@angular/router";
import { TableComponent } from "./core/table.component";
import { FormComponent } from "./core/form.component";
import { NotFoundComponent } from "./core/notFound.component";
import { ProductCountComponent } from "./core/productCount.component";
import { CategoryCountComponent } from "./core/categoryCount.component";
import { ModelResolver } from "./model/model.resolver";
import { TermsGuard } from "./terms.guard";

const childRoutes: Routes = [
    {
        path: "",
        canActivateChild: [TermsGuard],
        children: [{ path: "products", component: ProductCountComponent },
                   { path: "categories", component: CategoryCountComponent },
                   { path: "", component: ProductCountComponent }],
        resolve: { model: ModelResolver }
    }
];
```

```
const routes: Routes = [
    {
        path: "form/:mode/:id", component: FormComponent,
        resolve: { model: ModelResolver }
    },
    {
        path: "form/:mode", component: FormComponent,
        resolve: { model: ModelResolver },
        canActivate: [TermsGuard]
    },
    { path: "table", component: TableComponent, children: childRoutes },
    { path: "table/:category", component: TableComponent, children: childRoutes },
    { path: "", redirectTo: "/table", pathMatch: "full" },
    { path: "**", component: NotFoundComponent }
]

export const routing = RouterModule.forRoot(routes);
```

Child route guards are applied to a route using the canActivateChild property, which is set to an array of service types that implement the canActivateChild method. This method will be called before Angular activates any of the route's children. Listing 27-14 adds the canActivateChild method to the guard class from the previous section.

Listing 27-14. Implementing Child Route Guards in the terms.guard.ts File in the src/app Folder

```
import { Injectable } from "@angular/core";
import {
    ActivatedRouteSnapshot, RouterStateSnapshot,
    Router
} from "@angular/router";
import { MessageService } from "./messages/message.service";
import { Message } from "./messages/message.model";

@Injectable()
export class TermsGuard {

    constructor(private messages: MessageService,
        private router: Router) { }

    canActivate(route: ActivatedRouteSnapshot, state: RouterStateSnapshot):
        Promise<boolean> | boolean {

        if (route.params["mode"] == "create") {

            return new Promise<boolean>((resolve, reject) => {
                let responses: [string, (string) => void][] = [
                    ["Yes", () => resolve(true)],
                    ["No", () => resolve(false)]
                ];
                this.messages.reportMessage(
                    new Message("Do you accept the terms & conditions?",
                        false, responses));
```

693

```
            });
        } else {
            return true;
        }
    }

    canActivateChild(route: ActivatedRouteSnapshot, state: RouterStateSnapshot):
        Promise<boolean> | boolean {

        if (route.url.length > 0
            && route.url[route.url.length - 1].path == "categories") {

            return new Promise<boolean>((resolve, reject) => {
                let responses: [string, (string) => void][] = [
                    ["Yes", () => resolve(true)],
                    ["No ", () => resolve(false)]
                ];

                this.messages.reportMessage(
                    new Message("Do you want to see the categories component?",
                        false, responses));
            });
        } else {
            return true;
        }
    }
}
```

The guard only protects the categories child route and will return true immediately for any other route. The guard prompts the user using the message service but does something different if the user clicks the No button. In addition to rejecting the active route, the guard navigates to a different URL using the Router service, which is received as a constructor argument. This is a common pattern for authentication, when the user is redirected to a component that will solicit security credentials if a restricted operation is attempted. The example is simpler in this case, and the guard navigates to a sibling route that shows a different component. (You can see an example of using route guards for navigation in the SportsStore application in Chapter 9.)

To see the effect of the guard, click the Count Categories button, as shown in Figure 27-6. Responding to the prompt by clicking the Yes button will show the CategoryCountComponent, which displays the number of categories in the table. Clicking No will reject the active route and navigate to a route that displays the ProductCountComponent instead.

■ **Note**   Guards are applied only when the active route changes. So, for example, if you click the Count Categories button when the /table URL is active, then you will see the prompt, and clicking Yes will change the active route. But nothing will happen if you click the Count Categories button again because Angular doesn't trigger a route change when the target route and the active route are the same.

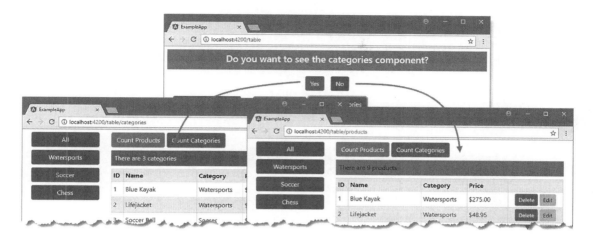

Figure 27-6. *Guarding child routes*

Preventing Route Deactivation

When you start working with routes, you will tend to focus on the way that routes are activated to respond to navigation and present new content to the user. But equally important is route *deactivation*, which occurs when the application navigates away from a route.

The most common use for deactivation guards is to prevent the user from navigating when there are unsaved edits to data. In this section, I will create a guard that warns the user when they are about to abandon unsaved changes when editing a product. In preparation for this, Listing 27-15 changes the FormComponent class to simplify the work of the guard.

Listing 27-15. Preparing for the Guard in the form.component.ts File in the src/app/core Folder

```
import { Component, Inject } from "@angular/core";
import { NgForm } from "@angular/forms";
import { Product } from "../model/product.model";
import { Model } from "../model/repository.model";
import { ActivatedRoute, Router } from "@angular/router";

@Component({
    selector: "paForm",
    templateUrl: "form.component.html",
    styleUrls: ["form.component.css"]
})
export class FormComponent {
    product: Product = new Product();
    originalProduct = new Product();

    constructor(private model: Model, activeRoute: ActivatedRoute,
        private router: Router) {

        activeRoute.params.subscribe(params => {
            this.editing = params["mode"] == "edit";
            let id = params["id"];
```

```
            if (id != null) {
                Object.assign(this.product, model.getProduct(id) || new Product());
                Object.assign(this.originalProduct, this.product);
            }
        })
    }

    editing: boolean = false;

    submitForm(form: NgForm) {
        if (form.valid) {
            this.model.saveProduct(this.product);
            this.originalProduct = this.product;
            this.router.navigateByUrl("/");
        }
    }

    //resetForm() {
    //    this.product = new Product();
    //}
}
```

When the component begins editing, it creates a copy of the Product object that it gets from the data model and assigns it to the originalProduct property. This property will be used by the deactivation guard to see whether there are unsaved edits. To prevent the guard from interrupting save operations, the originalProduct property is set to the editing product object in the submitForm method before the navigation request.

A corresponding change is required in the template so that the Cancel button doesn't invoke the form's reset event handler, as shown in Listing 27-16.

Listing 27-16. Disabling Form Reset in the form.component.html File in the src/app/core Folder

```html
<div class="bg-primary text-white p-2" [class.bg-warning]="editing">
    <h5>{{editing  ? "Edit" : "Create"}} Product</h5>
</div>

<div *ngIf="editing" class="p-2">
    <button class="btn btn-secondary"
            [routerLink]="['/form', 'edit', model.getPreviousProductid(product.id)]">
        Previous
    </button>
    <button class="btn btn-secondary"
            [routerLink]="['/form', 'edit', model.getNextProductId(product.id)]">
        Next
    </button>
</div>

<form novalidate #form="ngForm" (ngSubmit)="submitForm(form)">
    <div class="form-group">
        <label>Name</label>
        <input class="form-control" name="name"
               [(ngModel)]="product.name" required />
    </div>
```

```
<div class="form-group">
    <label>Category</label>
    <input class="form-control" name="category"
            [(ngModel)]="product.category" required />
</div>

<div class="form-group">
    <label>Price</label>
    <input class="form-control" name="price"
            [(ngModel)]="product.price"
            required pattern="^[0-9\.]+$" />
</div>

<button type="submit" class="btn btn-primary"
        [class.btn-warning]="editing" [disabled]="form.invalid">
    {{editing ? "Save" : "Create"}}
</button>
<button type="button" class="btn btn-secondary" routerLink="/">Cancel</button>
</form>
```

To create the guard, I added a file called unsaved.guard.ts in the src/app/core folder and defined the class shown in Listing 27-17.

Listing 27-17. The Contents of the unsaved.guard.ts File in the src/app/core Folder

```
import { Injectable } from "@angular/core";
import {
    ActivatedRouteSnapshot, RouterStateSnapshot,
    Router
} from "@angular/router";
import { Observable, Subject } from "rxjs";
import { MessageService } from "../messages/message.service";
import { Message } from "../messages/message.model";
import { FormComponent } from "./form.component";

@Injectable()
export class UnsavedGuard {

    constructor(private messages: MessageService,
                private router: Router) { }

    canDeactivate(component: FormComponent, route: ActivatedRouteSnapshot,
        state: RouterStateSnapshot): Observable<boolean> | boolean {

        if (component.editing) {
            if (["name", "category", "price"]
                .some(prop => component.product[prop]
                    != component.originalProduct[prop])) {
                let subject = new Subject<boolean>();

                let responses: [string, (string) => void][] = [
                    ["Yes", () => {
```

```
                    subject.next(true);
                    subject.complete();
                }],
                ["No", () => {
                    this.router.navigateByUrl(this.router.url);
                    subject.next(false);
                    subject.complete();
                }]
            ];
            this.messages.reportMessage(new Message("Discard Changes?",
                true, responses));
            return subject;
        }
    }
    return true;
}
}
```

Deactivation guards define a class called canDeactivate that receives three arguments: the component that is about to be deactivated and the ActivatedRouteSnapshot and RouteStateSnapshot objects. This guard checks to see whether there are unsaved edits in the component and prompts the user if there are. For variety, this guard uses an Observable<true>, implemented as a Subject<true>, instead of a Promise<true> to tell Angular whether it should activate the route, based on the response selected by the user.

■ **Tip**   Notice that I call the complete method on the Subject after calling the next method. Angular will wait indefinitely for the complete method is called, effectively freezing the application.

The next step is to register the guard as a service in the module that contains it, as shown in Listing 27-18.

Listing 27-18. Registering the Guard as a Service in the core.module.ts File in the src/app/core Folder

```
import { NgModule } from "@angular/core";
import { BrowserModule } from "@angular/platform-browser";
import { FormsModule } from "@angular/forms";
import { ModelModule } from "../model/model.module";
import { TableComponent } from "./table.component";
import { FormComponent } from "./form.component";
import { Subject } from "rxjs";
import { StatePipe } from "./state.pipe";
import { MessageModule } from "../messages/message.module";
import { MessageService } from "../messages/message.service";
import { Message } from "../messages/message.model";
import { Model } from "../model/repository.model";
import { RouterModule } from "@angular/router";
import { ProductCountComponent } from "./productCount.component";
import { CategoryCountComponent } from "./categoryCount.component";
import { NotFoundComponent } from "./notFound.component";
import { UnsavedGuard } from "./unsaved.guard";
```

```
@NgModule({
    imports: [BrowserModule, FormsModule, ModelModule, MessageModule, RouterModule],
    declarations: [TableComponent, FormComponent, StatePipe,
        ProductCountComponent, CategoryCountComponent, NotFoundComponent],
    providers: [UnsavedGuard],
    exports: [ModelModule, TableComponent, FormComponent]
})
export class CoreModule { }
```

Finally, Listing 27-19 applies the guard to the application's routing configuration. Deactivation guards are applied to routes using the canDeactivate property, which is set to an array of guard services.

Listing 27-19. Applying the Guard in the app.routing.ts File in the src/app Folder

```
import { Routes, RouterModule } from "@angular/router";
import { TableComponent } from "./core/table.component";
import { FormComponent } from "./core/form.component";
import { NotFoundComponent } from "./core/notFound.component";
import { ProductCountComponent } from "./core/productCount.component";
import { CategoryCountComponent } from "./core/categoryCount.component";
import { ModelResolver } from "./model/model.resolver";
import { TermsGuard } from "./terms.guard";
import { UnsavedGuard } from "./core/unsaved.guard";

const childRoutes: Routes = [
    {
        path: "",
        canActivateChild: [TermsGuard],
        children: [{ path: "products", component: ProductCountComponent },
                   { path: "categories", component: CategoryCountComponent },
                   { path: "", component: ProductCountComponent }],
        resolve: { model: ModelResolver }
    }
];

const routes: Routes = [
    {
        path: "form/:mode/:id", component: FormComponent,
        resolve: { model: ModelResolver },
        canDeactivate: [UnsavedGuard]
    },
    {
        path: "form/:mode", component: FormComponent,
        resolve: { model: ModelResolver },
        canActivate: [TermsGuard]
    },
    { path: "table", component: TableComponent, children: childRoutes },
    { path: "table/:category", component: TableComponent, children: childRoutes },
    { path: "", redirectTo: "/table", pathMatch: "full" },
    { path: "**", component: NotFoundComponent }
]

export const routing = RouterModule.forRoot(routes);
```

To see the effect of the guard, click one of the Edit buttons in the table; edit the data in one of the text fields; and then click the Cancel, Next, or Previous button. The guard will prompt you before allowing Angular to activate the route you selected, as shown in Figure 27-7.

Figure 27-7. *Guarding route deactivation*

Loading Feature Modules Dynamically

Angular supports loading feature modules only when they are required, known as *dynamic loading* or *lazy loading*. This can be useful for functionality that is unlikely to be required by all users. In the sections that follow, I create a simple feature module and demonstrate how to configure the application so that Angular will load the module only when the application navigates to a specific URL.

■ **Note** Loading modules dynamically is a trade-off. The application will be smaller and faster to download for most users, improving their overall experience. But users who require the dynamically loaded features will have wait while Angular gets the module and its dependencies. The effect can be jarring because the user has no idea that some features have been loaded and others have not. When you create dynamically loaded modules, you are balancing improving the experience for some users against making it worse for others. Consider how your users fall into these groups and be careful not to degrade the experience of your most valuable and important customers.

Creating a Simple Feature Module

Dynamically loaded modules must contain only functionality that not all users will require. I can't use the existing modules because they provide the core functionality for the application, which means that I need a new module for this part of the chapter. I started by creating a folder called ondemand in the src/app folder. To give the new module a component, I added a file called ondemand.component.ts in the example/app/ondemand folder and added the code shown in Listing 27-20.

■ **Caution**   It is important not to create dependencies between other parts of the application and the classes in the dynamically loaded module so that the JavaScript module loader doesn't try to load the module before it is required.

Listing 27-20. The Contents of the ondemand.component.ts File in the src/app/ondemand Folder

```
import { Component } from "@angular/core";

@Component({
    selector: "ondemand",
    templateUrl: "ondemand.component.html"
})
export class OndemandComponent { }
```

To provide the component with a template, I added a file called ondemand.component.html and added the markup shown in Listing 27-21.

Listing 27-21. The ondemand.component.html File in the src/app/ondemand Folder

```
<div class="bg-primary text-white p-2">This is the ondemand component</div>
<button class="btn btn-primary m-2" routerLink="/" >Back</button>
```

The template contains a message that will make it obvious when the component is selected and that contains a button element that will navigate back to the application's root URL when clicked.

To define the module, I added a file called ondemand.module.ts and added the code shown in Listing 27-22.

Listing 27-22. The Contents of the ondemand.module.ts File in the src/app/ondemand Folder

```
import { NgModule } from "@angular/core";
import { CommonModule } from "@angular/common";
import { OndemandComponent } from "./ondemand.component";

@NgModule({
    imports: [CommonModule],
    declarations: [OndemandComponent],
    exports: [OndemandComponent]
})
export class OndemandModule { }
```

The module imports the CommonModule functionality, which is used instead of the browser-specific BrowserModule to access the built-in directives in feature modules that are loaded on-demand.

Loading the Module Dynamically

There are two steps to set up dynamic loading a module. The first is to set up a routing configuration inside the feature module to provide the rules that will allow Angular to select a component when the module is loaded. Listing 27-23 adds a single route to the feature module.

Listing 27-23. Defining Routes in the ondemand.module.ts File in the src/app/ondemand Folder

```
import { NgModule } from "@angular/core";
import { CommonModule } from "@angular/common";
import { OndemandComponent } from "./ondemand.component";
import { RouterModule } from "@angular/router";

let routing = RouterModule.forChild([
    { path: "", component: OndemandComponent }
]);

@NgModule({
    imports: [CommonModule, routing],
    declarations: [OndemandComponent],
    exports: [OndemandComponent]
})
export class OndemandModule { }
```

Routes in dynamically loaded modules are defined using the same properties as in the main part of the application and can use all the same features, including child components, guards, and redirections. The route defined in the listing matches the empty path and selects the OndemandComponent for display.

One important difference is the method used to generate the module that contains the routing information, as follows:

```
...
let routing = RouterModule.forChild([
    { path: "", component: OndemandComponent }
]);
...
```

When I created the application-wide routing configuration, I used the RouterModule.forRoot method. This is the method that is used to set up the routes in the root module of the application. When creating dynamically loaded modules, the RouterModule.forChild method must be used; this method creates a routing configuration that is merged into the overall routing system when the module is loaded.

Creating a Route to Dynamically Load a Module

The second step to set up a dynamically loaded module is to create a route in the main part of the application that provides Angular with the module's location, as shown in Listing 27-24.

Listing 27-24. Creating an On-Demand Route in the app.routing.ts File in the src/app Folder

```
import { Routes, RouterModule } from "@angular/router";
import { TableComponent } from "./core/table.component";
import { FormComponent } from "./core/form.component";
```

```
import { NotFoundComponent } from "./core/notFound.component";
import { ProductCountComponent } from "./core/productCount.component";
import { CategoryCountComponent } from "./core/categoryCount.component";
import { ModelResolver } from "./model/model.resolver";
import { TermsGuard } from "./terms.guard";
import { UnsavedGuard } from "./core/unsaved.guard";

const childRoutes: Routes = [
    {
        path: "",
        canActivateChild: [TermsGuard],
        children: [{ path: "products", component: ProductCountComponent },
                   { path: "categories", component: CategoryCountComponent },
                   { path: "", component: ProductCountComponent }],
        resolve: { model: ModelResolver }
    }
];

const routes: Routes = [
    {
        path: "ondemand",
        loadChildren: "./ondemand/ondemand.module#OndemandModule"
    },
    {
        path: "form/:mode/:id", component: FormComponent,
        resolve: { model: ModelResolver },
        canDeactivate: [UnsavedGuard]
    },
    {
        path: "form/:mode", component: FormComponent,
        resolve: { model: ModelResolver },
        canActivate: [TermsGuard]
    },
    { path: "table", component: TableComponent, children: childRoutes },
    { path: "table/:category", component: TableComponent, children: childRoutes },
    { path: "", redirectTo: "/table", pathMatch: "full" },
    { path: "**", component: NotFoundComponent }
]

export const routing = RouterModule.forRoot(routes);
```

The loadChildren property is used to provide Angular with details of how the module should be loaded. The value of the property is the path to the JavaScript file that contains the module (omitting the file extension), followed by a # character, followed by the name of the module class. The value in the listing tells Angular to load the OndemandModule class from the ondemand/ondemand.module file.

Using a Dynamically Loaded Module

All that remains is to add support for navigating to the URL that will activate the route for the on-demand module, as shown in Listing 27-25, which adds a button to the template for the table component.

Listing 27-25. Adding Navigation in the table.component.html File in the src/app/core Folder

```
<div class="container-fluid">
    <div class="row">
        <div class="col-3">
            <button class="btn btn-secondary btn-block"
                    routerLink="/table" routerLinkActive="bg-primary"
                    [routerLinkActiveOptions]="{exact: true}">
                All
            </button>
            <button *ngFor="let category of categories"
                    class="btn btn-secondary btn-block"
                    [routerLink]="['/table', category]"
                    routerLinkActive="bg-primary">
                {{category}}
            </button>
        </div>
        <div class="col-9">

                < !-- ...elements omitted for brevity... -->

        </div>
        <div class="col-12 p-2 text-center">
            <button class="btn btn-primary" routerLink="/form/create">
                Create New Product
            </button>
            <button class="btn btn-danger" (click)="deleteProduct(-1)">
                Generate HTTP Error
            </button>
            <button class="btn btn-danger" routerLink="/does/not/exist">
                Generate Routing Error
            </button>
            <button class="btn btn-danger" routerLink="/ondemand">
                Load Module
            </button>
        </div>
    </div>
</div>
```

No special measures are required to target a route that loads a module, and the Load Module button in the listing uses the standard routerLink attribute to navigate to the URL specified by the route added in Listing 27-24.

To see how dynamic module loading works, restart the Angular development tools using the following command in the exampleApp folder, which rebuilds the modules, including the on-demand one:

```
ng serve
```

Now use the browser's developer tools to see the list of files that are loaded as the application starts. You won't see HTTP requests for any of the files in the on-demand module until you click the Load Module button. When the button is clicked, Angular uses the routing configuration to load the module, inspect its routing configuration, and select the component that will be displayed to the user, as shown in Figure 27-8.

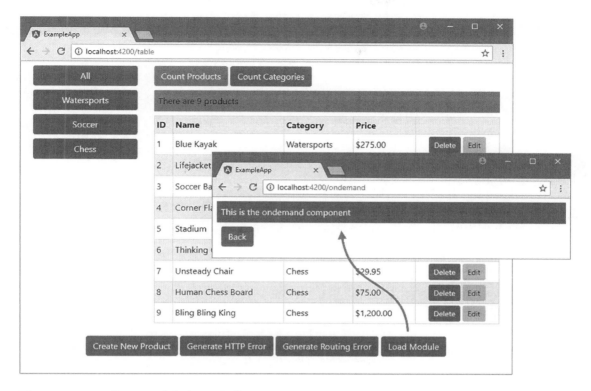

Figure 27-8. *Loading a module dynamically*

Guarding Dynamic Modules

You can guard against dynamically loading modules to ensure that they are loaded only when the application is in a specific state or when the user has explicitly agreed to wait while Angular does the loading (this latter option is typically used only for administration functions, where the user can be expected to have some understanding of how the application is structured).

The guard for the module must be defined in the main part of the application, so I added a file called load.guard.ts in the src/app folder and defined the class shown in Listing 27-26.

Listing 27-26. The Contents of the load.guard.ts File in the src/app Folder

```
import { Injectable } from "@angular/core";
import { Route, Router } from "@angular/router";
import { MessageService } from "./messages/message.service";
import { Message } from "./messages/message.model";

@Injectable()
export class LoadGuard {
    private loaded: boolean = false;

    constructor(private messages: MessageService,
                private router: Router) { }

    canLoad(route: Route): Promise<boolean> | boolean {
```

```
        return this.loaded || new Promise<boolean>((resolve, reject) => {
            let responses: [string, (string) => void] [] = [
                ["Yes", () => {
                    this.loaded = true;
                    resolve(true);
                }],
                ["No", () => {
                    this.router.navigateByUrl(this.router.url);
                    resolve(false);
                }]
            ];

            this.messages.reportMessage(
                new Message("Do you want to load the module?",
                    false, responses));
        });
    }
}
```

Dynamic loading guards are classes that implement a method called canLoad, which is invoked when Angular needs to activate the route it is applied to and which is provided with a Route object that describes the route.

The guard is required only when the URL that loads the module is first activated, so it defines a loaded property that is set to true when the module has been loaded so that subsequent requests are immediately approved. Otherwise, this guard follows the same pattern as earlier examples and returns a Promise that will be resolved when the user clicks one of the buttons displayed by the message service.

Listing 27-27 registers the guard as a service in the root module.

Listing 27-27. Registering the Guard as a Service in the app.module.ts File in the src/app Folder

```
import { NgModule } from "@angular/core";
import { BrowserModule } from "@angular/platform-browser";
import { ModelModule } from "./model/model.module";
import { CoreModule } from "./core/core.module";
import { TableComponent } from "./core/table.component";
import { FormComponent } from "./core/form.component";
import { MessageModule } from "./messages/message.module";
import { MessageComponent } from "./messages/message.component";
import { routing } from "./app.routing";
import { AppComponent } from "./app.component";
import { TermsGuard } from "./terms.guard"
import { LoadGuard } from "./load.guard";

@NgModule({
    imports: [BrowserModule, CoreModule, MessageModule, routing],
    declarations: [AppComponent],
    providers: [TermsGuard, LoadGuard],
    bootstrap: [AppComponent]
})
export class AppModule { }
```

Applying a Dynamic Loading Guard

Guards for dynamic loading are applied to routes using the canLoad property, which accepts an array of guard types. Listing 27-28 applies the LoadGuard class, which was defined in Listing 27-26, to the route that dynamically loads the module.

Listing 27-28. Guarding the Route in the app.routing.ts File in the src/app Folder

```
import { Routes, RouterModule } from "@angular/router";
import { TableComponent } from "./core/table.component";
import { FormComponent } from "./core/form.component";
import { NotFoundComponent } from "./core/notFound.component";
import { ProductCountComponent } from "./core/productCount.component";
import { CategoryCountComponent } from "./core/categoryCount.component";
import { ModelResolver } from "./model/model.resolver";
import { TermsGuard } from "./terms.guard";
import { UnsavedGuard } from "./core/unsaved.guard";
import { LoadGuard } from "./load.guard";

const childRoutes: Routes = [
    {
        path: "",
        canActivateChild: [TermsGuard],
        children: [{ path: "products", component: ProductCountComponent },
                    { path: "categories", component: CategoryCountComponent },
                    { path: "", component: ProductCountComponent }],
        resolve: { model: ModelResolver }
    }
];

const routes: Routes = [
    {
        path: "ondemand",
        loadChildren: "./ondemand/ondemand.module#OndemandModule",
        canLoad: [LoadGuard]
    },
    {
        path: "form/:mode/:id", component: FormComponent,
        resolve: { model: ModelResolver },
        canDeactivate: [UnsavedGuard]
    },
    {
        path: "form/:mode", component: FormComponent,
        resolve: { model: ModelResolver },
        canActivate: [TermsGuard]
    },
    { path: "table", component: TableComponent, children: childRoutes },
    { path: "table/:category", component: TableComponent, children: childRoutes },
    { path: "", redirectTo: "/table", pathMatch: "full" },
    { path: "**", component: NotFoundComponent }
]

export const routing = RouterModule.forRoot(routes);
```

The result is that the user is prompted to determine whether they want to load the module the first time that Angular tries to activate the route, as shown in Figure 27-9.

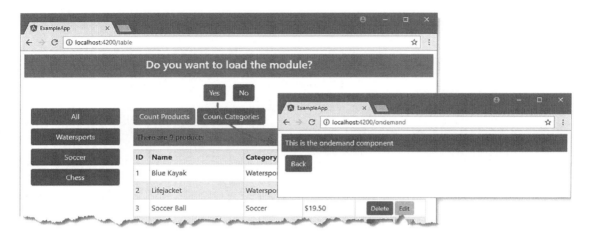

Figure 27-9. *Guarding dynamic loading*

Targeting Named Outlets

A template can contain more than one router-outlet element, which allows a single URL to select multiple components to be displayed to the user.

To demonstrate this feature, I need to add two new components to the ondemand module. I started by creating a file called first.component.ts in the src/app/ondemand folder and using it to define the component shown in Listing 27-29.

Listing 27-29. The first.component.ts File in the src/app/ondemand Folder

```
import { Component } from "@angular/core";

@Component({
    selector: "first",
    template: `<div class="bg-primary text-white p-2">First Component</div>`
})
export class FirstComponent { }
```

This component uses an inline template to display a message whose purpose is simply to make it clear which component has been selected by the routing system. Next, I created a file called second.component.ts in the src/app/ondemand folder and created the component shown in Listing 27-30.

Listing 27-30. The second.component.ts File in the src/app/ondemand Folder

```
import { Component } from "@angular/core";

@Component({
    selector: "second",
    template: `<div class="bg-info text-white p-2">Second Component</div>`
})
export class SecondComponent { }
```

This component is almost identical to the one in Listing 27-29, differing only in the message that it displays through its inline template.

Creating Additional Outlet Elements

When you are using multiple outlet elements in the same template, Angular needs some way to tell them apart. This is done using the name attribute, which allows an outlet to be uniquely identified, as shown in Listing 27-31.

Listing 27-31. Adding Outlets in the ondemand.component.html File in the src/app/ondemand Folder

```html
<div class="bg-primary text-white p-2">This is the ondemand component</div>
<div class="container-fluid">
    <div class="row">
        <div class="col-12 p-2">
            <router-outlet></router-outlet>
        </div>
    </div>
    <div class="row">
        <div class="col-6 p-2">
            <router-outlet name="left"></router-outlet>
        </div>
        <div class="col-6 p-2">
            <router-outlet name="right"></router-outlet>
        </div>
    </div>
</div>
<button class="btn btn-primary m-2" routerLink="/">Back</button>
```

The new elements create three new outlets. There can be at most one router-outlet element without a name element, which is known as the *primary outlet*. This is because omitting the name attribute has the same effect as applying it with a value of primary. All the routing examples so far in this book have relied on the primary outlet to display components to the user.

All other router-outlet elements must have a name element with a unique name. The names I have used in the listing are left and right because the classes applied to the div elements that contain the outlets use CSS to position these two outlets side by side.

The next step is to create a route that includes details of which component should be displayed in each outlet element, as shown in Listing 27-32. If Angular can't find a route that matches a specific outlet, then no content will be shown in that element.

Listing 27-32. Targeting Outlets in the ondemand.module.ts File in the src/app/ondemand Folder

```typescript
import { NgModule } from "@angular/core";
import { CommonModule } from "@angular/common";
import { OndemandComponent } from "./ondemand.component";
import { RouterModule } from "@angular/router";
import { FirstComponent } from "./first.component";
import { SecondComponent } from "./second.component";

let routing = RouterModule.forChild([
    {
        path: "",
        component: OndemandComponent,
```

```
        children: [
            { path: "",
              children: [
                  { outlet: "primary", path: "", component: FirstComponent, },
                  { outlet: "left", path: "", component: SecondComponent, },
                  { outlet: "right", path: "", component: SecondComponent, },
              ]},
          ]
      },
]);

@NgModule({
    imports: [CommonModule, routing],
    declarations: [OndemandComponent, FirstComponent, SecondComponent],
    exports: [OndemandComponent]
})
export class OndemandModule { }
```

The outlet property is used to specify the outlet element that the route applies to. The routing configuration in the listing matches the empty path for all three outlets and selects the newly created components for them: the primary outlet will display FirstComponent, and the left and right outlets will display SecondComponent, as shown in Figure 27-10. To see the effect yourself, click the Load Module button and click the Yes button when prompted.

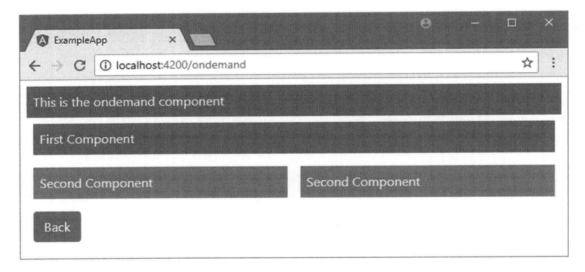

Figure 27-10. *Using multiple router outlets*

■ **Tip** If you omit the outlet property, then Angular assumes that the route targets the primary outlet. I tend to include the outlet property on all routes to emphasize which routes match an outlet element.

When Angular activates the route, it looks for matches for each outlet. All three of the new outlets have routes that match the empty path, which allows Angular to present the components shown in the figure.

Navigating When Using Multiple Outlets

Changing the components that are displayed by each outlet means creating a new set of routes and then navigating to the URL that contains them. Listing 27-33 sets up a route that will match the path /ondemand/ swap and that switches the components displayed by the three outlets.

Listing 27-33. Setting Routes for Outlets in the ondemand.module.ts File in the src/app/ondemand Folder

```
import { NgModule } from "@angular/core";
import { CommonModule } from "@angular/common";
import { OndemandComponent } from "./ondemand.component";
import { RouterModule } from "@angular/router";
import { FirstComponent } from "./first.component";
import { SecondComponent } from "./second.component";

let routing = RouterModule.forChild([
    {
        path: "",
        component: OndemandComponent,
        children: [
            {
                path: "",
                children: [
                    { outlet: "primary", path: "", component: FirstComponent, },
                    { outlet: "left", path: "", component: SecondComponent, },
                    { outlet: "right", path: "", component: SecondComponent, },
                ]
            },
            {
                path: "swap",
                children: [
                    { outlet: "primary", path: "", component: SecondComponent, },
                    { outlet: "left", path: "", component: FirstComponent, },
                    { outlet: "right", path: "", component: FirstComponent, },
                ]
            },
        ]
    },
]);

@NgModule({
    imports: [CommonModule, routing],
    declarations: [OndemandComponent, FirstComponent, SecondComponent],
    exports: [OndemandComponent]
})
export class OndemandModule { }
```

Listing 27-34 adds button elements to the component's template that will navigate to the two sets of routes in Listing 27-33, alternating the set of components displayed to the user.

Listing 27-34. Navigating to Outlets in the ondemand.component.html File in the src/app/ondemand Folder

```
<div class="bg-primary text-white p-2">This is the ondemand component</div>
<div class="container-fluid">
    <div class="row">
        <div class="col-12 p-2">
            <router-outlet></router-outlet>
        </div>
    </div>
    <div class="row">
        <div class="col-6 p-2">
            <router-outlet name="left"></router-outlet>
        </div>
        <div class="col-6 p-2">
            <router-outlet name="right"></router-outlet>
        </div>
    </div>
</div>
<button class="btn btn-secondary m-2" routerLink="/ondemand">Normal</button>
<button class="btn btn-secondary m-2" routerLink="/ondemand/swap">Swap</button>
<button class="btn btn-primary m-2" routerLink="/">Back</button>
```

The result is that clicking the Swap and Normal button will navigate to routes whose children tell Angular which components should be displayed by each of the outlet elements, as illustrated by Figure 27-11.

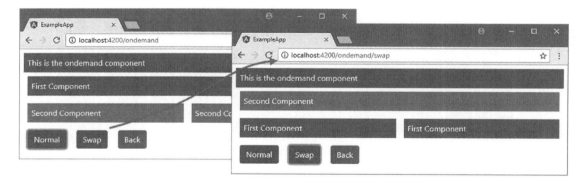

Figure 27-11. *Using navigation to target multiple outlet elements*

Summary

In this chapter, I finished describing the Angular URL routing features, explaining how to guard routes to control when a route is activated, how to load modules only when they are needed, and how to use multiple outlet elements to display components to the user. In the next chapter, I show you how to apply animations to Angular applications.

CHAPTER 28

Using Animation

In this chapter, I describe the Angular animation system, which uses data bindings to animate HTML elements to reflect changes in the state of the application. In broad terms, animations have two roles in an Angular application: to emphasize changes in content or to smooth them out.

Emphasizing changes is important when the content changes in a way that may not be obvious to the user. In the example application, using the Previous and Next buttons when editing a product changes the data fields but doesn't create any other visual change, which results in a transition that the user may not notice. Animations can be used to draw the eye to this kind of change, helping the user notice the results of an action.

Smoothing out changes can make an application more pleasant to use. When the user clicks the Edit button to start editing a product, the content displayed by the example application switches in a way that can be jarring. Using animations to slow down the transition can help provide a sense of context for the content change and make it less abrupt. In this chapter, I explain how the animation system works and how it can be used to draw the user's eye or take the edge off of sudden transitions. Table 28-1 puts Angular animations in context.

Table 28-1. *Putting Angular Animations in Context*

Question	Answer
What is it?	The animation system can change the appearance of HTML elements to reflect changes in the application state.
Why is it useful?	Used judiciously, animations can make applications more pleasant to use.
How is it used?	Animations are defined using functions defined in a platform-specific module, registered using the animations property in the @Component decorator and applied using a data binding.
Are there any pitfalls or limitations?	The main limitation is that it is fully supported on few browsers and, as a consequence, cannot be relied on to work properly on all the browsers that Angular supports for its other features.
Are there any alternatives?	The only alternative is not to animate the application.

© Adam Freeman 2018
A. Freeman, *Pro Angular 6*, https://doi.org/10.1007/978-1-4842-3649-9_28

Table 28-2 summarizes the chapter.

Table 28-2. *Chapter Summary*

Problem	Solution	Listing
Draw the user's attention to a transition in the state of an element	Apply an animation	1–9
Animate the change from one element state to another	Use an element transition	9–14
Perform animations in parallel	Use animation groups	15
Use the same styles in multiple animations	Use common styles	16
Animate the position or size of elements	Use element transformations	17
Use animations to apply CSS framework styles	Use the DOM and CSS APIs	18, 19

Preparing the Example Project

In this chapter, I continue using the exampleApp that was first created in Chapter 22 and has been the focus of every chapter since. The changes in the following sections prepare the example application for the features described in this chapter.

■ **Tip** You can download the example project for this chapter—and for all the other chapters in this book—from `https://github.com/Apress/pro-angular-6`.

Disabling the HTTP Delay

The first preparatory step for this chapter is to disable the delay added to asynchronous HTTP requests, as shown in Listing 28-1.

Listing 28-1. Disabling the Delay in the rest.datasource.ts File in the src/app/model Folder

```
import { Injectable, Inject, InjectionToken } from "@angular/core";
import { HttpClient, HttpHeaders } from "@angular/common/http";
import { Observable, throwError } from "rxjs";
import { Product } from "./product.model";
import { catchError, delay } from "rxjs/operators";

export const REST_URL = new InjectionToken("rest_url");

@Injectable()
export class RestDataSource {
    constructor(private http: HttpClient,
        @Inject(REST_URL) private url: string) { }

    getData(): Observable<Product[]> {
        return this.sendRequest<Product[]>("GET", this.url);
    }
}
```

716

```
    saveProduct(product: Product): Observable<Product> {
        return this.sendRequest<Product>("POST", this.url, product);
    }

    updateProduct(product: Product): Observable<Product> {
        return this.sendRequest<Product>("PUT",
            `${this.url}/${product.id}`, product);
    }

    deleteProduct(id: number): Observable<Product> {
        return this.sendRequest<Product>("DELETE", `${this.url}/${id}`);
    }

    private sendRequest<T>(verb: string, url: string, body?: Product)
        : Observable<T> {

        let myHeaders = new HttpHeaders();
        myHeaders = myHeaders.set("Access-Key", "<secret>");
        myHeaders = myHeaders.set("Application-Names", ["exampleApp", "proAngular"]);

        return this.http.request<T>(verb, url, {
            body: body,
            headers: myHeaders
        })
        //.pipe(delay(5000))
        .pipe(catchError((error: Response) =>
            throwError(`Network Error: ${error.statusText} (${error.status})`)));
    }
}
```

Simplifying the Table Template and Routing Configuration

Many of the examples in this chapter are applied to the elements in the table of products. The final preparation for this chapter is to simplify the template for the table component so that I can focus on a smaller amount of content in the listings.

Listing 28-2 shows the simplified template, which removes the buttons that generated HTTP and routing errors and the button and outlet element that counted the categories or products. The listing also removes the buttons that allow the table to be filtered by category.

Listing 28-2. Simplifying the Template in the table.component.html File in the src/app/core Folder

```
<table class="table table-sm table-bordered table-striped">
    <tr>
        <th>ID</th><th>Name</th><th>Category</th><th>Price</th><th></th>
    </tr>
    <tr *ngFor="let item of getProducts()">
        <td style="vertical-align:middle">{{item.id}}</td>
        <td style="vertical-align:middle">{{item.name}}</td>
        <td style="vertical-align:middle">{{item.category}}</td>
```

```
        <td style="vertical-align:middle">
            {{item.price | currency:"USD" }}
        </td>
        <td class="text-center">
            <button class="btn btn-danger btn-sm"
                    (click)="deleteProduct(item.id)">
                Delete
            </button>
            <button class="btn btn-warning btn-sm"
                [routerLink]="['/form', 'edit', item.id]">
                Edit
            </button>
        </td>
    </tr>
</table>
<div class="m-2">
    <button class="btn btn-primary" routerLink="/form/create">
        Create New Product
    </button>
</div>
```

Listing 28-3 updates the URL routing configuration for the application so that the routes don't target the outlet element that has been removed from the table component's template.

Listing 28-3. Updating the Routing Configuration in the app.routing.ts File in the src/app Folder

```
import { Routes, RouterModule } from "@angular/router";
import { TableComponent } from "./core/table.component";
import { FormComponent } from "./core/form.component";
import { NotFoundComponent } from "./core/notFound.component";
import { ProductCountComponent } from "./core/productCount.component";
import { CategoryCountComponent } from "./core/categoryCount.component";
import { ModelResolver } from "./model/model.resolver";
import { TermsGuard } from "./terms.guard";
import { UnsavedGuard } from "./core/unsaved.guard";
import { LoadGuard } from "./load.guard";

const routes: Routes = [
    {
        path: "form/:mode/:id", component: FormComponent,
        canDeactivate: [UnsavedGuard]
    },
    { path: "form/:mode", component: FormComponent, canActivate: [TermsGuard] },
    { path: "table", component: TableComponent },
    { path: "table/:category", component: TableComponent },
    { path: "", redirectTo: "/table", pathMatch: "full" },
    { path: "**", component: NotFoundComponent }
]

export const routing = RouterModule.forRoot(routes);
```

Open a new command prompt, navigate to the exampleApp folder, and run the following command to start the server that provides the RESTful web server:

```
npm run json
```

Open a separate command prompt, navigate to the exampleApp folder, and run the following command to start the Angular development tools:

```
ng serve
```

Open a new browser window and navigate to http://localhost:4200 to see the content shown in Figure 28-1.

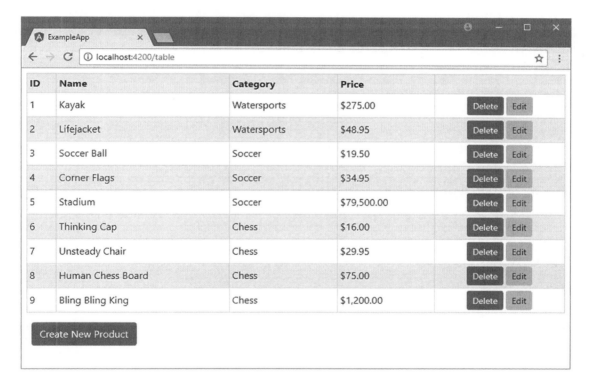

Figure 28-1. *Running the example application*

Getting Started with Angular Animation

As with most Angular features, the best place to start is with an example, which will let me introduce how animation works and how it fits into the rest of the Angular functionality. In the sections that follow, I create a basic animation that will affect the rows in the table of products. Once you have seen how the basic features work, I will dive into the detail for each of the different configuration options and explain how they work in depth.

But to get started, I am going to add a `select` element to the application that allows the user to select a category. When a category is selected, the table rows for products in that category will be shown in one of two styles, as described in Table 28-3.

Table 28-3. *The Styles for the Animation Example*

Description	Styles
The product is in the selected category.	The table row will have a green background and larger text.
The product is not in the selected category.	The table row will have a red background and smaller text.

Enabling the Animation Module

The animation features are contained in their own module that must be imported in the application's root module, as shown in Listing 28-4.

Listing 28-4. Importing the Animation Module in the app.module.ts File in the src/app Folder

```
import { NgModule } from "@angular/core";
import { BrowserModule } from "@angular/platform-browser";
import { ModelModule } from "./model/model.module";
import { CoreModule } from "./core/core.module";
import { TableComponent } from "./core/table.component";
import { FormComponent } from "./core/form.component";
import { MessageModule } from "./messages/message.module";
import { MessageComponent } from "./messages/message.component";
import { routing } from "./app.routing";
import { AppComponent } from "./app.component";
import { TermsGuard } from "./terms.guard"
import { LoadGuard } from "./load.guard";
import { BrowserAnimationsModule } from "@angular/platform-browser/animations";

@NgModule({
    imports: [BrowserModule, CoreModule, MessageModule, routing,
            BrowserAnimationsModule],
    declarations: [AppComponent],
    providers: [TermsGuard, LoadGuard],
    bootstrap: [AppComponent]
})
export class AppModule { }
```

Creating the Animation

To get started with the animation, I created a file called table.animations.ts in the src/app/core folder and added the code shown in Listing 28-5.

Listing 28-5. The Contents of the table.animations.ts File in the src/app/core Folder

```
import { trigger, style, state, transition, animate } from "@angular/animations";

export const HighlightTrigger = trigger("rowHighlight", [
    state("selected", style({
        backgroundColor: "lightgreen",
        fontSize: "20px"
    })),
    state("notselected", style({
        backgroundColor: "lightsalmon",
        fontSize: "12px"
    })),
    transition("selected => notselected", animate("200ms")),
    transition("notselected => selected", animate("400ms"))
]);
```

The syntax used to define animations can be dense and relies on a set of functions defined in the @ angular/animations module. In the following sections, I start at the top and work my way down through the detail to explain each of the animation building blocks used in the listing.

■ **Tip** Don't worry if all the building blocks described in the following sections don't make immediate sense. This is an area of functionality that starts to make more sense only when you see how all the parts fit together.

Defining Style Groups

The heart of the animation system is the style group, which is a set of CSS style properties and values that will be applied to an HTML element. Style groups are defined using the style function, which accepts a JavaScript object literal that provides a map between property names and values, like this:

```
...
style({
    backgroundColor: "lightgreen",
    fontSize: "20px"
})
...
```

This style group tells Angular to set the background color to lightgreen and to set the font size to 20 pixels.

CSS PROPERTY NAME CONVENTIONS

There are two ways to specify CSS properties when using the `style` function. You can use the JavaScript property naming convention, such that the property to set the background color of an element is specified as `backgroundColor` (all one word, no hyphens, and subsequent words capitalized). This is the convention I used in Listing 28-5:

```
...
style({
    backgroundColor: "lightgreen",
    fontSize: "20px"
})),
...
```

Alternatively, you can use the CSS convention, where the same property is expressed as `background-color` (all lowercase with hyphens between words). If you use the CSS format, then you must enclose the property names in quotes to stop JavaScript from trying to interpret the hyphens as arithmetic operators, like this:

```
...
state("green", style({
    "background-color": "lightgreen",
    "font-size": "20px"
})),
...
```

It doesn't matter which name convention you use, just as long as you are consistent. At the time of writing, Angular does not correctly apply styles if you mix and match property name conventions. To get consistent results, pick a naming convention and use it for all the style properties you set throughout your application.

Defining Element States

Angular needs to know when it needs to apply a set of styles to an element. This is done by defining an element state, which provides a name by which the set of styles can be referred to. Element states are created using the `state` function, which accepts the name and the style set that should be associated with it. This is one of the two element states that are defined in Listing 28-5:

```
...
state("selected", style({
    backgroundColor: "lightgreen",
    fontSize: "20px"
})),
...
```

There are two states in the listing, called `selected` and `notselected`, which will correspond to whether the product described by a table row is in the category selected by the user.

Defining State Transitions

When an HTML element is in one of the states created using the `state` function, Angular will apply the CSS properties in the state's style group. The `transition` function is used to tell Angular how the new CSS properties should be applied. There are two transitions in Listing 28-5.

```
...
transition("selected => notselected", animate("200ms")),
transition("notselected => selected", animate("400ms"))
...
```

The first argument passed to the `transition` function tells Angular which states this instruction applies to. The argument is a string that specifies two states and an arrow that expresses the relationship between them. Two kinds of arrow are available, as described in Table 28-4.

Table 28-4. *The Animation Transition Arrow Types*

Arrow	Example	Description
=>	selected => notselected	This arrow specifies a one-way transition between two states, such as when the element moves from the `selected` state to the `notselected` state.
<=>	selected <=> notselected	This array specifies a two-way transition between two states, such as when the element moves from the `selected` state to the `notselected` state and from the `notselected` state to the `selected` state.

The transitions defined in Listing 28-5 use one-way arrows to tell Angular how it should respond when an element moves from the `selected` state to the `notselected` state and from the `notselected` state to the `selected` state.

The second argument to the `transition` function tells Angular what action it should take when the state change occurs. The `animate` function tells Angular to gradually transition between the properties defined in the CSS style set defined by two element states. The arguments passed to the `animate` function in Listing 28-5 specify the period of time that this gradual transition should take, either 200 milliseconds or 400 milliseconds.

GUIDANCE FOR APPLYING ANIMATIONS

Developers often get carried away when applying animations, and the result is applications that users find frustrating. Animations should be applied sparingly, they should be simple, and they should be quick. Use animations to help the user make sense of your application and not as a vehicle to demonstrate your artistic skills. Users, especially for corporate line-of-business applications, have to perform the same task repeatedly, and excessive and long animations just get in the way.

I suffer from this tendency, and, unchecked, my applications behave like Las Vegas slot machines. I have two rules that I follow to keep the problem under control. The first is that I perform the major tasks or workflows in the application 20 times in a row. In the case of the example application, that might mean creating 20 products and then editing 20 products. I remove or shorten any animation that I find myself having to wait to complete before I can move on to the next step in the process.

The second rule is that I don't disable animations during development. It can be tempting to comment out an animation when I am working on a feature because I will be performing a series of quick tests as I write the code. But any animation that gets in my way will also get in the user's way, so I leave the animations in place and adjust them—generally reducing their duration—until they become less obtrusive and annoying.

You don't have to follow my rules, of course, but it is important to make sure that the animations are helpful to the user and not a barrier to working quickly or a distracting annoyance.

Defining the Trigger

The final piece of plumbing is the animation trigger, which packages up the element states and transitions and assigns a name that can be used to apply the animation in a component. Triggers are created using the trigger function, like this:

```
...
export const HighlightTrigger = trigger("rowHighlight", [...])
...
```

The first argument is the name by which the trigger will be known, which is rowHighlight in this example, and the second argument is the array of states and transitions that will be available when the trigger is applied.

Applying the Animation

Once you have defined an animation, you can apply it to one or more components by using the animations property of the @Component decorator. Listing 28-6 applies the animation defined in Listing 28-5 to the table component and adds some additional features that are needed to support the animation.

Listing 28-6. Applying an Animation in the table.component.ts File in the src/app/core Folder

```
import { Component, Inject } from "@angular/core";
import { Product } from "../model/product.model";
import { Model } from "../model/repository.model";
import { ActivatedRoute } from "@angular/router";
import { HighlightTrigger } from "./table.animations";

@Component({
    selector: "paTable",
    templateUrl: "table.component.html",
    animations: [HighlightTrigger]
})
export class TableComponent {
    category: string = null;

    constructor(private model: Model, activeRoute: ActivatedRoute) {
        activeRoute.params.subscribe(params => {
            this.category = params["category"] || null;
        })
    }
```

```
    getProduct(key: number): Product {
        return this.model.getProduct(key);
    }

    getProducts(): Product[] {
        return this.model.getProducts()
            .filter(p => this.category == null || p.category == this.category);
    }

    get categories(): string[] {
        return this.model.getProducts()
            .map(p => p.category)
            .filter((category, index, array) => array.indexOf(category) == index);
    }

    deleteProduct(key: number) {
        this.model.deleteProduct(key);
    }

    highlightCategory: string = "";

    getRowState(category: string): string {
        return this.highlightCategory == "" ? "" :
            this.highlightCategory == category ? "selected" : "notselected";
    }
}
```

The animations property is set to an array of triggers. You can define animations inline, but they can quickly become complex and make the entire component hard to read, which is why I used a separate file and exported a constant value from it, which I then assign to the animations property.

The other changes are to provide a mapping between the category selected by the user and the animation state that will be assigned to elements. The value of the highlightCategory property will be set using a select element and is used in the getRowState method to tell Angular which of the animation states defined in Listing 28-7 should be assigned based on a product category. If a product is in the selected category, then the method returns selected; otherwise, it returns notselected. If the user has not selected a category, then the empty string is returned.

The final step is to apply the animation to the component's template, telling Angular which elements are going to be animated, as shown in Listing 28-7. This listing also adds a select element that sets the value of the component's highlightCategory property using the ngModel binding.

Listing 28-7. Applying an Animation in the table.component.html File in the src/app/core Folder

```
<div class="form-group bg-info text-white p-2">
    <label>Category</label>
    <select [(ngModel)]="highlightCategory" class="form-control">
        <option value="">None</option>
        <option *ngFor="let category of categories">
            {{category}}
        </option>
    </select>
</div>
```

```
<table class="table table-sm table-bordered table-striped">
    <tr>
        <th>ID</th><th>Name</th><th>Category</th><th>Price</th><th></th>
    </tr>
    <tr *ngFor="let item of getProducts()"
            [@rowHighlight]="getRowState(item.category)">
        <td style="vertical-align:middle">{{item.id}}</td>
        <td style="vertical-align:middle">{{item.name}}</td>
        <td style="vertical-align:middle">{{item.category}}</td>
        <td style="vertical-align:middle">
            {{item.price | currency:"USD" }}
        </td>
        <td class="text-center">
            <button class="btn btn-danger btn-sm"
                    (click)="deleteProduct(item.id)">
                Delete
            </button>
            <button class="btn btn-warning btn-sm"
                    [routerLink]="['/form', 'edit', item.id]">
                Edit
            </button>
        </td>
    </tr>
</table>
<div class="m-2">
    <button class="btn btn-primary" routerLink="/form/create">
        Create New Product
    </button>
</div>
```

Animations are applied to templates using special data bindings, which associate an animation trigger with an HTML element. The binding's target tells Angular which animation trigger to apply, and the binding's expression tells Angular how to work out which state an element should be assigned to, like this:

```
...
<tr *ngFor="let item of getProducts()" [@rowHighlight]="getRowState(item.category)">
...
```

The target of the binding is the name of the animation trigger, prefixed with the @ character, which denotes an animation binding. This binding tells Angular that it should apply the rowHighlight trigger to the tr element. The expression tells Angular that it should invoke the component's getRowState method to work out which state the element should be assigned to, using the item.category value as an argument. Figure 28-2 illustrates the anatomy of an animation data binding for quick reference.

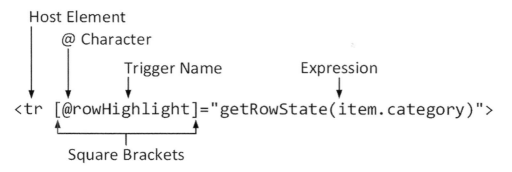

```
            Host Element
                 @ Character
                        Trigger Name              Expression
                            ↓                         ↓
<tr [@rowHighlight]="getRowState(item.category)">

            Square Brackets
```

Figure 28-2. *The anatomy of an animation data binding*

Testing the Animation Effect

The changes in the previous section add a select element above the product table. To see the effect of the animation, select Soccer from the list, and Angular will use the trigger to figure out which of the animation states each element should be applied to. Table rows for products in the Soccer category will be assigned to the selected state, while the other rows will be assigned to the notselected state, creating the effect shown in Figure 28-3.

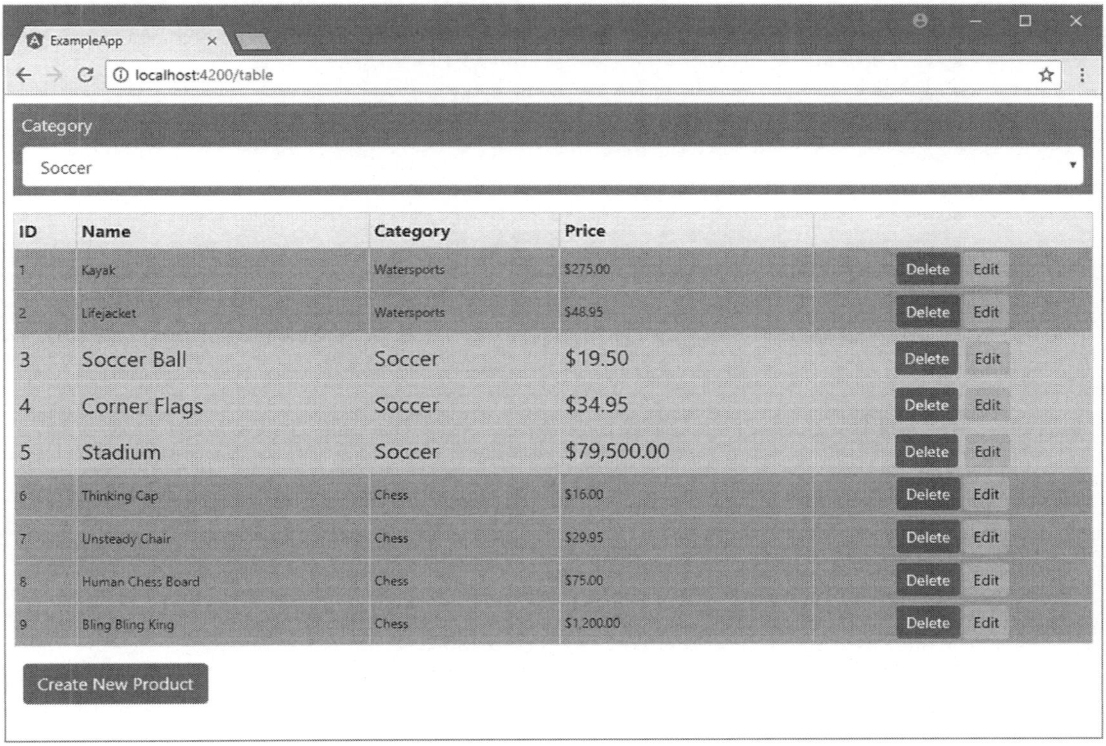

Figure 28-3. *Selecting a product category*

The new styles are applied suddenly. To see a smoother transition, select the Chess category from the list, and you will see a gradual animation as the Chess rows are assigned to the selected state and the other rows are assigned to the notselected state. This happens because the animation trigger contains transitions between these states that tell Angular to animate the change in CSS styles, as illustrated in Figure 28-4. There is no transition for the earlier change, so Angular defaults to applying the new styles immediately.

■ **Tip** It is impossible to capture the effect of animations in a series of screenshots, and the best I can do is present some of the intermediate states. This is a feature that requires firsthand experimentation to understand. I encourage you to download the project for this chapter from GitHub and create your own animations.

Figure 28-4. *A gradual transition between animation states*

To understand the Angular animation system, you need to understand the relationship between the different building blocks used to define and apply an animation, which can be described like this:

1. Evaluating the data binding expression tells Angular which animation state the host element is assigned to.

2. The data binding target tells Angular which animation target defines CSS styles for the element's state.

3. The state tells Angular which CSS styles should be applied to the element.

4. The transition tells Angular how it should apply CSS styles when evaluating the data binding expression results in a change to the element's state.

Keep these four points in mind as you read through the rest of the chapter, and you will find the animation system easier to understand.

Understanding the Built-in Animation States

Animation states are used to define the end result of an animation, grouping together the styles that should be applied to an element with a name that can be selected by an animation trigger. There are two built-in states that Angular provides that make it easier to manage the appearance of elements, as described in Table 28-5.

Table 28-5. *The Built-in Animation States*

State	Description
*	This is a fallback state that will be applied if the element isn't in any of the other states defined by the animation trigger.
void	Elements are in the void state when they are not part of the template. When the expression for an ngIf directive evaluates as false, for example, the host element is in the void state. This state is used to animate the addition and removal of elements, as described in the next section.

An asterisk (the * character) is used to denote a special state that Angular should apply to elements that are not in any of the other states defined by an animation trigger. Listing 28-8 adds the fallback state to the animations in the example application.

Listing 28-8. Using the Fallback State in the table.animations.ts File in the src/app/core Folder

```
import { trigger, style, state, transition, animate } from "@angular/animations";

export const HighlightTrigger = trigger("rowHighlight", [
    state("selected", style({
        backgroundColor: "lightgreen",
        fontSize: "20px"
    })),
    state("notselected", style({
        backgroundColor: "lightsalmon",
        fontSize: "12px"
    })),
    state("*", style({
        border: "solid black 2px"
    })),
    transition("selected => notselected", animate("200ms")),
    transition("notselected => selected", animate("400ms"))
]);
```

In the example application, elements are assigned only to the selected or notselected state once the user has picked a value with the select element. The fallback state defines a style group that will be applied to elements until they are entered into one of the other states, as shown in Figure 28-5.

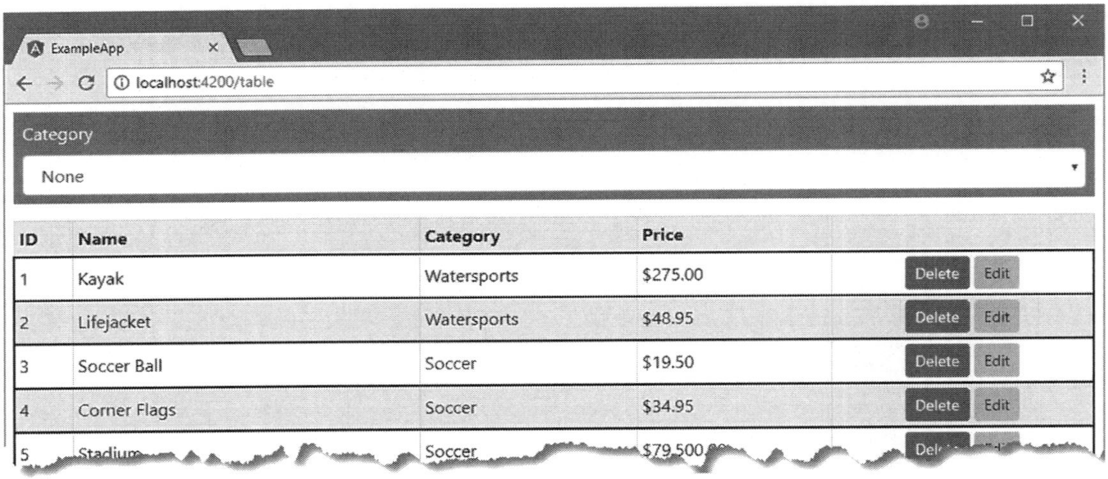

Figure 28-5. *Using the fallback state*

Understanding Element Transitions

The transitions are the real power of the animation system; they tell Angular how it should manage the change from one state to another. In the sections that follow, I describe different ways in which transitions can be created and used.

Creating Transitions for the Built-in States

The built-in states described in Table 28-5 can be used in transitions. The fallback state can be used to simplify the animation configuration by representing any state, as shown in Listing 28-9.

Listing 28-9. Using the Fallback State in the table.animations.ts File in the src/app/core Folder

```
import { trigger, style, state, transition, animate } from "@angular/animations";

export const HighlightTrigger = trigger("rowHighlight", [
    state("selected", style({
        backgroundColor: "lightgreen",
        fontSize: "20px"
    })),
    state("notselected", style({
        backgroundColor: "lightsalmon",
        fontSize: "12px"
    })),
    state("*", style({
        border: "solid black 2px"
    })),
    transition("* => notselected", animate("200ms")),
    transition("* => selected", animate("400ms"))
]);
```

The transitions in the listing tell Angular how to deal with the change from any state into the notselected and selected states.

Animating Element Addition and Removal

The void state is used to define transitions for when an element is added to or removed from the template, as shown in Listing 28-10.

Listing 28-10. Using the Void State in the table.animations.ts File in the src/app/core Folder

```
import { trigger, style, state, transition, animate } from "@angular/animations";

export const HighlightTrigger = trigger("rowHighlight", [
    state("selected", style({
        backgroundColor: "lightgreen",
        fontSize: "20px"
    })),
    state("notselected", style({
        backgroundColor: "lightsalmon",
        fontSize: "12px"
    })),
    state("void", style({
        opacity: 0
    })),
    transition("* => notselected", animate("200ms")),
    transition("* => selected", animate("400ms")),
    transition("void => *", animate("500ms"))
]);
```

This listing includes a definition for the void state that sets the opacity property to zero, which makes the element transparent and, as a consequence, invisible. There is also a transition that tells Angular to animate the change from the void state to any other state. The effect is that the rows in the table fade into view as the browser gradually increases the opacity value until the fill opacity is reached, as shown in Figure 28-6.

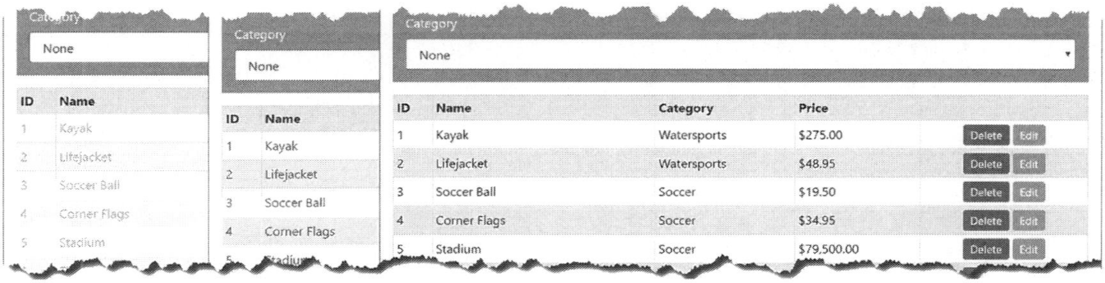

Figure 28-6. *Animating element addition*

Controlling Transition Animations

All the examples so far in this chapter have used to animate function in its simplest form, which is to specify how long a transition between two states should take, like this:

```
...
transition("void => *", animate("500ms"))
...
```

The string argument passes to the animate method can be used to exercise finer-grain control over the way that transitions are animated by providing an initial delay and specifying how intermediate values for the style properties are calculated.

EXPRESSING ANIMATION DURATIONS

Durations for animations are expressed using CSS time values, which are string values containing one or more numbers followed by either s for seconds or ms for milliseconds. This value, for example, specifies a duration of 500 milliseconds:

```
...
transition("void => *", animate("500ms"))
...
```

Durations are expressed flexibly, and the same value could be expressed as a fraction of a second, like this:

```
...
transition("void => *", animate("0.5s"))
...
```

My advice is to stick to one set of units throughout a project to avoid confusion, although it doesn't matter which one you use.

Specifying a Timing Function

The timing function is responsible for calculating the intermediate values for CSS properties during the transition. The timing functions, which are defined as part of the Web Animations specification, are described in Table 28-6.

Table 28-6. *The Animation Timing Functions*

Name	Description
linear	This function changes the value in equal amounts. This is the default.
ease-in	This function starts with small changes that increase over time, resulting in an animation that starts slowly and speeds up.
ease-out	This function starts with large changes that decrease over time, resulting in an animation that starts quickly and then slows down.
ease-in-out	This function starts with large changes that become smaller until the midway point, after which they become larger again. The result is an animation that starts quickly, slows down in the middle, and then speeds up again at the end.
cubic-bezier	This function is used to create intermediate values using a Bezier curve. See http://w3c.github.io/web-animations/#time-transformations for details.

Listing 28-11 applies a timing function to one of the transitions in the example application. The timing function is specified after the duration in the argument to the animate function.

Listing 28-11. Applying a Timing Function in the table.animations.ts File in the src/app/core Folder

```
import { trigger, style, state, transition, animate } from "@angular/animations";

export const HighlightTrigger = trigger("rowHighlight", [
    state("selected", style({
        backgroundColor: "lightgreen",
        fontSize: "20px"
    })),
    state("notselected", style({
        backgroundColor: "lightsalmon",
        fontSize: "12px"
    })),
    state("void", style({
        opacity: 0
    })),
    transition("* => notselected", animate("200ms")),
    transition("* => selected", animate("400ms ease-in")),
    transition("void => *", animate("500ms"))
]);
```

Specifying an Initial Delay

An initial delay can be provided to the animate method, which can be used to stagger animations when there are multiple transitions being performed simultaneously. The delay is specified as the second value in the argument passed to the animate function, as shown in Listing 28-12.

Listing 28-12. Adding an Initial Delay in the table.animations.ts File in the src/app/core Folder

```
import { trigger, style, state, transition, animate } from "@angular/animations";

export const HighlightTrigger = trigger("rowHighlight", [
    state("selected", style({
        backgroundColor: "lightgreen",
        fontSize: "20px"
    })),
    state("notselected", style({
        backgroundColor: "lightsalmon",
        fontSize: "12px"
    })),
    state("void", style({
        opacity: 0
    })),
    transition("* => notselected", animate("200ms")),
    transition("* => selected", animate("400ms 200ms ease-in")),
    transition("void => *", animate("500ms"))
]);
```

The 200-millisecond delay in this example corresponds to the duration of the animation used when an element transitions to the notselected state. The effect is that changing the selected category will show elements returning to the notselected state before the selected elements are changed.

Using Additional Styles During Transition

The animate function can accept a style group as its second argument, as shown in Listing 28-13. These styles are applied to the host element gradually, over the duration of the animation.

Listing 28-13. Defining Transition Styles in the table.animations.ts File in the src/app/core Folder

```
import { trigger, style, state, transition, animate } from "@angular/animations";

export const HighlightTrigger = trigger("rowHighlight", [
    state("selected", style({
        backgroundColor: "lightgreen",
        fontSize: "20px"
    })),
    state("notselected", style({
        backgroundColor: "lightsalmon",
        fontSize: "12px"
    })),
    state("void", style({
        opacity: 0
    })),
    transition("* => notselected", animate("200ms")),
    transition("* => selected",
```

```
        animate("400ms 200ms ease-in",
            style({
                backgroundColor: "lightblue",
                fontSize: "25px"
            }))
    ),
    transition("void => *", animate("500ms"))
]);
```

The effect of this change is that when an element is transitioning into the selected state, its appearance will be animated so that the background color will be lightblue and its font size will be 25 pixels. At the end of the animation, the styles defined by the selected state will be applied all at once, creating a snap effect.

The sudden change in appearance at the end of the animation can be jarring. An alternative approach is to change the second argument to the transition function to an array of animations. This defines multiple animations that will be applied to the element in sequence, and as long as it doesn't define a style group, the final animation will be used to transition to the styles defined by the state. Listing 28-14 uses this feature to add two additional animations to the transition, the last of which will apply the styles defined by the selected state.

Listing 28-14. Using Multiple Animations in the table.animations.ts File in the src/app/core Folder

```
import { trigger, style, state, transition, animate } from "@angular/animations";

export const HighlightTrigger = trigger("rowHighlight", [
    state("selected", style({
        backgroundColor: "lightgreen",
        fontSize: "20px"
    })),
    state("notselected", style({
        backgroundColor: "lightsalmon",
        fontSize: "12px"
    })),
    state("void", style({
        opacity: 0
    })),
    transition("* => notselected", animate("200ms")),
    transition("* => selected",
        [animate("400ms 200ms ease-in",
            style({
                backgroundColor: "lightblue",
                fontSize: "25px"
            })),
            animate("250ms", style({
                backgroundColor: "lightcoral",
                fontSize: "30px"
            })),
            animate("200ms")]
    ),
    transition("void => *", animate("500ms"))
]);
```

There are three animations in this transition, and the last one will apply the styles defined by the selected state. Table 28-7 describes the sequence of animations.

Table 28-7. *The Sequence of Animations in the Transition to the selected State*

Duration	Style Properties and Values
400 milliseconds	`backgroundColor: lightblue; fontSize: 25px`
250 milliseconds	`backgroundColor: lightcoral; fontSize: 30px`
200 milliseconds	`backgroundColor: lightgreen; fontSize: 20px`

Pick a category using the select element to see the sequence of animations. Figure 28-7 shows one frame from each animation.

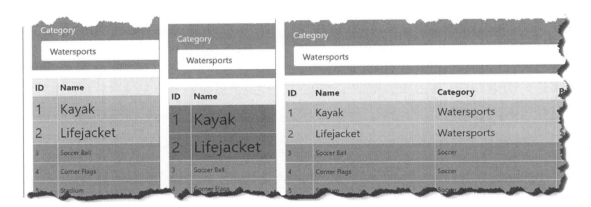

Figure 28-7. *Using multiple animations in a transition*

Performing Parallel Animations

Angular is able to perform animations at the same time, which means you can have different CSS properties change over different time periods. Parallel animations are passed to the group function, as shown in Listing 28-15.

Listing 28-15. Performing Parallel Animations in the table.animations.ts File in the src/app/core Folder

```
import { trigger, style, state, transition, animate, group }
    from "@angular/animations";

export const HighlightTrigger = trigger("rowHighlight", [
    state("selected", style({
        backgroundColor: "lightgreen",
        fontSize: "20px"
    })),
```

```
    state("notselected", style({
        backgroundColor: "lightsalmon",
        fontSize: "12px"
    })),
    state("void", style({
        opacity: 0
    })),
    transition("* => notselected", animate("200ms")),
    transition("* => selected",
        [animate("400ms 200ms ease-in",
            style({
                backgroundColor: "lightblue",
                fontSize: "25px"
            })),
        group([
            animate("250ms", style({
                backgroundColor: "lightcoral",
            })),
            animate("450ms", style({
                fontSize: "30px"
            })),
        ]),
        animate("200ms")]
    ),
    transition("void => *", animate("500ms"))
]);
```

The listing replaces one of the animations in sequence with a pair of parallel animations. The animations for the backgroundColor and fontSize properties will be started at the same time but last for differing durations. When both of the animations in the group have completed, Angular will move on to the final animation, which will target the styles defined in the state.

Understanding Animation Style Groups

The outcome of an Angular animation is that an element is put into a new state and styled using the properties and values in the associated style group. In this section, I explain some different ways in which style groups can be used.

■ **Tip** Not all CSS properties can be animated, and of those that can be animated, some are handled better by the browser than others. As a rule of thumb, the best results are achieved with properties whose values can be easily interpolated, which allows the browser to provide a smooth transition between element states. This means you will usually get good results using properties whose values are colors or numerical values, such as background, text and font colors, opacity, element sizes, and borders. See `https://www.w3.org/TR/css3-transitions/#animatable-properties` for a complete list of properties that can be used with the animation system.

Defining Common Styles in Reusable Groups

As you create more complex animations and apply them throughout your application, you will inevitably find that you need to apply some common CSS property values in multiple places. The `style` function can accept an array of objects, all of which are combined to create the overall set of styles in the group. This means you can reduce duplication by defining objects that contain common styles and use them in multiple style groups, as shown in Listing 28-16. (To keep the example simple, I have also removed the sequence of styles defined in the previous section.)

Listing 28-16. Defining Common Styles in the table.animations.ts File in the src/app/core Folder

```
import { trigger, style, state, transition, animate, group } from "@angular/animations";

const commonStyles = {
    border: "black solid 4px",
    color: "white"
};

export const HighlightTrigger = trigger("rowHighlight", [
    state("selected", style([commonStyles, {
        backgroundColor: "lightgreen",
        fontSize: "20px"
    }])),
    state("notselected", style([commonStyles, {
        backgroundColor: "lightsalmon",
        fontSize: "12px",
        color: "black"
    }])),
    state("void", style({
        opacity: 0
    })),
    transition("* => notselected", animate("200ms")),
    transition("* => selected", animate("400ms 200ms ease-in")),
    transition("void => *", animate("500ms"))
]);
```

The `commonStyles` object defines values for the `border` and `color` properties and is passed to the `style` function in an array along with the regular style objects. Angular processes the style objects in order, which means you can override a style value by redefining it in a later object. As an example, the second style object for the `notselected` state overrides the common value for the `color` property with a custom value. The result is that both the styles for both animation states incorporate the common value for the `border` property, and the styles for the `selected` state also use the common value for the `color` property, as shown in Figure 28-8.

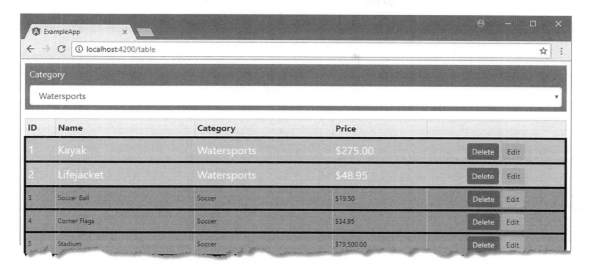

Figure 28-8. *Defining common properties*

Using Element Transformations

All the examples so far in this chapter have animated properties that have affected an aspect of an element's appearance, such as background color, font size, or opacity. Animations can also be used to apply CSS element transformation effects, which are used to move, resize, rotate, or skew an element. These effects are applied by defining a transform property in a style group, as shown in Listing 28-17.

Listing 28-17. Using an Element Transformation in the table.animations.ts File in the src/app/core Folder

```
import { trigger, style, state, transition, animate, group }
    from "@angular/animations";

const commonStyles = {
    border: "black solid 4px",
    color: "white"
};

export const HighlightTrigger = trigger("rowHighlight", [
    state("selected", style([commonStyles, {
        backgroundColor: "lightgreen",
        fontSize: "20px"
    }])),
    state("notselected", style([commonStyles, {
        backgroundColor: "lightsalmon",
        fontSize: "12px",
        color: "black"
    }])),
```

```
state("void", style({
    transform: "translateX(-50%)"
})),
transition("* => notselected", animate("200ms")),
transition("* => selected", animate("400ms 200ms ease-in")),
transition("void => *",  animate("500ms"))
]);
```

The value of the transform property is translateX(50%), which tells Angular to move the element 50 percent of its length along the x-axis. The transform property has been applied to the void state, which means that it will be used on elements as they are being added to the template. The animation contains a transition from the void state to any other state and tells Angular to animate the changes over 500 milliseconds. The result is that new elements will be shifted to the left initially and then slid back into their default position over a period of half a second, as illustrated in Figure 28-9.

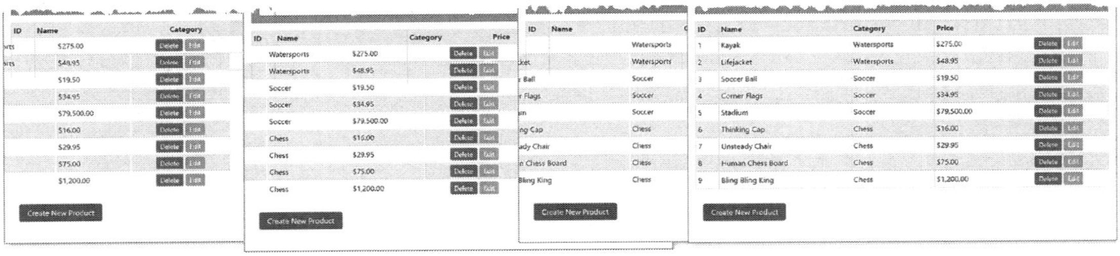

Figure 28-9. *Transforming an element*

Table 28-8 describes the set of transformations that can be applied to elements.

■ **Tip**   Multiple transformations can be applied in a single transform property by separating them with spaces, like this: transform: "scale(1.1, 1.1) rotate(10deg)".

Table 28-8. *The CSS Transformation Functions*

Function	Description
translateX(offset)	This function moves the element along the x-axis. The amount of movement can be specified as a percentage or as a length (expressed in pixels or one of the other CSS length units). Positive values translate the element to the right, negative values to the left.
translateY(offset)	This function moves the element along the y-axis.
translate(xOffset, yOffset)	This function moves the element along both axes.
scaleX(amount)	The function scales the element along the x-axis. The scaling size is expressed as a fraction of the element's regular size, such that 0.5 reduces the element to 50 percent of the original width and 2.0 will double the width.
scaleY(amount)	This function scales the element along the y-axis.
scale(xAmount, yAmount)	This function scales the element along both axes.
rotate(angle)	This function rotates the element clockwise. The amount of rotation is expressed as an angle, such as 90deg or 3.14rad.
skewX(angle)	This function skews the element along the x-axis by a specified angle, expressed in the same way as for the rotate function.
skewY(angle)	This function skews the element along the y-axis by a specified angle, expressed in the same way as for the rotate function.
skew(xAngle, yAngle)	This function skews the element along both axes.

Applying CSS Framework Styles

If you are using a CSS framework like Bootstrap, you may want to apply classes to elements, rather than having to define groups of properties. There is no built-in support for working directly with CSS classes, but the Document Object Model (DOM) and the CSS Object Model (CSSOM) provides API access to inspect the CSS stylesheets that have been loaded and to see whether they apply to an HTML element. To get the set of styles defined by classes, I created a file called animationUtils.ts to the src/app/core folder and added the code shown in Listing 28-18.

■ **Caution** This technique can require substantial processing in an application that uses a lot of complex stylesheets, and you may need to adjust the code to work with different browsers and different CSS frameworks.

Listing 28-18. The Contents of the animationUtils.ts File in the src/app/core Folder

```
export function getStylesFromClasses(names: string | string[],
        elementType: string = "div") : { [key: string]: string | number } {

    let elem = document.createElement(elementType);
    (typeof names == "string" ? [names] : names).forEach(c => elem.classList.add(c));

    let result = {};
```

```
    for (let i = 0; i < document.styleSheets.length; i++) {
        let sheet = document.styleSheets[i] as CSSStyleSheet;
        let rules = sheet.rules || sheet.cssRules;
        for (let j = 0; j < rules.length; j++) {
            if (rules[j].type == CSSRule.STYLE_RULE) {
                let styleRule = rules[j] as CSSStyleRule;
                if (elem.matches(styleRule.selectorText)) {
                    for (let k = 0; k < styleRule.style.length; k++) {
                        result[styleRule.style[k]] =
                            styleRule.style[styleRule.style[k]];
                    }
                }
            }
        }
    }
    return result;
}
```

The getStylesFromClass method accepts a single class name or an array of class names and the element type to which they should be applied, which defaults to a div element. An element is created and assigned to the classes and then inspected to see which of the CSS rules defined in the CSS stylesheets apply to it. The style properties for each matching style are added to an object that can be used to create Angular animation style groups, as shown in Listing 28-19.

Listing 28-19. Using Bootstrap Classes in the table.animations.ts File in the src/app/core Folder

```
import { trigger, style, state, transition, animate, group }
    from "@angular/animations";
import { getStylesFromClasses } from "./animationUtils";

export const HighlightTrigger = trigger("rowHighlight", [
    state("selected", style(getStylesFromClasses(["bg-success", "h2"]))),
    state("notselected", style(getStylesFromClasses("bg-info"))),
    state("void", style({
        transform: "translateX(-50%)"
    })),
    transition("* => notselected", animate("200ms")),
    transition("* => selected", animate("400ms 200ms ease-in")),
    transition("void => *", animate("500ms"))
]);
```

The selected state uses the styles defined in the Bootstrap bg-success and h2 classes, and the notselected state uses the styles defined by the Bootstrap bg-info class, producing the results shown in Figure 28-10.

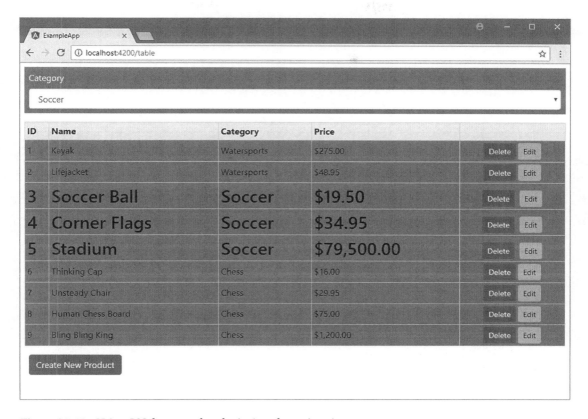

Figure 28-10. *Using CSS framework styles in Angular animations*

Summary

I described the Angular animation system in this chapter and explained how it uses data bindings to animate changes in the application's state. In the next chapter, I describe the features that Angular provides to support unit testing.

CHAPTER 29

■ ■ ■

Angular Unit Testing

In this chapter, I describe the tools that Angular provides for unit testing components and directives. Some Angular building blocks, such as pipes and services, can be readily tested in isolation using the basic testing tools that I set up at the start of the chapter. Components (and, to a lesser extent, directives) have complex interactions with their host elements and with their template content and require special features. Table 29-1 puts Angular unit testing in context.

Table 29-1. *Putting Angular Unit Testing Context*

Question	Answer
What is it?	Angular components and directives require special support for testing so that their interactions with other parts of the application infrastructure can be isolated and inspected.
Why is it useful?	Isolated unit tests are able to assess the basic logic provided by the class that implements a component or directive but do not capture the interactions with host elements, services, templates, and other important Angular features.
How is it used?	Angular provides a test bed that allows a realistic application environment to be created and then used to perform unit tests.
Are there any pitfalls or limitations?	Like much of Angular, the unit testing tools are complex. It can take some time and effort to get to the point where unit tests are easily written and run and you are sure that you have isolated the correct part of the application for testing.
Are there any alternatives?	As noted, you don't have to unit test your projects. But if you do want to unit testing, then you will need to use the Angular features described in this chapter.

DECIDING WHETHER TO UNIT TEST

Unit testing is a contentious topic. This chapter assumes you do want to do unit testing and shows you how to set up the tools and apply them to Angular components and directives. It isn't an introduction to unit testing, and I make no effort to persuade skeptical readers that unit testing is worthwhile. If would like an introduction to unit testing, then there is a good article here: https://en.wikipedia.org/wiki/Unit_testing.

I like unit testing, and I use it in my own projects—but not all of them and not as consistently as you might expect. I tend to focus on writing unit tests for features and functions that I know will be hard to write and that are likely to be the source of bugs in deployment. In these situations, unit testing helps

---

structure my thoughts about how to best implement what I need. I find that just thinking about what I need to test helps produce ideas about potential problems, and that's before I start dealing with actual bugs and defects.

That said, unit testing is a tool and not a religion, and only you know how much testing you require. If you don't find unit testing useful or if you have a different methodology that suits you better, then don't feel you need to unit test just because it is fashionable. (However, if you don't have a better methodology and you are not testing at all, then you are probably letting users find your bugs, which is rarely ideal.)

Table 29-2 summarizes the chapter.

Table 29-2. *Chapter Summary*

Problem	Solution	Listing
Perform a basic test on a component	Initialize a test module and create an instance of the component. If the component has an external template, an additional compilation step must be performed.	1–9, 11–13
Test a component's data bindings	Use the DebugElement class to query the component's template.	10
Test a component's response to events	Trigger the events using the debug element.	14–16
Test a component's output properties	Subscribe to the EventEmitter created by the component.	17, 18
Test a component's input properties	Create a test component whose template applies the component under test.	19, 20
Perform a test that relies on an asynchronous operation	Use the whenStable method to defer the test until the effect of the operation has been processed.	21, 22
Test a directive	Create a test component whose template applies the directive under test.	23, 24

Preparing the Example Project

I continue to use the exampleApp project from earlier chapters. I need a simple target to focus on for unit testing, so Listing 29-1 changes the routing configuration so that the ondemand feature module is loaded by default.

Listing 29-1. Changing the Routing Configuration in the app.routing.ts File in the src/app Folder

```
import { Routes, RouterModule } from "@angular/router";
import { TableComponent } from "./core/table.component";
import { FormComponent } from "./core/form.component";
import { NotFoundComponent } from "./core/notFound.component";
import { ProductCountComponent } from "./core/productCount.component";
import { CategoryCountComponent } from "./core/categoryCount.component";
```

```
import { ModelResolver } from "./model/model.resolver";
import { TermsGuard } from "./terms.guard";
import { UnsavedGuard } from "./core/unsaved.guard";
import { LoadGuard } from "./load.guard";

const routes: Routes = [
    {
        path: "ondemand",
        loadChildren: "./ondemand/ondemand.module#OndemandModule"
    },
    { path: "", redirectTo: "/ondemand", pathMatch: "full" }
]

export const routing = RouterModule.forRoot(routes);
```

This module contains some simple components that I will use to demonstrate different unit testing features. To keep the content shown by the application simple, Listing 29-2 tidies up the template displayed by the top-level component in the feature module.

Listing 29-2. Simplifying the ondemand.component.html File in the src/app/ondemand Folder

```
<div class="container-fluid">
    <div class="row">
        <div class="col-12 p-2">
            <router-outlet></router-outlet>
        </div>
    </div>
    <div class="row">
        <div class="col-6 p-2">
            <router-outlet name="left"></router-outlet>
        </div>
        <div class="col-6 p-2">
            <router-outlet name="right"></router-outlet>
        </div>
    </div>
</div>
<button class="btn btn-secondary m-2" routerLink="/ondemand">Normal</button>
<button class="btn btn-secondary m-2" routerLink="/ondemand/swap">Swap</button>
```

Open a new command prompt, navigate to the exampleApp folder, and run the following command to start the server that provides the RESTful web server:

```
npm run json
```

The RESTful web service isn't used directly in this chapter, but running it prevents errors. Open a separate command prompt, navigate to the exampleApp folder, and run the following command to start the Angular development tools:

```
ng serve
```

Open a new browser window and navigate to `http://localhost:4200` to see the content shown in Figure 29-1.

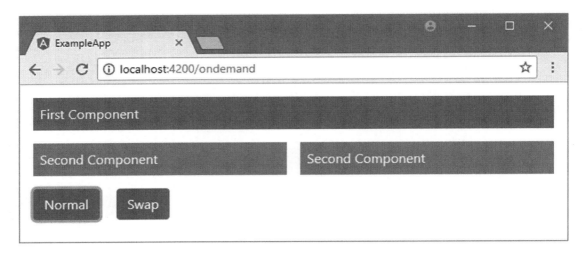

Figure 29-1. *Running the example application*

Running a Simple Unit Test

When a new project is created using the ng new command, all of the packages and tools required for unit testing are installed, based on the Jasmine test framework. The project also includes a sample unit test file, and in Listing 29-3 I have replaced the content of this file with a simple test that confirms that the unit tests are working.

Listing 29-3. Replacing the Contents of the app.component.spec.ts File in the src/app Folder

```
describe("Jasmine Test Environment", () => {
    it("is working", () => expect(true).toBe(true));
});
```

I explain the basics of working with the Jasmine API shortly, and you can ignore the syntax for the moment. Using a new command prompt, navigate to the exampleApp folder, and run the following command:

```
ng test
```

This command starts the Karma test runner, which opens a new browser tab with the content shown in Figure 29-2.

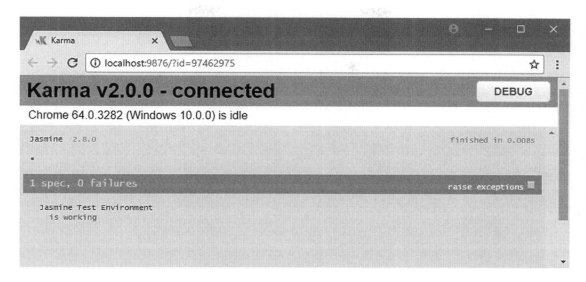

Figure 29-2. *Starting the Karma test runner*

The browser window is used to run the tests, but the important information is written out to the command prompt used to start the test tools, where you will see a message like this:

```
Chrome (Windows 10.0.0): Executed 1 of 1 SUCCESS (0.012 secs / 0.004 secs)
```

This shows that the one unit test in the project has been located and has been executed successfully. Whenever you make a change that updates one of the JavaScript files in the project, the unit tests will be located and executed, and any problems will be written to the command prompt. To show what an error looks like, Listing 29-4 changes the unit test so that it will fail.

Listing 29-4. Making a Unit Test Fail in the app.component.spec.ts File in the src/app Folder

```
describe("Jasmine Test Environment", () => {
    it("is working", () => expect(true).toBe(false));
});
```

This test will fail and will result in the following output, which indicates the test that has failed and what went wrong:

```
Chrome (Windows 10 0.0.0) Jasmine Test Environment is working FAILED
[1]     Expected true to be false.
...
Chrome (Windows 10.0.0): Executed 1 of 1 (1 FAILED) ERROR
```

Working with Jasmine

The API that Jasmine provides chains together JavaScript methods to define unit tests. You can find the full documentation for Jasmine at http://jasmine.github.io, but Table 29-3 describes the most useful functions for Angular testing.

Table 29-3. *Useful Jasmine Methods*

Name	Description
describe(description, function)	This method is used to group a set of related tests.
beforeEach(function)	This method is used to specify a task that is performed before each unit test.
afterEach(function)	This method is used to specify a test that is performed after each unit test.
it(description, function)	This method is used to perform the test action.
expect(value)	This method is used to identify the result of the test.
toBe(value)	This method specifies the expected value of the test.

You can see how the methods in Table 29-3 were used to create the unit test in Listing 29-4.

```
...
describe("Jasmine Test Environment", () => {
    it("is working", () => expect(true).toBe(false));
});
...
```

You can also see why the test has failed since the expect and toBe methods have been used to check that true and false are equal. Since this cannot be the case, the test fails.

The toBe method isn't the only way to evaluate the result of a unit test. Table 29-4 shows other evaluation methods provided by Angular.

Table 29-4. *Useful Jasmine Evaluation Methods*

Name	Description
toBe(value)	This method asserts that a result is the same as the specified value (but need not be the same object).
toEqual(object)	This method asserts that a result is the same object as the specified value.
toMatch(regexp)	This method asserts that a result matches the specified regular expression.
toBeDefined()	This method asserts that the result has been defined.
toBeUndefined()	This method asserts that the result has not been defined.
toBeNull()	This method asserts that the result is null.
toBeTruthy()	This method asserts that the result is truthy, as described in Chapter 12.
toBeFalsy()	This method asserts that the result is falsy, as described in Chapter 12.
toContain(substring)	This method asserts that the result contains the specified substring.
toBeLessThan(value)	This method asserts that the result is less than the specified value.
toBeGreaterThan(value)	This method asserts that the result is more than the specified value.

Listing 29-5 shows how these evaluation methods can be used in tests, replacing the failing test from the previous section.

Listing 29-5. Replacing the Unit Test in the app.component.spec.ts File in the src/app Folder

```
describe("Jasmine Test Environment", () => {
    it("test numeric value", () => expect(12).toBeGreaterThan(10));
    it("test string value", () => expect("London").toMatch("^Lon"));
});
```

When you save the changes to the file, the tests will be executed, and the results will be shown in the command prompt.

Testing an Angular Component

The building blocks of an Angular application can't be tested in isolation because they depend on the underlying features provided by Angular and by the other parts of the project, including the services, directives, templates, and modules it contains. As a consequence, testing a building block such as a component means using testing utilities that are provided by Angular to re-create enough of the application to let the component function so that tests can be performed against it. In this section, I walk through the process of performing a unit test on the FirstComponent class in the OnDemand feature module, which was added to the project in Chapter 27. As a reminder, here is the definition of the component:

```
import { Component } from "@angular/core";

@Component({
    selector: "first",
    template: `<div class="bg-primary text-white p-2">First Component</div>`
})
export class FirstComponent { }
```

This component is so simple that it doesn't have functionality of its own to test, but it is enough to demonstrate how the test process is applied.

Working with the TestBed Class

At the heart of Angular unit testing is a class called TestBed, which is responsible for simulating the Angular application environment so that tests can be performed. Table 29-5 describes the most useful methods provided by the TestBed method, all of which are static, as described in Chapter 6.

Table 29-5. *Useful TestBed Methods*

Name	Description
configureTestingModule	This method is used to configure the Angular testing module.
createComponent	This method is used to create an instance of the component.
compileComponents	This method is used to compile components, as described in the "Testing a Component with an External Template" section.

The configureTestingModule method is used to configure the Angular module that is used in testing, using the same properties supported by the @NgModel decorator. Just like in a real application, a component cannot be used in a unit test unless it has been added to the declarations property of the module. This means that the first step in most unit tests is to configure the testing module. To demonstrate, I created the src/tests folder and added to it a file called first.component.spec.ts, which is shown in Listing 29-6.

Listing 29-6. The Contents of the first.component.spec.ts File in the src/tests Folder

```
import { TestBed } from "@angular/core/testing";
import { FirstComponent } from "../app/ondemand/first.component";

describe("FirstComponent", () => {

    beforeEach(() => {
        TestBed.configureTestingModule({
            declarations: [FirstComponent]
        });
    });
});
```

The TestBed class is defined in the @angular/core/testing module, and the configureTestingModule accepts an object whose declarations property tells the test module that the FirstComponent class is going to be used.

■ **Tip** Notice that the TestBed class is used within the beforeEach function. If you try to use the TestBed outside of this function, you will see an error about using Promises.

The next step is to create a new instance of the component so that it can be used in tests. This is done using the createComponent method, as shown in Listing 29-7.

Listing 29-7. Creating a Component in the first.component.spec.ts File in the src/tests Folder

```
import { TestBed, ComponentFixture} from "@angular/core/testing";
import { FirstComponent } from "../app/ondemand/first.component";

describe("FirstComponent", () => {

    let fixture: ComponentFixture<FirstComponent>;
    let component: FirstComponent;
```

```
    beforeEach(() => {
        TestBed.configureTestingModule({
            declarations: [FirstComponent]
        });
        fixture = TestBed.createComponent(FirstComponent);
        component = fixture.componentInstance;
    });

    it("is defined", () => {
        expect(component).toBeDefined()
    });
});
```

The argument to the createComponent method tells the test bed which component type it should instantiate, which is FirstComponent in this case. The result is a ComponentFixture<FirstComponent> object, which provides features for testing a component, using the methods and properties described in Table 29-6.

Table 29-6. *Useful ComponentFixture Methods and Properties*

Name	Description
componentInstance	This property returns the component object.
debugElement	This property returns the test host element for the component.
nativeElement	This property returns the DOM object representing the host element for the component.
detectChanges()	This method causes the test bed to detect state changes and reflect them in the component's template.
whenStable()	This method returns a Promise that is resolved when the effect of an operation has been fully applied. See the "Testing with Asynchronous Operations" section for details.

In the listing, I use the componentInstance property to get the FirstComponent object that has been created by the test bed and perform a simple test to ensure that it has been created by using the expect method to select the component object as the target of the test and the toBeDefined method to perform the test. I demonstrate the other methods and properties in the sections that follow.

Configuring the Test Bed for Dependencies

One of the most important features of Angular applications is dependency injection, which allows components and other building blocks to receive services by declaring dependencies on them using constructor parameters. Listing 29-8 adds a dependency on the data model repository service to the FirstComponent class.

Listing 29-8. Adding a Service Dependency in the first.component.ts File in the src/app/ondemand Folder

```
import { Component } from "@angular/core";
import { Product } from "../model/product.model";
import { Model } from "../model/repository.model";

@Component({
    selector: "first",
    template: `<div class="bg-primary p-a-1">
                There are
                    <span class="strong"> {{getProducts().length}} </span>
                products
                </div>`
})
export class FirstComponent {

    constructor(private repository: Model) {}

    category: string = "Soccer";

    getProducts(): Product[] {
        return this.repository.getProducts()
            .filter(p => p.category == this.category);
    }
}
```

The component uses the repository to provide a filtered collection of Product objects, which are exposed through a method called getProducts and filtered using a category property. The inline template has a corresponding data binding that displays the number of products that the getProducts method returns.

Being able to unit test the component means providing it with a repository service. The Angular test bed will take care of resolving dependencies as long as they are configured through the test module. Effective unit testing generally requires components to be isolated from the rest of the application, which means that mock or fake objects (also known as *test doubles*) are used as substitutes for real services in unit tests. Listing 29-9 configures the test bed so that a fake repository is used to provide the component with its service.

Listing 29-9. Providing a Service in the first.component.spec.ts File in the src/tests Folder

```
import { TestBed, ComponentFixture} from "@angular/core/testing";
import { FirstComponent } from "../app/ondemand/first.component";
import { Product } from "../app/model/product.model";
import { Model } from "../app/model/repository.model";

describe("FirstComponent", () => {

    let fixture: ComponentFixture<FirstComponent>;
    let component: FirstComponent;

    let mockRepository = {
        getProducts: function () {
            return [
```

```
                new Product(1, "test1", "Soccer", 100),
                new Product(2, "test2", "Chess", 100),
                new Product(3, "test3", "Soccer", 100),
            ]
        }
    }

    beforeEach(() => {
        TestBed.configureTestingModule({
            declarations: [FirstComponent],
            providers: [
                { provide: Model, useValue: mockRepository }
            ]
        });
        fixture = TestBed.createComponent(FirstComponent);
        component = fixture.componentInstance;
    });

    it("filters categories", () => {
        component.category = "Chess"
        expect(component.getProducts().length).toBe(1);
        component.category = "Soccer";
        expect(component.getProducts().length).toBe(2);
        component.category = "Running";
        expect(component.getProducts().length).toBe(0);
    });
});
```

The mockRepository variable is assigned an object that provides a getProducts method that returns fixed data that can be used to test for known outcomes. To provide the component with the service, the providers property for the object passed to the TestBed.configureTestingModule method is configured in the same way as a real Angular module, using the value provider to resolve dependencies on the Model class using the mockRepository variable. The test invokes the component's getProducts method and compares the results with the expected outcome, changing the value of the category property to check different filters.

Testing Data Bindings

The previous example showed how a component's properties and methods can be used in a unit test. This is a good start, but many components will also include small fragments of functionality in the data binding expressions contained in their templates, and these should be tested as well. Listing 29-10 checks that the data binding in the component's template correctly displays the number of products in the mock data model.

Listing 29-10. Unit Testing a Data Binding in the first.component.spec.ts File in the src/tests Folder

```
import { TestBed, ComponentFixture} from "@angular/core/testing";
import { FirstComponent } from "../app/ondemand/first.component";
import { Product } from "../app/model/product.model";
import { Model } from "../app/model/repository.model";
import { DebugElement } from "@angular/core";
import { By } from "@angular/platform-browser";
```

```
describe("FirstComponent", () => {

    let fixture: ComponentFixture<FirstComponent>;
    let component: FirstComponent;
    let debugElement: DebugElement;
    let bindingElement: HTMLSpanElement;

    let mockRepository = {
        getProducts: function () {
            return [
                new Product(1, "test1", "Soccer", 100),
                new Product(2, "test2", "Chess", 100),
                new Product(3, "test3", "Soccer", 100),
            ]
        }
    }

    beforeEach(() => {
        TestBed.configureTestingModule({
            declarations: [FirstComponent],
            providers: [
                { provide: Model, useValue: mockRepository }
            ]
        });
        fixture = TestBed.createComponent(FirstComponent);
        component = fixture.componentInstance;
        debugElement = fixture.debugElement;
        bindingElement = debugElement.query(By.css("span")).nativeElement;
    });

    it("filters categories", () => {
        component.category = "Chess"
        fixture.detectChanges();
        expect(component.getProducts().length).toBe(1);
        expect(bindingElement.textContent).toContain("1");

        component.category = "Soccer";
        fixture.detectChanges();
        expect(component.getProducts().length).toBe(2);
        expect(bindingElement.textContent).toContain("2");

        component.category = "Running";
        fixture.detectChanges();
        expect(component.getProducts().length).toBe(0);
        expect(bindingElement.textContent).toContain("0");
    });
});
```

The ComponentFixture.debugElement property returns a DebugElement object that represents the root element from the component's template, and Table 29-7 lists the most useful methods and properties described by the DebugElement class.

Table 29-7. *Useful DebugElement Properties and Methods*

Name	Description
nativeElement	This property returns the object that represents the HTML element in the DOM.
children	This property returns an array of DebugElement objects representing the children of this element.
query(selectorFunction)	The selectorFunction is passed a DebugElement object for each HTML element in the component's template, and this method returns the first DebugElement for which the function returns true.
queryAll(selectorFunction)	Similar to the query method, except the result is all the DebugElement objects for which the function returns true.
triggerEventHandler(name, event)	This method triggers an event. See the "Testing Component Events" section for details.

Locating elements is done through the query and queryAll methods, which accept functions that inspect DebugElement objects and return true if they should be included in the results. The By class, defined in the @angular/platform-browser module, makes it easier to locate elements in the component's template through the static methods described in Table 29-8.

Table 29-8. *The By Methods*

Name	Description
By.all()	This method returns a function that matches any element.
By.css(selector)	This method returns a function that uses a CSS selector to match elements.
By.directive(type)	This method returns a function that matches elements to which the specified directive class has been applied, as demonstrated in the "Testing Input Properties" section.

In the listing, I use the By.css method to locate the first span element in the template and access the DOM object that represents it through the nativeElement property so that I can check the value of the textContent property in the unit tests.

Notice that after each change to the component's category property, I call the ComponentFixture object's detectChanges method, like this:

```
...
component.category = "Soccer";
fixture.detectChanges();
expect(component.getProducts().length).toBe(2);
expect(bindingElement.textContent).toContain("2");
...
```

This method tells the Angular testing environment to process any changes and evaluate the data binding expressions in the template. Without this method call, the change to the value of the category component would not be reflected in the template, and the test would fail.

Testing a Component with an External Template

Angular components are compiled into factory classes, either within the browser or by the Ahead-of-Time compiler that I demonstrated in Chapter 10. As part of this process, Angular processes any external templates and includes them as text in the JavaScript code that is generated similar to an inline template. When unit testing a component with an external template, the compilation step must be performed explicitly. In Listing 29-11, I changed the @Component decorator applied to the FirstComponent class so that it specifies an external template.

Listing 29-11. Specifying a Template in the first.component.ts File in the src/app/ondemand Folder

```
import { Component } from "@angular/core";
import { Product } from "../model/product.model";
import { Model } from "../model/repository.model";

@Component({
    selector: "first",
    templateUrl: "first.component.html"
})
export class FirstComponent {

    constructor(private repository: Model) {}

    category: string = "Soccer";

    getProducts(): Product[] {
        return this.repository.getProducts()
            .filter(p => p.category == this.category);
    }
}
```

To provide the template, I created a file called first.component.html in the exampleApp/app/ondemand folder and added the elements shown in Listing 29-12.

Listing 29-12. The first.component.html File in the exampleApp/app/ondemand Folder

```
<div class="bg-primary text-white p-2">
    There are
        <span class="strong"> {{getProducts().length}} </span>
    products
</div>
```

This is the same content that was previously defined inline. Listing 29-13 updates the unit test for the component to deal with the external template by explicitly compiling the component.

Listing 29-13. Compiling a Component in the first.component.spec.ts File in the src/tests Folder

```typescript
import { TestBed, ComponentFixture, async } from "@angular/core/testing";
import { FirstComponent } from "../app/ondemand/first.component";
import { Product } from "../app/model/product.model";
import { Model } from "../app/model/repository.model";
import { DebugElement } from "@angular/core";
import { By } from "@angular/platform-browser";

describe("FirstComponent", () => {

    let fixture: ComponentFixture<FirstComponent>;
    let component: FirstComponent;
    let debugElement: DebugElement;
    let spanElement: HTMLSpanElement;

    let mockRepository = {
        getProducts: function () {
            return [
                new Product(1, "test1", "Soccer", 100),
                new Product(2, "test2", "Chess", 100),
                new Product(3, "test3", "Soccer", 100),
            ]
        }
    }

    beforeEach(async(() => {
        TestBed.configureTestingModule({
            declarations: [FirstComponent],
            providers: [
                { provide: Model, useValue: mockRepository }
            ]
        });
        TestBed.compileComponents().then(() => {
            fixture = TestBed.createComponent(FirstComponent);
            component = fixture.componentInstance;
            debugElement = fixture.debugElement;
            spanElement = debugElement.query(By.css("span")).nativeElement;
        });
    }));

    it("filters categories", () => {
        component.category = "Chess"
        fixture.detectChanges();
        expect(component.getProducts().length).toBe(1);
        expect(spanElement.textContent).toContain("1");
    });
});
```

Components are compiled using the TestBed.compileComponents method. The compilation process is asynchronous, and the compileComponents method returns a Promise, which must be used to complete the test setup when the compilation is complete. To make it easier to work with asynchronous operations in unit tests, the @angular/core/testing module contains a function called async, which is used with the beforeEach method.

Testing Component Events

To demonstrate how to test for a component's response to events, I defined a new property in the FirstComponent class and added a method to which the @HostBinding decorator has been applied, as shown in Listing 29-14.

Listing 29-14. Adding Event Handling in the first.component.ts File in the src/app/ondemand Folder

```
import { Component, HostListener} from "@angular/core";
import { Product } from "../model/product.model";
import { Model } from "../model/repository.model";

@Component({
    selector: "first",
    templateUrl: "first.component.html"
})
export class FirstComponent {

    constructor(private repository: Model) {}

    category: string = "Soccer";
    highlighted: boolean = false;

    getProducts(): Product[] {
        return this.repository.getProducts()
            .filter(p => p.category == this.category);
    }

    @HostListener("mouseenter", ["$event.type"])
    @HostListener("mouseleave", ["$event.type"])
    setHighlight(type: string) {
        this.highlighted = type == "mouseenter";
    }
}
```

The setHighlight method has configured so that it will be invoked when the host element's mouseenter and mouseleave events are triggered. Listing 29-15 updates the component's template so that it uses the new property in a data binding.

Listing 29-15. Binding to a Property in the first.component.html File in the src/app/ondemand Folder

```
<div class="bg-primary text-white p-2" [class.bg-success]="highlighted">
    There are
    <span class="strong"> {{getProducts().length}} </span>
    products
</div>
```

Events can be triggered in unit tests through the `triggerEventHandler` method defined by the DebugElement class, as shown in Listing 29-16.

Listing 29-16. Triggering Events in the first.component.spec.ts File in the src/tests Folder

```
import { TestBed, ComponentFixture, async } from "@angular/core/testing";
import { FirstComponent } from "../app/ondemand/first.component";
import { Product } from "../app/model/product.model";
import { Model } from "../app/model/repository.model";
import { DebugElement } from "@angular/core";
import { By } from "@angular/platform-browser";

describe("FirstComponent", () => {

    let fixture: ComponentFixture<FirstComponent>;
    let component: FirstComponent;
    let debugElement: DebugElement;
    let divElement: HTMLDivElement;

    let mockRepository = {
        getProducts: function () {
            return [
                new Product(1, "test1", "Soccer", 100),
                new Product(2, "test2", "Chess", 100),
                new Product(3, "test3", "Soccer", 100),
            ]
        }
    }

    beforeEach(async(() => {
        TestBed.configureTestingModule({
            declarations: [FirstComponent],
            providers: [
                { provide: Model, useValue: mockRepository }
            ]
        });
        TestBed.compileComponents().then(() => {
            fixture = TestBed.createComponent(FirstComponent);
            component = fixture.componentInstance;
            debugElement = fixture.debugElement;
            divElement = debugElement.children[0].nativeElement;
        });
    }));

    it("handles mouse events", () => {
        expect(component.highlighted).toBeFalsy();
        expect(divElement.classList.contains("bg-success")).toBeFalsy();
        debugElement.triggerEventHandler("mouseenter", new Event("mouseenter"));
        fixture.detectChanges();
        expect(component.highlighted).toBeTruthy();
        expect(divElement.classList.contains("bg-success")).toBeTruthy();
        debugElement.triggerEventHandler("mouseleave", new Event("mouseleave"));
```

```
        fixture.detectChanges();
        expect(component.highlighted).toBeFalsy();
        expect(divElement.classList.contains("bg-success")).toBeFalsy();
    });
});
```

The test in this listing checks the initial state of the component and the template and then triggers the mouseenter and mouseleave events, checking the effect that each has.

Testing Output Properties

Testing output properties is a simple process because the EventEmitter objects used to implement them are Observable objects that can be subscribed to in unit tests. Listing 29-17 adds an output property to the component under test.

Listing 29-17. Adding an Output Property in the first.component.ts File in the src/app/ondemand Folder

```
import { Component, HostListener, Output, EventEmitter} from "@angular/core";
import { Product } from "../model/product.model";
import { Model } from "../model/repository.model";

@Component({
    selector: "first",
    templateUrl: "first.component.html"
})
export class FirstComponent {

    constructor(private repository: Model) {}

    category: string = "Soccer";
    highlighted: boolean = false;

    @Output("pa-highlight")
    change = new EventEmitter<boolean>();

    getProducts(): Product[] {
        return this.repository.getProducts()
            .filter(p => p.category == this.category);
    }

    @HostListener("mouseenter", ["$event.type"])
    @HostListener("mouseleave", ["$event.type"])
    setHighlight(type: string) {
        this.highlighted = type == "mouseenter";
        this.change.emit(this.highlighted);
    }
}
```

The component defines an output property called change, which is used to emit an event when the setHighlight method is called. Listing 29-18 shows a unit test that targets the output property.

Listing 29-18. Testing an Output Property in the first.component.spec.ts File in the src/tests Folder

```
import { TestBed, ComponentFixture, async } from "@angular/core/testing";
import { FirstComponent } from "../app/ondemand/first.component";
import { Product } from "../app/model/product.model";
import { Model } from "../app/model/repository.model";
import { DebugElement } from "@angular/core";
import { By } from "@angular/platform-browser";

describe("FirstComponent", () => {

    let fixture: ComponentFixture<FirstComponent>;
    let component: FirstComponent;
    let debugElement: DebugElement;

    let mockRepository = {
        getProducts: function () {
            return [
                new Product(1, "test1", "Soccer", 100),
                new Product(2, "test2", "Chess", 100),
                new Product(3, "test3", "Soccer", 100),
            ]
        }
    }

    beforeEach(async(() => {
        TestBed.configureTestingModule({
            declarations: [FirstComponent],
            providers: [
                { provide: Model, useValue: mockRepository }
            ]
        });
        TestBed.compileComponents().then(() => {
            fixture = TestBed.createComponent(FirstComponent);
            component = fixture.componentInstance;
            debugElement = fixture.debugElement;
        });
    }));

    it("implements output property", () => {
        let highlighted: boolean;
        component.change.subscribe(value => highlighted = value);
        debugElement.triggerEventHandler("mouseenter", new Event("mouseenter"));
        expect(highlighted).toBeTruthy();
        debugElement.triggerEventHandler("mouseleave", new Event("mouseleave"));
        expect(highlighted).toBeFalsy();
    });
});
```

I could have invoked the component's setHighlight method directly in the unit test, but instead I have chosen to trigger the mouseenter and mouseleave events, which will activate the output property indirectly. Before triggering the events, I use the subscribe method to receive the event from the output property, which is then used to check for the expected outcomes.

Testing Input Properties

The process for testing input properties requires a little extra work. To get started, I added an input property to the FirstComponent class that is used to receive the data model repository, replacing the service that was received by the constructor, as shown in Listing 29-19. I have also removed the host event bindings and the output property in order to keep the example simple.

Listing 29-19. Adding an Input Property in the first.component.ts File in the src/app/ondemand Folder

```
import { Component, HostListener, Input } from "@angular/core";
import { Product } from "../model/product.model";
import { Model } from "../model/repository.model";

@Component({
    selector: "first",
    templateUrl: "first.component.html"
})
export class FirstComponent {

    category: string = "Soccer";
    highlighted: boolean = false;

    getProducts(): Product[] {
        return this.model == null ? [] : this.model.getProducts()
            .filter(p => p.category == this.category);
    }

    @Input("pa-model")
    model: Model;
}
```

The input property is set using an attribute called pa-model and is used within the getProducts method. Listing 29-20 shows how to write a unit test that targets the input property.

Listing 29-20. Testing an Input Property in the first.component.spec.ts File in the src/tests Folder

```
import { TestBed, ComponentFixture, async } from "@angular/core/testing";
import { FirstComponent } from "../app/ondemand/first.component";
import { Product } from "../app/model/product.model";
import { Model } from "../app/model/repository.model";
import { DebugElement } from "@angular/core";
import { By } from "@angular/platform-browser";
import { Component, ViewChild } from "@angular/core";
```

```
@Component({
    template: `<first [pa-model]="model"></first>`
})
class TestComponent {

    constructor(public model: Model) { }

    @ViewChild(FirstComponent)
    firstComponent: FirstComponent;
}

describe("FirstComponent", () => {

    let fixture: ComponentFixture<TestComponent>;
    let component: FirstComponent;
    let debugElement: DebugElement;

    let mockRepository = {
        getProducts: function () {
            return [
                new Product(1, "test1", "Soccer", 100),
                new Product(2, "test2", "Chess", 100),
                new Product(3, "test3", "Soccer", 100),
            ]
        }
    }

    beforeEach(async(() => {
        TestBed.configureTestingModule({
            declarations: [FirstComponent, TestComponent],
            providers: [
                { provide: Model, useValue: mockRepository }
            ]
        });
        TestBed.compileComponents().then(() => {
            fixture = TestBed.createComponent(TestComponent);
            component = fixture.componentInstance.firstComponent;
            debugElement = fixture.debugElement.query(By.directive(FirstComponent));
        });
    }));

    it("receives the model through an input property", () => {
        component.category = "Chess";
        fixture.detectChanges();
        let products = mockRepository.getProducts()
            .filter(p => p.category == component.category);
        let componentProducts = component.getProducts();
        for (let i = 0; i < componentProducts.length; i++) {
            expect(componentProducts[i]).toEqual(products[i]);
        }
```

```
    expect(debugElement.query(By.css("span")).nativeElement.textContent)
        .toContain(products.length);
    });
});
```

The trick here is to define a component that is only required to set up the test and whose template contains an element that matches the selector of the component you want to target. In this example, I defined a component class called TestComponent with an inline template defined in the @Component decorator that contains a first element with a pa-model attribute, which corresponds to the @Input decorator applied to the FirstComponent class.

The test component class is added to the declarations array for the testing module, and an instance is created using the TestBed.createComponent method. I used the @ViewChild decorator in the TestComponent class so that I can get hold of the FirstComponent instance I require for the test. To get the FirstComponent root element, I used the DebugElement.query method with the By.directive method.

The result is that I am able to access both the component and its root element for the test, which sets the category property and then validates the results both from the component and through the data binding in its template.

Testing with Asynchronous Operations

Another area that requires special measures is dealing with asynchronous operations. To demonstrate how this is done, Listing 29-21 modifies the component under test so that it uses the RestDataSource class, defined in Chapter 24, to get its data. This isn't a class that was intended for use outside of the model feature module, but it provides a useful set of asynchronous methods that return Observable objects, so I have broken through the intended structure of the application so that I can demonstrate the test technique.

Listing 29-21. An Async Operation in the first.component.ts File in the src/app/ondemand Folder

```
import { Component, HostListener, Input } from "@angular/core";
import { Product } from "../model/product.model";
import { Model } from "../model/repository.model";
import { RestDataSource } from "../model/rest.datasource";

@Component({
    selector: "first",
    templateUrl: "first.component.html"
})
export class FirstComponent {
    _category: string = "Soccer";
    _products: Product[] = [];
    highlighted: boolean = false;

    constructor(public datasource: RestDataSource) {}

    ngOnInit() {
        this.updateData();
    }

    getProducts(): Product[] {
        return this._products;
    }
```

```
    set category(newValue: string) {
        this._category;
        this.updateData();
    }

    updateData() {
        this.datasource.getData()
            .subscribe(data => this._products = data
                .filter(p => p.category == this._category));
    }
}
```

The component gets its data through the data source's getData method, which returns an Observable object. The component subscribes to the Observable and updates its _product property with the data objects, which is exposed to the template through the getProducts method.

Listing 29-22 shows how this kind of component can be tested using the tools Angular provides for working with asynchronous operations in unit tests.

Listing 29-22. Testing an Async Operation in the first.component.spec.ts File in the src/tests Folder

```
import { TestBed, ComponentFixture, async, fakeAsync, tick } from "@angular/core/testing";
import { FirstComponent } from "../app/ondemand/first.component";
import { Product } from "../app/model/product.model";
import { Model } from "../app/model/repository.model";
import { DebugElement } from "@angular/core";
import { By } from "@angular/platform-browser";
import { Component, ViewChild } from "@angular/core";
import { RestDataSource } from "../app/model/rest.datasource";
import { Observable } from "rxjs";
import { Injectable } from "@angular/core";

@Injectable()
class MockDataSource {
    public data = [
        new Product(1, "test1", "Soccer", 100),
        new Product(2, "test2", "Chess", 100),
        new Product(3, "test3", "Soccer", 100),
    ];

    getData(): Observable<Product[]> {
        return new Observable<Product[]>(obs => {
            setTimeout(() => obs.next(this.data), 1000);
        })
    }
}

describe("FirstComponent", () => {

    let fixture: ComponentFixture<FirstComponent>;
    let component: FirstComponent;
    let dataSource = new MockDataSource();
```

767

```
    beforeEach(async(() => {
        TestBed.configureTestingModule({
            declarations: [FirstComponent],
            providers: [
                { provide: RestDataSource, useValue: dataSource }
            ]
        });
        TestBed.compileComponents().then(() => {
            fixture = TestBed.createComponent(FirstComponent);
            component = fixture.componentInstance;
        });
    }));

    it("performs async op", fakeAsync( () => {
        dataSource.data.push(new Product(100, "test100", "Soccer", 100));

        fixture.detectChanges();

        for (let i = 0; i < 1001; i++)  {
          tick(1);
        }

        fixture.whenStable().then(() => {
            expect(component.getProducts().length).toBe(3);
        });
    }));
});
```

The mock object in this example is more fully formed than the one I created previously, just to show different ways of achieving the same goal. The important point to note is that the getData method it implements introduces a one-second delay before it returns the sample data.

This delay is important because it means that the effect of calling the detectChanges method in the unit test won't affect the component immediately. To simulate the passage of time, I use the fakeAsync and tick methods, and to deal with the asynchronous changes, I call the whenStable method defined by the ComponentFixture class, which returns a Promise that resolves when all the changes have been fully processed. This allows me to defer the assessment of the outcome of the test until the Observable returned by the mock data source has delivered its data to the component.

■ **Note** At the time of writing, there is a bug in the tick method that means it must be called once for each millisecond that you want to simulate in the test.

Testing an Angular Directive

The process for testing directives is similar to the one required to test input properties, in that a test component and template are used to create an environment for testing in which the directive can be applied. To have a directive to test, I added a file called attr.directive.ts to the src/app/ondemand folder and added the code shown in Listing 29-23.

■ **Note**   I have shown an attribute directive in this example, but the technique in this section can be used to test structural directives equally well.

Listing 29-23. The Contents of the attr.directive.ts File in the src/app/ondemand Folder

```
import {
    Directive, ElementRef, Attribute, Input, SimpleChange
} from "@angular/core";

@Directive({
    selector: "[pa-attr]"
})
export class PaAttrDirective {

    constructor(private element: ElementRef) { }

    @Input("pa-attr")
    bgClass: string;

    ngOnChanges(changes: { [property: string]: SimpleChange }) {
        let change = changes["bgClass"];
        let classList = this.element.nativeElement.classList;
        if (!change.isFirstChange() && classList.contains(change.previousValue)) {
            classList.remove(change.previousValue);
        }
        if (!classList.contains(change.currentValue)) {
            classList.add(change.currentValue);
        }
    }
}
```

This is an attribute directive based on an example from Chapter 15. To create a unit test that targets the directive, I added a file called `attr.directive.spec.ts` to the `src/tests` folder and added the code shown in Listing 29-24.

Listing 29-24. The Contents of the attr.directive.spec.ts File in the src/tests Folder

```
import { TestBed, ComponentFixture } from "@angular/core/testing";
import { Component, DebugElement, ViewChild } from "@angular/core";
import { By } from "@angular/platform-browser";
import { PaAttrDirective } from "../app/ondemand/attr.directive";

@Component({
    template: `<div><span [pa-attr]="className">Test Content</span></div>`
})
class TestComponent {
    className = "initialClass"
```

```
    @ViewChild(PaAttrDirective)
    attrDirective: PaAttrDirective;
}

describe("PaAttrDirective", () => {

    let fixture: ComponentFixture<TestComponent>;
    let directive: PaAttrDirective;
    let spanElement: HTMLSpanElement;

    beforeEach(() => {
        TestBed.configureTestingModule({
            declarations: [TestComponent, PaAttrDirective],
        });
        fixture = TestBed.createComponent(TestComponent);
        directive = fixture.componentInstance.attrDirective;
        spanElement = fixture.debugElement.query(By.css("span")).nativeElement;
    });

    it("generates the correct number of elements", () => {
        fixture.detectChanges();
        expect(directive.bgClass).toBe("initialClass");
        expect(spanElement.className).toBe("initialClass");

        fixture.componentInstance.className = "nextClass";
        fixture.detectChanges();
        expect(directive.bgClass).toBe("nextClass");
        expect(spanElement.className).toBe("nextClass");
    });
});
```

The text component has an inline template that applies the directive and a property that is referred to in the data binding. The @ViewChild decorator provides access to the directive object that Angular creates when it processes the template, and the unit test is able to check that changing the value used by the data binding has an effect on the directive object and the element it has been applied to.

Summary

In this chapter, I demonstrated the different ways in which Angular components and directives can be unit tested. I explained the process of installing the test framework and tools and how to create the testbed through which tests are applied. I demonstrated how to test the different aspects of components and how the same techniques can be applied to directives as well.

That is all I have to teach you about Angular. I started by creating a simple application and then took you on a comprehensive tour of the different building blocks in the framework, showing you how they can be created, configured, and applied to create web applications.

I wish you every success in your Angular projects, and I can only hope that you have enjoyed reading this book as much as I enjoyed writing it.

Index

◼ A

@angular-cli package, 8, 211
@angular/forms package, 292
AngularJS, 38
Animations, 720
    adding and removing elements, 731
    applying framework styles, 741
    built-in states, 729
    defining, 721
    element states, 722
    enabling, 720
    guidance for use, 723
    parallel effects, 736
    style groups, 721, 737
    timing functions, 732
    transitions, 723, 730
    triggers, 724
app.component.ts file, 18
Applications
    jQuery, 32
    round-trip, 32
    single-page, 32
app.module.ts file, 21
Asynchronous JavaScript and XML (Ajax) web
    services, 32, 37, 39, 278, 593
Authentication, SportsStore, 171

◼ B

Bootstrap CSS framework, 10, 49
    angular.json file, 11
    basic classes, 50
    contextual classes, 50
    forms, 54
    grids, 55
        columns, 57
        responsive layout, 58
    margin classes, 51
    padding classes, 51
    size classes, 52
    tables, 53

Bootstrap file, 21
Building for production, 200
Business domain, 37

◼ C

Cascading Style Sheets (CSS), 49
Classes, 20
Code editor, 9
Code, examples, 6
Components, 18, 38, 229
    application structure, 403
    @Component decorator, 405
    content projection, 417
    creating, 404
    input properties, 412
    output properties, 415
    styles
        external, 422
        inline, 420
        shadow DOM, 423
        view encapsulation, 423
    template queries, 430
        @ViewChild decorator, 431
        @ViewChildren decorator, 431
    templates
        data bindings, 411
        external, 409
        inline, 408
Cross-Origin HTTP
    Requests (CORS), 607

◼ D

Data bindings
    attribute bindings, 244, 247
    classes, 249
    event binding, 29, 294
        dynamically defined properties, 297
        event data, 298
        filtering key events, 302
        template references variables, 300

Data bindings (*cont.*)
expressions, 240, 242
host element, 240, 244
live data updates, 258
one-way bindings, 26, 239
structure, 240
property bindings, 241, 244
restrictions
idempotent expressions, 283
limited expression context, 286
square brackets, 240, 243
string interpolation, 246
styles, 249
target, 240–241
two-way bindings, 26, 302
ngModel directive, 304
Data model, 16, 36, 115
Decorators, 19
@NgModule, 21
selector property, 19
templateUrl property, 19
Dependency injection services, 467, 474
Design pitfalls, 41
Development environment, 6, 7
@angular-cli package, 8
browser, 9
editor, 9
Git, 8
Node.js, 7
Directives
attribute directives, 343
data-bound inputs, 348
host element attributes, 345
custom directive, 130
custom events, 353
emit method, 355
@Directive decorator, 369
host element bindings, 357
host element content, 392
@ContentChild decorator, 393
@ContentChildren decorator, 395
@Input decorator, 349
lifecycle hooks, 350
micro-templates, 266
ngClass directive, 252
ngFor directive, 24, 270
even variable, 272
expanding micro-template syntax, 275
first variable, 272
index variable, 272
last variable, 272
let keyword, 271
minimizing changes, 277
odd variable, 272
of keyword, 271

trackBy, 279
using variables in child elements, 271
ngIf directive, 264
using literal values, 269
ngModel, 26, 304
ngStyle directive, 254
ngSwitch, 25, 267
ngSwitchCase, 25
ngSwitchDefault, 25
ngTemplateOutlet directive, 280
context data, 281
ng-template element, 281
@Output decorator, 353
structural directives, 367
collection changes, 381
concise syntax, 373
context data, 377
detecting changes, 369
iterating directives, 374
ngDoCheck method, 383
ng-template element, 370
property changes, 380
ViewContainerRef class, 369
using services, 483
Docker containers, 203

■ **E**

Editor, 9
Event bindings, 29, 294
Example code, 6

■ **F**

Forms, 305
model-based, 325
validation, 308
custom validators, 335
validation classes, 310
whole-form validation, 319

■ **G**

Git, 8

■ **H**

Hot module replacement, 222
HTML
attributes, 46
literal values, 47
without values, 46
document object model, 48
elements, 45
content, 47
hierarchy, 47

tags, 46
void elements, 46
HTTP methods, 40

■ I

index.html file, 12

■ J, K

JavaScript
    arrays, 81
        built-in methods, 83
        enumerating, 82
        literals arrays, 81
        modifying, 81
        reading, 81
        spread operator, 83
    classes, 90
        getters, 92
        inheritance, 92
        setters, 92
    closures, 74
    conditional statements, 77
    const keyword, 73
    defining variables, 72
    functions, 67
        as arguments to other functions, 71
        arrow functions, 71
        chaining, 71
        default parameters, 69
        hoisting, 68
        parameters, 69
        rest parameters, 69
        results, 70
    lambda functions, 71
    let keyword, 72
    literal values in directive expressions, 269
    modules, 93
        export keyword, 94
        import keyword, 94
        NPM packages, 95
        renaming imports, 96
        resolution, 95
    objects, 88
        classes, 90
        literals, 89
        methods, 89
    operators, 76
        equality *versus* identity operator, 78
    Promises, 574
    prototypes, 91
    statements, 67
        conditional, 77
    template strings, 75

truthy and falsy values, 251
types, 74
    booleans, 74
    converting explicitly, 79
    numbers, 76
    strings, 75
variable closure, 74
variables, 72
var keyword, 73
jQuery, 32
JSON Web Token (JWT), 171

■ L

Linting, 223
Listings
    complete listing, 4
    example code, 6
    interleaved listing, 5
    partial, 5
Live data model, 258

■ M

main.ts file, 21
Meta data,19 *See also* Decorators
Micro-templates
    use by directives, 266
Model-View-Controller, *See* MVC pattern
Modules, 21
    bootstrap property, 531
    declarations property, 530
    dynamic loading
        SportsStore, 166
        URL routing, 168
    feature modules, creating, 533
    imports property, 530
    @NgModule decorator, 529
    providers property, 531
    root module, 528
    using with JavaScript modules, 538
MVC pattern
    business domain, 37
    components, 38
    controllers, 38
    models, 36
    templates, 38
    view data, 38

■ N

ngFor directive, 24
ng lint command, 224
ngModel directive, 26
ng new command, 10, 211

ng serve command, 11, 221
ngSwitchCase directive, 25
ngSwitchDefault directive, 25
ngSwitch directive, 25
ngZone class, 616
Node.js, 7
node_modules folder, 216

■ O

One-way data bindings, 26

■ P, Q

Pipes
    applying, 439
        arguments, 440
    async pipe, 577
    combining, 444
    creating, 441
    formatting currency amounts, 453
    formatting dates, 458
    formatting numbers, 450
    formatting percentages, 456
    formatting string case, 462
    impure pipes, 446
    JSON serialization, 463
    @Pipe decorator, 442
    pure pipes, 445
    slicing arrays, 463
    using services, 480
Programmer's editor, 9
Progressive web applications, 33, 193
Projects
    app.component.html file, 18
    app.component.ts file, 18
    app.module.ts file, 21
    bootstrap, 21, 227
    bundles, 221
    components, 18, 229
    data model, 16, 231
    decorators, 19
    development HTTP server, 221
    development tools, 221
    hot module replacement, 222
    HTML document, 226
    index.html file, 12
    linting, 223
    main.ts file, 21
    modules, 21
    node_modules folder, 216
    packages, 216
        global packages, 219
        node package manager, 220

scripts, 219
    versions, 217
    Yarn package manager, 220
root module, 228
src/app folder, 215
src folder, 214
structure, 212
template, 18
webpack, 221

■ R

React, 34
Reactive extensions, 571
    async pipe, 577
    distinctUntilChanged method, 587
    filtering events, 583
    filter method, 583
    map method, 584
    Observable
        Promises, 574
        subscribe method, 572
    Observer, 574
    pipe method, 583
    receiving distinct events, 587
    skipping events, 589
    skipWhile method, 589
    Subject, 575
        types of, 576
    takeWhile method, 589
    transforming events, 584
REST,109 *See also* Web services
RESTful web services, 39
    HTTP methods, 40
    Sports Store example,160
        see also Web services
Root module, 228
Round-trip applications, 32

■ S

Services
    component isolation, 488
    dependency injection, 474
    @Host decorator, 522
    @Injectable decorator, 475
    local providers, 514
        providers property, 520
        viewProviders property, 521
    @Optional decorator, 523
    providers, 498
        class provider, 500
        existing service provider, 513
        factory provider, 510

multiple service objects, 507
  property, 477
  service tokens, 501
  value provider, 508
receiving services, 475
registering services, 477
services in directives, 483
services in pipes, 480
shared object problem, 469
@SkipSelf decorator, 523
Single-page applications, 32
SportsStore
  additional packages, 108
  authentication, 171
    JSON Web Token, 171
  bootstrap file, 114
  cart, 135
    summary component, 137
  category selection, 124
  containerizing
    create container, 205
    create image, 205
    deployment packages, 203
    Dockerfile, 204
    stop container, 207
  create project, 107
  data model, 115
    data source, 116
  data source, 116
  displaying products, 122
  dynamic module, 166
  navigation, 145
  orders, 153
  pagination, 126
  persistent data, 197
  production build, 200
  progressive features, 193
    caching, 194
    connectivity, 195
  project structure, 112
  REST data, 160
  root component, 113
  root module, 114
  route guard, 148
  stylesheets, 108
  URL routing, 142
  web service, 109

■ T

Templates, 18, 38
Two-way data bindings, 26
TypeScript
  access modifiers, 103
  any type, 101

indexable types, 103
multiple types, 101
tuples, 102
type annotations, 97

■ U

Unit testing
  components, 751
    asynchronous
      operations, 766
    configuring dependencies, 753
    data bindings, 755
    events, 760
    input properties, 764
    output properties, 762
    templates, 758
  directives, 768
  Jasmine, 748, 749
  Karma test runner, 748
  ng test command, 748
  TestBed class, 751
Updating data, 258
URL routing, 142, 623
  ActivatedRoute class, 632
  active elements, styles, 664
  basic configuration, 623
  change notifications, 662
  child routes, 669
    parameters, 673
    route outlets, 670
  dynamic modules, 700
    guarding, 705
    specifying, 702
    using, 703
  guards, 148, 679
    display loading message, 684
    preventing navigation, 687
    preventing route
      activation, 688
    resolvers, 680, 695
    URL entry problems, 686
  named outlets, 708
    routing to, 711
  navigating within component, 661
  navigation events, 643
  navigation links, 627
  optional URL segments, 639
  programmatic navigation, 632, 641
  redirections, 659
  route parameters, 635
  routerLink directive, 627
  router-outlet element, 625, 708
  Routes class, 623
  wildcard routes, 656

■ V

Vue.js, 34

■ W, X, Y, Z

Web services, 597
    cross-origin requests, 607
    errors, 613

HttpClient class
    consolidating requests, 606
    methods, 599
    responses, 600
HTTP verbs, 597
JSONP requests, 608
NgZone class, 616
request headers, 610